SOCIAL PROBLEMS

Most of the readers of this book are among the world's privileged people—those who have enough to eat, a comfortable place to sleep, and who have the special opportunity to study the human condition. I offer this book in the hope that it will stimulate thinking about the state of our world as well as action toward making it a better place.

John J. Macionis

Second Edition

SOCIAL PROBLEMS

JOHN J. MACIONIS
Kenyon College

PEARSON

Prentice
Hall

Upper Saddle River, New Jersey 07458

Library of Congress Cataloging-in-Publication Data
Macionis, John J.
Social Problems—2nd ed. / John J. Macionis
    p. cm.
Includes bibliographical references and indexes.
ISBN 0-13-189187-1 (alk. paper)
1. Social Problems.   2. Social Problems—United States.   I. Title

HN16.M24 2005
361.1—dc22

2003060874

Editorial Director: Leah Jewell
AVP, Publisher: Nancy Roberts
Editor-in-Chief of Development: Rochelle Diogenes
Development Editor: Karen Trost
VP, Director of Production and Manufacturing: Barbara Kittle
Production Editor: Barbara Reilly
Copy Editor: Carol Peschke
Proofreaders: Susan Plog, Alison Lorber
Supplements Editor: Erin Katchmar
Editorial Assistant: Lee Peterson
Director of Marketing: Beth Mejia
Senior Marketing Manager: Marissa Feliberty
Prepress and Manufacturing Manager: Nick Sklitsis
Prepress and Manufacturing Buyer: Mary Ann Gloriande

Creative Design Director: Leslie Osher
Art Director: Anne Bonanno Nieglos
Cover and Interior Design: Jill Lehan
Line Art Manager: Guy Ruggiero
Line Art Illustrations: Mirella Signoretto
Maps: Carto-Graphics, Inc.
Director, Image Resource Center: Melinda Reo
Manager, Rights and Permissions: Zina Arabia
Manager, Visual Research: Beth Brenzel
Manager, Cover Visual Research & Permissions: Karen Sanatar
Image Permission Coordinator: Debra Hewitson
Photo Researcher: Beaura Kathy Ringrose
Cover Art: Paul Schulenburg, Stock Illustration Source, Inc.
Media Editor: Kate Ramunda
Manager of Media Production: Lynn Pearlman

This book was set in 10.5/12 Janson by Lithokraft, and was printed and bound by Von Hoffman Press, Inc. The cover was printed by The Lehigh Press, Inc.

For permission to use copyrighted material, grateful acknowledgment is made to the copyright holders listed on page 502, which is considered an extension of this copyright page.

Pearson Education LTD.
Pearson Education Singapore, Pte. Ltd
Pearson Education, Canada, Ltd
Pearson Education—Japan
Pearson Education Australia PTY, Limited

Pearson Education North Asia Ltd
Pearson Educación de Mexico, S.A. de C.V.
Pearson Education Malaysia, Pte. Ltd
Pearson Education, Upper Saddle River, New Jersey

10 9 8 7 6 5 4 3 2
ISBN 0-13-189187-1

BRIEF CONTENTS

CONTENTS

Part III
PROBLEMS OF DEVIANCE, CONFORMITY,
AND WELL-BEING

CHAPTER 6
CRIME AND CRIMINAL
JUSTICE   134

Part V
GLOBAL PROBLEMS

CHAPTER 16
POPULATION AND GLOBAL
INEQUALITY 394

CHAPTER 17
TECHNOLOGY
AND THE ENVIRONMENT 422

MAPS

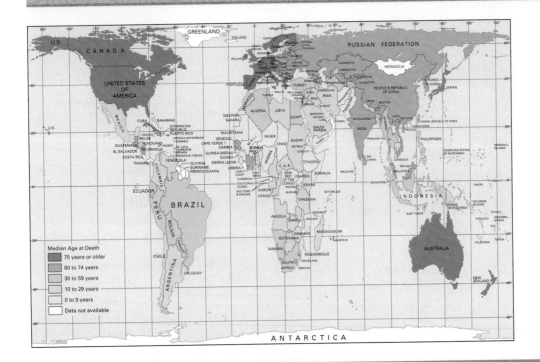

A WORLD OF DIFFERENCES

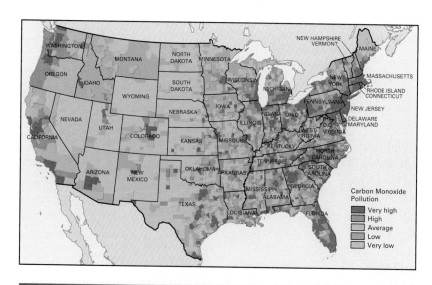

A NATION OF DIVERSITY

BOXES

Social Policy

Critical Thinking

A Global Perspective

Personal Stories

As this second edition of *Social Problems* is being published, the United States is in the midst of a presidential election campaign. Every day we hear the presidential candidates making claims about what is wrong with the United States (the "problems") and what we need to do to fix things (the "solutions"). Politics is an arena of competing claims about problems and solutions.

Almost everyone would agree that the outcome of such a contest makes a difference in shaping the kind of society—and world—in which we will live. Yet surveys tell us that most young people on campuses throughout the United States are not very interested in today's issues and that they rarely discuss politics. In fact, only about one-third of young women and men who are eligible even bother to cast a vote.

The discipline of sociology offers one way to connect people to the world of political ideas and action. For decades, U.S. colleges and universities have offered a course, typically titled "Social Problems," that applies the perspective, theory, and research findings of the discipline to current issues. *Social Problems* is a text that brings these issues to life in a most effective way.

CONNECTING TO POLITICS

The general purpose of this book is to connect readers with the political issues in the world around them. This is an important goal because *politics matters*. The candidates running for office in the United States represent a wide range of political positions—conservative, liberal, and left—each of which seeks a distinctive type of society. It is the responsibility of everyone as a citizen to learn enough about political issues to make a decision about which visions are worthy of support and then to become engaged in the political process, perhaps by speaking out, perhaps by volunteering in a campaign, perhaps by offering financial support, and certainly by voting.

Social Problems, Second Edition, does more than simply urge people to become politically active citizens. *It explains what politics is all about.* Beginning with Chapter 1 ("Studying Social Problems"), this text helps students understand the attitudes and values that define the conservative, liberal, and radical-left positions on the political spectrum. In every chapter that follows, these political points of view are applied to dozens of issues—from wealth and poverty in the United States to terrorism and war around the world—so that students become able to engage and analyze new issues on their own.

Politics involves several points of view. This text presents multiple political positions for four reasons. First, all are part of the political debate that goes on throughout the United States. Second, no one can formulate personal political beliefs with any conviction without understanding the arguments of those who disagree. In other words, in order to be, say, a good liberal, someone needs to understand not just liberal principles but the conservative and radical positions as well. Third, although anyone is likely to favor one position over others, each position offers some measure of truth. Fourth, by representing various political positions, this text invites all students to share their ideas, encouraging more lively class discussion.

THE SOCIAL-CONSTRUCTIONIST APPROACH

The most important reason to "put the politics in" when teaching a social problems course is that politics is the process by which segments of society define social problems. By incorporating politics (along with theory) as a foundation, this text differs from all the others in a basic and exciting way: Rather than using one (explicit or implicit) point of view that presents a sequence of "problems" and a sequence of "solutions" (as if everyone agreed on what these are), *Social Problems, Second Edition*, employs a multiperspective, *social-constructionist approach*.

With this approach, *Social Problems* focuses attention on how and why certain issues come to be defined as problems in the first place. Issues such as gender inequality, domestic violence, and AIDS have become defined as social problems only recently and as the result of social movements that have gained wide public support. Sometimes, as in the case of the September 11, 2001, terrorist attacks, specific events quickly thrust a new problem to the top of our national concerns.

Another benefit of the social-constructionist approach is alerting students to the fact that a society may not define something as a problem, *even when it causes great harm to many people.* As an example, Chapter 9 ("Alcohol and Other Drugs") points out that, although cigarette smoking results in more than 400,000 premature deaths in the United States each year—more than 100 times the September 11, 2001, death toll—tobacco use has yet to be defined as a serious social problem.

The social-constructionist approach also provides historical insights. As Chapter 4 ("Gender Inequality") explains, women a century ago had so few rights and opportunities that they lived as second-class citizens. But, back then, few people defined women and men as social equals; as a result, gender inequality was not widely defined as a social problem. Today's society, by contrast, has far greater gender equality. Yet, because most people *expect* women and men to have the same rights and opportunities, the inequalities that remain (even though they are much smaller today) are widely defined as a problem in need of a solution.

In sum, a social-constructionist approach is an excellent strategy for demonstrating the role of politics in the process of defining social problems and creating solutions.

FACTS—AND THEORY, TOO

Politics is not all there is to social problems. The discipline of sociology offers both hard facts and theoretical analysis of today's issues and controversies. In Chapter 2 ("Poverty and Wealth"), the analysis of poverty begins with important facts: How many poor people are there? What categories of the population are at greatest risk of poverty? Why, according to public opinion, are people poor? In addition, all chapters in *Social Problems, Second Edition,* contain *theoretical analysis*—guided by the structural-functional, symbolic-interaction, and social-conflict approaches. Theoretical analysis helps students understand the causes and consequences of poverty, gender inequality, crime, and other issues defined as problems today.

THIS TEXT AND WEB SITE

This text offers many ways to learn, because it is the heart of a complete learning package. Accompanying the textbook is a content-rich Companion Website™ that provides powerful support for learning and which is provided at no additional cost to the student. This

Companion Website ™ offers an interactive study guide with many helpful tools, including chapter quizzes, interactive maps, roll-over graphics, links to hundreds of Web sites, and self-grading practice tests for all the chapters of the book. To reach the Web site, go to http://www.prenhall.com/macionis and click on the cover of this book.

The textbook and the Companion Website ™ work together to make learning come alive. We invite you to examine them both!

THE ORGANIZATION OF *SOCIAL PROBLEMS*

Part I of this book, "Sociology and Social Problems," introduces students to the discipline of sociology and to the study of social problems. Chapter 1 ("Studying Social Problems") defines social problems and applies sociology's distinctive perspective to their study. It also acquaints students with commonly used methods for gathering facts and information, and illustrates the use of sociology's major theoretical approaches. In addition, this chapter explains the social construction of problems and solutions, highlighting the process of "claims making." The chapter explains the role of politics in this process, describes the various points on the political spectrum, and identifies what type of people are likely to hold particular points of view.

Part II addresses "Problems of Social Inequality." Chapter 2 ("Poverty and Wealth") explores the distribution of poverty and wealth in the United States, tracks trends in economic inequality, profiles the rich and the poor, highlights the challenges faced by low-income people, and examines the welfare system past and present. As in every chapter, conservative, liberal, and radical perspectives on economic inequality are included. Chapter 3 ("Racial and Ethnic Inequality") tackles two other dimensions of inequality—race and ethnicity. This chapter explains how societies construct racial and ethnic categories, explains the concept of "minority," surveys the social standing of various racial and ethnic categories of the U.S. population, and investigates the causes and consequences of prejudice and discrimination. Chapter 4 ("Gender Inequality") explains how societies construct gender and how gender distinctions are evident in the operation of the economy, the family, and the other social institutions; it notes the importance of gender as a dimension of social stratification, traces the feminist movement in the United States, and invites students to voice their opinions about all the political controversies involving gender. Chapter 5 ("Aging and Inequality") spotlights aging and inequality, explains how societies construct old age, examines the increasing share of older people in the United States, and provides both theoretical and political analysis of numerous issues linked to growing old, including social isolation, ageism, crime, poverty, poor housing, inadequate medical care, and the necessity of facing up to the ultimate reality of death.

Part III ("Problems of Deviance, Conformity, and Well-Being") begins with Chapter 6 ("Crime and Criminal Justice"), which explains how and why societies construct criminal law and how certain acts come to be defined as criminal. It uses crime statistics to track the extent of both violent and property crime and to profile "street" criminals. The chapter analyzes various types of crime, including juvenile delinquency, hate crime, white-collar crime, corporate crime, organized crime, and victimless crime, and concludes by surveying the operation of the police, courts, and correction system. As always, analysis reflects both sociological theory and various political perspectives. Chapter 7 ("Violence") extends this discussion, explaining how societies define some types of violence as necessary or even honorable while outlawing others. The chapter explores factors linked to criminal and family violence, including the influence of the mass media, poverty, drugs, gangs, and easy availability of guns. Chapter 8 ("Sexuality") explores sexuality as a biological process and as a cultural construction, then tackles political controversies surrounding sexual orientation, pornography, sexual harassment, prostitution, teenage pregnancy, abortion, and sexually transmitted diseases. Chapter 9 ("Alcohol and Other Drugs") begins by defining the concept "drugs," and goes on to examine how and why U.S. society endorses use of some drugs while outlawing the use of others. The chapter surveys the extent of alcohol and other drug use, discusses the link between drug abuse and problems of family life, homelessness, poor health, crime, and poverty, and concludes with theoretical and political analysis of drug abuse and policy responses. Chapter 10 ("Physical and Mental Health") begins with a global survey of human health and health care policies, highlighting how societies define being "healthy." The chapter investigates the U.S. health care system with an eye toward who has access to health care and who does not, surveys the challenges and policies relating to physical disabilities, and explains how U.S. society defines, and deals with, mental illness.

In Part IV ("Problems of Social Institutions"), Chapter 11 ("Economy and Politics") leads off investigating the economic and political systems by which U.S. society defines a just distribution of wealth and power. The chapter highlights the operation of corporations and the power of money to direct political life, and offers theoretical and political analysis of the U.S. political economy. Chapter 12 ("Work and the Workplace") explains the effects of the Information Revolution, deindustrialization, and the globalization of the economy on the U.S. labor force. The chapter identifies various workplace hazards, investigates unemployment during the recent economic downturn, and explores the experience of alienation and the rise of low-skill "McJobs" and temporary work. The chapter also discusses workplace barriers faced by women and other minorities and the decline of unions. There is theoretical and political analysis of all the issues. Chapter 13 ("Family Life") begins with a look at the changing definitions of "family," and then highlights current controversies surrounding cohabitation, single-parenting, work and family conflicts, child care, divorce, gay and lesbian families, and new reproductive technology. Chapter 14 ("Education") explains why societies come to define schooling as necessary and surveys educational inequality in the United States. Both theoretical and political analysis highlight issues including the performance of U.S. schools, dropping out, illiteracy, racial segregation, unequal funding, tracking, violence, schooling people with disabilities, and the challenges of schooling an increasingly diverse student population. Chapter 15 ("Urban Life") begins by surveying the changing problems faced by urbanites over the course of U.S. history, then tackles current issues including fiscal problems of today's cities, urban sprawl, urban poverty, urban housing, urban homelessness, and the uneven growth of Snowbelt and Sunbelt cities.

Part V ("Global Problems") begins with Chapter 16 ("Population and Global Inequality"), which charts the planet's population increase as well as trends in fertility and mortality around the world. The chapter also analyzes global poverty and hunger, with special focus on women and children, and discusses the continued existence of slavery. Various theoretical and political perspectives assess the likely future of global inequality. Chapter 17 ("Technology and the Environment") explores the emergence of the natural environment as a social problem. The chapter explains how technological advances, cultural patterns, and levels of consumption set the stage for environmental issues such as solid waste disposal, availability of fresh water, air pollution, diminishing rain forests, and global warming. Finally, Chapter 18 ("War and Terrorism") presents causes and consequences of war, explores the changing nature of warfare over time, tracks the spread of nuclear weapons, discusses the use of children as soldiers around the world, and explores strategies for peace. The chapter then provides theoretical and political analysis of terrorism as a new form of warfare.

ESTABLISHED FEATURES OF *SOCIAL PROBLEMS*

Social Problems has achieved remarkable success based on a combination of features found in no other text:

A writing style students say they love   This text excites students, motivating them to *read the book—* even beyond their assignments. The best evidence of this comes from the students themselves. Here are recent e-mail comments from students about the author's texts:

> I have just completed a class at [a Georgia college] using the book, *Social Problems*. It is an incredibly well-written book. I enjoyed the various points of view you included within the chapters.

> I am using your *Social Problems* textbook for my sociology course. I have never had a better book. It's so easy to follow. The stories and extra highlights are very interesting and I love to read them. It's a great book!

> I'm a college student in California and my sociology class used your book. It was by far the best textbook I have ever used. I actually liked to read it for pleasure as well as to study; anyway, just wanted to say it was great.

> Thanks for writing such a brilliant book. It has sparked my sociological imagination. This was the first textbook that I have ever read completely and enjoyed. From the moment that I picked the book up I started reading nonstop.

> I am a sociology major and my department and I live by your textbook. I just wanted to tell you that writing it was definitely a stroke of genius. You did a great job. I appreciate the time and effort you put into the book and I just wanted to let you know that you have touched a student across the United States.

> I have read four chapters ahead; it's like a good novel I can't put down! I just wanted to say thank you.

> I have been in college for three years now and I have not found a book as remarkable and thought-provoking as your text.

> Your book is extremely well written and very interesting. I find myself reading it for pleasure, something I have never done with college texts. It is going to be the only collegiate textbook that I ever keep simply to read on my own. I am also thinking of picking up sociology as my minor due to the fact that I have enjoyed the class as well as the text so much. Your writing has my highest praise and utmost appreciation.

> I am taking a sociology class using your book and I have told my professor it is the best textbook that I have ever seen, bar none. I've told her as well that I will be more than happy to take more sociology classes as long as there is a Macionis text to go with them.

> As an instructor, I can report that my students absolutely loved the *Social Problems* text. It is so readable, so clear, so colorful, so inviting. Their feedback made me glad I spent so much time choosing the best book for the course.

> Dude, your book *rocks!*

A social-constructionist approach   As we have explained, politics is the process by which a society debates and defines social problems and their solutions. This text "puts the politics in" with its social-constructionist approach that explains how societies come to define situations as social problems. Looking more closely, we also see how people's position on the political spectrum leads them to define certain issues as "problems" and certain policies as "solutions."

In every chapter, readers will find a major section titled "Politics: Constructing Problems and Defining Solutions." This discussion applies the political perspectives of conservatives, liberals, and radicals to the topic at hand. Doing this is an experience rather like (and here I am afraid I reveal my age) switching a sound system from "mono" to "stereo," because it adds new breadth as well as depth to political debates. By including multiple political perspectives, we encourage all students to become part of the debate and develop their own positions as they learn from others. Each chapter has a "Left to Right" table that summarizes the way the various political perspectives construct problems and define solutions.

Theoretical analysis in every chapter   Just as the world of politics involves different ways of looking at issues and events, so the discipline of sociology makes use of different theoretical approaches. The chapters of *Social Problems, Second Edition,* apply three major theoretical approaches—the structural-functional, symbolic-interaction, and social-conflict approaches. Each approach calls attention to different facts and provides worthwhile insights into the issues at hand.

Emphasis on critical thinking   Presenting students with different ways of thinking about issues is the best way to develop their critical-thinking abilities. In addition to its emphasis on political and theoretical analysis, this text uses a number of features to sharpen critical-thinking skills. These include Critical Evaluation sections following each theoretical discussion that point up the important contributions and limitations of that theoretical approach; Issues and Exercises questions at the end of each of the theme boxes that encourage students to formulate their own opinions about the issue at hand; a series of Thinking Critically: Questions and Issues items at the end of each chapter that prompts students to apply what they have learned; finally, many of the captions that accompany photographs and maps include thought-provoking questions that challenge students to actively engage the issues.

A focus on policy   *Social Problems, Second Edition*, is a text that focuses not only on problems but also on solutions. Therefore, a large part of every chapter of the text is devoted to social policy. The politics sections that conclude every chapter critically consider the policy approaches favored by conservatives, liberals, and radicals. In addition, a series of eighteen "Social Policy" boxes spread throughout the book provide multiple perspectives on important issues.

A national and global focus   *Social Problems, Second Edition*, takes both a national and a global focus. The two often go together, because looking at issues in international scope can suggest different ways to define problems and solutions. For example, most other high-income countries consider poverty to be a more significant problem than we do here in the United States, and their governments also do more to reduce economic inequality. Such comparisons, clearly, spark questions about *why* and stimulate students to think about how a condition that many people in this country define as "natural" could be defined as a "problem" by most people in another country.

Second, many issues are naturally global in scope. Population increase, hunger, the state of the natural environment, war, and terrorism are issues that must be studied in a global context and that demand global responses.

Readers will find information about not only the United States but also other countries in every chapter of this book. In addition, to help students learn more about the rest of the world, the text contains a series of ten A Global Perspective theme boxes, eighteen A World of Differences global maps, and numerous Dimensions of Difference comparison figures spread throughout the text.

National and global maps   *Social Problems, Second Edition*, includes thirty-four specially constructed sociological maps that engage students as they convey important information.

Seventeen A Nation of Diversity national maps highlight the state-by-state or county-by-county diversity of the United States with regard to such issues as poverty rates, life expectancy, divorce rates, air quality, voter apathy, popularity of cigarette smoking, access to personal computers, school dropout rates, the legality of carrying concealed weapons, the number of death row inmates, the geographical distribution of African American, Asian American, and Hispanic American people, total minority population, and other issues of interest.

In addition, seventeen A World of Differences global maps illustrate the planet's diversity with regard to women's political power, child labor, the size of the elderly population, the death penalty, prostitution, life expectancy, infant mortality, access to physicians, access to personal computers, extent of schooling, energy consumption, current military conflicts, and other issues of interest.

Boxes that highlight themes of the text   *Social Problems, Second Edition*, includes three or four boxes per chapter that highlight important themes. These include Critical Thinking boxes, which help students to assess arguments and form their own opinions; Social Policy boxes, which focus on controversial laws and public policies from different points of view; A Global Perspective boxes, which provides international comparisons of important issues; and Personal Stories boxes, in which individuals describe social issues in terms of their own life experiences.

"A Defining Moment"   New to this edition are the A Defining Moment box features in each chapter, which highlight a person or event that changed the way U.S. society looked at the particular social issue covered in that chapter.

A celebration of social diversity   In its photographs, maps, boxes, and coverage of issues, this text reflects the social diversity of the United States and the larger world. It makes special efforts to include the voices of all people—women and men, old and young, African American, Asian American, and those of Latino and European heritage—just as it presents all political points of view. In addition, while recognizing that some categories of the U.S. population face many more challenges than others, this text is careful to avoid treating minority populations as "problems" in and of themselves.

Engaging features that enhance learning This text provides a number of features that raise student interest and enhance learning. Getting the Picture is a listing of three or four facts on the opening page of each chapter that spark student interest. A chapter-opening vignette at the beginning of each chapter presents a real-world situation that generates interest and illustrates an important theme. Issues and Exercises questions and activities accompany every box in the text. At the end of each chapter, there are a number of helpful tools: A Chapter Summary highlights key facts and arguments and helps students assess their comprehension; a list of Key Concepts with clear definitions and page numbers helps students review (a full listing of concepts appears in the Glossary at the end of the book); Thinking Critically: Questions and Issues encourages students to form their own opinions and apply the chapter's lessons to new situations; Getting Involved: Learning Activities includes four suggestions for easy and worthwhile learning projects; Getting Connected: Useful Web Links are selected Internet sites that help students learn more about a topic; Getting Started on Your Own: Research Navigator™ is a new search engine that allows students to search journals, popular publications, and *The New York Times* by topic.

Recent research and the latest data All Macionis texts provide the most up-to-date content possible. Current events are used to illustrate important ideas throughout the book. All the statistical data are the most recent available. And the author reviews dozens of scholarly journals as well as government publications and Web pages to ensure that more than this book stands at the cutting edge of today's scholarship and political debates.

WHAT'S NEW
IN THE SECOND EDITION

The second edition of *Social Problems* represents a major revision of the book, and includes numerous changes and additions. The most significant changes are listed below.

"A Defining Moment" box features "A Defining Moment" refers to a person or event that went a long way to shaping the way we in the United States today define a social problem. In this revision, each chapter contains an A Defining Moment box feature that points to an important historical change.

Chapter 1   Ryan White: Changing the Face of AIDS

Chapter 2   U.S. Society Discovers Poverty

Chapter 3   Rosa Parks: Saying No to Segregation

Chapter 4   Elizabeth Cady Stanton: Claiming Women's Right to Equality

Chapter 5   Dr. Jack Kevorkian: Changing Our Ideas about Death

Chapter 6   Ralph Nader: Making Corporations More Accountable

Chapter 7   U.S. Society Discovers Child Abuse

Chapter 8   Alfred Kinsey: Talking Openly about Sex

Chapter 9   Bill Wilson: Alcoholics Can Learn to Be Sober

Chapter 10   Dorothea Dix: Changing Society's View of People with Mental Illnesses

Chapter 11   Doris Haddock: Sparking a Movement for Campaign Finance Reform

Chapter 12   Eugene Debs: Standing Up for the Union

Chapter 13   Axil and Eigil Axgil: Changing the Marriage Rules

Chapter 14   Linda Brown: Fighting to Desegregate the Schools

Chapter 15   Jacob Riis: Revealing the Horror of the Tenements

Chapter 16   Thomas Robert Malthus: Claiming Population Is a Problem

Chapter 17   Rachel Carson: Sounding an Environmental Wake-Up Call

Chapter 18   Mohandas Gandhi: Spreading a Message of Peace

These A Defining Moment box features not only teach students about important turning points in the way society defines social problems. They also illustrate the power of individuals to make a difference in the United States and the world.

More on claims making Since the first edition of *Social Problems* was published, the concept of claims making has gained importance in the field. This revision applies this concept, beginning in Chapter 1, expanding and strengthening the social-constructionist approach.

Rewriting for clarity and interest This revision in not simply updated in some places. It has been rewritten throughout in order to make the material as clear as possible and to boost reader interest.

More global material This revision includes an increase in the amount of global material. This increase is reflected in new chapter-opening vignettes, updated A World of Differences global maps, and also the new Dimensions of Difference figures found in most chapters.

The latest research Most instructors simply do not have the time to read all the sociological journals. By using *Social Problems, Second Edition*, students benefit from the latest research and developments in the field. This revision has been thoroughly updated from cover to cover: It contains almost 400 new research citations; a majority of the citations found in the text represent work published since 2000.

Web links The text encourages students to learn on their own through the new series of Web links that point to Internet sites relevant to the text discussion. There are four or five of these links throughout each chapter; in addition, at the end of each chapter is a list of five or six sites, with annotations, under the "Getting Connected: Useful Web Links" heading.

Research Navigator™ *Social Problems, Second Edition*, offers students a powerful new learning tool— Research Navigator™. This set of search engines— available at http://www.researchnavigator.com—can be easily accessed with the passcode that is included with every new copy of this textbook. By choosing relevant disciplines and entering keywords, the user can research topics through the ContentSelect™ database (powered by EBSCO), which includes more than 150 scholarly journals. In addition, *The New York Times* and *Financial Times* search engines do topic searches of all their issues published within the last eighteen months.

Updating in every chapter Finally, every chapter has new material. Here is a chapter-by-chapter listing of what's new in *Social Problems, Second Edition*:

Chapter 1: Studying Social Problems A new chapter-opening vignette describes the extent of obesity in the United States, which results in 300,000 premature deaths each year; there is new discussion of claims-making, part of an expanded focus on the social construction of social problems; a new figure analyzes the interplay of objective facts and subjective perceptions of situations; a new A Defining Moment feature describes the life and death of Ryan White, who helped define AIDS as everyone's problem; there are updates on all statistics and public-opinion poll data.

Chapter 2: Poverty and Wealth A new chapter-opening vignette describes the struggle facing people living in the poorest county in the United States; a new section discusses intersection theory, illustrating the multiple disadvantages attached to race, ethnicity, and gender; a new A Defining Moment box describes how presidents Roosevelt and Johnson led the country to define poverty as a national problem; there is a new discussion of political alienation among the poor; all data on the social standing of the U.S. population, distribution of income and wealth, and poverty rates are the latest available.

Chapter 3: Racial and Ethnic Inequality An expanded chapter opening describes the practice of racial profiling by police; new research discusses the social construction of race; the chapter contains a new section on multiracial people; a new A Defining Moment feature describes how Rosa Parks sparked a social movement to end desegregation of public transportation; a new discussion of prejudice includes recent data collected from college students in an updated social distance study modeled on classic research by Emory Bogardus; new statistics provide the latest on racial and ethnic inequality as well as the size and social standing of major minority categories.

Chapter 4: Gender Inequality A new A World of Differences global map provides data on the relative power of women and men around the world; a new section explores the status of women in the U.S. military; a new A Global Perspective box describes the practice of female genital mutilation in Africa, the Middle East, and the United States; a new A Defining Moment feature describes the efforts of Elizabeth Cady Stanton to challenge gender stratification; the latest survey research and government statistical data document the social standing of U.S. women, citing gender breakdowns in income and types of employment, and demonstrating the continuing presence of the glass ceiling in the corporate world.

Chapter 5: Aging and Inequality A new chapter-opening vignette highlights the plight of many of today's older people who lost much of their savings in the recent economic recession; there is an updated A World of Differences global map on child labor; find an updated A Nation of Diversity map on the elderly population; there is an updated discussion of intersection theory highlighting the combined disadvantages faced by people in minority categories who reach old age; there is more detail about the causes of elder abuse; a new discussion highlights the growing need for elder caregiving; find statistical updates on the social standing of seniors in the United States; a new A Defining Moment feature describes how Dr. Jack Kevorkian pushed the right-to-die movement onto the national stage; there is a new section on the hospice movement including a new Personal Stories box describing the work of one hospice volunteer.

Chapter 6: Crime and Criminal Justice   A new chapter-opening vignette explores recent cases of corporate crime, explaining that the costs involved far exceed that of ordinary property crime; a new A Defining Moment feature highlights Ralph Nader's efforts to make corporations more accountable to the public; a new section describes the principle of due process that underlies the criminal justice system; an updated global map shows which nations make use of capital punishment; this chapter now includes completely new sections on community-based corrections, including probation and parole.

Chapter 7: Violence   A new chapter-opening vignette relates the story of the 2003 "Beltway snipers," who shot twenty-one people in and around the nation's capital; a new A Defining Moment feature explains how one Colorado doctor helped define child abuse as a social problem; new data identify the most violent television shows and movies; and a new Social Policy box describes education programs to assist adults who have engaged in the sexual abuse of children.

Chapter 8: Sexuality   A new chapter-opening vignette describes the 2003 decision of the U.S. Supreme Court striking down a Texas sodomy law, which helped expand tolerance toward homosexuality and offered legal support for gay marriage; a new A Defining Moment feature profiles the work of Alfred Kinsey in establishing sex as a legitimate topic of social research; a new section provides the latest on gay marriage; there is an update on public support for abortion under various circumstances; a new Dimensions of Difference figure shows how race and ethnicity are linked to support for abortion.

Chapter 9: Alcohol and Other Drugs   A new chapter-opening vignette highlights the troubling consequences of alcohol use among college students; a reorganization of the chapter provides a more logical flow of topics; there are updates on the use of illegal drugs in the United States; a new section assesses the government's claim that buying illegal drugs finances terrorism; a new A Defining Moments feature profiles Bill Wilson and the organization he founded—Alcoholics Anonymous; the chapter includes an update on the war on drugs reflecting policy of the Bush administration.

Chapter 10: Physical and Mental Health   A new chapter-opening vignette suggests that people with a mental illness may well be the most stigmatized category in the United States; the chapter includes statistical updates on the state of health in the United States as well as how people pay medical costs; find an update on the global and national AIDS epidemic; a new A Defining Moment feature profiles the efforts of Dorothea Dix to change society's view of people with mental illnesses; there is a new discussion of the shortage of nurses in the United States; also included is a new section that points to the rising number of U.S. students with mental health problems.

Chapter 11: Economy and Politics   A new chapter-opening vignette examines the problem of voter apathy in the United States; find the latest on campaign finance reform including the 2003 reform law; there are new data showing the extent of voter apathy in the United States; a new A Defining Moment feature describes how one eighty-nine-year-old great-grandmother sparked national interest in campaign finance reform; a new discussion, including a new Social Policy box, explains how people on both the right and left support big government, although for different purposes.

Chapter 12: Work and the Workplace   A new chapter-opening vignette describes the movement of white-collar jobs overseas; a new Social Policy box highlights Barbara Ehrenreich's fieldwork doing low-wage jobs; a new A Defining Moment feature describes the work of Eugene Debs to strengthen unions and improve the lives of working people in the United States; the chapter includes updates on all workplace statistics, including unemployment rates.

Chapter 13: Family   A new chapter-opening vignette points to the increasing use of genetic screening to create "designer" children; a new figure shows the chances of children in various family arrangements living with both biological parents until age eighteen; a new Personal Stories box highlights the crisis of foster care in the United States; there are statistical updates on family patterns, including divorce, singlehood, and single-parenting.

Chapter 14: Education   The chapter provides an update on bilingual education in California in the wake of Proposition 227; discussion now includes recent developments in the school choice debate; a new national map shows average teacher salaries for all the states in 2002–2003; find the latest statistical data tracking the academic performance of U.S. students; there is also coverage of the 2002 education bill.

Chapter 15: Urban Life A new chapter-opening vignette highlights the failure of high-rise housing for the poor with a look at Chicago's Cabrini–Green project; new data show the latest population trends shaping central cities and suburbs as well as the continuing pattern of white flight away from central cities; a new section looks at the impact of terrorism on the city's future; a new A Defining Moment feature profiles how the writing and photography of Jacob Riis helped turn public opinion against the tenement housing of a century ago.

Chapter 16: Population and Global Inequality A new chapter-opening vignette describes the trend toward smaller and smaller families in Japan; a new A Global Perspective box exposes the dangers of working in sweatshops in low-income nations; the chapter contains statistical updates on social standing in all the world's nations as well as the latest on global stratification.

Chapter 17: Population and Global Inequality A new chapter-opening vignette highlights the waste produced by today's consumer-oriented culture; there is expanded discussion of the problem of water supply in the United States and around the world; the discussion of environmental deficit now includes use of the I = PAT formula (impact is a function of population, affluence, and technology).

Chapter 18: War and Terrorism A new chapter-opening vignette is part of the coverage of the War in Iraq; there is an updated global map showing where conflicts in the world took place in 2002–2003; find the latest statistics on global military spending, and global terrorism as well as updates on the U.S. war against terrorism; there is a new discussion of terrorism as a new form of warfare; a new Social Policy box outlines the controversy surrounding the USA PATRIOT Act.

A WORD ABOUT LANGUAGE

The commitment of this text to representing the social diversity of the United States and the world carries with it the responsibility to use language thoughtfully. In most cases, we prefer the terms "African American" and "person of color" to the word "black." We use the terms "Hispanic" and "Latino" to refer to people of Spanish descent. Most tables and figures in the text refer to "Hispanics" because this is the term the U.S. Census Bureau uses when collecting statistical data about our population.

Students should realize, however, that many individuals do not describe themselves using these terms. Although the term "Hispanic" is commonly used in the eastern part of the United States, and "Latino" and the feminine form "Latina" are widely heard in the West, throughout the country people of Spanish descent identify with a particular ancestral nation, whether it be Argentina, Mexico, some other Latin American country, or Spain or Portugal in Europe.

The same holds for Asian Americans. Although this term is a useful shorthand in sociological analysis, most people of Asian descent think of themselves in terms of a specific country of origin (say, Japan, the Philippines, Taiwan, or Vietnam).

In this text, the term "Native American" refers to all the inhabitants of the Americas (including the Hawaiian Islands) whose ancestors lived here prior to the arrival of Europeans. Here again, however, most people in this broad category identify with their historical society (for example, Cherokee, Hopi, or Zuni). The term "American Indian" designates only those Native Americans who live in the continental United States, not including Native peoples living in Alaska or Hawaii.

Learning to think globally also leads us to use language carefully. This text avoids the word "American"—which literally designates two continents—to refer to just the United States. For example, when referring to this country, the term "U.S. economy" is more correct than the "American economy." This convention may seem a small point, but it implies the significant recognition that we in this country represent only one society (albeit a very important one) in the Americas.

A WORD ABOUT WEB SITES

Throughout each chapter of *Social Problems, Second Edition*, are Web Links that identify Web sites related to the topic under discussion. In addition, an end-of-chapter list called "Getting Connected: Useful Web Links" provides additional sources of information on the Internet.

We have made every effort to check the sites listed for quality and currency, but they may not be updated in a timely way. In some cases, sites may change or disappear entirely. In addition, keep in mind that the suggested sites offer various points of view on the topic at hand and the author and the publisher do not necessarily agree with everything—or even anything—found at the site. Students should always be critical of what they encounter on the Internet.

SUPPLEMENTS

The ancillary materials that accompany *Social Problem, Second Edition*, are a part of a complete learning package and have been carefully created to enhance the topics discussed in the text.

For the Instructor

Instructor's Resource Manual   For each chapter in the text, this valuable resource provides a detailed outline, list of objectives, discussion questions, and classroom activities.

Test Item File   A test item file is available in both printed and computerized forms. The file contains 1800 items—100 per chapter—in multiple-choice, true/false, short answer, and essay formats; the answers to all questions are page-referenced to the text.

TestGEN-EQ   This computerized software allows instructors to create their own personalized exams, to edit any or all of the existing test questions and to add new questions. Other special features of this program include random generation of test questions, creation of alternate versions of the same test, scrambling question sequence, and test preview before printing.

ABCNEWS   *ABC News/Prentice Hall Video Library for Sociology*   Prentice Hall and *ABC News* are working together to bring to you the best and most comprehensive video material available in the college market. Through its wide variety of award-winning programs—*Nightline, This Week, World News Tonight*, and *20/20*—ABC offers a resource for feature and documentary-style videos related to the chapters in *Social Problems, Second Edition*. The programs have high production quality, present substantial content, and are hosted by well-versed, well-known anchors.

    Appropriate volumes for this course include:
Volume V: Social Problems (0-13-437823-7)
Volume IX: Social Problems (0-13-095774-7)
Volume XI: Race and Ethnic Relations II (0-13-021134-6)
Volume XII: Institutions (0-13-021133-8)

Prentice Hall Color Transparencies: Social Problems   Full-color illustrations, charts, and other visual materials from the text as well as outside sources have been selected to make up this useful in-class tool. Please see your Prentice Hall sales representative for more details.

Instructor Resource CD-ROM   Pulling together all of the print and media assets available to instructors, this interactive CD allows instructors to have all of the ancillaries in one place. In addition, they can insert media—PowerPoint® slides, graphs, charts, maps—into their interactive classroom presentations

Distance Learning Solutions   Prentice Hall is committed to providing our leading content to the growing number of courses being delivered over the Internet by developing relationships with the leading vendors. Please visit our technology solutions site at http://www.prenhall.com/demo

For the Student

SocNotes Plus   A useful and exciting super study guide, *SocNotes Plus* is Prentice Hall's one-stop resource for students studying social problems. Designed around the chapters in *Social Problems, Second Edition*, it helps students keep their course notes and lecture information in order.

    Easy-to-use and portable, *SocNotes Plus* includes the following for each chapter of this text:

- Chapter outline
- Learning objectives
- Key terms
- A note-taking section that includes key concepts and art from the chapter presented in PowerPoint® slide format
- Two chapter review tests that include multiple-choice and true/false questions

SocNotes is FREE when packaged with new copies of this text. Please see your local Prentice Hall representative for more details.

Companion Website™   This online study guide provides unique support to help students with their studies in social problems. Featuring a variety of interactive learning tools, including online quizzes with immediate feedback, this site is a comprehensive resource organized according to the chapters in **Social Problems, Second Edition**. It can be found at www.prenhall.com/macionis.

 **OneSearch with Research Navigator™: Sociology**   This guide focuses on using **Research Navigator™**, Prentice Hall's own gateway to databases including *The New York Times* Search-by-Subject Archive, *ContentSelect™* Academic Journal Database powered by EBSCO, *The Financial Times*, and the *Best of the Web* Link Library. It also includes extensive appendices on documenting online sources and

on avoiding plagiarism. This guide, along with the Research Navigator™ access code, is free to students when packaged with *Social Problems, Second Edition*.

TIME **TIME Special Edition: Sociology** Prentice Hall and *TIME* Magazine are pleased to offer you and your students a chance to examine today's most current and compelling issues in an exciting new way. *TIME Special Edition: Sociology* offers a selection of twenty *TIME* articles on today's most current issues and debates in sociology. *TIME Special Edition* provides your students the full coverage, accessible writing, and bold photographs that *TIME* is known for. Free when packaged with *Social Problems, Second Edition*, it is perfect for discussion groups, in-class debates, or research assignments. Please see your local Prentice Hall representative for more information.

"10 Ways to Fight Hate" brochure (0-13-028146-8)   Produced by the Southern Poverty Law Center, the leading hate-crime and crime-watch organization in the United States, this free supplement walks students through ten steps that they can take on their own campus or in their own neighborhood to fight hate everyday

 ***The New York Times*/Prentice Hall eThemes of the Times** *The New York Times* and Prentice Hall are sponsoring *eThemes of the Times*, a program designed to enhance student access to current information relevant to the classroom. Through this program, the core subject matter provided in the text is supplemented by a collection of timely articles downloaded from one of the world's most distinguished newspapers, *The New York Times*. These articles demonstrate the vital, ongoing connection between what is learned in the classroom and what is happening in the world around us. Access to *The New York Times*/Prentice Hall *eThemes of the Times* is available on the *Social Problems, Second Edition* Companion Website™.

IN APPRECIATION

Many talented and hard-working women and men have had a hand in this revision. At the top of the list are members of the Prentice Hall editorial, production, and marketing teams, including Yolanda de Rooy, division president and Nancy Roberts, publisher, for all that they have done to support this book and ensure its high quality.

I offer thanks to Jill Lehan for providing the interior design of the book, which was coordinated at Prentice Hall by Anne Nieglos. Photo research was provided by Kathy Ringrose. Karen Trost did a wonderful job as development editor, giving generously of her time and energy in many ways, large and small. Thanks are also due to Carol Peschke for copyediting the manuscript. Barbara Reilly, production editor, made an enormous contribution to this project, untangling language, checking facts, and helping to make this book so attractive to the eye. She works skillfully, enthusiastically, and manages to do all this on time (authors should be so virtuous!). Marissa Feliberty, senior marketing manager, led the marketing efforts for the book. In addition, to all the sales managers and their staffs across the country, thank you for your faith in the book.

As always, whatever wisdom that has found its way into this book is a gift from many of the people who have reviewed all or parts of the manuscript:

Patrick Donnelly	University of Dayton
Sheryl Donovan	Tri County Technical College
Keith Fernsler	Dickinson State University
Deborah Franzman	Allan Hancock College
Lee F. Hamilton	New Mexico State University
Simona Hill	Susquehanna University
Brenda Hoke	Agnes Scott College
Amy Holzgang	Cerritos College
Kim M. King	Hiram College
Kevin LaPoint	The University of New Mexico
D. L. Peck	The University of Alabama
Scott B. Potter	Marion Technology College
Deirdre Rogers	Bowling Green State University
Kimberley Saliba	Portland Community College—Sylvania
Timothy R. Tuinstra	Kalamazoo Valley Community College
Deidre Tyler	Salt Lake Community College
Susan Weaver	Miami University
J. Dennis Willigan	The University of Utah

I also wish to thank the following colleagues whose insightful comments and suggestions contributed to the success of the first edition of this text: Mark Abrahamson (University of Connecticut), Lynn L.

Anderson, (Navarro College), Paul Becker (Morehead State University), Walter F. Carroll (Bridgewater State College), William M. Cross (Illinois College), Patrick G. Donnelly (University of Dayton), Marna Drum (The University of Akron), Keith Fernsler (Dickinson State University), Lorna E. Foster (Clinton Community College), Chad Hanson (Northcentral Tech), Michael Hart (Broward Community College), Simona J. Hill (Susquehanna University), Brenda A. Hoke (Agnes Scott College), Jeanne Humble (Lexington Community College), A. Leigh Ingram (University of Colorado— Denver), Lee C. Jones (Broward Community College), Kim M. King (Hiram College), Robert McNamara (Furman University), Dennis L. Peck (The University of Alabama), Luis Posas (Minnesota State University— Mankato), Dianne Sykes (Marian College), Kenrick S. Thompson (Arkansas State University), J. Dennis Willigan (University of Utah), and especially, Patricia Gagné (University of Louisville).

A PERSONAL NOTE

This revision has been written in the hope that it will stimulate a spirit of community and compassion that exists within each of us. Most of the readers of this book are quite privileged. The greatest danger of privilege is that it makes us feel distant from those who fare less well, as if the suffering of others takes nothing away from our own lives. But it does. We are all part of a single human community just as we share membership in one universe struggling to find the moral direction that some people think of as God and others conceive in terms of Justice. Either way, the suffering of anyone diminishes each one of us. Likewise, any thought or action that helps lift up another raises us up as well. Four centuries ago, the English poet and priest John Donne (1573–1631) beautifully expressed this idea when he wrote:

"No man is an island, entire of itself;
Every man is a piece of the continent,
A part of the main . . .
Any man's death diminishes me,
Because I am involved in mankind.
And therefore never send to know
For whom the bell tolls;
It tolls for thee."

A course in social problems is an invitation to become involved in the effort to make society better, a process that begins by recognizing that all of us— throughout the United States and around the world—are connected. Looking at others, we see something of ourselves; when we think of ourselves, we need to learn to take account of others. I believe that this text will make a difference to the extent that it encourages readers to think this way, nudging people toward an ethic of service. Serving others is the most important and most worthwhile activity for any human being. It is a choice than can be made by anyone and everyone. In 1968, Reverend Martin Luther King, Jr., put it this way:

> Everybody can be great, because everybody can serve. You don't have to have a college degree to serve. You don't have to make your subject and your verb agree to serve. You don't have to know about Plato and Aristotle to serve. You don't have to know Einstein's Theory of Relativity to serve. You don't have to know the Second Theory of Thermal Dynamics in Physics to serve. You only need a heart full of grace, a soul generated by love, and you can be that servant.

With love for all and in the hope that each of us can make a difference,

John J. Macionis

CHAPTER 1

© Paul Marcus, Saturday, Studio SPM, Inc.

SOCIOLOGY: STUDYING SOCIAL PROBLEMS

*P*EOPLE AT THE TRUCKING COMPANY WERE SADDENED *to learn of the death of Marvin Walters, who had been a company driver for more than thirty-five years. Marvin was well liked, and he had a reputation for being a safe operator who had never had a driving accident. But most were not surprised to learn of his death. Over the last few years, Marvin had called in sick a number of days. Then, last spring, he suffered a stroke and was rushed from his home to a nearby hospital, where doctors performed coronary bypass surgery. He hung on for several months after the operation, but then his health rapidly declined. One close friend was heard to say that it was a shame when a man dies like that at age sixty-three but, after all, look at how he lived. Marvin was notorious for eating nothing but greasy fast food whenever he was on the road. As long as anyone could remember, he had been severely overweight and in poor physical condition.*

The story of Marvin Walters is not an isolated case. According to government statistics, being overweight is common in the United States: Sixty-five percent of adults weigh at least ten pounds too much, and 30 percent weigh more than thirty pounds too much. Obesity is linked to a number of serious illnesses, including diabetes, heart disease, and stroke. People who are significantly overweight die, on average, seven years earlier than people who maintain a healthy weight. More than 300,000 people in the United States die each year from illnesses brought on by being too fat (U.S. National Center for Health Statistics, 2002).

Sociologists point out that unhealthy eating habits are part of our way of life. We live in what some analysts have called a "fast-food nation" where the typical person grabs junk-food snacks and fast-food meals far too often and consumes portions that are far too large—and are getting larger (portions *and* people) as time goes on (Schlosser, 2001; Blumenthal, 2002; Nash, 2002; Bellandi, 2003).

GETTING THE PICTURE

✦ What makes some issue a social problem?

Social problems come into being as a concerned group defines an issue as harmful and in need of change.

✦ Aren't we always dealing with the same problems?

Most of today's problems are not those that most concerned the public several generations ago.

✦ Isn't a social problem any condition that is harmful?

Many conditions harmful to thousands of people are never defined as social problems.

1

People experience social problems such as poverty or poor health in personal ways. Can you easily imagine how this mother wishes she could do more for her children? Sociology's main insight is that the problems we face are not simply the results of choices we make, but reflect the operation of society itself.

SEEING PATTERNS: THE SOCIOLOGICAL PERSPECTIVE

Common sense might lead us to think of the case of Marvin Walters simply as a lifetime of bad choices made by a single individual. However, when we apply the **sociological perspective,** *a point of view that highlights how society affects the experiences of individuals,* the picture changes. Using the sociological perspective, we see that the operation of U.S. society encourages tens of millions of people to overeat and consume too much unhealthful food.

Sociology is *the systematic study of human societies.* By **society,** we mean *people who live within some territory and share many patterns of behavior.* As they study society, sociologists pay attention to **culture,** *a way of life including widespread values (about what is good and bad), beliefs (about what is true), and behavior (what people do every day).* Although cultural patterns in the United States are diverse, one widely shared value is the importance of individualism, the idea that, for better or worse, people are responsible for their own lives. In the case of Marvin Walters, it is easy to say, "Well, he died because he ate too much for a long time; he really brought it on himself." In other words, our common sense often defines deaths of this kind—even hundreds of thousands of them every year—as matters of *personal choice.* Without denying that people do make choices, sociologists point to ways in which society shapes our lives. Thinking sociologically, we see widespread obesity that causes early death as a *social issue.*

Sociology's key insight is that the troubles people face have causes far beyond themselves. As U.S. sociologist C. Wright Mills (1916–1963) explained, using what he called the sociological perspective helps us to recognize this important fact. The Critical Thinking box takes a closer look at Mills's arguments.

For more on C. Wright Mills,
visit the Gallery of Sociologists at
http://www.TheSociologyPage.com

By asking us to look at the world in a new way, the sociological perspective gives us power to bring about change. But a sociological viewpoint can also be disturbing. A course in social problems asks us to face the fact that many members of our society have no jobs, have been victims of crime, and go to bed hungry through no fault of their own. In fact, in this richest of nations, tens of millions of people—especially women and children—are poor. The study of social problems helps us both to see these truths more clearly and to play a part in shaping the future of our nation and the world.

SOCIAL PROBLEMS: THE BASICS

A **social problem** is *a condition that undermines the well-being of some or all members of a society and that is usually a matter of public controversy.* According to this definition, "condition" refers to any situation that at least some people define as troublesome, such as

Critical Thinking

C. Wright Mills: Turning Personal Troubles into Social Issues

ALL OF US STRUGGLE WITH OUR OWN PROBLEMS, which might include marital conflict, unemployment, financial debt, drug or alcohol abuse, poor health, or even prostitution. We experience these problems on a personal, sometimes gut-wrenching level. But C. Wright Mills believed that the roots of such "personal" problems lie in society itself, often involving the ways our economy and political system work. After all, it is society that favors some categories of people over others: the rich over the poor, white people over people of color, middle-aged people over the young and very old. But when people grapple with their troubles individually, and don't see the bigger picture of how society operates, they end up feeling that "their lives are a series of traps. They sense that within their everyday worlds, they cannot overcome their troubles" (1959:3). In short, we live in an individualistic culture that makes us quick to conclude that the troubles we experience are simply our own fault.

A more accurate and effective approach is to understand that it is society that shapes our lives. Using the sociological perspective, we transform our "personal troubles" into "social issues" by realizing that they affect not only us but also countless people *like* us. This knowledge gives us power because, joining with others, we can improve our lives—and break free of our traps—as we set out to change society.

ISSUES AND EXERCISES

1. Provide three examples of "personal problems" that Mills would define as "social issues."

2. Give one or more examples of people in the past coming together to address their problems through collective action.

3. Have you ever taken part in a movement for change? Which one? What were your reasons for participating?

Source: Based on Mills (1959).

having no job, lacking enough money, fearing crime, being overweight, or worrying about the effects of toxic wastes buried in the ground.

A condition that "undermines well-being" hurts people, either by causing them immediate harm or, perhaps, by limiting their choices. For example, poverty not only deprives people of nutritious food and safe housing but also takes away their dignity, leaving them passive and powerless.

Because any issue affects various segments of our population differently, social problems are seldom harmful to *everyone*. Wars that bring death to young soldiers and civilians also bring wealth to those who make and sell weapons. As a result, it is difficult to assess the exact consequences of a particular social problem.

Social problems spark public controversy. Sometimes a social problem (such as the poor performance of public schools in Philadelphia, Cleveland, or other large cities) disturbs a significant number of people. In other cases (such as the outbreak of severe acute respiratory syndrome, or SARS), a small number of significant people (researchers and public health officials) have the power to take action that affects the larger society (by, say, restricting travel to areas with many infected people).

Social Problems over Time

What are our country's most serious social problems? The answer depends on whom you ask. But, as shown in Table 1–1 on page 4, the public's view of problems changes. A survey of U.S. adults in 1935 identified the ten biggest problems facing the country back then (Gallup, 1935); a similar survey in 2003 identified the top ten problems then (Newport, 2003). The Depression was the major concern in the mid-1930s because 25 percent of U.S. adults were out of work. Not surprisingly, unemployment topped the list of problems that year. By 2003, the recession put economic problems high on the list once again. Likewise, in both years, the public expressed the fear of war. However, these are the only two issues that appear on both lists.

TABLE 1–1   SERIOUS SOCIAL PROBLEMS: 1935 AND 2003

1935	2003
1. Unemployment and a poor economy	1. Danger of war
2. Inefficient government	2. Feelings of fear
3. Danger of war	3. Poor economy
4. High taxes	4. Unemployment
5. Government too involved in business	5. Terrorism
6. Labor conflict	6. State of the world
7. Poor farm conditions	7. Health care
8. Inadequate pensions for the elderly	8. A decline in morals
9. High concentration of wealth	9. A decline in families
10. Drinking alcohol	10. Poor public schools

Sources: Gallup (1935) and Newport (2003).

The Social-Constructionist Approach

The fact that, over time, people define different issues as social problems is the foundation of the **social-constructionist approach,** which holds that *social problems arise as people define conditions as undesirable and in need of change.* Following this approach, social problems have a subjective foundation, reflecting the subjective judgments people make about their world. Even though health officials say that most U.S. adults are overweight, for example, the public has yet to

define obesity as a serious social problem. This is true despite the objective fact that illness brought on by obesity costs the lives of 300,000 people in the country each year (100 times the death toll of the September 11, 2001, terror attacks).

Figure 1–1 further illustrates the interplay of the subjective and objective foundations of social problems. Box A includes issues—such as homicide—that are objectively very harmful (more than 16,000 people are murdered each year in the United States) and that cause widespread concern (polls show that a majority of U.S. adults worry about this kind of violent crime) (NORC, 2003). Box B includes issues—such as the use of automobiles—that, objectively speaking, cause even greater harm (about 42,000 people in the United States die each year in auto accidents) and yet are not widely regarded as social problems. Of course, one reason people accept this high death toll is that we consider automobiles necessary to our way of life. Box C represents issues—such as school shootings—that, objectively speaking, cause relatively little harm (only a few dozen people have died from such incidents, fewer than die from bee stings in a given year), but are widely viewed as serious problems (Sowell, 1999; U.S. Federal Bureau of Investigation, 2001; U.S. National Center for Health Statistics, 2003).

Consider this curious pattern: A century ago, it was objectively true that the social standing of women was far below that of men. In 1900, nine out of ten adult men worked for income, whereas nine of ten adult women stayed home doing housework and raising children. Women could not even legally vote.

Although some condemned this blatant inequality, most people did not define this situation as a problem. Why not? Most people believed that

FIGURE 1–1   The Objective and Subjective Assessment of Social Issues

This figure shows that some issues (such as homicide) are both objectively harmful and widely seen as harmful. But many issues that are objectively harmful (the use of automobiles results in some 42,000 deaths each year) are not perceived as a serious social problem. Likewise, some issues that are viewed as serious social problems (school shootings, for example) actually harm a very small number of people.

For centuries, people in the United States have relied on animals for food and clothing. Organizations such as People for the Ethical Treatment of Animals claim that killing animals to produce fur coats is wrong. Do you agree? What about slaughtering animals to provide meat?

because women and men are biologically different, they must have different abilities. Therefore, it seemed natural for men go out to earn a living while women—thought to be the weaker sex—stayed behind to manage the home. Objectively, gender inequality was huge; subjectively, however, it was rarely defined as a social problem.

Today, although women and men are much closer to being socially equal than they were in 1900, awareness of a "gender problem" in the United States has actually become greater. Why? Our cultural standards have changed, so that most people now see the two sexes as mostly the same and so they *expect* women and men to be socially equal. As a result, they perceive even smaller instances of gender inequality as a problem.

In sum, when we investigate social issues, it is important to consider both objective facts and subjective perceptions. Both play a part in the social construction of social problems (Spector & Kitsuse, 1977; Best, 1995; Loseke, 1999).

Claims Making

In 1981, the U.S. Centers for Disease Control and Prevention began to receive reports of a strange disease that was killing people, mostly homosexual men. The disease came to be known as AIDS (acquired immunodeficiency syndrome). For several years, even as the numbers of cases in the United States climbed into the thousands, there was limited media coverage and little public outcry (certainly far less than in the 2003 outbreak of SARS). By 1985, however, the public had become concerned about AIDS, and this disease was defined as a serious social problem.

What brought about the turnaround? For any issue to be defined as a social problem, people—usually a small number at first—make claims that the issue *should be* defined this way. In the case of AIDS, the gay community in large cities (notably San Francisco and New York) mobilized to spread information about the dangers posed by this deadly disease. In addition, the infection of one young boy, Ryan White, helped convince the public that AIDS was a threat to everyone; the Defining Moment box on page 6 tells how.

Claims making is *the process of trying to convince the public (and important public officials) that a particular issue or situation should be defined as a social problem.* Ordinary people can join together to make claims more effectively. In 1980, women who had lost children in auto accidents caused by drunk drivers joined together to form MADD, Mothers against Drunk Driving. In recent decades, students on college campuses have called attention to the problem of violence against women, drawing support from organizations such as Take Back the Night.

For more on Mothers against Drunk Driving, visit
http://www.madd.org

Because the mass media can convey information to tens of millions of people, television, radio, and newspapers are extremely important in the process of claims making. Through extensive coverage of a topic—whether it is the story of Ryan White or the war against terrorism—newspapers or other media

A DEFINING MOMENT

Ryan White: Changing the Face of AIDS

Ryan White was a courageous young man whose life and death changed the way people in the United States thought about AIDS.

I N 1971, THREE DAYS AFTER RYAN WAYNE WHITE was born, doctors told his parents the boy was a hemophiliac, meaning that his blood did not clot, so he could easily bleed to death. Blood treatments twice a week were prescribed, which allowed Ryan to lead a mostly normal life.

But, in 1984, everything changed. The thirteen-year-old came down with pneumonia and was back in the hospital for lung surgery. Shortly after the operation, doctors realized that the blood Ryan had received was infected with HIV (human immunodeficiency virus). They predicted that he had six months to live.

Ryan White's next problem was not medical, but social. In the mid-1980s, people knew little about HIV and AIDS, and most thought that even being in the same room with an infected person posed a deadly risk. Officials at Ryan's school informed his family that the boy was no longer welcome. After his parents filed a lawsuit, the school agreed to let Ryan continue, but they insisted that he use a private bathroom. Restaurants in town threw away any dishes and silverware he had touched. Someone vandalized his locker, writing "FAG" on the door (reflecting the incorrect belief, common at the time, that HIV was a disease only of homosexual men). Someone fired a gun at Ryan's house.

The family decided they had no choice but to move. It was then that Ryan's situation caught the attention of ABC Television, which made a movie of his life (Ryan himself acted in the movie, playing one of his friends). His story appeared in newspapers and magazines, and he spoke on dozens of television shows. In each case, Ryan helped teach the entire country two important facts: (1) HIV is not spread through casual contact, and (2) the disease endangers everyone.

Ryan White was a fighter, proving his doctors' prediction wrong by living until 1990. When he died, he was celebrated as a hero, a courageous young man who had changed the face of a deadly disease.

---

can go a long way toward making an issue a matter of national concern (Altheide, 2002).

Success in claims making can occur quickly; after September 11, 2001, for example, the president and other government officials moved terrorism to the top of the list of social problems. In other cases, the process may take years. Although experts estimate the death toll from accidents caused by driving while talking on cellular telephones matches the September 11, 2001, death toll each year, only a few states have passed laws banning this practice (Seaman, 2001; Alonso-Zaldivar, 2002).

As claims making gains public attention, it is likely to prompt counterclaims from opponents. In other words, most controversial issues involve claims making from at least two different positions. In the abortion controversy, for example, one side of the debate claims that abortion is the wrongful killing of unborn babies. The other side claims that abortion is a reproductive choice that should be made only by a pregnant woman. Politics, then, involves claims and counterclaims about what should (or should not) be defined as a social problem (Loseke, 1999; Best, 2001).

Success in claims making often is a matter of passing a law, which not only is a clear statement that some behavior is wrong but also enlists the power of government to oppose it. The passage of laws against stalking and sexual harassment clearly defined these behaviors as problems and allowed the criminal justice system to act against offenders (Welch, Dawson, & Nierobisz, 2002).

Problems and Social Movements

The process of defining a condition as a social problem almost always involves the efforts of people working together. A **social movement** is *an organized effort*

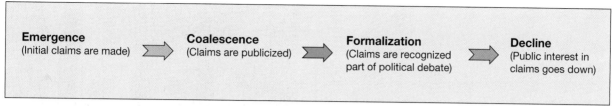

FIGURE 1–2 Four Stages in the Life Course of a Social Movement

Social movements typically pass through these four stages over time. How quickly this process unfolds varies from movement to movement.

to shape the way people think about an issue, thereby encouraging or discouraging social change. Over the last several decades, social movements have played a key part in the construction of numerous social problems, including the AIDS epidemic, sexual harassment, and family violence.

Stages in Social Movements   Typically, social movements progress through four distinct stages, shown in Figure 1–2, in their efforts to define a condition as a social problem (Blumer, 1969; Mauss, 1975; Tilly, 1978):

1. **Emergence.**   The emergence of a movement occurs when people (often few in number) engage in claims making about a particular issue. In the 1960s, for example, environmental leaders alerted the public to the fact that our way of life was harming the natural environment.

2. **Coalescence.**   The coalescence of a movement occurs as a new organization begins holding rallies and demonstrations, publicizing its beliefs, and engaging in political lobbying. A major step in the environmental movement occurred in 1970 as people across the United States joined in celebrating the first Earth Day.

3. **Formalization.**   Social movements become formalized as they become recognized players in political debate. At this point, the organization is no longer run entirely by volunteers but by a trained and salaried staff. The environmental movement became formalized when the government created the Environmental Protection Agency (EPA) in 1970 to monitor compliance with new environmental laws.

4. **Decline.**   Of course, becoming established is no guarantee of continuing success. Social movements may decline because they run out of money, because they fail to engage the public with their message, or because opposing organizations are more effective at claims making.

The environmental movement has lost some ground since 1980 because recent U.S. presidents have sought to limit government regulation of business.

Social Problems: Eight Assertions

Sociologists make eight important assertions about social problems. These statements form the foundation for everything that follows in this text.

1. **Social problems result from the ways in which society operates.**   Because U.S. culture stresses individualism, we tend to think that people are responsible for their own lives. But as C. Wright Mills (1959) pointed out, sociologists believe that social problems are caused less by personal failings than by the operation of society itself. In other words, a problem such as poverty results less from the fact that some people are lazy than it does from the way our economic and political systems operate. Correcting social problems, then, typically requires social change.

2. **Social problems are not caused by bad people.**   This is the flipside of the first assertion. It is true that individuals commit violent acts on the street, but the extent of crime depends not on individuals but on how society itself is organized. As Chapter 6 ("Crime and Criminal Justice") explains, a strong economy and the declining use of some dangerous drugs have brought the crime rate down over the last ten years.

3. **Social problems are socially constructed; that is, people come to define a condition as harmful and in need of change.**   Whatever the objective facts associated with a situation, people must come to see the condition as a serious problem.

4. **People see problems differently.**   Some issues such as the threat of terrorism in the wake

Compared with women fifty years ago, women today are much more equal to men in terms of rights and opportunities. Yet today's women are more likely to see gender inequality as a problem. Can you explain this apparent contradiction?

of the September 11, 2001, attacks are widely regarded as serious problems. But most issues are matters of controversy. For example, some people view President Bush's tax cut package as a good way to stimulate the economy, whereas others see the plan as a windfall for the rich.

5. **Definitions of problems change over time.** A century ago, the United States was a much poorer nation where no one was surprised to find people living on the streets of large cities. But as the country became richer, people began to think of safe housing as a basic right, and homelessness emerged as a social problem. Problems also go away as behavior norms change. Although most people defined premarital sex as a social problem fifty years ago, it raises far fewer eyebrows today.

6. **Problems involve (subjective) values as well as (objective) facts.** Today, almost half of all marriages end in divorce. But does this mean that there is a "divorce problem"? Facts are important, but so are subjective perceptions about any issue. People who value traditional families are likely to view a high divorce rate as a serious problem. But others who think family responsibilities limit the opportunities of individuals (especially women) may disagree.

7. **Many—but not all—problems can be solved.** One good reason to study social problems is to improve society. Sociologists believe that many

social problems can be reduced, if not eliminated entirely. Back in 1960, for example, 35 percent of elderly men and women in the United States lived below the poverty line. Since then, rising Social Security benefits and expanded pension programs provided by employers have reduced the poverty rate among seniors to less than one-third of what it used to be.

But sociologists do not expect that every social problem will be solved. As we have already noted, situations that are problems for some are advantageous to others, and sometimes those who benefit are powerful enough to prevent or slow the pace of change. For example, the United States remains the only industrial nation without a tax-funded system that helps pay for everyone's medical care. Although some 40 million people lack health insurance, political opposition to government-funded universal health care by organizations representing physicians and insurance companies has been a powerful barrier to change. Even problems that everyone wants to solve sometimes defy solution. For instance, just about everyone hopes that we will find for a cure for AIDS. But the research breakthrough that finally cures this disease may lie years in the future.

8. **Various social problems are related.** Many social problems are related to one another. This means that addressing one problem—say, reducing the number of children growing up in poverty—may in turn help to solve other

A Global Perspective

The Global Village: Problems around the World

To see just how desperate the lives of many of the world's 6.3 billion people really are, imagine the entire planet reduced to the size of a "global village" of 1,000 people. The global village contains 610 Asians, 130 Africans, 120 Europeans, 85 Latin Americans, 5 residents of Australia and the South Pacific, and just 50 North Americans, including 45 people from the United States.

The village is a very rich place with a vast array of goods and services. Yet anything beyond the basics is too expensive for almost everyone. This is because of economic inequality: The richest 100 villagers (10 percent) own half the entire village. By contrast, the worst-off 200 villagers (20 percent) are hungry every day and do not even have safe drinking water. Because of their deprivation, the poorest villagers have little energy to work and fall victim to life-threatening diseases.

Villagers boast of their fine schools. Yet only 75 people (7.5 percent) have a college degree (and just a few have doctorates), and about half the village's people cannot read or write.

As this example shows, half the world's people live with far less than those we in the United States call "poor." This harsh reality of suffering—detailed in Chapter 16 ("Population and World Hunger")—is one good reason to take a global perspective in our study of social problems.

ISSUES AND EXERCISES

1. Do any of the facts presented in this box surprise you? Which ones? Why?

2. Do people in rich nations have a responsibility to help solve problems in poor nations? Why or why not?

3. Research Navigator.com — Use Research Navigator™ to locate recent research and new stories about any country of interest to you (see the instructions on page 25).

Source: Data from the Population Reference Bureau and the United Nations, with calculations by the author.

---

problems, such as the high rate of high school dropouts, drug abuse, and crime.

It is also true that solving one problem may create a new problem that we did not expect. For example, a century ago the invention of the automobile helped people move about more easily, but soon automobiles were polluting the air and causing thousands of traffic deaths every year.

These eight assertions will help you gain a sociological understanding of social problems. In the following sections, we turn to another tool of analysis: sociological theory.

LOOKING BEYOND OURSELVES: A GLOBAL PERSPECTIVE

In recent years, the study of social problems has taken on a *global perspective*. A global outlook shows us, first, that harmful conditions often cross national boundaries. For example, Chapter 16 ("Population and World Hunger") explains that the problem

of population increase threatens the well-being of the entire planet. Chapter 17 ("Technology and the Environment") offers another example, showing how people (especially those living in rich countries) are consuming the planet's resources very quickly and polluting the planet's air and water.

Second, a global perspective shows us that many of the problems we face in this country are far more serious elsewhere. In a rich nation such as the United States, a baby born today can expect to live, on average, more than seventy-five years. But look at Global Map 1–1 on page 10 to see the typical age of death in poor regions of the world. Reaching sixty is common in the Asian nation of China; fifty years is typical in the South American nation of Brazil; in Africa, people in Libya average less than thirty years; and in the poor central African nation of Niger, more than half of people die before reaching the age of ten.

Many beginning students of sociology find it difficult to grasp the seriousness of social problems in places about which they know little. The Global Perspective box asks us to imagine the entire world as a

A WORLD OF DIFFERENCES

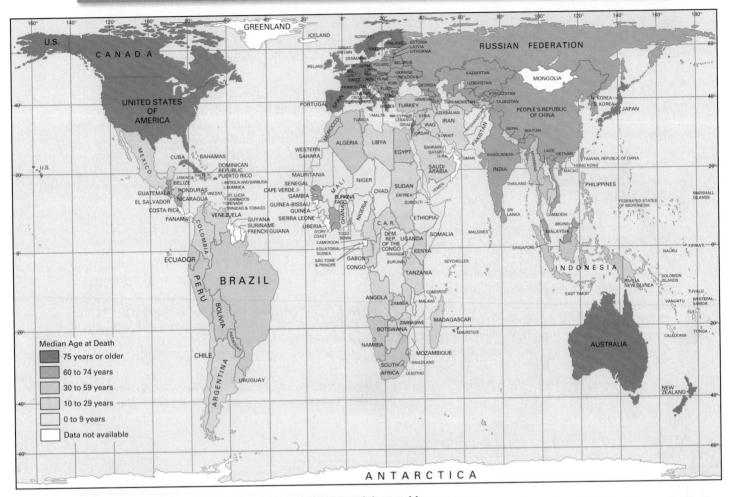

GLOBAL MAP 1–1   Median Age at Death around the World

By what age do half the people born at any given time die? In high-income nations including the United States, half the people born today will still be alive at seventy-five or beyond. In middle-income nations, including most of Latin America, most people die years or decades sooner. In low-income nations, including much of Africa, half of the population never lives to reach their tenth birthday.

Sources: The World Bank (1993) with updates by the author; map projection from *Peters Atlas of the World* (1990).

small village of 1,000 people in order to better understand the global problem of poverty.

ANALYZING SOCIAL PROBLEMS: THE ROLE OF THEORY

Sociologists weave various facts into meaning using **theory,** *a statement of how and why specific facts are related.* Building a theory, in turn, depends on a **theoretical approach,** *a basic image of one's subject matter* *that guides theory and research.* Using a particular theoretical approach leads sociologists to ask certain questions. The following sections present the discipline's three most widely used theoretical models: the structural-functional, social-conflict, and symbolic-interaction approaches.

The Structural-Functional Approach

The **structural-functional approach** is *a theoretical framework that sees society as a system of many interrelated* *parts.* Sociologists describe the main parts of this system as **social institutions,** *major spheres of social life, or societal subsystems, organized to meet a basic human need.* For example, the functionalist approach might explore how the family provides its members with a sense of belonging, how schools provide young people with the skills they need for adult life, how the economy produces and distributes material goods, how the political system sets national goals and priorities, and how religion gives our lives purpose and meaning.

Early Functionalism: Problems as Social Pathology

A century ago, functionalists looked on society as a living organism. This view gave rise to *social pathology theory,* a medical model that treats social problems as disruptions in society's normal operation. Crime, truancy, and premarital sex were all seen as "pathologies" (from a Greek word meaning "suffering" or "disease") that threatened the health of society. Because early functionalists saw society as good and healthy, they assumed that pathologies stemmed from deficient people.

English sociologist Herbert Spencer (1820–1903) used this approach, arguing that poverty resulted when people lacked personal ability and moral strength. Spencer based his thinking on the ideas of biologist Charles Darwin, who published a groundbreaking theory of evolution in 1859. Spencer's "social Darwinism" viewed the rich as society's most successful members and the poor as those who could not keep up. To Spencer, the harsh competition of the marketplace benefitted society by ensuring the "survival of the fittest." For this reason, Spencer opposed social welfare programs as harmful to society because they transfer wealth from what he saw as the most able people to the weakest ones.

Spencer enjoyed enormous popularity among rich industrialists of his day. But sociologists gradually turned against Spencer because there is no scientific basis to conclude that rich and powerful people are more worthy or able than others, nor that a competitive economy benefits everyone. Although social Darwinism commands little support among sociologists today, it still influences the thinking of many people (including politicians).

The "Chicago School": Problems as Disorganization

A second type of functionalist theory, often called the Chicago School because it originated at the University of Chicago (home of the first sociology department in the United States), linked problems not to deficient people but to social "disorganization" (Park

Disorganization theory claimed that a century ago, new industrial factories attracted many more immigrants than cities such as New York could readily absorb. More recently, social-conflict theories explain tenement housing as resulting from society's system of economic inequality. Which approach do you think better explains the plight of these New Yorkers back in 1900?

Jacob A. Riis, *Five Cents a Spot,* Unauthorized Lodging in Bayard Street Tenement, circa 1890. Museum of the City of New York, The Jacob A. Riis Collection (#155) (90.13.4.158).

& Burgess, 1921). *Social disorganization theory* holds that social problems arise when social change is so rapid that it overwhelms a society.

A century ago, the rapid growth of industrial cities and arrival of millions of immigrants seemed to disrupt neighborhoods, upset traditional family life, and filled schools to overflowing. Crime rose beyond what the police could control, and without enough housing for all the new arrivals, people lived on the streets.

In response to such problems, many Chicago sociologists in the 1920s and 1930s became active reformers. They supported local settlement houses, set up programs to teach English to immigrants, and, in a few cases, even ran for public office (Faris, 1967).

More Recent Functionalism: Problems as Dysfunctions

By about 1950, the functionalist approach changed its emphasis from activism to scientific analysis. Using this approach, many of today's sociologists study both positive functions (or *eufunctions*) and negative functions (*dysfunctions*),

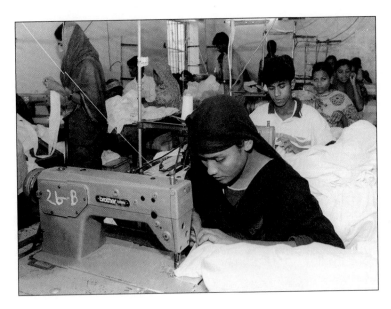

The structural-functionalist approach points to the contribution young people working in Bangladeshi factories make to their families' income. The social-conflict approach provides a different insight: Much of the clothing popular in the United States is made by young people in sweatshops that pay pennies an hour to workers.

pointing out that some functions are intended and widely recognized (called *manifest functions*) and others are unintended and less well known (called *latent functions*).

The explosive growth in the number of automobiles illustrates this approach. On the plus side, cars provide rapid transportation (a manifest function) and give young people the opportunity to get away from their parents' supervision (a latent function). On the minus side, some 225 million motor vehicles in this country cause environmental pollution, make our nation more dependent on foreign-produced oil, and result in some 42,000 highway deaths each year (U.S. National Center for Health Statistics, 2003).

Just as "good" things such as cars can have bad consequences, so "bad" things such as prostitution can sometimes do some good. Kingsley Davis (1971) argued that prostitution serves as a safety valve that relieves sexual strains on men and women in passionless marriages. In this way, Davis concludes, extramarital sexual activity can prevent some less-than-perfect marriages from breaking down entirely.

Critical evaluation. Although the structural-functional approach has been influential for more than a century, its importance has declined in recent decades. For one thing, many of today's sociologists have a renewed interest in activism and shy away from a "hands-off" approach that they think defends the status quo. For another, by viewing society as a well-operating system, the structural-functional approach glosses over social divisions based on race,

gender, and social class. Thus, since the 1960s, more attention has been paid to a second theoretical framework: the social-conflict approach.

The Social-Conflict Approach

The **social-conflict approach** is *a theoretical framework that sees society as divided by inequality and conflict.* In general, conflict theories claim that social problems arise from the fact that our society is divided into "haves" and "have-nots."

Marxism: Problems and Class Conflict   *Class conflict theory* is an explanation of social problems in terms of Karl Marx's theory of class struggle. Marx (1818–1883), a German-born thinker and social activist, was awed by how much the new industrial factories could produce. Yet Marx attacked the way society concentrated most of this wealth in the hands of a few. How, he wondered, could a society so rich contain so many who were so poor?

Marx devoted his life to analyzing *capitalism,* an economic system in which businesses are privately owned by people who operate them for profit. The business owners who make up the capitalist class are able to produce enough for everyone and therefore have the power to end human suffering. Yet Marx observed that capitalists care only about profit, not about the needs of people, creating social problems such as poverty.

Marx predicted that capitalism would bring about its own destruction. Under this economic system, Marx concluded, the rich would become ever richer, while the poor would endure rising misery. Industrial workers, whom he called the *proletariat*, performed hard labor in factories for low wages while facing the threat that machines eventually would strip them of their jobs. Marx was certain that workers, faced with little hope for the future, would join together and end this oppressive system.

As Chapter 2 ("Poverty and Wealth") explains, however, such a revolution has not yet happened, at least not in industrial-capitalist nations. But followers of Marx still advocate a radical restructuring of society as the best means to address many social problems.

Multiculturalism: Problems of Racial and Ethnic Inequality

Sociologists also see conflict based on color and culture. *Multicultural theory* is an explanation of social problems in terms of racial and ethnic inequality.

The great social diversity of the Western Hemisphere is the product of centuries of immigration. Every person who lives anywhere in the Americas, from the northern reaches of Canada to the southern tip of Chile, either migrated here or has an ancestor who did. Moreover, members of our society have always been keenly aware that race and ethnicity confer high prestige on some (especially the white Anglo-Saxon Protestants sometimes called WASPs) while devaluing others (especially people of color).

In 1865, the United States ended centuries of slavery, giving all people more equal standing before the law. Yet, as Chapter 3 ("Racial and Ethnic Inequality") points out, to this day minorities remain disadvantaged, at higher risk of poverty, poor health, street violence, and numerous other social problems. Just as important, the prejudice that persists in the United States means that some people see the very presence of minorities in their communities as a social problem.

Feminism: Problems and Gender Conflict

Feminism is *a political movement that seeks the social equality of women and men.* Feminists claim that women suffer more from poverty and many other social problems because society places men in positions of power over women. *Gender conflict theory* is the explanation of social problems in terms of men's dominance over women.

As Chapter 4 ("Gender Inequality") explains, the social standing of women and men has become more equal during this century. Even so, women working full time still earn just 77 percent as much as men do (U.S. Bureau of Labor Statistics, 2003). Also, in recent decades, a rising share of the poor are women

(especially single women) and their children. Just as important, from childhood to old age, women are subject to violence at the hands of men.

Critical evaluation. Offering a striking contrast to the functionalist vision of society as a well-integrated system, various social conflict approaches now dominate the study of social problems. But conflict theories, also have limitations.

Critics fault conflict analysis for overstating the significance of social divisions. They point out that members of our society have enjoyed a rising standard of living and therefore show little interest in Marxist class revolution. Moreover, although there is still much to be done, progress has been real: Women, African Americans, and other minorities have far more opportunities than they did in the past.

A second criticism is that social-conflict analysis seems to reject scientific objectivity in favor of political activism. Conflict theorists respond that in fact all theoretical orientations are politically "loaded"; they add that functionalism escapes some of this criticism only because it supports the status quo.

A final criticism, which applies to both the structural-functional and social-conflict approaches, is that these macro-level approaches make use of broad generalities that seem removed from how individuals actually experience their world. This concern has led to the development of a third major theoretical approach: the symbolic-interaction approach.

The Symbolic-Interaction Approach

The desire to describe society more in terms of how people experience the world underlies the **symbolic-interaction approach,** *a theoretical framework that sees society as the product of individuals interacting with one another.* We can apply this approach to social problems by asking two questions: (1) How do people become involved in problematic behavior? (2) More generally, how do people come to define issues as social problems in the first place?

Learning Theory: Problems and the Social Environment

Why do young people in one neighborhood get into more trouble than those who live in another neighborhood? *Learning theory* claims that people learn troublesome attitudes and behaviors from others around them. The point here is that

Reality is often less a matter of what people do than of how they define their own behavior. Studies show that many college students consume large amounts of alcohol on a regular basis. To these students, doing so may simply be "partying." College officials, however, may define such behavior as "binge drinking" and "alcohol abuse," which has serious consequences for a person's well-being.

no one sets out to become a burglar, a loan shark, a drug abuser, or an industrial polluter; rather, people gradually engage in such behavior as they learn skills and attitudes from others.

A learning approach guided Nanette Davis (1980, 2000) in her study of thirty women working as prostitutes. Interviewing these women, Davis discovered that no one simply decides to sell sex. Rather, she explains, a woman might turn to such a life for any number of reasons, perhaps as a way to cope with loneliness or a means of economic survival. Whatever the reason, Davis found, the women she studied typically "drifted" toward prostitution, usually taking years to learn the skills, norms, and attitudes that characterize the professional sex worker. In short, people learn such roles a little at a time, eventually reaching the point where the role becomes their livelihood as well as part of their social identity.

Labeling Theory: Problems and Social Definitions

The symbolic-interaction approach also explores how people socially construct reality. *Labeling theory* states that the reality of any particular situation depends on how people define it. For example, the spirited consumption of alcohol that young people view as normal partying may be labeled by college officials as dangerous binge-drinking.

The distinction between a "social drinker" and a "problem drinker" often depends on *which* audience is watching (do parents view drinking the same way that friends do?), *who* the actor is (do we view men who drink the same as women who do?), *where* the action takes place (is drinking in a park the same as drinking at a bar?), and *when* the action occurs (is drinking on Saturday night more acceptable than drinking on Sunday morning?). Obviously, many factors come into play as a people socially define a given situation.

Critical evaluation. The symbolic-interaction approach adds a micro or "real world" view of social problems. But by highlighting how individuals differ in their perceptions, this approach overlooks the extent to which social structure—say, class and race—shapes people's lives. In other words, pointing out that prostitution involves both learning and labeling is worthwhile, but we don't want to forget the broader issue of why men cast women into sexual roles in the first place.

This completes our introduction to the three basic theoretical approaches, summarized in Table 1–2. But sociologists not only use theory to analyze social problems, they also engage in research to gather relevant facts. Therefore, we turn to the ways in which sociologists conduct research.

FINDING THE FACTS: SOCIOLOGICAL RESEARCH

Many sociologists who devote their lives to investigating the nature and causes of social problems do so with the hope that they can help to make the world a better place. Barbara Ehrenreich (2001), for example, spent weeks working alongside low-wage workers in Florida, Maine, and Minnesota, documenting the many challenges faced by this country's "working poor." Simply being willing to work hard, she found, is sometimes not enough to escape poverty, a situation faced by millions of people in the United States.

Sociologist Lois Benjamin (1991) investigated the problem of racial prejudice. Is prejudice directed only at poor people, or are successful people also

TABLE 1–2 SOCIOLOGY'S THREE MAJOR THEORETICAL APPROACHES

THEORETICAL APPROACH	LEVEL	IMAGE OF SOCIETY	APPROACH TO PROBLEMS
Structural-functional	Macro	Society is a system of interrelated parts, all of which contribute to its overall operation	Claims that society is basically good; sees problems as the result of deficient people, too-rapid change, or dysfunctional consequences
Social-conflict	Macro	Society is a system of social inequality, whereby some benefit at the expense of others	Charges that problems stem from inequality in terms of class, race, and gender
Symbolic-interaction	Micro	Society arises from the ongoing interaction of individuals; people's perceptions of reality are varied and changing	Highlights how people learn attitudes and behavior and how people may or may not define situations as problems

victimized in this way? After interviewing 100 of the most successful African American men and women in the United States, Benjamin concluded that success provides no escape from prejudice. On the contrary, even black people at the top of their fields encounter the sting of racial hostility in their daily lives.

William Julius Wilson (1996) conducted interviews and examined available data in a major study of persistently poor people in Chicago. He found that these people contend with a host of social problems, including joblessness, unstable families, and, perhaps worst of all, a loss of hope. Wilson identified the key factor underlying these problems to be a rapid disappearance of work from the inner city.

These are just a few examples of the kinds of research being done by thousands of sociologists across the country. The following sections provide a brief description of the research methods used by Ehrenreich, Benjamin, Wilson, and many others to study social problems.

Research Methods

Sociologists use four major research methods in their investigation of social problems: surveys, field research, experimental research, and secondary analysis.

Survey Research: Asking Questions The most widely used research procedure is the **survey,** *a method by which a researcher asks subjects to respond to items in a questionnaire or interview.* A *questionnaire* is a series of items a researcher presents to subjects for their response. Researchers may deliver questionnaires in person, send them through the mail, or transmit questions using e-mail. Whatever technique

you use, the success of a project often rests on the ability to locate people. If you are studying, say, homeless people, identifying and tracking down subjects may be difficult because they may have no stable addresses. Alternatively, it would not be hard for researchers studying the medical system from the patient's point of view to find sick people in hospitals, but gaining access to them and getting them to complete a questionnaire might be more difficult.

The *interview* is a more personal survey technique in which a researcher meets face to face with respondents to discuss some issue. This interactive format allows an investigator to probe people's opinions with follow-up questions. Interviews are time-consuming, of course, which usually limits the number of people one can survey in this way. Whereas questionnaires offer the chance for greater *breadth* of opinion, interviews can provide greater *depth* of understanding.

Whether you use a questionnaire or an interview format, the key to a successful survey is selecting a sample of people that represents a larger population of interest. For example, researchers try to reach conclusions about all the police officers in a city by studying only a small number of them. To make a sample representative of a larger population, researchers usually select subjects randomly.

Sometimes, researchers pursue a *case study*, in which they focus on a single case: a person, an organization such as a college or gambling casino, or an event such as a rock concert or a hurricane. The advantage of this approach is that focusing on a single case allows greater detail and depth of understanding. However, because this strategy involves a single case, the researchers are less able to generalize their results.

Field Research: Joining In   Have you ever walked through an unfamiliar neighborhood and observed the people who lived there? If so, you have some experience with **field research** (also called "participant observation"), *a method by which researchers observe people while joining them in their everyday activities.* Field research might mean investigating a particular community to understand the problems and hopes of the people who live there. Elijah Anderson (1999) did this when he studied families in some of Philadelphia's poor African American neighborhoods. Anderson discovered that although most people in these neighborhoods had "decent" values, some had come to accept what Anderson calls "the code of the streets." Such people were likely to have weak family ties, to use drugs, and, especially among males, to engage in dangerous episodes of violence in an effort to maintain the respect of others.

Field studies involve several contradictions that researchers must resolve for themselves. For example, the researcher benefits from observing people in their natural surroundings. Yet as Anderson's work suggests, fieldwork can be dangerous, especially because it is typically carried out by a lone researcher. In addition, although this method is suitable for researchers with little money, it demands a sizable commitment of time, often a year or more. Finally, field researchers often experience a tension between the demands of being a *participant*, one who is personally involved in the setting, and an *observer*, one who adopts a more detached role in order to assess a setting or situation more objectively.

Experimental Research: Looking for Causes   Why are this country's prisons so violent? Philip Zimbardo and his colleagues investigated this question using an **experiment,** *a method by which a researcher investigates cause-and-effect relationships under highly controlled conditions.* Unlike field research, which takes place almost anywhere, most experiments are carried out in a specially designed laboratory. In this special setting, researchers alter one variable while keeping others the same; comparing outcomes allows them to track down specific causes of certain patterns of behavior.

To investigate the causes of jailhouse violence, Zimbardo built an artificial "prison" in the basement of the psychology building at Stanford University. He recruited male volunteers from among the university's students and then assigned the most physically and mentally healthy subjects to the roles of inmates and guards. After just a few days, Zimbardo was alarmed to see that on both sides of the bars,

people were becoming hostile and violent. In fact, the aggression was great enough that Zimbardo had to end the research for fear that someone would get seriously hurt.

Zimbardo's research highlights the responsibility researchers have for the safety and well-being of their subjects. His study also points to a fascinating conclusion: The prison system itself—not any personal problems on the part of inmates or guards—is the primary cause of prison violence (Zimbardo, 1972; Haney, Banks, & Zimbardo, 1973).

Secondary Analysis: Using Available Data   Sometimes all that is needed to study social problems is a trip to the local library. Easier still is logging onto the Internet, where a great deal of sociological information can be found. **Secondary analysis** is *a research method by which an investigator uses data originally collected by others.* In simple terms, why go to the trouble and expense of collecting information for yourself if suitable data already exist?

For many kinds of useful data,
visit the U.S. Census Bureau's Web site at
http://www.census.gov

The federal government collects a vast range of data about U.S. society. The Census Bureau continuously updates a statistical portrait of the U.S. population, counting people, tallying immigration, assessing patterns of health, and reporting levels of employment, income, education, and much more. Other government agencies also collect specific information; for example, the Federal Bureau of Investigation publishes a detailed account of crime in the United States.

Although secondary analysis often is quick and easy, this approach has its own problems. For one thing, a researcher who has not collected the data personally may be unaware of any bias or errors. Fortunately, however, the quality of government data typically is high, and the vast amount of material that is available will satisfy most researchers.

Truth, Science, and Politics

Whatever methods sociologists use to collect their data, there remains the crucial task of interpreting the results. It is one thing to collect facts but something else to explain what the facts mean. Sociologists turn to science in order to gather their data, but science offers no advice about how to use facts to address social problems. Although science can help us to learn, say, *how many* U.S. families are poor and

Critical Thinking
The Study of Social Problems: Science? Politics? Or Both?

How should sociologists tackle important and controversial issues such as poverty, family violence, and abortion? Should we simply try to discover the "facts"—reporting what is happening and why—and leave the political decisions to others? Or should we take a stand and actively try to change society for the better?

Sociologists have long debated how to square science and politics. No one wrestled more with this question than the German sociologist Max Weber (1864–1920), who urged his colleagues to focus on the "facts" in an effort to make research *value-free*. Weber knew that personal values lead people to choose one topic over another. But, Weber insisted, once research is underway social scientists should keep a professional objectivity in their work, holding their personal politics in check to avoid distorting results. In practice, this means that a researcher who personally supports the death penalty, for example, must be willing to accept results that might show that capital punishment has little or no effect on the murder rate. For Weber, the driving passion of sociology was to discover truth rather than to engage in politics and promote change.

In recent decades, however, an increasing number of sociologists have taken an opposing view. Many believe that sociology must be compassionate and that sociologists have a responsibility not just to learn about the world but to help people who suffer from poverty and prejudice. This might seem like taking sides—and it is. In defense of this value commitment, many sociologists (especially conflict theorists) argue that "objective" research is a myth because all theory and research data are bound to favor some category of people over another. If so, then all knowledge is political, and trying to be neutral is itself a political position that ends up favoring the status quo. In the end, they say, all sociologists must take one side or another on any issue they study. This activist orientation was the hallmark of Karl Marx, who summed up his view of this controversy (in words placed on his tombstone): "The philosophers have only interpreted the world in various ways; the point, however, is to change it."

ISSUES AND EXERCISES

1. Do you think researchers can be objective, or is all knowledge political? Give specific reasons for your position.

2. Some charge that standards of scientific correctness are being replaced by standards of "political correctness" on the campus and elsewhere. What is your view?

3. What about teaching? Should professors try to remain objective in front of a class (as Max Weber insisted), or should they express their personal values (as Karl Marx might have urged)? Ask several professors for their views.

---

even yield some insights as to *why* they are poor, science cannot tell us *what we should do* about poverty.

When we confront a social problem, we may use science to gather facts, which represent one kind of truth. But deciding how to respond to the problem always involves another kind of truth: our political values. The Critical Thinking box looks more closely at the relationship between facts and values in the study of social problems.

Truth and Statistics

Finally, a brief word about *statistics*, the numerical results that researchers include when they report their findings. Statistics are easy ways to characterize a large number of subjects, as when a professor announces that members of a class had an average grade of 85 on a midterm examination.

Many of us have been brought up to think of statistics as "facts." How often have we been told "the numbers don't lie"? But numbers may not always be so truthful, for two reasons.

First, like all research findings, numbers must be interpreted. A class exam average may be 85, but does that mean the students studied hard or that the exam was fairly easy? Or what? Similarly, one person can point out that the U.S. poverty rate was 12 percent in 2002 and interpret this as good news because

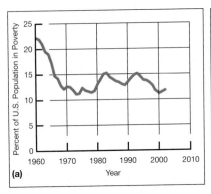
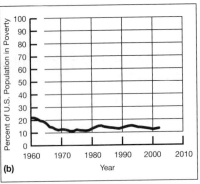
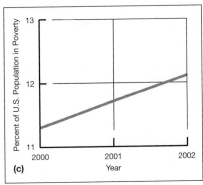

FIGURE 1–3   Do Statistics Lie?

Analysts, including sociologists, can "spin" their data to encourage readers to reach various conclusions. These three graphs are based on the same factual data. Yet the way we construct each graph suggests a different reality. The scale used in graph (a) gives the impression that, over time, the U.S. poverty rate has gone down. Graph (b) changes the scale to flatten the line, thus giving the impression that the poverty rate has changed little. Graph (c) presents data only for the years 2000, 2001, and 2002, giving the impression that the U.S. poverty rate is going up.

Source: Based on data from the U.S. Census Bureau (2003).

the rate has fallen in recent years. Another may see this as bad news because, in a rich country, tens of millions of people remain poor.

Second, organizations, politicians, and even sociologists often present their statistics in support of some preferred conclusion. How are we to know whether the statistics we read are presented in a misleading way? There is no easy answer, but here are three tips to make you a more critical reader:

1. **Check how people define their terms.** How people define terms affects the results. Even the most careful count of the poor will vary widely depending on how the researcher defines poverty.

2. **Remember that numbers are subject to error.** Even if we agree on how to define the poor, actually counting millions of poor women, men, and children is a very difficult task. This is especially true of those who are homeless and therefore difficult to contact. In most cases, government statistics end up undercounting poor, and especially homeless, people.

3. **People often "spin" their statistics.** What does a "steep decrease" in the homicide rate really mean? "Low unemployment" means low in relation to what? There are countless ways to select and present statistics, and you should expect people to do so in a way that advances the argument they are making.

Use special care when reading tables and graphs. Figure 1–3 illustrates the problem with three graphs showing changes in the official U.S. poverty rate. All are drawn from the same government data. Graph (a) might well be titled "Poverty Reduced!" because it has an expanded scale that makes the decline in poverty look big. Graph (b) uses a smaller scale to make change seem much smaller; one might label this figure "Poverty Holds Steady!" Graph (c), designed with a different scale, uses just three recent years to show a recent rise in poverty. Here we can announce "Poverty Going Up!"

Ideally, sociologists strive for accuracy, clarity, and fairness in their work and use statistical data with the intent to convey information rather than to mislead readers. But because researchers have to make choices about how to present their numbers, you should always think critically about statistical information, whether it appears in textbooks or anywhere else. Never assume statistics are the absolute truth.

RESPONDING TO SOCIAL PROBLEMS: SOCIAL POLICY

How does a society respond to social problems? This question brings us to the topic of **social policy,** *formal strategies to shape some dimension of social life.* Various organizations, including government agencies, create

Researchers have learned that the most effective policies to combat a social problem are those that are started early. That is, it makes more sense to try to teach youngsters, for example, the dangers of guns than to try to straighten out older men and women who use such weapons to commit crimes.

policy as a means to address social problems. Sociologists play an important role in formulating social policy. Over the years, sociologists have helped direct our nation's policy in dealing with racially segregated schools, poverty, pornography, health care, gun control, homelessness, racial discrimination, problems of family life, sexual harassment, and many other issues.

Policy Evaluation

How do we know whether a policy works? This important question is difficult to answer for three reasons (Weiss, 1972):

1. **How should we define "success"?**   There is more than one way to measure the success of any policy or program. Take, for example, a rehabilitation program for young people who abuse drugs. Does "success" mean that those completing the program stay "clean" for a year? Five years? Show a greater rate of completing high school? Or finding a job? Obviously, no single standard measures the success or failure of any policy or program. Therefore, researchers must assess different standards carefully, perhaps using more than one before deciding whether a particular program is a failure or a success.

2. **What are the costs of the policy or program?** In the real world of limited budgets and competing priorities, program evaluation involves weighing results against costs. It may be possible to greatly improve schools by increasing funding, for example, but a local community may not support raising property taxes.

    In addition to the financial costs of a program, there are ethical considerations. For example, installing surveillance cameras on public streets does reduce crime, or at least it drives criminal activity elsewhere. Yet many citizens object to having their every movement—including which stores they visit and with whom they strike up a conversation—recorded on videotape by public officials. In short, street surveillance may be "successful" in reducing crime yet involve an unacceptable cost by compromising people's privacy.

3. **Who should get the help?**   In assessing a social policy, another key question is whom the policy should target for assistance. To combat poverty, should agencies work with adults who need jobs? Provide a good breakfast to poor children in school? Provide prenatal care to pregnant women? All of these things may be helpful, but limited budgets rarely allow agencies to accomplish all their goals.

    One guideline for making decisions about whom to target for help is Benjamin Franklin's old saying that "An ounce of prevention is worth a pound of cure." Generally, the earlier the intervention, the more successful a policy is and the lower the costs. For example, helping young boys before they get into trouble costs far less—and does far more—than putting them in jail later on.

TABLE 1–3   THE POLITICAL SPECTRUM: A NATIONAL SURVEY, 2002

Survey Question: "We hear a lot of talk these days about liberals and conservatives. I'm going to show you a seven-point scale on which the political views people might hold are arranged from extremely liberal—point 1—to extremely conservative—point 7. Where would you place yourself on this scale?"

1	2	3	4	5	6	7
Extremely liberal	Liberal	Slightly liberal	Middle of the road	Slightly conservative	Conservative	Extremely conservative
3.4%	10.4%	11.6%	38.1%	15.2%	15.3%	3.0%

[Don't know/no answer 3.0%]

Source: General Social Surveys, 1972–2002: Cumulative Codebook (Chicago: National Opinion Research Center, 2003), p. 99.

Sherry Deane of the National Black Child Development Institute says that too many programs kick in too late: "We spend so much more money after the problem has occurred—after a baby is born at low birth weight, after a child begins to fail in school, after a child is in trouble with the law—instead of making an early investment in the child with prenatal care, preventive health care, early education" (cited in Goldman, 1991:5).

Policy and Culture

Social policy is also shaped by cultural values. That is, societies respond to a social problem in a particular way not necessarily because that approach is cheapest or works best but because a particular response seems like "the right thing to do."

As Chapter 2 ("Poverty and Wealth") explains, there are more than 30 million poor people in the United States, many living with inadequate nutrition, unsafe housing, and little or no medical care. Poverty persists in this country not because no one knows how to eliminate it; a policy to guarantee a minimum income for all U.S. families would end the problem very quickly. But because our way of life stresses self-reliance, there is not much support for "handout" policies of this kind. Guided by a culture that defines people as responsible for their social standing, we tend to see the poor as "undeserving" of assistance. As the next chapter describes in detail, such cultural values were at work when, in 1996, Congress and the White House acted with widespread public support to change public assistance programs so that fewer people were dependent on government support and more people took jobs.

Policy and Politics

The kinds of policies people favor depend on their political outlook. People with a politically conservative outlook usually try to limit the scope of societal change. Often, they favor policies that treat problems as shortcomings of particular individuals rather than as shortcomings of society. If the problem is unemployment, for example, conservatives might suggest helping jobless people get more schooling or learn new skills in order to make them more attractive to employers. In taking this more individualistic approach, conservatives are also saying that society is basically good the way it is; that is, they tend to support the status quo.

By contrast, people with more liberal views favor greater change in society. To combat unemployment, liberals might try to strengthen anti-discrimination laws, expand the power of labor unions, or call for government to create enough jobs to provide work for those who need it.

People with radical views seek policies that go beyond the reforms suggested by liberals. From their point of view, social problems are evidence that the entire system is flawed in some basic way. For example, Marxists see replacing the capitalist economy as the only real answer to unemployment. Because radical policies are, by definition, outside the political mainstream, they usually spark strong opposition. This is not to say that radical policies could not work; it simply means that they are usually very controversial.

We conclude this chapter—and each of the remaining chapters—with a discussion of how political attitudes lead people to define certain situations as problems in the first place and to define certain kinds of policies and programs as solutions to those problems.

Lower-income people tend to be very concerned about economic issues, for the simple reason that they lack economic security. Here, janitors in Long Beach, California, strike for higher wages. Higher-income people, by contrast, take economic security for granted. They are likely to be most concerned about social issues, such as women's rights. These suburban women are rallying in support of women's right to all forms of birth control.

POLITICS: CONSTRUCTING PROBLEMS AND DEFINING SOLUTIONS

We can illustrate the social-construction approach described earlier by exploring how political views guide people as they define social problems and devise solutions. We begin with a look at the political spectrum.

The Political Spectrum

Each of us becomes part of the political process as we form attitudes about various issues. Social scientists gauge people's opinions using a model called the **political spectrum,** *a continuum representing a range of political attitudes.* As shown in Table 1–3, attitudes on the political spectrum range from the far left at one extreme, through "middle of the road" views at the center, to the far right at the other extreme (Barone & Ujifusa, 1981; McBroom & Reed, 1990).

The data in Table 1–3 show that about 25 percent of people call themselves liberals (somewhat on the left), 38 percent consider themselves moderates (near the political center), and about 34 percent say that they are conservative (somewhat to the right). Just a small percentage describe themselves as being either extremely liberal (far to the left) or extremely conservative (far to the right) (NORC, 2003:99).

Over time, political attitudes may shift to the left (as they did in the 1960s) or to the right (as they did in the 1980s). But at any time there is always wide variation in people's political thinking. Some of this variation is regional: States such as Massachusetts and Minnesota almost always elect liberal candidates, whereas other states including Indiana and Texas usually elect conservatives. Similarly, some ethnic categories (such as Jews) historically have favored liberal positions, whereas others (such as Asian Americans) are more conservative.

What do terms such as "liberal" and "conservative" really mean? *Liberals* (from a Latin word for "free") think people should be free to decide, on their own, moral questions about how to live. On the other hand, *conservatives* look to the past for guidance about how to live and seek to conserve family and religious traditions.

Although liberals and conservatives differ in some important ways, both accept the existing political system. In contrast, people with more extreme views seek more basic change in society. Such attitudes are called *radical* (from Latin meaning "of the root") because they hold that the system must be changed right down to its roots.

Social and Economic Issues

People hold political attitudes on two kinds of issues. **Social issues** are *political debates involving* *moral judgments about how people should live.* Some of today's leading social issues include feminism, abortion, gay marriage, and the death penalty. People who lean to the left on social issues are called *social liberals.*

In general, social liberals think that people should shape their lifestyles for themselves. Thus, social liberals favor expanding opportunities for women, support the "pro-choice" side of the abortion controversy, and propose greater rights for gay and lesbian people, including legal marriage. Similarly, social liberals oppose the death penalty partly because, in the past, states have been more likely to execute African Americans than whites, as well as the poor compared with the rich, even for the same crimes.

People who lean to the right on social issues are called *social conservatives.* Social conservatives are respectful of traditional values and criticize what they see as too much individualism in today's society. Thus, social conservatives favor the "pro-life" side of the abortion controversy and support the traditional family in which women and men have different roles and responsibilities. Social conservatives also endorse the death penalty as a proper moral response to brutal criminal acts.

Economic issues are *political debates about how a society should distribute material resources.* Economic debates often focus on the degree to which the government should control the economy and reduce income disparity (Chapter 11, "Economy and Politics" tackles these issues in detail).

In general, *economic liberals* (leaning to the left on economic issues) favor government regulation of the economy in order to reduce inequality. A free-market system, they claim, too often works to the advantage of a select few and harms the many. For this reason, economic liberals support a higher minimum wage and high taxes on the rich to pay for social service programs that help the poor.

By contrast, *economic conservatives* (who lean to the right on economic issues) call for a smaller role for government in the economy. From their point of view, the market—not government officials—should set wage levels. Economic conservatives support lower tax rates in the belief that people should be able to keep more of their own earnings as they take responsibility for their own well-being.

Who Thinks What?

What types of people are likely to fall on each side of the political spectrum? Social standing is a good predictor, but it turns out that most people are

actually liberal on one kind of issue and conservative on the other.

People of high social position, with lots of schooling and above average wealth, tend to be liberal on social issues but conservative on economic issues. That is, highly educated people tend to be tolerant of lifestyle diversity (the liberal view), but many also seek to protect their wealth (the conservative position).

People with less education and wealth show the opposite pattern, taking a conservative stand on social issues and a liberal stand on economic issues. With a limited education, they tend to see moral issues more in clear-cut choices that are right or wrong (the socially conservative view). At the same time, poor people support government-enacted economic programs, which benefit them (making them economically liberal).

In sum, most people have a combination of liberal and conservative attitudes. This inconsistency helps explain why so many people call themselves "middle-of-the-roaders."

Finally, what about any differences between women and men? Research data suggest that if they are of the same social class, women and men hold roughly the same political attitudes. Even on abortion, which is often called a "woman's issue," men are as likely as women to support the liberal pro-choice position (NORC, 2003). However, political analysts have documented a "gender gap" in voting patterns: Men are somewhat more likely to vote for Republican candidates, whereas women favor Democrats. In the 2000 presidential election, for example, 54 percent of men but only 43 percent of women voted for Republican George W. Bush. Perhaps, in this age of social program cutbacks, women are more concerned about keeping an adequate social "safety net"—a Democratic position—to help those in need.

GOING ON FROM HERE

This chapter has presented the groundwork you will need for completing the rest of the book. Each chapter that follows presents research findings—information and statistical facts—related to the issue at hand. In addition, each chapter also applies sociology's major theoretical approaches—the structural-functional, social-conflict, and symbolic-interaction approaches—to understand the issues.

Most important to keep in mind, however, is that people socially construct social problems: What people define as a problem and what policies they are likely to favor as solutions depend on political attitudes. Therefore, instead of assuming what the "problems" are, this text will keep politics at center stage. In the remaining chapters, we will explain the different ideas conservatives, liberals, and radicals have about exactly what the "problem" is and what we ought to do about it. Indeed, one person's "solution" often turns out to be another's "problem."

What should you expect by the time you have finished reading this book? You will have learned a great deal about many social problems—in the United States and around the world—that command the attention of government officials and the public as a whole. Furthermore, you will be familiar with sociology's three theoretical approaches so that you can apply them to new issues as they arise. Finally, you will gain a firm grasp of the conservative, liberal, and radical views of society so that, as you encounter new issues in the future, you will be able to analyze them from each of these political perspectives. As you succeed in doing this, you will become an active participant in this nation's political process.

CHAPTER SUMMARY

1. Sociology is the systematic study of human society. The sociological perspective highlights how society shapes the lives of individuals.

2. A social problem is a condition that adversely affects all or part of a population, usually generating public controversy.

3. Both objective facts and subjective perceptions are important in people's understanding of social issues.

4. The social construction approach holds that problems arise as people define situations as harmful and in need of change.

5. Groups of people engage in claims making about social issues with the goal of influencing public opinion.

6. Social movements are important in the process of claims making, seeking to define certain issues as problems and certain policies as solutions.

7. Sociologists make a number of assertions about social problems, most importantly the idea that problems result less from the choices individuals make than from the operation of society.

8. A global perspective is important because many social problems cross national boundaries; in addition, many problems are more serious elsewhere in the world than they are in the United States.

9. Sociologists use theoretical approaches to guide their research and theory building. The major theoretical approaches—structural-functional, social-conflict, and symbolic-interaction—all provide insights into various social problems.

10. The structural-functional approach sees society as a complex system of many different parts. The early social pathology approach viewed problems as disruptions in society's normal operation. Later, functionalism developed a social disorganization approach that linked social problems to rapid change. Today, functionalism investigates both the functions and dysfunctions of all social patterns.

11. The social-conflict approach highlights social inequality. The class conflict approach, based on the ideas of Karl Marx, links social problems to the operation of a capitalist economic system. Multiculturalism spotlights problems arising from inequality between people in various racial and ethnic categories. Feminism links social problems to men's domination of women.

12. Unlike the macro-level structural-functional and social-conflict approaches, symbolic interaction is a micro-level approach. Here, we see how people experience social problems in their routine, everyday interaction. The learning approach links problems to learning skills and attitudes from others. The labeling approach investigates how and why people come to define certain behaviors as problematic and others as normal.

13. Sociologists use a variety of methods to investigate social problems: surveys (including questionnaires, interviews, and case studies), field research, experiments, and secondary analysis of existing data.

14. Although statistical data play an important part in the study of social problems, numbers can

mislead us. Readers need to be mindful of how researchers define concepts and how they choose to present their data.

15. Social policy consists of strategies to address problems. Societies enact certain policies based on results, costs, current political attitudes, and widespread cultural values.

16. The political spectrum is a model representing people's attitudes about social issues and economic issues.

17. Generally, people of high social position (highly educated and wealthy) are liberal on social issues and conservative on economic issues. People of low social position (with less schooling and little wealth) tend to be conservative on social issues and liberal on economic issues.

KEY CONCEPTS

sociological perspective   (p. 2) a point of view that highlights how society affects the experiences of individuals

sociology   (p. 2) the systematic study of human societies

society   (p. 2) people who live within some territory and share many patterns of behavior

culture   (p. 2) a way of life including widespread values (about what is good and bad), beliefs (about what is true), and behavior (what people do every day)

social problem   (p. 2) a condition that undermines the well-being of some or all members of a society and that is usually a matter of public controversy

social-constructionist approach   (p. 4) the assertion that social problems arise as people define conditions as undesirable and in need of change

claims making   (p. 5) the process of trying to convince the public (and important public officials) that a particular issue or situation should be defined as a social problem

social movement   (p. 6) an organized effort to shape the way people think about an issue, thereby encouraging or discouraging social change

theory   (p. 10) a statement of how and why specific facts are related

theoretical approach   (p. 10) a paradigm or basic image of one's subject matter that guides theory and research

structural-functional approach   (p. 10) a theoretical framework that sees society as a system of many interrelated parts

social institution   (p. 11) a major sphere of social life, or societal subsystem, organized to meet a basic human need

social-conflict approach   (p. 12) a theoretical framework that sees society as divided by inequality and conflict

feminism   (p. 13) a political movement that seeks the social equality of women and men

symbolic-interaction approach   (p. 13) a theoretical framework that sees society as the product of individuals interacting with one another

survey   (p. 15) a method by which a researcher asks subjects to respond to items in a questionnaire or interview

field research (participant observation)   (p. 16) a method by which researchers observe people while joining them in their everyday activities

experiment   (p. 16) a method by which a researcher investigates cause-and-effect relationships under highly controlled conditions

secondary analysis   (p. 16) a research method by which a researcher uses data originally collected by others

social policy   (p. 18) formal strategies to shape some dimension of social life

political spectrum   (p. 21) a continuum representing a range of political attitudes

social issues   (p. 21) political debates involving moral judgments about how people should live

economic issues   (p. 22) political debates about how society should distribute material resources

THINKING CRITICALLY: QUESTIONS AND ISSUES

1. Analyze the claims making expressed in the following slogans seen on bumper stickers: (a) "Guns don't kill people; people kill people"; (b) "It's a child, not a choice"; (c) "You can't make peace by preparing for war"; and (d) "No war for oil."

2. What kinds of questions might you ask about, say, poverty, using the structural-functional,

symbolic-interaction, and social-conflict approaches?

3. How would you describe your own views using the political spectrum? What are your views on social issues such as gay rights and on economic issues such as income inequality?

4. Explain how people's political attitudes affect the kind of issues they are likely to define as social problems. For example, what categories of people see "the breakdown of the traditional family" as a social problem? What categories of people are concerned about gender inequality?

GETTING INVOLVED: LEARNING ACTIVITIES

1. The sociological perspective can change the way we see the world around us. Take a "sociological tour" by walking around your own city. Where do rich and poor people live? What about people of different races or ethnic backgrounds? Note ways in which a sociological perspective changes the way you see your community.

2. Illustrate the importance of claims making by studying the history of domestic violence. One often-heard question is "Why doesn't the battered woman just leave?" Failing to provide an answer to this question may lead to the conclusion that women are to blame for their own victimization. How did the awareness of "battered women's syndrome"—a condition by which women learn to feel helpless and unable to change their situation—shift responsibility for the violence to abusive men? (For more, see Walker, 1984, and Rothenberg, 2002).

3. Every city and town contains many organizations engaged in community service. Pick one (ask family members or friends, or look through the Yellow Pages) and visit its local office. Ask about the organization's purpose and how it does its work. Is the organization making a difference in the community? How?

4. How much personal responsibility do you feel you have to help with social problems in your community? What about in the nation? The world as a whole? Have you ever taken specific action to address a social problem? If so, what did you do? If you have not, why not?

GETTING CONNECTED: USEFUL WEB LINKS

http://www.prenhall.com/macionis
Visit the interactive Companion Website™ that accompanies this text. Begin by clicking on the cover of your book. You will find a chapter-by-chapter study guide, practice tests, suggested Web links, and links to other relevant material.

http://www.TheSociologyPage.com
(or **http://www.macionis.com**)
This Web site offers information about the discipline of sociology, provides a sociological view of news events, lets you watch short videos about

sociology, and includes a full "Links Library" of Web destinations for organizations that provide sociological data and information.

http://www.gallup.org
This is the main page for the Gallup organization, where you can find information about political attitudes on various issues.

http://www.politicalresources.net
"Political Resources on the Web" is a site that describes political policies for a number of the world's nations.

GETTING STARTED ON YOUR OWN: RESEARCH NAVIGATOR™

Research Navigator.com
RESOURCES FOR COLLEGE RESEARCH ASSIGNMENTS

To access the full resources of Research Navigator™, please find the access code printed on the inside cover of *OneSearch with Research Navigator™: Sociology*. You may have received this booklet if your instructor recommended this guide be packaged with new textbooks. (If your book did not come with this printed guide, you can purchase one through your college bookstore). Visit our Research Navigator™ site at **http://www.ResearchNavigator.com** Once at this

site, click on REGISTER under New Users and enter your access code to create a personal Login Name and Password. (When revisiting the site, use the same Login Name and Password.) Browse the features of the Research Navigator™ Web site and search the databases of academic journals, newspapers, magazines, and Web links using keywords such as "social problems," "feminism," or "battered woman syndrome."

CHAPTER 2

© Paul Marcus, Upstairs–Downstairs, Studio SPM, Inc.

POVERTY AND WEALTH

*W*HERE IS THE POOREST PLACE IN THE *country? According to the U.S. Census Bureau, which collects information from people living in every one of the 3,066 counties that make up the United States, the unwelcome distinction of being poorest belongs to Loup County, Nebraska. How poor are the residents of this rural county near the center of that state? According to the latest government figures, the per capita (per person) income in Loup County was $6,606, far below the national average of about $30,000.*

The economy of Loup County is dying. The population has slipped downward to just 712 people. Why the decline? As big agricultural corporations buy up land, family farms are disappearing and there are no other jobs to be found. When asked how they manage to get by, people in town shake their heads. "About the only thing you can do," says one old-timer, "is wait for the welfare check. Or, [he cracks a faint smile] make drugs in your basement." A lack of jobs is one reason that both drug use and crime rates are rising rapidly in rural places such as Loup County. It is a sign that people are running out of options and running out of hope (Egan, 2002).

———————

GETTING THE PICTURE

✦ Is the United States a middle-class society?

The richest 20 percent of U.S. families earn almost as much as the remaining 80 percent of families combined; the richest 5 percent of U.S. families own about half of all privately held property.

✦ Do you think U.S. society is becoming more equal?

In recent decades, income inequality in the United States has increased.

✦ Are you on welfare?

Most government welfare does not go to the poor but to homeowners, farmers, corporations, and students.

The plight of people in Loup County, Nebraska, raises many questions that are all the more troubling because there are actually more than 30 million poor people in the United States. Why, in a nation that is rich, are so many people poor? Is poverty inevitable? Do people consider poverty a serious problem? What can be done about it?

This chapter examines poverty and wealth in the United States and provides answers to these questions. We begin by presenting some basic facts about the unequal distribution of economic resources in the United States.

People in the United States like to think that they live in a "middle-class society" in which everyone is, more or less, equal. In reality, however, almost half the income is earned by just 20 percent of U.S. families. Wealth is distributed even more unequally. What are some of the reasons that some enjoy luxuries while others lack even basic housing?

ECONOMIC INEQUALITY IN THE UNITED STATES

It doesn't take a sociologist to point out that some people have much more money than others. The evidence of economic inequality is everywhere: Large, fancy housing in one neighborhood stands in striking contrast to small, run-down homes across town; some children dress in the latest styles, eat nutritious meals, and have regular check-ups at the doctor, while others wear hand-me-downs, eat poorly, and go the emergency room only when they are badly injured or very sick.

These patterns are just some of the consequences of **social stratification**, *society's system of ranking categories of people in a hierarchy.* Stratification produces **social classes**, *categories of people who have similar access to resources and opportunities.* In other words, being born into a particular social class affects people's *life chances*, including how much schooling they receive, the kind of work they will do, and even how long they will live. Social stratification is a powerful system, and few people realize just how unequal people in the United States really are. We begin, then, with some important economic indicators.

Inequality of Income and Wealth

Any discussion of problems such as poverty must begin with a look at inequality in **income**, *salary or wages from a job plus earnings from investments or any*

other source. According to the U.S. government, the 2001 *median* family income—that is, the middle case if all families were ranked by income—was $51,407.

As Figure 2–1 shows, the highest-earning 20 percent of U.S. families (with income of at least $94,151 a year and averaging about $160,000) received 47.7 percent of all income. At the other end of the hierarchy, the lowest-paid 20 percent (with income below $20,000 a year and averaging $14,021) received just 4.2 percent of all income. In short, the high-income families earn more than ten times as much as the low-income families. Put another way, the highest-earning 20 percent of families earn almost as much as the remaining 80 percent of families combined.

Table 2–1 provides a more detailed look at the U.S. income distribution. Families in the top 10 percent earn at least $112,000 annually, those in the top 5 percent earn at least $164,000, and families in the top 1 percent receive more than $335,000 each year. At the very top, the highest-paid half of 1 percent of families earn more than $1.5 million each year. Thus, a small share of families earn as much money in a single year as a typical family earns in an entire lifetime.

Just as important, income inequality among U.S. families has been increasing. Between 1980 and 2001, the annual income of the highest-paid 20 percent of U.S. families (not necessarily the same actual families over the entire period) soared by 60 percent (from $100,000, on average, to about $160,000). During this period, people in the middle of the income distribution typically saw gains between 20 and

30 percent. Among the lowest-paid 20 percent of U.S. families, however, average income rose by just 7 percent. The overall pattern: All categories were better off, but the gains were huge for the rich and small for the poor, making income inequality greater than at any time in the last fifty years (U.S. Census Bureau, 2002). What do people think of this trend? The Critical Thinking box on page 30 provides some answers.

Inequality of income may be striking, but it is overshadowed by inequality of **wealth,** *the total economic assets owned by a person or family.* Wealth is made up of more than money earned; it also includes the value of homes, automobiles, stocks, bonds, real estate, and businesses. Figure 2–2 on page 31 shows that the wealthiest 20 percent of U.S. families own about 84 percent of all privately held wealth. Near the top, the very rich—those in the top 5 percent—own 60 percent of all wealth, and the super-rich in the top 1 percent control one-third of all private assets (Keister, 2000; Keister & Moller, 2000).

Given this extreme concentration of wealth, it is no surprise many ordinary people have little or no wealth at all. The second 20 percent of U.S. families owns about 11 percent of all wealth; although this includes some stocks and bonds, most is in the form of homes, automobiles, and other consumer goods. For about half of all U.S. families, wealth hardly exists at all. Ordinary families may own a home and other property, but these assets are roughly balanced by debts. Therefore, such families depend on their income and lack cash reserves to carry them through an emergency. In a world in which illness or unemployment can strike unexpectedly, many families are only one paycheck away from poverty.

Compare economic inequality in the United States with that found in Canada by visiting **http://www.ccsd.ca/facts.html**

Taxation

The government taxes people for three major reasons. First, and most important, taxes provide the government with the money it needs to operate. Second, the government uses taxes to discourage certain types of behavior; for example, the high taxes placed on cigarettes discourage smoking by making it more expensive. Third, and most important to this discussion, taxation is a means of reducing economic inequality.

The government reduces economic inequality through **progressive taxation,** *a policy that raises*

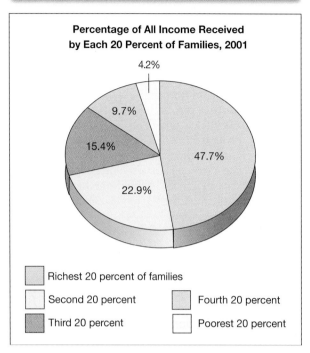

DIMENSIONS OF DIFFERENCE

Percentage of All Income Received by Each 20 Percent of Families, 2001

4.2%
9.7%
15.4%
22.9%
47.7%

Richest 20 percent of families
Second 20 percent
Third 20 percent
Fourth 20 percent
Poorest 20 percent

FIGURE 2–1 Distribution of Income in the United States

Income is unequally distributed, with the highest-earning one-fifth of U.S. families receiving 47.7 percent of all income. The lowest-earning one-fifth earn less than 10 percent as much: 4.2 percent of all income.

Source: U.S. Census Bureau (2002).

TABLE 2–1	U.S. FAMILY INCOME, 2001
HIGHEST PAID . . .	**ANNUALLY EARNS AT LEAST . . .**
0.5%	$1,500,000
1	335,000
5	164,000
10	112,000
20	94,000
30	74,000
40	63,000
50	53,000
60	41,000
70	31,000
80	24,000
90	10,000

Sources: Kennickell, Starr-McCluer, & Surette (2000), U.S. Census Bureau (2002), and author calculations.

Critical Thinking

"Haves" and "Have-Nots": Is Income Inequality a Problem?

IT IS A FACT THAT IN THE POOREST COMMUNITIES in the United States (such as Loup County, Nebraska; Chemung County, New York; and Bighorn County, Wyoming), people are lucky to clear $10,000 a year. In rich communities (such as Greenwich, Connecticut; Palm Beach, Florida; and Winnetka, Illinois) most people earn ten to twenty times that much. Should one person earn so much more than another? Is marked income inequality a problem? In a recent survey of a representative sample of U.S. adults, the National Opinion Research Center (NORC) asked about income inequality.

One item stated, *"Some people earn a lot of money, while others do not earn very much. In order to get people to work hard, do you think large differences in pay are necessary?"* In response, 67 percent of U.S. adults stated that large differences are necessary in order to get people to work hard; 27 percent disagreed, saying such differences are not needed (the remaining 6 percent had no opinion or did not answer). Rightly or wrongly, then, most people seem to think a lot of income inequality is needed to motivate people to do their best.

A second question asked, *"On the whole, do you think it should or should not be the government's responsibility to reduce the differences between the rich and the poor?"* In this case opinion was divided, with 43 percent saying the government should do this and 48 percent disagreeing (the remaining 9 percent were undecided or had no opinion). This item suggests that a significant share of people do think income differences are a problem.

A third item asked subjects to agree or disagree with the statement, *"Differences in income in America are too large."* In this case, 62 percent agreed, 20 percent said they neither agreed nor disagreed, and 12 percent disagreed (the remaining 6 percent had no opinion or did not respond).

The responses to these survey questions suggest that people do not think that income inequality has to be a problem and that people disagree about the government's role in reducing income inequality; however, two-thirds do think that differences in income in the United States are too big. In short, for many people, today's income inequality is a problem.

ISSUES AND EXERCISES

1. Do you think big differences in income are needed to motivate people to work hard? Why or why not?

2. Do the income differences we have presented seem too large to you? Why or why not?

3. Through taxes (higher on the rich than the poor) and social programs for those in need, government does lessen economic inequality. Should government do more? What should be done?

Source: NORC (2003):970, 1034, 1044.

---

tax rates as income increases. The idea is a modern-day version of Robin Hood, taking more from the rich (in taxes) and giving more to the poor (in assistance programs). As shown in Table 2–2, people with incomes between $15,000 and $25,000 pay, on average, 7.5 percent of their adjusted gross income in federal income tax; most receive government benefits that exceed their tax bill to boost their income. By contrast, people with incomes between $500,000 and $1,000,000 pay an average of 28.4 percent of their income, an amount that exceeds any benefits they may receive (U.S. Census Bureau, 2002).

Looking at dollars rather than rates, the same lower-income people (earning $15,000 to $25,000 a year) pay roughly $1,200 in federal income tax, whereas the higher-income people (with incomes from $500,000 to $1,000,000) pay an average of $192,428, or 160 times as much tax on incomes that are about forty times higher. At the high end, people earning more than $1 million per year (and averaging about $3 million) typically pay about $890,000 in income taxes (U.S. Census Bureau, 2002). Most high-income people also pay inheritance taxes as wealth passes from one generation to the next, which prompts them to use strategies such as annual gifts and trust funds to reduce these taxes (Bartlett, 2000).

Not all taxes are progressive. The tax on gasoline, for example, is *regressive* because, although the rate is the same for everyone, it ends up taking a bigger bite out of lower-income budgets. Moreover, many government tax policies (such as deductions for home mortgages, charitable contributions, and business expenses) typically benefit high-income people. Overall, our national tax policy does lessen income inequality somewhat, but when all tax policies are considered, it does not change the disparity very much.

THE RICH AND THE POOR: A SOCIAL PROFILE

Many families have roughly average income and wealth. But to sharpen our understanding of the extent of economic inequality in U.S. society, we now take a brief look at the two extremes: the rich and the poor.

The Rich

There is no standard definition of what it means to be "rich." We will define this category of the population in rough terms as falling in the top 10 percent of the income distribution. This means that a rich family has a six-figure income that, on average, is about $175,000 per year. Many men and women with high incomes are successful in business; others are distinguished physicians, lawyers, and college presidents (although, rarely, professors). Over their working lives, a good portion of the rich will become millionaires. Typically, they dress well, own large, comfortable homes, and command the respect of others. Many in this category are important decision makers, sitting on the boards of businesses and community organizations. In this elite category, we find a number of familiar names, such as Oprah Winfrey, one of the highest-paid people on television and a highly successful businesswoman.

At the very top of the income pyramid, wealth is truly staggering. One estimate placed the wealth of the ten richest families in the United States at about $225 billion, which is as much as 3.1 million average families, or the entire populations of Vermont, Arkansas, North Dakota, South Dakota, and Wyoming combined. One of these families—headed by Bill Gates, a founder and the largest shareholder in Microsoft Corporation—has roughly as much

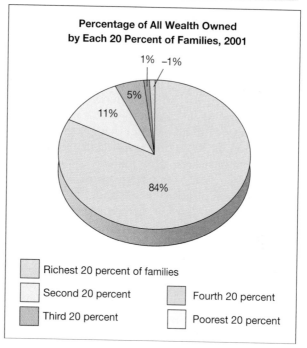

DIMENSIONS OF DIFFERENCE

Percentage of All Wealth Owned by Each 20 Percent of Families, 2001

1% –1%
5%
11%
84%

☐ Richest 20 percent of families

☐ Second 20 percent   ☐ Fourth 20 percent

☐ Third 20 percent   ☐ Poorest 20 percent

FIGURE 2–2 **Distribution of Wealth in the United States**

Wealth is distributed much more unequally than income is. Whereas the richest one-fifth of U.S. families control 84 percent of all privately owned wealth, the poorest one-fifth of families are in debt.

Source: Author estimates based on Keister (2000) and Russell & Mogelonsky (2000).

TABLE 2–2	PROGRESSIVE TAX ON INCOME, 2000	
ADJUSTED GROSS INCOME (AGI)	**AVERAGE TAX RATE (PERCENTAGE OF AGI)**	**AVERAGE INCOME TAX**
Less than $5,000	5.3%	$ 150
5,000–14,999	5.0	410
15,000–24,999	7.0	1,300
25,000–39,999	8.6	2,675
40,000–74,999	10.6	5,650
75,000–99,999	13.6	11,600
100,000–199,999	17.3	22,800
200,000–499,999	23.9	68,625
500,000–999,999	28.3	192,100
1,000,000 or more	29.2	920,000

Source: Author calculations from U.S. Census Bureau (2003) data.

money as 20 million "ordinary" people, equal to the population of Texas (*Forbes*, 2002).

What categories of people are most likely to be rich? In general, older people have more wealth because earnings rise through middle age. Men have more wealth than women do, as detailed in Chapter 4 ("Gender Inequality") because, on average, they earn one-third more than women. Married couples generally do better than single people because most benefit from double incomes. Finally, white people in the United States fare better than people of color. The Census Bureau (2003) reports that 33 percent of white families earn more than $75,000 annually, compared with just 16 percent of African American and 15 percent of Hispanic families.

Should we define the rich as a social problem? On one hand, the rich are successful people who are living out the "American dream," and many people see this as good. On the other hand, a society that distributes opportunity and wealth so unequally also leaves others behind: the poor.

The Poor

In a nation of great wealth, there are regions such as Loup County, Nebraska, described in the opening to this chapter, where people are lucky to find jobs. Indeed, across the United States millions of families struggle to get the food they need and to pay the monthly rent. The government counts one-fifth of all U.S. children as poor, and many of these children experience the same kind of hunger found in many low-income countries in Latin America, Africa, and Asia (a full discussion of global poverty and hunger is found in Chapter 16, "Population and Global Inequality").

TABLE 2–3	U.S. GOVERNMENT POVERTY THRESHOLD BY FAMILY TYPE, 2002
One person	9,183
Two persons	11,756
Three persons	14,348
Four persons	18,392
Five persons	21,744
Six persons	24,576
Seven persons	28,001
Eight persons	30,907
Nine or more persons	37,062

Source: U.S. Census Bureau (2003).

The Poverty Line

How many poor people are there in the United States? Back in 1964, when the federal government launched a "war on poverty," officials devised what they called the **poverty line,** *a standard set by the U.S. government for the purpose of counting the poor.* The poverty line is a level of annual income below which a person or family is defined as poor and therefore entitled to government assistance. In 2002, 34.6 million people out of a total 285 million—giving a *poverty rate* of 12.1 percent of the population—lived in a household with income (not counting government noncash benefits such as food stamps, Medicaid, and public housing) below the poverty line.

A report on food scarcity in the United States is found at
http://www.econ.ag.gov/epubs/pdf/fanrr2/fanrr2.pdf

The Department of Agriculture set the poverty line to represent an annual income three times what a family has to spend in order to eat a basic, nutritious diet. Every year, government officials adjust this dollar amount to reflect the changing cost of living. In 2002, the poverty line for a nonfarm family of four was $18,392; poverty thresholds by family size are shown in Table 2–3.

How easily can a family live on poverty line income? Many analysts claim it is difficult. Realistically, they suggest, it would take an income at least 25 percent higher to make a family economically secure. They add that the government sets the poverty line low to make the poverty problem seem smaller (Schwarz, 1992; Ehrenreich, 2001; Lichter & Crowley, 2002). The Personal Stories box lets you see for yourself how well a family can meet basic needs with income at the poverty line.

The Poverty Gap

Most poor families in the United States live on much less than the poverty line income. The **poverty gap** is *the difference between the actual income of the typical poor household and the official poverty line.* The poverty gap has been growing in recent years.

As the story of the Perkins family in the Personal Stories box suggests, it is hard enough to live on poverty line income. But in 2002 the average poor family in the United States had an income of about $11,000, which is a poverty gap of more than $7,000 (U.S. Census Bureau, 2003). In human terms, the greater the poverty gap, the greater the hardship caused by poverty.

Personal Stories — The Reality of Poverty: Living on the Edge

ZACH PERKINS, WHO LIVES IN RICHMOND, INDIANA, knows how hard it is to live at the poverty line. Zach had worked seven years building school buses in a nearby factory before he was laid off eighteen months ago. He now looks after seven-year-old twins Michael and Sonya while Sandy Perkins works in a fast-food restaurant. Sandy earns a little more than minimum wage—$6.25 an hour—for forty-eight hours each week year-round, for a yearly income of $15,600. Zach earns another $300 per month doing part-time work, which boosts the family's total annual earnings to about $19,000, just above the official poverty line for a family of four, which in 2002 was $18,392.

The Perkins family budgets $6,000, about one-third of their income, for food, which amounts to $16 per day. For this amount to provide three meals for four people, the family can spend just $1.25 per meal. "You know," says Sandy with a look of pain, "that's not even enough to eat in the Burger King where I work." Although it is enough to buy low-cost foods (such as spaghetti and eggs), it is not enough to ensure regular meals with meat and fresh vegetables.

If they manage to stay within their annual food budget, the Perkins family will have to meet all their other expenses for the year with $13,000, or about $1,100 per month. The monthly rent on a simple but adequate mobile home is $525 (they were lucky to find a rental house well below the national average rent level of about $700). But their utilities (gas, electricity, and water) add another $200 monthly. Then gasoline, insurance, and repair for the old car that Sandy uses to go to and from work add another $175 to their monthly total. So far, total expenses come to $900, leaving the Perkins family with $200 (about $7 per day) to cover the cost of clothes for the entire family, everyone's medical and dental care, repairs on their washing machine, television, and other home appliances, school supplies and toys for the children, and other household items. Obviously, at this income level, the family has little money for entertainment or child care, and they cannot even consider buying a new car, owning their home, giving music lessons to the children, saving for college, or taking a vacation (like many minimum-wage workers, Sandy gets no paid vacation). "I have to be very careful with my clothes," jokes Zach. "By the time I can afford new ones, these will probably be back in style."

Zach adds firmly: "This family will *never* ask for a handout." Seated across the room, Sandy nods in agreement. Like everyone else, the poor are proud, but Zach and Sandy are uneasy knowing that they are gradually falling behind in their bills.

Can a family survive at the poverty level? Yes, but only with careful attention to every dollar they spend. Getting by also depends of a good bit of luck: The family must face no unplanned expenses, which means they all must manage to stay healthy. "Am I sure we can get by?" says Zach, looking down at the floor. "I guess not. But I do know one thing: We have to try."

ISSUES AND EXERCISES

1. Do you think a family can survive with a poverty line income? Why or why not?

2. In what ways does growing up in a poor family limit the chances of children to succeed as adults?

3. Do you think society has some obligation to assist families such as this one? Why or why not?

The Poor: A Closer Look

In 2002, the federal government counted 34.6 million men, women, and children—12.1 percent of the U.S. population—as poor. As shown in Figure 2–3 on page 34, the poverty rate was 22 percent in 1960 and fell to about 12 percent by the mid-1970s, rising and falling since then.

As you might expect, the categories of people at risk of being poor are quite different from those likely to be rich. We can profile the U.S. poor according to age, race, gender, family patterns, and residence.

Age The age category at greatest risk of poverty is children, who make up 35 percent of the U.S.

DIMENSIONS OF DIFFERENCE

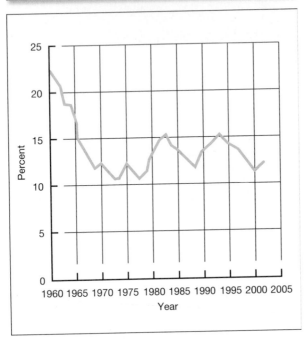

FIGURE 2–3   **The Poverty Rate in the United States, 1960–2001**

The poverty rate declined sharply in the 1960s, rising and falling since then but always staying above 10 percent of the U.S. population.

Source: U.S. Census Bureau (2002).

poor. In 2002, 12.1 million (16.7 percent) of young people under the age of eighteen were living in poor households. More seriously, almost half of these children live in families with incomes no more than *half* the poverty line ($9,000 or less). A generation ago, the elderly were most likely to be poor. Today, however, poverty wears a youthful face, as the Social Policy box explains.

Race   Many people in the United States link being poor with being African American or Hispanic. But there are more white people than black people who are poor, just as there are more non-Hispanic than Hispanic people living in poverty.

It is true that the *percentage* of minority people who are poor is higher than that of whites. In 2002, about 24.1 percent of African Americans, 21.8 percent of Hispanics, and 10.1 percent of Asian Americans were poor, compared to 8.0 percent of non-Hispanic whites. In other words, African Americans, Hispanics, and Asian Americans are at higher risk of being poor. This is why more than half of all poor people in the United States fall into these disadvantaged categories (Altonji et al., 2000; U.S. Census Bureau, 2003).

Gender   Women, too, are at greater risk of poverty: Fifty-six percent of all U.S. adults who are poor are women and 44 percent are men. The gender gap has become so large that sociologists have coined the term **feminization of poverty** to refer to *the fact that women represent an increasing share of the poor.* In 1960, most poor families contained both men and women; today, by contrast, 50 percent of poor families are headed by a woman with no husband present (U.S. Census Bureau, 2003).

Family Patterns   In general, marriage greatly reduces the risk of being poor. Whereas 5.3 percent of married couples are poor, 17.4 percent of single men and 22.6 percent of single women live in poverty (U.S. Census Bureau, 2003).

Single women with children are at even higher risk of poverty because, in order to care for their children, many do not work (or, in many cases, they cannot afford the child care they need to go to work). For all single mothers, the poverty rate in 2002 was 27 percent. Single African American or Hispanic mothers bear an added risk: About 35 percent have incomes below the poverty line. If the mother is also young and has not completed high school, poverty is almost a certainty (U.S. Census Bureau, 2003).

It is not surprising, then, that divorce raises the odds of poverty for adults and, especially, children. One study found that, within a year, one in eight children of divorcing parents had slipped below the poverty line. Once poor, such children usually live with their mothers and are likely to remain poor (Furstenburg & Cherlin, 1991).

Region   The official poverty rate varies from state to state, from a low of 5.8 percent in New Hampshire and 6.5 percent in Minnesota to a high of 18.4 percent in Mississippi and 19.8 percent in Arkansas. By region, the South (13.8 percent) and the West (12.4 percent) have higher poverty rates, followed by the Northeast (10.9 percent) and the Midwest (10.3 percent) (U.S. Census Bureau, 2003).

Many people link poverty with the inner city. Most poor people, just like most affluent people, live in urban areas today. But as National Map 2–1 on page 36 shows, average household income is lower in rural areas than urban areas. Indeed, poverty is widespread across Appalachia (including West Virginia and Kentucky), along the Texas border with

Social Policy   The United States: A Land of Poor Children

DESPITE THE ENORMOUS WEALTH OF THE UNITED STATES, one in six children under the age of eighteen (12 million boys and girls) is poor. Since the "war on poverty" began in 1964, the nation has managed to cut poverty among senior citizens by more than half. Yet the rate of child poverty is about the same today as it was then.

Most people have a distorted view of who poor children are. One stereotype is of African American children living in an inner city with a teenage mother who is on welfare. But in truth, two-thirds of poor children are white, and more than half live not in inner cities but throughout urban and rural areas.

Why so many poor children? Liberals point to the loss of good-paying jobs in the United States. In inner cities, where factories have closed, and in declining rural communities, many people simply cannot find good jobs. Conservatives note the role of family breakdown in the rising tide of poverty. They point out that about two-thirds of poor children live with a single parent, and 80 percent of these households have no adult working full time (U.S. Census Bureau, 2003).

Everyone agrees that children, wherever they live, are not to blame for their own poverty. Why, then, do we continue to tolerate their suffering? As a practical matter, isn't reducing the crushing experience of child poverty easier and less costly than dealing with the problems that come later, such as unemployment, drug use, crime, and violence?

ISSUES AND EXERCISES

1. Of the liberal and conservative explanations for the high rate of child poverty, which seems more correct? Why?

2. Few people think children themselves are responsible for being poor. Why, then, isn't there more popular support for increasing assistance to poor families with children?

3. [Research Navigator.com] Use Research Navigator™ to learn more about child poverty. (See instructions on page 25; keyword: "child poverty")

Sources: Children's Defense Fund (1995), Gilens (1999), Lichter & Crowley (2002), U.S. Census Bureau (2003).

Mexico (where many new immigrants live), and in parts of the Great Plains and the Southwest (especially on American Indian lands). In 2002, 14.2 percent of the rural population was poor, compared with 11.6 percent for people in urban areas or, looking more closely, 16.7 percent of people in central cities and 8.9 percent of people in suburbs (U.S. Census Bureau, 2003). Why do suburban areas show an advantage when it comes to income? By and large, poverty is lowest in areas that offer more jobs and more educational opportunity.

Working Families: Working Harder

Keep in mind that economic struggle is not limited to the poor. On the contrary, in recent decades, "the American Dream"—the belief that, with hard work, people can have a secure and improving way of life—has been shaken by some disturbing facts. Beginning about 1970, many U.S. families found themselves working harder than ever yet feeling that they were falling behind (Levy, 1987; Russell, 1995; Ehrenreich, 2001).

What's going on? For some families, of course, times have never been better. But for a large share of workers, income has nearly stalled. The earnings of a typical fifty-year-old man working full time jumped 50 percent between 1958 and 1973 in dollars controlled for inflation. Between 1973 and 2002, however, the same type of worker's income increased only half as much, so he had to work more hours to meet the rising costs of housing, college tuition, and medical care. Wage increases for younger workers have been very small over the last twenty years. This is the major reason that more than half (53 percent) of women and men between the ages of eighteen and twenty-four are living with their parents (Russell, 1995; U.S. Census Bureau, 2003).

A NATION OF DIVERSITY

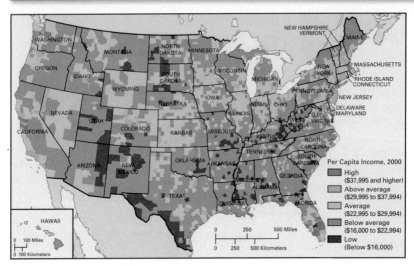

NATIONAL MAP 2–1

Per Capita Income across the United States

This map shows the median (middle case) personal income—that is, how much a person has to spend in a year—for counties across the United States in 2000. Counties shown in dark green are those with the highest personal income; counties shown in dark red are those where the typical person lives close to the poverty line. What can you say about the pattern of rich and poor counties? Does the map suggest a link between income and living in an urban versus rural county?

Source: American Demographics, April 2000, pp. 42–43. © 2000 *American Demographics* magazine. Courtesy of Intertec Publishing/A Primedia Company. All rights reserved.

Underlying this pattern of stalled earnings are changes in the economy detailed in Chapter 12 ("Work and the Workplace"). Through much of the twentieth century, the U.S. economy created jobs with *higher* pay; for example, low-paying farm jobs were replaced with higher-paying factory work. In recent decades, however, most new jobs have been in the service sector (including sales positions, computer data entry, and food service); jobs of this kind pay *less* than the factory jobs they are replacing.

The Working Poor

We introduced you to sociologist Barbara Ehrenreich in Chapter 1. She wanted to see for herself what it is like to be a low-wage worker, so she left her comfortable life as a writer to spend several months in Florida, Maine, and Minnesota, pretending to be in need of work, taking whatever jobs she could find, and trying to live on what she earned. Ehrenreich found that it was not easy. At the end of her journey, she explained (2001:220),

> I grew up hearing over and over . . . that hard work was the secret of success. "Work hard and you'll get ahead" or "It's hard work that got us where we are." No one ever said that you could work hard—harder than you ever thought possible—and still find yourself sinking ever deeper into debt and poverty.

In 2002, according to the government, 19 percent of the heads of poor families worked full time, at least fifty weeks during the year, yet remained below the poverty line. The reason is that low-wage work—Ehrenreich worked as a waitress, motel room cleaner, and sales clerk at a discount store—rarely pays much more than the federal minimum hourly wage of $5.15 per hour. At $7 per hour, even full-time, year-round work yields just $14,000, more than $4,000 below the poverty line for a nonfarm family of four (O'Hare, 2002; U.S. Census Bureau, 2003).

To learn more about the working poor, visit
http://www.bls.gov/cps/cpswp2000.htm

The Non-Working Poor

Many poor families do not have a steady income from work. Government data show that in 2002, 50 percent of the heads of poor families did not work at all; another 31 percent had part-time work (U.S. Census Bureau, 2003).

There are many reasons for not working. Some people have bad health; others lack the skills or self-confidence needed to hold a steady job. For many, however, the problem is a lack of available work. Most inner-city areas in the United States offer few jobs; similarly, in many rural areas and small towns in decline, stores and factories have closed their doors. To make matters worse, many parents cannot afford to pay for child care because it costs more than they would earn in a low-wage job (Schiller,

1994; Edin & Lein, 1996; Wilson, 1996; Pease & Martin, 1997; Duncan, 1999).

The Underclass

Poverty is most severe among the **underclass,** *poor people who live in areas with high concentrations of poverty and limited opportunities for schooling or work.* Much of the underclass lives in inner cities, often imprisoned by *hypersegregation,* meaning that these communities are cut off from the larger society, lacking good schools and, above all, good-paying jobs. Under such conditions, children grow up poor, and most remain poor as adults (Massey & Denton, 1989; Anderson, 1999).

Hypersegregation occurs in rural areas as well. Consider places such as Loup County, Nebraska, profiled in the opening to this chapter, which are just as isolated from the larger world as the inner cities. Across the United States, the underclass includes perhaps one in seven poor people, or 1 to 2 percent of the U.S. population. Although *persistent poverty* is the experience of some people, *temporary poverty* is more the rule. Overall, at some point during a ten-year period, about one-fourth of the U.S. population falls below the poverty line, usually because of unemployment, illness, or divorce. When this happens, the typical pattern is for a household to remain poor for only a year or two.

The underclass, then, is a small part of the poor population. But these men, women, and children receive a great deal of attention because their continuing poverty often brings on a wide range of additional struggles, as we now explain.

PROBLEMS LINKED TO POVERTY

Without the income needed for a safe and comfortable life, the poor suffer in many ways. We look briefly at five problems linked to poverty: poor health, substandard housing, homelessness, limited schooling, and crime.

Poor Health

There is a strong link between poverty and poor health. This is because many poor people cannot afford adequate nutrition; about 13 percent of poor households in the United States are undernourished. In addition, poverty is stressful, raising the risk of alcoholism, drug abuse, and violence. Further more, when illness or injury strikes, poor people have fewer

One way that we know that poverty is a social problem rather than simply an individual problem is by looking at poverty rates, which are very high in certain regions of the country. Economic opportunity is all but gone from a number of rural areas across the United States; as a result, entire communities suffer.

resources to fight back. At least one-third lack health insurance, so they simply cannot afford medical care (Center on Hunger and Poverty, 2000; Nord, Andrews, & Carlson, 2002; U.S. National Center for Health Statistics, 2002).

Poverty affects health from birth to old age. Among the poor, *infant mortality,* the risk of death during the first year of life, is twice the national average. Among the very poor, the death rate among newborns is four times the national average and about the same level as in low-income countries such as Honduras or Vietnam.

Income continues to shape health into adulthood. When asked to rate their personal health, 79 percent of people living in families with incomes over $35,000 replied "excellent" or "very good." But only 52 percent of people whose families had incomes of $20,000 or less could say the same (U.S. National Center for Health Statistics, 2002).

Finally, death comes sooner to the poor, who are more likely to die of infectious diseases and violence at any age. Most rich people, by contrast, die of cancer and heart disease which usually do not take their toll until old age. For this reason, life expectancy for whites is about 78 years; for their African American counterparts, who earn 82 percent as much, it is just 71 years (U.S. National Center for Health Statistics, 2003).

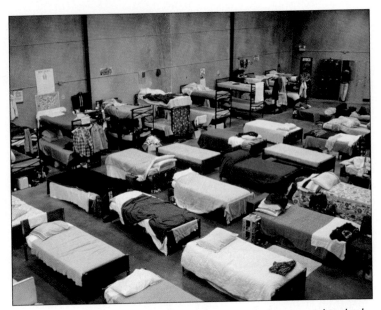

Homeless shelters provide necessary housing to hundreds of thousands of people across the United States. But the larger question is why do so many people lack affordable housing in the first place?

Substandard Housing

In the United States, better housing is available to those who can pay for it. For this reason, poor people take what is left: housing marked by crowded conditions, dangerous lead-based paint, lack of heat, faulty plumbing, and even collapsing walls and crumbling ceilings.

Just as important, recent years have seen a steady decline in the number of low-rent apartments in the United States. As a result, many poor families are forced to spend most of what they earn for housing, leaving too little for food, clothing, and other needs. Not surprisingly, in large cities across the United States, tens of thousands of poor people are on waiting lists for programs that will help them secure better housing (Adler & Malone, 1996; Ehrenreich, 2001).

Homelessness

In recent decades, the problem of **homelessness**, *the plight of poor people who lack shelter and live primarily on the streets*, has received a lot of attention. Experts estimate that 500,000 people are homeless in the United States on any given night, and as many as 2 million people are homeless at some point during a year (Kozol, 1988; Wright, 1989; Bohannan,

1991; U.S. Census Bureau, 2000; Wickham, 2000; Marks, 2001).

There are many causes of homelessness. Conservatives point to personal problems, noting that one-third of the homeless suffer from mental disorders, and many abuse alcohol and other drugs. Liberals counter that homelessness has less to do with personal shortcomings than with poverty, and they point to low-wage jobs and a lack of affordable housing as prime causes.

Whereas about half of homeless people do not work, half work at least part-time. Overall, average income for homeless individuals averages about $350 per month; for families, the figure is about $475. Such income is simply not enough to pay for housing (HUD, 1999; Ratnesar, 1999).

Read more about homelessness in this report:
http://www.usmayors.org/uscm/hungersurvey/hunger2000.pdf

Limited Schooling

Poor children are less likely than rich children to complete high school. Therefore, the odds of going to college (or completing an advanced degree) are low. Too often, underperforming public schools transform low-income children into low-achieving students who grow up to be low-income adults. In this way, schooling helps pass poverty from one generation to the next.

A key part of educational inequality is the practice of *tracking*, by which schools divide children into college-bound ("academic") tracks and job-oriented ("vocational") tracks. The stated goal of tracking is to teach children according to their academic abilities. But research suggests that school officials often label poor children as less able, just as they see privileged children as more talented. The result is that many poor children are taught by the least able teachers in crowded classrooms with fewer computers, books, and other learning equipment (Oakes, 1982, 1985; Hallinan & Williams, 1989; Kilgore, 1991; Gamoran, 1992; Kozol, 1992).

Crime and Punishment

Anyone who watches the popular television show *COPS* is bound to conclude that most criminals are poor people. Assault, robbery, burglary, auto theft—it is these "street crimes" that command the attention of the public and the mass media. As Chapter 6 ("Crime and Criminal Justice") explains, when it comes to street crimes, poor people are involved more often than affluent people, both as offenders and as victims. The public pays less attention to the types of crimes typically committed by wealthy people, including tax evasion, stock fraud, false advertising, bribery, and environmental pollution, even though such offenses almost certainly cause greater harm to society as a whole.

The greater public attention to street crime (compared with, say, fraud and other wrongdoing by corporate executives) means that it is the poor who are most likely to be arrested, go to trial, and face a prison sentence. Moreover, most poor people who enter the criminal justice system rely on public defenders or court-appointed attorneys, most of whom are underpaid and overworked. Wealthy people in trouble can enlist the help of private legal counsel and employ psychiatrists and other specialists, which greatly lowers the odds of conviction and prison time.

Finally, going to jail harms careers. Therefore, just as poverty raises one's risk of involvement with the criminal justice system, so experience within the criminal justice system raises a person's risk of staying poor (Western, 2002).

Political Alienation

Given the disadvantages faced by the poor, one might expect that such people would be politically active and involved in pressing for change. Sometimes poor people do organize politically, but typically they do not even vote. In the 2000 presidential election, about three-fourths of well-off families with incomes of $75,000 or more cast a ballot; by contrast, half of adults with family incomes of $35,000 did the same, and a large majority of poor adults did not vote at all. This pattern suggests that poor people feel alienated from a system that does not serve their interests (Samuelson, 2003).

RESPONDING TO POVERTY: THE WELFARE SYSTEM

To address the problem of poverty, all industrial nations rely on various kinds of **social welfare programs,** *organized efforts by government, private organizations, or individuals to assist needy people defined as worthy of assistance.* Social welfare takes many forms, including government unemployment insurance for workers, Red Cross benefits for flood victims, or simply people lending a hand after a disaster.

The poor are not the only people who benefit from government payments. Price supports and other subsidies paid to farmers across the United States are as great as assistance to the poor—although few call such payments "welfare." Although some of this money goes to family farmers, most is paid to large corporate farming operations.

But the largest welfare programs, run by the government, have three characteristics:

1. **Social welfare programs benefit people or activities defined as worthy.** The public and government officials debate and decide which categories of people or activities are worthy of support. Who benefits from social welfare programs changes over time.

2. **Social welfare programs benefit most people.** Welfare programs include not only assistance to poor families but also price supports for farmers, the oil depletion allowance to petroleum companies and tax relief to corporations, the homeowner's tax deduction for home mortgage interest, pensions paid to the elderly, benefits for veterans, and low-interest government loans for students.

3. **Overall, social welfare programs change income disparity only a little.** Some government programs take from the rich (in taxes) and others give to the poor (in benefits), thereby reducing economic inequality. But many programs in fact benefit wealthier individuals and

families. For example, the value of the tax deduction on home mortgage interest is worth about $50 billion annually to more affluent people, twice as much as the government provides in food stamps to low-income people (U.S. Census Bureau, 2000).

A Brief History of Welfare

Social welfare has a long and controversial history in the United States. The following discussion surveys welfare policies in three historical periods—the colonial era, the early industrial era, and the modern era after the Great Depression—and then highlights the 1996 welfare reforms (Trattner, 1980; Katz, 1986).

The Colonial Era   Europeans who came to the United States in the 1600s and 1700s settled in small communities where families and neighbors took responsibility for assisting the poor. Struggling to survive in a strange and uncertain world, most expected both poverty as a normal part of life. Some colonists, especially the early Puritans in New England, looked down on the very poor, seeing poverty as a sign of moral weakness. Free people looked down on slaves as inferior and therefore undeserving. In short during this period, "welfare" amounted to acts of personal kindness between neighbors.

The Early Industrial Era   As the Industrial Revolution took hold around 1800, U.S. cities swelled with immigrants. In addition, the new industrial capitalist economy fostered a spirit of individualism and self-reliance. As a result, attitudes toward the poor became more negative. Because most people expected others to pull their own weight, many claimed that charity only made people lazy by reducing their need to work. Organizations such as the Salvation Army (founded in 1865) offered food and shelter to the poor but also provided moral counseling in the belief that the poor were weak and of bad character.

However, not everyone shared this harsh view of the poor. In the 1870s, the *scientific charity* movement (really an early form of sociology) began studying who was poor, why they were poor, and what could be done to help them. Researchers soon learned that most poor people were not lazy but were men and women without jobs, children without parents, women without husbands, victims of factory accidents, and working people earning too little to support a family. In short, scientific charity defined poverty as the fault not of the poor but of society.

Such thinking was also part of the *settlement house movement*. Settlement houses were located in the worst slums of a city, where a staff of social scientists and reform-minded activists helped new immigrants get settled in their new surroundings. Members of this social movement also tried to make society as a whole more compassionate toward the poor.

The Twentieth Century   By 1900, tens of millions of immigrants had come to the United States, which fueled hostility among many better-off people toward the very poor. World War I (1914–18) made matters worse by raising suspicion of "foreigners."

Then, in 1929, the Great Depression rolled across the United States. One-fourth of the labor force lost their jobs, and millions of families fell into poverty. Banks closed, wiping out people's life savings, and families in debt lost their farms or their homes. Under such conditions, it was impossible to see poverty as caused by people who were "different" or lazy. It was then that poverty became widely viewed as a *social* problem.

Franklin D. Roosevelt became president in 1932 and proposed a "New Deal" to help the millions impoverished by the Depression. Through the 1930s, the federal government enacted a number of programs to fight poverty, the most important of which was Social Security. Today, this program provides monthly income to 45 million people, most of whom are elderly.

Roosevelt's reforms eased the suffering, and World War II (1939–45) not only helped end the Depression but also diverted public attention to other issues. Later, in the 1960s, researchers rediscovered poverty both in cities and across the rural countryside (Harrington, 1962), prompting President Lyndon Johnson to launch a "War on Poverty" in 1964. The Defining Moment box takes a closer look at U.S. society facing up to poverty.

A glance back at Figure 2–3 shows that the War on Poverty did work. The official poverty rate, which had stood at about 22 percent in 1960, fell to about 11 percent by the early 1970s. But in the 1980s, the mood of the country again turned against social welfare programs. Beginning with Reagan's administration, the federal government scaled back assistance programs, claiming (like critics a century earlier) that welfare programs were eroding personal initiative and creating "dependency."

A DEFINING MOMENT

U.S. Society Discovers Poverty

DURING THE FIRST CENTURIES OF U.S. HISTORY, many people lived in conditions that we today would consider unbearably primitive. However, people back then accepted their situation because when they looked around, everyone else they could see was living pretty much the same way.

When the Industrial Revolution came along, dramatically raising living standards for the majority of the population, the gap between rich and poor widened. Still, the poverty of those left behind failed to cause much public concern, probably because many of the poor were immigrants and were widely regarded as "different" by those who were more well off.

Then came the Great Depression in 1929, when people across all social classes lost whatever security they had previously taken for granted. Suddenly poverty was a serious social problem. Franklin D. Roosevelt became president in 1932, offering a "New Deal" to those he described as "one-third of a nation ill-clothed, ill-housed, and ill-fed." His economic programs—most

notably the various Works Progress Administration (WPA) projects and Social Security—put the unemployed to work and created a social "safety net" for the U.S. population.

With the end of World War II, the Depression had given way to a period of economic prosperity. But by the 1960s it was clear that a growing underclass of poor people—both in urban and rural areas—was negating the popular image of the United States as a rich society. Lyndon Baines Johnson, president from 1963 until 1968, mobilized the country to recognize the plight of this large segment of the U.S. population, and in 1964 he declared a "War on Poverty." He fought to get programs passed by Congress that would "strike at the causes, not the consequences" of poverty; these programs included Head Start for preschool children, Title I federal funding for public schools in low-income districts, and the Job Corps training program for adults.

Together, presidents Roosevelt and Johnson did more than any other U.S. leaders to define poverty as a social problem. Just as important, they directed the power of the government toward making the problem smaller.

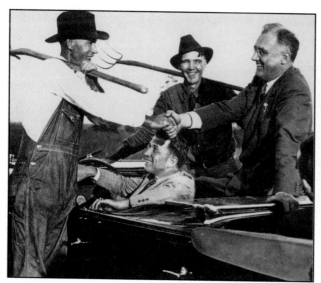

Franklin Delano Roosevelt, who was president from 1933 until 1945, established Social Security and other programs that provide a social "safety net" to the U.S. population. A generation later, Lyndon Baines Johnson, who was president from 1963 until 1968, declared a national "war on poverty" that succeeded in reducing the poverty rate.

Social Policy   An Undeserved Handout? The Truth about "Welfare"

ARE WELFARE ASSISTANCE CHECKS AND FOOD STAMPS just handouts for people too lazy to work? What are the facts? Here, we evaluate six widespread assumptions about public assistance.

1. **"Most welfare goes to the poor."** Not true. If we look at *all* government income programs, we find hundreds that offer financial benefits—cash transfers or reduced taxes—to many categories of people. Overall, no more than half of all government benefits go to poor people.

2. **"Most public assistance goes to able-bodied people."** Not true. Most assistance goes to people who are too old or too young to work. Some programs do assist poor mothers who do not work. But these funds are primarily for support of children, and they are provided only for a limited time.

3. **"Once on welfare, always on welfare."** Before the welfare reforms of 1996, there was some truth to this. Studies showed that half of families who ever enrolled in Aid for Families with Dependent Children received public assistance for four years or more (1991 Green Book). But because recent reforms limit lifetime benefits to five years, this is no longer the case.

4. **"Welfare recipients are African Americans and other minorities."** Not true. White households receive 64 percent of all food stamps and occupy 61 percent of public housing units (U.S. Census Bureau, 2002; U.S. Department of Agriculture, 2003). It is true that, in proportion to population size, minorities are more likely than whites to

receive income assistance. In the 1990s, about half of African American families received some kind of public assistance (the most common was school lunch programs), compared with 45 percent of Hispanic families and 16 percent of white families. These differences parallel the likelihood of being poor.

5. **"Welfare encourages single women to have children."** Not true. The average number of children among women without husbands is the same whether or not families receive welfare support. The case has also been made that welfare assistance enabled some women to support children without marrying. This may be so, but the trend toward more single parenting is found among people of all income levels and in all high-income nations.

6. **"Welfare fraud is a serious national problem."** Not really. Anyone who works at a social service agency will tell you that some people take advantage of the system, but most benefits go to people who are truly needy.

ISSUES AND EXERCISES

1. Did any of the facts presented in this box surprise you? Which ones? Why?

2. Why is the public as a whole ready to believe the worst about financial assistance to the poor?

3. Can you think of other false ideas about welfare and poverty? Refute them using what you have learned in this chapter.

Recent Welfare Reform

In the early 1990s, about 8 million poor households were receiving public assistance totaling some $40 billion annually, which averaged out to about $5,000 per family. The most important assistance program was Aid to Families with Dependent Children (AFDC), which provided income to poor mothers with children.

Changes in the welfare system began to take shape in 1992, when President Bill Clinton pledged

to "end welfare as we know it." In 1994, the Democratic president and a Republican Congress joined forces to produce the most sweeping welfare reform since the Roosevelt era. The purpose of the reform is suggested by its formal title: the 1996 Personal Responsibility and Work Opportunity Reconciliation Act. First, responsibility for helping the poor shifted from the federal government to the states. The old federal program, AFDC, was ended in favor of a state-level program called Temporary Assistance for Needy Families (TANF). The new rules are intended to increase the "personal responsibility" of the poor by requiring able-bodied people seeking benefits to find a job or enroll in job training. In addition, the program limits the period of time that families can receive benefits to two consecutive years with a lifetime cap of five years.

Supporters of welfare reform call the policy a success because the nation's welfare rolls have fallen by half. In addition, half of those who have left welfare now have jobs, and most of the remainder are in school or training programs. But critics counter that most people who have left welfare for work now have lower-wage jobs that leave them struggling to make ends meet. Therefore, they claim, although reform has reduced welfare assistance, it has not done much to reduce *poverty* (Dervarics, 1998; Lichter & Crowley, 2002).

The ongoing welfare debate points up a hard truth: People in the United States like to think they are compassionate, but because of society's cultural emphasis on personal responsibility, the public remains uneasy with giving the poor assistance. The Social Policy box evaluates six common assumptions about public assistance.

THEORETICAL ANALYSIS: UNDERSTANDING POVERTY

Why does poverty exist in the first place? We find some answers by applying sociology's major theoretical approaches to the issue of poverty.

Structural-Functional Analysis: Some Poverty Is Inevitable

Chapter 1 ("Studying Social Problems") identified a number of structural-functional approaches to social problems. Each has something to say about why poverty exists.

Social Pathology Theories: Personal Deficiency

Some early sociologists held a "bad apple" theory that claimed poverty was the result of personal flaws. For example, Herbert Spencer's "social Darwinism" viewed society as a competitive arena where the most able became rich and the least able fell into poverty. Spencer described this process as "the survival of the fittest."

The social pathology approach is also found in the work of anthropologist Oscar Lewis (1961, 1966). Lewis studied poor communities in San Juan (Puerto Rico), Mexico City, and New York City,

asking why some neighborhoods remained poor from generation to generation. His conclusion: They contain a **culture of poverty,** *cultural patterns that make poverty a way of life.* Lewis claimed that people *adapt* to poverty, accepting their plight and giving up hope that life can improve. Thinking this way, Lewis continued, people may turn to alcohol or drugs, become violent, neglect their families, and end up living just for the moment. Doing so, they pass on the culture of poverty from one generation to the next.

A recent social pathology theory is the "bell curve" thesis of Richard J. Herrnstein and Charles Murray (1994). Over the course of the twentieth century, they argue, the United States became more of a **meritocracy,** *a system of social inequality in which social standing corresponds to personal ability and effort.* In today's information age, intelligence is more valuable than ever. Therefore, the argument goes, the ranks of the rich increasingly are filled by smart people, whereas the poor are more likely to be those with limited intelligence. No wonder, Herrnstein and Murray argue, that it is so hard to improve the plight of the poor: As Herbert Spencer said a century earlier, they are capable of little more.

Social Disorganization Theory: Too Much Change

In the 1920s and 1930s, sociologists at the University of Chicago linked poverty to **social disorganization,** *a breakdown in social order caused by rapid social change.* Industrial factories drew tens of millions of people—rural Midwesterners, men and women from towns in Appalachia, African Americans from the South's Cotton Belt, and immigrants from Europe—to the rapidly growing cities.

People arrived too fast for neighborhoods, schools, and factories to absorb them. The result was overcrowded apartment buildings and classrooms, and people without work—in short, poverty and related social problems. Only with time could we expect the poverty problem to improve.

In recent years, the high rate of immigration to the United States, especially from Latin America, has contributed to high poverty rates in many regions of the Southwest and West where many new arrivals struggle to find housing and jobs. In time, according to the social disorganization approach, we would expect most of these families to improve their situation.

Recent Functional Theory: Inequality Is Useful

In 1945, Kingsley Davis and Wilbert Moore asked, "Why does inequality exist everywhere?" Their

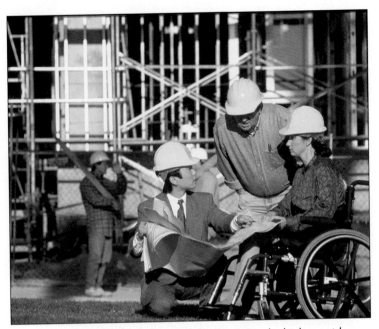

Engineers and architects are among the higher-paid workers in the U.S. labor force. From a structural-functional point of view, our society rewards work that requires rare skills and expensive education. As you read on, try to develop a critical response to this position based on social-conflict theory.

answer was that inequality is useful for the operation of society. Davis and Moore explain that some jobs (say, a security guard) are not very important and can be performed by just about anyone. But other positions (for example, a surgeon) require rare talents and extensive training. How can society motivate people to develop their abilities and gain the schooling they need for important jobs? Only by providing more rewards, including higher income, greater power, and more prestige. Of course, attaching greater rewards to some jobs necessarily creates social stratification, making some rich and others poor.

Davis and Moore point out that any society could reward everyone equally, but only if it made no difference who does what job or how well the task is done. A society with no differences in rewards, they continue, would not be very productive because it would give people little reason to excel. In sum, inequality actually helps society to be productive.

Another sociologist, Herbert Gans (1971) offers a different take, pointing out that inequality is useful but only to *affluent* people. The function of inequality, claims Gans, is to ensure that there is a supply of poor people willing to do almost any job, no matter how unpleasant. Other than poor people

(who have little choice in the matter), he asks, who would want to perform farm labor, pick up garbage, or clean other people's homes? In addition, the poor also buy things no one else wants, including run-down housing, old cars, rebuilt appliances, and second-hand clothing. In short, Gans suggests, poverty exists because many people benefit from it.

Critical evaluation.   All structural-functional theories share a key argument: Poverty is a natural, expected part of life that has some useful consequences. Critics, take issue with these theories, especially the idea that poor people are somehow inferior. As they see it, poverty is not something that people bring on themselves, nor is it inevitable. Rather, poverty has economic causes, including unemployment and wage levels that leave even full-time workers poor.

Why, then, have such theories been popular? Perhaps because locating the causes of poverty in poor people themselves justifies the status quo and turns attention away from flaws in society itself, as we now explain.

Symbolic-Interaction Analysis: Defining the Problem

Symbolic-interaction theory adds to our understanding of poverty by exploring how poor people are viewed by others and how those views contribute to very different analyses of who or what is responsible for poverty.

For instance, there's the view of poor people as lazy, lacking intelligence, or in some other way personally flawed, a notion mentioned earlier in connection with the functionalist approach. Given our society's individualistic culture, it's not surprising that many people are quick to view the poor as responsible for their own condition. William Ryan (1976) describes how this can happen. He explains that the process of **blaming the victim**, *finding the cause of a social problem in the behavior of people who suffer from it,* involves four simple steps:

1. **Pick a social problem.**   Almost any will do; here, our concern is poverty.

2. **Decide how people who suffer from the problem differ from everyone else.**   It is easy to see that poor people don't dress as well as others; many also don't speak English very well. Many have little schooling. They live in run-down housing. They sometimes get into trouble with the police. The list goes on and on.

3. **Define these differences as the cause of the problem.** Claim, "*Of course* those people are poor! Just look at them! Listen to them speak! See where they live! Who is surprised that people like that are poor? They *deserve* to be where they are."

4. **Respond to the problem by trying to change the victims, not the larger society.** Think to yourself that people would not be poor if only they would dress better, speak better, live in better neighborhoods—in short, be more like those who are well off.

However, if one sees the poor as people who are inherently no different from anyone else, the picture changes. Poor people become individuals who are struggling—often heroically—against unfair odds dealt them by society. When the poor are viewed this way, it is society—not any personal failings of poor people themselves—that is to blame for poverty.

William Ryan suggests that instead of shaking our heads at the run-down houses where poor people live, we should ask why U.S. society provides such housing to some people. Instead of making a remark about an ill-clothed person, we should ask why U.S. society does so little to meet some people's needs.

Critical evaluation. Symbolic-interaction analysis is useful in showing that poverty is not simply an issue about money; it is also a matter of meanings, or how we view the poor. Although this approach points to society as the cause of poverty, it says little about exactly how society makes some people poor. This issue brings us to the social-conflict approach.

Social-Conflict Analysis: Poverty Can Be Eliminated

Social-conflict theory takes the view that poverty is not natural and rejects the idea that it results from flaws in people. On the contrary, this approach claims that poverty is caused by flaws in society itself.

Marxist Theory: Poverty and Capitalism Karl Marx (1818–1883) could see how much the Industrial Revolution had increased economic production. At the same time, however, he objected to how all this wealth remained in the hands of a few.

Marx pointed to what he called an *internal contradiction* in capitalist economic systems: a system that produced so much ended up making so many so poor. From this observation, Marx went on to

There have always been poor children in the United States. Today, however, we might well ask whether child poverty should exist at all in a society that is so rich. What do the various sociological theories have to say about the reasons for child poverty? What would it take to end this serious problem?

encourage workers to band together to bring about the downfall of capitalism (for details about capitalist economic systems, see Chapter 11, "Economy and Politics").

In the more than 100 years since Marx's death, the United States and other high-income nations have seen living standards rise for all categories of people, a fact that goes a long way to explain why the workers' revolution that Marx predicted has not taken place. Even so, as noted earlier in this chapter, the lion's share of income and wealth still goes to a very small share of the people. Remember, too, that economic inequality has been increasing in recent years. Therefore, following Marx's thinking, although U.S. society has managed to hold off a workers' revolution, it continues to create the problem of poverty.

Poverty Involves More Than Money: Cultural Capital

In recent decades, analysts have explained that society not only provides some people with far more wealth than others but also provides some people with much more **cultural capital,** *skills, values, attitudes, and schooling that increase a person's chances of success.* Pierre Bourdieu and Jean-Claude Passeron (1977) argue that young people born into affluent families benefit from a cultural environment, both at home and at school, that ensures their success. On the other hand, those born to low-income families have few such advantages, so they are poor in more ways than one.

Multicultural Theory: Poverty, Race, and Ethnicity

The multicultural perspective highlights how poverty is closely linked to race and ethnicity. For example, the 2001 median income for non-Hispanic white families was $57,328. For African American families, it was $33,598, or 59 percent as much. Similarly, the figure for Hispanic families was $35,500, which was 62 percent of the white income level. Or, as noted earlier, both African Americans (24.1 percent) and Hispanics (21.8 percent) have almost three times the risk of poverty as non-Hispanic whites (8.0 percent). Asian American and Pacific Islander families have above-average income ($62,617 in 2000) and a poverty rate (10.1 percent) somewhat above that of non-Hispanic whites. Chapter 3 ("Racial and Ethnic Inequality") presents a full discussion of this issue.

Feminist Theory: Poverty and Patriarchy

Feminist theory adds to our understanding of poverty, explaining that women have a high risk of poverty. This is especially true of single mothers, who are more than six times as likely (50 percent) as single fathers (8 percent) to be poor (U.S. Census Bureau, 2003).

In 1960, just one in four poor families was headed by a woman; by 2002, half were. What explains the feminization of poverty? As feminists see it, the reason is simply that U.S. society provides more income, wealth, power, and prestige to men than to women. As Chapter 4 ("Gender Inequality") explains, our culture defines most high-paying jobs (as doctors, airline pilots, and college presidents) as "men's work" while expecting that lower-paying positions (as nurses, flight attendants, and clerical workers) will be filled by women.

Intersection Theory: Multiple Disadvantage

If African Americans and Hispanics are disadvantaged, and women are also disadvantaged, are African American or Hispanic women doubly disadvantaged? This question is the focus of **intersection theory,** *the investigation of the interplay of race, class, and gender often resulting in multiple dimensions of disadvantage.*

To illustrate how this works, we start by noting the disparities linked to race and ethnicity: The 2001 median income of non-Hispanic white men working full time was $43,194; African American men typically earned just $31,921, which is 74 percent as much; Hispanic men earned $25,271, or 59 percent as much.

Now add in gender. Compared with African American men, African American women (again, comparing just full-time workers) earned $27,297, or 86 percent as much. Hispanic women earned an average of $21,973, or 87 percent as much as Hispanic men. These disparities are linked to gender.

Now combine the two dimensions. Compared with non-Hispanic white men, African American women earned just 64 percent as much; Hispanic women earned only 51 percent as much. Therefore, we see that race or ethnicity and gender do not operate alone but combine so that certain categories of people are doubly disadvantaged (Bonilla-Santiago, 1990; St. Jean & Feagin, 1998; U.S. Census Bureau, 2002).

Critical evaluation.   Beginning with Karl Marx's observations that inequality involves struggle between the owners and workers in a capitalist society, more recent conflict theorists have extended this analysis to cultural capital as well as inequality involving race, ethnicity, and gender.

Marx argued that poverty is not an abnormal but a *normal* element of capitalist society. Yet critics point out that Marx did not foresee ways in which capitalist societies would improve living standards for working people and greatly reduce the extent of poverty.

Furthermore, critics ask, doesn't being rich or poor a least partly reflect the choices we make as individuals? If we take away people's responsibility for their situation, we all end up as passive victims of society. Indeed, there is probably more meritocracy—the ability to rise or fall based on individual talent and effort—in today's society than ever before.

Finally, multicultural and feminist theories, as well as intersection theory, point up how our society puts racial and ethnic minorities and all women at high risk for poverty. Yet, critics claim, these approaches ignore how opportunities for women and minorities have improved since the beginning of the twentieth century, when the segregation of African Americans was a matter of law and women of any color could not even vote.

POLITICS AND POVERTY: CONSTRUCTING PROBLEMS AND DEFINING SOLUTIONS

What are we to make of the fact that 34.6 million people in one of the richest nations on earth are poor? As with every issue we deal with in this book, poverty and wealth are controversial. Some people consider income inequality as inevitable and even good for society. Others are highly critical of income inequality and define poverty as a pressing national problem that can be reduced. We now examine how conservatives, liberals, and radicals construct the poverty problem and how they define solutions.

Conservatives: Personal Responsibility

Conservatives point out that almost all the poverty in the United States is *relative* poverty. That is, only a small percentage of those the government defines as poor are close to *absolute* poverty, where day-to-day survival is the issue. Rather, families are poor relative to what government officials claim people living in our rich society ought to have. Indeed, almost half of the poor own their homes, two-thirds have at least one car, and almost all have a television set and a personal computer (Rector, 1998; Gallagher, 1999). If we keep in mind that living standards have risen dramatically over the last century, conservatives argue, we can see that our society is doing pretty well at providing for the population.

Conservatives also value self-reliance, the idea that people should take personal responsibility for their well-being. It has long been a conservative belief that U.S. society offers plenty of opportunity to anyone who is willing to take advantage of it. Our way of life rewards both talent and effort so that, although a few inherit great wealth, most successful people (and even most rich people) are those who work hard in school and at their jobs (Stanley & Danko, 1996).

For example, U.S. Secretary of State Colin Powell speaks often about how, as a young boy, he began his working life with a broom. He explains that he always worked hard, doing his best and learning

Secretary of State Colin Powell is a good example of a self-made man, rising from a poor background to a position of national leadership. Conservatives see his story as evidence that the solution to poverty is hard work and personal responsibility. Liberals, however, point out that government needs to open doors and lend a hand to many people who face barriers that prevent them from succeeding on their own. Radicals on the left go even further, arguing that even though some people go from "rags to riches," U.S. society remains sharply divided between a rich and powerful elite and the working majority who are far from secure.

whatever he could from the job he had. As soon as he mastered one task, he asked for another one. He credits discipline and determination—learned from his parents—as the key to his success, rising to a top position in the U.S. military and a cabinet post in the Bush administration. In short, Powell argues, teaching our children personal virtue and responsibility is the most effective way to prevent poverty (Powell & Persico, 1995).

Is there a role for government in the fight against poverty? In general, because conservatives believe people are responsible for their own social standing, they support limited government and low taxes. Most conservatives support welfare programs that

Historically, U.S. culture has placed a strong emphasis on self-reliance, which is the idea that individuals are responsible for their own social standing. Such beliefs help explain why many people are "poor but proud"—needy but unwilling to ask for assistance. Is it reasonable to think that everybody who is poor can help themselves?

provide assistance to certain categories of people—those with disabilities, the elderly, and children—who are needy through no fault of their own. Most also think the government should provide a helping hand to veterans who have sacrificed for their country and short-term help to anyone thrown out of work. But government should never replace personal responsibility; as noted earlier, conservatives claim welfare programs can make poverty worse by fostering dependency. For this reason, most conservatives supported the 1996 welfare reform (Murray, 1984; Bennett, 1995; Connerly, 2000).

Liberals: Societal Responsibility

Whereas conservatives view personal responsibility as the way to defeat poverty, liberals claim that everyone shares responsibility for the poor. From a liberal point of view, poverty is more societal than individual. Most people become poor not because they are irresponsible but because of the way society operates. As Chapter 12 ("Work and the Workplace") explains, most unemployment is caused by economic recession or corporate mergers and downsizing that reduces the number of available jobs.

The structural roots of poverty are also evident in the fact that our society places specific categories of people at high risk of poverty. Because women, for example, are less likely than men to work for income, and because they earn less when they do, women are at higher risk of being poor.

Because poverty is a societal problem, liberals look for societal solutions. They reject the conservative arguments that individuals must take full responsibility for themselves. According to the liberal viewpoint, the U.S. economy may be highly productive, but it distributes income very unequally. Furthermore, many people are disadvantaged by racism and other forms of discrimination that prevent them from obtaining good jobs. Part of the liberal solution to poverty, then, is active enforcement of laws banning discrimination in education and the workplace.

In addition, liberals support government assistance programs that offer some measure of financial security to everyone—a "social safety net." Dismissing conservative worries about creating dependency, liberals view assistance programs as needed by millions of people (especially children) who are poor through no fault of their own. Liberals also support higher taxes, especially on the rich, to pay for such programs; whereas most conservatives supported the recent Bush tax cuts, most liberals opposed them. With the money raised through taxation, liberals would expand welfare programs to raise millions of poor families above the poverty line. Currently, support is so limited—the typical "welfare family" receives only about $600 per month—that people cannot improve their situation. For example, a poor working mother cannot afford to commute to a better job in a nearby suburb, to purchase better medical care so that she loses fewer days to illness, or to finish a high school diploma by taking night courses.

LEFT (TO) RIGHT

THE POLITICS OF INCOME INEQUALITY

	RADICAL LEFT VIEW	LIBERAL VIEW	CONSERVATIVE VIEW
WHAT IS THE PROBLEM?	Most of the country's wealth is controlled by a small share of the population.	Millions of men, women, and children have too little income and need assistance.	Some "worthy" people are poor and should be helped, but social welfare programs may discourage people's desire to work and may foster dependency.
WHAT IS THE SOLUTION?	The capitalist economic system must undergo fundamental changes.	Use higher taxes to expand government assistance programs and raise the income of the poor.	Provide short-term help to those who really need it; strengthen families and promote personal responsibility.

Join the debate . . .

1. Assess the 1996 welfare reform from the radical, liberal, and conservative points of view. From each political position, has the reform been helpful or harmful? To whom? Why?
2. During the 2004 presidential campaign, Democrats called for higher taxes to fund expanded social programs, primarily to assist disadvantaged people. Republicans defended a recent tax cut intended to create jobs and to give people more money to spend and invest. What arguments can you make for and against each position? What would be a radical response to this debate?
3. Which of the three political analyses of income inequality included here do you find the most convincing? Why?

Finally, liberals point out that millions of poor people never even apply for welfare benefits. Why not? In a culture that stresses personal responsibility, asking for help is a statement of personal failure and a source of shame (Wilson, 1996; Seccombe, 1999: Mouw, 2000; Murray, 2000).

Radicals: Change the System

Just as liberals are to the left of conservatives, so radicals are to the left of liberals. Radicals agree with liberals that poverty is a societal issue and that we cannot expect poor people to improve their situation on their own. But they differ by claiming that the problem of poverty is built in to a capitalist society (Liazos, 1982). That is, the normal operation of a capitalist economic system creates extremes of wealth and poverty so that the welfare programs supported by liberals are little more than a bandage applied to the body of a person with a deadly disease.

Karl Marx called poverty one of the *internal contradictions* of capitalism. Industrial capitalism produces great wealth, but production is controlled by the capitalist elite for their own benefit at the expense of working people. Thus, a very rich society can contain millions of people who are desperately poor.

Radicals claim that the way to solve the problem of poverty is to replace capitalism with a more just and humane economic system. The goal of such a system would be not to increase private profits but to meet social needs.

Radicals therefore share a distinctive definition of the problem and a particular solution. The Left to Right table sums up the views of all three political approaches.

GOING ON FROM HERE

This chapter describes the inequality of income and wealth that defines the rich and poor in the United States. We see that certain categories of people—women, children, and people of color—are at high risk of being poor and that all people who are economically disadvantaged contend with poor health, substandard housing, too little schooling, too few jobs, crime, and violence.

What can we expect in the future? Keep in mind that some trends are positive. Between 1960 and 2002, the official poverty rate fell by almost half, from 22 percent to just over 12 percent. Among the elderly, the poverty rate dropped by two-thirds from 33 percent to 10 percent (U.S. Census Bureau, 2003).

Even so, as shown in Figure 2–3 on page 34, most of the decrease in poverty occurred between 1960 and the early 1970s, and the overall trend has been slightly upward since then. Even more troubling, the age category at greatest risk of poverty is children: Overall, 16.7 percent are poor, with twice that rate among African American and Hispanic American youngsters. Thus, perhaps the most pressing question for the future is what to do about the "new poverty" in the United States involving households composed of women and children. The dramatic decline in the poverty rate among the elderly shows that this nation can reduce poverty when the public supports doing so. The question is whether we will do as much for our children as we have done for seniors.

There has always been controversy surrounding wealth and poverty in the United States, and this debate surely will continue. Conservatives focus on the need for personal responsibility and strong families, pointing out that single motherhood places women and their children at risk of poverty. Liberals call for raising the minimum wage, expanding child-care and job training programs, and combating workplace discrimination that harms women and people of color. Radical voices claim that a capitalist economic system always leaves many people behind. Whatever political position one favors, a focus of national attention in the decades to come will be the striking degree of economic inequality in the United States.

CHAPTER SUMMARY

1. Economic inequality involves both income and wealth; in the United States, wealth is distributed much more unequally than income.

2. In the United States, the richest 20 percent of families have incomes that average $160,000; most are, or will become, millionaires. Older people, white people, and men stand out among the rich.

3. The U.S. government defines "poverty" as family income below a poverty line roughly equal to three times the cost of food. By this measure, some 34.6 million people (12.1 percent of the population) are poor. The average poor family in the United States receives about $7,000 less than the poverty line in annual income, a difference called the poverty gap.

4. At greatest risk of poverty are children, women who head households, and racial and ethnic minorities. The rate of child poverty in the United States has remained high and now stands at 16.7 percent. What sociologists call the feminization of poverty means that, over time, women have made up a rising share (now 56 percent) of the poor.

5. The trend toward lower-paying service jobs means that many U.S. families are working harder than ever yet falling behind in terms of living standards.

6. The underclass consists of poor people trapped in areas where poverty is widespread. Such intense poverty involves a small share of the poor, most visible in inner cities but also in rural areas. The underclass has increased in size in recent years.

7. Poverty affects every aspect of life. The poor endure more illness, receive less schooling, experience more unemployment and crime, and are more likely to live in inadequate housing or to be homeless.

8. Public attitudes toward the poor and toward social welfare programs have varied over the course of this nation's history. In 1996, a harsher national mood led to reform of the current welfare system, pushing poor people toward work and sharply decreasing the number of people receiving benefits.

9. Structural-functional analysis offers various understandings of poverty. The social pathology

approach (including Spencer's social Darwinism, Lewis's culture of poverty thesis, and, more recently, Herrnstein and Murray's bell curve thesis) views poverty as the product of shortcomings on the part of the poor themselves.

10. Social disorganization theory, a second functionalist approach, views poverty as the product of rapid social change, which renders society unable to meet the needs of all its members.

11. More recent functionalism includes the Davis-Moore thesis, which argues that by attaching different rewards to various jobs, society encourages people with special talents to do the most important work. Herbert Gans adds that the poor serve the needs of the nonpoor in various ways, including doing work no one else wants to do.

12. The symbolic-interaction paradigm highlights meanings people attach to being poor. A common pattern is "blaming the victim," by which people blame the poor for their poverty.

13. Social-conflict theory offers additional insights about poverty. Karl Marx argued that a capitalist economy produced wealth for the few and poverty for the many. Marx held that the growing misery of the working class eventually would lead them to overthrow the capitalist system.

14. More recent conflict theorists explain that inequality involves not just money but cultural capital—advantages in skills, values, attitudes, and schooling—that are not available to those born into poverty.

15. The multicultural approach highlights how African Americans and people in disadvantaged racial and ethnic categories are at higher risk of poverty. Gender conflict theory links the higher poverty rate of women to patriarchy. Intersection theory highlights the fact that disparities based on race, class, and gender combine, resulting in greater disadvantage.

16. Conservatives argue that social standing should be a matter of personal responsibility; they criticize social welfare programs for fostering dependency. Liberals consider poverty a societal responsibility and support social programs that benefit the needy. Radicals claim that poverty is a necessary consequence of a capitalist economic system; therefore, they argue that nothing short of fundamental change in the nation's economy will solve the poverty problem.

KEY CONCEPTS

social stratification (p. 28) society's system of ranking categories of people in a hierarchy

social classes (p. 28) categories of people who have similar access to resources and opportunities

income (p. 28) salary or wages from a job plus earnings from investments or any other source

wealth (p. 29) the total economic assets owned by a person or family

progressive taxation (p. 29) a policy that raises tax rates as income increases

poverty line (p. 32) a standard set by the U.S. government for the purpose of counting the poor

poverty gap (p. 32) the difference between the actual income of the typical poor household and the official poverty line

feminization of poverty (p. 34) the fact that women represent an increasing share of the poor

underclass (p. 37) poor people who live in areas with high concentrations of poverty and limited opportunities for schooling or work

homelessness (p. 38) the plight of poor people who lack shelter and live primarily on the streets

social welfare program (p. 39) organized effort by government, private organizations, or individuals to assist needy people defined as worthy of assistance

culture of poverty (p. 43) cultural patterns that make poverty a way of life

meritocracy (p. 43) a system of social inequality in which social standing corresponds to personal ability and effort

social disorganization (p. 43) a breakdown in social order caused by rapid social change

blaming the victim (p. 44) finding the cause of a social problem in the behavior of people who suffer from it

cultural capital (p. 46) skills, values, attitudes, and schooling that increase a person's chances of success

intersection theory (p. 46) the investigation of the interplay of race, class, and gender, often resulting in multiple dimensions of disadvantage

THINKING CRITICALLY: QUESTIONS AND ISSUES

1. We hear many people refer to the United States as a "middle-class society." Based on what you now know about social inequality in this country, to what extent is this description accurate? Offer specific evidence to support your position.

2. At one level, social stratification is a matter of fairness: who should have what and why. What do conservatives, liberals, and radicals consider fair in terms of inequality of income? Why?

3. A disturbing fact is the high share of U.S. children living in poverty. What, in your opinion, explains this fact? What do you think can be done about it?

4. The 1996 welfare reform measures included cutting the number of people receiving assistance by about half, but the poverty rate has come down only slightly. In other words, many people are now working for income but remain poor because of low wages. Should the reform be considered a success? Why or why not?

GETTING INVOLVED: LEARNING ACTIVITIES

1. Find out more about the extent of poverty in your local area. U.S. Census Bureau reports are available from the local library, and you can find census data on the Internet at **http://www.census.gov/datamap/www** or by visiting a local social service agency.

2. Identify a social service agency in your community and ask to interview a caseworker about recent trends in poverty. Are the numbers up or down? How is change in the local economy evident in changing caseloads? How are local agencies responding to the time limitations for public assistance?

3. Have you ever had a low-wage job? If not, this is one good way to begin to understand what it means to be working but poor. Many low-wage jobs are available on or around campus. Whether you actually take such a job or not, work out a monthly household budget for a family of three and see how far a minimum wage job ($5.15 hourly) takes you toward supporting a family.

4. Do you tend to favor the Democratic party? The Republican party? Whichever you prefer, go to their national Web site (**http://www.democrats.org** or **http://www.rnc.org**) and learn about the party's policies toward poverty and related issues such as welfare reform and taxes.

5. Everyone can help in the fight against poverty and hunger. Many organizations on campus or in your local community welcome volunteers. Consider giving some of your own time, energy, and ideas in service to others. Perhaps your experiences could form the basis of a term paper.

GETTING CONNECTED: USEFUL WEB LINKS

http://www.prenhall.com/macionis
Visit the interactive Companion Website™ that accompanies this text. Begin by clicking on the cover of your book. You will find a chapter-by-chapter study guide, practice tests, suggested Web links, and links to other relevant material.

http://www.macionis.com
(or **http://www.thesociologypage.com**)
At the author's home page, you will find dozens of Internet links, many to organizations and agencies that offer information about poverty and policies to address this problem.

http://www.urban.org
This site offers analysis of the recent welfare reforms.

http://www.huduser.org/publications/homeless/ homelessness/contents.html
This report from the government's office of Housing and Urban Development (HUD) surveys programs for homelessness.

http://childstats.gov
http://www.bea.doc.gov
These two sites, the first run by the Federal Interagency Forum on Child and Family Statistics and the second by the government's Bureau of Economic Analysis, provide statistics and information about economic inequality, poverty, and the plight of poor children.

GETTING STARTED ON YOUR OWN: RESEARCH NAVIGATOR™

Follow the instructions found on page 25 of this text to access the features of Research Navigator™. Once at the Web site, enter your Login Name and Password. Then, to use the **Content Select** database, enter keywords such as "poverty," "homelessness," or "minimum wage," and the search engine will supply relevant and recent scholarly and popular press publications. Use the *New York Times* **Search-by-Subject Archive** to find recent news articles related to sociology and the **Link Library** feature to find relevant Web links organized by the key terms associated with this chapter.

CHAPTER 3

© Paul Marcus, Musical Chairs, oil painting on wood, 48 in. × 72 in., Studio SPM, Inc.

RACIAL AND ETHNIC INEQUALITY

I T WAS JUST AFTER DARK AS THE bronze Volvo turned the corner onto a quiet residential street in the Venice Beach community in Los Angeles. Cheryl Creighton, a southern California school administrator, had picked up two friends and was driving to a local restaurant for dinner. She glanced at the rear-view mirror and muttered, "Uh oh—what did I do now?" Behind her she could see the red lights on top of the police car.

She slowly pulled the car to the curb and turned off the engine. The doors of the police car opened; one officer walked up along the driver's side of the car, while another crouched down on the sidewalk. The first officer asked Creighton for her driver's license and registration and then told the three occupants to get out of the car, kneel, and then lie down in the street. The second officer came over and placed handcuffs on Ms. Creighton and her passengers. Allowing them to stand and move to the curb, the officers quizzed the three for ten minutes, asking where they had been and where they were going. One officer went back to the police car and ran several computer checks of the Volvo and its driver. Then the officers removed the handcuffs and told the three that they were free to leave.

For fifteen minutes after the police officers left, the three just sat in the car, shaken and getting angrier by the minute. No longer in the mood for dinner, they decided to drive to a nearby police station to complain about the way they had been treated. Mrs. Creighton and her friends walked into the precinct station and identified themselves to a sergeant behind the desk. Why had they been stopped? Why were they made to lie in the street and treated so roughly?

The sergeant made a short telephone call and then explained to them that Ms. Creighton's Volvo matched the description of an auto stolen shortly before the incident in the same neighborhood. But, she countered, the officers said nothing about that at the time. She asked sternly, "Would they have behaved the same way if we had been white instead of black?"

GETTING THE PICTURE

✦ Is race simply biological?

Race is a socially constructed category by which some people gain advantages over others.

✦ Who is a minority?

As early as 2060, white people will become a minority of the U.S. population.

✦ Is prejudice simply a matter of individual attitudes?

Prejudice and discrimination are also built into the operation of society.

Such cases are common enough in the United States that they have a name; the practice is now known as "racial profiling," the targeting of African Americans or other minorities as suspicious because of the color of their skin. Sometimes African Americans feel they have been guilty of nothing more than "driving while black" (Avril, Campbell, & Ginsburg, 1999).

Charges of racial profiling raise a number of important questions. What is "race"? How does race (and the associated concept of ethnicity) affect our everyday lives? How do they figure into problems of social inequality? This chapter will answer these questions and explore related issues of prejudice, discrimination, segregation, multiculturalism, and affirmative action. We begin with a closer look at the central concepts of race and ethnicity.

RACE AND ETHNICITY

Many people in the United States and other countries consider race and ethnicity to be important dimensions of social identity. They can be a source of great pride, yet they also drive people into savage conflict. The first step in understanding why is to clarify the meanings of the concepts.

Race

Race is *a socially constructed category of people who share biologically transmitted traits that a society defines as*

important. For hundreds of years, societies have divided humanity into categories based on skin color, hair texture, facial features, and body shape.

Race has nothing to do with being human; all people everywhere belong to a single biological species, *Homo sapiens* (Latin meaning "thinking person"), that emerged in Africa some 250,000 years ago. The physical variations that societies use to construct racial categories emerged over tens of thousands of generations among people living in different regions of the world. In tropical areas, humans living in the hot sun developed darker skin from a natural pigment called melanin; in cooler regions, humans developed lighter skin.

If people never moved from the place where they were born, we could expect everyone in one geographic area to look pretty much alike. But migration has spread physical traits (linked to our genes) the world over. This is especially true among people living in the world's "crossroads" regions, such as the Middle East. By contrast, historically isolated people are more physically similar; for example, almost all Japanese people have black hair.

The fact that race is a socially constructed category means that any distinctive physical traits may be used to assign people to a racial category. In the early decades of the twentieth century, public opinion turned against European immigrants as their numbers grew. For a time, many southern Europeans—such as Italians—were "racialized" and defined as nonwhite.

When Was Race Invented? Centuries ago, trade and global exploration brought the world's people into greater contact, boosting awareness of human diversity. By the late 1500s, Europeans began using the term *race*, and by about 1800 European scientists devised three broad classifications for humanity. They coined the term *Caucasian* (meaning European and Western Asian) to designate people with light skin and fine hair; *Negroid* (derived from Latin meaning "black") to refer to people with dark skin and the coarse, curly hair typical of sub-Saharan Africa; and *Mongoloid* (referring to the Mongolian region of Asia) to refer to people with yellow or brown skin and distinctive folds on the eyelids.

Are Races Real? Sociologists are quick to point out that, at best, racial categories are misleading and, at worst, they are a harmful way to divide humanity. First, biologically pure races simply do not exist. That is, human beings have migrated and reproduced throughout the world, resulting in physical diversity everywhere. For example, the Caucasian category includes both very light-skinned people (in Scandinavia) and very dark-skinned people (in southern India). Similarly, the Negroid category includes both dark-skinned people (common in Africa) and light-skinned people (the Australian Aborigines). Nor do physical traits line up in any consistent order. For instance, dark-skinned people can have kinky hair (common in Africa) or straight hair (common in India). Scientifically speaking, people from different racial categories differ in only about 6 percent of their genes, which is less than the genetic variation within each category. In short, from a scientific standpoint, physical variation is real, but racial categories simply do not fit that reality very well (Boza, 2002; Harris & Sim, 2002).

Should Races Exist at All? If racial categories are misleading, why do they exist? Some sociologists argue that dividing humanity into racial categories is simply a strategy to allow some people to dominate others (Bonilla-Silva, 1999; Johnson, Rush, & Feagin, 2000; Zuberi, 2001). That is, Europeans attached cultural traits to skin color (creating the "honest and rational" European versus the "beastlike" African and the "devious" Asian) in order to make themselves better than those they wanted to control. In this way, European colonists justified oppressing Latin Americans, Africans, and Asians. Similarly, North Americans defined Native peoples in less-than-human terms (as "red savages") to justify killing them and taking their land. Indeed, when people of English

Marriage between a woman and a man deemed to be of different races was illegal in much of the United States, although such laws were struck down by the end of the 1960s. Since then, the number of multiracial couples has risen dramatically, and studies show that about 5 percent of children consider themselves to be multiracial. Do you think that, a century from now, race will continue to be an important factor guiding romantic attachments?

ancestry needed Irish and Italian immigrants to work for little pay, they defined them as racially different (Ignatiev, 1995; Camara, 2000; Brodkin, 2001).

Well into the last century, many southern states legally defined as "colored" anyone having as little as 1/32 African ancestry (that is, one African American great-great-great grandparent). By 1970, such laws had been overturned by the courts, allowing parents to declare the race of their child as they wish (usually on the birth certificate). Even today, however, most people still consider racial identity important.

Multiracial People Today, more people than ever before identify themselves as multiracial. When completing the 2000 Census forms, almost 7 million people in the United States described themselves this way, checking more than one racial category.

In addition, marriage between people of different racial categories now accounts for 3 percent of all marriages. This, in turn, has tripled the official number of multiracial births over the last twenty years to 175,000 each year, accounting for about 5 percent of all births (U.S. Census Bureau, 2003). As time goes on, then, fewer people will see one another in terms of rigid racial categories.

TABLE 3–1	RACIAL AND ETHNIC CATEGORIES IN THE UNITED STATES, 2000	
RACIAL OR ETHNIC CLASSIFICATION*	**APPROXIMATE U.S. POPULATION**	**PERCENTAGE OF TOTAL POPULATION**
Hispanic descent	**35,305,818**	**12.5%**
Mexican	20,640,711	7.3
Puerto Rican	3,406,178	1.2
Cuban	1,241,685	0.4
Other Hispanic	10,017,244	3.6
African descent	**34,658,190**	**12.3**
Native American descent	**2,475,956**	**0.9**
American Indian	1,815,653	0.6
Eskimo	45,919	<
Other Native American	614,384	0.2
Asian or Pacific Island descent	**10,641,833**	**3.8**
Chinese	2,432,585	0.9
Filipino	1,850,314	0.7
Asian Indian	1,678,765	0.6
Vietnamese	1,122,528	0.4
Korean	1,076,872	0.4
Japanese	796,700	0.3
Cambodian	171,937	<
Hmong	169,428	<
Laotian	168,707	<
Other Asian or Pacific Islander	1,173,997	0.4
West Indian descent	**1,869,504**	**0.7**
Arab descent	**1,202,871**	**0.4**
Non-Hispanic European descent	**194,552,774**	**70.9**
German	42,885,162	15.2
Irish	30,594,130	10.9
English	24,515,138	8.7
Italian	15,723,555	5.6
Polish	8,977,444	3.2
French	8,325,509	3.0
Scottish	4,890,581	1.7
Dutch	4,542,494	1.6
Norwegian	4,477,725	1.6
Scots-Irish	4,319,232	1.5
Swedish	3,998,310	1.4
Russian	2,652,214	0.9
French Canadian	2,435,098	0.9
Welsh	1,753,794	0.6
Two or more races	**6,826,228**	**2.4**

*People of Hispanic descent may be of any race. Many people also identify with more than one ethnic category. Therefore, figures total more than 100 percent.

< Indicates less than 1/10 of 1 percent.

Sources: U.S. Census Bureau (2001, 2003).

Ethnicity

Whereas race revolves around biological traits, ethnicity is a matter of culture. **Ethnicity** is *a shared cultural heritage, which typically involves common ancestors, language, and religion.* Just as U.S. society is racially diverse, so the population contains hundreds of distinctive ethnic categories. Table 3–1 shows the breadth of this nation's racial and ethnic diversity.

Although race and ethnicity are different, the two may go together. For example, Korean Americans, Native Americans, and people of Italian or African descent share not only certain physical traits but also—at least among families maintaining cultural traditions—ethnic traits as well.

Immigration

This country's remarkable racial and ethnic diversity is a product of immigration. Everyone living in North America is descended from people who lived elsewhere.

The "Great Immigration"   What historians call the "Great Immigration" started at the end of the Civil War (1865) and lasted until the beginning of World War I (1914). New industrial factories offered many jobs, and East Coast cities were transformed as ships brought some 25 million people across the Atlantic Ocean in search of economic opportunity. In 1900, four-fifths of New Yorkers either had been born abroad or had foreign-born parents (Glaab & Brown, 1967).

Many people extended a welcome to the newcomers, but others—called *nativists*—feared that immigration might endanger this country's mostly English culture. Such opposition rose after 1900 when the tide of immigration shifted from northern Europe to southern and eastern Europe, where people had darker skin, spoke languages other than English, and were Catholic, Orthodox, or Jewish rather than Protestant. Pressured by nativists, Congress passed laws in the 1920s (especially the Immigration Act of 1924) that cut immigration by instituting a system of quotas for various nationalities. These laws, along with the economic depression that began in 1929, reduced immigration to a trickle by the 1930s, and the numbers stayed low until the mid-1960s.

Recent Immigration   Congress ended the quota system in 1965, leading to another wave of mass immigration. Once again, the arrival of immigrants—this time mostly from Mexico and other nations in Latin

America, and the Philippines, South Korea, and other Asian countries—has been controversial. In 1986, Congress enacted the Immigrant Control and Reform Act. The act also offered amnesty to illegal immigrants already in the country, but outlawed hiring of undocumented immigrants (now estimated to number about 7 million) to discourage further illegal immigration. Many workers produced fraudulent documents, however, and some companies avoided hiring *any* immigrants (or people who looked like they might be immigrants) for fear of criminal penalties (Portes, 2000; Gamboa, 2003).

California is the state with the largest immigrant population; about 40 percent of its people speak a language other than English at home. In 1994, Californians enacted Proposition 187, cutting off social service benefits including schooling and health care to illegal immigrants. The idea was to discourage illegal immigration, but this law also hurt people already in California.

Although Congress enacted additional laws during the 1990s to limit immigration, the number of people arriving each year is close to 1 million. This is more people each year than during the "Great Immigration" a century ago, although today's newcomers are joining a population five times larger. In 2003, of a total U.S. population of about 285 million, some 33 million (12 percent) are foreign born; about 21 percent have at least one parent born abroad.

Opposition to immigration continues today. In the Southwest, some landowners have used guns to threaten people who cross the border from Mexico and trespass on their land. Moreover, throughout the country fear of terrorism has made people wary of newcomers, even as the federal government monitors new arrivals—especially those from middle eastern countries—more closely (Ragavan, 2002).

Read more about current U.S. immigration at
http://www.immigration.gov

Minorities

Most immigrants to the United States have found more opportunities than they had in their homelands. But many have also discovered that their race and ethnicity stand as barriers to full participation in U.S. society. Social scientists use the term **minority** to refer to *any category of people, distinguished by physical or cultural traits, that a society subjects to disadvantages.*

During the Great Immigration, some 25 million people came to the United States, mostly from nations in Europe. Many were families that arrived with little more than their dreams.

Visibility Minorities share a *distinctive identity,* which may be racial (based on physical traits, which are difficult to change) or ethnic (including dress or accent, which people can change). For example, many people of Japanese ancestry in the United States have little knowledge of their native language, and more than half have non-Japanese spouses. Thus Japanese Americans are becoming less of an ethnic category and, by marrying with people of other backgrounds, they are becoming less of a racial category as well. A minority's ability to blend in with others depends on their desire to hold onto their traditions and on the willingness of other people to accept them. For instance, whites have shown a far greater willingness to marry people of Japanese ancestry than people of African descent (U.S. Census Bureau, 2003).

Power A second characteristic of minorities is *disadvantage.* In the United States, minorities have less schooling and lower-paying jobs, which means

A NATION OF DIVERSITY

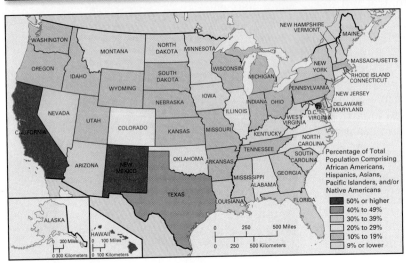

NATIONAL MAP 3–1
Where the Minority-Majority Already Exists

By 2000, minorities had become a majority in three states—Hawaii, California, and New Mexico—and the District of Columbia. With a 45 percent minority population, Texas is approaching a minority-majority. At the other extreme, Vermont and Maine have the lowest share of racial and ethnic minorities (about 2 percent). Why are states with high minority populations located in the South and Southwest?

Source: "America 2000: A Map of the Mix," *Newsweek*, September 18, 2000, p. 48. Copyright © 2000 Newsweek, Inc. All rights reserved. Reprinted by permission.

higher rates of poverty. Of course, not all people in any minority category are disadvantaged. In other words, despite the statistical averages some people of African, Asian, or Hispanic ancestry have very high social standing. But even the most successful individuals know that their membership in a minority category reduces their standing in some people's eyes (Benjamin, 1991).

Numbers　About one-fourth of the entire U.S. population falls into a minority racial or ethnic category. In Chapter 4 ("Gender Inequality"), we take up the question of whether women—of any race or ethnicity—should also be counted as a minority.

Minorities are a rising share of the U.S. population. In fact, minorities are a majority in half of the 100 largest U.S. cities (U.S. Census Bureau, 2002). As National Map 3–1 shows, a minority-majority already exists in three states, and more will soon follow. The Critical Thinking box asks at what point the entire nation will have a minority-majority.

PATTERNS OF MAJORITY-MINORITY INTERACTION

The way majority and minority populations interact can range from deadly to peaceful. In studying such patterns, sociologists use four models: genocide, segregation, assimilation, and pluralism.

Genocide

Genocide is *the systematic killing of one category of people by another.* Genocide is murder; even so, it has taken place time and again in human history, tolerated and sometimes even encouraged by governments and their people.

Beginning about 1500, the Spanish, Portuguese, English, French, and Dutch forcefully colonized North and South America, resulting in the deaths of thousands of native people. Although most native people fell victim to diseases brought by Europeans to which they had no natural defenses, many were killed outright (Matthiessen, 1984; Sale, 1990).

In the 1930s and 1940s, Adolf Hitler and his Nazi government murdered more than 6 million "undesirables," including homosexuals, people with disabilities, and most of Europe's Jewish population. Soviet dictator Josef Stalin slaughtered his country's people on an even greater scale, killing some 30 million real and imagined enemies during decades of violent rule. Between 1975 and 1980, Cambodia's Communist regime butchered millions whom they saw as enemies. More recently, Rwanda's Hutus massacred Tutsis in that African nation, and Serbs systematically killed Croats in Eastern Europe.

Segregation

Segregation is *the physical and social separation of categories of people.* Sometimes minority populations,

Critical Thinking   The Minority-Majority Debate

IN HALF OF THE 100 LARGEST U.S. cities, racial and ethnic minorities (people of African, Asian, and Latino descent) already make up a majority of the population. The Census Bureau predicts that the entire country will have a minority-majority by about 2060, within the lifetimes of many readers of this book.

Why? Because minority populations are rising rapidly. Whereas the number of non-Hispanic whites increased 5 percent between 1990 and 2000, during the same period the number of African Americans increased 16 percent, Native Americans rose by 19 percent, Hispanics jumped by 47 percent, and Asians and Pacific Islanders soared by 52 percent.

But predictions about the future are, at least to some extent, a matter of guesswork, and they are also guided by politics. Liberals look favorably upon the prediction of a minority-majority because it highlights the need for social programs to help minorities now—on campus, in the workplace, and in local communities. Regardless of exactly when the United States reaches a minority-majority, they argue, this country needs to make a greater effort to help disadvantaged minorities.

Conservatives, who oppose what they see as "special programs" for minorities, express doubt about the minority-majority prediction. Much of the current rise in the minority population, they point out, is caused by a high birth rate among recent immigrants. They predict that after immigrants have been in the United States for a number of years, their birth rates will fall into line with the national average, as has been the case with immigrants in the past. Moreover, who can be sure how many people will enter the United States in the decades ahead and from which nations they will come?

The United States probably will end up with a minority-majority. But exactly when that will occur remains a matter of debate. Even greater controversy surrounds the question of how U.S. society should prepare for this coming change.

ISSUES AND EXERCISES

1. What changes in U.S. culture would you expect to accompany a minority-majority? What might be the effects on film, music, television, religion, education, and language?

2. What problems are likely to accompany this trend toward greater social diversity?

3. Do you think this country needs to prepare now for a coming minority-majority? How?

Source: U.S. Census Bureau (2003).

---

especially religious orders such as the Amish, voluntarily segregate themselves. Usually, though, the majority population segregates minorities by forcing them to "stay with their own."

Racial segregation in the United States began with slavery and later included legally separate hotels, restaurants, schools, buses, and trains. A number of court cases have reduced de jure (Latin meaning "by law") segregation in the United States. However, de facto ("in fact") segregation continues; most neighborhoods, schools, hospitals, and even cemeteries still contain, for the most part, people of one race. For example, Livonia, Michigan, is 96 percent white; across the city line, Detroit is 83 percent African American (Emerson, Yancey, & Chai, 2001; Metzger, 2001; Krysan, 2002).

The most intense segregation occurs in inner-city areas. Douglas Massey and Nancy Denton (1989) documented the *hypersegregation* of African Americans who have little contact with people outside of their community. Whereas hypersegregation affects just a few percent of poor white people, it affects about one in five African Americans (Jagarowsky & Bane, 1990).

Because minorities, by definition, have little power, challenging segregation is not easy and may even be dangerous. Sometimes, however, the actions of even a single person can make a difference. The Defining Moment box on page 62 describes the actions of Rosa Parks, who sparked a social movement to end segregation on buses and other forms of public transportation.

A DEFINING MOMENT

Rosa Parks: Saying No to Segregation

IT ALL BEGAN SO ROUTINELY THAT NO one would have known history was being made. On December 1, 1955, Rosa Parks, a young black woman living in Montgomery, Alabama, boarded a city bus. At that time, city law required African Americans to ride in certain seats near the back of the bus, and Parks did exactly that. Slowly the bus filled with people. As the bus pulled to the curb to pick up some white passengers, the driver turned and asked four black people to give up their seats so that the white people could sit down. Three did as he asked. But Rosa Parks refused to move.

The driver left the bus and returned with a police officer, who arrested Parks for breaking the city's segregation law. She appeared in court, was convicted by a judge, and fined $14. But African Americans all over the city were telling one another about Parks's stand (or sitting) for justice, and a social movement was underway. Within days, African Americans in Montgomery had organized a boycott of all city buses. Soon after, the city agreed to end this form of segregation.

Today, Rosa Parks is in her nineties. But this well-known figure of the civil rights movement still appears

This photo shows Rosa Parks being fingerprinted by police in Montgomery, Alabama. At the time of her arrest, the law defined Rosa Parks as the "problem." But the bus boycott that followed her arrest soon changed that, defining racial segregation as the problem.

at public events to celebrate the power of people—even one at a time—to change the world.

Assimilation

Assimilation is *the process by which minorities gradually adopt cultural patterns from the majority population.* When minorities—especially new immigrants—assimilate, they change their styles of dress, language, cultural values, and even religion.

A common idea is that the United States is a "melting pot" where the different ways of life that people bring to this country from their homelands blend together to produce one national lifestyle. Although there is some truth to this image, U.S. history shows that minorities are the ones who do most of the changing as they adopt cultural patterns displayed by more powerful people who have been here longer. In some cases, the majority population forces change on minorities, as when public schools teach immigrant children English; in other cases, minorities imitate those they see as their "betters" in order to escape hostility and move up socially.

The amount of assimilation varies by category. For example, Germans and Irish have "melted" more than Italians, and the Japanese more than the Chinese or Koreans.

Pluralism

Pluralism is *a state in which people of all racial and ethnic categories have roughly equal social standing.* Pluralism represents a situation in which no minority category is subject to disadvantage. The United States is pluralistic to the extent that—officially, at least—all people have equal standing under the law. But in reality, tolerance for diversity (majority tolerance for minorities and one minority population's tolerance for another) is limited. For example, half the states have passed laws designating English as their official language. Furthermore, as we now explain, the social standing of most minority populations is below that of the white, European majority.

THE SOCIAL STANDING OF U.S. MINORITIES

The United States is a nation of racial and ethnic diversity. It is important to know something of the history of the largest minorities in order to understand today's racial and ethnicity inequality.

Native Americans

Native Americans are descendants of Asians, the first people to come to North America across the Bering Strait from Asia. Over thousands of years, they spread throughout the hemisphere, forming hundreds of distinct societies, including the Inca of South America, the Aztec of Central America, the Aleuts and Eskimos of Alaska, and a number of American Indian societies, including the Cherokee, Zuni, Sioux, and Iroquois.

By 1500, the arrival of European explorers and colonizers marked the beginning of centuries of conflict. What some Europeans called bringing civilization to "the New World" was for Native Americans the destruction of their ancient and thriving civilizations. From a population in the millions at the time of European contact, the number of "vanishing Americans" soon fell to barely 250,000 by 1900 (Dobyns, 1966; Tyler, 1973).

At first, the U.S. government viewed native peoples as independent nations and tried to gain land from them through treaties. But the government was quick to use its superior military power against any who resisted. Soldiers forcibly removed the Cherokee from their homelands in the southeastern United States, causing thousands of deaths along what came to be known as the Trail of Tears. By 1800, few Native people remained along the East Coast.

In 1871, the United States declared American Indians wards of the federal government. At this point, the goal was assimilation. This meant remaking Native peoples as "Americans" by placing them

Despite media reports of the financial success that legal gambling on reservations has brought to some American Indians, the majority of Native people in the United States are greatly disadvantaged. Scenes such as this one from the Hopi reservation near Tuba City, Arizona, are more the rule than the exception.

on reservations where they were forced to adopt Christianity in place of their ancestral religions and where schools taught children English in place of ancestral tongues.

Reservations still operate today even as the government tries to help American Indians strike out on their own. Since gaining full citizenship in 1924, a growing number of American Indians have assimilated into the larger society, many marrying people of other backgrounds. But as Table 3–2 shows, American Indians remain disadvantaged, with below-average income, a high poverty rate, and low educational achievement.

TABLE 3–2 THE SOCIAL STANDING OF NATIVE AMERICANS, 2000

	MEDIAN FAMILY INCOME	PERCENTAGE LIVING IN POVERTY	PERCENTAGE WITH FOUR OR MORE YEARS OF COLLEGE (AGES 25 AND OVER)
Entire U.S. population	$50,891	11.3%	25.6%
Native Americans	$31,064	27.1%	9.3%*

*Author estimate based on latest available data.

Source: U.S. Census Bureau (2002).

In the 1990s, American Indian organizations reported a tide of new membership applications, and many children are learning to speak native languages better than their parents (Fost, 1991; Johnson, 1991; Nagel, 1996; Martin, 1997). Many American Indians operate a wide range of successful businesses, and some tribes have used the legal autonomy of reservations to build casinos. But the enormous profits from these casinos actually enrich few Native peoples, with most profits going to non-Indian investors (Raymond, 2001; Bartlett & Steele, 2002). In sum, while some prosper, most American Indians remain severely disadvantaged and share a profound sense of historical injustice suffered at the hands of their conquerors.

People of African Descent

People of African ancestry arrived in the Americas along with the first European explorers. After 1619, however, when a Dutch trading ship delivered twenty Africans to Jamestown, Virginia, to work for whites, people gradually began to see dark skin as a sign of inferiority. In 1661, Virginia enacted the first slave law (Sowell, 1981). In 1776, the year the United States declared its independence from Great Britain, slavery was legal in every state.

The Southern plantation system depended on slaves to work the cotton and tobacco fields. To meet the demand for slave labor, slave traders (including Arabs and Africans as well as Europeans and North Americans) legally transported human beings across the Atlantic Ocean, in chains and under horrific conditions, until 1808. In all, slave traders brought 10 million Africans to the Americas, including 500,000 to the United States. This was just half the number who left Africa—the other half died during the brutal journey (Tannenbaum, 1946; Franklin, 1967; Sowell, 1981).

Slave owners could make any demands on their workers and discipline them in whatever way they wished. Slaves could not attend school, and owners routinely broke apart families as they traded men, women, and children for profit.

Not all people of African descent were slaves. Roughly 1 million free persons of color lived in the North and the South, most farming small parcels of land, working at skilled jobs in cities, or operating small businesses.

How could slavery exist in a society with a Declaration of Independence that declared "all men are created equal" and entitled to "life, liberty, and the pursuit of happiness?" Rather than making all people free, our society decided that African Americans were not really people. In the 1857 Dred Scott case, the U.S. Supreme Court stated that people of color were not citizens entitled to the rights and protections of U.S. law.

The Civil War brought slavery to an end. The northern states, where slavery had less economic value, had already ended the practice. As the guns roared, President Abraham Lincoln declared slavery abolished in the southern Confederacy on January 1, 1863. When the fighting ended in 1865, Congress banned slavery with the Thirteenth Amendment to the Constitution. In 1868, the Fourteenth Amendment reversed the Dred Scott decision, giving citizenship to

The mass media played a powerful role in the civil rights movement of the 1950s and 1960s. Televised scenes such as this one in Birmingham, Alabama, in which police turned dogs and fire hoses on demonstrators, changed the mood of the nation in favor of the idea that all people should have equal opportunity and equal standing before the law.

TABLE 3-3 THE SOCIAL STANDING OF AFRICAN AMERICANS, 2001

	MEDIAN FAMILY INCOME	PERCENTAGE LIVING IN POVERTY	PERCENTAGE WITH FOUR OR MORE YEARS OF COLLEGE (AGES 25 AND OVER)
Entire U.S. population	$51,407	11.7%	26.7%
African Americans	$33,598	22.7%	16.6%

Source: U.S. Census Bureau (2002).

all people, regardless of color, born in the United States. But the end of slavery did not bring with it the end of racial discrimination; so-called Jim Crow laws were soon enacted, barring black people from voting and sitting on juries, and segregating trains, restaurants, hotels, and other public places (Woodward, 1974).

After World War I, when Congress closed the doors to further immigration, the need for labor in the booming factories sparked the "Great Migration," which drew tens of thousands of men and women of color from the rural South to the industrialized North. These were times of great achievements in African American life as, for example, the Harlem Renaissance (centered in the large African American community in New York City) produced writers such as Langston Hughes. Even so, racial segregation in neighborhoods, schools, and jobs remained across the country.

But change was coming. In 1948, President Harry Truman declared an end to segregation in the military. Black legal scholars, including Thurgood Marshall (1908–1993), who served for thirty years on the U.S. Supreme Court, led an attack on school segregation, leading to the 1954 case, *Brown v. The Board of Education of Topeka* (Kansas). In this landmark decision, the Supreme Court rejected the claim that black and white children could receive "separate but equal" schooling.

One year later, the heroic action of Rosa Parks sparked the bus boycott that desegregated public transportation in Montgomery, Alabama. Soon after, the federal government passed the Civil Rights Act of 1964 (prohibiting segregation in employment and public accommodations), the Voting Rights Act of 1965 (banning voting requirements that prevented African Americans from having a political voice), and the Civil Rights Act of 1968 (which outlawed discrimination in housing). Together, these laws brought an end to most legal discrimination in public life.

But African Americans' struggle for full participation in U.S. society is far from over. People of

African descent are still disadvantaged in U.S. society, as shown in Table 3–3. African American families still have below-average income, and the black poverty rate is three times higher than the white poverty rate. Although about 85 percent of African Americans now complete high school, the college graduation rate is well below the national average.

By 2000, half of all African American families earned at least $35,000 a year; one-third earned more than $50,000 (U.S. Census Bureau, 2002). But whereas most white families are in the middle class, most black families remain in the working class (Horton et al., 2000). Indeed, for some African American families, income has declined as factory jobs, especially important to people living in central cities, have moved to countries with lower labor costs. Moreover, unemployment among African Americans stands at 10.3 percent—more than twice the rate among white people (Wilson, 1996; U.S. Department of Labor, 2003).

For more on the social standing of U.S. minorities, go to http://www.access.gpo.gov/eop/ca/index.html

People of Asian Descent

Asian Americans include people with historical ties to dozens of Asian nations. The largest number have roots in China (2.4 million), the Philippines (2.0 million), India (1.7 million), South Korea (1.1 million), and Japan (925,000). In all, Asian Americans number more than 10 million (4 percent of the total population) and over the last decade have increased in number faster than any other minority category (U.S. Immigration and Naturalization Service, 2002).

The first Asians to migrate to North America in the modern era came more than 150 years ago from China and Japan. The Gold Rush of 1849 created a demand for laborers in California. Chinese men answered the call, numbering 100,000 within a generation, and they were joined by a small number of

Japanese immigrants. As long as cheap labor was needed, whites welcomed them. But when economy slowed, these workers were seen as an economic threat by whites who labeled them the Yellow Peril."

Legislatures and courts were pressured to bar Asians from certain work. In 1882, the federal government passed the Chinese Exclusion Act, which ended the flow of new immigrants from China. A similar action against Japan took place in 1908. These laws caused the Asian population in the United States to fall because almost all the people already here were men, and racial hostility prevented Asian men from marrying non-Asian women. After 1920, California and other states enacted laws banning interracial marriage outright.

Many Asians formed urban neighborhoods where they could help one another. Chinatowns soon flourished in San Francisco, New York, and other large cities, with Chinese-owned restaurants, laundries, and other small businesses. Self-employment has been popular not only among the Chinese but among all minorities who find few employers willing to hire them for good wages.

World War II brought important changes to both the Japanese American and Chinese American populations. The war in the Pacific began when Japan attacked Hawaii's Pearl Harbor naval base. The military strike stunned the United States, and many people wondered which side Japanese Americans would take in the conflict. From the outset, Japanese Americans demonstrated their loyalty to the United States. But fear of Japan's industrial and military might, coupled with racial hostility, pushed President Franklin Roosevelt to issue Executive Order 9066, forcibly relocating all people of Japanese ancestry to military camps located in remote inland areas. The order forced more than 100,000 Japanese Americans to sell their businesses, homes, and farms for a fraction of their true value. Taken to camps, they lived under the watchful eyes of armed soldiers until 1944, when the U.S. Supreme Court declared the policy unconstitutional. (It is interesting to note that although the United States was also at war with Germany, no such policy was used against people of German ancestry.) In 1988, Congress admitted this action was wrong and awarded a symbolic compensation of $20,000 to each surviving camp inmate.

Learn more about the problems and achievements of Japanese Americans at this site: **http://www.jinjapan.org**

Because China joined the United States in the fight against Japan, in 1943 the federal government ended the 1882 ban on Chinese immigration and gave citizenship to Chinese Americans born abroad. The same offer was made after the war, in 1952, to foreign-born Japanese Americans.

After the war, people of Chinese and Japanese descent flocked to college, believing that more schooling was the key to success. By the 1980s, Asian Americans were finding themselves touted as the "model minority," based on their cultural commitment to study and hard work and their outstanding record of achievement.

From 1942 until 1944, more than 100,000 men, women, and children of Japanese ancestry were forced to live in military detention camps. This policy took away not just Japanese Americans' liberty but also most of their property, as families were forced to sell homes and businesses for a small share of what they were really worth. Why do you think no people of German or Italian ancestry (the United States was at war with those nations, too) were ever treated this way?

TABLE 3-4 THE SOCIAL STANDING OF ASIAN AMERICANS, 2001

	MEDIAN FAMILY INCOME	PERCENTAGE LIVING IN POVERTY	PERCENTAGE WITH FOUR OR MORE YEARS OF COLLEGE (AGES 25 AND OVER)
Entire U.S. population	$51,407	11.7%	26.7%
All Asian Americans	$60,158	10.2%	47.2%
Chinese Americans	$57,174*	10.2%*	51.0%*
Japanese Americans	$71,336*	5.1%*	43.2%*
Korean Americans	$46,924*	9.9%*	43.2%*

*Author estimates based on latest available data.

Source: U.S. Census Bureau (2002, 2003).

There is some truth to the "model minority" notion. As Table 3–4 shows, both Chinese and Japanese Americans now have above-average income and education. Poverty rates also are below the national average. But many Asian families work long and hard in low-paying jobs. Although the Chinatowns and Little Tokyos found in some large cities may offer social support, they may limit job opportunities by discouraging their residents from learning English (Portes & Jensen, 1989; Zhou & Logan, 1989; Kinkead, 1992; Gilbertson & Gurak, 1993).

Today, about half of all immigrants to the United States each year are from an Asian nation. Many Asian Americans, especially those with high social standing, have assimilated into the larger cultural mix. For example, few third- and fourth-generation Japanese Americans (the *Sansei* and *Yonsei*) live in segregated neighborhoods. Indeed, most people of Japanese ancestry marry someone of another racial and ethnic background.

Many Koreans and Indians, on the other hand, follow the example of immigrants a century ago and settle in ethnic neighborhoods, sometimes for protection from racial and ethnic hostility. Although Asian Americans have fared better than most minorities, anti-Asian prejudice is strong (Chua-Eoan, 2000; Parrillo, 2003). Many Asian Americans remain socially marginal, living in two worlds and fully belonging to neither one.

Hispanic Americans

Hispanic Americans are people with cultural roots in the nations of Central and South America, the Caribbean, and Spain. As a result, there are many Hispanic or Latino cultures. Racially, eight in ten Hispanic Americans consider themselves to be white, although these diverse people have a range of skin colors and physical features.

On Census Bureau forms, people of any race may identify themselves as being of Hispanic origin. In 2000, more than 35 million people did so, making Hispanics the largest U.S. minority, with 12.5 percent of the population (exceeding African Americans at 12.3 percent).

National Map 3–2 on page 68 shows the concentration of Hispanic Americans—as well as African Americans and Asian Americans—across the United States. Many Hispanic Americans reside in the Southwest because about two-thirds (more than 20 million) are Mexican Americans, commonly referred to as Chicanas (females) and Chicanos (males). Next in terms of numbers are Puerto Ricans (3 million) and Cuban Americans (1.2 million), with smaller numbers from dozens of other countries. Overall, Hispanic Americans are so numerous and their cultural contributions so great that Spanish has become the second language of the United States.

Many Mexican Americans have lived for centuries on land that, after the Mexican War (1846–1848), became what is now Texas, New Mexico, Arizona, Nevada, Utah, California, and Colorado. Of course, others are new arrivals, drawn to the United States by a desire for greater economic opportunity.

Puerto Rico, an island controlled by the Spanish beginning in the sixteenth century, became a U.S. territory at the end of the Spanish-American War in 1898. Since 1917, all island residents have been U.S. citizens, although Puerto Rico is a commonwealth (not a state). The largest Puerto Rican community off the island is New York's Spanish Harlem, home to roughly 800,000 people. In recent years, about as many people have returned to the island from New York as have come to New York from Puerto Rico (Navarro, 2000).

A NATION OF DIVERSITY

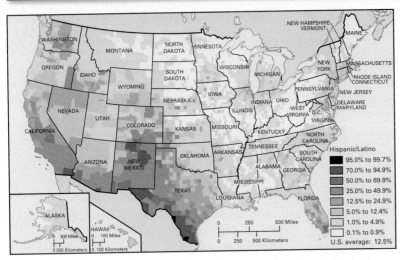

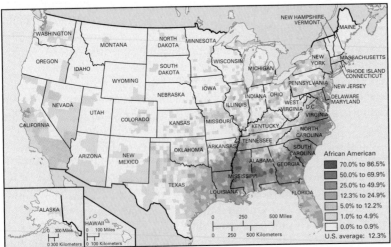

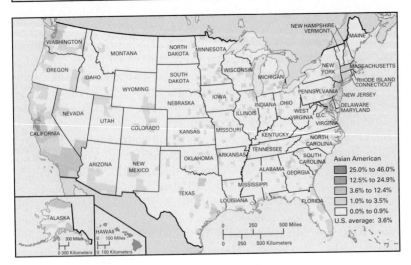

NATIONAL MAP 3–2

The Concentration of Hispanics/Latinos, African Americans, and Asian Americans, by County, 2000

In 2000, Hispanic Americans became the largest minority, with 12.5 percent of the U.S. population, compared with 12.3 percent for African Americans and 3.6 percent for Asian Americans. These three maps show the geographic distribution of these categories of people in 2000. Comparing them, we see that the southern half of the United States is home to far more minorities than the northern half. But do the three concentrate in the same areas? What patterns do the maps reveal?

Source: U.S. Census Bureau (2001).

Many Cubans fled to the United States after Fidel Castro gained control of Cuba in 1959. These men and women, numbering several hundreds of thousands, included affluent businesspeople and professionals. Most settled in Miami, building a vibrant Cuban American community.

Table 3–5 shows that the social standing of Hispanic Americans is below the U.S. average. However, various categories of Latinos have very different rankings. The most well-off are Cuban Americans, who have higher income and more schooling. Chicanos occupy a middle position in terms of income, although those who are immigrants have a low rate of high school completion. Puerto Ricans have the lowest relative ranking, with median family income at barely half the national average. One reason for this disadvantage is that many Puerto Ricans continue to speak only Spanish and not English, which can limit job opportunities.

Although one-third of Hispanic American families now earn more than $50,000 annually, many suffer from schools that deal poorly with Spanish speakers. Chapter 14 ("Education") reports that 28 percent of Latinos between ages fourteen and twenty-four leave school without a high school diploma. Furthermore, their cultural difference—and dark skin—still spark hostility.

PREJUDICE

As the preceding accounts show, minorities face the problem of **prejudice,** *any rigid and irrational generalization about an entire category of people.* Prejudice is a prejudgment, an attitude one develops *before* interacting with the specific people in question. Because such attitudes are not based on direct experience, prejudices are difficult to change.

Positive prejudices lead us to assume certain people (usually those like ourselves) are better or smarter. Negative prejudices include seeing someone who is different from us as less worthy. Prejudices—both positive and negative—involve social class, gender, religions, age, and sexual or political orientation. But probably no dimensions of difference involve as many prejudices as race and ethnicity.

Test your own degree of prejudice at
http://www.tolerance.org/hidden_bias/index.html

Stereotypes

A concept closely linked to prejudice is **stereotype,** *an exaggerated description applied to every person in some category.* The word *stereo* comes from Greek meaning "hard" or "solid," suggesting that people adhere rigidly to stereotypes when they are at odds with reality. Our culture contains stereotypes about every racial and ethnic minority. What stereotypes are conveyed in common phrases such as "Dutch treat," "French kiss," "Russian roulette," and "gypping" someone (a reference to gypsies)?

Of course, we all form opinions about the world, distinguishing, say, "good" and "bad" people and interesting and dull subjects. Generalizations of this kind usually cause no harm to anyone. But stereotypes are more of a problem because they assume that an entire racial or ethnic category of people shares particular traits, as when a white person thinks all African Americans are dishonest or a person of color thinks every white person is hostile. There is nothing wrong with forming a judgment about another individual on the basis of actual personal experience. But when we place people in a category before we have a chance to judge them as individuals, stereotypes dehumanize people.

TABLE 3–5 THE SOCIAL STANDING OF HISPANIC AMERICANS, 2001

	MEDIAN FAMILY INCOME	PERCENTAGE LIVING IN POVERTY	PERCENTAGE WITH FOUR OR MORE YEARS OF COLLEGE (AGES 25 AND OVER)
Entire U.S. population	$51,407	11.7%	26.7%
All Hispanics	$34,490	21.4%	11.1%
Mexican Americans	$33,533	22.8%	7.5%
Puerto Ricans	$30,095	26.1%	14.0%
Cuban Americans	$35,217	16.5%	18.6%

Source: U.S. Census Bureau (2002).

Prejudice can stand between people of different racial or ethnic categories as effectively as a wooden fence. Do you think prejudice is weakening among college students, as recent research suggests? Why or why not?

Racism

The most serious example of prejudice is **racism,** *the assertion that people of one race are less worthy than or even biologically inferior to others.* Over the course of human history, people the world over have assumed they were superior whereas outsiders were lesser human beings.

Why is racism so widespread? Because the claim that people are *biologically* inferior (although entirely wrong) can be used to justify making them *socially* inferior. For example, Europeans used racism to support the often brutal colonization of much of Latin America, Asia, and Africa. Colonizers spoke of the "white man's burden," meaning they (allegedly superior beings) had the obligation to help others (allegedly inferior beings) to become more like them.

Even today, hundreds of hate groups in the United States continue to claim that minorities are inferior. In addition, subtle forms of racism are common in everyday life (Feagin, 1991). The Critical Thinking box uses national survey data to reveal the extent of racist thinking.

Measuring Prejudice: The Social Distance Scale

Prejudice guides social interaction by drawing people toward some categories of people and away from others. Early in the twentieth century, Emory Bogardus (1925) developed the *social distance scale* to measure prejudice among students at U.S. colleges and universities. Bogardus asked students how closely they were willing to interact with people in thirty racial and ethnic categories. Figure 3–1 on page 72 shows the seven-point scale used by Bogardus. At one extreme, people express very high social distance (high negative prejudice), saying that some category of people should be barred from the country (point 7 in the figure); at the other extreme (little or no negative prejudice), people say they would accept members of some category into their family through marriage (Bogardus, 1925, 1967; Owen, Elsner, & McFaul, 1977).

Bogardus found that students (regardless of their own race and ethnicity) were most prejudiced toward Hispanics, African Americans, Asians, and Turks; they were willing to have these people as co-workers but not as neighbors, friends, or family members. At the other extreme, they were most accepting of the English, Scots, and Canadians, whom they were willing to have marry into their families.

Recently, Vincent Parrillo (2003)[1] repeated the social distance study to see how today's students felt about various minorities. There were three major findings:

[1]Parrillo dropped seven of Bogardus's original categories (Armenians, Czechs, Finns, Norwegians, Scots, Swedes, and Turks), because they are no longer visible minorities, and added nine new categories (Africans, Arabs, Cubans, Dominicans, Haitians, Jamaicans, Muslims, Puerto Ricans, and Vietnamese). This change probably encouraged higher social distance scores, making the downward trend all the more significant.

Critical Thinking   Attitudes toward Race and Intelligence

ALMOST EVERY YEAR, AS PART OF THE General Social Survey, researchers ask a representative sample of U.S. adults to rank racial and ethnic categories with regard to overall intelligence. They ask people to use a seven-point scale that ranges from 1 (very low intelligence) to 7 (very high intelligence). The figure at the right shows the average score respondents gave to each category of people.

Apparently, the U.S. public believes some racial and ethnic categories are smarter than others. Whites, the majority category, rank themselves high in intelligence. Notice, however, that southern whites—who historically have had less education than those in other regions—get a lower rating. The national opinion is that most minorities are less bright. An exception is Jewish people, most of whom are white and non-southern, with above-average education. Asian Americans also are ranked slightly above whites. The survey data place African Americans and Latinos further down the scale.

Almost all scientists agree that some individuals are smarter than other individuals. But just a few researchers argue that entire categories of people are innately smarter than others. For example, Richard Herrnstein and Charles Murray (1994) review research on intelligence and report that the average intelligence quotient (IQ) of white people (of European ancestry) is about 100, whereas the average IQ for people of East Asian ancestry is a bit higher at 103, and IQ for people of African descent is somewhat lower at 90.

Most sociologists claim that such differences are misleading. For example, Thomas Sowell argues that differences in IQ scores reflect not innate ability but differences in environment. Sowell found that early in the last century, immigrants from Poland, Lithuania, Italy, Greece, China, and Japan scored ten to fifteen points below the U.S. average on IQ tests. Today, Sowell adds, people in these same categories have IQ scores that are average or above. Among Italian Americans, for example, average IQ jumped almost ten points in fifty years; among Polish and Chinese Americans, the rise was almost twenty points.

Sowell found a similar pattern among African Americans. Black people living in the North outscore black people living in the South on IQ tests by about ten points, a difference that cannot result from biology. Similarly, African Americans who migrated from the South to the North after 1940 soon performed much better on IQ tests.

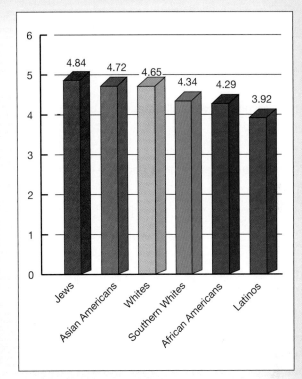

Source: NORC (2003:392–3).

Sowell concludes that cultural patterns are the main cause of IQ differences between categories of people. Asians score higher on tests not because they are smarter but because their cultures value learning and excellence. African Americans score lower because they carry a legacy of disadvantage that can undermine self-confidence and discourage achievement.

ISSUES AND EXERCISES

1. Why do you think U.S. adults rank racial and ethnic categories differently with regard to intelligence?

2. Do you think what we call "intelligence" is real? Can it be measured?

3. What value do you see in the use of IQ tests? Do you think the use of IQ tests can fuel unfair prejudice? Why or why not?

Sources: Sowell 1994, 1995; Herrnstein & Murray, 1994; NORC, 2003.

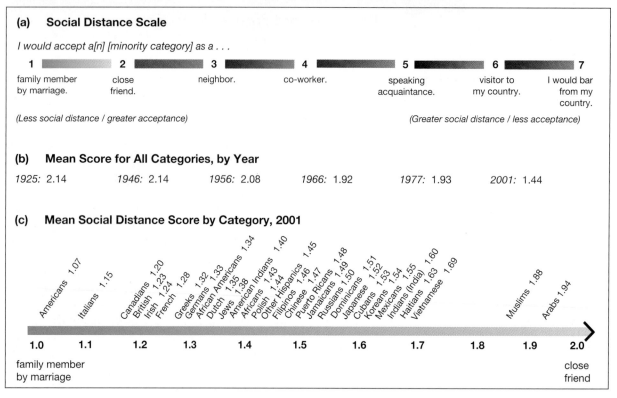

FIGURE 3–1   Bogardus Social Distance Scale

Using this seven-point scale, Emory Bogardus and others have shown that people feel much closer to some categories of people than they do to others. Between 1925, when the study was first carried out, and the most recent study in 2001, the average social distance response has dropped from 2.14 to 1.44, showing increasing tolerance of diversity.

Source: Parrillo (2003).

- **Today's students are more accepting of minorities.** Today's students express greater acceptance of all minorities compared to students decades ago. Figure 3–1 shows that the average (mean) response on the social distance scale was 2.14 in 1925 and 1946, dropping to 2.08 in 1956, 1.92 in 1966, 1.93 in 1977, and just 1.44 in 2001. In the most recent study, students (81 percent of whom were white) expressed much more acceptance of African Americans: Placed near the bottom in 1925, this category was near the top in 2001.

- **Today's students see less difference between the various minorities.** In the earliest studies, although students were very accepting of some people, they gave some

minorities average scores almost three points higher (between 4 and 5). In 2001, students gave no minority an average score greater than 1.94.

- **Today's students express the most prejudice toward Arabs and Muslims.** The most recent study was done just weeks after the terrorist attacks that took place on September 11, 2001. Perhaps the fact that the nineteen men who attacked the World Trade Center and the Pentagon were Arabs and Muslims helps to explain why students expressed the greatest social distance toward these categories. Even so, not one student in the study said that Arabs or Muslims should be barred from the United States. Also, even the most prejudiced score by today's students (Arabs at 1.94) shows greater tolerance than students expressed toward eighteen of the thirty categories of people used in 1977.

Institutional Racism: The Case of Racial Profiling

The studies we have just looked at involve prejudice in terms of individual attitudes. But if it is widespread, we should expect prejudice to be built into the operation of society itself. This idea underlies the work of Stokely Carmichael and Charles Hamilton (1967), who described **institutional racism** as *racism at work in the operation of social institutions, including the economy, schools, hospitals, the military, and the criminal justice system.*

Read about charges that banks practice institutional discrimination in their lending policies:
http://www.hud.gov/library/bookshelf18/presrel/subprime.html

Racial profiling, described in the opening to this chapter, illustrates the operation of institutional racism. It is one thing for an individual police officer to be prejudiced and to think most African Americans are criminals. But critics charge that there is a nationwide pattern of police jumping to the conclusion that a black person is engaged in wrongdoing. Furthermore, because some police consider a black person more dangerous than a white person, they may be quicker to draw their weapons. In recent years, a number of African Americans—who turned out to be neither armed nor guilty of any crime—have been killed by police who may well have reacted partly to their color.

Challenging cases of institutionalized racism is difficult. Police departments are part of society's power structure and claim to serve the public interest. Therefore, institutional racism of this kind is often ignored.

Causes of Prejudice

What causes people to become prejudiced in the first place? Researchers point to two key factors: The personality of individuals and the structure of society itself.

Personality Factors T. W. Adorno (1950) and his colleagues claimed prejudice is strong in people with an *authoritarian personality*. Such people rigidly conform to conventional norms and see the world in stark contrasts of "right" versus "wrong" and "us" versus "them." What creates such a personality?

Adorno places much of the blame on cold and demanding parents who fill their children with insecurity and anger. Such children, especially when they lack schooling, develop little tolerance of others and are quick to reject people who differ from themselves.

Societal Factors Prejudice also results from the structure of society itself. *Scapegoat theory* for example says that prejudice develops among people who are frustrated at their lack of control over their lives (Dollard, 1939). Working-class whites in southwest Texas, for example, may feel anxious and angry at their lack of economic security, but whom should they blame? The poor, illegal immigrants from Mexico who are willing to grab any job they can find, often at less than minimum wage? Or the bosses who take advantage of the immigrants' desperate situation to keep more money for themselves? Scapegoat theory suggests that people direct their hostility at safe, less-powerful targets—the illegal immigrants in our example. Because many of society's least powerful people are minorities, they are blamed for a host of troubles that are, of course, not their fault.

In addition, *cultural theory* claims prejudice is built into our culture. An example is the research using the social distance scale by Emory Bogardus noted earlier in this chapter. Bogardus showed that most people turn out to have the same kinds of prejudice, favoring certain categories of people and avoiding others. The fact that these attitudes are so widely shared suggests that prejudice is not a trait of deviant individuals as much as it is a part of culture itself.

Multiculturalism

Is there a way to address prejudice deeply rooted in our culture? One strategy for change is **multiculturalism,** *educational programs designed to recognize cultural diversity in the United States and to promote respect for all cultural traditions.*

Multiculturalism claims, first, that U.S. society has long played down its cultural diversity. That is, schools have taught generations of children that the United States is a cultural "melting pot" that blends human diversity into a single culture we call "American." However, multiculturalism maintains, our diverse population has "melted" far less than many people think. On the contrary, race and ethnicity have always formed a hierarchy. At the top, Europeans (and especially the English) represent the cultural ideal of the well-informed, well-groomed, and well-behaved man and woman. What we call assimilation, then, is really a process of *Anglicization*, as

Wouldn't most people assume that the hand holding the wine glass is white? Despite the outlawing of racial discrimination, there is still considerable social inequality beween white and black people in U.S. society. The widespread pattern of people of color providing personal service to members of the dominant white majority goes all the way back to the beginnings of slavery.

immigrants try to become more like the privileged white Anglo-Saxon Protestants (WASPs).

In addition, U.S. institutions—including schools, law, and the economy, as well as dominant religions and family forms—are all modeled along Western European lines. Multiculturalists describe this bias as **Eurocentrism,** *the practice of using European (particularly English) cultural standards to judge everyone.* To multiculturalists, in short, U.S. culture is itself an expression of prejudice against those who differ from the dominant model. Multiculturalism thus asks that we rethink our national heritage and recognize the accomplishments of everyone regardless of race or ethnicity.

Although there is strong support for multiculturalism (especially among liberals) as giving more visibility and power to minorities, others (especially conservatives) claim this approach divides society by downplaying what we have in common. The Latin phrase that appears on all U.S. currency—*E Pluribus Unum*—literally means "out of many, one." The controversy over multiculturalism is really about how much we should stress a single national identity and how much we should highlight differences.

DISCRIMINATION

Discrimination means *unequal treatment of various categories of people.* Whereas prejudice is a matter of *attitudes*, discrimination is a matter of *actions*. Like prejudice, discrimination can be positive or negative. We discriminate in a positive way when we single out people who do especially good work or when we provide special favors to friends or family members. We discriminate in a negative way when we put people down or exclude entire categories of people from our lives.

Few people would object to an employer who favors an applicant with more schooling over one with less. But what if an employer favors one category of people (say, Christians) over another (say, Jews)? Unless the job is directly related to a person's religion (for example, if a church is hiring a priest), ruling out an entire category of people is wrongful discrimination, which violates the law.

Institutional Discrimination

As in the case of prejudice, some discrimination involves the actions of individuals. For example, a restaurant owner might refuse to serve students with tattoos. Most people condemn discrimination of this kind; moreover, in public settings such as a restaurant, it violates the law.

Institutional discrimination is *discrimination that is built into the operation of social institutions, including the economy, schools, and the legal system.* A well-known example of institutional discrimination is this nation's history of placing black and white children in separate schools. Not until 1954 did civil rights activists succeed in overturning the legal doctrine of "separate but equal." But racial segregation is widespread in U.S. society; for example, fifty years after the 1954 *Brown* decision by the U.S. Supreme Court, most children still sit in classrooms surrounded by students of the same race.

Prejudice and Discrimination: A Vicious Circle

Because prejudice and discrimination reinforce each other, they can form a vicious circle that harms minorities. Take racial profiling, which illustrates how prejudice can lead to discrimination:. If prejudiced white police officers think that most African Americans are criminals, they may well engage in racial profiling, stopping a disproportionate number of black motorists and being quicker to arrest black citizens on the street. Such discrimination, in turn, can overly criminalize African Americans, reducing their chances of finding good jobs and raising their risk of living in neighborhoods marked by poverty, drug abuse, and crime. As this happens, discrimination leads to justification of the original prejudice. And so it goes, around and around.

Affirmative Action: Reverse Discrimination or Antidote for Prejudice?

One strategy aimed at breaking the vicious cycle of prejudice and discrimination is **affirmative action,** *policies intended to improve the social standing of minorities subject to historic prejudice and discrimination.* Affirmative action policies have changed over time, as we now explain, and they will continue to change in response to court rulings.

History of Affirmative Action After World War II, the government assisted veterans by funding education, and minorities who might not otherwise have gone to college took advantage of the "G.I. Bill" and entered classrooms across the country. By 1960, almost 350,000 African Americans had drawn on government funds to obtain college degrees, but these men and women were not ending up with the kinds of jobs for which they were qualified. The Kennedy administration concluded that education alone could not overcome deep-seated prejudice and discrimination against people of color, so they devised the policy of affirmative action to require employers to "throw a wider net" to identify and hire qualified minority applicants. In the years that followed, employers hired thousands of African American women and men for good jobs, helping to build the black middle class.

By the 1970s, affirmative action was extended to include college admissions, and many policies took the form of "quota systems" in which employers or colleges set aside a certain number of places for minorities, which by then included women, Hispanics, veterans, and, in some cases, people with physical disabilities. In 1978, the Supreme Court heard the case of *University of California Regents v. Bakke*, brought by Allen Bakke, a white man who was rejected for admission to medical school at the University of California at Davis. The medical school had a policy of setting aside 16 places (of 100) for African Americans, Asian Americans, Native Americans, and Hispanic Americans. Such rigid quotas were ruled to be illegal, but the court did endorse the use of race and ethnicity as part of the overall process of admitting students or hiring employees in order to increase minority representation in settings from which minorities historically had been excluded.

By the mid-1990s, opposition to affirmative action programs grew stronger. In 1995, the University of California system declared it would no longer consider race and gender in admission, hiring, and contract decisions. In 1996, California voters passed Proposition 209, which required state agencies to operate without regard to race, ethnicity, or gender. A similar proposition passed in the state of Washington. Also in 1996, a federal district court (*Hopwood v. Texas*) declared that race and gender could no longer be considered by public colleges and universities in Texas, Louisiana, and Mississippi.

Seeking socially diverse enrollments, many colleges and universities have tried to find a way around the new regulations. In Texas, for example, public universities admit anyone in the top 10 percent of their high school class, a policy that benefits students from predominantly African American and Hispanic schools.

In 2003, the U.S. Supreme Court once again addressed the issue of affirmative action. The case involved admission policies at the University of Michigan, a state university. In the undergraduate admissions process at the University of Michigan, applicants of underrepresented minorities had received a numerical bonus that was added to a total score, which also reflected grades and college board scores. The Supreme Court struck down this point system as too similar to the racial quota systems rejected by the Court in the past. However, the Court did allow the University of Michigan Law School to continue its policy of taking account of applicants' race in the interest of creating a racially diverse student body. In this administrative process, rather than a rigid point system, race was treated as one of several variables used in giving each applicant individual

Should race be used as a factor in admissions policies at U.S. colleges and universities? On one side of the issue, people argue that all applicants should be treated equally on the basis of their achievement. On the other, people argue that applicants from historically disadvantaged categories of the population deserve a leg up; moreover, doesn't everyone benefit from a campus that is racially and ethnically diverse?

consideration. In these decisions, the Court was affirming the national importance of allowing colleges and universities to build racially diverse classes, while at the same time stating that all applicants must be considered as individuals (Stout, 2003).

The United States continues to wrestle with affirmative action. Most people agree that society needs to give real opportunity to people in every racial and ethnic category. But disagreement remains as to whether affirmative action is part of the problem or part of the solution (Fetto, 2002; Fineman & Lipper, 2003; Kantrowitz & Wingert, 2003; NORC, 2003).

THEORETICAL ANALYSIS: UNDERSTANDING RACIAL AND ETHNIC INEQUALITY

Why do the various racial and ethnic categories of the U.S. population have unequal social standing? The following discussion draws answers from sociology's three major theoretical approaches: the structural-functional, symbolic-interaction, and social-conflict approaches.

Structural-Functional Analysis: The Importance of Culture

Structural-functional theory places great importance on culture. To the extent that various racial and ethnic categories have different cultural orientations—for example, more or less emphasis on education or

achievement—unequal social standing is the likely result.

The Culture of Poverty   Chapter 2 ("Poverty and Wealth") introduced the "culture of poverty" thesis of Oscar Lewis (1966). Lewis explained the typically low social standing of the Puerto Rican population in San Juan and New York in terms of a cultural orientation he called "fatalism," which leads people to accept their situation with little hope that life will get better. Growing up poor and learning fatalistic values, young people develop low self-esteem and a sense of hopelessness and eventually grow into adults who are not well prepared to take advantage of whatever opportunities society offers them.

Joan Albon made a similar claim about American Indians, whose traditional cultures tend to be cooperative and thus "in direct opposition to the principles of the modern, competitive, capitalistic order" (1971:387). Some African American peer groups also have been described is having an "oppositional culture" that discourages members from excelling by defining school achievement as "acting white" (Fordham & Ogbu, 1992). In such an environment, adds Shelby Steele (1990), a successful man or woman of color risks the charge of not being a "real" African American.

Critical evaluation.   Although few doubt that culture matters, critics claim that this approach defines people as responsible for their own disadvantage—what Chapter 2 ("Poverty and Wealth") described as "blaming the victim." People who live in individ-ualistic societies such as the United States find it easy to blame people for their own poverty. But do poor people really deserve to live as they do? If disadvan-taged people lack some of the optimism and confi-dence found among people who are better off, critics suggest, this is more the *result* than the *cause* of low social standing.

Symbolic-Interaction Analysis: The Personal Meaning of Race

Forty years after the end of slavery in the United States, pioneering sociologist W. E. B. Du Bois (1903) published *The Souls of Black Folk*, an analysis of the social standing of black people. As Du Bois saw it, despite the end of slavery, there had been lit-tle real change and most African Americans re-mained second-class citizens.

Every time black people and white people met, said Du Bois, race hung in the air, defining each in the eyes of the other. From the African American perspective, race produces

> a peculiar sensation, [a] double-consciousness, [a] sense of always looking at oneself through the eyes of others, of measuring one's soul by the tape of a world that looks on in amused contempt and pity. (2001:227; orig. 1903)

In effect, Du Bois said, U.S. society makes whites the standard by which others (including African Americans) should be measured. In daily encoun-ters, race operates as a *master status*, a personal trait that ends up defining and devaluing any person of color.

Today, a century after Du Bois wrote, race con-tinues to shape the everyday lives of everyone, re-gardless of their color. Manning Marable sums it up this way:

> As long as I can remember, the fundamentally defin-ing feature of my life, and the lives of my family, was the stark reality of race. (1995:1)

Critical evaluation.   Symbolic-interaction analysis investigates how we use color (or, in the case of eth-nicity, cultural background) as we define ourselves and other people. In other words, race and ethnici-ty are part of the reality of our everyday lives.

At the same time, race involves more than per-sonal understandings. Race is also an important struc-ture of society, a dimension of social stratification. This insight brings us to the social-conflict approach.

Social-Conflict Analysis: The Structure of Inequality

Social-conflict analysis argues that the unequal standing of minorities reflects the organization of society itself. Class, race, and ethnicity are closely linked dimensions of inequality.

The Importance of Class   For Karl Marx, the roots of social inequality lie in a society's economy. As ex-plained in Chapter 2 ("Poverty and Wealth"), Marx criticized capitalism for concentrating wealth and power in the hands of a small elite. He charged that this capitalist elite, realizing that the strength of the working class lies in its greater numbers, tries to di-vide the workers by playing up racial and ethnic dif-ferences. Marx's colleague Friedrich Engels (Marx & Engels, 1959; orig. 1893) pointed to the racial and ethnic diversity of the United States as the reason U.S. workers had not come together to form a so-cialist movement. "Immigration," Engels wrote,

> divides the workers into two groups: the native born and the foreigners, and the latter in turn into (1) the Irish, (2) the Germans, (3) the many small groups, each of which understands only itself: Czechs, Poles, Italians, Scandinavians, etc. And then the Negroes. To form a single party out of these requires unusual-ly powerful incentives. (1959:458)

Both Marx and Engels hoped the increasing misery of workers would eventually unify them into a po-litically active class. To some degree, this has hap-pened; however, racial and ethnic differences still divide the U.S. work force as they do workers around the world.

Multicultural Theory   Social-conflict theory also notes the importance of culture. A multicultural per-spective claims that U.S. culture provides privileges to the European majority while pushing minorities to the margins of society.

Cultural bias against minorities has distorted ac-counts of U.S. history. When Christopher Columbus landed in the Bahamas in 1492, he encountered Na-tive Americans who were, on the whole, peaceful. In-deed, this gentleness led to their subjugation by the more competitive and aggressive Europeans. Yet most historical accounts portray Europeans as heroic ex-plorers and Native Americans as thieves and mur-derers (Unruh, 1979; Josephy, 1982; Matthiessen, 1984; Sale, 1990).

As W. E. B. Du Bois noted, biases about race and ethnicity are still part of everyday life. Take the common case in which people assume that "classical music" refers only to European compositions of a certain period (not to music by Chinese, Indian, or Zulu composers). Biases also lead people to apply the term "ethnic" to anyone not of English background, or even to speak of "whites and blacks," placing the dominant category first (as we do for "males and females"), even though an alphabetical ordering would flip them the other way around.

Critical evaluation.   One criticism of social-conflict theory is that this approach understates what people in the United States have in common. Whatever their color or cultural background, most people identify themselves as being "Americans," and they have joined together over and over again to help each other in bad times and to celebrate, in good times, the principle of individual freedom that defines our way of life.

A second problem is that painting minorities as victims runs the risk of taking away people's responsibility for their own lives. It is true that minorities confront substantial barriers, but we need to remember that people also make choices about how to live and can act to raise their social standing and join together to improve their communities.

Third, and finally, conflict theory tends to minimize the significant strides this nation has made in dealing with its social diversity. Over time, U.S. society has moved closer to the ideals of political participation, public education, and equal standing before the law for everyone. As a result, the share of minorities who are well schooled, politically active, and affluent is on the rise. Although much remains to be done there is also reason for pride and optimism.

POLITICS, RACE, AND ETHNICITY: CONSTRUCTING PROBLEMS AND DEFINING SOLUTIONS

Should racial and ethnic inequality be defined as a problem? What should be done about it? Conservative, liberal, and radical viewpoints produce different answers to these questions.

Conservatives: Culture and Effort Matter

Conservatives support the idea that everyone should have equal standing before the law and the chance to improve their lives. Believing that this is mostly true in the United States, conservatives also believe that people are largely responsible for their own social standing.

If some racial and ethnic minorities prosper more than others, it is likely that cultural differences are at work. On average, people in various racial and ethnic categories place different emphasis on schooling, aspire to different kinds of jobs, and even think differently about financial success. For instance, Italians have long worked in the building trades, the Irish lean toward public service occupations, Jews have long dominated the garment industry and are well represented in most professions, and many Koreans operate retail businesses. Such differences make no one "better" than anyone else. But as conservatives see it, they do produce social inequality.

According to the conservative view, social standing should reflect ambition, education, and hard work. In a society such as ours, people are free but also unequal. Favoring freedom over equality, conservatives oppose government efforts to engineer social equality.

This is the reason conservatives typically oppose affirmative action policies. They argue that instead of being an effective way to give everyone an equal chance—a path toward the goal of a color-blind society—affirmative action is really a system of "group preferences." In practice, as they see it, such policies amount to "reverse discrimination" that favors people based not on their qualifications and performance but on their race, ethnicity, or gender. If treating people according to color was wrong in the past, how can it be right today?

Conservatives add that affirmative action harms minorities by calling into question their accomplishments: How would you feel, for example, if other people thought you had been admitted to college not just because of your abilities but because of your race?

Finally, conservatives point out that affirmative action helps the minorities who need it least. Minorities on college campuses and in the corporate world are, by and large, already well off; affirmative action does less for the minority poor, who need help the most (Gilder, 1980; Murray, 1984; Sowell, 1987, 1990; Carter, 1991; Steele, 1990; Stone, 2000).

Liberals: Society and Government Matter

Liberals do not believe that cultural differences are the main reason for inequality, and they do not believe that everyone has the same chance to get ahead. On the contrary, liberals believe that racial

Until the 1960s, sights such as this were common. The federal government brought an end to formal segregation during this decade of change; even so, many residential areas and public settings today are still used mainly by people of one racial category. How far, in your opinion, has U.S. society come towards ending racial segregation?

and ethnic inequality come from prejudice and discrimination built into society's institutions.

Liberals urge people to reject the idea that minorities themselves are the problem. Although categories of people do differ in terms of culture, liberals see these differences as the *result* rather than the *cause* of social inequality.

Society, not people, is the problem, and we cannot expect minorities acting as individuals to improve their situation. Liberals look to government as the solution, supporting policies—including antidiscrimination laws—that reduce racial and ethnic inequality.

This view helps explain why liberals support affirmative action. As they see it, affirmative action is a necessary correction for historical prejudice and discrimination against minorities. African Americans today face the legacy of two centuries of slavery and an additional century and a half of segregation. In short, this nation's history has been a policy of *majority* preference, one reason the social standing of whites is higher than that of blacks and other minorities. Therefore, minority preference is both necessary and fair as a step to help level the playing field.

Moreover, liberals claim, affirmative action has been good for the country. Where would minorities be today without the affirmative action that began in the 1960s? After all, major employers in government and corporate business began hiring large numbers of minorities (and women) only because of affirmative action, resulting in the growth of the African American middle class (Feagin & Feagin, 1986; Orfield & Ashkinaze, 1991; Johnson, Rush, & Feagin, 2000).

Radicals: Fundamental Changes Are Needed

Radicals claim that more than liberal reforms are needed to end the problem of racial and ethnic inequality. Following Marx, radicals point out that as long as a capitalist society defines workers simply as a supply of labor, there is little reason to expect an end to exploitation and oppression, whether based on class or race. Therefore, the radical position is that the best way to reduce racial and ethnic inequality is to attack the source of *all* inequality: capitalism itself (Liazos, 1982).

A more recent radical idea focuses not on economics but on culture. In recent years, a growing number of activist-scholars have concluded that the way to end racial inequality is to eliminate entirely the concept of race because its only purpose is to divide people and justify giving advantages to some at expense of others. Can we abandon the notion of race, which is so basic to conventional ways of thinking? In time, perhaps. But one thing is certain: Doing so will demand basic changes to the current white power structure. As one group of sociologists claims (Johnson, Rush, & Feagin, 2000:101);

LEFT TO RIGHT

THE POLITICS OF RACIAL AND ETHNIC INEQUALITY

	RADICAL LEFT VIEW	LIBERAL VIEW	CONSERVATIVE VIEW
WHAT IS THE PROBLEM?	Striking inequality and racism are built into the very institutions of U.S. society.	Social and economic inequality places minorities at the margins of U.S. society.	Some people are still prejudiced and discriminate against minorities; some minority communities need to improve their standing.
WHAT IS THE SOLUTION?	There must be fundamental change in economic, political, and other social institutions to eliminate racial hierarchy.	Government programs must attack prejudice and discrimination and provide assistance to minorities.	Although all people need to treat others as individuals, some minorities must overcome cultural disadvantages through individual effort in order to realize higher achievement.

Join the debate . . .

1. Explain how supporters of each of the three political perspectives would respond to this assertion: "Over the course of its history, the United States has moved closer to the ideal of being a color-blind society." Do you agree or disagree with this statement? Why?

2. Do you think that, a century from now, racial and ethnic inequality will be greater, about the same, or less than it is now? Why?

3. Which of the three political analyses of racial and ethnic inequality included here do you find most convincing? Why?

A useful place to begin undoing racism is to address the social, economic, and political embeddedness of white racism within the foundation of the U.S. political system. . . . Thus, [we] call for a new constitutional convention, one that will represent fairly and equally, for the first time, all major groups of U.S. citizens. What might the social, political, and economic landscape of the United States look like if we started with a social system constructed to actually meet the needs of democracy and humanity rather than the goals of privilege-maintenance and racial hierarchy?

The Left to Right table provides a summary of the three political perspectives applied to the issue of racial and ethnic inequality.

GOING ON FROM HERE

In lower-income nations of the world, people typically define each other in terms of a kin group, a tribe, or a religion. In high-income countries, by contrast, people break free of traditional categories as they come to believe that their lives should be guided by personal choices, talents, and efforts. Thus, most members of our society view categorizing people on the basis of their color or cultural heritage as wrong—a matter of unfair prejudice and discrimination.

Social institutions in the United States have changed over time to reflect these new beliefs. Slavery was abolished (1865); soon after, African Americans gained citizenship (1868), followed by Native Americans (1924), Chinese immigrants (1943), and Japanese immigrants (1952).

Even so, this chapter has shown that racial and ethnic inequality persists. Minorities still endure the sting of prejudice and discrimination. These harmful biases exist not only in the attitudes and actions of individuals but in the operation of society itself. Thus, the inequality described in this chapter is carried from generation to generation, as too many young Hispanic Americans, African Americans, and Native Americans grow up poor.

In 1913, W. E. B. Du Bois predicted that race would be the defining problem of the twentieth century. He was right. Could we say the same for the twenty-first century? What are the prospects for change over the next 100 years? The conservative solution amounts to adopting a set of "color-blind" attitudes: Treat people as individuals and demand that people take responsibility for their own social standing. Liberals also endorse the long-range "color-blind" goal but argue that, to reach it, government action (including programs that take into account people's race and ethnicity) is needed to guarantee full participation by all categories of people. Radicals weigh in with a greater challenge: Racism is too deeply entrenched in U.S. institutions to expect well-meaning individuals or government reform to level the playing field; on the contrary, institutions must undergo fundamental change.

Throughout its history, U.S. society has debated issues related to racial and ethnic inequality. Let us hope that, by the end of this century, we find answers that satisfy all categories of people.

CHAPTER SUMMARY

1. Race is a socially constructed category based on physical traits a society defines as significant. Ethnicity is a shared cultural heritage. Both race and ethnicity are dimensions of inequality in the United States.

2. Minorities are categories of people that a society sets apart and subjects to disadvantages because of physical or cultural traits.

3. Pluralism is a state in which racial and ethnic categories, though distinct, have equal social standing. Assimilation is a process by which minorities adopt social patterns of the dominant culture. Segregation is the social and physical separation of some category of a population. Genocide is the deliberate killing of a category of people.

4. Native Americans suffered greatly at the hands of Europeans over the course of five hundred years. Even today, Native Americans have relatively low social standing.

5. African Americans came to the United States as cargo transported by slave traders. Despite substantial gains, African Americans are still, on average, disadvantaged.

6. Asian Americans have lived in the United States for more than a century. Although their social standing is average or above average today, they still suffer from prejudice and discrimination.

7. Hispanic Americans are a diverse category of people sharing a Latin American and Spanish heritage. Some categories, such as Puerto Ricans, have low social standing; others, such as Cuban Americans, are better off.

8. Prejudice consists of rigid prejudgments about some category of people. A stereotype is an exaggerated and unfair description. The study of prejudice using the social distance scale shows a trend toward greater tolerance on the part of U.S. college students.

9. Racism is the assertion that people of one race are innately superior to people of another. Racism has been used throughout human history to justify the social inferiority of some category of people.

10. Researchers have linked prejudice to individual traits (the authoritarian personality) and to social structure (scapegoat theory) and patterns of belief (cultural theory).

11. Discrimination consists of actions that treat various categories of a population differently. Institutionalized discrimination is bias built into the operation of the economy, legal system, or other social institution.

12. Structural-functional analysis explains racial and ethnic inequality in terms of cultural values. One example is the "culture of poverty" theory developed by Oscar Lewis.

13. Symbolic-interaction analysis highlights how race often operates as a master status in everyday interaction.

14. Social-conflict analysis highlights how racial and ethnic inequality is built into the structure of society. Marxist theory argues that elites encourage racial and ethnic divisions as a strategy to weaken the working class. More recently, multicultural theory notes ways in which much U.S. culture is biased against minorities.

15. Conservatives point to cultural patterns, such as the importance given to education, as a cause of racial and ethnic inequality. Conservatives claim that individuals should be responsible for their social standing and oppose government policies that treat categories of people differently.

16. Liberals point to social structure, including institutional prejudice and discrimination, as the cause of racial and ethnic inequality. Liberals endorse government efforts to promote equality, including enforcement of antidiscrimination laws and affirmative action.

17. Radicals claim that the goal of racial and ethnic equality will require basic change to U.S. social institutions, including the capitalist economic system and the political system, so that they operate in the interests of all categories of people.

KEY CONCEPTS

race (p. 56) a socially constructed category of people who share biologically transmitted traits that a society defines as important

ethnicity (p. 58) a shared cultural heritage, which typically involves common ancestors, language, and religion

minority (p. 59) any category of people, distinguished by physical or cultural traits, that a society subjects to disadvantages

genocide (p. 60) the systematic killing of one category of people by another

segregation (p. 60) the physical and social separation of categories of people

assimilation (p. 62) the process by which minorities gradually adopt cultural patterns from the majority population

pluralism (p. 62) a state in which people of all racial and ethnic categories have roughly equal social standing

prejudice (p. 69) any rigid and irrational generalization about an entire category of people

stereotype (p. 69) an exaggerated description applied to every person in some category

racism (p. 70) the assertion that people of one race are less worthy than or even biologically inferior to others

institutional racism (p. 73) racism at work in the operation of social institutions, including the economy, schools, hospitals, the military, and the criminal justice system

multiculturalism (p. 73) educational programs designed to recognize cultural diversity in the United States and to promote respect for all cultural traditions

Eurocentrism (p. 74) the practice of using European (particularly English) cultural standards to judge everyone

discrimination (p. 74) unequal treatment of various categories of people

institutional discrimination (p. 74) discrimination that is built into the operation of social institutions, including the economy, schools, and the legal system

affirmative action (p. 75) policies intended to improve the social standing of minorities subject to historic prejudice and discrimination

THINKING CRITICALLY: QUESTIONS AND ISSUES

1. What does the following statement mean: "Race is not a simple matter of skin color but a socially constructed category"?

2. How do prejudice and discrimination reinforce each other? How do assertions of biological inferiority and social inferiority reinforce each other?

3. What sets an unfair stereotype apart from a fair generalization? For example, would it be wrong to say, "White people are racist"? What about saying, "Black children are more likely than white children to grow up without fathers in the home"? Explain your answer.

4. Do you think all minority categories should benefit from affirmative action? Should all members—even those who are well off—benefit? Why or why not?

GETTING INVOLVED: LEARNING ACTIVITIES

1. Take a trip to the campus library and locate several books on the history of various racial or ethnic categories of the U.S. population. Based on your reading, trace the history of legal discrimination in the United States.

2. An easy and enlightening research project is to watch ten or twenty hours of television over the next week or two while taking notes on the race of TV actors and what kinds of characters they play. Although your sample may not be representative of all shows, it might get you thinking about racial stereotypes in the mass media.

3. The Census Bureau collects data on interracial marriage: See the *Statistical Abstract* or other documents in the library. Since 1970, how has the percentage of interracial marriages changed? What other patterns can you find?

4. Do you know a couple who represent two different racial or ethnic categories? If so, ask to interview them about the role that race and ethnicity play in their everyday lives.

GETTING CONNECTED: USEFUL WEB LINKS

http://prenhall.com/macionis
Visit the interactive Companion Website™ that accompanies this text. Begin by clicking on the cover of your book. You will find a chapter-by-chapter study guide, practice tests, suggested Web links, and links to other relevant material.

http://www.aclu.org/profiling
What does the American Civil Liberties Union have to say about racial profiling?

http://www.US-English.org
US English is an organization that believes only English should be the official language of the United States. Why do they take this position? Do you think a recent immigrant who does not speak English would agree?

http:www.naacp.org
http://www.adl.org
http://www.iprnet.org/IPR/
Many organizations seek to raise the social standing of U.S. minorities. Can you identify strategies used by the National Association for the Advancement of Colored People, the Anti-Defamation League, and the Institute for Puerto Rican Policy?

http://www.civilrights.org/lcef/hate/toc.html
How does prejudice mix with crime? This site investigates hate crimes in the United States.

http://www.access.gpo.gov/eop/ca/index.html
Want to learn more about the social standing of minorities? Visit this government site.

http://www.collegeboard.com/repository/ minorityhig_3948.pdf
This report, by the College Board's National Task Force on Minority High Achievement, analyzes racial and ethnic differences in higher education.

GETTING STARTED ON YOUR OWN: RESEARCH NAVIGATOR™

Follow the instructions found on page 25 of this text to access the features of Research Navigator™. Once at the Web site, enter your Login Name and Password. Then, to use the **Content Select** database, enter keywords such as "race," "ethnicity," and "racial profiling," and the search engine will supply relevant and recent scholarly and popular press publications. Use the *New York Times* **Search-by-Subject Archive** to find recent news articles related to sociology and the **Link Library** feature to find relevant Web links organized by the key terms associated with this chapter.

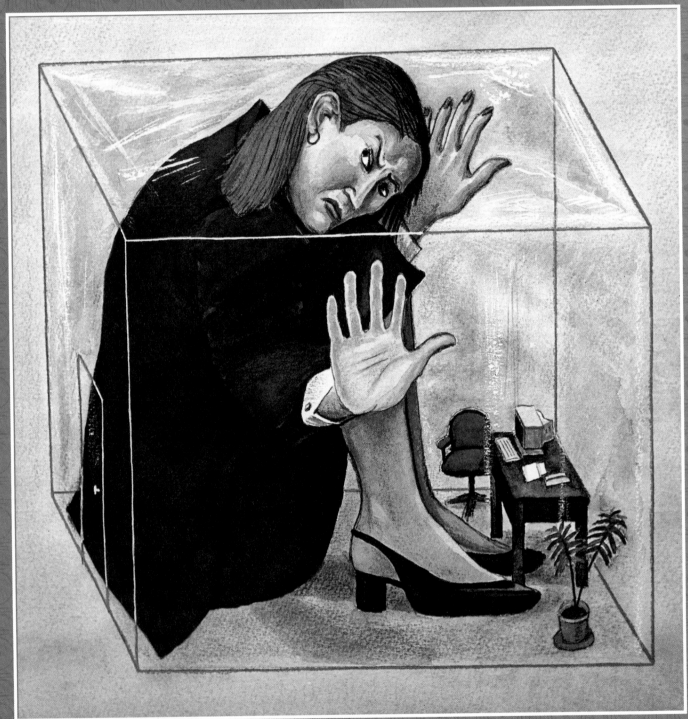

GENDER INEQUALITY

FATMA MINT MAMADOU SMILES AND SHAKES HER head when the social worker asks her age. She has no idea when she was born. Nor does she know how to read or write. All she knows is the work she does every day: tending camels, herding sheep, hauling bags of water, sweeping, and serving tea to her owners. This young woman is a slave, one of roughly 100,000 slaves who live today in north Africa's Islamic Republic of Mauritania.

In the central region of Mauritania, people link being a woman with dark brown skin to being a slave to an Arab owner. Fatma accepts this for the simple reason that she knows nothing else. "I am a slave," she explains in a matter-of-fact voice, "just as my mother was a slave before me. And her mother before that." The social worker's steady gaze prompts her to continue: "Just as God created a camel to be a camel, he created me to be a slave."

Fatma lives with her mother, three sisters, and a brother outside Nauak-chott, Mauritania's capital city. They live in a 9-by-12-foot hut built from wood scraps and other material taken from construction sites. The roof is simply a piece of cloth. The home has no plumbing and no furniture. The nearest drinking water comes from a well a mile down the road.

Slavery is illegal in Mauritania. But laws mean little in a place where traditions have supported slavery for more than 500 years. During that time, Arab and Berber tribes have been roving across the region raiding local villages and making slaves of the people, especially poor women. As a result, Fatma and others like her have no idea what freedom to choose means.

The social worker then asks a more personal question: "Are you and other girls ever raped?" Again, Fatma hesitates. With no hint of emotion, she responds, "Of course, in the night the men take us to breed us. Is that what you mean by rape?" Burkett (1997).

GETTING THE PICTURE

✦ Are women and men equal in U.S. society?

Not in terms of income, with women earning 76 percent as much as men.

✦ Do you believe in marriage?

Research suggests marriage improves health more for men than for women.

✦ Is beauty simply about looking good?

A concern about beauty ends up giving men power over women.

85

Patriarchy means that men have power to control the behavior of women. This young Pakistani woman was mutilated by the men in her family, who declared that her behavior had dishonored them.

Poor people in countries all over the world have little idea of the personal freedom that most of us take for granted. But women in poor and rich countries alike face special hardships. In low income countries such as Mauritania, many women are literally the property of men. Less than a century ago, U.S. women were also second-class citizens, with no right to vote, with little or no chance to go to college, and expected to serve men in the home.

In the United States, much has changed in the last hundred years. But compared with men, women still have fewer job opportunities and less economic security. In addition, women still contend with unwanted sexual overtures and even outright violence. To understand many of the issues facing women and men today, we begin by looking at the importance that gender plays in how society operates.

WHAT IS GENDER?

In societies around the world, women and men lead different lives. Sociologists explore this difference using the concept of **gender,** *the personal traits and life chances that a society links to being female or male.* Gender is not the same as **sex,** *the biological distinction between females and males.* Sex is determined biologically as an embryo is conceived. As Chapter 8 ("Sexuality") explains, these biological differences allow the human species to reproduce. Gender is a social construction that shapes the lives of women and men throughout the life course, affecting the amount of schooling they receive, the kind of work they do, and their income. To varying degrees, all societies define men and women as different types of people, creating the inequality.

Patriarchy

Gender is an important dimension of *social inequality.* **Gender stratification** is *the unequal distribution of wealth, power, and privilege between men and women.* Around the world, we find various degrees of **patriarchy** (literally, "the rule of fathers"), *a social pattern in which males dominate females.* **Matriarchy,** *a social pattern in which females dominate males*, is extremely rare. Two centuries ago, the North American Seneca (an American Indian nation) assigned to their women the job of providing most of the food, and they required men to obtain women's permission for any military campaign or other important decision (Lengermann & Wallace, 1985; Arrighi, 2001; Freedman, 2002).

Global Map 4–1 surveys women's power around the world. Typically, women in poor countries have less power than those in high-income nations.

Explanations of Patriarchy   Is patriarchy just a matter of men's greater body size? On average, says Barbara Ehrenreich (1999:58), males "are 10 percent taller, 20 percent heavier, and 30 percent stronger" than females. However, she notes that women are catching up to men in almost every test of physical performance. And, although physical strength may have been crucial to our cave-dwelling ancestors, muscles are far less important in today's high-technology societies.

Nor does the puzzle of patriarchy rest on brain power. Young men perform visual-spatial tasks better than young women, and boys usually outscore girls on math tests. But girls do better than boys on tests of verbal ability. All in all, scientists find no significant differences in intelligence between men and women (Maccoby & Jacklin, 1974; Baker et al., 1980; Lengermann & Wallace, 1985; Tavris & Wade, 2001).

Another theory links patriarchy to greater aggressiveness in males based on their higher levels of sex hormones (Maccoby & Jacklin, 1974; Goldberg,

A WORLD OF DIFFERENCES

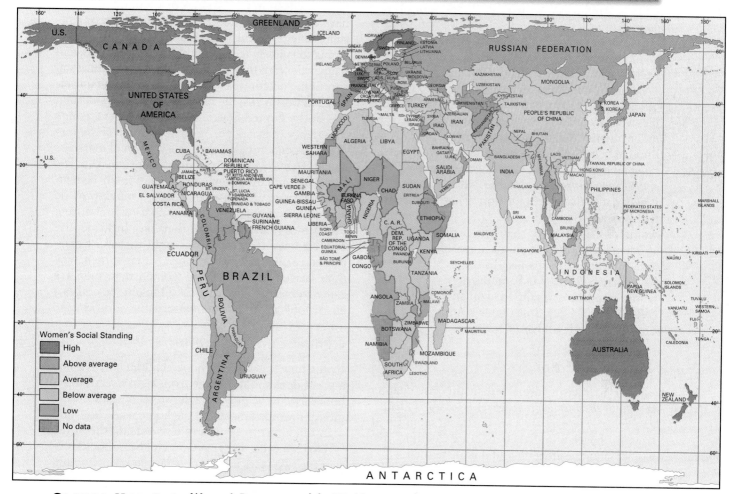

GLOBAL MAP 4–1 Women's Power around the World

The social power of women in relation to that of men varies around the world. In general, women are closer to equality with men in high-income nations, and men have more control over women's lives in low-income nations. Where are women and men most equal? The answer is in the Nordic nations of Norway, Sweden, and Finland.

Source: Data taken from Seager (1997) with updates by the author.

1974, 1987; Popenoe, 1993; Udry, 2000, 2001). Chapter 7 ("Violence") reports that most murders are the work of young males, who generally have high levels of testosterone. But not everyone agrees with the testosterone theory. Barbara Ehrenreich (1999) counters that the male hormone testosterone and the female hormone estrogen are found in both sexes, and scientists have yet to show any clear link between either hormone and aggressive behavior.

Most sociologists reject the idea that *any* behavior is "hard-wired" into human biology. On the contrary, they believe that patriarchy and all the behaviors linked to a particular gender are mostly creations of society. In short, whatever biological forces are at work, societies can and do shape the social differences between the sexes.

Prejudice and Discrimination Like race and ethnicity, gender shapes the kind of people we become. Familiar stereotypes cast women as dependent, sensitive, and emotional while portraying men as independent, rational, and competitive. Notice that gender stereotypes divide humanity by constructing femininity and masculinity in opposing terms.

Such stereotypes overlook the fact that most women and men exhibit a mixture of traits, being more "feminine" in some respects and more "masculine" in others. Also, does the capacity for showing emotions make anyone less rational? In short, gender stereotypes do not describe real people very well (Bernard, 1980; French, 1985).

Our culture also assigns more worth to what we call masculine than what we call feminine. For example, would anyone prefer being dependent to being independent? Being passive to being active? Being timid to being brave? Taken together, gender stereotypes amount to a form of *prejudice* against women.

Given that society devalues what is feminine, it is no wonder that discrimination against women is so widespread. For centuries, U.S. society defined women as little more than the property of men. Women had to respect the authority of their fathers and, later, their husbands. To some degree, times have changed: Most U.S. adults now say that they would support a qualified woman for president (NORC, 2003:222). Still, of our country's forty-four presidents so far, all have been men.

The Problem of Sexism

Similar to racism, discussed in the last chapter, **sexism** is *the assertion that one sex is less worthy than or even innately inferior to the other.* Sexism supports patriarchy by claiming that men are "better" than women and therefore should dominate them.

Sexism involves not just individual attitudes but also the operation of social institutions. As the following sections explain, the notion of male superiority is institutionalized in the workplace (men run most companies and women perform most of the clerical support work), in politics (although women are more likely to vote, most elected leaders are men), and even in religious life (although women attend religious services more often, most religious leaders are men).

GENDER AND SOCIAL INSTITUTIONS

Like class, race, and ethnicity, gender shapes all aspects of our lives. The importance of gender can be seen in the operation of all the social institutions, which we survey now, beginning with the family.

Gender and the Family

Do parents value boys more than girls? Traditionally, parents in the United States valued boys more, although this bias has weakened in recent decades. In poor countries around the world, however, a pro-male bias is strong. In rural areas of India, for example, families benefit from the earnings of a son, whereas they have to pay a dowry to marry off a daughter. As a result, many pregnant women undergo ultrasound examinations solely to find out the sex of the fetus, and many who learn they are carrying a female request an abortion. Sometimes families may even kill an unwelcome newborn girl, the practice of *female infanticide.*

In the United States, gender shapes everyone's experience of marriage. As Jessie Bernard (1982) explained, gender makes the male version of marriage a matter of providing economic support, making key decisions, and often remaining emotionally distant. In the female version of marriage, women provide emotional support to husbands and raise children, sometimes to the point that they have little identity of their own. If Bernard was right that most marriages are unequal partnerships that favor men, why does it seem that far more women than men are eager to marry? The Critical Thinking box takes a closer look at this curious pattern.

Gender and Education

By the time they begin school, children have learned a great deal about gender from books. Children's books used to be full of gender stereotypes, showing girls and women mostly in the home while boys and men did almost everything else outside the home (Weitzman et al., 1972). Newer children's books present the two sexes in a more balanced way, although some antifemale bias remains (Purcell & Stewart, 1990; Taylor, 2003).

And what of school itself? Today's primary and secondary schools do a pretty good job of providing equal education to both boys and girls. In fact, 56 percent of all college students are now women. Even so, gender stereotyping still steers women toward majors in English, dance, drama, or sociology while pushing men toward physics, economics, biology, mathematics, and computer science (Correll, 2001; U.S. National Center for Education Statistics, 2003).

Gender and College Sports Gender is at work on the playing fields as much as in the classroom. In the past, extracurricular athletics was a male world in which females had little chance to play. In 1972, Congress passed Title IX, the Educational Amendment to the Civil Rights Act, banning sex discrimination in any educational program receiving federal funding. In recent years, colleges and universities have also tried to provide an equal number of sports to both women and

Critical Thinking

Marriage: Life Gets Better (But for Whom?)

AT COUNTLESS BRIDAL SHOWERS, WOMEN CELEBRATE A friend's upcoming marriage by showering her with useful gifts. But the scene is very different at bachelor parties, where men give their friend one last fling before he must settle down to the humdrum routines of married life. We find the same pattern among singles: Contrast the positive image of a carefree bachelor with the negative one of an aging spinster,[1] resigned to her loneliness.

On the face of it, it seems that marriage is a *solution* for women and a *problem* for men. But is this really the case? Research indicates that, in general, marriage is good for people, not only raising levels of personal happiness, but improving health and raising income, too (Waite & Gallagher, 2000). But Jessie Bernard (1982) points out that the benefits of marriage are greater for men than for women. Indeed, she states, there is no better prescription for a man's long life, good health, and overall happiness than having a wife devoted to caring for him and keeping an orderly home. That is why divorced men are less happy than divorced women and are more eager to remarry.

But for many women, Bernard claims, marriage reduces happiness and increases the risk of depression or other personality disorders. Why? Bernard claims the problem is not marriage in general but the fact that

[1]The term "spinster" originally referred to a woman who worked at spinning thread in a New England textile mill in the early nineteenth century. People assumed that a working woman was also single.

many marriages are based on conventional ideas about gender. That is, marriage in which men are in charge and women are saddled with most of the housework is not healthy for women.

In the past, marriages based on conventional ideas about gender were more common than they are today. So why have women always seemed so eager to marry? Bernard explains that, at a time when women were all but shut out of the labor force, "landing a man" was the only path to economic security.

Today, however, women with more economic opportunity also have more choices about marriage. This is one reason that more couples are looking closely at their relationships with a eye toward sharing responsibilities more equally. Doing so means breaking away from conventional ideas about gender and making both women and men happier and healthier.

ISSUES AND EXERCISES

1. Throughout the past century, women moved into the labor force in ever greater numbers. In your opinion, how has this trend changed marriage?

2. In your opinion, what elements of today's marriages might be called "gendered"? Why?

3. What share of today's marriages would you describe as "conventional" with regard to (a) men being in charge? (b) men contributing all the income? (c) women doing all the housework?

---

men. Even so, men benefit from higher-paid coaches and enjoy greater interest from spectators. In short, despite the federal policy outlawing gender bias, in few athletic programs is gender equality a reality.

Gender and the Mass Media

With more than 245 million televisions in the United States and, on average, people watching a household TV set for four and one-half hours each day (U.S. Bureau of the Census, 2003), who can doubt the importance of the mass media in shaping how we think and act? What messages about gender do we find on TV?

When television became popular in the 1950s, men had almost all the starring roles. Only in recent decades have television shows featured women as central characters. But we still find fewer women than men cast as talented athletes, successful stock traders, brilliant detectives, and skilled surgeons. More often than not, women have supporting roles as wives, assistants, and secretaries. Music videos also come in for criticism: Performing groups are mostly all male, and when women do appear on stage, they are clearly there for their sex appeal. Moreover, song lyrics often reinforce men's power over women.

TABLE 4–1   POLITICAL "FIRSTS" FOR U.S. WOMEN

1869   Law allows women to vote in Wyoming territory; Utah follows suit in 1870.

1872   First woman to run for the presidency (Victoria Woodhull) represents the Equal Rights party.

1917   First woman elected to the House of Representatives (Jeannette Rankin of Montana).

1924   First women elected state governors (Nellie Taylor Ross of Wyoming and Miriam ["Ma"] Ferguson of Texas); both followed their husbands into office. First woman to have her name placed in nomination for vice-presidency at the convention of a major political party (Lena Jones Springs).

1931   First woman to serve in the Senate (Hattie Caraway of Arkansas); completed the term of her husband upon his death and won reelection in 1932.

1932   First woman appointed to the presidential cabinet (Frances Perkins, secretary of labor in the cabinet of President Franklin D. Roosevelt).

1964   First woman to have her name placed in nomination for the presidency at the convention of a major political party (Margaret Chase Smith, a Republican).

1972   First African American woman to have her name placed in nomination for the presidency at the convention of a major political party (Shirley Chisholm, a Democrat).

1981   First woman appointed to the U.S. Supreme Court (Sandra Day O'Connor).

1984   First woman to be successfully nominated for the vice-presidency (Geraldine Ferraro, a Democrat).

1988   First woman chief executive to be elected to a consecutive third term (Madeleine Kunin, governor of Vermont).

1990   First woman of color elected to Congress (Patsy Takemoto Mink of Hawaii).

1992   Political "Year of the Woman" yields record number of women in the Senate (six) and the House (forty-eight), as well as (1) first African American woman to win election to U.S. Senate (Carol Moseley-Braun of Illinois), (2) first state (California) to be served by two women senators (Barbara Boxer and Dianne Feinstein), and (3) first woman of Puerto Rican descent elected to the House (Nydia Valasquez of New York).

1996   First woman appointed secretary of state (Madeleine Albright).

2000   Record number of women in the Senate (thirteen) and the House (sixty).

2000   First former First Lady to win elected political office (Hillary Rodham Clinton, senator from New York).

2002   First woman to serve as minority whip in House of Representatives (Nancy Pelosi, representative from California).

What about advertising? In the early years of television, advertisers targeted women during the day because so many women were at-home wives (the fact that most of the commercials advertised laundry and household products is the reason daytime TV dramas are still called "soap operas"). On television and in newspaper and magazine advertising, most ads still use male models to pitch products such as automobiles, banking services, travel, and alcoholic beverages to men, whereas female models sell products such as clothing, cosmetics, cleaning products, and food to women. Moreover, ads typically show men in offices or in rugged out-door scenes, while placing women in the home (Courtney & Whipple, 1983; Davis, 1993).

Gender biases in advertising can be subtle. Research shows that ads almost always present men as taller than women, and women (but never men) often lie on sofas and beds or sit on the floor like children. Furthermore, men's facial expressions suggest competence and authority, whereas women laugh, pout, or strike childlike poses. Finally, men in advertising focus on the products they are promoting; women, as often as not, pay attention to men (Goffman, 1979; Cortese, 1999).

Gender and Religion

Religions also teach us about gender. When people in a national sample of U.S. adults were asked whether they tend to think of God as "Mother" or "Father," 6 percent replied they envision God more as "Mother." Two-thirds—eleven times as many—favored "Father," with the remaining one-fourth imagining God equally in these terms (NORC, 2003:146).

The fact that most of us think of God as male is no surprise because societies attribute power and wisdom to men. Thus, all the Western religious traditions see the divine being as male. The Qur'an

A NATION OF DIVERSITY

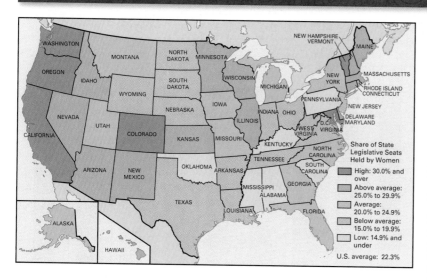

NATIONAL MAP 4–1
**Women's Political Power
across the United States**

Women represent slightly more than half of U.S. adults. Even so, in 2002, women held just 23 percent of seats in the state legislatures across the country. The map provides the state-by-state percentages. Looking at the map, what pattern can you detect? What factors can you think of that might account for this pattern?

Source: Center for American Women and Politics, Eagleton Institute of Politics, Rutgers University, "Women in State Legislatures 2002." [Online] Available August 30, 2002, at http://www.cawp.rutgers.edu/pdf/stleg.pdf

(Koran), the sacred text of Islam, clearly endorses patriarchy with these words:

> Men are in charge of women. . . . Hence good women are obedient. . . . As for those whose rebelliousness you fear, admonish them, banish them from your bed, and scourge them. (quoted in Kaufman, 1976:163)

Paul, perhaps the most influential leader of the early Christian church, also supported the social dominance of men over women:

> A man . . . is the image and glory of God; but woman is the glory of man. For man was not made from woman, but woman from man. Neither was man created for woman, but woman for man. (I Corinthians 11:7–9)
>
> Wives, be subject to your husbands, as to the Lord. For the husband is the head of the wife as Christ is the head of the church. . . . As the church is subject to Christ, so let wives also be subject in everything to their husbands. (Ephesians 5:22–24)

Judaism also has a long history of supporting the social power of men. A daily prayer among Orthodox Jewish men includes the following words:

> Blessed art thou, O Lord our God, King of the Universe, that I was not born a gentile.
>
> Blessed art thou, O Lord our God, King of the Universe, that I was not born a slave.
>
> Blessed art thou, O Lord our God, King of the Universe, that I was not born a woman.

In recent decades, more liberal denominations in the United States (including Episcopalians and Presbyterians) have moved toward greater gender equality. This liberal trend includes not only the revision of prayers, hymnals, and even the Bible to reduce sexist language, but also the ordination of both women and men as priests and ministers. Not all religious organizations embrace this spirit of change. Orthodox Judaism, Islam, and Roman Catholicism have retained traditional male leadership. But throughout the religious community, a lively debate surrounds the question of whether patriarchal traditions represent God's will or merely reflect "times gone by."

Gender and Politics

Patriarchy is about power. Therefore, women have played only a marginal role in U.S. political history. As Table 4–1 shows, the first woman to win election to the United States Congress joined the House of Representatives in 1917, 128 years after that body came together for the first time. In 1920, the country reached a political milestone with the passage of the Nineteenth Amendment to the U.S. Constitution, which permitted women to vote in national elections.

Winning the right to vote brought women only so far into the U.S. political mainstream. At the local level, thousands of women now serve as mayors of cities and towns and as members of other governing boards across the country. In 2002, 23 percent of state legislators were women (up from just 4 percent in 1970), and 6 of the 50 state governors were women (12 percent). National Map 4–1 compares regions of

DIMENSIONS OF DIFFERENCE

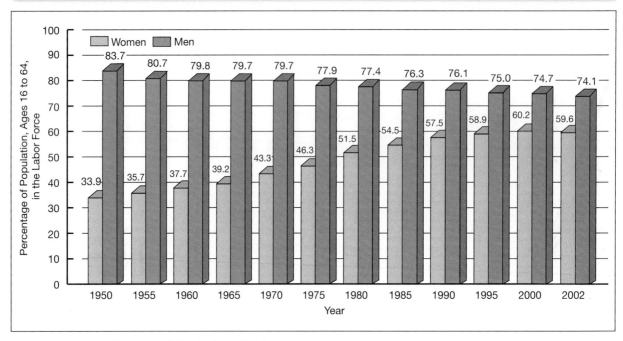

FIGURE 4–1   Women and Men in the U.S. Labor Force

Over the last fifty years, the share of men in the labor force has gone down (with men retiring earlier and living longer), while the share of women working for income has gone up rapidly.

Source: U.S. Department of Labor (2003).

the United States in terms of women's power in state government.

In national government, the picture is similar. In 2002, 59 of 435 members of the House of Representatives (14 percent) and 13 of 100 senators (13 percent) were women (Center for American Women in Politics, 2003).

Around the world, the pattern is much the same: Women hold just 14.7 percent of seats in the world's 179 parliaments. Only in the Nordic nations of Norway, Sweden, Finland, and Denmark (38.9 percent), and Iceland (34.9 percent) does women's share of parliamentary seats even approach their share of the population (Inter-Parliamentary Union, 2003).

For more on women in U.S. politics, visit
http://www.rci.rutgers.edu/~cawp

Gender and the Military

Women have been part of the military since the Revolutionary War. As recently as World War II, however, women made up just 2 percent of the armed forces.

By the Gulf War in 1991, that share rose to almost 7 percent, and 5 of the 148 soldiers killed were women. In the 2003 War in Iraq, women were 15 percent of the U.S. military, and one woman was included among the 550 fatalities (as of February 1, 2004).

Whereas all Coast Guard positions are open to both sexes, the Army, Navy, Air Force, and Marine Corps all restrict opportunities for women. The traditional explanation is that women are not as strong as men, although this argument makes little sense in a high-technology military. The real reason certainly has more to do with gender itself. Many people have difficulty with the idea of women—those our culture defines as nurturers—being put in a position to kill and be killed (McNeil, 1991; Wilcox, 1992; Kaminer, 1997).

Gender and Work

In most societies, people think of different kinds of jobs as either "men's work" or "women's work." A century ago in the United States, in fact, most people did not think women should work at all (at least not for pay); it was said that a woman's place was in the home. In 1900, just one in five women worked for income. By 2002, as Figure 4–1 shows, this share jumped to three in five (60 percent), even as the share of adult men in the labor force declined. Moreover, three-fourths of women in the labor force now work full time (U.S. Department of Labor, 2003).

Why this dramatic change? Many factors are involved. At the beginning of the twentieth century, a majority of the U.S. population lived in rural areas, where women typically spent long hours cooking, doing housework, and raising large families. Today's typical home has a host of appliances, including washers, vacuums, and microwaves, that have dramatically reduced the time needed for housework. In addition, today's average woman bears just two children, half the number of a century ago. It is not surprising, then, that women have joined men working outside the home. Indeed, in two-thirds of all married couple households, both partners are employed.

In the past, the few women who did work for pay typically had no children. But no longer: Sixty-two percent of married women with children under age six work, as do 80 percent of women with children six to seventeen years old (U.S. Census Bureau, 2002).

Even though more women now work for pay, the range of jobs open to them is still limited (Bellas & Coventry, 2001; van der Lippe & van Dijk, 2002) because our society still labels most jobs as either feminine or masculine. "Masculine jobs" are those that involve physical danger (such as firefighting and police work), strength and endurance (construction and truck driving), and leadership roles (clergy, judges, and business executives). "Feminine jobs," shown in Table 4–2, include support positions (secretarial work or medical assisting) or work requiring nurturing skills (child care and teaching young children).

Gender discrimination was outlawed by the federal Equal Pay Act of 1963 and Title VII of the Civil Rights Act of 1964. This means that employers cannot discriminate between men and women in hiring or pay. But gender inequality is deeply rooted in U.S. society; officials investigate thousands of discrimination complaints every year, and few doubt that the real number of cases is far higher.

GENDER STRATIFICATION

Gender stratification is *the unequal distribution of wealth, power, and privilege between men and women.* Women's inequality is evident in many aspects of

TABLE 4–2	GENDER SEGREGATION IN THE WORKPLACE: JOBS DEFINED AS "FEMININE"
OCCUPATION	PERCENTAGE IN OCCUPATION WHO ARE WOMEN
1. Family child-care provider	99.4
2. Secretary	98.7
3. Dental assistant	98.1
4. Dental hygienist	98.1
5. Prekindergarten and kindergarten teacher	97.7
6. Private household child-care worker	97.6
7. Receptionist	97.1
8. Stenographer	95.2
9. Licensed practical nurse	94.9
10. Speech therapist	94.2

Source: U.S. Department of Labor, Bureau of Labor Statistics.

life, including income, responsibility for housework, patterns of violence, and even issues related to reproduction.

Income

Income is a one important dimension of gender inequality. As we have explained, women and men perform different kinds of work, with women generally holding clerical and service jobs and men having most executive and professional positions. The predictable result is that women and men receive different levels of pay.

Median 2002 pay for full-time male workers was $39,429, whereas women working full time earned $30,203, or 77 percent as much. Almost 40 percent of full-time women workers earned less than $25,000 in 2002, compared to 24 percent of men. The pattern is reversed for high-income positions: Three times as many men (16 percent) as women (5 percent) earned more than $75,000 (U.S. Census Bureau, 2003).

Most women who live in high-income households depend on the earnings of a man. For this reason, after separation, divorce, or death of a husband, a woman's income may fall, placing her at high risk of poverty, especially if she has young children.

Such gender inequality is found around the world to differing degrees. In Japan, despite a recent rise in the number of working women (because of

In global perspective, high-income countries vary dramatically in the economic opportunities they offer to women. In Sweden (left), most women work for income; in Japan (right), by contrast, most women do not. In this regard, the United States falls somewhere between traditional Japan and progressive Sweden.

that country's stalled economy), a majority of women still do not work for income (French, 2002). At the other extreme, even in Norway, Sweden, Finland, and Denmark, where a larger share of women work for pay than in the United States, women earn only about 85 percent as much as men.

In the United States, why do men earn so much more than women? The first and biggest reason, noted earlier, is that men and women typically hold different types of jobs. A second reason is that U.S. society assigns women primary responsibility for raising children. For this reason, pregnancy, childbirth, and raising small children limit women's careers more than men's. Even if everything else were equal, men would have more workplace seniority than women because women devote more time to the family matters (Fuchs, 1986). Indeed, many employers still look on a woman's attention to family concerns as evidence that she has less commitment to the job. Furthermore, some women with young children or aging parents seek out work that does not tie up their evenings and weekends or require them to travel far from home. Still other mothers (but rarely fathers) choose a job because it is nearby, offers a flexible schedule, or provides child-care facilities, even if it does not provide the best pay or the best chance for advancement. One recent study of college professors found that women with at least one child were 22 percent less likely to have tenure than comparable men in the same field (Shea, 2002). In short, the net effect of family life is that *even if*

both sexes start out with exactly the same jobs, women typically fall behind their male colleagues.

The third reason for gender inequality is that women suffer from gender discrimination. This means that many employers pay women less than men simply because they can get away with it. This practice is illegal, and equal opportunity laws have reduced the blatant discrimination that was common in the past. But more subtle discrimination continues, as in this case, in which one company

> frequently invited [men] to out-of-town business meetings and social functions from which [women] were excluded. These occasions were a source of information on business trends and store promotions and were a rich source of potentially important business contacts. When [one woman] asked why she had not been invited to these meetings and social gatherings, the response was that her employer thought it was "too dangerous for her to be driving out of town at night by herself." (Benokraitis & Feagin, 1995:85)

The Glass Ceiling   Today, when a company is looking to fill a top job, no one is likely to come right out and say, "Let's promote a man." But cultural bias against women affects promotion all the same. Sociologists use the term **glass ceiling** to refer to *subtle discrimination that effectively blocks the movement of women into the highest positions in organizations*. According to one recent survey, the top executives in Fortune 500 corporations include 2,162 men (96 percent of the total) and 93 women (4 percent).

Just 11 of the 1,000 largest U.S. corporations (and including Pearson Education, the publisher of this text), have a woman as their chief executive officer (Catalyst, 2003).

Housework

Just as patriarchy gives men control of the workplace, it also assigns women most of the housework. In Japan, probably the most patriarchal of all high-income nations, women do almost all the shopping, cooking, cleaning, and child care. In the United States, although the two-income married couple is now the norm, women still do most of the housework (or they pay other women to do it). Figure 4–2 shows that the amount of housework people do depends on whether they are single or married, working for pay or staying at home. In every one of these categories, however, women spend much more time doing housework than men—one reason that housework is sometimes called women's "second shift" (Presser, 1993; Keith & Schafer, 1994; Harpster & Monk-Turner, 1998; Stapinski, 1998; Stratton, 2001).

Violence against Women

Perhaps the most serious problem linked to patriarchy is men's physical violence against women. Assault, rape, and even murder are common enough that many see them as one dimension of men's domination of women.

Read a report about violence against women around the world:
http://www.unicef-icdc.org/publications/pdf/digest6e.pdf

The government estimates that about 2 million nonsexual physical assaults against women take place each year, with an additional 400,000 sexual assaults, including 200,000 rapes or attempted rapes (U.S. Bureau of Justice Statistics, 2001). On campus, the government estimates that in 2000, 1.7 percent of female college students were victims of rape and another 1.1 percent were victims of attempted rape (U.S. Department of Justice, 2001).

Read a report about sexual violence on campus:
http://www.ncjrs.org/pdffiles1/nij/182369.pdf

Why is violence a gender issue? First, physical aggressiveness is part of our cultural definition of masculinity. Put simply, "real men" take control of a situation and do not allow themselves to be pushed around, one reason most violent crimes are

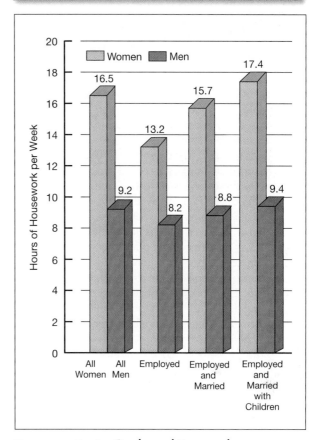

FIGURE 4–2 Gender and Housework

Regardless of employment or family status, women do more housework than men.
Source: Stapinski (1998).

committed by males (see Chapter 7, "Violence"). Second, people often treat with contempt what a patriarchal society labels as "feminine" (Goetting, 1999; Herman, 2001).

Gender violence ranges from annoying actions (such as a wolf whistle when a woman walks down a city street) to unwanted physical contact (such as "cornering" a woman against a wall in a dorm hallway) to outright violence (an angry punch in a suburban home). In all cases, these assaults are not so much *sexual*—as is commonly thought—as they are expressions of male *power* over women (Griffin, 1979; Herman, 2001).

Looking over the statistics, the most dangerous setting for women turns out not to be the dark alley but the well-lit home. This is exactly the place people are supposed to find peace and support (Straus &

A Global Perspective

Female Genital Mutilation: Using Violence to Control Women

IN A POOR HOME IN THE EAST AFRICAN NATION of Ethiopia, a little girl huddles in the corner. Only eighteen months old, she does not understand what has happened; all she feels is pain.

Her suffering was caused by a surgical clitoridectomy, sometimes mistakenly called female circumcision, whereby the clitoris is cut away. In its more extreme form, the clitoris is cut away entirely and the vagina is sewed almost completely shut, to be cut open again only on a woman's wedding night. This procedure—sometimes performed by a doctor but more often by a midwife or a tribal practitioner, and usually without anesthesia—is common in Ethiopia, Nigeria, Togo, Somalia, Egypt, and three dozen other nations in Africa and the Middle East. More than 100 million girls worldwide have endured a clitoridectomy, now widely called female genital mutilation.

This so-called medical procedure is not about illness; it is a means to control women. In highly patriarchal societies, men demand that the women they marry be virgins and that wives remain sexually faithful thereafter. Without the clitoris, a woman loses some of her ability to experience sexual pleasure, which, people expect, will make her more likely to live by the rules of her society.

In the United States, although this procedure is illegal, thousands of girls in immigrant families undergo clitoridectomy each year. In fact, some immigrant mothers believe that this procedure is *more* necessary once they are living in the United States, where sexual norms provide women with more freedom.

ISSUES AND EXERCISES

1. How is the practice of female circumcision used to control the behavior of women?
2. What steps should be taken—in the United States and elsewhere—to eliminate this practice?
3. [Research Navigator.com] Use Research Navigator™ to learn more about this practice. (See instructions on page 25; keyword: "female circumcision")

Sources: Based on Crossette (1995) and Boyle, Songora, & Foss (2001).

Gelles, 1986; Schwartz, 1987; Gelles & Cornell, 1990; Smolowe, 1994).

In a number of countries, including the United States, families use violence to control the behavior of women. The Global Perspective box looks at the dramatic case of female genital mutilation.

Sexual Harassment

Sexual harassment refers to *unwanted comments, gestures, or physical contact of a sexual nature*. Awareness of sexual harassment as a social problem emerged in the 1980s as a challenge to the traditional male practice of viewing women in sexual terms. If men think of women in sexual terms, men cannot accept women as equals in the workplace, on the campus, or elsewhere. Just as important, in the absence of rules against sexual harassment, men in positions of power can coerce sex from women they supervise. Surveys show that about 50 percent of women claim they have received unwanted sexual attention (Paul, 1991; NORC, 2003).

Some sexual harassment is blatant and direct: A professor solicits sexual favors from a student, threatening a poor grade if she refuses. The law defines such quid pro quo sexual harassment (the Latin phrase means "one thing in return for another") as a violation of civil rights. But sexual harassment can involve subtle behavior—sexual teasing or off-color jokes—that someone may not even intend as harassment. Such behavior is still wrong if it has the effect of creating a *hostile environment* that prevents people from doing their work (Cohen, 1991; Paul, 1991). In such cases, the offender and the victim may well define the behavior in question differently. For example, a man may think that a compliment to a co-worker about her appearance is simply a friendly gesture, but she may find that such behavior gets in the way of her job performance.

Sexuality, Beauty, and Reproduction

A patriarchal culture teaches men to assess women not according to their abilities but simply on the basis of their sexual attractiveness. Women also learn these lessons. Social norms encourage girls and women to wear figure-flattering clothing and shoes (whether or not they are comfortable or even safe) and to flirt with and be attentive to men.

In recent years, sociologists have pointed out that beauty is not simply about looking good; it is about power and inequality. The Critical Thinking box on page 98 takes a closer look.

Another concern involves control of sexual reproduction. In the past, physicians and legislators (almost all of them men) restricted access to birth control technology. As late as the 1960s, state laws controlled even the sale of condoms and other birth control devices. As Chapter 8 ("Sexuality") explains, controversy continues today over new birth control technology, such as RU-486.

Abortion also remains a highly divisive issue. Conservatives see abortion as a moral question the need to protect unborn children. Liberals (especially feminists) see abortion as an issue of power and choice. Restricting access to abortion places the decision about whether to continue a pregnancy in the hands of men—that is, fathers, husbands, physicians, and legislators—rather than with the women whose bodies and lives will be affected by such a decision. In the liberal view, access to birth control and safe abortion expands women's choices about their lives, including their ability to work, and it reduces gender inequality.

In low-income nations, boys have more economic value than girls because they can earn more money. Therefore, many poor families engage in sex-selective abortion to avoid giving birth to a daughter. In villages in India, clinics provide sonograms that usually reveal the sex of a fetus; they also provide abortions to women who choose to "try again" in the hopes of having a son.

Women: A Majority Minority?

Chapter 3 ("Racial and Ethnic Inequality") defined a minority as any distinctive category of people who are socially disadvantaged. Does that make women a minority? Numerically, women are a slight majority (51.1 percent) of the U.S. population. Even so, in a patriarchal society they meet the test of being physically distinctive and disadvantaged.

Even so, researchers have long noted that most women do not think of themselves as a minority (Hacker, 1951; Lengermann & Wallace, 1985). One reason is that many women feel they are more or less privileged based on their color, ethnicity, and class position rather than their sex. Also, our society teaches women to think that they *should* defer to men, defining a husband's career, for example, as more important than their own.

Objectively speaking, however, even relatively privileged women have less income, wealth, and power than men. Therefore, it seems reasonable to conclude that women are a minority.

Minority Women: Intersection Theory

If racial and ethnic minorities are disadvantaged, and women are, too, what about minority women? Are they doubly disadvantaged? Intersection theory, discussed in Chapter 3, claims that the answer is "yes."

In 2001, the median income for non-Hispanic white women working full time was $31,794. Comparable African American women earned $27,297, 86 percent as much, and Hispanic women earned $21,973, or 69 percent as much as non-Hispanic whites. For women, then, race and ethnicity are one source of disadvantage.

Then there is the second disadvantage based on gender. Within racial and ethnic categories, we see that in 2001, African American women earned 86 percent as much as African American men, and Hispanic women earned 87 percent as much as Hispanic men.

Combining these two dimensions of inequality, African American women earned 63 percent as much

Critical Thinking   Beauty: What's It Really About?

BEAUTY IS ABOUT GOOD LOOKS—what could be more obvious? But beauty is also about gender and power.

Naomi Wolf (1990) claims that our culture's ideas about beauty put men in a position of power over women. Women, she says, learn to measure their personal importance in terms of their physical appearance, thereby discouraging other avenues of personal development. Furthermore, the standards by which society encourages women to judge themselves are those created by the multimillion-dollar fashion, cosmetics, and diet industries. These standards (in the form of the *Playboy* "playmate" or the 100-pound New York fashion model) have little to do with the reality of most women's bodies or lives.

In addition, a focus on beauty teaches women to try to please men. The pursuit of beauty makes women highly attuned to how men react to them and encourages them to view other women not as allies but as competitors.

Taken together, our cultural ideas about beauty amount to an effective strategy to maintain patriarchy. Much advertising directed at women on television and in magazines and newspapers is not simply about what women should buy and use. Rather, it is about what women *should be*. This cultural "beauty myth," Wolf charges, is a form of gender bias that is harmful to women.

ISSUES AND EXERCISES

1. The Duchess of Windsor once said, "A woman cannot be too rich or too thin." Does this advice apply to men as well? Why or why not?

2. Look ahead to Chapter 10 ("Physical and Mental Health"), which explains that almost all people suffering from eating disorders are women. Why do you think this is the case?

3. To what extent is the current "fitness craze" about gender as much as about health?

---

as white men and Hispanic women earned 51 percent as much as white men (U.S. Census Bureau, 2002). Therefore, the intersection of gender with race and ethnicity does result in even greater disadvantages for some categories of the U.S. population.

THEORETICAL ANALYSIS: UNDERSTANDING GENDER INEQUALITY

Each of sociology's three major theoretical orientations—the structural-functional, social-conflict, and symbolic-interaction approaches—offers insights into gender stratification. As we have seen in earlier chapters, each approach highlights different facts and reaches different conclusions.

Structural-Functional Analysis: Gender and Complementarity

According to the functionalist approach, gender is society's recognition that women and men differ in some useful ways. In this approach, society defines gender in terms of *complementarity*, as if to say, " Differences between men and women help build families and integrate society as a whole."

Talcott Parsons: A Theory of Complementary Roles

The best known theory of this kind was developed by Talcott Parsons (1942, 1951, 1954). To understand his ideas, it is helpful to begin with a historical look at gender.

Among early hunters and gatherers, biological differences between the sexes were very important. Our distant ancestors had no way to control reproduction, so women experienced frequent pregnancies and had to care for children through much of the life course. As a result, such societies expected women to build their lives around the home, gathering vegetation and raising the young. Men's greater size and strength meant that they took charge of hunting and warfare, tasks that took them away from the home. Over many generations, this sex-based division of labor became *institutionalized*, meaning it was built into the culture and passed from generation to generation.

By the time of the Industrial Revolution, the division of labor based on gender had become less necessary. For one thing, societies had devised effective means of birth control. As Chapter 8 ("Sexuality") explains, rubber condoms, which appeared around 1850, were a fairly reliable method of contraception. Industrial technology also greatly reduced the importance of physical strength in the labor force, opening more jobs to women.

Talcott Parsons argued that gender differences are getting smaller because, over the course of human history, the biological facts of sex—physical size and strength—matter less and less. Still, Parsons suggested, some gender differences remain functional today because gender still serves to integrate people into a smoothly functioning society. By defining the two sexes in *complementary* ways, society ensures that men and women need each other and benefit from joining together as families. In the family, women still bear the children, of course, and they take more responsibility for the household. By contrast, men do more to link the family to the larger world, mostly through their greater participation in the labor force.

Given this pattern, society urges parents to raise their boys and girls differently. Masculinity, explains Parsons, involves an *instrumental* orientation, emphasizing rationality, competition, and goal orientation. Femininity involves an opposing *expressive* orientation: emotional responsiveness, cooperation, and overall concern for other people and relationships.

Young people soon learn that straying too far from the masculine or feminine ideal can bring disapproval from others. As they grow older, boys and girls also learn that failure to display the right social patterns may result in loss of sexual appeal. In short, society teaches men to favor women who are feminine, just as it teaches women to favor men who are masculine. The end result is that men and women bring different elements to a relationship, and each needs the other.

Critical evaluation. Structural-functional analysis of gender was quite influential fifty years ago, but it is far less so today. Why? Because the functionalist argument that "gender differences work" strikes those doing research in this area today as very conservative. Many of today's sociologists (who, for the most part, have more liberal views) see what Talcott Parsons called "complementary roles" as little more than male domination.

But there are other problems with this approach. First, by arguing that society benefits from conventional ideas about gender, the structural-functional approach ignores how men and women can and do relate to one another in a variety of ways that do not fit any norm. We cannot assume that everyone will fit into either the "instrumental" or "expressive" category. Also, the majority of both men and women now have "instrumental" roles in the labor force.

A second problem cited by critics is that functional thinking glosses over personal strains and social conflicts produced by rigid gender patterns (Giele, 1988). They argue that gender may be more dysfunctional than functional. Such concerns bring us to symbolic-interaction analysis, which explores the ways people experience gender in their everyday lives.

Symbolic-Interaction Analysis: Gender in Everyday Life

The symbolic-interaction approach provides a micro-level analysis of gender, which highlights gender at work in the everyday lives of individual people.

Personal Behavior How does gender shape daily behavior? As we have seen, gender involves power; more powerful people have more choices about how to behave. In general, our society gives men greater freedom in personal behavior. For example, would you react the same way to a man who uses foul language and to a woman who does the same thing? Similarly, researchers have documented men's tendency to interrupt others (especially women) in conversation, whereas women are more likely to listen politely, especially to men (Smith-Lovin & Brody, 1989; Henley, Hamilton, & Thorne, 1992; Johnson, 1994).

The same gender pattern is evident in facial expression. In addition to symbolizing pleasure, smiling shows respect and a desire to make peace. Not surprisingly, then, researchers note that women tend to smile more than men (Henley, Hamilton, & Thorne, 1992).

Use of Space In general, the more power people have, the more space they command. In the classroom, for example, it is the professor who can pace around the room while speaking, whereas students are expected to remain in their seats. Because men have greater social power, they typically use more space than women, whether they are speaking in front of a group at work or relaxing on the sidelines of a sporting event. We gauge masculinity by how much space a man uses (the standard of "turf"), and we assess femininity by how little space a woman uses (the standard of "daintiness").

In addition, men's greater power gives them the option of moving closer to others, even to the point of violating what we consider our personal space. Women have to be more careful in this regard because "moving in on a man" is likely to be treated as a sexual overture (Henley, Hamilton, & Thorne, 1992).

Language   Finally, gender is at work in the language we use. When speaking fondly of possessions, most people use female pronouns, as when young men gaze at a new car and one asks, "Isn't she a beauty?" Using a male pronoun in this case ("Isn't *he* a beauty?") seems wrong; this reflects the fact that in a patriarchal culture, men control women, not the other way around.

People's names show the same pattern. Among newlyweds, the conventional practice is for the woman to take her husband's last name. The opposite pattern—a man taking his wife's last name—is extremely rare. Although few would claim this pattern means that a man actually owns a woman, it does suggest that men expect to have control over women's lives.

Finally, notice how the English language tends to give what is masculine more value than what is feminine. Traditional titles associated with men—such as *king* and *lord*—have positive meanings, whereas the corresponding titles associated with women—such as *queen*, *madam*, and *dame*—often have negative meanings.

Critical evaluation.   The strength of symbolic-interaction analysis lies in putting a human face on gender, showing how gender is at work in familiar dimensions of everyday life. It is clear that gender is an important building block of social reality.

At the same time, a limitation of this approach (and, indeed, of all micro-theories) is that it overlooks gender as a broad structure of society. We now turn to social-conflict theory to examine broad issues of gender inequality and gender conflict.

Social-Conflict Analysis: Gender and Inequality

Social-conflict analysis switches the focus from functionalism's horizontal image of gender differences as complementary to a more vertical view of gender as a dimension of social inequality. Rather than promoting social integration, conflict theory argues, gender generates conflict between male "haves" and female "have-nots."

Friedrich Engels: The Rise of Patriarchy   Friedrich Engels (1820–1895), a lifelong friend and collaborator of Karl Marx, expanded Marx's ideas about class conflict to include gender (Engels, 1902; orig. 1884). Engels argued that the same process that allows a ruling class to dominate workers places men in a dominant position over women.

Early hunting and gathering societies assigned women and men different daily routines, but both sexes made vital contributions to daily life. That is, men may have done most of the hunting, but women collected the vegetation that provided most of the food (Leacock, 1978; Ehrenreich, 1999).

As societies gained the ability to raise their own animals and crops, surpluses resulted. As some families gained most of this surplus for themselves, social classes were born. Once some people had much more than others, the idea of private property gained importance, at least to the elites. At the same time, men began controlling the behavior of women. Why? Because men with property are concerned about passing their wealth to their heirs, and they need to make sure who their offspring are. Therefore, wealthy men devised the family as a way to control the sexuality of women, who were to remain faithful and raise a man's children. In Engels's view, patriarchy is a system by which wealthy men transmit property to their sons.

With the rise of capitalism, Engels continued, patriarchy became stronger than ever, taking the form of a male-dominated capitalist class. In addition, capitalism created an ever-expanding market. To ensure demand for the products of capitalist production, society teaches women that personal happiness lies in marriage and the domestic role as a consumer of products and services. Finally, because capitalism forced most men to work long hours in factories, men expected their wives to do all the housework. To Engels, the double problem of capitalism lies in exploiting men in factories (for low pay) and exploiting women in the home (for no pay at all) (Eisenstein, 1979; Barry, 1983; Jagger, 1983; Vogel, 1983).

Critical evaluation.   Social-conflict analysis shows how gender became part of social stratification. Engels's work also highlights the close link between gender and class.

But conflict theory has its critics. First, families may be patriarchal, but they perform the vital task of raising children. Second, the lives of men and women may be different, but not everyone defines these differences as unjust. In other words, critics

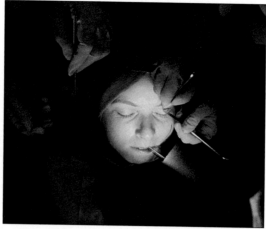

From head to toe, women have long endured great discomfort in pursuit of cultural standards of beauty. In centuries past, many Chinese women tightly bound their feet in childhood to achieve the "dainty" size that culture defined as feminine. Today, tens of thousands of U.S. women undergo surgery on their faces and elsewhere to increase their physical attractiveness to men.

claim, conflict theorists minimize the extent to which women and men live together cooperatively and, often enough, quite happily. Third, some challenge Engels's assertion that capitalism is at the heart of gender stratification. After all, patriarchy is also strong in socialist nations, including Cuba and the People's Republic of China.

FEMINISM

Since the 1960s, feminism has gained great importance in sociology. Formally defined, **feminism** is *the study of gender with the goal of changing society to make women and men equal.* Feminism therefore involves both theory and action.

Read more about feminism at **http://www.feminist.org**

The history of feminism in the United States spans more than 150 years. The movement's first wave began in the 1840s as a spinoff of efforts to abolish the slavery of African Americans. Women including Lucretia Mott (1793–1880) and Elizabeth Cady Stanton (1815–1902) saw parallels between whites oppressing people of color and men subjugating women (Randall, 1982). The Defining Moment box on page 102 takes a closer look.

Feminist Foundations

There is more than one version of feminism. But almost all feminists agree on the following six general points:

1. **The importance of gender.** Men and women can understand their lives, feminists claim, only by recognizing how gender shapes life experience. Men don't decide to be competitive any more than women decide to be deferential; this kind of behavior has much to do with how our society defines masculine and feminine behavior.

2. **The importance of change.** Because U.S. society elevates men and subordinates women, feminists oppose the status quo. Feminism seeks both to understand and to change the social world.

   Feminists claim that everyone—women and men—would benefit from gender equality. For one thing, patriarchy limits the development of women, who make up half the population. But men also suffer from a system that drives them to seek control of others, a pattern that results in high risk of death from suicide, violence, accidents, heart attacks, and other diseases related to stress. Isn't what psychologists call the

A DEFINING MOMENT

Elizabeth Cady Stanton: Claiming Women's Right to Equality

Here we see the beginnings of the feminist movement in the United States: Elizabeth Cady Stanton speaks to people who traveled great distances to attend the first women's rights convention in Seneca Falls, New York, in June 1848.

IT MAY BE HARD TO IMAGINE, but just 150 years ago, women in the United States were legally second-class citizens. Women could not vote, own property, or enter into legal contracts. It was rare for women to earn income, and the few who did typically turned the money over to their husbands or fathers.

Therefore, it is hardly surprising that many people brought together by their opposition to the slavery of African Americans soon began to compare it to the standing of white women. Elizabeth Cady Stanton (1815–1902) understood the second-class standing of women and decided to do something about it. In 1848, Stanton and her friend Lucretia Mott (1793–1880) began the process of change by organizing a meeting in Seneca Falls, New York.

Some 300 women gathered at Wesleyan Chapel in the small upstate New York town to hear more about "women's rights." Stanton led the meeting, asking why women should not have the same rights and opportunities as men, including the right to vote. Even many of those who thought women deserved something more were shocked by the suggestion that they should have a political voice equal to men's. Stanton's husband, Henry, convinced that his wife had gone too far, rode out of town in protest.

Even though Stanton lived for another half-century, she never saw her dream come to pass. Women finally gained the right to vote in 1920, eighteen years after Stanton's death. Even after women won the right to vote, many people realized that women remained unequal to men in many other ways. As a result, a "second wave" of the feminist movement continues to this day—addressing issues such as equality in the workplace and reproductive rights.

Type A personality—marked by impatience, driving ambition, and competitiveness, all of which increase the risk of heart disease—the same thing as behavior our culture defines as masculine (Ehrenreich, 1983)?

3. **The importance of choice.** Feminists see gender as a cultural creation that imposes a narrow set of opportunities on both women and men. Only if we abandon conventional ideas about the kind of lives women and men "ought" to lead will we all be free to decide the direction of our own lives.

4. **Eliminating patriarchy.** Feminism opposes all forms of sexism and gender inequality. One important step in this process, as feminists see it, is for U.S. society to affirm that women and men have equal standing before the law. This is

why, since its introduction in Congress in 1923, feminists have supported passage of the Equal Rights Amendment (ERA) to the U.S. Constitution. The ERA states, *"Equality of rights under the law shall not be denied or abridged by the United States or any State on account of sex."*

5. **Eliminating violence against women.** As noted earlier in this chapter, feminists see violence against women as a pressing social problem (Millet, 1970; J. Bernard, 1973; Dworkin, 1987; Herman, 2001). Feminists claim that violence against women can end only when society places women and men on the same level.

6. **The importance of sexual autonomy.** Feminists claim that women have the right to control their sexuality. Feminists support the wide availability of birth control technology, and

oppose legal restrictions on abortion. Many feminists also support the gay rights movement. As some feminists see it, lesbians, even more than gay men, are targets of prejudice and discrimination because they violate both the norm of heterosexuality and the expectation that men should control the sexuality of women (Deckard, 1979; Barry, 1983; Jagger, 1983; Hadley, 1996; Jackson & Scott, 1996; Benokraitis, 1997).

Types of Feminism

All feminists agree on the general goals just noted, but they recognize various paths to achieving them. Generally speaking, there are three feminist solutions to the problem of patriarchy: liberal feminism, socialist feminism, and radical feminism (Barry, 1983; Jagger, 1983; Vogel, 1983; Phillips, 1987; Lindsay, 1994; Armstrong, 2002; Freedman, 2002).

Liberal Feminism *Liberal feminism* seeks a society in which all people are treated as individuals so that both women and men can freely develop their talents and pursue their interests. Liberal feminism is a reform approach, meaning that it seeks change within existing social institutions. The goal of liberal feminism is for women to enjoy the same rights, opportunities, and rewards as men.

Passage of the Equal Rights Amendment is one objective. In addition, liberal feminists support laws to combat prejudice and discrimination against women. Furthermore, they endorse policies such as maternity leave for women workers and child-care facilities in the workplace so that family responsibilities do not prevent women from holding jobs.

Finally, liberal feminists do not expect that all women will have the same social standing. Individual talent and effort will always elevate some people above others. The liberal feminist position is that society should place no barriers in people's way simply because they are women or men; people should be treated as individuals.

Socialist Feminism Further to the political left, other feminists doubt that existing social institutions will ever end patriarchy. Supporters of *socialist feminism* claim that Marxist class revolution is needed to secure equality for all people. Recall from our earlier discussion that Friedrich Engels pointed to the roots of patriarchy in capitalist private property. That is, capitalism oppresses women by forcing them to do housework (a situation Engels called "domestic slavery") and hold low-wage jobs. Without the ability to earn enough to support themselves, women are dependent on men for economic security.

From a socialist perspective, abolishing the capitalist class system means replacing private property (including the private household) with collective living arrangements in which people come together to share tasks such as cooking and child care. If work is shared in this way, there will be no classes, nor will men dominate women.

In short, socialist feminism sees class revolution as necessary for gender revolution. Whereas liberal feminism accepts the basic institutions of U.S. society, socialist feminism does not. From this point of view, women's liberation can be achieved only through elimination of the broader economic conditions that historically have oppressed all humanity.

Radical Feminism A third strategy calls for the most basic change of all. *Radical feminism* argues that patriarchy is built into the concept of gender itself; therefore, nothing short of erasing gender will bring about equality. Why? Radical feminists begin with what may seem to be a surprising assertion: The roots of gender are the biological differences by which women carry and bear children. In other words, motherhood is the main reason women have always been unequal to men. From this point of view, the family is not so much an economic relationship (as Friedrich Engels and socialist feminists claim) as it is a form of institutionalized heterosexuality that limits women to child-care and home responsibilities.

But if the problem of patriarchy is rooted in human biology, what hope is there for change? Until recently, radical feminists explain, there was none, because societies had little control over reproduction. But that is no longer true. Technological advances now give people power over reproduction, and the newest technology even raises the possibility of reproduction in the absence of conventional heterosexual parenting. In vitro fertilization (meaning that a woman's ovum is fertilized "in glass," outside of her body) is already a reality, which means that neither heterosexuality nor the historical family is necessary to reproduce the human species (see the discussion of new reproductive technologies in Chapter 13, "Family Life").

The future imagined by radical feminism is more revolutionary than that seen by socialists. Here we consider abolishing not only the traditional family but also all differences between women and men, and perhaps even ending heterosexual relationships entirely.

Could this ever happen? Certainly, social institutions would be very different from those we know today. The economy and political systems would have to evolve toward greater social equality. Families would take a new form, with collective responsibility for raising children. Some have suggested that in order for adults not to be defined by the task of parenting, children must gain greater rights and responsibilities for themselves (Jagger, 1983). Others, who see heterosexuality as necessarily patriarchal, claim that equality for all would require new thinking about sexuality itself. Andrea Dworkin (1987), for example, argues that an equal society would be one that gave up all sexual norms, including those that currently discourage masturbation, homosexuality, and sex outside marriage.

In the end, we can only imagine what a gender-free society would be like. But for many feminists, that is exactly the point. Whether or not one agrees with this view, radical feminism certainly helps us see how deeply gender is woven into all aspects of our lives.

Critical evaluation.   Because feminism has become a powerful social movement throughout the United States, it is a major force in sociology. The contributions of feminism lie in showing how gender affects almost every aspect of our lives and in bringing about change toward greater equality of women and men.

Like any successful social movement, feminism is controversial. Some critics claim that academic feminists focus attention on ways in which women remain unequal to men, ignoring the enormous progress women have made and the opportunities they now enjoy (Sommers, 2003). Other opposition to feminism comes from men who sense that this movement targets their power and privileges. But there are also men and women who reject the idea that all differences between the sexes are unjust and oppressive. Some critics claim that differences between men and women (whether biological or cultural) provide useful ways to organize social life (this was the view of Talcott Parsons, noted earlier). Others suggest that, despite the trend toward young mothers working for pay, women's steady presence in the home makes a crucial contribution to the well-being of their children (Baydar & Brooks-Gunn, 1991; Popenoe, 1993). Still others argue that feminism has wrongly sought to deny any differences between women and men; by contrast, we need to recognize the special strengths of women and build on them (Ehrenreich, 1999).

In the end, of course, the view one takes of feminism—or of any issue related to gender—is a matter of values and politics. We now explore how politics shapes what people define as the social problems and solutions related to gender.

POLITICS AND GENDER: CONSTRUCTING PROBLEMS AND DEFINING SOLUTIONS

According to the Declaration of Independence, "All men are created equal." Historians claim that our founding fathers did not intend to include women in this statement. Women had no political voice at that time, and this nation's political leaders were men. But the issue of gender inequality has sparked controversy ever since.

Conservatives: The Value of Families

Generally speaking, conservatives accept the wider social role of women today. They realize that most families depend on the income of both wives and husbands, and a rising number of women are political leaders in both the Democratic and Republican parties.

But many conservatives are uneasy about today's more gender-equal society. They define the trend toward gender equality as a problem to the extent that it weakens the family. In this view, conservatives agree with Talcott Parsons, whose structural-functional analysis described gender as a pair of complementary roles that encourage men and women to depend on each other and form strong families. Since the 1960s, as women have entered college and the labor force in record numbers, divorces and people living alone have become more common (see Chapter 13, "Family Life").

A second important issue for conservatives involves child care. Now that most mothers have joined fathers in the workplace, who's minding the kids? Evidence suggests that today's children are getting less—some say much too little—attention from adults (Popenoe, 1993; Blankenhorn, 1995; Shapiro & Schrof, 1995). In an age of two-career couples, home life often involves weary men and women with little time and energy for their children. No one doubts that most parents do their best to raise their daughters and sons, but conservatives point out that popular ideas such as a little "quality time" with the kids amount to excuses for fathers and mothers who do too little parenting (Dizard & Gadlin, 1990).

Although most conservatives are willing to support women in the workplace and even in positions of national leadership, most also support policies to strengthen families. One conservative proposal to end the "marriage penalty"—referring to the fact that many people pay less tax if they file their tax returns as individuals rather than as a married couple—was part of President Bush's tax cuts in 2003. Conservatives continue to support policies that will raise the importance of families in our national life and encourage women and men to make their partners and children their highest priority. In sum, conservatives argue that, especially for parents, people's choices about how to live should recognize the importance of families for our way of life.

Liberals: The Pursuit of Equality

Liberals point out that, at the time of the Declaration of Independence, the U.S. political system did not even define women (or African Americans and many other minorities) as full human beings. Liberals applaud the slow but steady progress this country has made to expand the rights and opportunities available to women.

However, liberals claim, there is still much work to do. As this chapter has shown, in the United States women still fill most of the country's low-income jobs. Furthermore, more than eighty years after gaining the right to vote, only a token number of women sit in the highest political circles (accounting for just 14 percent of House members and 13 percent of Senators). In short, liberals conclude, patriarchy is alive and well in the United States, and gender inequality is a serious social problem.

Liberals take exception to the conservative claim that the trend toward gender equality has weakened families. First, as liberals see it, conservatives have a nostalgic—and distorted—view of some "golden age" of family life built around visions of family life in the 1950s. Although television shows such as *Leave It to Beaver* celebrated the stay-at-home moms of that era, should we conclude that most women wanted to live that way? Furthermore, liberals believe that families have changed in recent decades largely because most families *need* two working adults to make ends meet (Stacey, 1990).

A liberal profamily agenda seeks government support for the kinds of families that actually exist today. One pressing need is affordable child care. Liberals support the expansion of child-care programs by both employers and government so that women can have the same opportunities as men to pursue their careers.

Conservatives argue that strong families and effective parenting depend on at least one parent spending much of the day in the home with young children. Liberals counter that most women want the chance to pursue careers just as men do. In your opinion, how should men and women balance the responsibilities of work and parenting?

Second, liberals believe that men must take greater responsibility for the home and for children. Liberals counter conservative claims that working women neglect their children by asserting that working men should do more parenting and perform their fair share of housework.

Third, liberals place a high priority on policies that will raise the earning power of women. Enforcing laws to eliminate workplace discrimination against women is part of the solution. In addition, liberals support affirmative action (see Chapter 3, "Racial and Ethnic Inequality") as an effective strategy to increase the presence of women in workplace settings (such as executive positions) that historically have excluded them. Moreover, the U.S. economy has long provided lower pay for some jobs simply because they are performed mostly by women. For example, laundry workers who wash clothes (typically women) are paid less than the laundry truck drivers (mostly men) who transport the laundry, showing how our culture values "women's work" less than "men's work." To counter this form of institutionalized discrimination, some liberals support a policy of *comparable worth*, by which women and men would receive the same pay not just for doing the

LEFT ⓣⓞ RIGHT

THE POLITICS OF GENDER INEQUALITY

	RADICAL LEFT VIEW	LIBERAL VIEW	CONSERVATIVE VIEW
WHAT IS THE PROBLEM?	Serious gender inequality is built into not only the institutions of U.S. society but also the biological task of childbearing.	Although U.S. society has made strides toward greater equality for women and men, women still have lower social standing.	The trend toward gender equality has boosted incomes but has weakened families and reduced the importance of parenting in people's eyes.
WHAT IS THE SOLUTION?	There must be fundamental change in economic, political, and family institutions in order to eliminate gender inequality. Some suggest that reproduction, too, must change to liberate women from childbearing.	Government programs (including passing the ERA) can combat prejudice and discrimination; affirmative action will open more doors to women; a comparable worth policy would reduce income differences between women and men.	Cultural values should encourage people to strengthen their commitment to marriage partners and children.

Join the debate . . .

1. Can you identify areas on which the three political perspectives agree? What are they?

2. Do you think that, a century from now, gender inequality will be greater, about the same, or less than it is now? Why?

3. Which of the three political analyses of gender inequality included here do you find most convincing? Why?

same work but for doing different work that has the same value. In other words, supporters of a comparable worth policy claim that it is possible to measure the worth of different jobs in objective terms, and they note that women currently earn about 25 percent less than men for work of equal value. Although courts have debated this policy, the United States—unlike Great Britain and Australia—has no comparable worth laws (Parcel, Mueller, & Cuvelier, 1986; Blum, 1991; England, 1992; Bellas, 1994; Huffman et al., 1996; England, Hermsen, & Cotter, 2000).

Liberals claim that all these efforts at increasing gender equality have the support of a majority of U.S. adults. Indeed, survey data show that most U.S. adults are committed, in principle, to equal rights for women and men (NORC, 2003:254).

Radicals: Change the System

Most people who support feminism identify with its liberal form; that is, they seek greater gender equality within the bounds of current social institutions. But, as we have already noted, others believe that more basic change is needed before U.S. society will ever approach gender equality.

For some, the target of basic change is the family. For example, Judith Stacey (1990:269–70) states, "'The family' is *not* 'here to stay.' Nor should we wish it were. On the contrary, I believe that all democratic people, whatever their kinship preferences, should work to hasten its demise." The reason, Stacey explains, is that families perpetuate traditional forms of inequality based on class, race, and gender.

How should families change? What are the alternatives? Most radicals argue that, at a minimum, basic change must come to the economic and political systems. The socialist feminist solution to gender inequality, described earlier, begins with change from a capitalist economy towards a socialist system. This transformation would allow people to perform economic and domestic work collectively to the benefit of everyone. The end result would be movement away from class inequality as well as the patriarchy that has subordinated women throughout history.

Radical feminism offers an ever more far-reaching vision of the elimination of gender itself. From this point of view, complete equality between women and men depends on liberating women from their historical task of childbearing and nurture. As we have explained, new reproductive technology makes such a vision at least possible.

The Left to Right table summarizes this discussion of gender inequality.

GOING ON FROM HERE

Imagine people living in the United States back in 1850—when the feminist movement began—arriving in our society today. No doubt many would be startled to learn that most women work for pay, that women vote and hold elected office, and that women outnumber men on college campuses.

Just as important, in the United States today, very few women die in childbirth. On the contrary, women are far healthier and live much longer than ever before (and longer than men). Visitors from a past era, when electricity was unknown, would expect most women to spend all day doing housework. Moreover, they would recall an average woman having about five children. Today, housework is far easier, and mothers average just two children.

In light of such great changes, perhaps our visitors from the past would be surprised to find that the social standing of women is still controversial. One reason is that people's expectations have changed. Almost no one today accepts the centuries-old belief that women belong in the home. Yet, as we have seen, women are still unequal to men.

Where are we likely to be 150 years from now? Will the controversies surrounding gender inequality continue? This seems all but certain. Women still earn less than men, partly because many people still assume men and women will do different work and partly because many people think women's lives should focus on their family responsibilities. Given such widespread beliefs, it seems unlikely that women will do the same work as men, earn as much as men, and share domestic work equally with men anytime soon. Keep in mind that gender equality has not been realized in a single one of the world's 191 countries.

At the same time, the worldwide trend is unmistakable: Women are moving closer to equality with men, and all indications are that the trend will continue. However, ensuring that women become full participants in society will require continuous effort as we move through the new century.

CHAPTER SUMMARY

1. Sex is the biological distinction between females and males. Gender refers to the personal traits and life chances that a society associates with each sex, creating the cultural concepts of "feminine" and "masculine."

2. Gender is an important dimension of social stratification. All societies display some degree of patriarchy, they differ in the degree of gender stratification.

3. Sexism is the assertion that one sex is less worthy than or even innately inferior to the other.

4. Gender affects the operation of all social institutions, including the family, schools, the mass media, religion, politics, the military, and the workplace. In each case, gender operates to provide privileges to men and to subordinate women.

5. Gender stratification, found in the United States and elsewhere, is the unequal distribution of wealth, power, and privilege between men and women.

6. Women working full time earn 76 percent as much as men do. The biggest reason for this disparity is that many women have low-paying clerical or service jobs.

7. Despite entering the labor force in record numbers, women continue to do most of the housework.

8. Violence against women is a serious national problem in the United States and throughout the world. U.S. government agencies receive about 2 million reports of nonsexual assaults and 400,000 sexual assaults against women each year.

9. Sexuality, beauty, and reproduction are also important issues. Women's ability to control reproduction has consequences for their freedom to work outside the home.

10. Because women have a subordinate position in relation to men, they should be considered a minority group. Intersection theory points out that women who are also racial or ethnic minorities contend with multiple disadvantages.

11. The structural-functional approach views gender in terms of complementary roles that link men and women, building families and integrating society as a whole.

12. Symbolic-interaction analysis highlights how gender influences people's actions and use of space in everyday situations. Language also reflects the social dominance of males.

13. Social-conflict theory sees gender as a dimension of social inequality, with men having greater wealth, power, and privileges than women. Friedrich Engels linked gender stratification to men's desire to pass on property to their offspring.

14. Feminism is an important social-conflict approach in sociology. Liberal feminism seeks reform within existing institutional arrangements. Socialist feminism links gender equality to broader class revolution, following Marxist principles. Radical feminism calls for the elimination of gender itself, partly through the use of new reproductive technologies to liberate women from childbearing.

15. Conservatives place great importance on the traditional family. From this political perspective, the trend toward gender equality has weakened families and reduced the importance of parenting.

16. Liberals look to government to raise the social standing of women by opposing gender discrimination and increasing women's economic opportunities.

17. Radicals claim that gender stratification is deeply rooted in present social institutions. According to the radical view, reaching the goal of gender equality requires basic change in the economy, political system, and family life.

KEY CONCEPTS

gender   (p. 86) the personal traits and life chances a society links to being female or male

sex   (p. 86) the biological distinction between females and males

patriarchy   (p. 86) a social pattern in which males dominate females

matriarchy   (p. 86) a social pattern in which females dominate males

sexism   (p. 88) the assertion that one sex is less worthy than or even innately inferior to the other

gender stratification   (p. 93) the unequal distribution of wealth, power, and privilege between men and women

glass ceiling   (p. 94) subtle discrimination that effectively blocks the movement of women into the highest positions in organizations

sexual harassment   (p. 96) unwanted comments, gestures, or physical contact of a sexual nature

feminism   (p. 101) the study of gender with the goal of changing society to make women and men equal

THINKING CRITICALLY: QUESTIONS AND ISSUES

1. What do racism and sexism have in common? How do they differ?

2. Do you think women of all colors and cultures should be considered a minority? Why or why not?

3. Explain how gender shapes the operation of major social institutions, including family, religion, politics, the mass media, the military, and the economy.

4. Do you think men's lives have changed as much as women's over the last century? Give specific reasons for your answer.

GETTING INVOLVED: LEARNING ACTIVITIES

1. A walk around your campus with an eye toward gender can be revealing. Identify spaces (buildings, rooms, activities) that are dominated by men or women. Which are the men's and women's spaces? Which sex controls more space?

2. Visit a magazine rack in your local bookstore or supermarket. Example popular magazines aimed at women. What images are on the covers? What topics—stories, features, and photographs—do magazines consider "women's issues"?

3. Most communities (and many campuses) have organizations that deal with violence against women. Identify such an organization and arrange a site visit. What are its goals and strategies to achieve them?

4. Does popular music contain bias against women? Listen to at least two kinds of music (rap, rock, country, and so on) and see what messages about the life goals and relative power of males and females you can find.

GETTING CONNECTED: USEFUL WEB SITES

http://www.prenhall.com/macionis
Visit the interactive Companion Website™ that accompanies this text. Begin by clicking on the cover of your book. You will find a chapter-by-chapter study guide, practice tests, suggested Web links, and links to other relevant material.

http://www.now.org
Visit the Web site for the National Organization of Women (NOW). Which issues does this organization consider important? What are NOW's strategies for change?

http://www.iwpr.org
Another informative site is run by the Institute for Women's Policy Research. What issues does this organization find most important? Would you characterize this site as feminist? Why or why not?

http://www.frc.org
The Family Research Council supports what they describe as "family values." Visit this site to determine what those values are. Specifically, what goals does this organization have for women's and men's lives?

http://www.ojp.usdoj.gov/bjs/pub/press/svcw.pr
Here is a 2001 Justice Department report on the extent of sexual violence against women on the campus.

http://www.feminist.org
Learn more about feminism from the Feminist Majority Foundation Online.

GETTING STARTED ON YOUR OWN: RESEARCH NAVIGATOR™

 Follow the instructions found on page 25 of this text to access the features of Research Navigator™. Once at the Web site, enter your Login Name and Password. Then, to use the **Content Select** database, enter keywords such as "gender," "sexual harassment," and "feminism," and the search engine will supply relevant and recent scholarly and popular press publications. Use the *New York Times* **Search-by-Subject Archive** to find recent news articles related to sociology and the **Link Library** feature to find relevant Web links organized by the key terms associated with this chapter.

© Paul Marcus, *The Mourning After, oil on panel, 30 in. × 24 in. Studio SPM, Inc.*

AGING AND INEQUALITY

"*I THOUGHT THIS WAS THE BEGINNING OF THE 'golden years,'*" *says sixty-five-year-old Margaret Parry to her long-time friend Sarah Williams as the two sit and stir their coffee, catching up with each other on a rainy morning. "I just got the statements on my 401k retirement accounts," Perry continues. "It's now more like a 201k," she jokes, trying hard to grin. "In the last three years, my savings has fallen to half what it was!"*

Back in 2000, Margaret Parry sold her small company and had about $1 million to carry her into retirement. She looked forward to travel, playing golf, and an active social life. But the economic downturn has slashed the value of her investments so that, even counting her Social Security check, she now has to get by on about $25,000 a year.

She looks down at the table and sums up her plight. "I had it made. I was so sure. Now everything is on hold. I have to start looking for a part-time job." After a pause, she adds, "Maybe it'll end up being a full-time job."[1]

[1]Based on Kadlec (2002).

Over the course of the twentieth century, the share of older people in the labor force steadily declined as many people happily moved into retirement. In recent years, however, the trend has changed as millions of people who had retired have seen their incomes fall, forcing them back to work. Millions more who hoped to retire are staying on the job, wondering whether they will have a chance to enjoy their own "golden years."

The story of Margaret Parry highlights one challenge for people entering old age. As this chapter explains, the final decades of life raise the risks of poverty, illness, and disability. Then, sooner or later, older people need to face up to their lives coming to an end.

GROWING OLD

Old age is the final stage in the **life course,** *socially constructed stages that people pass through as they live out their lives.* In our culture, we commonly recognize many stages of the life course, including childhood, adolescence, adulthood, and old age. The last of these stages is the focus of **gerontology,** *a branch of the social sciences dealing with aging and the elderly* (Holmes & Holmes, 1995; Elash, 1997; Kosterlitz, 1997; Wise, 1997; Costa, 1998).

Visit the National Institute on Aging's Web site at
http://www.nih.gov/nia

People refer to the gradual physical, mental, and social changes that occur during the first half of the life course as "growing up." After midlife, however, aging is perceived in more negative terms, as if people start "growing *down*." Physical strength declines, hair turns gray or falls out, and the skin becomes wrinkled. Among older men and women, injuries come more easily and take longer to heal, the body loses some resistance to disease, and the senses (including sight, taste, hearing, and smell) are less sharp. Compared with thirty-year-olds, people at age seventy-five have a metabolism that has slowed by one-sixth; their heart and kidney functions are reduced by one-third; and their breathing capacity has fallen by half (Leaf, 1973; Holmes & Holmes, 1995).

The elderly suffer more from chronic (long-term) illnesses such as arthritis that, though not life threatening, cause pain and make movement difficult. The odds of contracting a deadly disease (such as cancer, stroke, or heart disease) keep going up with advancing age. Also, older people can fall seriously ill with an infection such as the flu that a younger person would shake off in a day or two (Holmes & Holmes, 1995; Posner, 1995; Treas, 1995).

People with high income usually have better health because they can spend more for safe housing, good nutrition, and high-quality health care. Well-being also reflects lifestyle and personal choices: Factors such as good diet, regular exercise, not smoking, and moderation in alcohol intake all contribute to good health at any age (Manheimer, 1994; Medina, 1996).

Industrialization and Aging

Growing old involves more than the biological changes just described. How a culture defines this stage of life makes a great deal of difference in the experience of old age.

Preindustrial Societies: Elders as Social Elite   In traditional, rural societies where many people engage in farming, ways of life change slowly. In a slowly changing society, the knowledge gained by the oldest members of society remains valuable, so younger people look up to elders as wise and deserving of respect. In addition, the oldest people (typically the oldest men) own most of the land, which gives them not only wisdom but also real power. Therefore, preindustrial societies take the form of a **gerontocracy,** *a social system that gives a society's oldest members the most wealth, power, and prestige.*

In farming societies, seniors typically remain active working and leading the family until they are physically unable to continue, at which point they can expect to be well cared for by their children for the rest of their lives. Even after death, they will remain objects of respect and devotion through the religious pattern of ancestor worship.

Industrial Societies: Elderly as Social Problem   The Industrial Revolution did much to raise living standards, but it reduced the social power and prestige of older people. This is because industrial technology greatly increases the pace of cultural change, which leads people to dismiss the knowledge and skill of seniors as unimportant to the lives of the young. Indeed, the word "elder," used in preindustrial societies as a term of respect, has given way to the term "elderly," which has a more negative meaning. It is not far off the mark to say that in modern, industrial societies, many younger people tend to regard older people as something of a social problem.

In the nineteenth century, industrialization in the United States drew workers from rural farming to jobs in urban factories, so that young people had less reason to look to their elders for guidance. In fact, as many headed off for the growing cities, they left their aging parents behind. It was at this time that a rising proportion of the elderly began to fall into poverty. Some ended up in poorhouses, where they passed their final days in wretched, rat-infested structures in the company of criminals and people suffering from mental and physical illnesses (Powell et al., 1996).

Fortunately, in the twentieth century the plight of the elderly in the United States began to improve. The poorhouses closed their doors, in part because of a social movement demanding better treatment for older people. A milestone was reached in 1935 when

A Global Perspective

Will the Golden Years Lose Their Glow? Growing Old in Japan

SIXTY-TWO-YEAR-OLD TAIZO KOMURASAKI GREW up during the turbulence of World War II, went to college, and found a job with a trading company, where he spent his whole career. At age sixty, he retired with a pension and looked forward to another fifteen or twenty years of security.

But his golden years have already lost some of their glow. For one thing, his pension equals only $1,625 per month ($19,500 per year) in a country where the cost of living is one of the highest in the world. Moreover, pension programs by corporations and government are straining under the twin burden of an economic recession and an elderly population increasing faster than in any country in the world. In 2000, almost 20 percent of Japanese people were over age sixty-five (compared with 13 percent in the United States); in 2025, when about 17 percent of the U.S. population will have reached age sixty-five, Japan's share will approach 30 percent. At the same time, the Japanese birth rate is among the world's lowest, so Japan's total population will actually decline in decades to come. The predictable outcome? The demand for pension funds will go up as the number of workers paying into these systems will go down.

A Japanese tradition requires children (especially daughters) to care for aging parents. But most of today's Japanese couples live in small apartments with little space for another person. As more women join the labor force, there is less time to devote to elder care.

One sign of changing times is that the Japanese are now building facilities that were long unknown in that nation: nursing homes. As elders live longer, as pensions run low, and as families find they have less to offer to aging parents, the cultural taboo against placing them in nursing homes is breaking down.

ISSUES AND EXERCISES

1. In both Japan and the United States, the number of retired seniors is outpacing the number of younger workers. What do you think should be done to head off a crisis?

2. What responsibilities should families have for their elder members?

3. [Research Navigator.com] Use Research Navigator™ to learn more about the debate over supporting older people in Japan. (See instructions on page 25; keyword: "elderly in Japan")

Source: Based on Strom (2000).

---

the federal government passed the Social Security Act, which provides a monthly pension to everyone over sixty-five. In addition to providing needed income, this program makes the statement that older people are worthy of support (Wallace & Williamson, 1992; Watkins, 1993; Powell et al., 1996).

Older people may be better off economically, but many still find they are devalued by today's "youth culture." The fashions and attitudes that dominate the mass media feature young people, making the lives of older people seem hopelessly old-fashioned. Also, because U.S. culture values self-reliance, many elders try hard to stay independent; the result is that many do not get the help they need (Holmes & Holmes, 1995; Kosterlitz, 1997; Wise, 1997).

Read a global report on aging at
http://www.census.gov/prod/2001pubs/p95-01-1.pdf

Not all industrial societies are so hard on their oldest members. Japan stands out as a country that retains much of its centuries-old respect for old people (Kiefer, 1990; Powell, Branco, & Williamson, 1996). But even in Japan, older people face challenges, as the Global Perspective box explains.

Life Expectancy

Life expectancy is *the number of years, on average, people in a society can expect to live.* In the earliest hunting and gathering societies, most people died in childhood; someone who lived to thirty was considered to have reached a "ripe old age." In the poorest nations today (most of which are found in central and southern Africa), life expectancy is about forty years.

Life expectancy is much greater in high-income nations, which have better nutrition and sanitation. Today, males born in the United States can expect to live 74 years, and females can expect to live 80 years (U.S. National Center for Health Statistics, 2003).

What's more, life expectancy is increasing, which means that these societies must plan to meet the needs of an increasing number of older people. This is especially true for the United States, as we now explain.

THE GRAYING OF THE UNITED STATES

When the United States won its independence in 1776, half the new country's population was under age sixteen, and it was the rare for someone to live to age sixty. Thus, despite the familiar image of gray-haired "founding fathers," the great leaders of that time were surprisingly young by today's standards.

George Washington (about to become our nation's first president) was in his early forties, and Thomas Jefferson (who wrote the Declaration of Independence) had just passed his thirtieth birthday.

Find a statistical profile of the U.S. elderly at
http://www.agingstats.gov

By 1900, as the Industrial Revolution was re-shaping this country, the 3 million seniors past age sixty-five made up just 4 percent of the population. But, as shown in Figure 5–1, that share doubled by 1950 and will double again by 2020, with an elderly population of about 55 million (Kausler & Kausler, 1996; U.S. Census Bureau, 2003). While the elderly population increases rapidly, the number of young people is staying about the same. This trend is called "the graying of the United States." National Map 5–1 shows that the share of the U.S. population over age sixty-five is projected to reach 20 percent by about 2030.

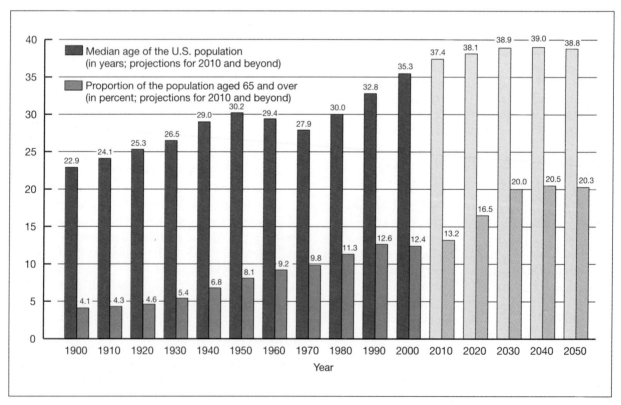

FIGURE 5–1   The Graying of U.S. Society

The Census Bureau projects that people aged sixty-five and older will reach 20 percent of the U.S. population by 2030. At that point, almost half the U.S. population will be over the age of forty.

Source: U.S. Census Bureau (2003).

A NATION OF DIVERSITY

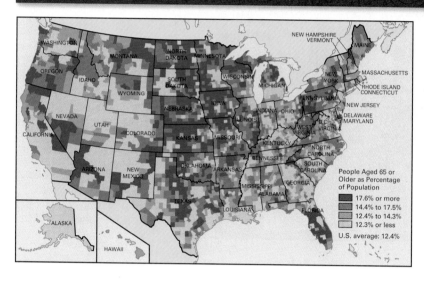

NATIONAL MAP 5–1
The Elderly Population across the United States

Many people think that most elderly people like to live in warm retirement areas, such as southern Florida and the Southwest. There is some truth to this belief, but most of the counties with high proportions of older people are actually in the Plains states. To see why, consider this: Which regions of the country are younger people likely to leave to attend college and find a job?
Source: U.S. Census Bureau (2001).

People Aged 65 or Older as Percentage of Population
- 17.6% or more
- 14.4% to 17.5%
- 12.4% to 14.3%
- 12.3% or less

U.S. average: 12.4%

Elders: A Diverse Population

Sociologists conduct research to help us understand the size, needs, and problems of the elderly population of the United States. The evidence shows that elders are quite diverse socially.

Three Levels of "Old"   One way in which older people differ from one another is age itself. Researchers divide the elderly into three categories. Most people sixty-five to seventy-four years of age—the "younger old"—enjoy good health and live independently. People aged seventy-five to eighty-four, who are more likely to need support services, are called the "older old." Finally, researchers call elders eighty-five and older, who need the most help, the "oldest old" (Neugarten, 1982; Riley & Suzman, 1985; Schick & Schick, 1994). Of the three categories, the oldest old are increasing most rapidly in number. From a mere 0.1 percent in 1900, they made up 2 percent of the U.S. population in 2000, a twenty-fold increase over the last century.

Class, Race, Ethnicity, and Gender   Social inequality shapes the lives of people of all ages. Older men and women who are well-off financially, especially the "young old," have many choices about where and how they want to live. For many who no longer need to work, traveling provides both adventure and learning. Their *wanderlust* is summed up by a popular bumper sticker, seen on many recreational vehicles, that says, "We're spending our children's inheritance." Other well-off "young old"

people retire to Florida, Arizona, or other Sunbelt states to enjoy the mild weather and low cost of living. But just one in twenty older people ends up making such a move. Why? Many (especially those with health problems) want to stay close to family members. For most, however, the reason is money: They simply cannot afford it (Manheimer, 1994; Schick & Schick, 1994; Kausler & Kausler, 1996; Neugarten, 1996).

The elderly are also racially and ethnically diverse, but less so than the younger population. The reason is that much racial and ethnic diversity in the United States results from immigration, and immigrants, on average, are young. Thus, whereas 40 percent of children under five years of age are minorities (including African, Asian, Hispanic, and Native Americans), this is true of just 17 percent of those over age sixty-five (U.S. Census Bureau, 2002).

A final dimension of diversity among the elderly involves gender. Women, on average, live longer than men. Therefore, although women are a slight majority of the total population (51 percent), they represent 58 percent of all people over the age of sixty-five. Among this country's 60,000 centenarians—people aged 100 years or older—83 percent are women (U.S. Census Bureau, 2003).

PROBLEMS OF AGING

People confront change at every stage of life. But most people find that the changes of old age present the greatest challenges. Although the physical health of

Elderly people in the United States point to loneliness as their most serious social problem. What factors increase the social isolation of older people?

the elderly is, on the whole, better than stereotypes of "frail old people" suggest, many older women and men live with pain from various ailments. Just as important, they must learn to accept depending on others. And as loved ones die, older people face loneliness and the knowledge that the end of their own lives is drawing near. We now take a closer look at problems common to society's oldest members.

Social Isolation

At any age, being alone can cause anxiety and depression. But isolation is most common among older people. Retirement from work closes off an important source of contact with others. As people age, declining health limits their ability to get around, and negative stereotypes of the elderly as sickly, old-fashioned, or "out of touch" may keep younger people away.

Few human experiences are as painful and isolating as the death of a close friend and, especially, a spouse. One study of older men and women who had lost their spouse found that three-fourths cited loneliness as their most serious problem. Undoubtedly this is why older people are likely to die—sometimes by suicide—in the months following the death of a spouse (Benjamin & Wallis, 1963; Lund, 1989).

Social isolation is a problem more common among elderly women than men. Among people over sixty-five, 74 percent of men live with a wife; by contrast, just 42 percent of women live with a husband. From another angle, 16 percent of elderly men live alone, compared with 40 percent of older women (U.S. Census Bureau, 2002). In part, these differences

reflect the fact that women typically outlive men. But they also reflect the fact that widowers are more likely to remarry than widows are. Men's chances of finding another spouse are higher than women's because U.S. culture supports the pairing of older men and younger women while frowning on the pairing of older women with younger men.

Many elderly people look to community services such as senior citizen centers and "meals on wheels" programs as a source of social contact. Still, for most seniors, families are the primary support systems. Most elderly people have at least one adult child who lives within ten miles. About half of adult children who live nearby visit their parents at least once a week, although research confirms that daughters are more likely than sons to visit regularly (Stone, Cafferata, & Sangl, 1987; Lin & Rogerson, 1994; Rimer, 1998).

Retirement

As industrialization made societies more productive, not everyone had to work. In time, child labor became defined as wrong, and young people spent more of their lives in school. Similarly, it became common for old people to retire from the labor force so they could spend their remaining years doing as they wished.

Most working people start to think about withdrawing from paid work by the age of sixty-five. Over the last fifty years, the median age for retirement fell from sixty-eight (in 1950) to sixty-two (in 2000). Yet as the opening to this chapter explained, this trend reversed in the last few years because of the recent recession. A loss of savings has forced many people to delay retirement. Some now find it more financially sound to give up work in steps, a process called *staged retirement*. And some retirees, who have not worked in years, are now being pushed back into the labor force for economic reasons (Gendell, 2002; Kadlec, 2002).

Sociologists suggest that people need to prepare themselves for the challenge of retirement. One way to begin is to ask yourself what you think you will miss about no longer going to work and then consider whether new activities can provide some of the same pleasures. Of course, people differ in their visions of a satisfying retirement. Although some may look eagerly for new activities, others are satisfied with spending much more time with children and grandchildren, and just as many others are content simply to sit back and relax. Of course, what people can and cannot do in retirement also depends on health and finances (Neugarten, 1996; Gall, Evans, & Howard, 1997).

Some employers can ease the transition to retirement by allowing those who retire to keep some of their activities and privileges. For example, colleges and universities give retiring faculty members the title "emeritus professor" so that they keep their faculty standing and perhaps even their parking space. Many retired professors stay involved in their disciplines by continuing to write and by attending professional meetings. But in an era of corporate downsizing, companies may push older (and often higher-paid) workers to retire; such unplanned retirement usually offers the greatest challenges.

What is the government's retirement policy? Back in the 1930s, the U.S. government set the retirement age at sixty-five, which was about how long people lived at that time. But today, on average, people live fifteen years longer. Because of the increase in life span, in 1987 Congress passed legislation that required employers to phase out mandatory retirement policies by 1994. (Bosworth & Burtless, 1998; Wyatt, 2000).

Ageism

Whether they are still working or happily retired, older people may find that others look down on them simply because of their age. **Ageism** is *prejudice and discrimination directed against the elderly* (Butler, 1975, 1994; Cohen, 2001). Like racism and sexism, ageism defines physical traits—in this case, graying hair, wrinkled skin, and a stooped posture—as signs of being less of a person. Certainly, ageism helps explain the

A rising number of older women and men are in the paid labor force, a trend that increased during the recent economic downturn. How does ageism affect the types of jobs older people hold?

tendency of many older people to exercise hard, take medications (such as Viagra), and even undergo cosmetic surgery in order to lessen the effects of aging on their appearance and behavior.

Because people judge women more than men by their physical appearance, ageism often harms women more. But whenever people portray elders of either sex as if they were all senile, narrow-minded, or old-fashioned, they devalue them as human beings.

Age-Based Prejudice Ageism involves prejudice: negative prejudgments about the elderly. Such prejudice can be blatant, as when college officials pass over a job application from an older person because they prefer hiring a younger person. Prejudice can also be subtle, as when a doctor assumes that an ailment is caused simply by a patient's age, as described in the Critical Thinking box on page 118.

Prejudice directed towards the elderly may take the form of stereotypes depicting older people as "sick, senile, useless, sexually impotent, ugly, isolated, poor, or miserable" (Palmore, 1998:30–31). Such stereotypes are wrong because most elderly people are none of these things: Eighty percent of people age sixty-five and older live healthy and independent lives, and just 5 percent have health problems that force them to be institutionalized. Most seniors work

Critical Thinking   Is Aging a Disease?

A seventy-five-year-old man who loved to square dance suddenly had a sharp pain in his left knee. He went to his doctor to find out what the trouble was. The doctor noted his age, gave his knee a fairly superficial examination, and said, "I can't find anything obviously wrong with your knee. It must be due to your age." The man asked the doctor to explain. The doctor launched into a discussion of various theories of aging and how they might explain his knee problem, and concluded, "Now do you understand?" The old man replied, "No, I don't, because my right knee is just as old as my left knee, and it's not giving me a bit of trouble!"

MEDICAL SOCIOLOGIST ERDMAN PALMORE (1998:29) TELLS THIS story to make a point about subtle forms of ageism. Had this patient been twenty-five years old, Palmore explains, the doctor would never have treated him this way. The doctor probably would have ordered an X-ray or some other procedure immediately to find out what was causing the pain. But with elderly patients, doctors sometimes engage in a subtle form of ageism by acting as if aging itself were the disease. This response is based more on stereotypes than sound scientific evidence and therefore is bad medical practice.

ISSUES AND EXERCISES

1. People do suffer more illnesses as they age, so what's wrong with treating aging as a disease?

2. Can you point out other subtle forms of ageism? What about age-related stereotypes?

3. ![Research Navigator.com] Use Research Navigator™ to learn more about ageism. (See instructions on page 25; keywords: "age discrimination," "ageism")

Sources: Based on Butler (1994) and Palmore (1998).

---

as effectively as younger workers, and employers rate older workers as more trustworthy and loyal. Just as important, most elderly men and women can and do have satisfying sexual relationships (U.S. National Center for Health Statistics, 2002).

Age-Based Discrimination   Prejudiced thinking often leads to unfair treatment (Palmore, 1998). For this reason, Congress passed the Age Discrimination in Employment Act in 1967, banning employers from discriminating against people because of their age. Because the work force in the United States is aging—more than 56 million workers (40 percent of the total) will be age forty-five or older in 2005—the number of complaints of age-based discrimination is rising, a trend that is likely to continue in years to come. Data show that the typical complaint of age discrimination now comes from workers in their forties, not their sixties (Kelley-Moore, 2002).

Age discrimination may be illegal, but this law is difficult to enforce because many older people turned down for a job never know exactly why. In addition, companies can legally lay off higher-salary workers, even though this usually hurts older people the most (McNaught, 1994; Kosterlitz, 1997; Palmore, 1998; Labaton, 2000).

Elderly Minorities: Greater Disadvantage   Sooner or later, ageism affects everyone—or at least those lucky enough to grow old. Ageism also combines with racism, sexism, and other forms of prejudice and discrimination. The result is that minorities, including women and people of color, who reach old age face greater disadvantage.

Think about the older women and men you have seen on television and in films. When older people appear on screen, it is almost always in stereotypical roles. In the Oscar-winning film *Driving Miss Daisy*, for example, Jessica Tandy played an old, lonely woman unable to cope with change. By contrast, older men are seen on screen much more often—think of the many roles played by Harrison Ford, Sean Connery, and Clint Eastwood—and they usually appear (both on- and off-screen) in leading roles opposite women half their age. Twenty-nine-year-old actress Mary McCormack recalled her excitement playing opposite Clint Eastwood:

I only shot one scene with Clint, but I got to make out with him. He's sixty-eight and completely sexy. It's a man's world, because when I'm sixty-eight, there's not going to be a twenty-nine-year-old actor saying, "And then I got to make out with Mary McCormack." (*Vanity Fair*, 1998, p. 63)

Much the same can be said for people of color. African Americans are visible on television and in movies featuring young people, but are far less likely to be cast in roles that portray characters over the age of sixty-five.

Victimization of the Elderly

In the 1980s, U.S. society began to define *elder abuse* as a social problem. Elder abuse ranges from passive neglect to active verbal, emotional, and physical mistreatment. Experts estimate that about 1 million elderly people (about 3 percent) suffer serious abuse each year, with three times as many (about 10 percent) experiencing less severe mistreatment. Of cases reported to Adult Protective Services (APS), the government agency responsible for this problem, half involve neglect of elderly people who cannot care for themselves. The remainder involve active physical abuse, psychological abuse, or wrongfully taking an older person's money or other property. Only in rare cases are the elderly subject to sexual abuse (Bordreau, 1993; Tatara, 1993; Barnett, Miller-Perrin, & Perrin, 1997; Thompson, 1997, 1998).

Like other forms of family violence (discussed in Chapter 13, "Family Life"), elder abuse often is undetected because victims are afraid to speak out. Many worry that if they report bad treatment, their abusers will become more violent or will try to have them institutionalized. Thus, APS estimates that only 10 percent of all actual abuse cases are reported (Pillemer, 1988; Tatara, 1993; Holmstrom, 1994; Barnett et al, 1997).

Causes of Elder Abuse What would cause someone to neglect or abuse an older person? People who abuse family members often have problems of their own: They may be poor, be addicted to alcohol or other drugs, or have problems holding a job. But any middle-aged person caught between the demands of working, caring for young children, and looking after an aging parent may feel out of control and slip into abusive behavior (Hinrichsen, Hernandez, & Pollack, 1992; Barnett et al., 1997).

Another important research finding is that many abusers were themselves abused as children. Because they learned to respond to problems with violence in

Perhaps 1 million elders in the United States are victims of serious abuse every year. Countless others suffer from neglect and from treatment that robs them of their dignity. What are some of the causes of this problem? What do you think should be done about it?

the past, abusers carry this pattern into the care of aged parents (Anetzberger, 1987; Stone et al., 1987; Fulmer & O'Malley, 1987; Kosberg, 1988; Godkin, Wolf, & Pillemer, 1989; Greenberg, McKibben, & Raymond, 1990; Bendick, 1992; Barnett et al., 1997).

Read a report on nursing home abuse at
http://www.heaton.org/nursinghomeabuse.pdf

Abuse also occurs in institutional settings such as nursing homes. Sometimes this problem results from efforts to cut costs. For example, nursing home owners may try to operate their businesses with fewer workers or replace nurses with less-trained aides, resulting in shoddy care or neglect (Manheimer, 1994). Like family members, staff members who face constant patient demands and complaints may reach a point of frustration that triggers abuse. The Social Policy box on page 120 describes a recent government investigation of nursing home abuse.

Social Policy   Nursing Home Abuse: What Should Be Done?

FEW PEOPLE WOULD DISAGREE WITH THE IDEA that a society should treat its oldest members with kindness. Yet in a recent investigation of nursing homes, the U.S. House of Representatives concluded that one-third of homes nationwide had been cited for violations of proper care standards; in one-third of these cases (that is, about 10 percent of all nursing homes), the violations were serious enough to endanger the lives of residents.

Many—and perhaps even most—nursing homes provide good care to their residents. But a substantial share are not doing their job well enough. One witness before a congressional investigating committee was Leslie Olivia, who had been caring for her aging mother at home. When her mother began to suffer from a degenerative brain disease, she needed much more care than Olivia could provide, so Olivia turned to a nursing home for help. Within months of moving in, her mother suffered bruises, bedsores, and a broken pelvis. Sometimes attendants simply left a meal tray at the end of her bed, out of reach; without adequate nutrition, she quickly lost weight. Olivia moved her to another home, but the abuse continued. Again, she suffered from bedsores and severe dehydration. Soon after Olivia moved her a second time, nursing home officials called Olivia to report that her mother had choked to death on her food. Given her disturbing experience at the other homes, Olivia did not believe them, and she backed up her position with evidence that her mother was attached to a feeding tube.

Was this disturbing story an isolated case? Unfortunately, congressional officials heard many similar stories. Even nursing home workers testified that abuse is widespread and often covered up. Although care of residents improves when government inspectors visit a nursing home, they explained, the pattern of abuse resumes soon after they leave.

Other surveys suggest that elder abuse can be found in nursing homes across the United States. It is especially likely to occur in homes that are understaffed and where employees are underpaid and have little training. The bottom line is that tens of thousands of our society's oldest members are suffering needlessly, and many are in danger.

ISSUES AND EXERCISES

1. Why do you think the public is not more outraged at the kind of abuse described here?
2. What changes in the operation of nursing homes might prevent cases like that of Leslie Olivia's mother?
3. [Research Navigator.com logo] Use Research Navigator™ to learn more about elder abuse in nursing homes. (See instructions on page 25; keyword: "nursing home abuse")

Sources: Based on Thompson (1998) and U.S. House of Representatives (2001).

The Growing Need for Caregiving

The share of the U.S. population over age sixty-five is increasing; slightly more than half will never live in a nursing home or care facility. Therefore, more and more seniors have a need for caregiving by other people. **Caregiving** is *informal and unpaid care provided to a dependent person by family members, other relatives, or friends* (Lund, 1993; Spillman, 2002).

In the United States and other high-income nations, today's middle-aged people are a "sandwich generation" who will spend as much time caring for their aging parents as they did raising their young children. In most cases, care for an aging person is provided by one particular family member. Most caregivers are women, typically a wife (if the older person is a married man), a daughter living nearby, or a daughter-in-law (Himes, 2001).

Because caregiving usually is the job of one person, the demands of time and energy can be great. Most caregivers have their own families to think about, and half of them also have jobs. The typical caregiver provides help for about three hours a day, usually on top of what is already a full day's work.

Poverty

About 10 percent of the U.S. population over age sixty-five—about 3.6 million women and men—live below the government's poverty line. The good news is that the elderly poverty rate has dropped from a high of almost 30 percent in 1965 (U.S. Census Bureau, 2003).

Why the positive trend? The main reason is that seniors now receive better retirement benefits, especially Social Security payments with automatic cost-of-living adjustments (COLAs) (Meyer & Bellas, 1995; Morris, 1996). The reduction of poverty among the elderly is a success story that shows how social problems can be improved. But, of course, there is still much to be done.

James Schulz (1997) points out that the current poverty statistics do not include elders who are institutionalized, most of whom are poor. He adds that officials set the poverty line for an older person (in 2002, $8,628 for a single person over sixty-five) below the line for everyone else ($9,359 for a single person below age sixty-five). A more accurate poverty rate, Schultz claims, might be much higher than the official number.

Age Stratification Age stratification is *social inequality among various age categories within a society.* As we have already explained, in preindustrial societies elders have more wealth and power than younger people. In modern industrial societies, the opposite is true.

Figure 5–2 shows the average income and the official poverty rate by age for the U.S. population. Notice that average income rises throughout the life course, peaks at about age fifty, and falls as people enter old age. By contrast, the poverty rate falls as people move through adulthood until about age fifty and then rises with increasing age.

Intersection Theory: Age, Race, Ethnicity, and Gender

Social stratification involves not only age but also other dimensions of social inequality, including race and gender. As intersection theory points out, people with multiple minority standing—such as elderly people who are also African American or women—experience even greater disadvantages. Figure 5–3 on page 122 contrasts the poverty rate for various categories of the elderly population in the United States. The poverty rate among elderly African Americans is

DIMENSIONS OF DIFFERENCE

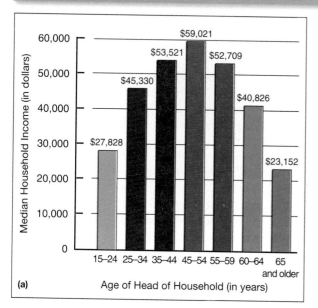
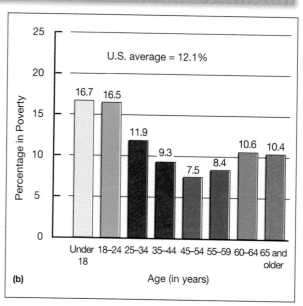

FIGURE 5–2   U.S. Household Income and Poverty Rate, by Age, 2002

In part (a), we see that median household income typically rises over the life course, peaking at around age fifty and falling as people enter old age. Part (b) shows that poverty rates go down as people get older, reaching a low point at about age fifty and rising as people enter old age.

Source: U.S. Census Bureau (2003).

DIMENSIONS OF DIFFERENCE

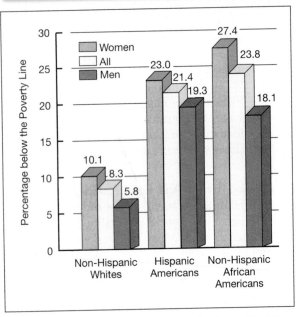

FIGURE 5–3   U.S. Poverty Rates by Race, Ethnicity, and Gender, Age 65 and Older, 2002

Among those over age sixty-five, Hispanic Americans and African Americans are more than twice as likely to be poor as non-Hispanic whites are. In every category, older women are more likely to be poor than older men.
Source: U.S. Census Bureau (2003).

23.6 percent, almost three times as high as the 8.3 percent rate among elderly whites (U.S. Census Bureau, 2003).

As people reach old age, the risk of poverty goes up. But among older people, the highest poverty rates are for minorities, who are more likely to be poor at any point in the life course.

A closer look at the case of elderly women shows the interaction of age and gender stratification. First, gender stratification (which puts the burden of family responsibilities on women) makes it harder for women to join the paid labor force so that, especially after they become mothers, women have less opportunity for paid work. Second, as Chapter 4 ("Gender Inequality") explains, women who do work earn, on average, just 76 percent as much as men (comparing full-time workers). Third—and here is where age stratification comes in—both these factors disadvantage older women more than younger women. Whereas women twenty-five to thirty-four years old earn 86 percent as much as comparable men, women fifty-five to sixty-four years old earn just 68 percent as much as men. Why the age

difference in earnings? Today's older women grew up at a time when social norms kept many women out of college and the workplace; with less education and job seniority, they now have lower earnings.

In the future, as a larger share of women graduate from college and remain employed throughout their adult lives, the income disparity between older women and older men may go down. But because women's wages probably will still lag behind men's, and more women than men will work in jobs lacking pension benefits, gender inequality in old age is likely to continue for some time (Davis, Grant, & Rowland, 1992; Manheimer, 1994; Neugarten, 1996; U.S. Census Bureau, 2003).

Housing

Between 2000 and 2010, the U.S. elderly population will grow by almost 5 million, with one-third of the growth among people eighty-five and older. Yet many policy makers and social service providers believe that there is not enough suitable housing for them (Katsura, Struyk, & Newman, 1989; Pynoos & Liebig, 1995; U.S. Census Bureau, 2003).

In the United States, both elders and younger people view keeping a home as central to an independent and satisfying life. Today, about three-fourths of the nation's elderly population live independently. More than 80 percent of elders own their own homes, and 73 percent own them mortgage-free. Even so, these homeowners must pay taxes, insurance, maintenance, and utility bills, a situation that leaves many "asset rich but income poor" (Rowles, 1993; Manheimer, 1994; Kontos, 1998; U.S. Census Bureau, 2003).

Because most elders prefer to "age in place," staying in the homes where they lived while working and raising their children, only 15 percent of elders live in housing specifically designed for older people. Physical changes that occur with aging, including loss of strength, slower reaction time, and weaker eyesight, require safety modifications to a home such as grab bars near toilets and bathtubs or extra lighting. Stairways in multistory houses can also pose a hardship.

Moreover, like the people who live in them, these homes tend to be older than average. This means that many elders' homes need repairs, insulation, and updating of heating and air conditioning systems. Such housing problems are especially common among categories of elders at higher risk of poverty: African Americans, women, and rural as well as inner-city people.

When housing is not up to date, the risk of accident or injury goes up. For example, a fall on dangerous stairs may cause a broken hip, landing an otherwise healthy senior citizen in a nursing home. Trying to heat a drafty home with a space heater raises the risk of fire or death by asphyxiation. This is why programs such as Medicare pay for some nonmedical equipment such as safety seats for showers and tubs. But many elders are unaware of the federal programs that can help make their homes safer (Manheimer, 1994; Gilderbloom & Markham, 1996).

Access to shopping is another issue important to seniors. Suburban communities have few buses and require the use of cars, yet many older people no longer drive. As a result, aging people may find stores, businesses, churches, and recreational facilities out of reach.

In one study of a declining neighborhood in southern California, Barbara Myerhoff (1979) found that elderly residents wanted, above all, to remain independent. But dressing, shopping, cooking, and cleaning an apartment are not easy for those challenged by arthritis in the hands or failing eyesight. Furthermore, Myerhoff found that the neighborhood had no large grocery store, forcing residents to take the bus, but the bus's high steps were hard to climb and prevented the use of a wheeled shopping cart. Night was another matter: Fear of crime kept older people behind locked doors.

Housing Programs for Older People Across the United States, many retirement communities offer comfortable, accessible homes with on-site health care services and help with cleaning, meals, and transportation. But costs, including entrance fees of as much as $250,000 plus high monthly fees, put such housing within reach of only a very limited number of older people.

To make safe, accessible housing available to those with lower incomes, the Department of Housing and Urban Development (HUD) operates the largest senior housing program. This program provides rental subsidies tied to income. Elderly people occupy one-third of the 500,000 public housing units managed by HUD. In 1990, Congress passed the National Affordable Housing Act, making additional money available for housing frail elders, a population that will increase quickly in the years to come as more seniors live past age eighty-five (Manheimer, 1994; Lawton, 1995; Binstock, 1996; U.S. Census Bureau, 2002).

Passage of the National Affordable Housing Act also made available "reverse mortgages," financial

Many elderly people prefer to "age in place." But homes that were comfortable for middle-aged people can become challenging to those who are entering old age. Alterations to make a home suitable for an older person can be very expensive, and alternatives such as moving to a retirement community can be more expensive still. Do you think U.S. society should expect individuals to meet these challenges for themselves?

arrangements that allow qualified elders to borrow against home equity without making monthly mortgage payments. The cash can be used as they wish— say, for home repairs, medical care, or housekeeping services. Eventually, the loan is paid back from the proceeds of the sale of the house after the person dies or moves elsewhere. Many seniors are not comfortable borrowing against their most important asset, although one study estimated that this program could reduce the elder poverty rate by 25 percent (Kutty, 1998).

Finally, faced with the high cost of housing and declining income, many elders cut costs by sharing a home. About 15 percent of U.S. seniors share a home with an unrelated adult (Doress-Worters & Siegal, 1994; U.S. Census Bureau, 2002).

Medical Care

People need much more medical care as they grow old. Since 1965, the federal government has provided benefits to seniors through Medicare, a program that pays for hospital care and 80 percent of other medical care costs for people over age sixty-five. In 2003, Congress added prescription drug subsidies to the Medicare program.

The cost of medical care has been rising steadily in the United States. To help cover the expenses not covered by Medicare, three-quarters of elders purchase private health insurance. When all the costs are added together, seniors typically spend more than 20 percent of their annual income on health care.

Costs skyrocket for people who move to a nursing facility. Although just 5 percent of U.S. elders live in a nursing home at any given time, almost 50 percent will at some point. Here, again, Medicare and insurance typically pay for just some of the costs, and the rest can easily overwhelm many people (Meyer & Bellas, 1995; Spillman, 2002; Espo, 2003; Fetto, 2003).

Death and Dying

Eventually, everyone faces the reality of death. One of the most important challenges of growing old is coming to terms with the end of life.

Culture shapes attitudes toward death and dying. In low-income nations, people learn to accept death as a common element of everyday life. Many infants die at birth, and—due to accident or illness—perhaps half of the remainder die before reaching age ten. In most cases, people in such societies die in the company of family and friends.

Advancing technology changes people's view of death. More precisely, modern societies remove death and dying from everyday life. Have you ever seen a person die? Most people have not because family members and friends approaching death are whisked away to die behind closed doors in the company of medical specialists. Even in hospitals, morgues are well out of the sight of patients and visitors (Sudnow, 1967; Ariès, 1974; Lee, 2002).

Moreover, professional morticians now prepare bodies for burial or cremation, a task once performed by family members. Typically, death rituals take place in funeral homes, not in a family home, as in years past.

In short, U.S. culture treats death as a topic to avoid. However, a new social movement with elders leading the way, is trying to bring death and dying out in the open, raising some important questions.

Euthanasia and the Right to Die   Advances in medical technology, better nutrition, and a safer environment allow people to live far longer than in the past. Yet the power to extend life also changes death from an event into a decision. The recent right-to-die movement claims that dying people—not doctors and hospital personnel—should decide when, where, and how they die (Morris, 1997; Ogden, 2001).

Although it is not possible to escape death, many believe that people with terminal diseases should be able to guide the process of dying and to ask for help from others. This belief has led to growing support for **euthanasia** (from Greek meaning "a good death"), *assisting in the death of a person suffering from an incurable disease.*

Euthanasia has two forms. *Passive euthanasia* involves doctors ending the treatment of a terminally ill person by, say, turning off respirators or other life-support machines. Passive euthanasia is generally accepted by lawmakers and is widely practiced by doctors. Indeed, about 25 percent of U.S. adults have prepared a *living will* stating which treatments they do and do not want if they are facing death and unable to speak for themselves.

Active euthanasia, on the other hand, involves a physician or other person actively causing the death of a person. For example, a doctor might administer a lethal injection to a dying person to bring a painless end to life.

A middle ground between passive and active euthanasia is called *physician-assisted suicide*. In this case, a patient requests help in dying from a physician who, typically, writes a prescription for lethal drugs. The doctor does nothing more; the patient is the one who actually takes the drugs. In the United States, Dr. Jack Kevorkian has been an activist pushing for laws to allow physician-assisted suicide. The Defining Moment box tells how he has tried to change people's thinking about the process of dying.

Euthanasia in the Netherlands   Since 1981, the Netherlands has permitted active euthanasia under specific circumstances. The rules say that patients must be dying with no hope of recovery, they must be suffering, and they must understand all the medical options available. At this point, they must clearly request help in dying from a doctor. The doctor, in turn, must consult with another doctor before acting

A DEFINING MOMENT

Dr. Jack Kevorkian: Challenging Our Ideas about Death

N O PERSON HAS PLAYED A GREATER ROLE in the debate over how people in the United States should die than Michigan doctor Jack Kevorkian. He supports the "right-to-die" side of the debate, believing that people should be able to make decisions about their own deaths, including having the help of a physician. In 1990, Kevorkian turned his beliefs into action when he first helped a terminally ill person who wanted to die. In the decade that followed, he assisted in the deaths of another 130 women and men.

Assisting in the deaths of his patients—and making the deaths public—created a firestorm of controversy: Kevorkian became a national figure when his picture appeared on the cover of *Time* magazine. Supporters applauded his courage in forcing U.S. society to confront the fact that many people wanted professional help in dying. Opponents called him "Dr. Death" and claimed that what he was doing amounted to murder.

In response to Kevorkian's actions, his home state of Michigan stripped him of his license to practice medicine. In 1999, the controversy reached a peak when Kevorkian assisted in a patient death, taped the entire event, and had the tape aired on the television program *60 Minutes*. Soon after, Michigan officials acted again,

Dr. Jack Kevorkian, who was convicted of murder and is currently serving a prison sentence, claims that people have a right to die with the assistance of a physician.

this time charging Kevorkian with second-degree murder. Kevorkian was found guilty and sentenced to a prison term of up to twenty-five years. He remains in prison, not eligible for parole until 2007.

Probably no one has done more to advance the "right-to-die" position than Dr. Jack Kevorkian. Currently, only one state—Oregon—permits this practice, and Kevorkian believes that all other states will pass such a law eventually, although maybe not in his lifetime.

to end a life (della Cava, 1997; Mauro, 1997). Dutch authorities report that about 4,500 people a year die with a physician's help.

Most people in the Netherlands support this policy. Yet there is evidence that doctors do not always follow the rules. A 1999 article in the *Journal of Medical Ethics* reported that, of the 4,500 cases of active euthanasia in the Netherlands in 1995, doctors administered lethal drugs to 900 patients (20 percent of the total) who never explicitly asked to die. In such cases, doctors went ahead because, in their view, death was in the patient's best interest. Moreover, in most of these cases, the doctors made no report to local medical examiners (Gillon, 1999).

A Web site advocating a right to die is http://www.finalexit.org

What about the United States? The right-to-die debate continues in the United States with people lining up to support or oppose active euthanasia. In 1997, the U.S. Supreme Court ruled (in *Vacco v. Quill* and *Washington v. Glucksberg*) that people have no legal right to die, a decision that set back the movement to legalize active euthanasia and physician-assisted suicide. Yet a majority of voters in one state, Oregon, endorsed a "Death with Dignity" law (1994 and 1997), which permits physicians to assist people in dying, providing the patients have less than six months to live (Capron, 1997; Cain, 2001).

The right-to-die movement remains controversial. Supporters claim that people should have a choice about when and how to die, including help from doctors to bring about a "good death." Opponents ask

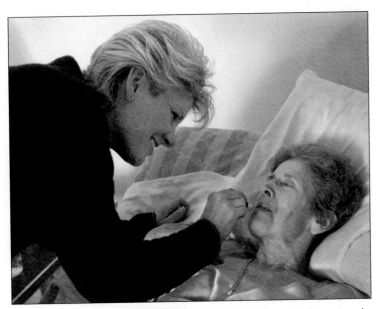

Hospice organizations provide assistance to dying people and their families. Unlike a hospital, where doctors and nurses try to prevent death, hospice workers try to make the process of dying as comfortable as possible.

whether a request for a quick death may sometimes be prompted not by pain or even a terminal condition but by sadness and depression. National surveys show that people have sympathy for both sides: A majority of adults support doctors helping terminally ill patients who, with family agreement, request help in dying, but an even larger majority opposes allowing doctors to cause death just because a patient is "tired of living" (NORC, 2003:238–9). Another concern is that a "right-to-die" law will create a "slippery slope" that makes active euthanasia more likely to be abused as it becomes more common. Who can be sure that a decision to end a life is not prompted by family members who, eager for an inheritance or fearful of high medical bills, pressure old or sick people into a quick death? Furthermore, health insurance companies would certainly make bigger profits by ending lives rather than treating dying patients. Finally, what about the poor? Doctors and hospitals treating poor patients or those without health insurance would have a financial incentive to "get it over with." In short, opponents of active euthanasia point out that it is very difficult to set moral guidelines for such cases and even harder to prevent abuse (Kleinman, 1997).

In 1999, a report from health officials in Oregon claimed that in 1998, physicians provided lethal drugs to patients in just twenty-three cases (*New England Journal of Medicine*, February 18, 1999). Of those who received prescriptions, six died of their illnesses before taking the drugs, fifteen took the lethal drugs and died, and two people did not take the drugs and were still alive at the end of the year. These numbers suggest that the concerns raised by critics of right-to-die laws may be overstated. But as the elder population rapidly increases, this debate is sure to continue.

Hospice   Another important development that affects patterns of death is the increasing use of **hospice**, *homelike care that provides physical and emotional comfort to dying people and their families.* The first hospice facility in the United States opened in 1974. Today, there are more than 3,000 hospice organizations caring for almost 750,000 people each year. Unlike a hospital, where medical personnel work to save lives, a hospice staff helps people to die in comfort and with dignity. In some cases, a hospice organization operates a home where dying people go; in many cases, hospice workers go to the homes of dying people to assist them and their families.

The hospice movement is growing because many people want to avoid the impersonal and highly regimented environment of a hospital. Typically, hospice personnel work with a doctor and family members to ensure that a dying person is comfortable, using drugs as necessary to control pain but making no efforts to extend the life of the dying person. In short, the work of a hospice is to help the patient and family members accept death in an environment that is as comfortable as possible. The Personal Stories box profiles one hospice volunteer in a Midwestern town.

THEORETICAL ANALYSIS: UNDERSTANDING AGING AND INEQUALITY

We can better understand the social problems of aging through the use of theoretical analysis. In the following sections, we apply the structural-functional, social-conflict, and symbolic-interaction approaches to many of the issues raised in this chapter.

Structural-Functional Analysis: The Need to Disengage

The structural-functional approach highlights how societies operate smoothly. Given the realities of aging and death, all societies must devise ways to replace old workers with young ones. In other words, society solves the problem of people's physical

Personal Stories   A Hospice Volunteer: "I Take Away More than I Give"

"No, I'M NOT AFRAID OF DEATH," SAYS Kim as she talks about her work helping others die. But then she pauses and adds, "But, then again, it's not me who's dying." Kim is a middle-aged woman living in a small town in Ohio. She works as a massage therapist and is a wife and a mother to a grown daughter. For more than three years, she has been a hospice volunteer and has helped more than 100 people reach the end of life. Kim shares something of her experiences:

The typical case begins when the hospice volunteer director calls. She tells me I have been matched with a patient. I call the patient's home and arrange the first visit. I might give patients a bed bath, make lunch, maybe just give the spouse an hour or so break and a chance to get out of the house.

You get to know each other pretty fast. Something about dying strips away all the pretenses and, within a month or so, I get to be like one of the family. That doesn't mean it's always easy. Some family members don't like a stranger in the house. Once I even had kids in the family stealing drugs from the mother who was dying.

The work becomes more intense as the time of death gets close. The problem is that most people have never experienced death up close. They need someone to be there to let them know what to expect, how to help, and to tell them when it is time to let go.

Letting a loved one die is very hard for most people. People's first reaction is to fight death, but, when it's going to happen soon, they can also end up making death harder for themselves and for the person who is dying.

Of course, the people who *really* fight death don't use hospice at all—they send the dying person to the hospital. Hospitals try to prevent death. But when there's no more to be done, hospitals make death antiseptic. They use drugs to sedate the patient to the point that people die smoothly and quickly. It's also very expensive. The hospice approach is more natural. It's like letting the body just shut down on its own. We use drugs for pain, but that's all. But, this way, dying sometimes takes hours and, near the end, a dying person might go two or three minutes between each breath. That can go on for five or six hours! This is the point when the hospice worker—there is often a doctor or nurse there, too—is most helpful telling people what is happening. We are really just guides. When someone is close to death, we have a saying, "Don't just do something, stand there!" The most important thing is just being there with the family and the dying person, helping them to understand and accept the coming death.

We try to stay away from the debate over physician-assisted suicide. But, in reality, a doctor and family members usually talk about if and when to use a drug to bring the dying process to an end. Whether you are in a hospital, at a hospice facility, or in the patient's home, dying almost always involves a decision.

I wish there had been someone like me available years ago when my own father died. I know I do good for people. But I always take away more than I give.

ISSUES AND EXERCISES

1. What do you see as the advantages of hospice care? What about disadvantages?

2. Would you volunteer to do this kind of work? Why or why not?

3. [Research Navigator.com] Use Research Navigator™ to learn more about hospice. (See instructions on page 25; keyword: "hospice")

Source: Based on interview by the author, 2003.

decline by *disengaging* the elderly, transferring their workplace roles and other responsibilities to younger people. Disengagement, then, is a strategy to ensure that the aging of the population does not disrupt the performance of important tasks.

Retirement is the main strategy for easing aging people out of productive roles while they are still capable of performing them. Retirement occurs in rapidly changing societies, where older workers lack recent knowledge and many up-to-date skills; younger workers, by contrast, have the benefit of the latest training. **Disengagement theory,** then, is *the idea that modern societies operate more smoothly by removing people from positions of responsibility as they enter old age.*

Disengagement is not only functional for society as a whole. It can also provide older people with the reward of rest, relaxation, and opportunities for travel after years of hard work (Cumming & Henry, 1961; Voltz, 2000).

Critical evaluation.   The eventual disengagement of elderly people may be necessary for society as a whole, but not all aging people are ready to retire from jobs or other responsibilities. Many enjoy their work, and most look to their jobs for needed income. Therefore, a criticism of this approach is that disengagement of the elderly carries personal costs, including loss of status and income as well as social isolation. The need for people to remain active in old age points us to the symbolic-interaction approach.

Symbolic-Interaction Analysis: Staying Active

The symbolic-interaction approach focuses on the meaning people find in their everyday lives. If aging people must withdraw from some activities (especially those that are physically challenging), most will want to seek out new ones. For example, many older people retire from paid work but expand their hobbies, travel, and volunteer work. The importance of finding new activities is especially important in light of the fact that people in the United States who reach age sixty-five typically can look forward to about twenty more years of life (Robinson, Werner, & Godbey, 1997; Smart, 2001; U.S. National Center for Health Statistics, 2003).

Researchers have found that personal satisfaction in old age depends on remaining socially active (Havinghurst, Neugarten, & Tobin, 1968; Neugarten, 1996). **Activity theory** states that *people enhance personal satisfaction in old age by keeping a high level of social activity.*

Activity theory accepts the fact that aging people need to disengage from some kinds of work (especially jobs that are physically challenging). But this theory adds that people usually try to replace old roles with new ones. In addition, we need to remember that older people (like people of any age) have diverse needs, abilities, and interests. Thus, we should expect that seniors will seek out a wide variety of activities (Havinghurst et al., 1968; Neugarten, 1977; Palmore, 1979).

Critical evaluation.   Activity theory overlooks the fact that at least some older people are not physically able to maintain a busy schedule. Even healthy older people do not always have a great deal of choice about their lives. In nursing homes, for example, many elders would welcome the chance to be more active but find limited recreational opportunities. Similarly, companies may pressure older workers to retire (or avoid hiring them in the first place). Many elders find that low incomes limit their choices. In sum, as long as seniors are disadvantaged in various ways, they cannot shape their lives as they may wish. This concern brings us to social-conflict theory.

Social-Conflict Analysis: Age and Inequality

Social-conflict analysis highlights age stratification, pointing out ways in which society limits the opportunities and resources available to older people. By and large, it is middle-aged people who have the most power and privileges in our society. As we have explained, modern societies tend to define elderly people in negative terms, causing both prejudice and discrimination. In the workplace, age discrimination is against the law, but companies usually prefer hiring younger workers all the same. Similarly, the law forbids forcing older workers to retire, but companies commonly replace older employees with younger, lower-paid employees in order to contain costs. In short, some analysts conclude that capitalist societies turn older people into second-class citizens as a means of increasing profits (Atchley, 1982; Phillipson, 1982).

Social-conflict analysis also shows us that some categories of elders face greater disadvantages than others. Social class, gender, and race all affect one's range of opportunities. For example, many of the low-skill service jobs commonly filled by women and African Americans rarely provide pensions and were only recently covered by Social Security. Therefore, minorities who earn lower wages to begin with, as well as women who interrupt their working lives to have children, have the hardest time in retirement.

Critical evaluation.   Age is certainly an important dimension of social stratification, one that combines with other dimensions of inequality including class, race, and gender. Yet by focusing on the plight of some elders, the social-conflict approach overlooks the economic gains achieved by seniors, on average, in recent decades. In addition, seniors have a lot of political clout because most of them vote (at three times the rate of people ages eighteen to twenty-four), and they support politically active organizations such as the American Association of Retired Persons (AARP). Thus, although some elders live in poverty and many encounter prejudice and discrimination, the system does seem to meet the needs of the aging population fairly well.

POLITICS AND AGING: CONSTRUCTING PROBLEMS AND DEFINING SOLUTIONS

As with other areas of social life, exactly how people view the social problems of the elderly is guided by politics. We turn now to how politics shapes our view of issues related to aging.

Conservatives: More Family Responsibility

As conservatives see it, a healthy society is built on strong families that care for their members. Conservatives also claim that today's society suffers from weaker family ties. In an age that celebrates individualism and independence, the age-old system by which a family takes care of its own is breaking down, they say, just at the time when the elderly population is increasing and caregiving is needed more than ever. A number of social problems, including poverty, social isolation, and abuse among the elderly, is the result.

Because people today are living longer and longer, many families face the task of raising young children and caring for aging parents (Roots, 1998). But, conservatives point out, we must reject a "me-first" culture that makes many younger people unwilling to take on family responsibilities.

Another important conservative value is planning for the future. Conservatives argue that people should take responsibility for their own old age by planning and saving throughout their working lives. Ideally, at least, elder people's own resources, perhaps with help from their families, should provide for a comfortable old age.

All this is consistent with the conservative desire for limited government. Almost all conservatives support Social Security, and many Republicans as well as Democrats supported the recent extension of Medicare to help pay for prescription drugs. At the same time, conservatives claim we need to control government spending for all social programs. One way to do this is to limit or even cut off government benefits to well-off seniors who do not need

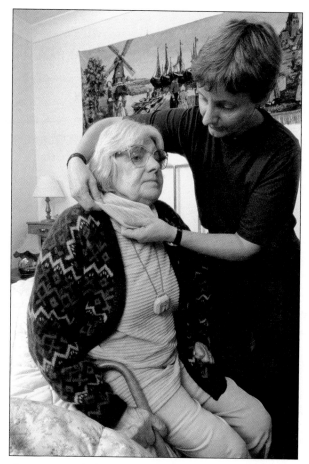

Conservatives believe that families should provide care as their members grow old. Liberals look to government to expand social programs that benefit seniors. Which political viewpoint do you think seniors themselves prefer? Why?

them. In the process, they argue, this policy would strengthen the future of Social Security for those who do need it as the number of seniors rises in the decades to come.

Liberals: More Government Assistance

As liberals see it, there are many serious problems related to aging in the United States. Liberals reject the conservative position that these are problems people should be able to solve for themselves by saving wisely or relying on family members. On the contrary, they say, many older people have trouble finding work, and many have faced racial and gender discrimination all their lives. It is no wonder, then, that many seniors have little security in their old age.

LEFT TO RIGHT

THE POLITICS OF AGING

	RADICAL LEFT VIEW	LIBERAL VIEW	CONSERVATIVE VIEW
WHAT IS THE PROBLEM?	Age stratification is one dimension of the striking social inequality caused by the capitalist U.S. economy.	Elders face a higher risk of poverty, as well as prejudice and discrimination based on their age, sometimes in combination with disadvantages based on class, race, and gender.	Although some seniors are poor, in general, older people do not face a host of social problems. In the United States, elders are more prosperous and live longer than they did in the past.
WHAT IS THE SOLUTION?	Replacing the capitalist economy with a socialist, system would end the practice of devaluing less productive people. Government must provide for the well-being of people of all ages.	Government programs (including Social Security and laws banning age discrimination) are crucial to meeting the needs of the rising elder population.	A culture of self-reliance will encourage most people to provide for their own old age; families should support elder members as necessary, and government programs should be a last resort.

Join the debate . . .

1. To what extent, as radicals, liberals, and conservatives see it, are elders disadvantaged in U.S. society today? What specific kinds of problems do you find most important?

2. Overall, how do the scope and severity of age-based inequality in the United States compare with

those of inequality based on class, race, and gender? Provide specific facts to support your argument.

3. Which of the three political analyses of aging and inequality included here do you find most convincing? Why?

Liberals are also quick to point out that many of today's families depend on the earnings of both women and men just to meet their own needs. How, then, can we expect them to care for aging parents as well? In addition to the financial burdens, many younger adults (especially women) come home tired from a day of work and are stretched to the limit trying meet the needs of their children, never mind their aging parents.

For their part, few older people want to depend on their children. On the contrary, the greatest fear of many older people is becoming a burden to their children. To help seniors remain independent, liberals conclude, the solution is not to limit social programs for the elderly but to expand them. Programs that lower the cost of medical care and housing and those that provide transportation to doctors' appointments and shopping centers would dramatically improve the quality of life for elders and their children.

Radicals: Capitalism and the Elderly

Radicals on the left have focused more on inequality based on class, race, and gender than on age stratification. But one radical analysis of aging is offered by Steven Spitzer (1980). Following Karl Marx, Spitzer argues that capitalist societies have an overriding focus on profits. For this reason, the culture of capitalism devalues any category of people that is economically less productive. To the extent that elderly people are not working—and to the extent that they depend on pensions and other benefits—they are a costly burden to the capitalist economy. This is the reason we tend to view elderly people in negative terms and push them to the margins of society.

From this point of view, the solution to ageism and other problems of inequality is to take the radical step of replacing the capitalist economy with one that values all people. In short, a socialist economy would lessen all dimensions of inequality, including age stratification. The Left to Right table summarizes how each political perspective defines age-related problems and solutions.

GOING ON FROM HERE

In this chapter, we have explained how older people suffer from a number of problems, including prejudice and discrimination, social isolation, poverty, and inadequate housing. Historically, as industrial societies raised living standards for everyone, they reduced the social standing of the oldest members of society. Given this trend, what can we expect in the future?

Looking ahead, perhaps the most important fact to keep in mind is the steadily rising share of elderly people in the U.S. population. Perhaps even more than women, African Americans, and other disadvantaged categories of the U.S. population, elders are well organized and very active politically. We noted earlier that people over age sixty-five are three times more likely to vote than those aged eighteen to twenty-four. It is no surprise, then, that politicians listen to the concerns of older people (Wallace & Williamson, 1992; Powell et al., 1996; U.S. Census Bureau, 2002).

The greatest test for the elderly of tomorrow is likely to be the Social Security system. It seems simple enough: Working people pay into the system, and retired people draw out benefits. Yet with the rapid increase in the elderly population of the United States, the demands on Social Security are going up as well. In 1950, there were six workers for every retired person. By 2050, projections indicate that there will be just two workers for every retiree, which threatens Social Security with bankruptcy. The challenge is to ensure the financial security of older people without placing an unfair burden on the young (Costa, 1998; Riche, 2000; Gendell, 2002).

As government officials debate the future of Social Security, some critics—especially conservatives—point out that many older people are well-off and do not need government help. As a result, their solution is to cut future Social Security benefits to well-off people. Liberals counter that more money will be needed to keep this vital system operating. Most seniors (knowing what is in their own interest) offer strong support for Social Security. With their substantial political clout, today's seniors—and those of tomorrow—may have the power to bring about changes needed to improve their lives.

CHAPTER SUMMARY

1. The life course refers to the socially constructed stages that people pass through as they live out their lives. Gerontology is the study of old age, the final stage in the life course.

2. Aging is a biological fact of life, but the experience of growing old—and how people define "old"—is shaped by society. Preindustrial societies give most wealth and power to elders. By contrast, industrial societies confer lower social standing on the elderly.

3. People sixty-five to seventy-four—the "younger old"—are typically active and in good health. "Older old" people—from seventy-five to eighty-four—contend with more health-related problems and need more assistance. For the "oldest old"—people over eighty-five—staying healthy is the greatest problem.

4. The "graying of the United States" refers to the increasing share of the U.S. population over age sixty-five.

5. One social problem affecting many elderly people is isolation, which is often made worse by retirement and by the death of a spouse.

6. Ageism is prejudice and discrimination directed against the elderly. Ageism involves not just stereotypes but also discrimination in employment and housing.

7. Every year, about 1 million elderly people in the United States suffer serious neglect or abuse. The rising number of elders in the United States makes caregiving a responsibility for more and more people.

8. Although the poverty rate among senior citizens in the United States has fallen in recent

decades, poverty is still a problem for many seniors, especially for older women and other minorities.

9. The United States lacks enough suitable and affordable housing to meet the needs of this nation's surging elder population.

10. Medical expenses rise with advancing age. Government programs such as Medicare cover only some of the costs of medical care and nursing homes.

11. Advances in medical technology that extend life now make death a decision. The right of very ill people to decide when to die is at the heart of the debate over euthanasia and physician-assisted suicide.

12. Disengagement theory, a structural-functional approach, argues that society must disengage elders from important roles, passing responsibilities from one generation to the next.

13. Activity theory, a symbolic-interaction approach, states that elders who remain involved in many social activities have greater life satisfaction.

14. The social-conflict approach highlights age as a dimension of social stratification. Older women and other minorities, subject not only to ageism but also to sexism and perhaps also racism, may be much more disadvantaged.

15. Conservatives point out that seniors are doing better than ever; they look to people's own savings and support from families to provide for a secure old age.

16. Liberals focus on how poverty and ageism increase in old age and claim that these problems are beyond most people's control. As a result, liberals look to government to provide all people with a secure old age.

17. Radicals take issue with capitalism's emphasis on efficiency and profit, claiming that this is why many look down on older people who are no longer economically productive.

KEY CONCEPTS

life course (p. 112) the socially constructed stages that people pass through as they live out their lives

gerontology (p. 112) a branch of the social sciences dealing with aging and the elderly

gerontocracy (p. 112) a social system that gives a society's oldest members the most wealth, power, and prestige

life expectancy (p. 113) the number of years, on average, people in a society can expect to live

ageism (p. 117) prejudice and discrimination directed against the elderly

caregiving (p. 120) informal and unpaid care provided to a dependent person by family members, other relatives, or friends

age stratification (p. 121) social inequality among various age categories within a society

euthanasia (p. 124) assisting in the death of a person suffering from an incurable disease

hospice (p. 126) homelike care that provides physical and emotional comfort to dying people and their families

disengagement theory (p. 127) the idea that modern societies operate more smoothly by removing people from positions of responsibility as they enter old age

activity theory (p. 128) the idea that people enhance personal satisfaction in old age by keeping a high level of social activity

THINKING CRITICALLY: QUESTIONS AND ISSUES

1. Everyone knows that aging is a biological fact of life. How is aging also a cultural issue?

2. A minority is a category of people who have a distinctive appearance and who are socially disadvantaged. Based on the information presented

in this chapter, should the elderly be considered a minority in the United States? Why or why not?

3. Technology often advances faster than our cultural understanding of it—an example of what

sociologists call cultural lag. How has the development of life-sustaining medical technology outpaced our understanding of how to use it?

4. As the number of seniors continues to rise, what are some of the changes you expect in U.S. society? Do you expect old age to get better? Why or why not?

GETTING INVOLVED: LEARNING ACTIVITIES

1. Try to talk to someone who grew up in a culture outside the United States. Ask about conceptions of the life course, including how childhood and old age differ in that society.

2. Just about every town has a senior citizen center. Visit to ask about the social problems common to older people in your community. Why not volunteer to help out at the center once a week? This is an excellent way to get to know older people. Your efforts can be a wonderful learning experience for all involved.

3. Ask your grandparents or other older people you know about their own experiences with

aging. What do they say are the joys and sorrows of aging? What can they teach you about the experience of retirement?

4. Although there is more attention to death and dying today, this issue is still something of a social taboo. Are there any courses on your campus that deal with death and dying? Is there any "death and dying" organization, such as a hospice, in your community? If so, contact the organization to discover the range of services it provides.

GETTING CONNECTED: USEFUL WEB LINKS

http://www.prenhall.com/macionis
Visit the interactive Companion Website™ that accompanies this text. Begin by clicking on the cover of your book. You will find a chapter-by-chapter study guide, practice tests, suggested Web links, and links to other relevant material.

http://www.aarp.org
Visit the home page of the American Association of Retired Persons (AARP). What issues does this organization consider to be important? What services do they provide for older people?

http://www.nho.org
http://www.hospicefoundation.org
Here are two Web sites that provide information about the hospice movement. What range of services

do they provide? What part could you play in helping others in need?

http://www.aoa.gov
The government's Department of Health and Human Services operates this site. Visit here to learn more about trends and issues that affect older people across the United States.

http://www.seniornet.org
Of all age categories, seniors are the least likely to have computer skills. Seniornet is an organization trying to bring information age skills to elders. What are their objectives and programs? What can you do to help?

GETTING STARTED ON YOUR OWN: RESEARCH NAVIGATOR™

Follow the instructions found on page 25 of this text to access the features of Research Navigator™. Once at the Web site, enter your Login Name and Password. Then, to use the **Content Select** database, enter keywords such as "elderly," "ageism," and "hospice," and the

search engine will supply relevant and recent scholarly and popular press publications. Use the *New York Times* **Search-by-Subject Archive** to find recent news articles related to sociology and the **Link Library** feature to find relevant Web links organized by the key terms associated with this chapter.

© *Paul Marcus, [detail from]* Yvonne's Story: Maze of AIDS, *oil on wood,*
12 × 14 in. Studio SPM, Inc.

CRIME AND CRIMINAL JUSTICE

TYCO INTERNATIONAL SEEMED LIKE ONE BIG SUCCESS *story: A global corporation operating in one hundred countries, Tyco was growing rapidly and reporting ever-increasing earnings. The company's chief executive officer (CEO), Dennis Kozlowski, was buying new companies so fast he had earned the nickname "Deal-a-Month Dennis."*

But in 2002 everything changed. After the mass media reported that the company was improperly reporting its earnings, CEO Dennis Kozlowski promptly resigned. He faces charges of falsifying business records, grand larceny, and enterprise corruption. Simply put, he is accused of improperly using $600 million in company money for his own benefit, including millions for lavish parties, a 130-foot yacht, and a New York apartment filled with a fortune in artwork (Lavella, 2002; Sloan, 2002; Smart, 2003).

Now indicted by a criminal court, Kozlowski has joined a growing number of CEOs in trouble with the law. The companies they have left behind—including Enron, Global Crossing, WorldCom, and Adelphia Communications—are struggling to survive, and public confidence in large corporations has fallen sharply. Even Martha Stewart, the country's symbol of stylish living and head of her own corporations, was charged with misdeeds and faced trial in 2004.

This chapter examines the problem of crime in the United States: what crime is, how much it costs, who the offenders are, and how the criminal justice system responds to violations of the criminal law. We begin by defining several important terms.

GETTING THE PICTURE

✦ Do you feel safe from crime?

Despite a downward trend in crime rates, it is likely that more than 30 million serious crimes occur each year in the United States.

✦ Does crime pay?

In 75 percent of all robberies in the United States, the police never make an arrest.

✦ Do trials provide justice?

More than 90 percent of people in the United States charged with a crime never get a trial at all, but are sentenced through the process of plea bargaining.

Crime represents a special category of wrongdoing—the breaking of formally enacted law. The response to crime is also formal, typically involving citizen reports to police. Here a young woman who witnessed a hit-and-run accident gives information to police.

NORMS, LAW, AND CRIME

All societies make rules defining what people can and cannot do. **Norms** are *rules and expectations by which a society guides the behavior of its members.* Many norms are informal, enforced with just a comment or facial expression in everyday life. Yet another type of norms is **law,** *norms formally created through a society's political system.* The main source of law is a legislature (such as Congress), although laws are also enacted by executive orders (by a local mayor, state governor, or national president) and by international treaties.

Law includes both civil and criminal statutes. *Civil law* defines the legal rights and relationships involving individuals and businesses. Civil law is involved when, say, one person sues another after an automobile accident. *Criminal law,* on the other hand, defines people's responsibilities to uphold public order. After an accident, for example, a driver who is found to be drunk is likely to face arrest for a criminal violation. So whereas civil law involves harm or loss leading to a settlement, violations of criminal law involve arrest and punishment.

Crime, then, is *the violation of the criminal laws enacted by federal, state, or local governments.* Federal laws apply everywhere in the United States, whereas state and local laws apply within limited jurisdictions. There are two major categories of crimes. A **misdemeanor** is *a less serious crime punishable by less than one year in prison.* A **felony,** on the other hand, is *a more serious crime punishable by at least one year in prison.*

In deciding whether a person has committed a crime, courts must establish not only what the person did but also the person's *intent,* that is, what the person meant to do. For example, a court could classify a killing in many ways, ranging from self-defense (in which someone acts with deadly force but only to escape serious injury or death) to murder in the first degree (in which someone plans and carries out the killing of another person).

CRIME: THE EXTENT OF THE PROBLEM

Surveys show that most people in the United States think crime is a serious problem (NORC, 2003). Police record some 12 million serious crimes each year. At some time, most people in the United States are victimized by crime (U.S. Federal Bureau of Investigation, 2003). The high number of crimes, combined with extensive reporting of serious crime in the mass media, promotes widespread fear of crime. Indeed, fear of crime is itself a social problem because it limits the things people do and the places they go. For example, one-third of U.S. adults say they are afraid to walk alone at night in their own communities (NORC, 2003:244).

Crime Statistics

Police departments across the country make regular reports to the Federal Bureau of Investigation (FBI), which compiles an annual book titled *Crime in the United States: The Uniform Crime Report* (UCR). This book includes data on felonies or serious crimes of two kinds. The first is **crime against property,** *crime that involves theft of property belonging to others.* Crimes against property include burglary, larceny-theft, motor vehicle theft, and arson. The second type is **crime against persons,** *crime that involves violence or the threat of violence against others.* Crimes against persons include murder and manslaughter, aggravated assault, forcible rape, and robbery. Table 6–1 defines all of these serious crimes.

TABLE 6–1 SERIOUS CRIME IN THE *UNIFORM CRIME REPORT*

CRIMES AGAINST PROPERTY	
Burglary	The unlawful entry of a structure to commit a serious crime or a theft
Larceny-theft	The unlawful taking, carrying, leading, or riding away of property from the possession of another
Motor vehicle theft	The theft or attempted theft of a motor vehicle
Arson	Any willful or malicious burning or attempt to burn the personal property of another
CRIMES AGAINST PERSONS	
Murder or manslaughter	The willful killing of one human being by another
Aggravated assault	An unlawful attack by one person on another for the purpose of inflicting severe or aggravated bodily injury
Forcible rape	The carnal knowledge of a female forcibly and against her will
Robbery	Taking or attempting to take anything of value from the care, custody, or control of a person or persons by force or threat of force or violence or putting the victim in fear

Source: U.S. Federal Bureau of Investigation (2000).

There are two reasons to treat the *Uniform Crime Reports* with caution. First, the *UCR* includes only crimes known to the police. But, how many crimes are *not* reported? To answer this question, the FBI conducts the annual National Crime Victimization Survey. Researchers ask a random sample of the U.S. population whether they have been victims of serious crime within the past year. A comparison of survey responses with official crime reports suggests only about one-third of serious crimes are reported to the police. Realistically, then, a complete tally might show that 30 to 35 million offenses actually occur each year.

Information and statistics about U.S. crime can be found at
http://www.ojp.usdoj.gov/bjs

A second concern about the *UCR* is that it gathers statistics on "street crimes" but not more "elite crimes," which include business fraud, corruption, price fixing, and illegal dumping of toxic wastes, all likely to be committed at the direction of corporate executives. Overall, then, the *UCR* not only underestimates the extent of street crime but also gives a biased picture of the typical criminal based only on one kind of crime (Reiman, 1998).

Violent Crime: Patterns and Trends

Violent crimes, that is, crimes against persons, account for only 12 percent of all serious offenses;

crimes against property account for the remaining 88 percent. Put another way, the crime rate for property offenses is about seven times higher than that for violent crimes against persons (U.S. Federal Bureau of Investigation, 2003). Figure 6–1 on page 138 shows the rates (the number of reported crimes per 100,000 people) for both crimes against persons and crimes against property.

From 1960 until the early 1990s, violent crime rose quickly. After that, the trend turned downward. (The rate of property offenses also rose quickly after 1960, with a downturn in the early 1980s and further decline through 2001.) Why the drop in crime rates? Analysts point to a number of factors, including a strong economy during the 1990s, a drop in the use of crack cocaine, the hiring of more police, and tougher sentences for criminal convictions (Boggess & Bound, 1997; Zimring & Hawkins, 1997; Blumstein & Rosenfeld, 1998; Fagan, Zimring, & Kim, 1998; Witkin, 1998; Johnson, 2000). We now take a closer look at trends for each offense covered by the *UCR*.

Murder In 2002, police recorded 16,204 murders, which amounts to one every thirty-two minutes. Even so, since 1993 the U.S. murder rate been falling, and it is now at about the same level as in 1960 (U.S. Bureau of Justice Statistics, 2003).

The FBI also tracks the percentage of murders that are "cleared," meaning the police arrested someone for the crime, whether or not that person later was found guilty. In 2002, police made arrests in

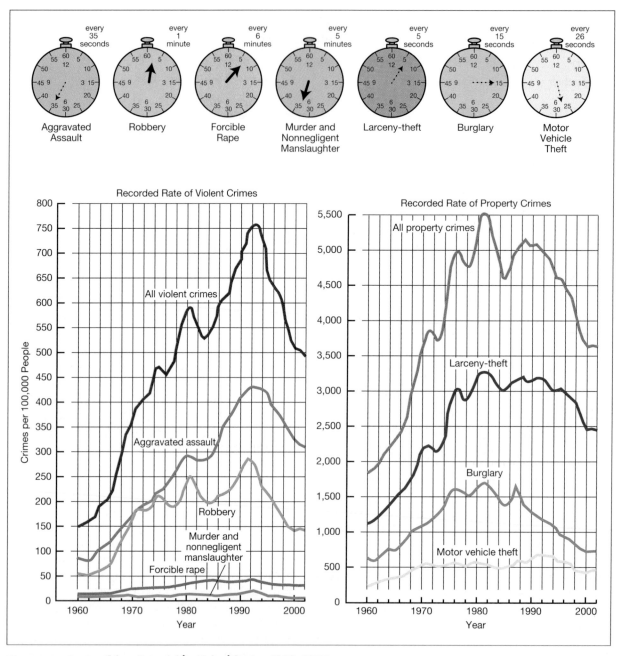

FIGURE 6–1   Crime Rates in the United States, 1960–2002

The graphs represent crime rates for various violent crimes and property crimes between 1960 and 2002. "Crime clocks," shown at the top of the figure, are another way of describing the frequency of crimes.

Source: U.S. Federal Bureau of Investigation (2003).

64 percent of all reported murders (U.S. Federal Bureau of Investigation, 2003).

Most murder victims (77 percent in 2002) are males. African Americans (about 12 percent of the population) are at especially high risk: The FBI reports that 48 percent of murder victims are black, 48 percent are white, and 3 percent are of other races. The statistics also show that murder is an intraracial crime, meaning that offenders and victims typically are of the same race. In 91 percent of cases

Social Policy   Stalking: Prelude to Violence

DARLENE LIVED WITH RICHARD FOR TWO YEARS. Early in the relationship, she found him charming and kind. But gradually he changed, to a point where he tried to control her every move and often erupted in fits of anger. Afraid for her safety, Darlene moved out, staying with relatives in an attempt to steer clear of Richard. But he always managed to track her down, threatening to harm her if she did not come back to him. Darlene called the police, but they explained that they could arrest Richard only if he actually became violent.

The threats continued, and Darlene called the police again and again. But the police kept insisting there was nothing they could do as long as Richard was only "talking." One day Richard called to say he was leaving town and wanted to pick up some things from Darlene. With a sense of relief, she agreed to meet him in front of her aunt's house. When Richard arrived, she walked to the street and handed him a box. Suddenly, he exploded with rage. As Darlene turned and ran, Richard jumped into his van and ran her down, pinning her against the house. Her family looked on in horror as bricks from the house tumbled down around her lifeless body (Walker, 1989).

Darlene's murder took place in the 1980s, when there were no laws allowing police to protect victims of stalking. But as people concerned about stalking came together to form a social movement, they were able to lobby lawmakers so that, in 1990, California passed the nation's first antistalking law. Groups across the country took up the cause, and soon every state had similar laws. Today, victims of stalkers can obtain police protection and court orders demanding that the person stay away from them or face arrest and jail.

ISSUES AND EXERCISES

1. Provide several arguments in support of antistalking laws. Do you think such laws might threaten the freedom of law-abiding people? Why or why not?

2. Why, in your opinion, did no law of this kind exist before 1990?

3. [Research Navigator.com] Use Research Navigator™ to find additional material on stalking. (See instructions on page 25; keyword: "stalking")

Sources: Walker (1989), Tjaden (1997), and Tjaden & Thoennes (1998).

---

involving an African American victim, the arrested suspect is of the same race; the same is true in 84 percent of cases involving a white victim (U.S. Federal Bureau of Investigation, 2003).

FBI data show that half of all murder victims knew the offender; furthermore, in 13 percent of the cases, victim and offender were related. A relationship between the victim and the offender is especially likely when the murder victim is a woman. Whereas just 3 percent of male victims were killed by wives, ex-wives, or girlfriends, 32 percent of female victims were slain by husbands, ex-husbands, or boyfriends (U.S. Federal Bureau of Investigation, 2003).

In many cases, a killer begins by stalking the victim for a period of time (Lowney & Best, 1995). **Stalking** is defined as _persistent efforts by someone to establish or reestablish a relationship against the will of the victim._ About 2 percent of men and 8 percent of

women report being stalked at some time. Whereas men (typically celebrities) usually are stalked by strangers, women are almost always stalked by people they know—in most cases, former husbands or boyfriends. Most stalkers threaten their victims, and some vandalize property, harm or kill pets, or engage in deadly violence. The Social Policy box takes a closer look at how stalking came to be defined as a serious social problem.

The high murder rate in the United States demands that we take a critical look at the role of handguns. Two-thirds of murder victims die as a result of shootings. There are as many guns as adults in the United States—some 200 million in all—one-third of which are handguns. Those who favor stricter gun control argue that easy availability of guns explains why violence in the United States is so deadly. Opponents of gun control, on the other

In the early 1990s, every state passed laws making stalking a crime. Research reveals that most people who experience this frightening crime are women; typically, stalkers are ex-husbands or boyfriends. Why, in your opinion, was stalking defined as a problem only recently?

hand, claim that background checks and waiting periods (required by the 1993 Brady Bill) only inconvenience law-abiding citizens and do little to keep weapons out of the hands of criminals, who typically get guns illegally. Some go even further and argue that gun ownership actually reduces crime by discouraging criminals from preying on people who may be armed. In any case, gun control is no magic bullet: The number of Californians killed each year by knives is greater than the number of Canadians killed by all weapons (Currie, 1985; Wright, 1995; Loth, 2000).

Forcible Rape   In 2002, the FBI recorded 95,136 rapes in the United States, which amounts to one every six minutes. The fact that most attackers are known to their victims explains why police are able to make arrests in half of reported rape cases.

As explained in Chapter 7 ("Violence"), the shame and fear associated with this crime means that many women do not report being victimized. Efforts by colleges and universities to educate women and men about "date rape"—sexual assault in which the offender and victim know one another—have encouraged more victims to come forward in recent years. Even so, across the country, only half of women who are raped make a report to the police.

The FBI statistics do not include attempted rape, nor do they include sex with a minor (typically a person under eighteen) when no force is used (an offense known as statutory rape). In addition, rape statistics do not reflect attacks on males, despite research showing that male rape victims suffer greater physical injury than women (Mezey & King, 1989; Calhoun & Atkeson, 1991). The Personal Stories box takes a closer look at the problem of rape in men's prisons.

This is the site for Stop Prisoner Rape, Inc.: **http://www.spr.org**

Human Rights Watch has issued a report on rape in prison: **http://www.hrw.org/reports/2001/prison/**

Aggravated Assault   Aggravated assault accounts for nearly two-thirds of all reported violent crime. Despite a downward trend in the assault rate after 1991, police recorded 894,348 aggravated assaults in 2002, which works out to one every 35 seconds. Police make arrests in 57 percent of reported cases. Aggravated assault is a very male crime: A large majority of both victims and offenders are young men (U.S. Federal Bureau of Investigation, 2003).

Robbery   Robbery involves both stealing and threatening another person, making this both a property crime and a violent crime. In 2002, there were 420,637 robberies, with one occurring every minute. Since 1991, the trend in the robbery rate has been downward.

Because the victims usually do not know the robbers, this crime is the least likely of all violent offenses to result in an arrest: In 2001, police cleared just 26 percent of robberies. Again, almost all offenders are males, and most are under age twenty-five. Race is also a factor in robbery: In 2002, African Americans accounted for 54 percent of arrests, whites represented 44 percent, and the remaining 1 percent were classified in some other racial category (U.S. Federal Bureau of Investigation, 2003).

What are your chances of becoming a victim of violent crime? National Map 6–1 on page 142 rates the risk of violent crime for counties across the United States.

Property Crime: Patterns and Trends

Law enforcement agencies recorded 10.5 million property crimes in 2002, seven times the number of violent crimes. Nationwide, a property crime occurs every three seconds, with annual losses of $17 billion (U.S. Federal Bureau of Investigation, 2003).

Personal Stories   Rape: Memories That Don't Go Away

DAVID PITTMAN WAS EIGHTEEN THE FIRST TIME he went to jail for robbing a convenience store. A big man (6' 1" tall and 180 pounds), David entered prison thinking he could take care of himself. He was wrong. Within days of being jailed while awaiting his trial, David was gang raped over and over again. He felt ashamed and powerless, and his rage grew. Eighteen years later—and back in jail again—he has joined a therapy group with others who have endured a similar ordeal. The following is based on the story he posted on the Internet in the hope that it might help others.

Prison life is so negative and repressive that prisoners look anywhere to relieve loneliness and despair. Some guys decide it's better to be an abuser than a victim. To them survival and dominance are everything. They get pleasure by dominating and humiliating others. But their victims are traumatized for life.

When I got to jail there were twenty guys in my "tank," which was split into two ten-man "pods." Each pod had five bunks with a day room between them. My first night in jail, three men approached me. Two were about my size; the third was twenty pounds lighter and six inches shorter. They asked what I was in for. I told them, and the biggest guy asked if I had ever been f_____ed. I said, "No, and I'm not planning on it." He said, "We're gonna f_____ you." I was scared out of my mind. I swung at him, but he blocked my punch and his buddy knocked me down. They grabbed me by the hair and slammed my head into the floor, knocking me out.

When I came to, I was on my stomach. They had pulled my pants off and spread my legs wide apart. One guy was sitting on each leg, and the biggest guy was lying on my back. He was slapping me in the face to wake me up. He said, "I want you to feel this." When I was fully conscious, he raped me. I never felt such pain in my life. I tried to get away, but it was no use. It seemed like he took forever. When he was finished, he switched places with another guy. When it was over, all three had raped me. When they were done, they held me in a head lock while they debated whether to kill me. They asked if I was going to snitch. I knew they'd kill me if I said yes, so I said, "No." They threatened to kill me if I said anything. I thought my life was over.

I was completely numb inside. I didn't know what to do. My father always taught me to handle my own problems. Navy boot camp reinforced that lesson. I was from another state and didn't know

a soul in California. I was terrified and filled with shame. I had no choice but to keep my mouth shut. I was paralyzed with fear.

That night the same three guys came to my bunk. I was their "punk" now, and fighting wouldn't do any good. They'd just beat me up worse than before. I was like a robot. I did exactly what they told me to do. I didn't think about it. I just did it. Going along was better than getting killed. After that, other guys started waking me up at night, demanding sex. It was established in the tank that I was a sex toy. I just did what I was told to avoid a beating. I figured I better make the best of things and try to endure it the best I could. Finally, I went to trial. I was found guilty and sent to prison.

In prison, I'd fight anyone at the drop of a hat and got in a lot of trouble. After I got out of prison, I was just as bad on the street. I wasn't going to be anybody's punk again. Today I'm doing life for killing a guy who threatened me. I'm 6' 2" tall and weigh 250 pounds. I'm a power lifter and I run with some of the meanest guys in the joint. None of my friends would believe I'd ever been a punk. It's been eighteen years since that experience in county jail.

Rape is a horrible act, whether it's of a man or a woman. I know the helplessness, shame, guilt, self-doubt, self-blame, and terror. But for me, the greatest fear was that someone I knew would find out. In some ways, male rape is worse than female rape, because men have no one they can talk to. Even my wife laughed at me when I tried to tell her about my experiences. Most guys bottle everything up inside, where it just turns to rage. Male rape probably causes a lot of alcohol and drug abuse, and it's probably led to the murder of men who have threatened a male rape victim.

ISSUES AND EXERCISES

1. Why, in your opinion, does our society do little to combat the problem of rape in prison?
2. What policies can you suggest to address the problem of prison rape?
3. [Research Navigator.com] Use Research Navigator™ to learn more about prison rape. (See instructions on page 25; keyword: "prison rape")

Source: Adapted from Pittman (2001) with permission of Stop Prisoner Rape, Inc.

A NATION OF DIVERSITY

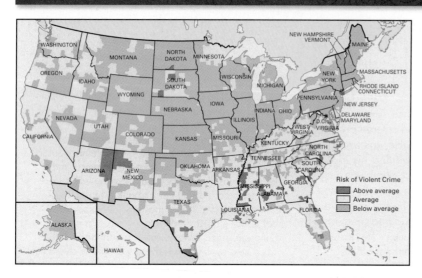

NATIONAL MAP 6–1
The Risk of Violent Crime across the United States

The map shows the risk of falling victim to violent crime—in this case, including murder, rape, and robbery, but not aggravated assault—for all counties across the United States. In most places, the risk is below the national average, suggesting that violent crime is concentrated in certain areas of the country. Can you explain the pattern?

Source: American Demographics, December 2000. © 2000 *American Demographics* magazine. Reprinted by permission.

In most property crimes, the victim never sees the offender. Thus, whereas police make an arrest in about half of reported violent crimes, they clear only 18 percent of property crimes (U.S. Federal Bureau of Investigation, 2003). We now take a brief look at each property crime.

Burglary   Despite a decade-long decline in the burglary rate, police recorded more than 2 million burglaries in 2002. This translates to one crime every fifteen seconds and an annual total property loss of more than $3 billion (the average loss per burglary is about $1,500).

In 2002, police cleared just 13 percent of burglary cases. Of those arrested, 87 percent were male and 63 percent were under the age of twenty-five (U.S. Federal Bureau of Investigation, 2003).

Larceny-Theft   Larceny-theft includes familiar forms of stealing such as shoplifting, pick pocketing, purse-snatching, theft from a motor vehicle, and bicycle theft. Such cases do not involve "breaking and entering," and typically offenders use no force or violence.

Larceny-theft is the most common of all the serious crimes that are tracked by the FBI, accounting for 60 percent of the total. In 2002, the FBI reported 7 million incidents of larceny-theft, which averages one crime every 5 seconds. The larceny-theft rate in 2002 was ten times as high as it was in 1960, despite a recent downward trend. In 2002, the value of lost property from such crimes nationwide

was $4.9 billion (an average loss of about $700 per incident).

In 2002, law enforcement agencies cleared 18 percent of larceny-theft cases. Most of those arrested were male (63 percent), with females making up the rest (37 percent) (U.S. Federal Bureau of Investigation, 2003).

Motor Vehicle Theft   Despite a downward trend in recent years, the number of motor vehicle thefts—including stealing cars, trucks, buses, motorcycles, and snowmobiles—exceeded 1.2 million in 2002. Nationally, one such theft took place every 25 seconds. The FBI reports that losses in 2002 exceeded $8 billion (an average loss of $6,700).

In 2002, police cleared just 14 percent of motor vehicle thefts. Two-thirds of those arrested were under age twenty-five, and 84 percent were males (U.S. Federal Bureau of Investigation, 2003).

Arson   Fire investigators determine whether a suspicious fire was caused by arson. The FBI does not have complete national data on arson, but some studies suggest that as many as 15 million cases of arson may occur annually, a rate that has not changed significantly in recent years. The FBI reports that the average loss in arson cases comes to about $11,000.

In 2002, police cleared 17 percent of known cases of arson. Again, of those arrested, 85 percent were male, and 68 percent were under age twenty-five (U.S. Federal Bureau of Investigation, 2003).

"STREET" CRIME: WHO ARE THE CRIMINALS?

Based on FBI data, we can create a profile of the typical "street criminal" in terms of several important variables: age, gender, social class, race, and ethnicity. Keep in mind that this profile is based not on courtroom convictions but on arrest data.

Age

For all offenses, there is strong link between arrest and youth. Arrest rates for both violent crime and property crime peak in the late teens and decline steadily thereafter. In the United States, people aged fifteen to twenty-four make up just 14 percent of the population, but in 2002 they accounted for 39 percent of arrests for violent crimes and 47 percent of arrests for property crimes. In recent years, young people have been responsible for a rising share of serious crime (U.S. Federal Bureau of Investigation, 2003).

Gender

Men, who make up about half of the general population, accounted for 69 percent of arrests for property crimes in 2002. This means that men are arrested for property crimes more than twice as often as women. For violent crimes, gender plays an even greater role. Men are arrested in 83 percent of cases, five times as often as women.

Women do figure prominently in the arrest data for certain crimes, however, including larceny-theft (37 percent of arrests are of women), fraud (45 percent), embezzlement (50 percent), runaway youth (60 percent), and prostitution (66 percent). Moreover, for all serious crimes the gender gap is narrowing: From 1993 to 2002, the number of arrests of women *increased* 14 percent, whereas the arrests of men *fell* by 6 percent (U.S. Federal Bureau of Investigation, 2003).

Social Class

Because there is no precise way to measure someone's social class, the FBI does not track the class standing of those arrested for serious crime. But sociological research shows that people of lower social position are involved in most arrests for street crime (Braithwhite, 1981; Thornberry & Farnsworth, 1982; Wolfgang, Thornberry, & Figlio, 1987; Reiman, 1998).

Crime and violence are serious problems in many poor neighborhoods. But it is important to remember that most people who live in poor neighborhoods

Larceny-theft—including shoplifting—is the most common of all serious crimes tracked by the FBI. In many cases, stealing is motivated by the "kicks" young people get if they are able to beat the system. Because of the high-tech surveillance equipment used by stores today, the odds of getting caught are high. How do you think courts respond to offenders who claim that their actions were "only a game"?

obey the law. Sociologist Elijah Anderson (1994, 2002) has shown that inner-city neighborhoods contain mostly decent, hard-working families. Most crime is committed by a small number of repeat offenders. Keep in mind also that the link between class and criminality depends on the type of crime we are talking about. If we consider not just street crime but the types of crimes that cause corporations to collapse—such as the case described in the opening to this chapter—our profile of the "common criminal" suddenly includes more rich people.

Race and Ethnicity

Both race and ethnicity are linked to crime rates. With regard to property crime, whites represent 68 percent of all arrests, and African Americans account for 30 percent. In the case of violent crime, whites represent 60 percent of arrests, and African Americans 38 percent. In terms of actual numbers, then, most arrests involve white offenders. But in proportion to their share of the population (12 percent), African Americans are more likely than whites to be arrested (U.S. Federal Bureau of Investigation, 2003).

The plight of African American men in the United States is a serious problem: Blacks are more than five times more likely than whites to spend time in jail (U.S. Bureau of Justice Statistics, 2003). In fact, one study found that one-third of black men between the ages of twenty and twenty-nine were either in jail, on probation (sentenced to spend time under court supervision), or on parole (under court supervision after being released from prison) (The Sentencing Project, 2000).

Why does race play such a large part in the crime picture? First and most important, African Americans have a high poverty rate. Half of all black children grow up in poverty, compared with one in eight white children. For some, such deprivation breeds hostility toward police and other aspects of "the system." As a result, some young people adopt what Anderson calls "the code of the streets," which emphasizes violence as a way to survive in a dangerous society.

The second reason is closely related to the first: Police are more likely to patrol poor neighborhoods, which are disproportionately home to African Americans. Prejudice based on race—and sometimes class—can prompt people to suspect blacks of criminal behavior simply on the basis of skin color (the practice of "racial profiling" discussed in Chapter 3, "Racial and Ethnic Inequality"). Research suggests that such biases lead police to be more quick to arrest African Americans than whites (Holmes et al., 1993; Covington, 1995; Tonry, 1995; Reiman, 1998; Chiricos, McEntire, & Gertz, 2001; Quillian & Pager, 2001).

A third factor involves family patterns. Two-thirds of black children are born to single mothers, compared with one-fourth of white children. Single mothers and single fathers have less time to supervise children, and they earn less money (especially single mothers), which adds to family pressures. For these reasons, children who grow up without fathers are at higher risk for criminality (Kratcoski & Kratcoski, 1986; Popenoe, 1988, 1992, 1993; Piquero, MacDonald, & Parker, 2002).

When considering all these patterns that link crime with race, remember that "street crime" rates focus on offenses more likely to be committed by poor people. When we examine white-collar, corporate, and organized crime, the picture of the typical criminal changes dramatically to include many more white people.

A final racial pattern is that Asian Americans are underrepresented in street crime statistics. Making up 3.6 percent of the population, they figured in just 1.1 percent of all arrests in 2002. This lower criminality is due to higher income levels and also a strong cultural emphasis on family, discipline, and honor, all of which tend to discourage criminal behavior.

OTHER DIMENSIONS OF THE CRIME PROBLEM

Although street crimes command the greatest attention of the U.S. public, there are many additional types of crime. In the following sections, we address problems of juvenile delinquency, hate crimes, white-collar crime, corporate crime, organized crime, and victimless crimes.

Juvenile Delinquency

The discussion so far suggests that young people have a big part in the U.S. crime problem. **Juvenile delinquency** is *the violation of the law by young people* (the precise age varies from state to state but is generally less than eighteen). Any violation of criminal law can lead a court to declare a young person delinquent. In addition, some laws—such as curfews and truancy statutes that require school attendance—apply only to the young. Cases involving children are heard in a *juvenile court*, where the focus is on helping children straighten out rather than simply punishing them. Similarly, imprisonment, when applied in juvenile cases, usually is stipulated only until the legal age of adulthood (typically between eighteen and twenty-one), and the term is served in a juvenile detention center rather than a prison. The assumption here is that, given the will and the opportunity, young people can reform. Thus, the juvenile justice system has an eye toward not just the protection of the community but also the best interests of the young offender.

In cases of serious offenses such as robbery or murder, however, officials may decide to charge a young person as an adult. This means that the suspect is tried in an adult court, sentenced as an adult, held in juvenile detention centers until reaching the legal age of adulthood, and then transferred to an adult prison to serve out the rest of the sentence. U.S.

courts have also sentenced young people to death. In 2001, across the United States, seventy-seven offenders who were seventeen or younger when they committed their crime were on death row awaiting execution (U.S. Bureau of Justice Statistics, 2002).

Hate Crimes

The term *hate crime* did not exist until the mid-1980s, when civil rights groups began campaigning for states to pass laws creating a new category of crime (Jenness & Grattet, 2001). By 2002, forty-three states had passed hate-crime statutes, which mandate additional penalties for offenses if they also meet the criteria of a hate crime. According to the FBI, a **hate crime** is *a criminal offense against a person, property, or society motivated by the offender's bias against a race, religion, disability, sexual orientation, or ethnicity or national origin.*

In 1990, Congress passed the Hate Crime Statistics Act, directing the U.S. Attorney General to collect data from law enforcement agencies about bias-motivated crimes. In 2002, the government recorded 9,462 hate crimes. Figure 6–2 shows that almost half of hate crimes on record (48.8 percent) involve racial bias.

Most hate crimes are not reported. For one thing, many agencies do not record or submit hate-crime data; for another, many victims—particularly gay men and lesbians—are reluctant to report their victimization. Therefore, the true extent of the hate-crime problem is far greater than official statistics indicate.

The odds of becoming a victim of a hate crime are especially high for people with multiple disadvantages, such as gay men of color. Even so, hate crimes can victimize anyone: One recent study found that 25 percent of the hate crimes based on race targeted white people (Jenness & Grattet, 2001).

Debate surrounds hate-crime laws. Critics argue that because crimes such as assault are already illegal, special hate-crime laws are unnecessary. Moreover, because such laws end up punishing offenders for their attitude toward their victims, critics consider such laws a step in the direction of government control over not just what we do but also how we think (Sullivan, 2002). Supporters of hate-crime laws counter that the government must take extra steps to protect categories of people who are targets of hostility and violence. Moreover, they argue, because hate crimes harm not just a single victim but entire communities, they warrant more severe penalties.

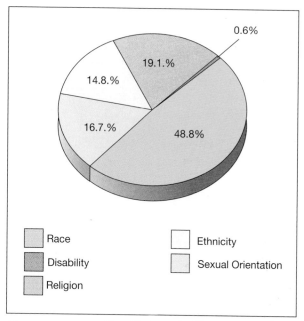

FIGURE 6–2 Bias-Motivated Offenses, 2002

Although the motivations for hate crimes vary, about half of all such crimes express racial bias.

Source: U.S. Federal Bureau of Investigation (2003).

White-Collar Crime

If we were to base our knowledge of crime on television shows like *COPS*, we would think almost every person arrested for a crime was poor. But there is another side to crime that typically involves people who are much more well off. **White-collar crime** refers to *illegal activities committed by people during the course of their employment or regular business activities.* White-collar crime occurs in banks and corporations and often involves important members of a community. As compared with "crime on the streets," then, white-collar crime is better described as "crime in the suites."

Edwin Sutherland (1940), who pioneered the study of white-collar crime, noted that crimes such as fraud (obtaining money under false pretenses) and embezzlement (taking money illegally from one's employer) are far more common than people imagine. Another example of white-collar crime is insider trading, whereby a person uses company information not available to the public to profit (or avoid loss) by buying (or selling) company stock or by advising others to do the same.

Overall, annual losses due to white-collar crime in the United States exceed $100 billion, not to mention billions more spent for security products and

The arrest and prosecution of a number of corporate executives following the recent corporate accounting scandals reminds us that criminals are found at all class levels within U.S. society.

services to protect individuals and businesses from such crimes. Some analysts claim that white-collar offenses represent the biggest share—in terms of dollars—of the U.S. crime problem (Cunningham, Strauchs, & Van Meter, 1990; Reiman, 1998).

Sutherland pointed out more than sixty years ago that the public usually pays little attention to white-collar offenses. Moreover, such cases usually are heard in a civil court rather than a criminal court. Therefore, the person may have to pay damages but is not labeled a criminal. When white-collar offenders do face criminal charges, jail time is far from certain. One study showed that just 55 percent of embezzlers convicted in the U.S. District Court system received any jail time at all; the remainder were fined or placed on probation, requiring them to report regularly to a court official (U.S. Bureau of Justice Statistics, 2002). However, because of recent corporate scandals such as the one described in the opening to this chapter, attitudes toward white-collar crime are growing more critical, and the odds of offenders going to jail are rising.

Corporate Crime

Business crime can involve not only the actions of individuals but the policies and actions of entire companies. **Corporate crime** is an *illegal act committed by a corporation or others acting on its behalf.* One example of corporate crime is *gross negligence:* knowingly producing faulty or dangerous products. In one well-known case from the 1970s, Ford Motor Company continued to produce the subcompact Pinto automobile despite knowledge that its gas tank could explode in a rear-end collision. Even after deadly accidents took place, Ford refused to support a recall that would have saved lives, deciding it would be cheaper to pay the legal claims that would result from future accidents. Eventually, lawsuits and public demands forced the recall and brought an end to the Pinto (Kitman, 2003).

One individual who has done a great deal to raise public awareness of wrongdoing by corporations is Ralph Nader. The Defining Moment box profiles Nader's career.

Read more about the life and work of Ralph Nader at **http://www.nader.org**

As noted at the beginning of this chapter, law enforcement officials recently have charged a number of corporate leaders with corporate crimes including accounting fraud, misleading of investors, and other wrongdoings. The collapse of companies such as Enron, Tyco, and WorldCom has led to the layoffs and loss of pension funds of tens of thousands of workers as well as financial losses to millions of investors. In 2001, Enron corporation employees and stockholders lost approximately $50 billion, more than three times the nation's loss that year from all the property crimes (burglary, larceny-theft, motor vehicle theft, and arson) described earlier in this chapter (Lavella, 2002). A handful of Enron executives have since been charged with crimes, the penalty for which, in at least one case, would involve years in jail. Prosecutions are likely to continue for several years.

Organized Crime

Organized crime is *a business operation that supplies illegal goods and services.* Such businesses profit from selling goods and services that people want—including gambling, sex, or drugs—but that are in violation of the law.

Organized crime has a long and violent history in the United States, beginning in the early twentieth century. During Prohibition (from 1919 to 1933), when the government outlawed the manufacture and

A DEFINING MOMENT

Ralph Nader: Making Corporations More Accountable

Ralph Nader has had a long career as a lawyer, consumer advocate, and presidential candidate.

TODAY, MOST PEOPLE KNOW RALPH NADER as the unsuccessful presidential candidate of the Green Party in the 2000 election. But Nader first walked on to the public stage in 1963, when he left his law practice, hitchhiked to Washington, D.C., and began a career as a consumer advocate and political activist.

Nader gained national attention when he charged that the U.S. automobile industry was building cars with little concern for public safety and in the process was contributing to tens of thousands of highway deaths each year. His book *Unsafe at Any Speed* was an important wake-up call that helped mobilize the consumer rights movement, which sought to make corporations accountable to consumers.

Nader has targeted a wide range of industries, from Maine's paper mills (for causing environmental pollution) to West Virginia's coal mines (for hazards to workers) to the hot dog industry (for using unhealthy ingredients). Over the course of his forty years in public life, he has helped to found dozens of organizations (nicknamed by the press "Nader's raiders") that seek to make large corporations more accountable for their actions and more responsive to the public interest.

---

sale of alcoholic beverages, the Mafia or *La Cosa Nostra* (Italian for "our thing") gained both wealth and power by making and distributing liquor to an eager public. Criminal gangs often used violence to force legitimate businesses to deal with them, to intimidate law enforcement officials, and to kill members of opposing gangs.

The Mafia became a huge business enterprise, demanding absolute loyalty from members. The Mafia code of conduct (*omerta*) gives control of the business to the crime boss and calls on underlings to do almost anything the boss orders.

In the fight against organized crime, in 1970 Congress passed the Racketeer Influenced and Corrupt Organization Act (RICO). The law gives police the authority to seize property such as cars or homes used in the commission of crimes such as gambling, prostitution, loan sharking, narcotics, and labor racketeering.

Today, organized crime has become an international problem. The Global Perspective box on page 148 takes a closer look.

Victimless Crime

Victimless crimes are *offenses that directly harm no one but the person who commits them*. Sometimes called *public order crimes*, victimless crime includes gambling, prostitution, public drunkenness, drug use, and vagrancy. Laws prohibit such activities mostly because they violate widespread norms and values, although few who engage in these activities think of them as criminal. Still, these crimes can and do cause harm. A large share of prostitutes encounter violence at the hands of clients or pimps, just as many "johns" who visit prostitutes contract a sexually transmitted disease that they pass on to their wives or others (Jenness, 1993).

Laws regulating victimless crime vary from place to place. Gambling is legal in certain places in eleven states and on Native American reservations in twenty-nine states, prostitution is legal in parts of rural Nevada, and use of marijuana is legal in a few communities on the East and West coasts. But in most places, the enforcement of laws banning

A Global Perspective — Organized Crime: All over the World

THE WORLD IS BECOMING ONE VAST MARKETPLACE, with multinational corporations doing business almost everywhere. Organized crime, too, has "gone global," raking in profits that the early gangsters of Chicago or New York could never have imagined.

Organized crime's major activity is drug trafficking, which generates tens of billions of dollars annually, making some drug gangs richer than many countries. Gangs also carry out acts of terrorism, sell weapons, engage in murder-for-hire, smuggle illegal immigrants, counterfeit money, and illegally copy and sell compact discs and computer software.

Organized crime operates in most parts of the world. From their bases in Colombia, drug cartels control 75 percent of the global cocaine production and work with other criminal organizations from the United States to China.

The Russian *mafiya* deals in arms trafficking, car theft, extortion, murder for hire, money laundering, the manufacture and sale of illegal drugs, and even human slavery. Since the collapse of the Soviet Union in 1991, Russian crime organizations have expanded and have linked with criminal organizations around the world.

China's Six Great Triads are centuries-old organizations; today, with more than 100,000 members, they are the world's largest criminal organizations. Working in Chinese communities in many countries, the Triads deal in drugs, weapons, and stolen cars. They smuggle illegal migrants, pirate electronics and software, and profit from gambling, loan sharking, prostitution, and pornography. Japan, too, has a vast organization: The 60,000 member *Yakuza* engages in the same wide range of criminal activities.

These organizations affect the United States by smuggling guns, illegal migrants and drugs across the border. In addition, bootlegged software, videos, books, and compact discs cost U.S. businesses billions of dollars annually in lost income. Moreover, great wealth gives organized crime the means to bribe public officials. All in all, many experts consider global organized crime a serious threat to the security of the United States.

ISSUES AND EXERCISES

1. Do you think criminal organizations simply meet a demand, or are they a real threat to the United States? Why?
2. What actions—both here and abroad—should the United States take to combat organized crime?
3. [Research Navigator.com] Use Research Navigator™ to learn more about organized crime. (See instructions on page 25; keyword: "organized crime")

Sources: Based on Sullivan (1996) and Valdez (1997).

---

victimless crimes is far from consistent; it usually amounts to occasional crackdowns.

THE CRIMINAL JUSTICE SYSTEM

The **criminal justice system** is *society's organized means to enforce the law through the use of police, courts, and prisons.* In the following sections, we briefly survey the U.S. criminal justice system.

Due Process

The Constitution states that U.S. society must respond to crime using *due process;* that is, the criminal justice system must operate within the bounds of law. No person, the Constitution states, can be "deprived of life, liberty, or property without due process of law." In part, this means that if you are charged with a crime you have a right to defend yourself and to confront your accusers; you have a right to legal counsel and a speedy, impartial, and public trial, with a jury if desired; you can refuse to testify against yourself; and you cannot be tried twice for the same crime. Furthermore, the Constitution gives all people protection against excessive bail as well as protection against cruel and unusual punishment if found guilty (Inciardi, 2000).

Read the U.S. Bill of Rights at this Web site:
**http://www.archives.gov/exhibit_hall/charters_of_freedoms/
bill_of_rights/bill_of_rights.html**

Police

The United States has about 665,000 police officers (U.S. Federal Bureau of Investigation, 2003). Still, even this many officers cannot monitor the actions of 290 million people. Therefore, police have to make decisions which situations are serious enough to warrant their attention. In a study of police discretion in five cities, Douglas Smith and Christy Visher (1981; Smith, 1987) noted six factors that guided police in deciding whether to make an arrest:

1. **How serious is the crime?** The more serious a situation seems, the more likely police are to make an arrest.

2. **What does the victim want?** If a victim demands that an arrest be made, police are more likely to do so.

3. **Is the suspect cooperative?** Police are more likely to arrest an uncooperative suspect.

4. **Does the suspect have a record?** Police are more likely to arrest someone they know has been arrested before.

5. **Are bystanders watching?** Police are more likely to make an arrest when people are watching. This gives police more control by moving the situation off the street.

6. **What is the suspect's race?** Smith and Visher argue that, all other factors being equal, police are more likely to arrest African American and Hispanic suspects than whites.

Two recent changes in police work are thought to have contributed to the recent downturn in crime rates in U.S. cities. First, the practice of community policing makes police more visible, as some officers have moved from cars to riding bicycles or patrolling on foot. The idea is for officers to get to know local neighborhoods and work with citizens to prevent crime. A second innovation is a zero-tolerance policy by which police are instructed to respond to any offense, no matter how minor. In recent years, New York City police began ticketing or arresting people for urinating in public, jumping subway turnstiles, and jaywalking. Supporters claim that this approach deters crime because fewer people will risk carrying a weapon, knowing that any minor infraction may cause police to stop and search them. Critics, however, counter that this policy causes police to waste time harassing law-abiding people instead of concentrating on solving major crimes.

Recent debate has centered on the practice of "racial profiling," by which police are more likely to stop and investigate African Americans than white people. Some police, in other words, consider skin color to be a clue as to whether a person is a criminal or not. If you were a chief of police, what action would you take to address this issue? Why?

Courts

Approximately half of suspects arrested are later released for lack of evidence, and half are charged and tried in a court of law. In principle, the U.S. court system is *adversarial process* by which the prosecutor presents the state's case against the suspect and the suspect's attorney presents a defense.

But the reality of justice often is altogether different. About 90 percent of cases are settled through **plea bargaining,** *a negotiation in which the state reduces a defendant's charge in exchange for a guilty plea.* Plea bargaining saves the time and expense of a trial, allowing courts to focus on the most serious cases. But efficiency may not mean justice. A public defender is provided by law to all defendants who are unable to pay for a lawyer themselves. But, because public defenders usually are young lawyers with limited experience, who are overworked and underpaid,

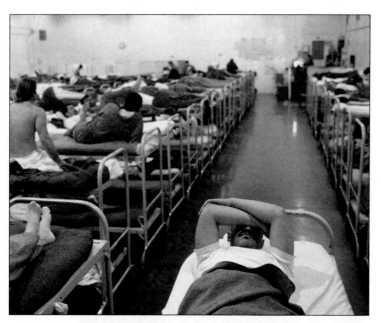

In recent years, the United States has imprisoned record numbers of people with the goal of controlling the crime problem. What arguments can you point to in support of this policy? On balance, do you think this policy works or not? Why?

they are often eager to resolve a case quickly. As a result, low-income defendants often feel that they have little choice but to plea bargain, also known as "copping a plea." (Novak, 1999). The problem with plea bargaining is that overuse of it threatens the principle of due process by undercutting the Constitutional right to a trial in which a defendant is presumed innocent until proven guilty.

Punishment

Currently, more than 2 million people are incarcerated in the United States (U.S. Bureau of Justice Statistics, 2003). The criminal justice system can enforce a range of punishment, ranging from fines, to jail time, to death. But how is the crime problem solved by punishment? There are four answers to this question: retribution, deterrence, rehabilitation, and societal protection.

Retribution The oldest reason to punish is a sense of revenge. **Retribution** is *moral vengeance by which society inflicts suffering on an offender comparable to that caused by the offense*. Retribution is based on the idea that the moral order of society is upset by crime. But this order can be restored by declaring the offender

guilty and exacting a punishment fitting the crime. The biblical dictum "an eye for an eye" expresses this vision of justice.

Deterrence A second reason to punish is **deterrence**, *using punishment to discourage further crime*. Deterrence is a more modern idea, emerging as the eighteenth-century Enlightenment portrayed people as rational decision makers. If society ensures that the pain of punishment will outweigh the pleasure of the offense, people will realize that "crime does not pay."

Punishment provides *specific deterrence* on an individual level by convincing the offender to avoid future crime. At the same time, it provides *general deterrence* by teaching everyone a lesson about what happens to people who break the law. For deterrence to work, of course, people must believe that there is a strong chance that offenders will be caught (which, at least in the case of property crimes, is not the case in the United States today).

Rehabilitation A third reason to punish is **rehabilitation**, *reforming the offender to prevent future offenses*. The idea of rehabilitation developed in the nineteenth century along with the social sciences. The idea here is that if a bad environment pushes people toward crime, rehabilitation programs can turn them back into law-abiding citizens.

Rehabilitation differs from retribution and deterrence in its positive character: helping people improve rather than making them suffer. Rehabilitation also differs in another way: Whereas retribution and deterrence demand that the punishment fit the crime, rehabilitation means tailoring treatment to the needs of a specific offender.

Societal Protection The fourth reason for punishment is **societal protection**, *protecting the public by rendering an offender incapable of further offenses through incarceration or by execution*. For the last decade, the United States has been building prisons at the rate of a new 1,000-bed facility every week. Few doubt that the growing number of people in prisons has played a part in bringing down the crime rate (Johnson, 2000).

Does Punishment Work? Is punishment a solution to the crime problem? The answer is far from clear. Retribution is based on Durkheim's insight that, by responding to crime, a society strengthens public morality. Yet some argue that punishment—especially the death penalty—further brutalizes a society already fraught with violence.

A WORLD OF DIFFERENCES

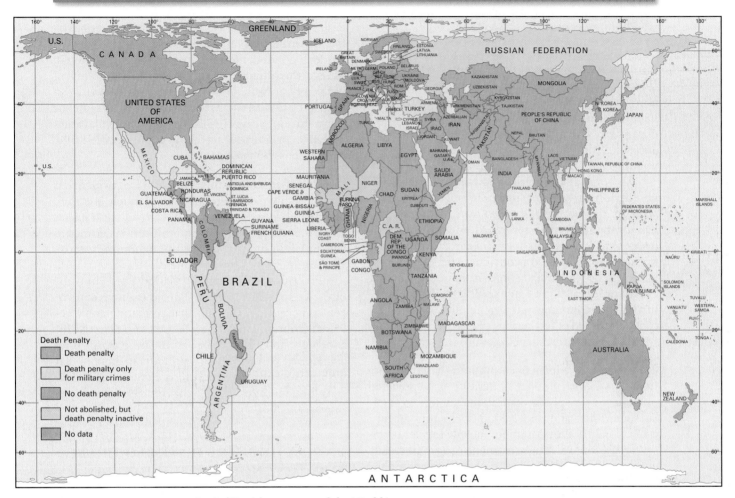

GLOBAL MAP 6–1   Capital Punishment around the World

This map shows the eighty-four countries and territories in which the law provides for the death penalty for ordinary crimes; in fifteen other countries, the death penalty is reserved for special crimes under military law or during times or war. In twenty more, the death penalty is on the books but has not been used for at least ten years. There is no death penalty in seventy-four countries and territories. Looking at the map, what general patterns do you see? In what way do the United States and Japan stand out?

Source: Amnesty International Website against the Death Penalty. Available August 27, 2003, at http://web.amnesty.org/pages/deathpenalty-countries-eng

Deterrence, too, is controversial. Although common sense suggests that punishment discourages crime, this country has a high rate of **criminal recidivism,** *subsequent offenses by people previously convicted of crimes.* A recent government study reported that two-thirds of state prison inmates released from jail in 1994 were rearrested for a serious crime within three years (U.S. Department of Justice, 2002). Such data cast doubt on the idea that putting people in prison deters further crime. Indeed, some critics argue that by stigmatizing inmates and allowing them to share their knowledge with one another, prisons may actually make further crime more likely (McNulty, 1994; Wright, 1994; Petersilia, 1997; DeFina & Arvanites, 2002).

What about rehabilitation? Again, prison may help some offenders "straighten out." But the high recidivism rate suggests that successful rehabilitation is the exception rather than the rule.

In recent years, the greatest debate concerning punishment has centered on the death penalty. As Global Map 6–1 shows, the United States is one of the few high-income nations in the world that puts convicted offenders to death. The Social Policy box takes a closer look at the recent controversy over whether innocent people may be executed.

Community-Based Corrections

Prisons keep convicted criminals off the streets. But as we have already explained, they may do little to rehabilitate most offenders. Furthermore, prisons are expensive: The cost of maintaining one inmate is about $25,000 per year (not including the cost of building the prison in the first place).

An alternative to prison is **community-based corrections,** *correctional programs located in society at large rather than behind prison walls.* Community-based corrections have several advantages, including lower cost, a reduction in prison overcrowding, and the ability to supervise a convicted offender without applying the stigma that comes from imprisonment. However, because this approach lets offenders remain in the community, it is generally used only for those convicted of less serious crimes who seem likely to avoid future criminal violations (Inciardi, 2000).

Probation   One form of community-based corrections is *probation,* a policy of permitting a convicted offender to stay in the community subject to regular supervision and under conditions imposed by a court. These conditions might include regular counseling sessions, a drug treatment program, steady employment, and avoidance of known criminals. Should the probationer fail to meet regularly with the probation officer, fail to comply with other conditions set by the court, or commit another crime, the court may end probation and send the offender to prison.

Shock Probation   A related strategy is *shock probation,* by which a judge sentences a convicted offender to prison for a substantial length of time but then explains that only a portion of the sentence will be served in actual incarceration, with the remainder to be served on probation. Shock probation is thus a mix of prison and probation that impresses on the offender the seriousness of the situation without a long prison term. In some cases, shock probation takes place in a special "boot camp" facility, where offenders might spend several months in a military-style setting intended to teach discipline and respect for authority (Cole & Smith, 2002).

Parole   *Parole* is a policy of releasing inmates from prison to serve the remainder of their sentences in the local community under supervision. Most inmates become eligible for parole after serving a specified portion of a sentence. At this time, a parole board evaluates the offender's chances of staying out of trouble; if parole is granted, the court monitors the offender's conduct until the sentence is completed. Should the offender not comply with conditions of parole or be arrested for another crime, the board can return the person to prison to complete the sentence there. In some cases (usually serious crimes), courts sentence an offender to prison for a specified time without possibility of parole.

Do Probation and Parole Work?   The evidence is mixed. Probation and parole cost much less than prison and do reduce prison overcrowding. It makes sense to send people who commit serious crimes to prison while monitoring in the community those who commit less serious crimes.

Probation and shock probation do seem to be effective for some people. Parole is more controversial because of the fact that so many people released from prison on parole are soon arrested for another crime. For this reason, some states have abandoned parole. Yet this policy remains popular with prison officials because the chance to be released encourages good behavior among inmates (Inciardi, 2000).

EXPLAINING CRIME: BIOLOGICAL AND PSYCHOLOGICAL THEORIES

Having examined various kinds of crimes, we now turn to a basic question: Why does crime exist at all? In the following sections, we first review biological and psychological theories and then turn to sociological explanations.

Biological Causes

In the nineteenth century, an Italian doctor named Cesare Lombroso (1876) came up with the idea that criminals were physically different from law-abiding people. Studying the physical features of men in prison, Lombroso pointed to several distinctive traits: low foreheads, prominent jaws and cheekbones, protruding ears, excessive hairiness, and unusually long arms. Putting these traits together, Lombroso concluded that criminals appeared apelike. But Lombroso's work was flawed. He failed to see that the physical traits he found among prisoners were just as likely to be found in the general population.

Social Policy   The Death Penalty: Is Justice Served?

EARLY IN 2000, GOVERNOR GEORGE RYAN OF Illinois made the startling announcement that his state would stop all executions until officials could ensure that no innocent people would be put to death. Ryan had good reason for concern: Between 1987 and 2000, thirteen inmates in his state were released from death row after courts reviewed their cases and declared them to be innocent. Ryan, a long-time supporter of the death penalty, concluded that Illinois "had a shameful record of convicting innocent people and placing them on death row." So deep was Governor Ryan's concern about the possibility of executing innocent people that before he left office in January 2003, he commuted the sentences of all 167 inmates on death row in Illinois to life in prison (Babwin, 2003; Levine, 2003).

The death penalty controversy quickly spread to all thirty-eight states with death penalty laws on the books. Nationwide, between 1973 and 2003, almost two thousand people have had their death sentences overturned by the courts, including people found to have been innocent all along (U.S. Bureau of Justice Statistics, 2003). National Map 6–2 shows where the more than 3,500 people throughout the country await execution.

A majority of U.S. adults support the death penalty in cases of very serious crime. Supporters argue that the death penalty is rare—in less than 1 percent of murder cases is a convicted offender executed—but is a just response to the most serious crimes. Critics counter that there is little evidence that the death penalty deters crime. Even more important, there is mounting evidence that people—especially the poor, who rely on public defenders—are being sentenced to death despite being innocent. In light of the evidence that errors do occur, the question remains: Does the death penalty serve justice?

ISSUES AND EXERCISES

1. Does the fact that we live in an imperfect world—in which juries can make mistakes—mean there should be no death penalty (a penalty that, once inflicted, cannot be withdrawn)? Why or why not?

2. Does the policy of providing defendants with public defenders ensure legal protection for all (as originally intended) or perpetuate "second-class justice" for the poor? Explain your answer.

3. **Research Navigator.com** Use Research Navigator™ to learn more about the death penalty. (See instructions on page 25; keywords: "capital punishment," "death penalty")

Source: U.S. Bureau of Justice Statistics (2003).

A NATION OF DIVERSITY

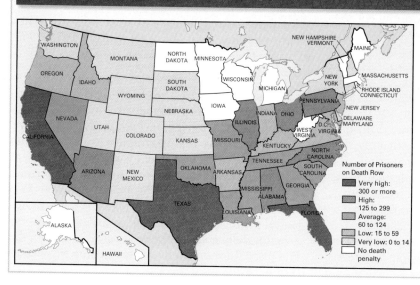

NATIONAL MAP 6–2

Inmates on Death Row across the United States

In the United States, thirty-eight states have laws permitting the death penalty. But some states apply these laws frequently, and others do not. For this reason, half of all prisoners on death row are in just five states. What regional pattern do you see for states that have condemned the most people? Can you explain the pattern?

Source: U.S. Bureau of Justice Statistics (2000).

Number of Prisoners on Death Row

Very high: 300 or more
High: 125 to 299
Average: 60 to 124
Low: 15 to 59
Very low: 0 to 14
No death penalty

According to Emile Durkheim, one of the key functions of crime is bringing people together with a shared sense of outrage. Can you think of such a case that might have taken place on your campus?

Still, biological research continued. In the mid-twentieth century, William Sheldon (1949) examined the body types of hundreds of young men, some criminal, some not. Sheldon found that men with athletic builds (*mesomorphs*) were more likely to be criminals than fat, round people (*endomorphs*) or thin, wiry people (*ectomorphs*). These results were later confirmed by Sheldon Glueck and Eleanor Glueck (1950). But the Gluecks cautioned that a muscular build may not be the *cause* of criminal behavior. A more likely explanation, they thought, was that athletic boys become more independent. With more emotional distance from parents and others, perhaps muscular boys grow up less sensitive to others. The Gluecks also pointed out that people may expect muscular boys to act like bullies and treat them accordingly, creating a self-fulfilling prophecy that accounts for a higher rate of criminal behavior.

By the 1960s, researchers began looking for a link between genetics and criminal behavior. An interesting finding is that men with an extra Y chromosome (XYY, a rare pattern compared with the normal XY pattern) may have a greater chance of becoming criminals (Taylor, 1984; LaFree, 1998). But the evidence linking criminality to any specific genetic trait is far from conclusive.

Critical evaluation.   Biological theories have yet to show that they can explain criminality. What is more likely is that genes, together with social influences, will eventually explain some types of criminality. At best, most researchers think, biological factors may turn out to have a small effect on criminal behavior (Wilson & Herrnstein, 1985; Brennan, Mednick, & Volavka, 1995; Pallone & Hennessy, 1998). A major problem with this approach is that most people convicted of crimes turn out to be biologically just like the rest of us.

Psychological Causes

Like biological research, psychological study of crime focuses on individual traits—in this case, abnormal personalities. Walter Reckless and Simon Dinitz explain delinquency in terms of a boy's degree of moral conscience. These researchers began by asking teachers to identify twelve-year-old male students who were likely to get in trouble with the law and those who were not. They then interviewed all the boys and their mothers, trying to assess the boys' personalities and how they related to others. They found that the boys whom the teachers had identified as nondelinquent had a more positive self-concept and a stronger conscience; that is, they held to conventional norms and values and could handle frustration without becoming angry or violent. By contrast, the boys whom the teachers thought were prone to delinquency had weak belief in conventional norms and values and reacted angrily when frustrated (Reckless, Dinitz, & Murray, 1956, 1957; Dinitz, Scarpitti, & Reckless, 1962; Reckless & Dinitz, 1972; Reckless, 1973).

Critical evaluation.   Social workers and law enforcement officers give much attention to psychological theories. Indeed, few doubt that personality traits play a part in encouraging or discouraging criminality. But one problem with this approach, as with biological theories, is that many serious crimes are committed by people who are quite normal (Vito & Holmes, 1994). A second problem is that psychological theories focus on the individual, ignoring why a society defines some people as rule-breakers in the first place. In short, to understand crime we need to turn to sociological theories.

EXPLAINING CRIME: SOCIOLOGICAL THEORIES

According to the sociological approach, the organization of society itself gives rise to certain laws and certain patterns of criminality. The following discussions apply sociology's three major theoretical approaches to the issue of crime.

Structural-Functional Analysis: How Society Creates Crime

The structural-functionalist approach highlights the importance of any social pattern to the operation of society as a system. Four notable theories of crime use this approach.

Emile Durkheim: The Functions of Crime

Emile Durkheim (1964a, orig. 1895; 1964b, orig. 1893), one of the first great sociologists, began his study of crime by pointing out that it exists everywhere. If so, he reasoned, crime must somehow be useful to society. He went on to identify four functions of crime:

1. **Crime affirms a society's norms and values.** People cannot have a belief in what is good without having a corresponding belief in what is bad. In short, societies must recognize crime as they go about upholding a sense of morality.

2. **Recognizing crime helps everyone clarify the line between right and wrong.** When a college convicts a student of cheating, that community is educating everyone about behavior that will not be tolerated.

3. **Reacting to crime brings people together.** When someone in a neighborhood is victimized by crime, others are likely to share a sense of outrage.

4. **Crime encourages social change.** Deviant members of a community suggest alternatives to the status quo. What people condemn at one point in time (whether it is rock and roll music or use of a particular drug) may end up being the norm later on.

Notice how Durkheim's theory shifts the focus, asking not why some individual would engage in crime but why society must recognize some behavior as criminal. This insight explains the pattern noted earlier, that most people who are defined as criminals are quite normal. Indeed, as Durkheim concluded, crime is a normal part of society.

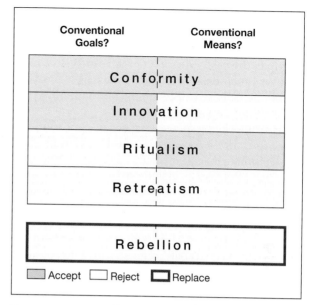

FIGURE 6–3 Merton's Strain Theory of Deviance

Source: Merton (1968).

Robert Merton: Strain Theory

Robert Merton (1938, 1968) agrees that crime is a product of society itself. His theory explains why rule-breaking takes various forms. Merton begins by saying that society defines being successful in terms of certain goals (such as financial security) but does not always provide the means (including schooling and good jobs) to reach these goals. Therefore, Merton continues, patterns of rule-breaking depend on whether people accept society's goals and whether they have the opportunity to reach them. Merton identified five specific outcomes shown in Figure 6–3.

Conformity is likely when people accept society's goals and have the approved means to get there. But what if legitimate means to success are not available? Children growing up in Appalachia, for example, may see how the rich live on television but then find that their communities offer few good jobs. As a result of the strain between cultural goals and limited means to achieve them, people may engage in what Merton calls *innovation*, the use of unconventional means to achieve a conventional goal. For example, some poor people in the Appalachian region have turned to growing marijuana to make a living. Many property crimes can be explained in this way.

Another option for people who lack legitimate means to achieve success is *ritualism*, which Merton defined as living almost obsessively by the rules. Doing this does not bring great success, but it does offer some measure of respectability. A ritualist—for example, the clerk who takes exactly forty-five minutes for lunch every day and never makes personal telephone calls at work—might not be highly paid but is proud of playing by the rules.

Still another response to a lack of opportunity is *retreatism*, turning away from both approved goals and legitimate means; in effect, retreatists "drop out" of society. Retreatists include some alcoholics, drug addicts, street people, and backwoods survivalists.

Finally, *rebellion* involves not just rejecting conventional goals and means but also advocating some new system. Instead of dropping out of society the way retreatists do, rebels come up with a new system, playing out their ideas as religious zealots, political terrorists, or revolutionaries.

Richard Cloward and Lloyd Ohlin: Opportunity Structure
Richard Cloward and Lloyd Ohlin (1966) extended Merton's theory, arguing that whether or not one becomes a criminal depends not only on the lack of legitimate opportunity (such as schooling or jobs) but also on the presence of illegitimate opportunity. In other words, people cut off from conventional opportunity are likely to engage in crime only if they have opportunities to do so. In short, patterns of conformity and criminality depend on what Cloward and Ohlin call people's *relative opportunity structure*.

Among people who have little (legitimate) opportunity to get to college but who do have (illegitimate) opportunity to make money through, say, prostitution or drug dealing, criminality is likely. People who are cut off from both legitimate and illegitimate opportunity may express their frustration through violence.

Travis Hirschi: Control Theory
Perhaps the best-known theory of crime is Travis Hirschi's *control theory*. Hirschi (1969) argues that what discourages crime is social ties, that is, connections to others. Hirschi points out four kinds of social ties that operate to control crime:

1. **Attachment to other people,** especially parents but also teachers, coaches, and friends

2. **Commitment to conformity,** a belief that playing by the rules pays off in the long run

3. **Involvement in conventional activities,** including team sports or religious groups

4. **A belief in the rightness of cultural norms and values,** which leads one to think that society is basically good

If these four kinds of social ties are strong, people are likely to resist the temptation of crime. To the extent that they are weak, the risk of criminality rises.

Critical evaluation. The strength of structural-functional theories lies in showing, first, that the consequences of crime are good as well as bad. In addition, this approach explains that crime cannot be understood simply by looking at individuals; on the contrary, the organization of society itself causes criminality.

At the same time, these theories have limitations. Durkheim may be right about crime being necessary, but at what level? Similarly, looking at Merton's theory, not everyone defines "success" in the same way or agrees on the "right" and "wrong" ways to get there. Cloward and Ohlin's theory seems unable to explain white-collar offenses committed by people who already have so much going for them. Finally, although Hirschi's theory is supported by other research (cf. Langbein & Bess, 2002), it says little about how and why society defines some people who break the law as criminal while ignoring others. We turn now to symbolic-interaction theories, which address this last point.

Symbolic-Interaction Analysis: Socially Constructing Reality

Symbolic-interaction analysis examines how people construct reality in their everyday interactions. From this point of view, people learn criminal behavior as they learn everything else: from their surroundings. In addition, what becomes a crime and who becomes a criminal result from a process of social definition that may vary from time to time and from place to place.

Edwin Sutherland: Differential Association Theory
Edwin Sutherland (1940) pointed out that learning takes place in social groups. Therefore, he continued, whether a person moves toward conformity or deviance depends on the extent of contact with others who encourage, and those who discourage, conventional behavior. This is Sutherland's theory of *differential association*.

For example, take the use of alcohol and other drugs by young adults in the United States. Researchers studying why high school students started using various drugs discovered a close connection between drug use and the degree to which students' peer groups encouraged such activity. The young people most likely to become regular drug consumers were those whose friends defined this behavior in positive rather than negative terms (Akers et al., 1979).

Howard S. Becker: Labeling Theory When does behavior "cross the line"? Howard S. Becker (1966:9) states that the only real definition of rule-breaking is "behavior that people so label." **Labeling theory** is *the assertion that crime and all other forms of rule-breaking result not so much from what people do as from how others respond to those actions.* In other words, no action is right or wrong in any absolute sense. Take the case of consuming alcohol: Is drinking likely to get a teenager into trouble? The answer depends on any number of factors, including whether anyone saw it; if so, how the observer defined it (taking into account *when* the drinking took place, *where* it took place, and *who* was doing the drinking); and whether the observer decided to do anything about it.

Labeling theory states that the "reality" of drinking, taking something that belongs to someone else, or any other behavior is a matter of how people label that behavior. Crime turns out to be a matter of socially constructed reality, a highly variable process of detection, definition, and response. From Becker's point of view, the line separating crime from conformity is both thin and ever-changing.

Edwin Lemert: Primary and Secondary Deviance Edwin Lemert (1951, 1972) explored how individuals can be changed by the labels others apply to them. To begin, many norm violations—skipping school, underage drinking, experimenting with drugs—bring little reaction from others. Lemert refers to these incidents, which may have only passing significance, as *primary* acts of deviance.

But what if minor norm violations are defined as important? People might define a young man who tries an illegal drug as a "user" and keep their distance from him. Or a young woman who has a love affair might find herself defined as "easy" by others on campus. Such reactions often provoke confusion and anger and may have long-term consequences, such as the loss of friends. The person may then seek the company of people who are more accepting, who perhaps have experienced rejection for similar behavior themselves. In this way, the reaction of others to *primary* deviance can provoke *secondary* deviance in

A criminal trial has been described as a public "degradation ceremony" in which a person receives the powerful stigma of being a criminal. Why do you think society goes to such lengths to impose such labels on those convicted of crime? Once people have paid the price for their crime and are released from prison, why is there no ceremony to declare them "redeemed"?

which the person begins to change, taking on a deviant identity.

Erving Goffman: The Power of Stigma Growing up, we hear people say, "Sticks and stones can break your bones, but names can never hurt you." Erving Goffman (1963), for one, disagrees. Calling someone a "criminal" can be a form of **stigma,** *a powerful negative social label that radically changes a person's self-concept and social identity.* Once stigmatized, a person may find that friends and legitimate opportunities begin to disappear. In some cases, being stigmatized by others may launch a person on what sociologists call a *deviant career,* marked by an increasing identity and deeper involvement in rule-breaking behavior.

Criminal prosecution is a powerful ritual that stigmatizes a person. The person stands before the community, a prosecutor states the case against the person, and if he or she is found guilty, a judge or jury may well declare the person unfit to remain in society. The stigma attached by this "degradation ceremony" may be very hard to lose (Garfinkel, 1956). How do people feel about someone who they learn is an "ex-con?"

Critical evaluation. Symbolic-interaction theories help us to understand how people may come to define certain criminal behavior in positive terms and how some people end up defined as "criminal" by others. In short, the reality of crime is socially constructed.

Even so, there is little disagreement that some behavior—such as intentionally killing another—is a serious crime. Labeling theory therefore may best be applied to milder offenses such as drug use or prostitution. Another problem is that by making crime seem highly relative, symbolic-interaction theory misses the fact that some categories of people are always at higher risk of being called "criminal." This concern brings us to the third theoretical approach: social-conflict theory.

Social-Conflict Analysis: Crime and Inequality

The social-conflict approach highlights how social inequality shapes who and what is defined as "criminal." How laws are written, which neighborhoods police patrol, who ends up being arrested—all these reflect who has power and who does not.

Karl Marx: Class and Crime Karl Marx understood social problems in terms of class conflict. He believed that in a capitalist society, the legal system protects the property of the capitalist class. Capitalists gain wealth legally by "doing business"; ordinary people who threaten capitalists' wealth risk arrest as "political revolutionaries" or "common criminals." Furthermore, with little wealth of their own, some members of the working class turn to crime in order to survive (Spitzer, 1980).

From a Marxist point of view, then, the solution to the crime problem is to eliminate capitalism in favor of a more egalitarian system that serves the interests of everyone (McClellan, 1985; Vito & Holmes, 1994).

Feminist Theory: Gender and Crime As Chapter 4 ("Gender Inequality") explains, gender stratification is the pattern by which men have power over women. Feminists argue that gender stratification is also evident in patterns of crime.

All feminists agree that U.S. society subordinates women to men. Therefore, as second-class citizens, many women look to crime, including fraud, drug dealing, and prostitution, to increase their opportunity to make a living. To support their position, feminists point out that when law enforcement officials combat crimes such as prostitution, they are far more likely to arrest women (working as prostitutes) than

men (who also break the law as their clients) (Daly & Chesney-Lind, 1988; Simpson, 1989; Jenness, 1993). Some feminists—especially socialist feminists who support the ideas of Karl Marx—argue that capitalism exploits both men and women, who must turn to crime in their struggle to get by. Here, again, the solution to the crime problem begins with eliminating capitalism.

Critical evaluation. All social-conflict theories argue that the criminal justice system serves the interests of powerful segments of the population. But this approach has limitations. For one thing, it has little to say about why well-off people engage in white-collar, corporate, and organized crime—and sometimes land in jail for doing so. Moreover, if capitalism is the cause of crime, why do socialist societies have so many prisons? Furthermore, if feminist analysis is correct, why are men many times more likely than women to be arrested for crime and to end up in jail (Doyle, 1980; Scanlon, 1992)?

POLITICS AND CRIME: CONSTRUCTING PROBLEMS AND DEFINING SOLUTIONS

Crime has long been an issue of great public concern. But like so many social issues, how people see the crime problem and its solutions depends on their political viewpoints. We now examine the crime problem from the conservative, liberal, and radical perspectives.

Conservatives: Crime and Morality

Conservatives believe that some controls are needed to keep people from engaging in criminal behavior. The most effective control, as they see it, is "conscience": a person's own sense of right and wrong. For this reason, conservatives emphasize the need for young people to learn moral values from families and the church, school, and local community. People raised in families that teach them respect for the law, strong religious values, and the importance of active involvement in their communities are unlikely to get into trouble.

Conservatives see the rise in crime rates beginning in the 1960s as the result of a growing "permissiveness" in society. Crime rates went up, they claim, because of a decline in the number of two-parent families, a weakening of religious values, and the erosion of neighborhood ties. It is no surprise to conservatives that a majority of young people arrested for violent crimes do not have a father living at home.

If some families fail to raise children with proper values, conservatives continue, society must turn to tougher laws, more aggressive policing, and harsher penalties to keep crime in check. But conservatives doubt that the criminal justice system, by itself, can ever solve the crime problem. The key to controlling crime always lies with parents who teach their children to make the right choices in a world filled with pressures to do the wrong thing.

Liberals: Crime and Jobs

Liberals believe that although most people try to do the right thing, many live in situations that pressure them to break the law. Thus, as liberals see it, crime is caused by a harmful environment, especially one twisted by poverty. Millions of U.S. children are born into poor families, pass through substandard schools, and find few jobs waiting for them. It should be no surprise that in such surroundings, some young people lose hope, adopt an "oppositional culture" that rejects authority figures, and end up joining criminal gangs (Anderson, 1994, 2002).

Liberals agree with conservatives that crime is a serious social problem, but they disagree about the solution. To begin, whole districts of our cities and many rural regions need economic renewal. If jobs are available, liberals argue, families will be stronger, youngsters will not lose hope, and fewer people will turn to crime. Indeed, liberals point to the strong economy of the 1990s as the main reason for the drop in crime rates throughout that decade. Likewise, they predict that the recent recession will push the crime rate up in the years to come (several types of crime did post an increase in 2002).

Finally, without more jobs, liberals see the criminal justice system as a revolving door: People leave prison only to return because there is simply no opportunity to make it through honest work.

Radicals: Crime and Inequality

The real crime in this society, from a radical-left perspective, is the shocking extent of economic inequality, an already vast gap that keeps growing. Although the news is full of stories trumpeting the success of the few, radical critics see an economic system that is failing to meet the needs of tens of millions of people. Radicals, like liberals, claim that many people resort to crime because there may be no other way to get by.

Young people growing up in low-income, urban neighborhoods are at higher risk for getting into trouble with the law. How do conservatives, liberals, and radicals differ over the reasons for this pattern?

Radicals accuse conservatives of "blaming the victims" by pointing to single parents as the source of the crime problem. Likewise, they fault liberals for seeking mere reform measures without recognizing that the lack of jobs, which paralyzes so many communities, is built into the capitalist system. Radicals see the "get tough" policies of the criminal justice system—including adding to the numbers of police and prisons—as simply one more way to oppress poor people. The radical solution begins with restructuring the economic and political system toward an egalitarian social order that can make a real claim to justice. The Left to Right table on page 160 sums up the various political views of the crime problem and its solutions.

GOING ON FROM HERE

Crime has been part of the human story since people first devised laws thousands of years ago. Although some crime helps society operate, as Durkheim explained, few doubt that today's high crime rate is a serious social problem. Indeed, we have seen that the debates over crime take into account not only street crimes (property crimes and violent crimes) but also white-collar crime, corporate crime, and crime motivated by hate. Moreover, today's organized crime operates on a global scale.

L E F T to R I G H T

THE POLITICS OF CRIME AND CRIMINAL JUSTICE

	RADICAL LEFT VIEW	LIBERAL VIEW	CONSERVATIVE VIEW
WHAT IS THE PROBLEM?	The great economic inequality of a capitalist society promotes criminal activity by the underclass, those unable to succeed by legitimate means; the criminal justice system is used to maintain order and protect the interests of capitalist elites.	A lack of jobs is the major factor that forces people to break the law, often as a means to survive and support their families.	The moral order of society is breaking down; because of weakening religious values and the decline of the two-parent family, children are not being taught to behave responsibly.
WHAT IS THE SOLUTION?	Crime can never be controlled until class differences cease to exist. Therefore, the capitalist economy should be eliminated in favor of a more equitable system.	Government needs to use resources not to build more prisons but to expand economic opportunity in poor urban and rural areas where people are in desperate need of work.	The single most significant step toward reducing crime is to strengthen families and increase the culture's emphasis on good parenting; tougher law enforcement is also necessary when a crime has occurred.

Join the debate . . .

1. About three-fourths of men in federal prisons grew up without a father present in the home. How would conservatives interpret this fact? How might liberals and radicals interpret it differently?

2. What trends in crime would people across the political spectrum expect to see in the coming decades? Provide reasons for these predictions.

3. Which of the three political analyses of crime included here do you find most convincing? Why?

What is the likely future of crime? As we have seen, a strong economy, decline in drug use, and more police and prisons have pushed the rates down in recent years. Crime rates may rise in coming years, reflecting the loss of jobs caused by the recent economic recession.

Responding to this increase, conservatives point to the need to strengthen families, but how to do that has never been very clear. Liberals point to the need for more jobs, yet even with a strong economy, crime rates are high. Radicals call for a complete overhaul of the economic system, although even countries with far more economic equality than the United States still have high crime rates.

For the foreseeable future, the burden of crime control is likely to remain squarely on the shoulders of the criminal justice system. Without doubt, the most popular idea in the United States when it comes to solving the problem of crime is to "get tough," which means adding more police, more prisons, and tougher sentences for people convicted of serious crimes. So strong is this public opinion that no politician today can afford to be viewed as being "soft on crime." However, the idea that the criminal justice system can solve the crime problem on its own has little support in research or in practice.

We can hope that the recent downward trend in the U.S. crime rate will continue. Economic recovery will certainly be needed for this to happen. In addition, the share of the U.S. population in the "high-crime years" between the middle teens and middle twenties will fall in the coming decades. Perhaps this trend will help control crime—at least until U.S. society develops a more effective solution.

CHAPTER SUMMARY

1. Societies formally enact some norms in the form of law. Crime, which is the violation of criminal law, includes more serious felonies and less serious misdemeanors.

2. Police record some 12 million serious crimes each year; the actual total probably exceeds 30 million. Serious offenses are of two kinds: crimes against the person (violent crimes including murder, rape, aggravated assault, and robbery) and crimes against property (including burglary, larceny-theft, motor vehicle theft, and arson).

3. Crime rates went up quickly after 1960 but began to decline in the early 1990s.

4. Thirty-nine percent of arrests for violent crimes and 47 percent of arrests for property crimes involve young people between fifteen and twenty-four years of age.

5. For property crimes, 69 percent of arrests involve males; in the case of violent crime, males figure in 83 percent of arrests.

6. Whites represent 68 percent of those arrested for property crimes and 60 percent of those arrested for violent crimes. In relation to population size, African Americans have higher arrest rates than whites.

7. Juvenile delinquency is the violation of the law by young people. The juvenile justice system seeks to reform rather than simply punish offenders.

8. Forty-three states and the federal government have hate-crime laws that provide more severe penalties for crimes motivated by bias based on a victim's race, religion, disability, sexual orientation, or ethnicity or national origin.

9. White-collar crime is committed by people in the course of their employment. Corporate crime involves illegal activity committed by a company or individuals acting on its behalf. Typically, such wrongdoing is handled in civil courts, but a recent trend is toward more frequent filing of criminal charges.

10. Organized crime, which has a long history in the United States, also operates throughout most of the world. Victimless crimes are offenses that directly harm only the offender.

11. Police are the most visible part of the criminal justice system. Courts determine the innocence or guilt of those charged with crimes, typically through plea bargains. In principle, societies punish offenders for four reasons: retribution, deterrence, rehabilitation, and societal protection.

12. Community-based corrections include probation and parole. These programs cost less than keeping offenders in prison. Probation is effectively used for those who commit less serious crimes. Whether offenders spend time on probation or in prison, the odds of recidivism (later arrest for another crime) are high.

13. Biological theories of crime point to physical differences between criminals and law-abiding citizens. Yet little evidence supports the conclusion that biological factors cause people to commit crime.

14. Psychological theories highlight characteristics of individual offenders. Although personality factors play a part in some types of criminality, most offenders are psychologically normal.

15. Durkheim's structural-functional theory argues that crime contributes to the operation of society. Other functional theories highlight the role of opportunity in explaining patterns of rule-breaking among segments of a society's population. Hirschi's control theory argues that social ties are important in helping a person resist temptation to break the law.

16. Sutherland's differential association theory states that people learn criminal or noncriminal attitudes from others in groups. Labeling theory, another key contribution of the symbolic-interaction approach, argues that crime results less from what people do than from how others respond to the behavior. Being stigmatized as a rule-breaker may deepen a person's deviant identity.

17. Social-conflict theory links crime to social inequality. Marxist theory highlights how capitalism oppresses people and uses the criminal justice system to deal with those who challenge the system. Feminist theory points to male domination of society as limiting women's opportunity and forcing women into lives of crime.

18. Conservatives highlight the importance of families in teaching young people proper behavior. Liberals highlight a lack of jobs as the major cause of crime. Radicals point to the injustice of economic inequality in capitalist societies and advocate a more egalitarian social system.

KEY CONCEPTS

norms   (p. 136) rules and expectations by which a society guides the behavior of its members

law   (p. 136) norms formally created through a society's political system

crime   (p. 136) the violation of the criminal laws enacted by federal, state, or local governments

misdemeanor   (p. 136) a less serious crime punishable by less than one year in prison

felony   (p. 136) a more serious crime punishable by at least one year in prison

crime against property   (p. 136) crime that involves theft of property belonging to others

crime against persons   (p. 136) crime that involves violence or the threat of violence against others

stalking   (p. 139) persistent efforts by someone to establish or reestablish a relationship against the will of the victim

juvenile delinquency   (p. 144) the violation of the law by young people

hate crime   (p. 145) a criminal offense against a person, property, or society motivated by the offender's bias against a race, religion, disability, sexual orientation, or ethnicity or national origin

white-collar crime   (p. 145) illegal activities committed by people during the course of their employment or regular business activities

corporate crime   (p. 146) an illegal act committed by a corporation or others acting on its behalf

organized crime   (p. 146) a business operation that supplies illegal goods and services

victimless crimes   (p. 147) offenses that directly harm no one but the person who commits them

criminal justice system   (p. 148) society's organized means to enforce the law through the use of police, courts, and prisons

plea bargaining   (p. 149) a negotiation in which the state reduces a defendant's charge in exchange for a guilty plea

retribution   (p. 150) moral vengeance by which society inflicts suffering on an offender comparable to that caused by the offense

deterrence   (p. 150) using punishment to discourage further crime

rehabilitation   (p. 150) reforming the offender to prevent future offenses

societal protection   (p. 150) protecting the public by rendering an offender incapable of further offenses through incarceration or by execution

criminal recidivism   (p. 151) subsequent offenses by people previously convicted of crimes

community-based corrections   (p. 152) correctional programs located in society at large rather than behind prison walls

labeling theory   (p. 157) the assertion that crime and all other forms of rule-breaking result not so much from what people do as from how others respond to those actions

stigma   (p. 157) a powerful negative social label that radically changes a person's self-concept and social identity

THINKING CRITICALLY: QUESTIONS AND ISSUES

1. Why must we use caution when using arrest data from the *Uniform Crime Reports?* Why, in your opinion, are white-collar and corporate offenses not included in the government's definition of "serious crime"?

2. Based on FBI arrest data, what is the profile of someone arrested for property crime? What about violent crime? What explanation can you provide for these patterns?

3. Why do you think crime rates rose quickly after 1960? What explanation can you offer for the downward trend in crime in the 1990s?

4. Do you think popular "get tough" policies are the best way to address the crime problem? Why or why not?

GETTING INVOLVED: LEARNING EXERCISES

1. Do some research about the developing pattern of computer crime. How big a problem is computer crime now? What do analysts predict about the future? What new tactics will law enforcement need to control computer offenses?

2. See whether a local law enforcement agency (such as local or campus police) will let you accompany an officer on duty. Note how a police officer's view of crime and law enforcement may differ from your own.

3. Watch several episodes of the television show *COPS*. How does this show portray the typical offender? Does this portrayal seem fair to you in light of what you have learned in this chapter? Why or why not?

4. Find reports of the prison study at Stanford University by psychologist Philip Zimbardo (see Chapter 1, "Studying Social Problems"). One report is on the Web at **http://www.prisonexp.org**. What conclusions about prison does this research suggest?

GETTING CONNECTED: USEFUL WEB LINKS

http://www.prenhall.com/macionis
Visit the interactive Companion Website™ that accompanies this text. Begin by clicking on the cover of your book. You will find a chapter-by-chapter study guide, practice tests, suggested Web links, and links to other relevant material.

http://www.ojp.usdoj.gov/bjs/
The U.S. Department of Justice site offers the latest crime trends and information on the criminal justice system. Can you find trends not discussed in this chapter?

http://www.ojp.usdoj.gov/bjs/abstract/ hvvc00.htm
This government report examines Hispanic victims of crime. How does ethnicity affect patterns of victimization?

http://www.ojp.usdoj.gov/bjs/abstract/ pjim01.htm
This report from the U.S. Bureau of Justice Statistics surveys the U.S. prison population.

http://www.cybercrime.gov
Here is a government Web site that provides information on computer crime.

http://www.crime.com/info/jailcam.html
Have you ever seen the inside of a prison? View life in the Maricopa County, Arizona, jail.

GETTING STARTED ON YOUR OWN: RESEARCH NAVIGATOR™

Follow the instructions found on page 25 of this text to access the features of Research Navigator™. Once at the Web site, enter your Login Name and Password. Then, to use the **Content Select** database, enter keywords such as "crime," "probation," and "death penalty," and the search engine will supply relevant and recent scholarly and popular press publications. Use the *New York Times* **Search-by-Subject Archive** to find recent news articles related to sociology and the **Link Library** feature to find relevant Web links organized by the key terms associated with this chapter.

CHAPTER 7

© Paul Marcus, Quality Time, Studio SPM, Inc.

VIOLENCE

I N 2002, JOHN MUHAMMAD INTRODUCED HIS YOUNG *friend, Lee Malvo, to an old army buddy. "This is Lee," he said with a straight face, "He's a sniper." Think-ing back on that meeting, the friend, Robert Holmes, recalled that Muhammad was being perfectly serious. Muhammad was not using the term "sniper" as if it were a nickname, explained Holmes, "It was more like a job description."*

In a matter of weeks, the entire country learned how horribly true these words were. John Muhammad, age 42, and the young Lee Malvo, just 17, car-ried out twenty-one sniper shootings in six states and the District of Columbia, killing fourteen of their victims. The deadly and apparently random violence of the "Beltway snipers" terrorized people in the entire region for weeks.

After the two were caught, questions remained, especially about young Malvo. A court found that he played an active part in the killing spree and even pulled the trigger in several of the shootings. How could this young boy become such a cold-blooded killer, even before he had become a man? (Peraino & Thomas, 2003)

There are no easy answers to this question. Family ties—or lack of them—may have played a part. Muhammad was a drifter; Malvo's father aban-doned him early in his life, and his mother soon did the same. But this extreme case makes one wonder about the a broader pattern of widespread violence in U.S. society, a pattern evident in television, movies, musical lyrics, and, of course, police records. This chapter begins its exploration of the many factors linked to violence with a basic definition.

WHAT IS VIOLENCE?

Violence is *behavior that causes damage to property or injury to people.* Al-though violence is always destructive, it may or may not be defined as a so-cial problem. Many people think some acts of violence are quite normal and even desirable. Polls show that a majority of people in the United States

✦ Are people in the United States safer from crime than people in other countries?

The U.S. murder rate is almost twice as high as that in Canada, three times higher than in most European nations, and five times higher than in Japan.

✦ Can television teach children to be violent?

Each year, a typical U.S. youngster watches 12,000 acts of violence on television.

✦ Is the United States a well-armed nation?

There are more than 200 million guns in the United States, enough to arm every person over age thirteen.

165

Many examples of violence exist within our society. The crash of a football tackle is certainly violent, yet few people consider this to be a problem. Under what conditions is violence likely to be defined as a social problem?

accept the war in Iraq as necessary, for example, just as most people support the death penalty for certain violent criminals. Moreover, there is no arguing the popularity of violent movies or sports.

Violence as a Social Problem

According to labeling theory (see Chapter 6, "Crime and Criminal Justice"), the reality of an action has less to do with the behavior itself than with how it is defined by its audience. Following this approach, then, the significance of violent behavior depends on how people perceive it.

In deciding whether violence is a problem, people take into account several factors, including the following:

1. **What do the actors intend by their actions?** A car crash is violent, but in most cases people assume the event was an accident, that is, the driver involved did not want the crash to happen. On the other hand, a driver who intentionally runs down a pedestrian probably would face a criminal prosecution.

2. **Does the violence conform to or violate social norms and values?** Many sports are violent without being seen as social problems. As sociologist Harry Edwards (2000) explains, football is about as violent as hand-to-hand combat, causing personal harm including spinal cord injuries and brain damage. Even so, football fans crave the bone-crushing hits between rival teams. Why? Football, as Edwards explains, is a national ritual that upholds cultural values of competitiveness, toughness, and masculinity.

3. **Does the violence support or threaten the social order?** Football may be violent, but it is also big business. Because it supports the social order, most people celebrate rather than condemn it. In contrast, a number of Chicago area high school students who engaged in a violent hazing incident in 2003 attracted national attention, even though the resulting injuries were minor, and the young women involved ended up in front of a judge.

4. **Is the violence committed by or against the government?** In general, people accept violence such as war, capital punishment, and the action of police SWAT teams because these are government-sanctioned actions that they assume are done for good reasons. In general, there is widespread support for **institutional violence,** *violence carried out by government representatives under the law.* People believe that a certain amount of violence is necessary to keep society operating, whether it is used to oppose criminals or defend against foreign enemies. This does not mean that police violence is always lawful, of course, but there are laws in place that limit an officer's use of deadly force.

On the other hand, people are quick to condemn **anti-institutional violence,** *violence directed against the government in violation of the law.* The war on terrorism, which began after the attacks on the World Trade Center and the Pentagon in 2001, has clearly defined any violence directed against the U.S. government or its citizens as a serious threat. In the United States, most people were outraged by the anti-institutional violence of the nineteen September 11 terrorists yet supported the institutional violence of the United States' military response in Afghanistan and, later, Iraq.

CRIMINAL VIOLENCE

There is widespread agreement that criminal violence is a serious social problem. In terms of the factors listed earlier, criminal offenders intend to harm others, their actions break social norms (by violating the law), they threaten the social order, and they oppose government officials (the police). It is not surprising, then, that most people see criminal offenses as the biggest part of the general problem of violence in our society.

Chapter 6 explained that crime involves breaking criminal laws enacted by federal, state, or local government. **Violent crime** (also called "crimes against persons") is *crime that involves violence or the threat of violence against others.* The violent crimes tracked by the Federal Bureau of Investigation (FBI) include murder and manslaughter ("the willful killing of one human being by another"), aggravated assault ("the unlawful attack by one person upon another for the purpose of inflicting severe or aggravated bodily injury"), forcible rape ("the carnal knowledge of a female forcibly and against her will"), and robbery ("taking or attempting to take anything of value from the care, custody, or control of a person or persons by force or threat of force or violence and/or putting the victim in fear").

The rate of violent crime in the United States rose dramatically after 1960, falling back through the 1990s and through 2002, the most recent data available (see Figure 6–1 on page 138). In 2002, police recorded some 1.4 million violent crimes, which is only about half of the violent crime that actually took place. If we figure in *all* cases (whether reported to the police or not), a violent crime took place somewhere in the country every ten seconds around the clock (U.S. Federal Bureau of Investigation, 2003).

Fear of crime has made violence an important political issue. In the following sections, we investigate patterns surrounding two of the most serious violent crimes: murder and rape.

Murder

Every society has laws that forbid people from killing one another; typically, societies treat this as one of the most serious of all crimes. Killings not only take a life but also severely harm families, friends, and local communities (Rogers et al., 2001).

At the same time, intentional killings are not all viewed as the same. This is because criminal law not only takes into account a person's *action* but also

Everyone agrees that the level of violence in U.S. society is too high. But people have very different ideas about the causes of this problem and what the solutions should be. For example, some believe easy access to handguns is the problem—as they see it, banning such weapons would make everyone safer. Others, however, view handguns as necessary protection—from this point of view, learning the safe use of a gun is the solution to the violence problem.

weighs the person's *intent* (in legal terms, *mens rea*, or "guilty mind") in carrying out the act.

Murder involves *the unlawful, intentional killing of one person by another,* as in the case of a killing for hire or a person who kills a relative in order to gain an inheritance. **Manslaughter,** by contrast, involves *the unlawful, unintentional killing of one person by another,* as in the case of a person who fires a gun into the air to scare another person only to learn that the bullet struck and killed someone else. Because the shooter did not intend to kill anyone, the state treats the offense as less serious than murder; at the same time, because the state expects people to know the reasonable consequences of their actions, this dangerous (and ultimately deadly) act is still a serious crime. In some cases, officials may declare a killing to

TABLE 7–1	NUMBER OF MURDERS FOR SELECTED CITIES, 1990 AND 2002		
	1990	**2002**	**CHANGE**
Atlanta	231	152	−34%
Chicago	851	642*	−25
Dallas	447	196	−56
Denver	67	51	−24
District of Columbia	472	264	−44
Los Angeles	983	654	−33
Miami	129	65	−50
New Orleans	304	258	−15
New York	2,245	587	−74
Seattle	53	26	−51

*Data for 2001.

Source: U.S. Federal Bureau of Investigation (2003).

be neither murder nor manslaughter but a case of purely accidental death, in which no blame is attached to anyone. An example of accidental death might be a fatal highway crash on an icy road, in which no one is charged with any driving violation. Obviously, there is often a fine line between one category of killing and another; making these determinations is a matter for police, prosecutors, and courts.

The murder rate in the United States over the past forty years has followed the general pattern of violent crime noted earlier. After climbing steadily from 1960 to 1993, the murder rate fell sharply, although it turned slightly upward again in 2001. Still, the 16,204 cases of murder recorded in 2002 reflect only a slightly higher murder rate than was recorded back in 1960. The overall decline in the murder rate since the early 1990s has been particularly notable in many of the largest cities, as shown in Table 7–1.

Murder reveals a number of important patterns. First, two-thirds of murders are committed with handguns. This is the major reason for the current public attention to the issue of gun control.

Second, men are involved in most murders, both as offenders (65 percent of those arrested for murder in 2002 were men) and as victims (77 percent of victims were men). These facts underscore the strong link between gender and violence in the United States (U.S. Federal Bureau of Investigation, 2003).

Third, most murders are not the cold, calculated acts commonly portrayed in murder mysteries. On the contrary, most murders are unplanned, resulting from arguments between acquaintances that suddenly turn violent. In most cases, drinking or the use of other drugs is a factor in deadly violence. This pattern leads analysts to characterize many murders as *crimes of passion*.

Fourth, the majority of murders involve offenders and victims of the same race. In 91 percent of cases involving an African American victim, police arrested a black suspect; similarly, in 84 percent of cases involving a white victim, police arrested a white suspect. These figures reflect the fact that offender and victim are often acquainted, and they also remind us that many whites and blacks still live in separate worlds. At the same time, the problem of violent crime is greater for African Americans than for whites. Although blacks represent 12 percent of the U.S. population, they accounted for 48 percent of murder victims in 2002. Whites, 75 percent of the population, accounted for 48 percent of murder victims (U.S. Federal Bureau of Investigation, 2003).

Read a government report on Hispanic victims of violent crime at
http://www.ojp.usdoj.gov/bjs/abstract/hvvc00.htm

Fifth, and finally, the United States remains the most violent high-income nation on earth. Even with the decline in murder rates in the 1990s, the rate of killing (murder and manslaughter) is still almost twice as high as it is in Canada, three times higher than in the European nations of France, Germany, and the United Kingdom, and five times higher than in Japan.

Mass Murder   The United States has not only a very high rate of murder but also a high frequency of **mass murder,** *the intentional, unlawful killing of four or more people at one time and place.* The killing of thirteen people at Colorado's Columbine High School, which grabbed the attention of the country in 1999, illustrates the horror of mass murder. In the 1990s, deadly shootings occurred at a dozen other schools across the country. Workplaces also have been targets, as disgruntled workers vent their rage against people they feel have wronged them.

Terrorism, too, can result in mass murder. The September 11, 2001, attacks killed about 3,000 people. In more typical years, however, mass murder in the United States generally involves no more than about fifty killings—less than 1 percent of the 16,204 murders in 2002 (U.S. Bureau of Justice Statistics, 2003). But cases of mass murder are of great concern to the public because, for one thing, they receive extensive media attention. Just as important, mass murders typically occur in public places, such as schools or businesses, where people assume they are safe from violence.

What do mass murderers have in common? Almost all are men, and many collect firearms. School shootings typically involve young men—students or ex-students—who have experienced rejection by their peers. Mass murder in the workplace usually involves employees or ex-employees, many of whom abuse alcohol or other drugs (Dietz, 1986; Holmes & Holmes, 1993).

Serial Murder Another type of killing that captures a great deal of public attention is **serial murder,** *the killing of several people by one offender over a period of time*. In 2003, Derrick Todd Lee was arrested and charged with the murder of five women in Louisiana; the killings had made women throughout the Baton Rouge area fearful for over a year (Deslatte, 2003).

A number of convicted serial killers gained notoriety for their crimes. Ted Bundy, who killed as many as thirty people, was executed in 1989; John Wayne Gacy was convicted of killing thirty-three young men and was executed in 1994; Jeffrey Dahmer was convicted of fifteen murders and later died in a prison attack in 1994; Ted Kaczynski, the convicted "Unabomber," killed three people and seriously injured twenty-three more and is currently serving a life sentence without parole in prison.

Serial killers probably are the best known of all deadly offenders, and fictitious killers such as Hannibal "the Cannibal" Lecter have thrilled millions of movie-goers. Yet, keep in mind that serial killing represents only a small fraction of all murders.

Most serial killers are somewhat older than those who commit single murders. Almost all are men, but some serial killers target men whereas other target women. Most are mentally ill, suffering from psychotic disorders that distort their sense of reality. Researchers note that some serial killers say they hear voices or receive messages urging them to kill; others have an irresistible desire to control other people; still others lack any compassion and strike out violently at those who get in their way (Jenkins, 1994; Holmes & Holmes, 1998; Warf & Waddell, 2002).

Combating Deadly Violence Nearly three out of four adults in the United States think that the criminal justice system is not doing enough to combat violent crime (NORC, 2003:101). Such concern has led to "three strikes and you're out" policies that mandate a sentence of life in prison for a third felony conviction. Another "get tough" policy is mandatory prison sentences for a number of crimes, especially

Gary Leon Ridgway, of Washington state, was recently convicted of serial murder and will spend the rest of his life behind bars. His admission that he killed at least forty-eight women makes him the most deadly serial killer in U.S. history.

drug offenses. Policies such as these, which have been adopted in many places, are the main reason the U.S. prison population has swelled to more than 2 million, its highest level in history.

Another important change has been an increasing number of police across the United States, from 400,000 in 1990 to about 670,000 in 2002. Much of this increase was in the police departments of large cities: For example, the number of New York City police officers soared from 26,844 to 37,240 (U.S. Department of Justice, 2003).

Finally, police procedures are changing. New York City's "zero tolerance" policy allows patrol officers to stop and investigate any offense—even jaywalking—to check people for concealed weapons. Supporters applaud such policies for dramatically cutting the rate of violent crime. Critics, however, counter that more aggressive policing threatens personal freedoms and opens the door to *racial profiling*, by which police direct their attention toward certain categories of the population—especially young black

Personal Stories — Police Abuse of Power: When Violence Wears a Badge

ON A SUMMER EVENING IN 1997, THIRTY-YEAR-OLD Abner Louima, a Haitian immigrant, was relaxing at a Brooklyn nightclub. Suddenly, a fight broke out and, within minutes, police moved through the club making arrests. Louima was taken into custody and was soon sitting in a police van.

Louima, a married father who works as a bank security guard, claims that police beat him as they drove to the station house (Farley & McLaughlin, 1997). But only after they arrived at the station did Louima's real nightmare begin. First, he was strip-searched. Then, with his pants still around his ankles, he explains, "They take me to the bathroom and they threw me to the ground. One started beating me up and then one of them—there was two of them—one picked up something on the floor. I don't know what it was, but it looked like a plunger to me, and just, you know, push it in my ass and then it come out with shit and blood and then after that he put it in my mouth" (Noel, 1997:47).

Later, four white officers—Justin Volpe, Charles Schwarz, Thomas Weise, and Thomas Bruder—were charged with beating Louima, who is black. Volpe confessed to being the one who brutally sodomized the prisoner in the bathroom. The investigation showed that, after the attack, Volpe warned Louima, "If you tell anybody about this, I'll find you and kill you" (White, 1999:63). Volpe then walked around the station house, showing the bloodied stick to other officers and bragging that he "brought a man down" that night (Marks, 1999:4). The police left Louima writhing in pain for more than an hour before calling for help.

Louima required medical treatment for broken teeth, a ruptured bladder, and a torn rectum. Louima's cousin, Samuel Nicolas, said of the incident, "They were trying to kill him. Abner . . . may never be able to urinate normally again. He has a bag which he has to urinate in. He has a bag which he has to defecate in" (Noel, 1997:47).

Volpe was convicted of this crime and will spend up to thirty years in prison. Although they were initially tried and convicted for their role in the attack, a federal appeals court in 2002 reversed the convictions of officers Schwarz, Wiese, and Bruder, claiming that the evidence against them did not support the specific charges brought against them. Mr. Louima also sued the city and the police union and received a settlement of $8.75 million. Although this case shows that abusive police risk ending up in jail, critics claim that abuse is common, and successful prosecutions are rare. Indeed, many see New York's aggressive policing as a two-edged sword: The crime rate has fallen, but police feel freer to take matters into their own hands and, as a result, the city has seen more than 5,000 complaints of police brutality filed annually. In short, the fear of crime may be down in New York and many other cities, but, especially in minority communities, fear of the police has gone up.

ISSUES AND EXERCISES

1. Do you think that more aggressive policing will help solve the problem of violent crime in the United States? Why or why not?

2. Do you think a case such as Abner Louima's is an isolated incident (as New York's mayor claimed) or part of a larger pattern of misconduct? Explain your position.

3. [Research Navigator.com — RESOURCES FOR COLLEGE RESEARCH ASSIGNMENTS] Use Research Navigator™ to investigate police brutality. (See instructions on page 25; keywords: "racial profiling," "police violence")

Sources: Based on Marks (1999), White (1999), and McFadden (2002).

men—whom they view as likely offenders (White, 1999). Moreover, critics continue, aggressive policing encourages some officers to engage in unwarranted violence, especially against minorities. The Personal Stories box provides an account of one recent case of such abuse of power.

Rape

The FBI defines **forcible rape** as *"the carnal knowledge of a female forcibly and against her will."* In reality, of course, men as well as women can be victims of rape. Men raping other men is a serious problem in the U.S. prison system, as noted in Chapter 6 ("Crime and Criminal Justice"). Still, official statistical data include only cases of men raping women.

Children, too, are raped. Everywhere in the United States, it is against the law for an adult to have sex with a child, even if no force is used and the young person does not object. In effect, the law says "no" for a young person below the age of consent, which varies from state to state but is usually between sixteen and eighteen. Violation of this law is called *statutory rape*, which typically carries a somewhat lesser penalty than forcible rape.

FBI records show that almost 100,000 rapes are reported each year (more than five times the number of recorded murders), but just as many rapes are never reported to police. There are several reasons for the low reporting rate in cases of forcible rape. Some people still believe that rape is a matter of sex rather than a violent crime. Victims of rape may also be paralyzed by the thought that they, rather than the rapist, are somehow responsible for the crime. Still other victims do not make a report because they are reluctant to make trouble for an offender whom they know or because they do not want to go through a lengthy legal proceeding. The rate of reporting is rising, however, and because most victims can identify their attackers, police made arrests in 45 percent of all reported cases in 2002 (well below the two-thirds of reported cases of murder cleared by arrest).

Combating Rape Historically, as Susan Brownmiller (1975) points out, rape laws did little more than protect men from false accusations of rape and offer compensation to husbands and fathers if their wives or daughters were violated. In short, rape laws served the interests of men rather than women.

But a different view of rape emerged as women gained a greater political voice in the 1960s. Since then, with more women voting, more women holding elected office, and more women's organizations speaking out, U.S. public policy now better reflects women's interests. For example, no longer must women prove that they are innocent victims who have done nothing to lead on or seduce the attacker. No longer is a previous sexual relationship with the attacker or anyone else grounds to dismiss a rape charge; on the contrary, the terms *acquaintance rape* and *date rape* have been added to our language in recognition of the fact that victims typically know their attackers.

Nowhere is date rape more widely discussed than on college and university campuses. Life on a

Colleges and universities throughout the country are studying the role of alcohol as a cause of violence, especially sexual violence. Do you think drinking plays a part in patterns of violence on your campus? Why or why not?

college campus encourages a feeling of safety and trust, which can leave students vulnerable to sexual violence. To counter the problem, college officials and concerned students across the country are speaking out about sexual violence, emphasizing that both partners must consent to sexual activity and pointing out that consuming alcohol or other drugs can make consent impossible.

Finally, the law now addresses sex forced on wives by their husbands. Historically, people assumed—and the courts agreed—that when a woman said "I do" she gave up the right to say "I won't" (Russell, 1990). In other words, marriage was understood to give men unlimited sexual access to their wives, whether the wives wanted to have sex or not. Today, however, all states have laws against *marital rape* (Violence against Women Online Resources, 2001).

FAMILY VIOLENCE

Most of us like to think of the family as a source of protection and support in the face of an uncertain and sometimes cruel world. But the family is also a source of conflict and a widespread pattern of **family violence,** *emotional, physical, or sexual abuse of one family member by another.* Indeed, for many people in the United States, being at home is more

A DEFINING MOMENT

U.S. Society Discovers Child Abuse

IN 1958, DR. C. HENRY KEMPE WAS working as a physician in Denver's Colorado General Hospital. Dr. Kempe became concerned that some children's injuries were not the "accidents" children and parents said they were but were really caused by violence. Kempe began to study x-rays to determine the real causes of children's injuries.

Convinced by his own investigations that many children were victims of violence at home, Kempe set up the hospital's first "child protection team" to investigate children's injuries. Three years later, he presented a paper reporting on the extent of violence against children, drawing the nation's attention to a problem he called *battered child syndrome*. Not only does family violence harm children physically, he concluded, but it also results in psychological harm—including poor self-image and depression—and makes it difficult for injured children to form trusting relationships.

Dr. Kempe's research was truly a defining moment in helping U.S. society to look upon violence against children as a social problem rather than a private, family matter. He also set the stage for people to

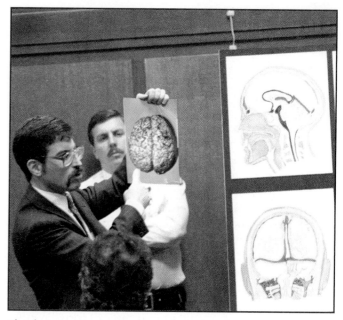

Thanks to Dr. Kempe, doctors today routinely review medical data with an eye toward identifying cases of child abuse. This physician is using autopsy charts to describe the brain damage suffered by an abused six-year-old.

recognize and combat two other types of family violence: violence against women and violence against the elderly.

Source: Kempe et al. (1962).

---

dangerous than walking the streets at night (Gelles & Straus, 1988; Jasinski & Williams, 1998). Sociologists focus on family violence directed at children, women, and elders.

Violence against Children

Not until the 1960s did people in the United States begin to define violence toward children as a social problem. This was not because children never experienced violence. Rather, it was because U.S. society considered what went on in the home—including parental violence directed at children—as a private, family matter.

The pioneer in changing this attitude was Dr. C. H. Kempe (Kempe et al., 1962). The Defining Moment box explains how U.S. society came to define **battered child syndrome** as *a pattern of physical and psychological injury to a child caused by the action (or neglect) of another person.*

By 1966, thanks to Dr. Kempe's work, every state in the country passed laws making child abuse a crime and requiring medical personnel to report suspected cases of child abuse to authorities. Each year, about 3 million cases are reported, and 1 million turn out to be serious. Researchers add, though, that most child abuse may not be reported at all. Most seriously, almost 1,500 children across the United States are murdered each year, half at the hands of family members (Melton & Barry, 1994; Wallace, 1996; U.S. Federal Bureau of Investigation, 2003).

Children also suffer from *sexual abuse*. As noted earlier, the law forbids sexual activity involving an adult and a child because children are too young to consent to sex or to defend themselves from unwanted sexual advances. Sexual child abuse covers a wide range of offenses: exposing one's genitals to a child; encouraging children to engage in sexual acts together; oral, anal, or genital sex with a child; and

Social Policy Child Sexual Abusers: Step Forward

THE TALL, THIN, SEVENTY-ONE-YEAR-OLD MAN walks slowly to the front of the room of about 100 people in the city of Burlington, Vermont. He pauses, looked around the room, and then says slowly but firmly, "I am a recovering child sexual abuser. For several years in the early 1990s, I sexually abused three of my granddaughters."

The people in the room listen in silence. The man, who does not use his real name, continues, "After each of the incidents, I felt guilty and hated myself. I vowed to stop, but I didn't. My stepdaughter confronting me is what finally stopped me."

The conventional thinking has been that we must teach children—with programs such as "good touching, bad touching" in schools—to protect themselves. But the extent of sexual abuse of children—and the public attention given to the recent scandal involving sexual abuse of children by priests in the Roman Catholic Church—is prompting people to try something new. The man described here represents a new approach, which is to teach adults to protect children. It is hoped that by having actual abusers speak to groups, adults will come to understand what the sexual abuse of children is, that it is more common than most people think, and that they must be alert for any indications of possible abuse in their communities and in their own families.

In recent years, the Centers for Disease Control has begun funding programs like the one in Burlington. Experts claim that such programs help recovering abusers straighten out their lives. In addition, they also help families learn about this problem so they are better able to stop abuse, perhaps even before it happens.

ISSUES AND EXERCISES

1. What are some reasons children may be reluctant to report being sexually abused?

2. Do you think programs such as the one described here are likely to be effective? Why or why not?

3. Use Research Navigator™ to learn more about the sexual abuse of children. (See instructions on page 25; keywords: "child abuse," "sexual abuse")

Source: Based on Villarosa (2002).

---

filming or photographing children for pornographic purposes. Estimates suggest that about 500,000 U.S. children are sexually abused each year, with only about half of all cases ever being reported. Research indicates that about 90 percent of child sexual abusers are men and, despite the common idea that children can avoid trouble by "watching out for strangers," at least three-fourths of offenders are known to the child. In about 20 percent of cases involving boys and 40 percent of cases involving girls, the abuser is a family member (Villarosa, 2002).

Many schools now teach young children (as early as preschool) the difference between "good touching" and "bad touching" and emphasize the need to tell a grown-up if someone acts toward them in a manner that they think is wrong. The Social Policy box describes another new approach in the fight against the sexual abuse of children.

Which children are at greatest risk of sexual abuse? There is no simple answer to this question because abusive families come from all walks of life. But research shows that the risk is greatest among children who (1) are young (most sexually abused children are between seven and thirteen years of age); (2) are girls, who have twice the rate of abuse as boys; (3) live in poverty; (4) live with a stepparent or a single mother with a cohabiting male; (5) have parents or other family members who abuse alcohol or other drugs; or (6) have parents or stepparents who were themselves abused as children (Van Biema, 1994; Daly & Wilson, 1996; Barnett et al., 1997; Murray, 2001; Villarosa, 2002).

Combating Child Abuse The 1974 Federal Child Abuse Prevention and Treatment Act requires local officials to respond to all reports of child abuse; it also established Child Protection Services (CPS) to investigate abuse cases and to help parents stop abusive behavior. When officials determine a child is in extreme danger, CPS has the authority to remove a child from a home.

Yet CPS has limited resources, and investigators cannot always keep up with heavy caseloads. A more efficient approach to child abuse may well be prevention, which is why many communities offer classes in effective parenting techniques for pregnant teenagers, day-care centers that provide relief to stressed parents, and home visits by social workers trained to work with at-risk parents so that they do not become abusive.

The greatest challenge is that many abused children have grown into adults who view violence as normal. As they respond to their own troubles with violence, the abuse cycle passes from one generation to the next (Gelles & Straus, 1988; Groves, 1997).

Violence against Women

Of about 55 million married couples in the United States, 15 million experience at least some violence in the home each year, and about 3 million endure serious episodes of assault (U.S. Bureau of Justice Statistics, 2000). Among the roughly 6 million unmarried partners living together, the rate of domestic violence is even higher (Stets & Straus, 1989; Popenoe & Whitehead, 1999). Because U.S. women are more likely to be injured in the home than anywhere else, domestic violence is a serious national problem.

Although men also suffer from family violence, in 85 percent of all cases women are the victims. More than one-third of all women who are murdered (about 1,300 women annually, nationwide) die at the hands of a partner or ex-partner (Warshaw, 1990; U.S. Federal Bureau of Investigation, 2003).

Combating Domestic Violence The public began to recognize violence against women as a social problem in the 1970s. Much credit for this change goes to the women's movement, which began establishing emergency shelters for battered women in communities across the country. In addition, activists succeeded in prompting all states to enact stalking laws that prohibit a partner or ex-partner from following and otherwise threatening someone and make it easier for people who experience domestic violence to obtain court orders that require partners to stay away (Schechter, 1982; Tierney, 1982; Gagné, 1998).

Some people still consider domestic violence a private matter, which is one reason that domestic

violence is likely to go unreported unless a third party is involved. But public support for victims of domestic violence is growing, in part because the work of sociologists confirms the fact that women are more likely to be injured by a partner or current family member than they are to be mugged, raped by a stranger, or hurt in an automobile accident (Shupe, Stacey, & Hazlewood, 1987; Blankenhorn, 1995; Buzawa & Buzawa, 1996; Felson, 2000).

Violence against Elders

Another kind of family violence is *elder abuse*. In such cases, family members or other caregivers victimize older people in ways that range from passive neglect to active assault. How extensive is elder abuse? Experts estimate that some 4 million people aged sixty-five or older in the United States (about 10 percent of the total) suffer some form of abuse each year. Of these, more than 1 million (3 percent) suffer serious physical abuse and injury (National Center for Elder Abuse, 2004).

The highest rate of elder abuse is found among poor families and families whose members are addicted to alcohol or other drugs or who were themselves victimized as children. But it does not stop there. Millions of adults in otherwise healthy families feel the pressures of going to work, caring for young children, and looking after one or more aging parents. Because seniors are living longer than ever before, today's middle-aged people have become a *sandwich generation* who often spend as much time caring for parents as for their young children. Pressed from two directions, people sometimes find they simply cannot cope, and frustration may lead to violence (Greenberg, McKibben, & Raymond, 1990; Bendick, 1992; Hinrichsen, Hernandez, & Pollack, 1992; Barnett et al., 1997).

Combating Elder Abuse The recognition of elder abuse as a social problem emerged in the 1980s, building on the awareness of other types of family violence and fueled by the growing activism of seniors. A major challenge in combating this problem is uncovering the abuse itself. As is true of other kinds of family violence, much of the problem of elder abuse exists behind closed doors. Many abused elders are ashamed to call out for help, anxious about losing what care they have and fearful of reprisals from the abuser. Some abused elders living in private homes keep quiet, convinced that speaking out will cause family members to send them to a nursing home. At present, experts say, barely one in ten cases of elder

TABLE 7–2 MOST VIOLENT MEDIA PROGRAMMING, 2001–2002

	Name of Show (Network)	Number of Scenes with Serious Violence	Rating
TV Series	Xena: Warrior Princess (SYN)	63	PG
	Walker: Texas Ranger (CBS)	53	PG-14
	Sheena (SYN)	47	PG
	Cleopatra 2525 (SYN)	38	PG
	Andromeda (SYN)	33	PG
Movies*	The Patriot	159	R
	Gladiator	110	R
	Mission Impossible II	108	PG-13
	Shanghai Noon	99	PG-13
	Romeo Must Die	88	PG-13

SYN = first-run syndication.
*Based on fifty top-grossing films.
Source: Center for Media and Public Affairs (2002).

abuse comes to the attention of Adult Protective Services (APS), the federal agency charged with controlling this problem. But as public awareness of this problem grows, there is little doubt that the number of reports will increase (Pillemer, 1988; Tatara, 1993; Holmstrom, 1994; Barnett et al., 1997).

SOCIAL DIMENSIONS OF VIOLENCE

How is it that violence has become part of so many people's lives in the United States? Sociologists look for clues by linking violence to other dimensions of social life. The following sections briefly investigate the mass media, drugs, poverty, gangs, and guns.

The Mass Media and Violence

The mass media—radio, television, movies, and the Internet—have a great influence on the way people, especially young people, view the world around them. No one claims that the high level of U.S. violence has a single cause, but most believe that the mass media are part of the problem.

Violence is central to today's mass-media culture. Children encounter far more media violence than their parents or grandparents did, especially from the most popular medium: television. The typical youngster in the United States watches about four hours of television each day and, over the course of a year, observes some 12,000 violent acts (Barry, 1993; Groves, 1997). Anyone who spends time in

theaters knows that movies, on average, are even more violent. One sign of how serious the problem has become is the declaration by the American Medical Association (AMA) that the mass media are a hazard to our health (AMA, 1997). Many people seem to agree: The AMA reports that three-fourths of U.S. adults say they have either turned off a television program or walked out of a movie because of disturbing levels of violence.

A recent study documents the extent of violence in television shows and movies. Studying all television shows during the 2000–2001 season, the Center for Media and Public Affairs counted an average of fifteen scenes involving serious violence (defined as murder, aggravated assault, rape, and kidnapping) per hour, and they observed the same level of violence in movies. Table 7–2 shows which television shows and movies topped the list for violence.

According to the researchers, recent criticism of violence in the mass media may be having some effect. When comparing today's level of media violence with that found by a similar survey in 1998–1999, the researchers noted a 17 percent decline in the rate of serious violence on television during the 2000–2001 season. In the movies, however, there was no such decline. In addition, the researchers point to the need for a more effective rating system, especially for television programming: Of the five most violent TV shows in the study, four were given the mild PG ("Parental Guidance") rating (Lichter, 2002).

Critical Thinking   Media-Based Violence: Playing Out a Fantasy?

AT ABOUT MIDNIGHT ON MARCH 8, 1995, a slight young woman named Sarah Edmonson entered a convenience store in Ponchatoula, Louisiana, forty miles northwest of New Orleans. Edmonson picked up two candy bars and placed a $20 bill on the counter. The cashier, Patsy Ann Byers, a thirty-seven-year-old mother of three, picked up the bill and opened the register drawer. Just then, Edmonson pulled a gun from her pocket and fired point-blank at Byers. Then she reached over the counter, grabbed all the cash, and fled the store, jumping into a waiting car driven by her boyfriend, Ben Darrus.

Byers was hospitalized but survived the shooting. Edmonson and Darrus, both eighteen years of age, were soon arrested and charged with robbery and attempted murder. Police learned that the two had shot and killed a man just days before. During the investigation, Edmonson bragged that she and Darrus had decided to go on a killing spree after watching Oliver Stone's 1994 film *Natural Born Killers*.

The recent wave of school shootings across the United States also raises concerns about the effects of violence in the mass media. In the 1999 Columbine High School massacre in Colorado, two young men killed twelve students and one teacher before turning their guns on themselves. In a tape the two shooters made before the attack, they pointed to the many hours they had spent playing violent video games and watching violent movies and talked about how they planned to kill classmates at school as if that, too, were a game. Then the pair laughed, claiming that once the massacre was over, Hollywood studios would fight over the rights to make a movie of their lives.

ISSUES AND EXERCISES

1. Why, in your opinion, is there so much violence in the mass media, including television, movies, video games, and even popular music?

2. Limiting violence in the mass media raises the issue of free speech. Do you think that policies to restrict violence in the mass media threaten free expression? Or do you think the level of violence in U.S. society threatens everyone in an even more serious way? Explain your answers.

3. **Research Navigator.com** Use Research Navigator™ to learn more about violence in the media. (See instructions on page 25; keyword: "mass media violence")

Sources: Based on Gibeaut (1997), Cowley (1998), and Gibbs & Roche (1999).

But does viewing violence make people commit violence? Some studies conclude that the more children watch media violence, the more they engage in rough play and the more likely they are to resort to violence as adults (Zimring & Hawkins, 1997; Ritter, 2003). Furthermore, media violence seems to cause some adults to act out violent fantasies. The Critical Thinking box provides two examples.

Watching violence in the mass media, then, seems to encourage some people to engage in deadly violence. But what about the rest of us? Most analysts agree that watching violence in the mass media affects everyone by *desensitizing* us to violence; that is, we get so used to media violence that the idea of people deliberately harming each other no longer bothers us. Moreover, evidence suggests that exposure to media violence also encourages young and old alike to view the world as unsafe and unjust (Donnerstein, Slaby, & Eron, 1994; Gerner et al., 1994; Sege & Dietz, 1994; Groves, 1997; Kromar & Valkenburg, 1999).

Drugs and Violence

The use of alcohol and other drugs is linked to violence. A government study shows that more than 60 percent of people in prison for violent offenses report having been under the influence of drugs, alcohol, or both when they committed their crimes (U.S. Department of Justice, 1994). In addition, researchers have long noted the role that alcohol and other drugs play in most cases of family violence (Gelles & Cornell, 1990; Goldstein, 1995; Mendelson & Mello, 1995; Gelles, 1997; Kantor & Jasinski, 1998).

Across the United States, about 1 million young people are members of youth gangs, some of which routinely engage in violence. What are the reasons that many young people are drawn to gangs in the first place? What are some of the causes of gang violence?

How do drugs encourage violence? Drugs distort judgment and reduce inhibitions. The combined result is that a person already inclined to violent behavior is more likely to lose control when "under the influence" (Gelles & Straus, 1988; Gelles, 1997). In addition, some drugs are addictive. An addiction can cause cravings so strong that the search for the next high may cause some people to resort to violence or even to abandon their children. In short, the damage goes beyond just the drug abuser. Children or others living in a home where drugs are abused are often neglected and grow up at higher risk of abusing drugs, dropping out of school, having trouble with police, and engaging in violent behavior. Drugs create a cycle of violence that spills from one generation to another.

Drug use may contribute to violence in another, indirect way. As Chapter 9 ("Alcohol and Other Drugs") explains, national policy to combat drug abuse focuses on criminal prosecution, including mandatory prison sentences for users as well as dealers. As some see it, locking up nonviolent drug users exposes them to serious violence in prison, which may well turn minor offenders into hardened criminals.

Some people suggest that legalizing drugs might reduce violence on the street. They argue that a good deal of crime results from drug abusers' need for large amounts of ready cash to buy drugs, a need that would be much smaller if drugs were made available at low cost from a government-controlled treatment program. Moreover, by outlawing drugs, society ensures that drugs make huge profits for dealers, who will use any means necessary to protect their interests (Goldstein, 1995; Bertram et al., 1996; Inciardi, 1996).

Poverty and Violence

Violence is also linked to poverty. Low-income people are disadvantaged by poor nutrition, limited schooling, substandard housing, and lack of employment opportunities, all of which raise everyday stress. Indeed, some analysts view poverty itself as a form of violence that afflicts tens of millions of people (Gilligan, 1996). It is not surprising, then, that low-income people are highly represented among both offenders and victims of violent crime (Wolfgang, Thornberry, & Figlio, 1987; Reiman, 1998; Parler & Pruitt, 2000).

Despite these findings, most poor families are neither violent nor criminal. Although it is true that poor neighborhoods have higher rates of violent crime than affluent communities, most such crime is the work of a small number of repeat offenders (Elliott & Ageton, 1980; Harries, 1990).

Youth Gangs and Violence

Another factor contributing to violence, especially in the poor neighborhoods of large U.S. cities, is **youth gangs,** *groups of young people who identify with*

A NATION OF DIVERSITY

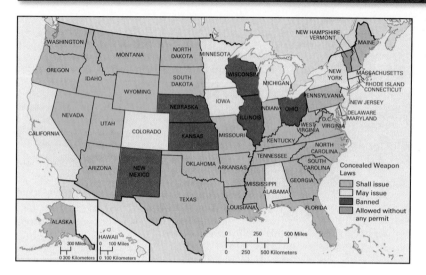

NATIONAL MAP 7–1
Who's Packin'? Concealed Weapon Laws across the United States

In only one state (Vermont), any person can carry a concealed weapon without a permit. In just seven states, no one can do so by law. Fourteen states (identified as "May issue" states) issue concealed weapon permits in cases of demonstrated special need. But in most states ("Shall issue" states)—twenty-nine in all—permits are available to most people without special need. What regional pattern do you see? Can you explain this pattern?

Source: Handgun Control (2001).

one another and with a particular territory. Not all gangs are violent, of course. Just as important, not all groups of young people end up being called "gangs." Many people have a tendency to call middle-class groups "clubs" while calling groups of poor young people "gangs," regardless of the behavior of their members.

A recent federal government study identified more than 24,500 street gangs with almost 1 million members in some 4,000 cities across the United States (U.S. Office of Juvenile Justice and Delinquency Prevention, 2003). These gangs range from nonviolent groups, to groups that sometimes clash over turf, to all-out criminal organizations that engage in drug dealing, robbery, extortion, and even murder.

Who is most likely to join a gang? The typical violent gang member comes from a poor, single-parent family in a neighborhood with a high rate of crime, drug abuse, and unemployment, and many have experienced violence in their own homes. Often, young people look to gangs for protection and a positive self-image that they cannot find elsewhere (Howell, 1996; Zimring, 1998; Hixon, 1999). According to the "culture of the streets" in many poor communities, if you are tough, others will leave you alone. In other words, a tendency to resort to violence can be a strategy to avoid becoming a victim (Anderson, 1994, 2002).

Because gang activity is often linked to drug dealing, the level of gang violence went down along with the decline in the use of crack and cocaine in the late 1980s. However, in recent years, it has been on the rise again. In all U.S. cities with 100,000 or more people, there were 1,334 gang-related killings in 2001. Two cities—Los Angeles and Chicago—accounted for more than half of the total (U.S. Office of Juvenile Justice and Delinquency Prevention, 2003). Many of the dead were innocent victims of stray bullets fired by people they never even saw (McCarthy, 2001).

Guns and Violence

In recent years, the factor contributing to violent crime that has received the most attention is the easy availability of guns. Without doubt, U.S. society is awash in guns: About 40 percent of households have one or more guns, for a total of some 200 million firearms, enough to arm everyone over age twelve. About 64 percent of these weapons are handguns, and many find their way into the hands of criminals or curious children (U.S. Bureau of Justice Statistics, 2000). Therefore, some people define gun ownership itself as a serious social problem and support more extensive laws to make guns harder to get and mandatory devices such as trigger locks to make guns harder to use. National Map 7–1 shows where in the United States people can and cannot carry a concealed weapon.

For their part, gun owners point to the Second Amendment to the U.S. Constitution, which guarantees citizens the right to "keep and bear arms"; they believe that government efforts to regulate gun ownership violate this basic right. In addition, supporters of gun ownership claim that the fact that so many U.S. households have guns actually discourages violent crime (Lott, 2000). As they see it, to take guns out of the hands of law-abiding people would leave everyone more vulnerable to armed criminals. According to the saying on a popular bumper sticker, "If guns are outlawed, only outlaws will have guns."

Read a government report on gun violence in public housing at
http://www.huduser.org/periodicals/rrr/rrr_3_2000/0300_1.html

---

On the other hand, supporters of gun control look to countries such as Canada, where the government is aggressive in restricting ownership of guns (Canada has just 1 million handguns, compared with more than 100 million in the United States). Canada's tough policy does seem to work: The rate of handgun deaths is one-seventh that of the United States (Burns et al., 2000).

From another angle, Figure 7–1 shows the various types of weapons typically involved in cases of murder. More than 50 percent of murder cases involve handguns, which suggests that in the absence of guns, violence might be reduced. In other words, many fights that ended up with someone being killed might have remained nonfatal assaults had there not been a gun at hand. In short, the easy availability of guns is certainly not the only cause of violence in the United States, but it is certainly one reason that violence in this country is so often deadly (Zimring & Hawkins, 1997).

EXPLAINING VIOLENCE: BIOLOGICAL AND PSYCHOLOGICAL THEORIES

Do societies have to be violent? What causes violence? To answer these questions, we turn to theories that try to explain violence. We look first at biological theories, then consider psychological theories, and, in the next section, present sociological theories.

The Biological Approach

The basic idea behind biological theories is that violence is somehow part of human nature. Sigmund Freud (1856–1939), a medical doctor who gained a

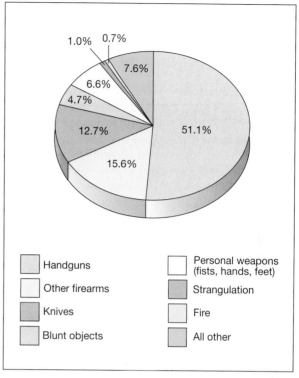

FIGURE 7–1 Murder: Type of Weapon Used

Firearms are used in almost two-thirds of all murders. Handguns are involved in more killings than all other weapons combined.

Source: U.S. Federal Bureau of Investigation (2003).

global reputation for developing the theory of psychoanalysis, claimed that a tendency to act aggressively is part of human nature (rooted in the drives he called the *id*). If so, we should expect some level of violence in any society.

Freud pointed to culture as the means by which societies restrain human aggression. In other words, cultural values and norms, taught through social institutions such as the family, operate in the individual (in the form of conscience or *superego*) to rein in aggressive impulses and maintain social order. Even so, Freud concluded, culture can never curb human aggression entirely. The best we can hope for is that society can convert human aggression into socially constructive activity (through a process Freud called *sublimation*); in U.S. society, football and other rough sports serve this purpose.

Beyond this general theory, biological conditions such as brain injury can make certain people especially likely to engage in violence. Specifically, injury to the limbic system—especially the amygdala, a small part of the brain that controls aggression—may cause people to react violently to frustration (Kassin, 2001).

Critical evaluation.   Many—but not all—experts accept Freud's theory that aggression is part of the biological foundation of human beings (Lorenz, 1966). Yet even if the theory is true, it says little about why some categories of people have higher rates of arrest for violent crime. Nor does the theory offer much help in explaining why some nations (such as the United States) have rates of criminal violence much higher than others (such as Japan). In addition, although it may be that certain injuries or disorders can make a person more likely to be violent, most of the problems we have described in this chapter are caused by people who are clinically quite normal. In the end, then, biological theories offer a limited explanation for violence.

The Psychological Approach

A psychological approach links violence to the individual personality. The most well-established psychological approach to violence is *frustration-aggression theory* (Dollard et al., 1939). In its simplest terms, this theory has three parts: (1) People pursue important goals; (2) when people cannot achieve their goals, they become frustrated; and (3) frustrated people are likely to direct aggression at those they believe are preventing them from achieving their goals.

Of course, people may not know exactly who is to blame for their frustration, and so they often select a safe target—one without the power to fight back—called a *scapegoat*. For example, take the case of young white men living in a working-class community with few jobs. They may feel frustration at not having a more secure life. However, rather than confronting the powerful political officials responsible for letting the community run down, they may direct their aggression at the small minority population living in the community, whom they wrongly blame for their situation.

Another psychological approach claims that the violence common to some people comes from an *antisocial personality* (such people sometimes are called "sociopaths" or "psychopaths"). Most such people are males who get into trouble by the time they are teenagers. In common language, these individuals lack a conscience, so they can lie, steal, or harm others without regret or remorse. Charles

Manson, who led a small group of followers on a killing spree in 1969 that took the lives of nine people, is a well-known example of a person with an antisocial personality (Black, 2000; Myers, 2001).

Critical evaluation.   Frustration-aggression theory makes sense, but it also raises as many questions as it answers. For example, why does frustration lead to aggression in some cases but not in others? Why is the aggression violent in some cases but not in others? As noted earlier in this chapter, how people deal with frustration depends on how they have learned to solve their problems. People who have grown up in violent families typically are the ones most likely to turn to violence themselves. In addition, whether weapons are close at hand can make all the difference as to whether aggression turns deadly (Berkowitz, 1993; Berkowitz & LePage, 1994).

Psychologists are convinced that the antisocial personality explains many cases of extreme violence, including serial killings. But sociologists counter that psychological abnormalities explain at best a small share of the violence in the United States; from their point of view, violence is more *normal* than *abnormal* and has roots in society itself.

EXPLAINING VIOLENCE: SOCIOLOGICAL THEORIES

Whereas biological and psychological theories focus on individuals, sociological theories highlight how society itself encourages or restrains violence. As in past chapters, we apply the structural-functional, symbolic-interaction, and social-conflict approaches to this issue.

Structural-Functional Analysis: The Culture of Violence

Structural-functionalists highlight how culture defines the rules of everyday behavior. Although no culture accepts any and all violence, every culture points to certain situations in which violence is acceptable and perhaps even desirable. In a classic study, Marvin Wolfgang and Franco Ferracuti (1967) examined the traditional culture of Sicily, where families jealously protect their honor. If a man were to dishonor a family—perhaps by running off with a daughter—cultural norms demand a swift response that might well include violence. Such violence might break the law in the United States, Wolfgang

Sociologists point out that people learn violent behavior just like they learn everything else—from their environment. When adults express anger in ways that turn violent, they harm not only themselves but also the young people who learn these social patterns from them.

and Ferracuti point out, but it might be *necessary* in a different cultural setting.

There is evidence that U.S. culture has become more accepting of violence. One recent survey of high school students found that 19 percent of girls and 43 percent of boys claimed it is all right to hit or threaten someone who makes you angry; 60 percent of girls and 75 percent of boys admitted they had done so in the past year (Tippit, 2001).

The *culture of violence* thesis states that a society's level of violence depends on cultural values. In the same way, the culture of a particular group—that is, a *subculture*—can encourage or discourage violence. Many researchers have noted that some young men (and, less often, young women) living in low-income, urban neighborhoods come to see violence as an acceptable, even necessary element of everyday life. With few chances for completing college and getting a good job, such people may use physical aggression to gain prestige. Moreover, in communities where violence is all too common, the ability to act quickly and violently may well be a good strategy for survival (Miller, 1970; Cohen, 1971; Anderson, 1994, 2002).

Critical evaluation. Structural-functional theory highlights the importance of culture, which goes a long way to explain why one society, or one segment of a population, would engage in violence more readily than another. But why do some people living in a particular neighborhood adopt patterns of violent behavior while others do not? In addition, what is it about certain neighborhoods that makes violence a

means of gaining respect in the first place? We can find answers to these questions by turning to sociology's other theoretical approaches.

Symbolic-Interaction Analysis: Learning Violence

The symbolic-interaction approach highlights how violence emerges from the interaction of individuals in their everyday lives. *Social learning theory* states that lessons about how to act—including whether or not to become violent—are learned from the earliest years of life as children observe and imitate their parents and others who are important to them. Research shows that children are especially likely to learn aggressive and violent behavior when people reward them for their violent actions and when they are targets of violence (Huesmann, 1986).

Later on, *peer groups*—people like us with whom we interact—can be a source of learning. On the college campus, men living together in dorms or fraternities sometimes come to define sex as a form of sport, in which "scoring" is the all-important goal. Learning to think of women in terms of sexual conquest, especially in a setting that also encourages alcohol abuse, contributes to the campus problem of sexual violence (Bandura, 1983; Herman, 2001).

Critical evaluation. The symbolic-interaction approach points out how each individual learns from living in a particular environment. This approach is useful in showing how people in some situations come to define violence as acceptable while those in some other setting do not. But this approach says little about why entire categories of people (such as men) are more likely to use violence whereas other categories of people (such as women) are common targets of violence. To understand such patterns, we turn to social-conflict analysis.

Social-Conflict Analysis: Violence and Inequality

The social-conflict approach investigates the causes and consequences of social inequality. This approach understands violence in terms of the power of certain categories of people over others.

As earlier chapters explained, Karl Marx described capitalist societies as divided into two main classes: the ruling capitalists (or bourgeoisie) and the majority who are workers (or the proletariat). As Marx saw it, the capitalist elite imposes its will on everyone else, forcing people to work in order to survive and using the police (or the national guard) to repress opposition. Thus, **structural violence,** *the use of violence by elites to protect their power and privileges,* is common in capitalist societies. From the social-conflict perspective, the greatest violence is not the occasional disruptions of the system by criminals or those seeking change but the normal operation of a system that brutalizes the majority by forcing them to live in poverty and with little control over their lives (Chambliss, 1995; Elias, 1997).

Social-conflict theory treats riots and criminal acts less as law-breaking than as a form of *rebellion,* that is, an effort by the powerless to strike back at a corrupt system. Perhaps it should not be surprising that some people in the poorest communities reject both the law and agencies of law enforcement as parts of the system that oppresses them (Agnew, 1992, 1994; Unnithan et al., 1994; Anderson, 2002).

Critical evaluation.   A strength of the social-conflict approach is that it shows how the system, under the banner of "justice," uses violence to protect the interests of the rich and powerful. Seen from this perspective, violence takes on a political character as an act of rebellion and an effort to bring about change. In support of social-conflict theory, note that some countries with less economic inequality than the United States—notably the Scandinavian nations of Norway, Sweden, and Denmark—also have less violent crime and very little rioting and other civil unrest. Yet, there are also

nations with high economic inequality—Australia is one example—where violent crime is much lower than in the United States (United Nations Development Programme, 2002). Perhaps the biggest problem with social-conflict theory is that it fails to explain why nations with socialist systems, including the People's Republic of China and Cuba, make extensive use of police and military power to repress dissent and why the prisons in these countries are full.

POLITICS AND VIOLENCE: CONSTRUCTING PROBLEMS AND DEFINING SOLUTIONS

Almost everyone considers violence, especially deadly violence, to be a problem. But the exact nature of the problem, what people see as its causes, and what they think U.S. society should do to solve it differ according to a person's political attitudes. Here we review the issue of violence from conservative, liberal, and radical perspectives.

Conservatives: Violence and Morality

Conservatives claim that human beings are prone to violence; they agree with Freud that aggression is part of human nature. As a result, it is up to the institutions of society—especially the family, religious groups, schools, and local communities—to control people's behavior. What lifts civilization above the "rule of the jungle" is that people often forgo what they *want* to do in favor of what they know they *ought* to do. In short, civilization depends on people learning and applying a set of moral standards that distinguish right from wrong.

What social arrangements make this likely? From a conservative point of view, children raised in two-parent, law-abiding, hard-working families, who are also guided by religious beliefs and are well integrated into their communities, are more likely to know right from wrong and less likely to engage in criminal violence. Conservatives claim the rise of criminal violence after 1960 was caused by a rising rate of divorce and out-of-wedlock births. This was also the time when schools relaxed strict discipline policies and dress codes, and the U.S. Supreme Court decided that prayer had no place in public schools. Moreover, conservatives claim that in the 1960s, Hollywood stopped making movies with positive moral messages and real heroes in favor of films that criticize the system and give the public ever-larger

During the 1960s, many inner cities erupted in violence. What conservatives denounced as a breakdown of law and order, liberals saw as a reaction to racial injustice, and radicals on the left viewed as rebellion on the part of ordinary people against a corrupt society run by the rich. Which view do you find most convincing? Why?

doses of sex and violence. Finally, women joined men in the work force, leaving fewer adults at home to supervise children, who often had to fend for themselves after school. Conservatives argue that the combination of these factors caused a decline of civility in everyday life and a rapid rise in the rates of crime and violence in the decades that followed (Carter, 1998).

Most conservatives favor tougher laws, more aggressive policing, and more severe penalties in response to the rising tide of violence. But they point out that the criminal justice system can do only so much to curb crime. The key to controlling violent crime lies not in reacting to criminals after violence happens but in preventing violence in the first place. This puts the greatest responsibility for an orderly society squarely on the shoulders of parents, who must teach their children to make the right moral choices in a world that tempts them to do the wrong thing.

Liberals: Violence and Opportunity

Liberals have a more positive view of human nature. They assume that people tend to be nonviolent unless twisted by a poor social environment. Therefore, liberals see violence as one consequence of the social problem of poverty. From this point of view, the problem of violence is greatest where economic opportunity is lowest: in many inner-city communities that have few jobs to offer (Wilson, 1996). Indeed, as we have explained, in the most depressed areas of large U.S. cities, a significant share of young people simply give up on a system that has failed them, greatly raising the odds that they will become involved in crime and violence (Anderson, 1994, 2002).

Learn more about racial differences between victims of violence at
http://www.ojp.usdoj.gov/bjs/abstract/vvr98.htm

Liberals agree with conservatives that today's families are under greater pressure than ever before. But liberals see the problem in economic terms: Many jobs pay so little that most families need at least two working adults just to get by. Equally important, many communities just don't have enough jobs to go around. From a liberal perspective, a true profamily policy would include a higher minimum wage and programs to create jobs in areas that need them. In short, whereas conservatives treat violence as a moral problem and look to families for a solution, liberals consider violence an economic problem and look to government to provide more job opportunities.

Liberals point to one other dimension of the violence problem: the easy availability of guns. To reduce the level of deadly violence in the United States, liberals argue, the government must do a better job of controlling firearms. One step was the 1993 Brady Bill, which requires a waiting period before a firearm can be purchased, during which time the dealer must conduct a background check of the buyer. Liberals also support the federal ban on sales of assault weapons and press for more restrictions on ownership of guns, especially the handguns that are used in more than half the murders in the United States.

Radicals: Violence as Insurrection

Radicals at both ends of the political spectrum reject society in its present form and demand fundamental change in social institutions. As those on the far right see it, the basic problem with the United States is the ever-growing power and reach of government. Right-wing radicals accept the conservative view that the rise in crime and violence is caused by the decline of the traditional family and a weakening of religious beliefs. They hold the government directly responsible for what they see as the collapse of society; programs and policies such as welfare, affirmative action, and the ban on prayer in public schools have transformed the United States into a nation in which people do less and less for themselves and look more and more to government to do things for them. Should this trend continue, right-wing radicals predict, government elites (and the corporate executives who work closely with them) will end up running everyone's lives, telling people what to do and even what to think. The recent war on terrorism has increased government power over everyone's lives more than ever. Just as important, they argue, with the government taking measures to ban guns, the average person will have no chance to fight back. Such thinking helps to explain why right-wing radicals are so passionate about the right to own firearms. Moreover, they argue, the government has already used military force against those who are determined to resist; the Critical Thinking box provides details of two important cases.

People on the far left of the political spectrum have not been involved in violent antigovernment actions to the same degree as people on the far right. But the radical left shares the view that violence directed against the system may be justified.

Radicals on the far left accept the liberal view that a harmful social environment is generally the cause of violence. But whereas liberals believe that U.S. society has the power to expand economic opportunities and thereby reduce violence, radicals claim that only the overthrow or collapse of the capitalist economic system will bring meaningful change. The problem, from the point of view of the far left, is that capitalism generates such economic disparities that tens of millions of families live in or near poverty, without quality schooling and with little chance to better their lives.

The far left's formula for a violence-free society begins with an economic system that meets the basic needs of all and a political system that is not dominated by the rich. Marx imagined that this goal could be accomplished by organizing economic production communally rather than through a system of private property. Once the United States has rid itself of the extremes of wealth and poverty, the argument continues, it will be possible to build a society with a far lower level of violence. The Left to Right table on page 186 views the problem of violence and possible solutions from the various political perspectives.

GOING ON FROM HERE

In this chapter, we have described the problem of violence, including murder, rape, and violence within the family. Numerous factors, including the mass media, drugs, poverty, gangs, and the easy availability of guns, play a part in this country's violence problem.

The United States has struggled with violence from the earliest contact between European colonizers and native peoples, through the "Wild West" era, gangster violence during Prohibition, periodic urban rioting, and the soaring rates of violent crime after 1960, as well as terrorism coming both from abroad and from within. Even so, there are some hopeful signs that the violence is declining, especially the overall downward trend in violent crime since the early 1990s.

As we look to the future, will this trend continue? The rates of violent crime have declined over the last decade, and the drop in the number of young people in the age category most prone to violence may keep these rates from rising much higher. But a long-term solution to the violence problem is likely to require some basic changes in society itself. Here is where differences of opinion arise. Conservatives

Critical Thinking

Ruby Ridge and Waco: The View from the Far Right

RANDY WEAVER VIEWED THE UNITED STATES from the radical right, believing the government interfered in every aspect of his life. In response, he moved his wife and children to a remote cabin on Ruby Ridge, high in Montana's Rocky Mountains.

But government officials suspected Weaver of illegally selling guns and monitored his movements. FBI agents tried several times to buy weapons from him and, in 1992, Weaver sold an undercover agent an illegal sawed-off shotgun. Soon after, FBI agents surrounded Weaver's cabin and demanded that he surrender. Weaver refused to come out. When Weaver's fourteen-year-old son, Samuel, dashed from a shed toward the house, agents opened fire, killing the boy. Before the standoff ended, Weaver killed a government agent, and agents killed Weaver's wife and infant son.

A second case, in 1993, brought agents from the government's Bureau of Alcohol, Tobacco, and Firearms (ATF) to the headquarters of the Branch Davidian religious cult in Waco, Texas. ATF officials believed that the Branch Davidian leader, David Koresh, was stockpiling weapons and possibly harming children. After Koresh refused the agents' demands that he surrender, some 100 agents approached the compound, sparking an exchange of gunfire in which four agents and six Branch Davidian members died. The agents retreated.

The FBI entered the case and and tried to negotiate with Koresh, who refused to cooperate with authorities. As time went on, agents managed to obtain the release of thirty-four people, including twenty-one children. But days turned to weeks and FBI agents decided to take action. On April 19, 1993—fifty-one days after the siege began—the FBI rammed a tank through the wall of the main building of the compound, firing flammable tear gas inside. The building quickly became an inferno that claimed the lives of Koresh and eighty-six Branch Davidian members. The FBI found hundreds of weapons in the compound; evidence suggests that many who died were shot at close range, perhaps by Koresh himself.

To many people, Randy Weaver and David Koresh were simply kooks and criminals. But to some on the radical right, their stories are clear evidence of the government's determined efforts to subdue people who resist government control. Such thinking provides some insight into Timothy McVeigh's deadly bombing of the Alfred P. Murrah Federal Building—a symbol of government power—in Oklahoma City on April 19, 1995, killing 168 people. McVeigh, a member of a radical right-wing group who was later convicted and executed for the crime, destroyed the building on the two-year anniversary of the Waco tragedy.

ISSUES AND EXERCISES

1. Do you think a free society should allow people to stockpile weapons? Do such actions threaten public safety and justify police action? Explain your view.

2. In the wake of the September 11, 2001, terror attacks, are you more or less supportive of police action against allegedly dangerous people? Why?

3. Research Navigator.com — Use Research Navigator™ to learn more about the Ruby Ridge and Waco incidents. (See instructions on page 25; keywords: "Ruby Ridge," "radical right")

Sources: Kantrowitz (1993), Barnes (1995), Bovard (1995).

consider violence a moral and family issue, whereas liberals argue that a violence-free society depends on economic opportunity; moderates (including both conservatives and liberals) believe reforms can make a difference, whereas radicals (on the far right and the far left) advocate nothing less than basic change in society's institutions. The great differences between the various political positions suggest that the national debate over a solution to the problem of violence is likely to go on for some time.

LEFT ⓣⓞ RIGHT

THE POLITICS OF VIOLENCE

	RADICAL LEFT VIEW	LIBERAL VIEW	CONSERVATIVE VIEW	RADICAL RIGHT VIEW
WHAT IS THE PROBLEM?	While agreeing with the general liberal analysis, radicals on the left see the structure of the capitalist system as the source of the greatest violence and suffering.	People tend to be nonviolent unless their social environment encourages antisocial behavior. Many U.S. communities lack economic opportunities, which encourages crime and violence.	A tendency toward violence is part of human nature, which society must control. In recent decades, a weakening of families and religion means less moral education and a rising tide of violence.	While agreeing with the general conservative analysis, radicals on the right see the expanding power of government as the biggest threat to society. Gun control amounts to a government strategy to disarm society and repress opposition.
WHAT IS THE SOLUTION?	Fundamental change in our political and economic institutions is needed to create a more egalitarian system. Crime and violence are forms of rebellion by the powerless.	Government must expand economic opportunity for those who need it most by creating jobs and raising the minimum wage; gun control is also needed.	The criminal justice system can do only so much to control crime and violence; society must reaffirm the importance of teaching children to make sound moral choices.	People's rights to act free of government control—especially the right to bear arms—must be protected. Crime and violence against the government are acts of political rebellion.

Join the debate . . .

1. If you were put in charge of a national commission to end violence, what new policies would you enact to address this problem?

2. How would people using each political perspective view the issue of rape? What about family violence?

3. Which of the four political analyses of violence included here do you find most convincing? Why?

CHAPTER SUMMARY

1. Violence is behavior that causes damage to property or injury to people. Whether people view violence as a problem depends on the intentions of the actor, whether the action conforms to cultural norms and values, whether the action threatens the social order, and whether the actions are carried out by or against the government.

2. Violent crime is common in the United States. Most murders are committed by male offenders using guns; in most cases, offender and victim are of the same race; many murders are unplanned crimes of passion.

3. Although accounting for just a tiny fraction of all murders, mass murder causes great public

concern because it usually occurs in public places. Serial killing is also rare, and it, too, attracts much media attention. Most serial killers are considered mentally ill.

4. Responses to violent crime include get-tough policies, such as "zero tolerance" policing and "three strikes and you're out" sentencing, backed up by an increase in the number of police officers and resulting in a sharp rise in the number of people sent to prison.

5. As women have gained a strong political voice, rape has been defined as a serious social problem. Police now make an arrest in 44 percent of all reported cases; other responses to rape include laws forbidding marital rape and stalking, as well as education programs about acquaintance rape.

6. Problems of family violence gained public attention beginning with child abuse in the 1960s, violence against women in the 1970s, and elder abuse in the 1980s.

7. The mass media expose people to a great deal of violence. Research suggests that watching media violence increases aggressiveness in everyone and raises the risk of deadly violence in some people.

8. Drugs play a part in many violent crimes: Sixty percent of inmates imprisoned for violent offenses claim they were under the influence of alcohol, an illegal drug, or both when they committed their crime.

9. Poverty is linked to violence because it generates both frustration and stress.

10. Government studies suggest there are more than 26,000 youth gangs in the United States, which range from nonviolent groups to full-fledged criminal organizations.

11. There are some 200 million guns in the United States; 40 percent of households have at least one gun.

12. Biological theories of violence argue that the human species has a tendency toward aggression that culture must restrain. In addition, certain brain injuries raise the likelihood that a person will become violent.

13. Psychological explanations of violence include frustration-aggression theory, which states that people may strike out at others whom they think are preventing them from achieving their goals.

14. Among sociological theories, the culture of violence thesis is a structural-functional approach stating that some societies encourage violence much more than others. Within a society, a subculture may encourage violent behavior.

15. Social learning theory is a symbolic-interactional approach stating that people learn violence, often early in life, just as they learn other patterns of behavior.

16. The social-conflict approach highlights structural violence, the use of violence by elites to protect their power and privileges.

17. Conservatives define violence as a moral issue, highlighting the responsibility of families to raise children with strong values emphasizing self-control. Liberals see violence as an economic issue, claiming that a lack of jobs in many communities weakens families and generates widespread frustration and anger. Radicals treat violence as a form of rebellion, with those on the far right condemning government for seeking to control people's lives and those on the far left condemning capitalism for exploiting people.

KEY CONCEPTS

violence (p. 165) behavior that causes damage to property or injury to people

institutional violence (p. 166) violence carried out by government representatives under the law

anti-institutional violence (p. 166) violence directed against the government in violation of the law

violent crime (p. 167) crime that involves violence or the threat of violence against others

murder (p. 167) the unlawful, intentional killing of one person by another

manslaughter (p. 167) the unlawful, unintentional killing of one person by another

mass murder   (p. 168) the intentional, unlawful killing of more than four people at one time and place

serial murder   (p. 169) the killing of several people by one offender over a period of time

forcible rape   (p. 170) the carnal knowledge of a female forcibly and against her will

family violence   (p. 171) emotional, physical, or sexual abuse of one family member by another

battered child syndrome   (p. 172) a pattern of physical and psychological injury to a child caused by the action (or neglect) of another person

youth gangs   (p. 177) groups of young people who identify with one another and with a particular territory

structural violence   (p. 182) the use of violence by elites to protect their power and privileges

THINKING CRITICALLY: QUESTIONS AND ISSUES

1. Form your own definition of violence. What do you see as the differences between individual violence and institutional violence?

2. Do you think that the mass media present too much violence? Why or why not?

3. Perception of a social problem usually depends on how power is distributed among various categories of people. Why was violence (including lynching) by white people against black people not a treated as a crime during much of U.S. history? Why did men's violence against women become a visible problem only in recent decades? Can you think of a type of violence accepted today that may be defined as a serious problem in decades to come?

4. What specific changes might conservatives, liberals, and radicals make to U.S. society in an effort to address many of the violence issues raised in this chapter? Which changes would you support? Why?

GETTING INVOLVED: LEARNING ACTIVITIES

1. Watch several episodes of prime time television programming (perhaps including some of the shows listed in Table 7–2), noting all acts of violence. To gauge the extent of the TV violence, count instances of violence and assess its severity using a simple measure called TIP: your estimate of the total years in prison someone would serve for committing the violent acts you see.

2. Almost every community has a shelter for battered women. Find one in your area and speak to the people who run it about the problem of domestic violence and about the shelter's programs and goals. Consider volunteering at the shelter.

3. Almost all colleges and universities keep track of violent crime that occurs on the campus. Check with campus security and see what kinds of data they collect. Also, many campuses have organizations (such as "Take Back the Night") from which you can learn more about the problem of sexual violence.

4. One of the hottest issues on the U.S. political scene involves gun control. Use Research Navigator™ (see instructions on page 25; keyword: "gun control") or visit your library to find material on gun control. Look for scholarly research studying the link between guns and violence and find out more about groups that support gun ownership (such as the National Rifle Association) and support gun control (such as Handgun Control, Inc.).

GETTING CONNECTED: USEFUL WEB LINKS

http://www.prenhall.com/macionis
Visit the interactive Companion Website™ that accompanies this text. Begin by clicking on the cover of your book. You will find a chapter-by-chapter study guide, practice tests, suggested Web links, and links to other relevant material.

http://www.who.int/violence_injury_prevention
For a global perspective on problems of violence, visit the World Health Organization's Violence Prevention Web site, where links will lead you to statistics, studies, and current efforts to reduce violence worldwide. What are some anti-violence strategies?

http://www.iir.com/nygc
This is the Web site for the National Youth Gang Center, which offers information, statistics, policy, and programs to combat gang-related violence. Based on this site, what factors encourage the formation of violent gangs?

http://www.ojp.usdoj.gov/bjs/abstract/svcw.htm
Are you concerned about campus violence? This site contains a recent report from the Bureau of Justice Statistics on sexual violence directed against college women.

GETTING STARTED ON YOUR OWN: RESEARCH NAVIGATOR™

Follow the instructions found on page 25 of this text to access the features of Research Navigator™. Once at the Web site, enter your Login Name and Password. Then, to use the **Content Select** database, enter keywords such as "mass murder," "rape," and "family violence," and the search engine will supply relevant and recent scholarly and popular press publications. Use the *New York Times* **Search-by-Subject Archive** to find recent news articles related to sociology and the **Link Library** feature to find relevant Web links organized by the key terms associated with this chapter.

© *Paul Marcus, [detail from]* Yvonne's Story: Maze of AIDS, *Studio SPM, Inc.*

SEXUALITY

JOYFUL SINGING FLOWED FROM THE WARM KITCHEN on a cold winter day. Julie and Hillary Goodridge were spending a happy afternoon with their young daughter, Annie, as the Beatles song "All You Need Is Love" boomed in the living room. As the song ended, Julie asked Annie whether she knew any people who loved each other. "Sure," Annie replied, and she rattled off the names of a dozen of her mother's friends, all heterosexual married couples.

"What about Mommy and Ma?" asked Julie.

"Well," the child thought about it, "If you loved each other, you'd get married."

Suddenly the joy was gone from the room. Julie and Hillary looked at each other, feeling both sad and angry.

The next day the couple drove off to the Massachusetts Department of Public Health to see about getting a marriage license. Nervously approaching the counter, they asked for an application.

"No, you're not allowed to," said the woman working there. "I'll need two grooms first." They asked to speak to the department supervisor. But the woman snapped, "No, you can't get married, and there is nothing you can do about it."

Julie and Hillary Goodridge decided there was something they could do. With the help of a gay and lesbian activist group, they filed a lawsuit demanding that the state of Massachusetts allow them to marry. Their case led to a landmark decision by the Massachusetts Supreme Judicial Court affirming the right of homosexual people to legal marriage (Thomas, 2003).

Controversy over gay marriage is on the rise in the United States. In 2003, the U.S. Supreme Court overturned a Texas gay couple's sodomy conviction for sexual acts in the privacy of their own apartment. The high court's decision, which struck down all sodomy laws across the country, was applauded by many who saw it as opening the door to gay marriage. In 2004,

GETTING THE PICTURE

✦ Is U.S. society open about sex?

For most of our history, people did not discuss sex, and most considered sex other than intercourse by married partners to be wrong.

✦ Does love naturally lead to marriage?

Not for same-sex couples, who are legally barred from marrying in the United States.

✦ Do you know all the dangers of sexual activity?

They include the risk of infection by more than fifty diseases, including AIDS.

191

Before the sexual revolution, U.S. society tolerated little in the way of public displays of sexuality, as this visiting day for World War II military personnel suggests.

in fact, thousands of same-sex couples were married in San Francisco and several other cities.

Some conservatives, however, were dismayed at the Supreme Court ruling and at the possibility of gay marriage becoming a reality. In their view, sex and marriage should be between a man and a woman. Currently, the law in every state bans gay marriage, but for how long?

This chapter explores the controversy over gay marriage, prostitution, pornography, and many other issues involving human sexuality. We begin with some basic definitions.

WHAT IS SEX?

Sex reflects the influences of both biology and culture. To understand this concept, then, we need to examine sex from a biological and a cultural perspective.

Sex: A Biological Issue

Sex is *the biological distinction between females and males.* The two sexes have different *genitals*, the organs used for reproduction, which are also called *primary sex characteristics*. In addition, when people

mature they typically display different physical traits, called *secondary sex characteristics:* Females develop breasts and wider hips, and males develop more muscle and body hair.

The term **sex** also refers to *sexual activity that leads to sexual gratification and possibly reproduction.* From a biological point of view, reproduction is vital to the survival of a species. Among humans, a female provides an ovum, or egg, which is fertilized by a male's sperm through sexual intercourse to form a fertilized embryo. The embryo contains twenty-three pairs of chromosomes, which are the biological codes that determine a child's sex and other physical traits.

Sex: A Cultural Issue

Sociologists point out that sex is also guided by culture and, as such, varies from one place to another. In every society, cultural norms influence the selection of sexual partners. These norms involve *age* (some societies accept sexual activity on the part of children, for example, whereas others define such behavior as a serious problem), *marital status* (some societies restrict sexual activity to married partners, but others are more permissive), and *the sex of partners* (societies differ dramatically in their attitudes toward sexuality involving people of the same sex). In the United States, the cultural norm historically has been adult, male–female married partners engaging in vaginal intercourse. In reality, of course, much sexual behavior in our society does not conform to this model. People have sex within and outside marriage, sexual relationships involve both different-sex and same-sex partners, and sexual activity includes anal as well as vaginal intercourse, oral–genital contact, and masturbation alone or with a partner. Moreover, some people (whether by choice or circumstance) engage in little or no sexual activity (Laumann et al., 1994).

SEXUAL ATTITUDES IN THE UNITED STATES

How people think and act regarding sex has changed over the course of this nation's history. During the colonial era, the European settlers had no effective means of birth control. Therefore, most communities had strict norms limiting sex to married couples for the purpose of reproduction. For example, the New England Puritans condemned sex outside marriage and regarded as sinful any sex (including masturbation) that was not intended to result in

A DEFINING MOMENT

Alfred Kinsey: Talking Openly about Sex

ALFRED KINSEY (1894–1956) ASKED PEOPLE TO TALK about sex. In today's society, this may not seem very controversial, but in Kinsey's day, people did not consider sex a topic for polite conversation, much less scientific research.

Kinsey founded the Institute for Sex Research at Indiana University in 1942, and in the years that followed, he and a dozen research assistants interviewed more than 11,000 men and women about their sexual practices. His first book, *Sexual Behavior in the Human Male* (1948), is a fairly dry, scientific work; yet it sold more than half a million copies. A second volume, *Sexual Behavior in the Human Female* (1953), was equally popular. Clearly, people in the United States were more interested in sex than they were willing to let on.

Some of Kinsey's findings made news headlines, especially his conclusion that people in the United States were far less conventional about sex than popularly believed. Kinsey's subjects reported breaking many cultural taboos of that time: Almost half of female subjects reported having sexual intercourse before marriage, and one-third of married men said that, while married, they had a sexual relationship with someone other than their wives.

Reports of Alfred Kinsey's survey of human sexual practices caused nothing less than a sensation in the news media in the mid-1900s.

Critics pointed out flaws in Kinsey's study, noting that his subjects may not have been representative of the U.S. population (Masters et al., 1992): In his eagerness to find people willing to talk about their sexual experiences, he had ended up using far too many college students and prisoners while almost totally ignoring people who were older, rural, or poor. Nevertheless, Kinsey's research was a defining moment in our nation's history because it brought sex out of the closet and put it on the table as a topic of people's everyday conversation.

---

conception. They believed that without strict rules to control people's behavior, and even their dress, the ever-present temptation of sex would lead to unwanted pregnancy and also prostitution.

Gradually, advances in technology gave people more control over reproduction and thus more choices about their sexual practices. Other factors played a part, too. After 1920, millions of people migrated from farms and small towns across the United States to industrial cities, where many young men and women lived on their own and also worked together. The result was more sexual freedom, which is one of the reasons that decade was dubbed the Roaring Twenties.

A landmark in the nation's changing view of sexuality came after World War II in the research of Alfred Kinsey (1894–1956). Perhaps the most remarkable thing about Kinsey was that he investigated

sex, which had never been the focus of a major research project. The Defining Moment box explains how Kinsey changed a whole nation's way of thinking.

The Sexual Revolution

From the growing sexual freedom of the Roaring Twenties to the Kinsey research of the 1940s and 1950s, sexual attitudes evolved throughout the twentieth century. But it was not until the late 1960s,—when young people embraced a culture of freedom summed up in the cry, "Sex, drugs, and rock and roll!"—that people began to speak of a "sexual revolution."

A major factor in the sexual revolution was the introduction of the birth control pill in 1960. Unlike condoms and diaphragms, which had to be used at the time of intercourse, "the pill" could be taken at

DIMENSIONS OF DIFFERENCE

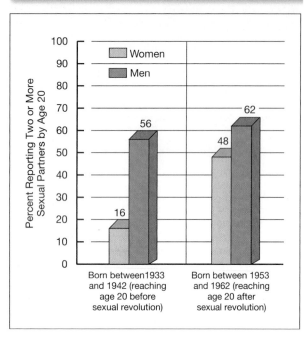

FIGURE 8–1   The Sexual Revolution: Moving Away from the Double Standard

Among people who came of age before the sexual revolution (shown on the left), a smaller share had two or more sexual partners by age 20 compared with people who came of age after the sexual revolution (shown on the right). The difference is especially marked between the two categories of women.

Source: Laumann et al. (1994).

a woman's convenience, and she could have sex anytime. This fact, combined with the pill's high effectiveness, dramatically reduced the connection between heterosexual intercourse and pregnancy.

Figure 8–1 confirms that the U.S. population became more free and easy about sex in the 1960s. Among those born between 1933 and 1942—who reached age twenty before 1962—only 56 percent of men and 16 percent of women said they had two or more sexual partners before they were twenty. But one generation later, among those born between 1953 and 1962, 62 percent of men and 48 percent of women reported two or more sexual partners by age twenty (Laumann et al., 1994:198). The smaller difference in male–female responses in the latter group also suggests that U.S. society was moving away from the traditional *double standard* by which men enjoyed sexual freedom while women

were expected to delay sex until marriage and then remain faithful to their husbands.

The Sexual Revolution and Gender   The revolutionary 1960s was about more than "good lovin'." This was the decade in which homosexual men (commonly called "gays") and homosexual women (or "lesbians") launched a social movement to combat prejudice and discrimination against people of their sexual orientation. The 1960s also saw a renewed effort by women to end their historical domination by men. In fact, many feminists argued that sexuality was at the heart of male domination. Kate Millet (1970) summed up the argument, saying that sex is really about power: As long as men view women as sexual creatures, and women accept this definition of themselves, men will dominate women. The word "sexism" came into people's vocabulary, thereby defining a new social problem.

Feminists challenged male power by demanding, equal pay for equal work and by taking a stand against pornography, rape, and incest. In addition, they demanded the rights to contraception (which was illegal in some parts of the country as late as the 1960s) and abortion (which was illegal everywhere until 1973). In short, out of the sexual revolution emerged the idea that the only person with a right to control a woman's body is the woman herself.

The Sexual Counterrevolution

The movements toward freer sexuality, greater power for women, and acceptance of gays and lesbians found many supporters but also sparked opposition. By the 1970s, a sexual counterrevolution was underway as conservatives called for a return to traditional "family values." As conservatives saw it, what people needed was not more freedom but stronger families and more personal responsibility.

The conservative backlash to the sexual revolution did not succeed in turning back the clock. Since the 1960s, a majority of U.S. adults have remained convinced that people should decide for themselves whether and with whom to have sex. Such beliefs are evident in the rising share of people—about three-fourths of men and two-thirds of women—who have sexual intercourse by their senior year in high school (Laumann et al., 1994). Yet many issues involving sexuality remain controversial, as later sections of this chapter will explore. We begin with the matter of sexual orientation.

SEXUAL ORIENTATION

Sexual orientation refers to *a person's romantic, emotional, and sexual attraction to another person.* Sexual orientation can include partners of the same sex, the other sex, either sex, or neither sex (that is, no sexual partners at all).

Many people have a vague or confused idea of what specific sexual orientations are. The most common sexual orientation, one approved by cultures the world over, is **heterosexuality** (*hetero* is Greek meaning "the other of two"), *sexual attraction to someone of the other sex.* Even so, in all societies a small but significant share of people favor **homosexuality** (*homo* is Greek meaning "the same"), which is *sexual attraction to someone of the same sex.*

Many people mistakenly believe that heterosexuality and homosexuality are opposites, with every person falling neatly into one category or the other. But as Kinsey (1948) explained, many people have varying degrees of both sexual orientations. Also, keep in mind that sexual *attraction* is not the same as sexual *behavior.* Although most people have experienced some attraction to a person of the same sex, far fewer have engaged in homosexual behavior. The fact that many people do not act on their attraction is due to cultural norms that discourage same-sex relationships.

Kinsey's finding that sexual orientation often is not clear-cut called attention to the existence of **bisexuality,** *sexual attraction to people of both sexes.* Some bisexual people experience equal attraction to females and males; others have a stronger attraction to one sex than to the other. Of course, bisexuals may experience attraction to both sexes but limit their sexual behavior to partners of one sex. Finally, not everyone experiences sexual attraction at all. **Asexuality** is *the absence of sexual attraction to people of either sex.*

We now take a closer look at issues related to homosexuality.

Homosexuality

Because most people endorse heterosexuality as a norm, homosexual people—gay men and lesbians—are pushed to the margins of society. To the extent that homosexuality is defined as deviant, it can itself be viewed as a social problem. This attitude was—and to some degree still is—common in U.S. society, which is the major reason that gay men and lesbians have long experienced prejudice and discrimination.

Today, as acceptance of homosexuality grows, laws have been passed banning many forms of discrimination based on sexual orientation; for example, it is illegal to withhold housing or a job from people based on their sexual orientation. But other forms of discrimination are legal: The military can and does lawfully discharge homosexual men and women who openly display their sexual orientation, and many religious organizations refuse to ordain gay men or lesbians as leaders. In addition, as noted in the opening to this chapter, although the movement supporting same-sex marriage is gaining ground, it remains illegal everywhere in the United States.

Prejudice against gay men and lesbians is also found on the college campus. One recent study found that one-third of gay and lesbian students reported that they had experienced harassment in the past year (Rankin, 2003).

Sometimes hostility toward gay men and lesbians leads to violence. The FBI records some 1,250 hate crimes against gays each year, and the true number is certainly far higher. Many of these violent acts—including assault and even murder—are directed at people simply because of their sexual orientation. According to the National Gay and Lesbian Task Force, one in five gay men and lesbians reports being physically assaulted, and almost all homosexual people report verbal abuse (National Gay and Lesbian Task Force, 1998; U.S. Federal Bureau of Investigation, 2003).

The Extent of Homosexuality What share of the U.S. population has a homosexual orientation? This is a hard question to answer because, as already noted, sexual orientation is not a matter of neat categories. The extent of homosexuality depends on exactly how one defines the term.

In his pioneering work, Alfred Kinsey (1948) found that most women and men experience at least some same-sex attraction. Although most do not act on it, many do: Kinsey estimated that one-third of men and one-eighth of women have at least some homosexual experience; that is, they engage in some homosexual acts at some point (often in adolescence). Furthermore, Kinsey estimated that 4 percent of men and 2 percent of women were exclusively homosexual in orientation, meaning they had only same-sex desires, engaged in only same-sex sexual activity, and thought of themselves as gay men or lesbians.

More recent research by Edward Laumann and his colleagues (1994) provides a more scientific estimate of homosexuality. Figure 8–2 on page 196 shows that 9.1 percent of men and 4.3 percent of women (some 20 million people in all) report at least

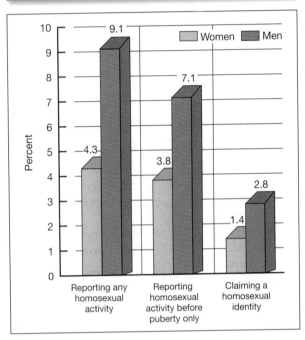

FIGURE 8–2   **Measuring Homosexual Orientation**

How one defines "homosexual orientation" affects the number of people considered to be homosexual.

Source: Laumann et al. (1994).

some homosexual activity, typically in adolescence; 2.8 percent of men and 1.4 percent of women (about 6 million people) define themselves as homosexual or bisexual (Laumann et al., 1994).

What Gives Us Sexual Orientation?

If sexual orientation is hard to define, it is also difficult to explain. Sexual orientation results from many factors, including genetics, brain structure, hormones, life experiences, and culture. Not surprisingly, then, experts point out that both culture and biology have a part to play in sexual orientation.

Cultural Factors   People did not always pay much attention to sexual orientation. French social philosopher Michel Foucault (1990) notes that there was little historical existence of homosexuals as a category until scientists began defining people that way in the late nineteenth century. This is not to say that, in earlier times, people did not have same-sex experiences. The point is simply that cultural systems took little note of it. But once societies socially constructed

the categories of "heterosexual," and "homosexual," people who had homosexual experiences were set apart as different and became targets of prejudice and discrimination (D'Emilio, 1984; Weeks, 1985).

Different meanings attached to sexual behavior are also evident in the fact that same-sex behavior varies considerably from culture to culture. Among the Chukchee Eskimo of Siberia, for example, a man may take on the role known as a *berdache*, dressing and acting like a Chukchee woman, doing women's work and perhaps even marrying another man. Among the Sambia of New Guinea, by contrast, most boys engage in a sexual ritual in which they perform oral sex on older men in the belief that ingesting semen will enhance their masculinity. Given such diversity of sexual expression in the world, it is easy to conclude that sexual orientation has much to do with society itself (Herdt, 1993; Murray & Roscoe, 1998; Blackwood & Wieringa, 1999).

Finally, some sociological studies suggest that sexual orientation is rooted in socialization. One recent study of opposite-sex twins (one girl and one boy) found a higher likelihood of homosexual orientation among people raised in a gender-neutral environment than among those raised according to conventional ideas of masculine and feminine behavior (Bearman & Bruckner, 2002).

Biological Factors   On the individual level, most evidence suggests that sexual orientation is rooted in human biology. Like being left- or right-handed, sexual orientation appears to be largely fixed at birth.

Neurobiologist Simon LeVay (1993) claims that the key to sexual orientation is found in the human brain. Le Vay studied the brains of both homosexual men and heterosexual men and noted a difference in the hypothalamus, an organ of the brain that regulates the body's hormone levels. Biologists have established that hormone levels (especially testosterone levels in men) affect sexual orientation. Thus, they conclude, small differences in the brain play a significant part in establishing a person's sexual orientation (Grady, 1992).

Genes, as well as hormones, may affect sexual orientation. In a study of forty-four pairs of brothers—all homosexual—researchers found that thirty-three of the pairs had a unique feature on the X chromosome (one of the genetic components that affects human sexuality). Could this be evidence of a "gay gene"? Some researchers think so, noting that the gay brothers had an unexpectedly high number of gay male relatives on their mother's side, the source of the X chromosome (Hamer & Copeland, 1994).

Critical evaluation. Scientists continue to debate the social and biological causes of sexual orientation. The evidence to date suggests that biology plays a major part in how people experience sexual attraction (Weinrich, 1987; Troiden, 1988; Isay, 1989; Angier, 1992; Gelman, 1992). But keep in mind that many people do not fit into simple categories as being "gay" or "straight."

Finally, why does it matter whether sexual orientation is caused by society or human biology? The point is that if sexual orientation is biological, it is as much beyond our control as the color of our skin. Therefore, gay people cannot be blamed for their sexual orientation and are entitled to the same legal protection from discrimination as African Americans (Herek, 1991; Schmalz, 1993).

Even so, a biological foundation of sexual orientation may pose dangers as well, given the rapid pace of advancements in medical technology. For example, if someday parents are able to learn that their future child has a gay gene, they might decide to abort the fetus; another possibility is that doctors might try to develop surgical techniques in an effort to "correct" the brains of gay men and lesbians (Zicklin, 1992).

Homosexuality and Public Policy

In 1960, homosexuality was widely regarded as wrong in the United States. Many people also considered it a sickness; even the American Psychiatric Association included homosexuality in its list of mental disorders. Discrimination against gay men and lesbians was common, as companies, schools, government agencies, and the military routinely refused to hire people thought to be homosexual. Just as important, employees found to be gay or lesbian were fired for no other reason than their sexual orientation. Given this hostile environment, it is easy to see why most lesbians and gay men stayed "in the closet," that is, kept their homosexuality secret from all but a few close friends.

The American Psychological Association posts answers to commonly asked questions regarding sexual orientation at
http://www.apa.org/pubinfo.html

In recent decades, attitudes toward homosexuality have become more tolerant (Loftus, 2001). In 1973, the American Psychiatric Association removed homosexuality from its list of mental disorders. Public attitudes, too, have become more accepting. As

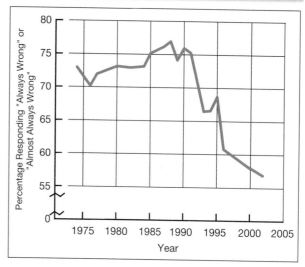

DIMENSIONS OF DIFFERENCE

FIGURE 8–3 U.S. Attitudes toward Homosexual Relations, 1973–2002

Survey Question: "What about sexual relations between two adults of the same sex? Do you think it is always wrong, almost always wrong, wrong only sometimes, or not wrong at all?"

Source: NORC (2003).

shown in Figure 8–3, the percentage of U.S. adults who claim homosexuality is wrong was well over 70 percent twenty years ago; today, it has dropped to about 57 percent (NORC, 2003:234). Moreover, such surveys show that whatever they think about homosexuality, a majority of U.S. adults now believe that homosexual people should have the same job opportunities and basic civil rights as everyone else.

The growing acceptance of homosexuality appears to have been on the minds of the justices of the U.S. Supreme Court when, in 2003, they handed down the landmark ruling (*Lawrence et al. v. Texas*) that struck down the Texas law banning sodomy ("unnatural sex, especially anal intercourse") between same-sex couples. This ruling, described in the opening to this chapter, ended similar laws that remained in other states.

Gay Marriage

To many people, the Supreme Court's decision in the Texas case suggests that legal marriage for gay people may not be too far in the future. Some states—notably Vermont and Massachusetts—have taken steps toward legalizing gay marriage. In addition, dozens of cities—from San Francisco to New York—permit gay couples to register their "domestic partnerships." Such policies provide many of the same benefits, including family health care and inheritance rights. Recently, mayors in several cities permitted thousands of same-sex partners to marry, ignoring state laws banning such unions.

Should one state enact a law allowing gay marriage, it could have nationwide consequences because the Constitution requires states to honor each other's laws. In effect, if gay marriage becomes legal in one state, it would become legal everywhere. For this reason, thirty-eight states have passed laws stating that they will not recognize gay marriages, and in 1996 Congress passed the Defense of Marriage Act, which allows states to ignore a same-sex marriage performed in any other state. In the meantime, hundreds of business corporations—including a growing number of colleges and universities as well as the "big three" automakers—have decided to extend the same employee benefits they give to married spouses to domestic partners. Around the world, Denmark, Norway, and Sweden recognize gay marriage with limited rights, and the Netherlands, Belgium, and, most recently, Canada, provide full legal marriage rights to gays and lesbians.

Many conservatives oppose any steps toward gay marriage, claiming that the traditional idea of marriage in the United States has always been a union between a man and a woman (Thomas, 2003). But some people who support conservative "family values" *do* favor gay marriage—as well as the right of gay couples to adopt children—on the grounds that because families are good for people and good for society, we should encourage families for everyone, whether straight or gay (Sullivan, 2002).

The Gay Rights Movement

The social gains made by gay men and lesbians have resulted largely from efforts by the gay rights movement. Although the first gay rights group was formed in Chicago in 1924, the movement became influential in the 1950s (Chauncy, 1994). Rather than accepting the conventional definition of homosexuality itself as a problem, activists turned the tables by defining the problem as prejudice and discrimination against gay people.

Despite the risks of being identified as homosexual, in the 1960s more and more lesbians and gay men stepped forward to bring about change. A turning point occurred on June 27, 1969, when police raided the Stonewall Inn, a bar in New York's Greenwich Village. Police knew this was a gay bar; conducting a raid meant taking people's names, which usually ended up in the newspaper. This time, however, the patrons of Stonewall openly resisted what they believed was a clear case of unlawful harassment. Joined by others, they battled police for the better part of two days. This event, which came to be known as the Stonewall Riot, marked a new militancy in the gay rights movement.

Soon after the Stonewall Riot, the gay rights movement began using the term **homophobia** to describe *an aversion or hostility to people thought to be gay, lesbian, or bisexual.* This concept reinforced the idea that the problem was not homosexuality but people who would not accept others simply because of their sexual orientation (Weinberg, 1973). The success of the gay rights movement is evident in the widespread condemnation of homophobia as a social problem today.

PORNOGRAPHY

Pornography consists of *words or images intended to cause sexual arousal.* But there is little agreement about precisely what is and what is not pornographic. For one thing, sexual material comes in many forms. *Erotica* includes the artistic portrayal of nudity, although not necessarily sexual activity. Then there is *soft-core pornography*, which shows or describes nudity and suggests sexual activity. Finally, *hard-core pornography* contains explicit descriptions or images of sexual acts, as in films that carry an X rating.

But exactly when does sexual material break the law and become *obscenity?* Recognizing that what is acceptable in one place may be objectionable in another, the U.S. Supreme Court allows communities to ban sexual material as obscene if it violates community standards of decency and lacks any redeeming social value. Even so, in any community, not everyone agrees about standards of decency, making the issue of pornography complex and divisive.

But there is little doubt that sexually explicit material is readily available in the United States. Most people are familiar with sexually explicit magazines, books, movies, and videos; people can also purchase sexual conversation by telephone. In recent years, hundreds of thousands of Web sites have opened that portray every imaginable type of sexual behavior. In all, the sale of material amounts to a $10-billion-a-year industry, which is more than the total economic output of some countries.

Pornography is an unusual issue in that both liberals and conservatives oppose it, although for different reasons. Liberals condemn pornography as degrading to women, while conservatives condemn it because they see pornography as morally wrong, a violation of strict codes of acceptable sexual conduct.

Is Pornography a Social Problem?

Pornography is big business in the United States and throughout the world. But is the sale of sexually explicit material a social problem? There is widespread agreement that pornography showing children under age eighteen in sexual situations is wrong; police enforce federal and state laws against child pornography. There is also widespread concern about the effects of pornography involving adults. Yet, as we shall see, various categories of people object to pornography for different reasons.

Conservatives: The Moral Issue Conservatives treat sex as a moral issue; from their point of view, pornography is a social problem because it goes against morality. Pornography encourages lustful behavior, which has become an addiction for several million people in the United States. Thus, at the very least, pornography weekens a society's moral virtue; at worst, it threatens the stability of marriage and family. About 60 percent of U.S. adults echo conservative concerns, claiming that "sexual material leads to a breakdown of morals" (NORC, 2003:235).

Liberals: Issues of Freedom and Power Liberals are divided over whether pornography is a social problem. Some liberals believe that what people choose to read or view is their own business. Therefore, without claiming that pornography is good, liberals seek to protect the freedoms of expression and privacy. Liberals who share this position have been outspoken in defending government support of the arts, including art that is highly controversial. The Social Policy box on page 200 takes a closer look.

Although some liberals defend pornography on the grounds of protecting free speech, a growing share of liberals object to pornography as demeaning to women. They see pornography as a power issue, noting that sexually explicit material typically turns women into the playthings of men. After all, they note, the word itself comes from the Greek word *porne*, which means "sexual slave" (Dworkin, 1991; MacKinnon, 2001).

In sum, although some people continue to defend the right of free expression and the idea that people should be free to choose whatever entertainment they want, opposition to pornography has increased. In this case, conservatives (who object to sexually explicit material on moral grounds) have joined with liberals (who object on political grounds) in their opposition to pornography.

Pornography and Violence

Another widespread concern is that pornography promotes violence. In 1985, President Ronald Reagan appointed the U.S. Attorney General's Commission on Pornography (commonly called the Meese Commission after attorney general Edwin Meese) to investigate how people reacted to sexually explicit materials. The commission (1986) concluded that exposure to pornography not only causes sexual arousal but also increases people's sexual activity, encourages aggression in males, and makes men more accepting of violent acts such as rape. In addition, concluded the researchers, pornography involving children encourages some men to desire sexual activity with them (a crime known as *pedophilia*). Critics challenged some

Social Policy   Does the Government Fund Obscenity?

IN 1990 A SMALL CINCINNATI, OHIO, art gallery displayed photographs by Robert Mapplethorpe, a talented and openly gay artist. The exhibit soon sparked a national controversy. Although many of Mapplethorpe's photographs are widely regarded as beautiful and quite conventional, some depict homosexual acts as well as sadism (acts that provide pleasure by dominating or hurting another person) and masochism (acts that provide pleasure by being dominated or hurt by another person or by oneself). For example, one photograph shows the artist, in the nude, with the handle of a bullwhip inserted in his anus.

Images of this kind sparked a national debate over the relationship between art and obscenity. Moreover, because Mapplethorpe received a grant from the National Endowment for the Arts (NEA), many critics charged that the government was using taxpayers' money to fund pornography.

Taking a conservative position, Cincinnati's district attorney filed charges against the gallery's owner, claiming that some of Mapplethorpe's work was obscene according to the Supreme Court guidelines (*Miller v. California*, 1973). Using what they felt were standards of decency common to people in Cincinnati, city officials claimed that some of the pieces on exhibit met the test of (1) appealing to prurient (lustful) interests, (2) depicting sexual conduct in a patently offensive way, and (3) lacking serious artistic, literary, political, or scientific merit. Liberals (including most of the city's gays and

lesbians) rushed to Mapplethorpe's defense, countering that his work, though sexual, is serious art. In the end, courts sided with the liberals, dismissing the obscenity charges and permitting the gallery to reopen.

By the end of the 1990s, the question of government funding for the arts took a turn in favor of conservatives. In 1998, the U.S. Supreme Court (*National Endowment for the Arts v. Finley*) ruled that the government can apply standards of decency to decisions about funding the arts. In its decision, the court stated that although artists enjoy freedom of expression, the public and public officials have the right to judge their work to be obscene. Furthermore, the court concluded that artists have no right to expect government to support their work if they violate public standards of decency.

ISSUES AND EXERCISES

1. Do you think works can be both artistic and obscene? Why or why not?

2. Should public officials try to protect the public from obscenity, or should people decide for themselves what they want to see or to avoid? Explain your position.

3. Develop arguments for and against the policy that the government should consider standards of decency in deciding which artistic projects to fund.

of these conclusions, but this report found widespread acceptance among both conservatives and liberals. One national survey confirms that about half of U.S. adults believe that pornography does encourage people to commit rape (NORC, 2003:235).

SEXUAL HARASSMENT

As explained in Chapter 7 ("Violence"), sexual violence—ranging from verbal abuse to forced sex—is a problem for both women and men. Indeed, as the Critical Thinking box explains, some critics contend that U.S. culture closely links sex and violence.

In recent years, people have come to recognize an additional aspect of sexual violence: **sexual**

harassment, *unwanted comments, gestures, or physical contact of a sexual nature.* Fifty years ago, sexual harassment of women on the street, on the campus, and on the job was routine; few defined such behavior as a social problem.

But this situation gradually changed with the rise of the women's movement in the 1960s. In 1964, Congress passed the Civil Rights Act, with the goal of protecting African Americans from employment discrimination. The women's movement successfully lobbied to extend the bill to include not just race but also sex. Thus, Title VII of the Civil Rights Act prohibits discrimination in the terms, conditions, and privileges of employment on the basis of sex and race. In 1972, Congress extended these protections

Critical Thinking   Sex and Violence: Linked by Culture

SOCIOLOGIST DIANNE HERMAN (2001) CHARACTERIZES the United States as a "rape culture." By this, she means that our way of life links sex and violence. Can you see how?

First, think about language. Common slang phrases such as "Screw you!" have both sexual and aggressive overtones. Second, most young men imagine themselves in the glamorous roles performed by violent, sexually active characters in the mass media. Take, for example, British super-agent James Bond: What is Bond's claim to being a "real man"? The answer, presumably, is the ease with which he "alternately whips out his revolver and his [penis]" (Griffin, 1971, cited in Herman, 2001:38). For James Bond, sex and violence are two sides of the same coin.

To the extent that this is a "rape culture," Dianne Herman concludes, the problem of sexual violence is not caused by "weirdos" but rather by men who are well adjusted to a flawed cultural system that equates sex and violence. In short, when you mix males brought up to think this way and females brought up to submit to males, you get a recipe for widespread sexual violence.

ISSUES AND EXERCISES

1. Do you agree with Herman that our culture links masculinity, sexuality, and violence? If so, can you think of ways other than those mentioned here? If not, why not?

2. Why, in your opinion, is there a link between sex and violence?

3. Make a list of film characters who fit the pattern of combining sex and violence.

---

to schools, colleges, and universities when it passed Title IX of the Higher Education Amendment, which banned sex discrimination in institutions receiving federal funds. Congress then set up the Equal Employment Opportunity Commission (EEOC) to investigate complaints of racial or sexual discrimination. In 1976, a federal court (*Williams v. Saxbe*) declared that sexual harassment amounted to illegal sex discrimination. This decision brought sexual harassment to public attention, and it was soon considered a serious problem.

Check the latest EEOC data on workplace harassment at
http://www.eeoc.gov/stats/harass.html

According to the EEOC, there are two types of sexual harassment. The first is *quid pro quo* (Latin meaning "one thing for another") harassment, in which a person makes sexual advances or requests for sexual favors to an employee or other subordinate as a condition of employment. That is, a boss might demand or imply that sex is a condition for an employee's promotion. The second type of harassment is subtle behavior, such as telling sexual jokes, displaying nude photos, offering compliments on someone's good looks, or engaging in unnecessary touching, that

the offender may not intend to be harassing. The law is concerned with *effects*, not just the offender's intent. It considers unlawful any behavior that has the effect of creating a *hostile environment*, regardless of what the offender's intentions might have been. The point of the law is to protect people who are trying to do their jobs from having unwanted sexuality imposed on them (Cohen, 1991; Paul, 1991).

Who Harasses Whom?

Because men hold most positions of power in U.S. society, about 85 percent of harassers are men who harass women (Equal Employment Opportunities Commission, 2003). But not all harassment follows this pattern. In 1998, the U.S. Supreme Court declared that a person can be sexually harassed by someone of either sex (*Oncale v. Sundowner Offshore Services, Inc.*, 1998). In that case, when male co-workers threatened a married man with rape, he reported the incident to his supervisor. When the company did not respond to the situation, the man quit his job and filed a successful lawsuit against the company. In some cases, men sexually harass other men who do not display what the harassers consider to be typical masculine behavior. In this way, sexual harassment is a form of control used by men to force others to conform to gender stereotypes (Lee, 2000).

Must Harassment Harm Victims? Recent Court Cases

Does sexual harassment exist only when a victim suffers clear harm? In two recent cases, the U.S. Supreme Court addressed this question. In the first case (*Ellerth v. Burlington Industries, Inc.*, 1998), a woman complained that her supervisor made sexual advances in which he stated that he could make her job very easy or difficult depending on whether she "loosened up." Although she resisted his advances, she did not report the behavior, and the evidence suggests that her career was not harmed. Soon after, she quit her job and then filed suit, claiming she had been the victim of sexual harassment.

In the second case (*Faragher v. City of Boca Raton*, 1998), three women who worked as lifeguards claimed they had endured a hostile environment for years, based on physical touching and sexual comments by their supervisors. Their employer, the city of Boca Raton, had a sexual harassment policy in place, but no one had informed the women of the policy. Subsequently, the women filed a lawsuit against the city, charging that they had been harassed on the job.

In considering the two cases, the Supreme Court ruled that employees can be harassed even if they were not harmed by, say, losing out on a promotion. The court also stated that employers are responsible when a supervisor harasses another employee—even if the company was not aware of the behavior—unless the company can demonstrate that it had a well-publicized sexual harassment policy in place that the employee failed to use.

PROSTITUTION

The cultural ideal of sex involves companionship and intimacy between two people. Therefore, although it may be "the world's oldest profession," **prostitution,** or *the selling of sexual services*, has always been controversial. Prostitution, as well as soliciting the services of a prostitute, is against the law everywhere in the United States except in parts of rural Nevada.

Legal or not, prostitution is common. There is no accurate count of the number of people who work as prostitutes in the United States, but national surveys reveal that about 15 percent of men say that they have paid for sex at least once (NORC, 2003:1226). In global perspective, as Global Map 8–1 shows, prostitution is most common in low-income nations where women's economic opportunities are most limited.

Prostitutes: A Profile

Most prostitutes—or, as many prefer, sex workers—are women. But they are a diverse category, with better or worse working conditions depending on their physical attractiveness, age, and level of education.

The most well-off prostitutes are *call girls*, who arrange appointments with clients by telephone. Typically, these women are youthful, attractive, well educated, and highly paid. Most call girls work independently rather than for a manager. Many advertise their services in the classified ads of big-city papers, typically as an "escort," which is a polite way of saying they offer an evening of charming company, gracious conversation, and, in most cases, sex.

In the middle are prostitutes who work in brothels, large "escort services," or "massage parlors." These women are employees who must follow the direction of their superiors; in addition, most turn over half or more of their earnings.

The worst-off prostitutes, and also the majority, are *street walkers*. These prostitutes work the streets, offering sex to people who pass by in cars. Street walkers earn the lowest incomes, typically 10 to 15 percent as much as top call girls. Although some work on their own, most give most of their earnings to managers, or pimps, who "look after them." With little control over who their customers are, street walkers are at high risk for violence and other abuse as well as sexually transmitted diseases (STDs). Researchers estimate that the majority of street walkers have been victims of rape, incest, or other forms of sexual abuse, often going back to childhood (Gordon & Snyder, 1989; Estes, 2001; Williamson & Cluse-Tolar, 2002).

Prostitutes typically offer the sexual service that appeals to the client. Research suggests that the most common sexual act performed by prostitutes is oral sex, followed by sexual intercourse (Monto, 2001).

What about men who work as prostitutes? About 10 percent of prostitutes are men, and almost all sell sex to other men. They, too, are a diverse category, ranging from well-paid "escorts" to young runaways trying to survive on the streets (Boyer, 1989; Strong & DeVault, 1994).

Arrests for Prostitution

Although prostitution is against the law almost everywhere in the United States, law enforcement is

A WORLD OF DIFFERENCES

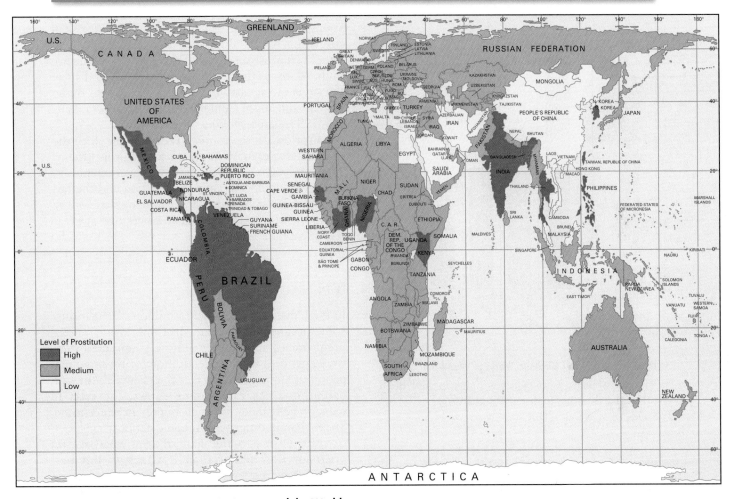

GLOBAL MAP 8–1   **Prostitution around the World**

The map shows that prostitution occurs worldwide. Even so, the level of prostitution tends to be higher in regions of the world where people are poor and where the social standing of women is low in relation to that of men. Latin America, a region of widespread poverty and pronounced patriarchy, shows a high level of prostitution. In the Islamic nations of northern Africa and the Middle East, patriarchy is also strong, but Islam appears to discourage prostitution.

Source: Peters Atlas of the World (1990); updated by the author.

selective. About two-thirds of the roughly 60,000 people arrested for prostitution in 2002 were women; the remaining one-third were men (including both male prostitutes and male clients) (U.S. Federal Bureau of Investigation, 2003). Furthermore, according to COYOTE (Call Off Your Old Tired Ethics), a sex workers' rights organization founded in 1973, 90 percent of women arrested for prostitution are street walkers; very few are high-status call girls. Race also figures into the picture: COYOTE reports that

although most prostitutes are white, most of those arrested are African Americans (COYOTE, 2000).

Visit the COYOTE Web site at
http://www.bayswan.org/COYOTE.html

Should police and the courts do more to punish people involved in prostitution? In a recent survey, only 39.1 percent of respondents agreed with the statement, "There is nothing inherently wrong with

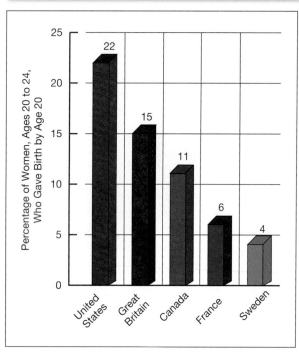

FIGURE 8–4   Births to Teenage Women

The rate of teenage pregnancy is higher in the United States than in other high-income countries.

Source: Darroch et al. (2001).

prostitution as long as the health risks can be minimized. If consenting adults agree to exchange money for sex, that is their business" (NORC, 2003:605). The health risks of prostitution include the danger of spreading sexually transmitted diseases, including AIDS. In addition, it is likely that even fewer people would approve of prostitution if they knew the extent of violence and drug abuse that often accompanies this way of life.

Child Prostitution

Few defend prostitution when it involves children. In global perspective, as many as 100 million children live on the streets, selling sex to survive. Some of these boys and girls have families nearby, and others were orphaned by AIDS or war; almost all are desperately poor.

The Southeast Asian nation of Thailand, which has become a center for the global "sex tourism" industry, has some 2 million prostitutes, accounting for almost 10 percent of the country's female population. In countless brothels and sex shows on the streets of Bangkok, Thailand's capital city, half the women have not yet passed their teens. Why the popularity of child prostitutes? Customers favor young women in the belief that they pose less risk of spreading AIDS. But given the fact that half of Bangkok's prostitutes are HIV-positive, the risks are high. Many of these girls and women also display the signs of various others diseases, brought on by neglect and abuse (Anderson & Moore, 1993; Santoli, 1994; Janus, 1996).

Worldwide, sex tourism is on the rise, with the fastest increases in Africa and Eastern Europe (Remy, 1996). In response, many national governments are calling for an end to child prostitution and the entire sex tourism industry. Still, in many parts of the world, being young and female places one at great risk of exploitation.

TEENAGE PREGNANCY

In the United States, almost 1 million teenagers become pregnant each year. Most did not plan their pregnancies, and neither did the young men they were involved with. Indeed, most of these young people are unprepared to face the responsibilities of parenthood. As Figure 8–4 shows, the rate of teenage pregnancy is much higher in the United States than in other high-income nations.

Fifty years ago, the share of teens who became pregnant was higher than it is today. But because people married younger, most teens who became pregnant in 1950 were young wives starting families with their husbands. Moreover, given the pressure to avoid having an "illegitimate" child, unmarried couples expecting a baby married quickly (the so-called "shotgun marriage," often held at the insistence of the woman's father), or the woman quietly moved away and, after the birth, put the child up for adoption. In some cases, women obtained abortions, although it was against the law almost everywhere.

Today, most young women who become pregnant are not married. Rarely do teenage girls who become pregnant rush to get married, and few put their babies up for adoption. Rather, about one-third have abortions and two-thirds keep their babies (Voydanoff & Donnelly, 1990; Holmes, 1996; Alan Guttmacher Institute, 2003).

Another recent trend is that the pregnancy rate for girls in their early teens has been rising. The reason is simply that girls and boys are becoming sexually active at a younger age. Some are having sex

A NATION OF DIVERSITY

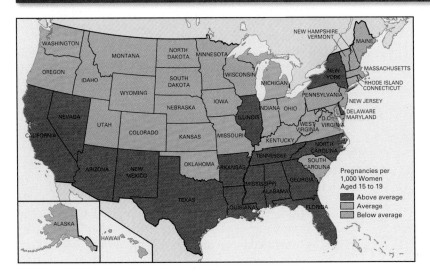

NATIONAL MAP 8–1
Teenage Pregnancy Rates across the United States

The map shows pregnancy rates for women aged fifteen to nineteen across the United States in the mid-1990s. What can you say about the regions of the country where rates are high? Where they are low? Can you explain these patterns?

Source: U.S. Centers for Disease Control and Prevention (2000).

before their bodies are mature and before they understand how their reproductive systems work.

Teenage girls at highest risk for pregnancy are from poor families. Compared with those from richer families, these girls are also more likely to keep their babies. Why? Researchers point out that most poor girls and boys consider college and a good career to be beyond their reach. As a result, having a baby—being a parent—seems to be the only way they can prove their adulthood. Single motherhood is particularly common among poor African Americans, who are doubly disadvantaged by poverty and racism. For all racial and ethnic categories, becoming an unmarried teenage mother makes it harder to finish school and work, raising the risks of remaining poor (Staples & Johnson, 1993; Kaplan, 1997; Alan Guttmacher Institute, 2002). National Map 8–1 shows the rate of teenage pregnancy across the United States.

The Costs of Teenage Pregnancy

At its best, parenthood is a source of great joy. But for men and women who are young and poor, parenthood can turn into a nightmare of economic pressures that they simply cannot handle. As a result, the financial cost of medical care, welfare, and other support for pregnant teenagers in the United States probably exceeds $35 billion each year (Brindis & Davis, 1998).

The greatest burden, however, is borne by the babies themselves. On average, infants born to teens have lower birth weight and higher risk of physical and developmental problems. Many such infants face

Read a new report from the Alan Guttmacher Institute on trends in teenage sex and pregnancy:
http://www.agi-usa.org/pubs/ib_1-02.pdf

a life of problems that accompany poverty, including poor nutrition, violence in the local neighborhood, little schooling, and inadequate health care. To make matters worse, most face these challenges with little or no help from their fathers. Not surprisingly, these children grow up at high risk for becoming single parents themselves.

Sex Education: A Solution?

What can society do to combat the problem of teenage pregnancy? One strategy looks to schools. Sex education programs explain to young people how their bodies grow and change, how reproduction occurs, and how to avoid pregnancy by using birth control or abstaining from sex altogether.

Today, "sex ed" is found in most public schools. Still, this program remains controversial. Critics (typically conservatives) point out that as more schools have adopted sex education programs over the past two decades, the level of sexual activity among teenagers has gone up. Researchers tell us that half of today's boys have sexual intercourse by their sixteenth birthday, and half of all girls do so by age seventeen. Although such data do not necessarily mean that schools are making the problem worse, they do raise doubts about whether sex ed programs are making things better.

TABLE 8–1	U.S. ATTITUDES TOWARD ABORTION

Survey Question: It should be possible for a woman to obtain a *legal abortion . . ."*

	Percentage Answering "Yes"
"if the woman's own health is seriously endangered by the pregnancy"	89.3%
"if she becomes pregnant as a result of rape"	78.0%
"if there is a strong chance of a serious defect in the baby"	76.1%
"if the family has a very low income and cannot afford any more children"	42.9%
"if she is not married and does not want to marry the man"	42.9%
"if she is not married and does not want any more children"	43.3%
"for any reason"	41.9%

Source: NORC (2003: 206–7)

Supporters of sex education (mostly liberals) counter that the biggest cause of high teen pregnancy is ignorance. It makes sense, they say, to teach young people—many of whom are sexually active—about birth control methods and the risks of contracting sexually transmitted diseases.

Disagreement is strongest over the issue of distributing condoms in school. Critics claim that this policy only encourages young people to rush headlong into sexual activity. Supporters respond that most young people will be sexually active one way or another; the point is to give them what they need to avoid pregnancy and sexually transmitted disease (Stodghill, 1998; Alan Guttmacher Institute, 2002).

ABORTION

Perhaps the most divisive issue involving sexuality in the United States is **abortion,** *the deliberate termination of a pregnancy.* Each year, about 860,000 abortions are performed in the United States, about one for every three live births. The typical woman receiving an abortion is in her twenties and has never had an abortion before; 56 percent are white, and 81 percent are unmarried (U.S. Centers for Disease Control and Prevention, 2002).

Abortion: Looking Back

Abortion is an ancient practice that was common among the ancient Egyptians, Romans, and Greeks (Luker, 1984; Tannahill, 1992). In the United States, from the colonial era until the mid-nineteenth century, early term abortion was legal. After its founding in 1847, the American Medical Association (AMA) pressed to outlaw the procedure, in part to put out of business midwives and other traditional healers who performed abortions. By the early twentieth century, every state in the country had enacted laws banning abortion (Luker, 1984). Such laws did not end the practice, however. Women with money could find a doctor willing to perform a safe abortion; poor women either endured an unwanted pregnancy or submitted to a "back alley" procedure performed by an unlicensed practitioner, with sometimes deadly results.

By the 1960s, a social movement was underway to repeal abortion laws in the United States. The movement succeeded when, in 1973, the U.S. Supreme Court struck down all state abortion laws (*Roe v. Wade, Doe v. Bolton*). Ever since, "pro-choice" people (typically liberals) have fought to keep abortion available to women. "Anti-abortion" people (typically conservatives) are working just as hard to reverse the high court decision and once again make abortion illegal.

The Abortion Controversy Today

Since 1973, various laws and court decisions have limited women's access to abortion in certain circumstances. In 1977, for example, Congress passed the Hyde Amendment prohibiting the use of Medicaid funds for abortions, except to save the life of the mother. In 1980, the Supreme Court ruled that state and federal governments need not provide poor women with taxpayer-funded abortions (*Harris v. McRae*). In 1989, the Supreme Court upheld a state law that banned public employees or public facilities from performing abortions, except to save the mother's life. The Court has also upheld state laws that require doctors to perform medical tests to see whether the fetus could survive outside the mother's body (*Webster v. Reproductive Health Services,* 1989). In 1992, the Court reaffirmed that states had wide latitude in setting abortion policy (*Planned Parenthood of Southeastern Pennsylvania v. Casey*). Later in the 1990s, Congress twice proposed laws banning so-called "partial birth" abortions performed in the third trimester of pregnancy, but President Clinton vetoed both bills. Finally, twenty-nine states have enacted laws requiring minors to have parental consent before they can have an abortion. The Bush administration has been less supportive of abortion rights than the Clinton administration, and in 2003 Congress again acted to restrict later-term abortion. Even so, few analysts expect any basic change in current law in the near future (Klein, 2003).

The issue of abortion remains both complex and controversial. Table 8–1 shows the share of U.S. adults who support abortion under various circumstances. Although a large majority (89.3 percent) support legal abortion if a woman's health is threatened by her pregnancy, less than half (41.9 percent) support legal abortion for any reason at all (NORC, 2003:206–7). Attitudes toward abortion also vary by race and ethnicity. Figure 8–5 shows that, overall, people of Arab and Italian descent are more conservative on this issue, with only 29 percent supporting abortion for any reason. At the liberal end of the political spectrum, 62 percent of Jewish Americans support abortion for any reason (Zogby International, 2001).

Why is the abortion controversy so intense? Because, from everyone's point of view, a great deal is at stake. Anti-abortion activists claim that abortion is the killing of unborn children; as a matter of life and death, many will not compromise their beliefs. Yet pro-choice activists, too, have reason to stand firm. As they see it, legal access to abortion is the key to women having control over not only childbearing but their whole lives. Unless they can avoid unwanted pregnancy, women lose much of their opportunity to earn income and establish their independence from men. In short, without legal abortion women lose ground in their efforts to achieve social equality (Luker, 1984; Simon, 2003).

SEXUALLY TRANSMITTED DISEASES

There are more than fifty types of **sexually transmitted diseases (STDs),** which are *diseases spread by sexual contact.* Rates of infection of most sexually transmitted diseases, including gonorrhea, syphilis, and genital herpes, began to rise during the sexual revolution of the 1960s. In recent decades, the danger of STDs has played a part in the sexual counterrevolution described earlier. The following sections briefly describe several common STDs.

Gonorrhea and Syphilis

Gonorrhea and syphilis, among the oldest diseases to afflict humans, result from microscopic organisms

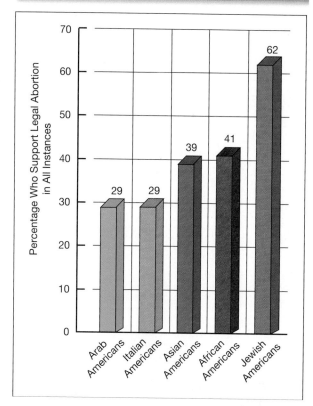

DIMENSIONS OF DIFFERENCE

FIGURE 8–5 Support for Legal Abortion by Race and Ethnicity

In the United States, race and ethnicity are linked to attitudes about abortion.

Source: Zogby International (2001).

typically transmitted during sexual activity. Untreated, gonorrhea can cause sterility; syphilis can result in blindness, mental disorders, and even death.

Officials record some 361,000 cases of gonorrhea and 32,000 cases of syphilis annually in the United States, although the actual totals probably are much higher. Official data show that most cases involve African Americans (75 percent), with lower numbers among whites (16 percent), Latinos (7 percent), and Asian Americans and Native Americans (1 percent each) (Masters, Johnson, & Kolodny, 1988; Moran et al., 1989; U.S. Centers for Disease Control and Prevention, 2003).

Doctors treat gonorrhea and syphilis effectively with antibiotics, such as penicillin. Therefore, neither disease is considered a major U.S. health problem today.

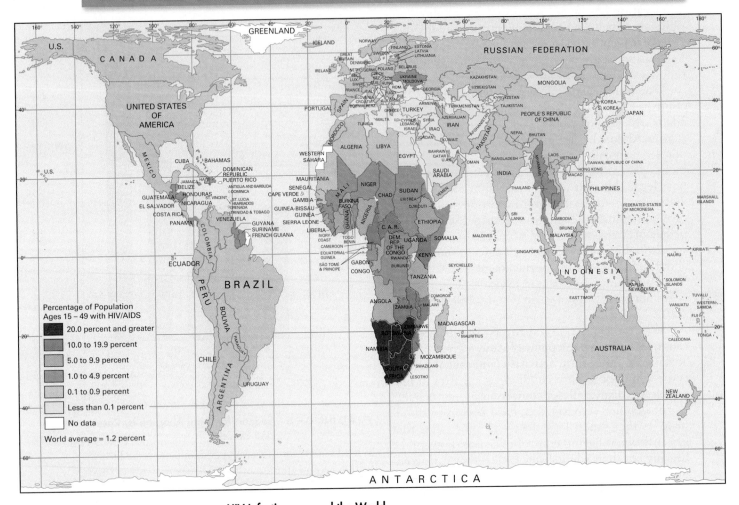

GLOBAL MAP 8–2   **HIV Infections around the World**

The nations of sub-Saharan Africa contain more than two-thirds of the world's cases of HIV. Currently, however, it is Southeast Asia that shows the fastest increase in HIV infections, accounting for about 20 percent of global cases. Infection rates are fairly low in North and South America, which together account for 8 percent of global cases of HIV.

Sources: Population Reference Bureau (2003); map projection from *Peters Atlas of the World* (1990).

Genital Herpes

Genital herpes is a virus that infects as many as 45 million adults in the United States, or one in five (U.S. Centers for Disease Control and Prevention, 2003). Although herpes poses less danger than gonorrhea and syphilis, it is incurable. Some people with this disease have no symptoms at all; others experience periodic, painful blisters on the genitals accompanied by fever and headache. One serious concern is that women with active genital herpes can transmit the disease to infants during a vaginal

delivery, and it can be deadly to a newborn. Therefore, doctors usually advise infected women to give birth by cesarean section.

AIDS

The most serious of all sexually transmitted diseases is *acquired immuno deficiency syndrome*, or *AIDS*. Soon after identifying this disease in 1981, doctors concluded that it is incurable and, if untreated, almost always fatal. AIDS is caused by a virus: the *human immunodeficiency virus* or *HIV*, which destroys the body's immune system. AIDS itself does not kill; it makes a person unable to fight off a wide range of other diseases that eventually cause death.

The Extent of the AIDS Problem

Although the rate of AIDS deaths is decreasing, officials recorded 16,371 deaths due to AIDS in the United States in 2002. Officials also noted 26,464 new cases that year, pushing the number of people who have contracted AIDS in the United States to almost 890,000. Of these, about 501,669 have died (U.S. Centers for Disease Control and Prevention, 2003).

Non-Hispanic white people (71 percent of the population) account for 41 percent of patients with AIDS, and African Americans (12 percent of the population) account for 39 percent of people with AIDS. Moreover, about 60 percent of women and children with the disease are African Americans. Latinos also show high infection rates: They represent 13 percent of the population but 18 percent of people with AIDS and 20 percent of all women with AIDS. Asian Americans and Native Americans (together almost 5 percent of the population) account for less than 1 percent of people with AIDS (U.S. Centers for Disease Control and Prevention, 2003).

In many regions of the world, AIDS is a medical catastrophe. In 2000, U.S. President Bill Clinton declared that the death toll from AIDS had grown so high that it threatens to undermine national economies and destabilize political systems. He concluded that global AIDS was a threat to the national security of the United States.

How great is the global toll? Around the world, HIV infects some 60 million people, half under age twenty-five. Moreover, the numbers keep rising. Global Map 8–2 shows that the countries with the highest rates of HIV infection are in Africa, where 70 percent of global cases are found. According to the United Nations, in much of sub-Saharan Africa, teenagers have a 50 percent chance of becoming infected with HIV. In these nations, girls are at higher risk than boys, because HIV is more easily transmitted from males to females than the other way around. President George W. Bush traveled to countries hard hit by AIDS in 2003, pledging $15 billion in assistance (United Nations Development Programme, 2001; Whitelaw, 2003).

The Spread of HIV

Because people who become infected with HIV display no symptoms at all for a year or even longer, most remain unaware of their condition and may unknowingly spread the disease.

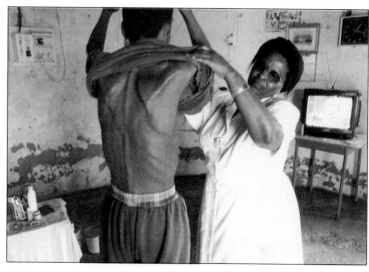

AIDS is a medical catastrophe in many countries in sub-Saharan Africa. Not only do young people have a fifty-fifty chance of becoming infected with HIV, but the medical treatment that is available in poor countries does little to prolong life.

Within five years, one-third of infected people develop full-blown AIDS; half do so within ten years, and almost all become sick within twenty years.

Although HIV is infectious, it is not contagious. This means that HIV is transmitted from person to person only in specific ways: through blood, semen, or breast milk. It is not transmitted through casual contact such as shaking hands, hugging, sharing towels or dishes, or swimming together, or even by coughing and sneezing. The risk of transmitting the virus through saliva (as in kissing) is extremely low. One effective strategy to greatly reduce the risk of transmitting HIV through sexual activity is for males to use a latex condom. However, only abstinence or an exclusive relationship with an uninfected person can eliminate the risk entirely.

Specific behaviors put people at high risk for HIV infection:

1. **Anal sex.** This practice is dangerous because it can cause rectal bleeding, which permits easy passage of HIV from one person to another. For this reason, homosexual and bisexual men account for 46 percent of U.S. AIDS cases.

2. **Sharing needles.** Sharing a needle used to inject drugs is a high-risk behavior because users come into contact with each other's blood. Intravenous drug users account for 25 percent of people with AIDS. For this reason, sex with an

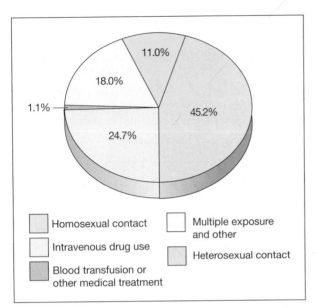

FIGURE 8–6   **Types of Transmission for Reported U.S. AIDS Cases, 2002**

Almost half the people with AIDS in the United States were infected through homosexual activity. However, there are many other ways to become infected.

Source: U.S. Centers for Disease Control and Prevention (2003).

intravenous drug user is also a high-risk behavior. Because the rate of intravenous drug use is high among poor people in the United States, AIDS is becoming a disease of the economically disadvantaged.

3. **Using any drug.**   The use of any drug, including alcohol, can harm one's judgment. Even people who understand the risks may act less responsibly if they are under the influence of alcohol, marijuana, or some other drug.

As Figure 8–6 shows, 11 percent of people with AIDS in the United States became infected through heterosexual contact (although heterosexuals, infected in various ways, account for 30 percent of AIDS cases). The risk goes up along with the number of sexual partners, especially if they fall into high-risk categories. Around the world, heterosexual activity accounts for two-thirds of all infections.

Combating AIDS   In the early 1980s, the gay community was the first to call attention to the problem of AIDS. The government was slow to respond, however, perhaps because it was gay men who were most affected by the epidemic. Activists pressed for greater government funding for AIDS research and

more social services for people with AIDS. By the mid-1980s, when the epidemic had spread into the heterosexual population through infected blood being used for transfusions, officials gave the problem greater attention; they began screening the nation's blood supply for HIV (Shilts, 1987).

As the death toll mounted, the gay and lesbian community came together to begin safer-sex outreach programs, spreading the word about what HIV is and how it is spread. These efforts succeeded as gay men began to reduce the number of sexual partners and avoid high-risk behavior.

In recent years, new drug therapies have extended the lives of people with HIV. This is good news, but the high cost of treatments—many of which are not covered by health insurance—is a burden many people simply cannot afford (Pear, 1997).

THEORETICAL ANALYSIS: UNDERSTANDING SEXUALITY

Sociological theory helps explain various social problems. In the following sections, we apply the three major approaches to issues of sexuality.

Structural-Functional Analysis: Controlling Sexuality

One function of sexuality is human reproduction. *Controlling sexuality* is important because social order depends on people reproducing according to social norms. To see why, imagine for a moment that people reproduced again and again with just anybody. If this were the case, the family as we know it would not exist because people would not observe kinship. Without families, no one would have any particular relationship to anyone else, and society itself would collapse.

Incest and Legitimacy   One important norm guiding reproduction is the *incest taboo*, which bans sex and reproduction between certain close family members. Every society in the world observes the incest taboo, although it is not applied to exactly the same kin. Why is this norm important? Again, if close kin (other than husband and wife) were to reproduce, social relationships would soon become hopelessly confusing (if a father and a daughter reproduced and had a son, what would the boy's relationship be to each of them?).

In the same way, the traditional norms favoring *legitimate* offspring—meaning children born to married couples—is a strategy to ensure both that children are cared for and that they establish legal ties, including rights to inheritance, with their biological parents. In short, structural-functional analysis helps explain why inappropriate sexual relationships, including incest and childbearing out of wedlock, have long been viewed as social problems.

The Functions of Prostitution If certain sexual relationships cause social problems, it is also true that some sexual problems are not entirely bad for society. Take the case of prostitution. As explained earlier in this chapter, most people view prostitution as a problem because it spreads disease and exploits women (NORC, 2003). But as Kingsley Davis (1971) pointed out, prostitution also performs several useful, if less noticed, functions.

Some members of society—including soldiers, sailors, and travelers—do not have ready access to sex. Prostitution, explains Davis, is one way to meet their sexual needs. Moreover, Davis continues, the fact that sex is available without commitment may even help to support some marriages that might otherwise fall apart.

Critical evaluation. The structural-functional approach shows that sexuality plays an important role in the organization of society. At the same time, now that modern technology has largely separated sex from reproduction, does society need to regulate sex as much as it once did?

This approach also implies that everyone observes the same set of sexual norms, which in a multicultural society is not really the case. The various ways people understand sexuality bring us to the symbolic-interaction approach.

Symbolic-Interaction Analysis: Defining Sexuality

The symbolic-interaction approach highlights the variable meanings people attach to sexuality. In other words, members of a society socially construct sexuality just as they create all reality. Different ways of understanding sex are easy to see if we look back in history.

The Meaning of Virginity A good example of the changing meanings attached to sex is the idea of *virginity*, that is, never having had sexual intercourse. Through most of this nation's history, strong cultural norms have demanded that people—or, more precisely, women—remain virgins until marriage. Before modern methods of birth control were developed, the norm of virginity was the only assurance men had that they were not marrying a woman who was carrying another man's child.

Effective birth control separated sexuality from reproduction, which greatly weakened the norm of virginity. Indeed, one study shows that among people born in the decade after 1963, 84 percent of men and 80 percent of women reported that they were not virgins at first marriage. In fact, fifty years ago many people defined premarital sexual intercourse as a social problem; today, however, it is considered the norm (Laumann et al., 1994; NORC, 2003).

Learning Sexual Roles: The Case of Topless Dancers
The symbolic-interaction paradigm not only points up the relative nature of sexual norms but also offers insights into how people learn and interpret their own sexual behavior. For example, how do women become topless dancers? How do such women think of themselves?

In a study of forty topless dancers in a southwestern city, researchers found that women came to this kind of work gradually, in stages, just as people

Are so-called "gentlemen's clubs" and other "strip joints" a problem? Conservatives tend to oppose this sort of thing on moral grounds. Many liberals support the idea that adults should be free to behave as they wish as long as they do not harm others. But other liberals—and most radicals—condemn selling sex as encouraging traditional gender stereotypes that harm women.

enter any other kind of career (Thompson & Harrod, 1999). Most of the women explained that they first danced topless in response to a dare from someone else, and only after having a few drinks. The women received encouragement for their efforts and, more important, they soon realized that they could earn more money dancing than through other "straight" work.

Although the women went on to earn a living doing what many people consider deviant, most insisted they did nothing wrong. Their clubs helped them think well of themselves by having strict "look but don't touch" policies, which allowed the women to maintain that they were entertainers, not prostitutes. Furthermore, all used stage names so that customers knew nothing of their "real world" identities. Likewise, most women told only a few people what their job actually was; to the rest, including parents, they were simply "in the nightclub business."

Finally, almost all the women working as topless dancers learned to see their work as useful, pointing out that they provided entertainment without hurting anyone. In sum, the women gradually built a world of meanings that both protected them and made them comfortable with their work (Thompson & Harrod, 1999).

Critical evaluation.   The symbolic-interaction approach highlights how people construct reality in their everyday lives, a fact that applies to sexuality as it does to other forms of behavior. But although many aspects of sexuality vary over time and from place to place, some patterns are remarkably consistent, such as men's tendency to devalue women as sex objects. To understand this pattern, we turn to the social-conflict approach.

Social-Conflict Analysis: Sex and Power

The social-conflict approach highlights social inequality. Sexuality involves inequality, both between women and men and between homosexuals and heterosexuals.

Women as Sexual Objects   A social-conflict approach points out that many aspects of sexuality reflect men's social domination of women. Pornography, prostitution, and even topless dancing degrade women, casting them in the role of sexual objects that exist only for men's pleasure. Indeed, if men value women only for their looks and submissiveness, the two sexes can never participate in society on equal terms. This is the major reason that the movement for gender equality has helped define sexuality in the workplace

as a social problem, prompting companies to enact anti-harassment policies.

Male domination involves not just inequality but also violence. As we have already explained, U.S. culture weaves sex and violence together, evident in expressions such as "hitting on," a phrase that can refer to either sexuality or physical violence. It is for this reason that social-conflict theory—and especially feminism—has been sharply critical of sexuality. Some feminists reject sexual relations with men entirely, claiming that women who sleep with men are like slaves having sexual relationships with their masters (Dworkin, 1987).

Queer Theory   Social-conflict theory criticizes not only sexual relationships between men and women but also U.S. culture's heterosexual bias. Alongside feminism, then, is the recent development of **queer theory,** *a body of theory and research that challenges the heterosexual bias in U.S. society.*

Feminism characterizes U.S. society as *sexist.* Queer theory claims society is characterized by **heterosexism,** that is, *bias that treats heterosexuality as the norm while stigmatizing anyone who differs from this norm as "queer."* The heterosexism of U.S. society condemns not only gay men and lesbians but also bisexual people, asexual people, and transsexuals who alter their sexuality surgically. Heterosexist norms are common in everyday life, as when the mass media celebrate the "sex appeal" of popular movie stars, almost all of whom are heterosexual. In 1998, comedian and actress Ellen DeGeneris sparked controversy when she "came out" as a lesbian on her television show. Yet in 2004, shows like *Queer Eye for the Straight Guy* and *Boy Meets Boy* suggest that attitudes are changing.

Although discrimination against women and African Americans is now illegal, bias against people who differ in their sexuality is not only common but, in many cases, legal. Organizations from the Boy Scouts to the U.S. military still exclude anyone who displays behavior considered "queer."

Critical evaluation.   Social-conflict theory highlights how closely sexuality is tied to social inequality. But critics of this approach point out that not everyone thinks of sexuality as a power issue; indeed, most people find that sexuality strengthens their relationship to another person. In addition, social-conflict theory tends to give little attention to the many steps U.S. society has taken to attack bias against women, gay men, and lesbians, including antidiscrimination policies and hate-crime laws.

POLITICS AND SEXUALITY: CONSTRUCTING PROBLEMS AND DEFINING SOLUTIONS

As we have shown in earlier chapters, what people define as a sexual problems and what strategies they support as solutions depend on their political values. Here we sum up the issues raised in this chapter from the conservative, liberal, and radical points of view.

Conservatives: The Value of Traditional Morality

The basic principle that defines the conservative view of sexuality is that people should be guided not by selfish desires but by established moral principles of right and wrong. If traditional virtues of "gentlemanly" and "ladylike" behavior are promoted, conservatives argue, most of the problems noted in this chapter can be avoided (Sommers, 2003).

Many conservatives support the conventional norms that claim sexuality belongs within the traditional bonds of marriage. From this point of view, premarital sex and extramarital sex are social problems linked to other problems such as teenage pregnancy and sexually transmitted diseases. Conservatives also condemn prostitution and pornography not only because they violate traditional standards of decency but also because they can threaten marriages.

Conservatives oppose a policy of abortion on demand because this gives one person the power to end the life of another who is innocent and helpless: the unborn child. Rather than ending 860,000 unwanted pregnancies each year by aborting them, conservatives advocate greater sexual responsibility so that fewer unwanted pregnancies occur in the first place.

Conservatives do not agree on every issue, of course. Homosexuality is a case in point. Some conservatives condemn homosexuality as an immoral lifestyle and oppose gay marriage as a violation of tradition and biblical scripture. Other (more moderate) conservatives believe that sexual orientation is not a moral issue because it is not a matter of choice; they support gay marriage as a means of bringing the benefits of family life to all people, gay and straight alike.

This site presents the ideas of Andrew Sullivan, a gay man who describes himself as conservative: http://www.andrewsullivan.com

Overall, the conservative answer to sexual social problems is strong social institutions—including churches, schools, and, especially, families—that teach young people to struggle against temptation and peer pressure in the interest of doing what is right. Today, conservatives support a number of policies that promise to strengthen families, such as tougher child support laws, laws requiring parental notification in cases of young women who seek abortions, and policies giving parents time away from work to care for family members. Most of all, conservatives claim, U.S. society would greatly benefit from a national effort to see that as many children as possible are born to a home with both a father and a mother.

Liberals: Sex and Individual Choice

Whereas conservatives emphasize the importance of traditional morality, liberals stress the importance of individual freedoms. As liberals see it, all people should be free to choose how they express their sexuality. Thus, their attitude is one of tolerance. In the case of sexual orientation, for example, liberals avoid making harsh judgments that a particular behavior is always right or wrong; they favor respecting the right of individuals to decide for themselves how they wish to behave. In the same way, liberals are

In 2004, the Massachusetts Supreme Court demanded nothing less than full legal marriage for gay and lesbian couples in that state. How far will this ruling advance gay marriage across the United States?

LEFT to RIGHT

THE POLITICS OF SEXUALITY

	RADICAL VIEW	LIBERAL VIEW	CONSERVATIVE VIEW
WHAT IS THE PROBLEM?	Men dominate women, just as heterosexuals dominate people with other sexual orientations.	Prostitution and pornography harm women, teen pregnancy is linked to poverty, and sexual harassment prevents people from doing their jobs.	Premarital sex, extramarital sex, and homosexuality violate traditional principles of right and wrong; abortion, too, is morally wrong.
WHAT IS THE SOLUTION?	Because sexism and hetero-sexism are deeply rooted in the existing system, queer theory argues that equality for people of all sexual orientations will require a basic change in culture and the U.S. power structure; similarly, radical feminism advocates change in the direction of a gender-free society.	Government must combat prostitution and pornography, keep sexuality out of the workplace, ensure that abortion is available to all women, and pursue a cure for AIDS.	Families—preferably with two active, involved parents—must teach children traditional virtues, such as self-restraint in matters of sexuality. To the extent that they do, problems such as teen pregnancy and sexually transmitted diseases will decline.

Join the debate . . .

1. In your opinion, which issues discussed in this chapter are the most serious social problems? Why?

2. Overall, do you think sexual social problems are getting better or worse? Why?

3. Which of the three political analyses of sexuality included here do you find most convincing? Why?

tolerant of premarital sex as long as the people in-volved have the maturity and the knowledge to make responsible choices.

The limits of liberal tolerance come when some-one threatens another with harm. Liberals define sexual violence, AIDS, and teenage pregnancy as so-cial problems for this reason. Similarly, although lib-erals defend freedom of expression, many express concern that pornography and prostitution end up harming women.

Liberals look to government to address various social problems. Schools can take the lead in teach-ing young people what they need to know to make responsible choices about sex. They see the criminal justice system as a vital weapon against domestic vi-olence and rape. In their view, government agencies must continue to monitor the workplace to be sure companies protect employees from sexual harass-ment. Finally, only the resources available to the government are likely to bring an eventual end to the AIDS epidemic.

Following the principle that individuals should decide for themselves how to behave, liberals sup-port making abortion available to all and leaving the decision on any individual case up to the woman involved. Indeed, most liberals support government funding for abortions so that all pregnant women have choices, regardless of their ability to pay.

Radicals: Go to the Root of the Problem

Radicals point out that a common element among the issues raised in this chapter—including sexual orientation, pornography, sexual violence, and pros-titution—is social inequality. As they see it, each problem comes about because some category of peo-ple has power over another.

On one level, as queer theory argues, U.S. soci-ety privileges heterosexuality while dismissing any-one who differs from that norm as "queer." So deep is the heterosexual bias, queer theory claims, that nothing less than challenging the roots of power can produce an egalitarian society in which all people are equal participants in social life.

On another level, as radical feminists explain, U.S. society is deeply patriarchal. Because male power runs deep into the structure of U.S. society, radical feminists doubt that efforts at reform will ever create a society in which women and men stand together as equals. As a result, radical feminists seek the elimination of gender itself. As noted in Chapter 4 ("Gender Inequality"), many radical feminists believe that, to do this, society must challenge the biological facts of reproduction. Perhaps, they suggest, new reproductive technologies will liberate women from their historical link to childbearing, which will open up the possibility of equal participation in social life. In the short term, many radical feminists encourage women to work together to achieve political aims and to avoid dependency on men. Some even call for ending sexual ties to men, offering a strong voice on behalf of lesbians. It is lesbians, after all, who defy two basic structures of U.S. society: They challenge the heterosexual norm by being homosexual, and they challenge male power by choosing to live without men. The Left to Right table outlines the three political perspectives on sexuality.

GOING ON FROM HERE

If anything is a sure bet to be around a century from now, it is sex. However societies may change, sex seems to remain a steady element of human experience.

But is it? This chapter has traced remarkable change in sexual practices and attitudes in the United States. From the rigid, "sex as reproduction" view of the earliest European settlers to the open, "anything goes" views of the sexual revolution, ideas about sex have been anything but static.

Change is also evident in the definition of sexual problems. At the beginning of the twentieth century, homosexuality was treated as a serious problem: No one talked about it, many saw it as a sin or a sickness, and homosexual behavior was against the law almost everywhere. As the gay rights movement gained strength, the idea of sexual diversity entered U.S. culture. Today, it is now possible to be openly gay, as millions of people are.

Several decades ago, few considered sexual harassment to be a problem, believing that men should think of women primarily in sexual terms. As women have gained economic, political, and educational clout in the United States, such thinking has been replaced by the idea that women as well as men should be evaluated on the basis of their abilities rather than their looks. In the last decade, the widespread enactment of sexual harassment policies has sought to remove sex from working relationships.

Going on from here, what changes should we expect in the future? Although continued controversy is certain, the trend toward greater tolerance of homosexuality seems all but certain. In fact, it seems only a matter of time until gay men and lesbians gain the ability to form legal marriages. Likewise, efforts to bring an end to the AIDS epidemic are likely to intensify. With time, this disease, which has cost hundreds of thousands of lives in the United States, will be tamed. But what about the poor nations of the world, where meanwhile the death toll is expected to reach hundreds of millions? And, back at home, what about the divisive issue of abortion? All that is certain is that this controversy will continue well into the twenty-first century.

In sum, sex may always be part of social life. But, in this case, the more things stay the same, the more they change.

CHAPTER SUMMARY

1. Although sociologists recognize the biological aspects of sexuality, they focus on how sexuality is shaped by society.

2. Sexual attitudes have changed over the course of U.S. history. Early colonists viewed sex rigidly in terms of reproduction; in recent decades, sex has also become more a matter of intimacy and personal pleasure.

3. The sexual revolution, which was pronounced in the late 1960s, encouraged people to be freer and more open about sexuality; by the 1980s, a sexual counterrevolution arose in response to conservative political goals and fears about sexually transmitted diseases.

4. Although the norm in all societies is heterosexuality, other sexual orientations—including homosexuality, bisexuality, and asexuality—are found as well.

5. Pornography consists of words or images that cause sexual arousal. Conservatives oppose pornography on moral grounds; many liberals object to it as demeaning to women.

6. In recent years, sexual harassment has been defined as a social problem; today, laws protect people from sexual harassment, especially in the workplace.

7. Prostitution has long been widespread in the United States; law enforcement usually targets female prostitutes rather than male clients and poor street walkers rather than more affluent call girls. The extent of prostitution is even greater in Asia and many other poor regions of the world.

8. More than 1 million U.S. teens become pregnant each year. Most teens who become pregnant are not married, and about half decide to keep their babies. Babies born to teens, especially girls who are poor, are at high risk for poverty as adults.

9. Abortion is among the most divisive issues in the United States. Abortion rights involve not just unintended pregnancy but also the social standing of women.

10. Unprotected sexual activity transmits some fifty diseases, including deadly AIDS. In global perspective, AIDS is becoming a medical catastrophe.

11. The structural-functional approach emphasizes society's need to control sexuality through the incest taboo and norms regarding "legitimate" childbirth. In addition, sexual patterns such as prostitution, though regarded as deviant, also have positive functions.

12. The symbolic-interaction approach highlights the relativity of sexual norms, such as those involving virginity. This paradigm also helps explain how people take on what many people define as deviant sexual careers.

13. The social-conflict approach explores sexuality in terms of men's social dominance over women. In addition, queer theory investigates heterosexual bias in U.S. culture.

14. In general, conservatives believe sexuality should be guided by traditional morality. Liberals argue sexuality should be a matter of individual choice. Radical feminism and queer theory argue the need for basic changes in U.S. society in pursuit of equality for all, female and male, gay and straight.

KEY CONCEPTS

sex   (p. 192) the biological distinction between females and males; also, sexual activity that leads to physical gratification and possibly reproduction

sexual orientation   (p. 195) a person's romantic, emotional, and sexual attraction to another person

heterosexuality   (p. 195) sexual attraction to someone of the other sex

homosexuality   (p. 195) sexual attraction to someone of the same sex

bisexuality   (p. 195) sexual attraction to people of both sexes

asexuality   (p. 195) the absence of sexual attraction to people of either sex

homophobia   (p. 198) an aversion or hostility to people thought to be gay, lesbian, or bisexual

pornography   (p. 198) words or images intended to cause sexual arousal

sexual harassment   (p. 200) unwanted comments, gestures, or physical contact of a sexual nature

prostitution   (p. 202) the selling of sexual services

abortion   (p. 206) the deliberate termination of a pregnancy

sexually transmitted diseases (STDs)   (p. 207) diseases spread by sexual contact

queer theory   (p. 212) a body of theory and research that challenges the heterosexual bias in U.S. society

heterosexism   (p. 212) bias that treats heterosexuality as the norm while stigmatizing anyone who differs from this norm as "queer"

THINKING CRITICALLY: QUESTIONS AND ISSUES

1. Explain the following statement: Although sex seems to be a biological issue, it is mostly a matter of culture.

2. What changes in U.S. society over the course of the last century are connected to a freer attitude toward sexuality (and homosexuality)? Consider changes in the role of women, the growth of

   the mass media, and the fact that children are no longer economic assets but economic liabilities.

3. Cite several sexual issues that were defined as social problems several generations ago but are not now. Contrast these with aspects of sexuality that have been defined as a problem only in recent decades. Can you explain these shifts?

4. Where do liberals and conservatives agree and disagree on sexual issues such as pornography, prostitution, teenage pregnancy, homosexuality, and abortion? Explain why "one person's social problem is likely to be another person's solution."

GETTING INVOLVED: LEARNING EXERCISES

1. Almost every campus has student organizations involved in sexual issues discussed in this chapter, including gay rights, sexual violence, and abortion. See which organizations operate on your campus. What are their goals? What changes do they seek? How would you characterize them politically?

2. Ask an official in your college's student services office about the extent of sexual violence on campus. See what you can learn about the percentage of crimes reported and the policies and procedures to assist and protect victims.

3. Visit the office of Planned Parenthood that serves your community and see what policies and programs the organization supports to address the problems of teenage pregnancy and the dangers of sexually transmitted diseases.

4. Do some research in the library and on the Internet to learn more about past and present laws in your state and local community regarding prostitution, sodomy, sexual violence, stalking, and sexual harassment.

5. In recent years, "hooking up" has emerged as a pattern of sexual behavior on college campuses. Organize a class discussion that explores what people think "hooking up" means, why this pattern has emerged, and what problems it involves.

GETTING CONNECTED: USEFUL WEB LINKS

http://www.prenhall.com/macionis
Visit the interactive Companion Website™ that accompanies this text. Begin by clicking on the cover of your book. You will find a chapter-by-chapter study guide, practice tests, suggested Web links, and links to other relevant material.

http://www.now.org
http://www.frc.org
These two Web sites discuss issues involving sexuality from different political viewpoints. Visit the site for the National Organization for Women, a liberal organization, and also visit the site for the Family Research Council, which is conservative. Which issues does each organization find most important? Can you find any areas of agreement?

http://www.gay.com
http://www.qrd.org
These sites address a wide range of issues concerning homosexuality and sexual orientations.

http://www.teenpregnancy.org
The National Campaign to Prevent Teen Pregnancy operates this site to educate young people about responsible sexual behavior. Visit the site and identify the organization's goals and strategies.

http://www.agi-usa.org
The Alan Guttmacher Institute carries out a great deal of research about issues involving sexuality.

GETTING STARTED ON YOUR OWN: RESEARCH NAVIGATOR™

Follow the instructions found on page 25 of this text to access the features of Research Navigator™. Once at the Web site, enter your Login Name and Password. Then, to use the **Content Select** database, enter keywords such as "sexual orientation," "sexually transmitted diseases," and "sexual harassment," and the search engine will supply relevant and recent scholarly and popular press publications. Use the *New York Times* **Search-by-Subject Archive** to find recent news articles related to sociology and the **Link Library** feature to find relevant Web links organized by the key terms associated with this chapter.

CHAPTER 9

© Paul Marcus, Junk in the Hole, Studio SPM, Inc.

ALCOHOL
AND OTHER DRUGS

I T IS A BUSY SATURDAY NIGHT AT the Twin Oaks, a local campus bar in Geneva, New York, where about 100 students are having fun listening to music, talking with friends, and drinking alcohol. Scenes like this can be found on or near almost every campus in the United States, and probably few people would define partying like this as a social problem. Indeed, as a researcher who studies alcohol use by U.S. college students put it, "I think there has been the view that whatever college students are doing, it's not that serious a problem; it's a rite of passage."

But a recent government-funded study by the National Institutes of Health (2002) presents some disturbing findings. Each year, about 1,400 college students die and 500,000 are injured in alcohol-related accidents, which often involve drinking and driving. In addition, 400,000 students report having had unprotected sex as a result of drinking alcohol, and alcohol contributes to 70,000 cases of sexual assault or "date rape."

Alcohol, as well as many other drugs, can be a source of pleasure. Yet drug use harms people of all ages across the country. This chapter explains what drugs are and how they work and examines the consequences of their use. We begin with a basic definition.

WHAT IS A DRUG?

Broadly defined, a **drug** is *any chemical substance other than food or water that affects the mind or body* (Goldstein, 1994). For thousands of years, people have used various natural substances to cause changes in the human body. In fact, most people use a number of drugs every day, from the aspirin that eases a headache to a cup of morning coffee that helps them wake up.

But most people in the United States define other drugs, such as crack cocaine and heroin, as dangerous and view their use as a serious social problem (Blendon & Young, 1998; NORC, 2003:101). In the case of still other drugs,

GETTING THE PICTURE

✦ Why are some drugs legal but others are not?

Until 1903 cocaine was one ingredient of Coca-Cola; from 1920 until 1933, all alcoholic beverages were illegal throughout the United States.

✦ Are students responsible drinkers?

A recent survey found that 44 percent of U.S. college students reported abusing alcohol in the past two weeks.

✦ Is illegal drug use a victimless crime?

Each year more people die from using illegal drugs than from gunshots, car accidents, and AIDS combined.

219

such as marijuana, there is less agreement as to whether use of the drug is a serious social problem (Stein, 2002). When and why are drugs defined as good or as harmful? To answer this question we need to explore the link between drugs and culture.

Drugs and Culture

How people view a particular drug varies from society to society. For example, Europeans have enjoyed drinking alcohol for thousands of years. But Native Americans, who were introduced to wine and liquor by European colonists five centuries ago, had no customs to guide their use. As a result, many Native Americans fell into drunken stupors, causing tribal leaders to declare alcohol a serious problem (Mancall, 1995; Unrau, 1996).

On the other hand, for centuries Native American people have used peyote as part of their religious rituals. When they shared it, many Europeans became terrified by the hallucinations it produces and soon pronounced peyote a dangerous drug.

Such diverse cultural views of drugs continue today. Coca, the plant used to make cocaine, is grown legally in the South American nations of Bolivia, Peru, and Colombia, as it has been for thousands of years. In those nations, many local farmers chew the plant as they work to give them a "lift." But in the United States, the growing of coca and the sale or possession of cocaine are illegal. Indeed, in the United States most people view this drug as a cause of violence and crime (Léons & Sanabria, 1997).

Drugs and Social Diversity

The definition of drugs changes over time and across cultures. A century ago, almost no one in the United States thought there was a "cocaine problem." On the contrary, famous people such as Sigmund Freud used cocaine openly, and anyone could enjoy the popular new "brain tonic" called Coca-Cola, which included cocaine as one of its ingredients (Inciardi, 1996; Léons & Sanabria, 1997).

People's attitudes toward various drugs also has much to do with their view of racial and ethnic categories who they think may be using the drug. A century ago in the South, many white people feared that easily available cocaine would fall into the hands of African Americans, who might then break the law and even become violent toward whites. Such fears were an important reason that, in 1903, the Coca-Cola company stopped putting cocaine in its beverage. In the years that followed, state after state outlawed the use of cocaine (Goode, 1993; Bertram et al., 1996).

Public opinion about other drugs shows a similar pattern. In the nineteenth century, as immigrants came to the United States in ever-increasing numbers, they brought not only their dreams but also their favored drugs. In the 1850s, for example, many Chinese immigrants in California smoked opium (a practice they learned from the British). Anti-Chinese feelings prompted eleven western states to ban opium. At the same time, in the East, obtaining opium was as easy as picking up a Sears Roebuck mail-order catalogue.

As the number of immigrants climbed, the U.S. Congress acted in 1914 to pass the Harrison Act,

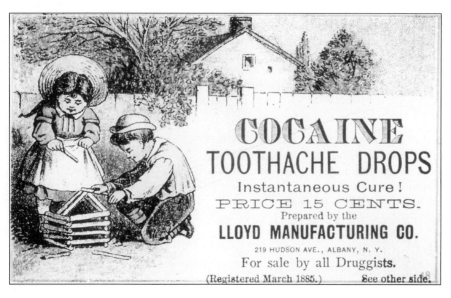

Whether a society defines a substance as a "useful medication" or a "dangerous drug" varies over time. It would surprise many people to learn that, a century ago, cocaine was an ingredient in a number of readily available products, such as this remedy for toothaches.

restricting the sale of cocaine and heroin. By 1919, not even doctors could write prescriptions for these drugs. Then, in 1920, the nation's attention turned to a much more widely used drug: alcohol.

Changing Views of Alcohol

The history of alcohol use in the United States is also linked to popular views of minorities. Although alcohol was popular since Europeans first settled this land, as the tide of immigration increased throughout the nineteenth century, public opinion about drinking began to turn negative. Why? Common stereotypes linked the Germans with beer, the Irish with whiskey, and the Italians with wine. In short, many people thought a million immigrants entering the country each year was bad enough, but so many immigrants drinking alcohol added up to a serious social problem (Pleck, 1987; Unrau, 1996).

As opposition to immigration increased (see Chapter 3, "Racial and Ethnic Inequality"), so did support for the Temperance Movement, a national organization seeking to ban alcohol. In 1920, the movement reached its goal when Congress passed the Eighteenth Amendment to the Constitution, which outlawed the manufacture and sale of alcohol across the country.

But many people—regardless of race and ethnicity—liked to drink. Therefore, although Prohibition reduced alcohol consumption, it did not end it. Moreover, with a limited supply, prices quickly went up. With so much money to be made, people began smuggling illegal liquor from Canada or distilling it themselves. In the rural South, for example, the poor made "moonshine" in local stills in the mountains. In the urban North, notorious gangsters such as Al Capone made fortunes smuggling and distributing liquor to "speakeasy" nightclubs.

Because Prohibition gave organized crime more power and money than ever before, the public gradually came to see Prohibition not as a solution but a problem itself. In 1933, Congress repealed the Eighteenth Amendment, bringing "the Great Experiment" to an end.

THE EXTENT OF DRUG USE

What is the extent of drug use today? The answer depends on which drugs one is talking about. If we define drugs in a broad way to include substances such as aspirin and caffeine, almost everyone is a "user." Parents give analgesics to teething infants and Ritalin to overactive school children, college students

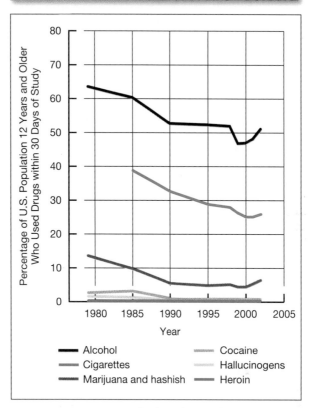

FIGURE 9–1 Use of Selected Drugs by the U.S. Population, 1979–2002

The most commonly used of the drugs listed here is alcohol, followed by cigarettes. The trend in overall drug use has been downward, with an upward turn in the last few years.

Source: U.S. Department of Health and Human Services (2003).

take appetite suppressants to control their weight, and adults reach for antidepressants, tranquilizers, and even pills to restore sexual functioning. In short, most people in the United States look to drugs to go to sleep, to wake up, to relax, or to ease pain.

With such a widespread reliance on chemicals, we might well describe our way of life as a "drug culture." Even so, most people do not define this kind of drug use as a problem, simply because it is so routine. On the contrary, most people define the drug problem as the use of *illegal* drugs.

In 2000, according to government surveys, nearly 14 million people in the United States, which represents 6 percent of the population aged twelve and older, had used some illegal drug at least once in the past thirty days. As Figure 9–1 shows, the trend in

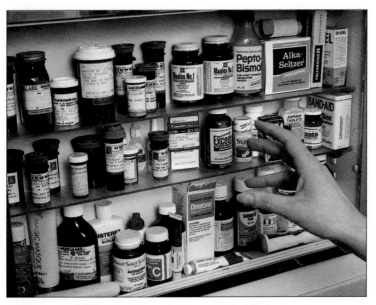

Drugs are part of our way of life, a fact that is evident in the collection of pills, capsules, and liquid medications found in most household bathrooms.

illegal drug use (and legal use of alcohol and cigarettes) declined in the 1980s, held about steady in the 1990s, and rose slightly after 2000 (U.S. Department of Health & Human Services, 2002). For the most part, illegal drug use goes up among people in their late teens and early twenties as they gain personal freedom, and it declines as people get older and take on family and job responsibilities.

Why Do People Use Drugs?

There are a number of reasons that people use drugs. First, some drugs have *therapeutic* uses, offering medical benefits such as controlling seizures or depression. Second, people use drugs for *recreational* reasons; that is, drugs such as beer or wine taste good and make the user feel more relaxed. Third, drugs (especially when used often or in large dosages) offer a form of *escape;* many people whose lives are troubled turn to alcohol or other drugs. Fourth, because drugs can alter human consciousness, some people use them for *spiritual* or *psychological* reasons; consider the use of peyote by Native American societies described earlier in this chapter. Fifth, and perhaps most important, people use drugs for *social conformity,* that is, to fit in. Peer pressure may lead young people to start smoking cigarettes or to try some illegal drug, for example.

Of course, many of these factors often operate at once. When dining at a restaurant with business associates, people may have a glass of wine with dinner to help them relax (recreational) and also because it is expected of them (social conformity). Whether they realize it or not, they may also be improving their health (therapeutic); doctors report that consuming small amounts of red wine each day can reduce the risk of heart disease.

Use and Abuse

What is the difference between *using* drugs and *abusing* them? These terms mark a socially constructed boundary between acceptable and unacceptable behavior. Most people use the term *drug abuse* to refer to use of any illegal substance or to use of a legal substance (such as a prescription drug) in a way that violates accepted medical practice (Abadinsky, 1989).

But some people distinguish use from abuse with an eye toward the *effect* of a drug. In other words, whereas people who *use* a drug may manage to function well, those who *abuse* a drug suffer physical, mental, or social harm (Weil & Rosen, 1983; White, 1991). From this point of view, any drug, whether illegal or legal, can be abused. After all, even a few (legal) drinks of alcohol can endanger a person who gets behind the wheel of a car (Goode, 1993).

In addition, people often disagree about whether a drug causes harm. For example, a person who is a regular user of marijuana may be convinced that this practice poses no danger. Friends may shake their heads, noting that this drug use—or, from their point of view, abuse—keeps the person from attending classes or meeting other daily responsibilities and raises the risk of trouble with the law.

Addiction and Dependency

This brings us to **addiction,** *a physical or psychological craving for a drug.* When doctors first began using this term in the nineteenth century, they considered people "addicted" if they suffered physical symptoms— sometimes called *withdrawal symptoms*—when they stopped using the drug. Withdrawal symptoms that accompany use of drugs such as opium and cocaine include chills, fever, diarrhea, twitching, nausea, vomiting, cramps, aches, and pains. The only quick way to end such symptoms is to take more of the drug.

Addiction is a complex state, one that depends not only on the dosage and length of time a drug is used but also on the physical and mental health of

A NATION OF DIVERSITY

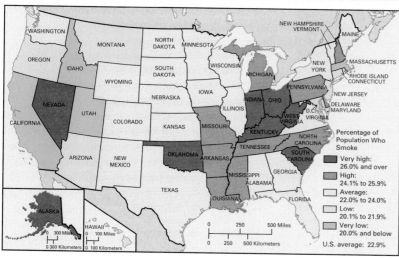

NATIONAL MAP 9–1

Cigarette Smoking across the United States

The highest percentage of smokers is found in Kentucky (30.8 percent), a tobacco-growing state and also a state where unemployment and poverty are serious problems. By contrast, Utah, with its high Mormon population, has the fewest smokers (13.7 percent) of all states. In general, what pattern can you see when it comes to smoking across the country? Hint: States with very few smokers generally have affluent populations who are concerned about health.

Source: U.S. Centers for Disease Control and Prevention (2003).

---

the user. In recent years, researchers have learned more about how addictive drugs affect the brain, raising levels of a substance called dopamine, which gives the drug user feelings of euphoria (Begley, 2001).

Addiction also involves **dependency,** *a state in which a person's body has adjusted to regular use of a drug.* People who have a drug dependency experience a need to continue taking the drug in order to feel comfortable. Such dependency is the reason that people sometimes talk about someone having a drug "habit." In recent years, the terms *addiction* and *dependency* have become used more loosely to refer to the use of just about any substance—including food—over which a person seems to have little or no control (Goode, 1993; Milkman & Sunderwirth, 1995).

TYPES OF DRUGS

One way to classify drugs is according to the effects they have on the body and brain. Here we briefly describe six types of drugs: stimulants, depressants, hallucinogens, cannabis, steroids, and prescription drugs.

Stimulants

Stimulants are *drugs that elevate alertness, changing a person's mood by increasing energy.* Because U.S. culture values action and achievement, stimulants are widely used in the United States.

Caffeine Probably the most popular drug of all in the United States is caffeine, which is available in many products, including coffee, tea, soft drinks, chocolate, and "stay alert" pills. At times, at least, almost everybody—from long-distance truck drivers to college students facing an exam to anyone trying to wake up before getting to work—depends on caffeine to stay alert.

Nicotine Although nicotine is legal in the United States and almost everywhere else in the world, this stimulant is both toxic and highly addictive. The most common way to use nicotine is to smoke cigarettes, a practice that became popular among men in the United States during World War I, when the army issued cigarettes to soldiers. Within a generation, the health hazards of cigarette smoking were becoming clear, but there were few efforts by government to discourage cigarette smoking until the 1960s. By then, 45 percent of U.S. adults smoked, including almost as many women as men. Since then, as people have become aware of the health hazards of smoking, the numbers have been going down. By 2001, just 22.9 percent were lighting up; National Map 9–1 gives a state-by-state survey of smoking.

Worldwide, the share of adults who smoke is higher than in this country—about 30 percent—and the figure is climbing. Figure 9–2 on page 224 shows that in many other countries, a majority of men smoke, often with little awareness of the harm it causes to the heart, lungs, and other bodily organs.

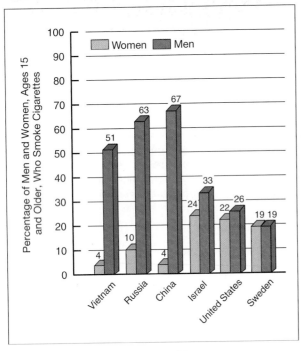

FIGURE 9–2 Cigarette Smoking in Selected Countries

In many of the world's low-income nations, cigarette smoking is more widespread among men than in the United States. At the same time, in these strongly patriarchal countries, gender norms limit the extent of smoking among women.

Sources: World Health Organization (2002).

In the United States, cigarette smoking remains by far the single greatest preventable cause of death. Each year, about 440,000 people die prematurely due to tobacco use, a death toll that far exceeds that caused by the use of alcohol and illegal drugs combined (U.S. Centers for Disease Control, 2003). In 1998, the U.S. tobacco companies reached a settlement with a number of states that gave them protection from mounting lawsuits in exchange for billions of dollars toward medical care for past smokers and a ban on cigarette advertising directed at young people. Even so, thousands of young people start smoking every day, and unless they quit, smoking will both harm them and place an enormous burden on our heath care system. Although some researchers warn that smoking during adolescence can damage lungs permanently, a decade after quitting most ex-smokers have health as good as that of people who never lit up in the first place (Recer, 1999).

Cocaine and Crack Cocaine and crack are powerful stimulants that heighten alertness as they raise blood pressure and pulse rate. These drugs keep users awake, reduce appetite, and cause many people to become agitated.

Cocaine, in a powder form, can be snorted up the nose. It is very addictive, and cocaine use leads to about 3,500 deaths each year in the United States (U.S. Department of Health & Human Services, 1995). Cocaine's popularity peaked in the 1980s, when it was the drug of choice among many young urban professionals ("yuppies"). Even though its popularity waned in the 1990s, the typical cocaine user is well-to-do, a fact that breaks the stereotype of drug abusers as "down and out" (U.S. Department of Justice, 1997; U.S. Department of Commerce, 1998).

Crack is a hardened form of cocaine usually smoked in a pipe. Although most people think crack is stronger than cocaine and more likely to provoke violence, current research indicates that the effects of the two drugs are very similar (Inciardi, 1992; Wren, 1996; Gómez, 1997).

Crack hit large cities in the United States with a vengeance in the 1980s, pushing crime rates sharply higher. As in the case of powdered cocaine, crack's popularity declined in the 1990s. However, experts estimate that about 1.5 million people use crack each year. African Americans have been about four times as likely as whites to use crack (U.S. Department of Health & Human Services, 2003).

Amphetamines Amphetamines were first developed for the medical treatment of personality disorders and obesity. These drugs increase alertness, cause an excited sense of well-being, and reduce the desire to sleep and eat. Because amphetamines are easy to make, many underground chemists operate highly profitable businesses selling drugs known on the street as "crank," "speed," "crystal," "go," "meth," or "ice."

After cocaine, amphetamines are the most popular illegal stimulants. Officials statistics suggest that about 12.5 million people have tried amphetamines. Many become dependent on them, including patients who begin taking amphetamines under a doctor's supervision. Such users typically experience withdrawal symptoms such as apathy, depression, irritability, and disorientation (U.S. Department of Health & Human Services, 2003). As the usage increases, amphetamines carry greater risk of causing agitation, fever, hallucinations, and convulsions and can even cause death. The Personal Stories box provides a look at the tragic effects of the use of amphetamines in the life of one young woman.

Personal Stories — "My Life Is Gone": One Crank User's Story

It is a warm Friday evening in Billings, Montana, and a bright moon shines overhead. But twenty-five-year-old Jennifer Smith couldn't tell you whether it's night or day. A regular user of "crank" (methamphetamine), Smith has been wide awake for five days. On Monday night, she left her three-year-old daughter at a friend's house, promising to be right back. Then the drug ride started. Crank produces a high that keeps the user madly active to the point of forgetting about food—and even children.

Now, Jennifer sits on a barstool, gulping shots of bourbon to help calm her nerves. She looks around for her boyfriend, forgetting that he ditched her two days ago. She wonders, too, what happened to her purse, in which she had a child-support check she hoped would pay for more drugs.

Smith strikes up a conversation with a man she has known for several years. He can see that she is out of control. "Crank makes you lose everything," she stammers, reaching for the rest of her bourbon. What has she lost? The list begins with her purse and her boyfriend and includes her good looks, her job, her hopes for the future, and, most important, the girl she calls "her little angel."

"I'm not afraid, though," she says, shaking her head. "I've cranked for seven years. . . . I'm getting pretty used to losing everything."

ISSUES AND EXERCISES

1. Do you think there is much public sympathy for women like Jennifer Smith? Why?
2. What policies might reduce the number of cases of this kind?
3. If Jennifer Smith were arrested, would she be better off or worse off? What about her child?

Source: Adapted from Kirn (1998).

Ritalin Ritalin, or methylphenidate hydrochloride, is a legal drug prescribed by doctors to treat children with attention deficit hyperactivity disorder (ADHD) or attention deficit disorder (ADD). These are disorders in which children become hyperactive, have trouble concentrating, or cannot pay attention to a teacher or another adult. In recent years, the use of Ritalin has increased sharply in the United States: More than 10 percent of school-age boys and 5 percent of school-age girls (a total of about 6 million youngsters) take the drug. In fact, medication use is rising faster among young people than among the elderly. Many college students take the drug, obtained from others who have a doctor's prescription, in order to concentrate more effectively on their studies (Livingston, 1997; Diaz, 2001; Novak, 2001; U.S. Department of Health and Human Services, 2003).

This widespread use of Ritalin has sparked controversy. On one side of the debate, defenders of the drug (including drug companies and many parents) claim that Ritalin helps children stay calm in school and focus on their work. Critics, though, reject the idea of using drugs to control children's behavior. Speaking for critics, pediatrician Lawrence Diller (1998) contends that U.S. children are being unnecessarily medicated by parents who are overworked or overly concerned with their children's achievement.

Depressants

Depressants are *drugs that slow the operation of the central nervous system.* In this sense, depressants have an effect opposite to stimulants.

Analgesics One class of depressants is analgesics, drugs that dull pain. The most widely used analgesics include familiar over-the-counter pain relievers such as aspirin, ibuprofen (Motrin), and acetaminophen (Tylenol). Although these drugs can be abused, they present little problem when used according to directions (Goode, 1993).

More problematic are naturally occurring narcotics, or *opiates* such as opium and drugs derived from opium, including morphine, codeine, and heroin. All are dangerous drugs that are highly addictive, disrupting the lives of abusers.

Heroin is made from morphine, which comes from the seed pods on poppy plants. A synthetic form of the drug is merperidine (marketed as Demerol).

Although most people have heard of heroin, only 0.1 percent of the U.S. population are current users (look back at Figure 9–1). When injected, sniffed, or smoked, this drug quickly causes euphoria and drowsiness. Because heroin is highly addictive, the law bans its use for any purpose. Addicts who stop using heroin experience strong cravings and physical withdrawal symptoms. Because users can never be sure how pure their heroin is, overdoses are common and can be fatal (U.S. Department of Health & Human Services, 2000; Leinwand, 2001).

Sedatives, Hypnotics, and Alcohol   Other depressants with a more wide-ranging effect on the central nervous system are sedatives and hypnotics. These drugs help people relax and, at higher dosages, cause drowsiness and sleep. Examples of sedatives and hypnotics include barbiturates, such as secobarbital (Seconal) and pentobarbital, and tranquilizers, including alprazolan (Xanax), diazepam (Valium), and triazoland (Halcion). Overuse of these drugs, especially when mixed with alcohol or other drugs, can be fatal.

Alcohol is the most widely used depressant in the United States. As noted in Figure 9–1, about half the adult population aged twelve and over (and about one-third of teens) in the United States consumes alcohol regularly. For many who drink responsibly and in moderation, alcohol poses no problem. But more than four in ten people in this country have been affected directly or indirectly (through the struggle of a close friend or family member) by **alcoholism,** *an addiction to alcohol.* Estimates place the number of U.S. adults who have a drinking problem at about 18 million (about 10 percent of the adult population); about 30 million people have such a problem at some point in their lives (about 17 percent). Yet only 1.5 million people seek help for a problem related to alcohol each year (U.S. Department of Health and Human Services, 2003). For every person who battles alcoholism, four people face the challenge of living or working with an alcoholic person. With the exception of nicotine, alcohol is the most addictive drug available legally with no prescription. Analysts put the total cost of alcoholism in the United States (reflecting everything from accidents to lost days at work) at about $200 billion per year (Kalb, 2001).

As explained in the opening to this chapter, alcohol abuse is a serious problem at U.S. colleges and universities. A study of college students by the National Institutes of Health (2002) found that about 40 percent said they had engaged in binge drinking—which the researchers defined at having at least five drinks in a row for men or four drinks for women—at least once in the past two weeks. Furthermore, half of these students fell into the "extreme binge drinker" category, with three or more such drinking episodes in the past two weeks. The 20 percent of students who are heavy drinkers consume 70 percent of the alcohol used by all U.S. students. By contrast, only about 20 percent of students said they had no alcoholic drink in the past year.

As noted earlier, the researchers found that consuming alcohol—especially "drink 'til you drop" binge drinking—causes 1,400 student deaths and 500,000 injuries each year. In addition, 400,000 students claim they had unprotected sex after drinking alcohol, which can lead to a number of problems, including unwanted pregnancy and sexually transmitted diseases including AIDS. Finally, by affecting people's judgment, alcohol also plays a part in about 70,000 cases of date rape each year.

Throughout the population, the use of alcohol is related to crime: In 2002, police made about 600,000 arrests for public drunkenness and disorderly conduct involving alcohol. More seriously, another 1.5 million arrests are made each year for driving a motor vehicle while under the influence of alcohol; police records show that alcohol is involved in about 41 percent of the 57,000 motor vehicle deaths on U.S. roads each year. In addition, about 40 percent of people jailed for violent offenses report that they were under the influence of alcohol when they committed their crimes (U.S. Department of Transportation, 2002; U.S. Federal Bureau of Investigation, 2003).

Finally, although an occasional alcoholic beverage may provide some health benefits, heavy drinking is a health hazard. For one thing, drinking provides many calories but no nutrition, causing weight gain and, as consumption increases, harm to the heart and the liver. Finally, pregnant women who consume alcohol put their unborn child's health at risk (U.S. Department of Health and Human Services, 1995; U.S. Census Bureau, 2003).

Antipsychotics   Antipsychotics, including lithium and haloperidol (Haldol), are powerful drugs that doctors prescribe to people with serious personality disorders such as schizophrenia. Although these pills can be overused, causing harm, these drugs are effective in reducing psychotic symptoms such as paranoia, visual hallucinations, and hearing voices. Supervised use of antipsychotic drugs allows hundreds of thousands of people who might otherwise need hospitalization to live independently (Goode, 1993).

Hallucinogens

Hallucinogens are stimulants, generally taken in pill or capsule form, that cause hallucinations. In the United States, the most commonly used hallucinogens include LSD, peyote, mescaline, psilocybin, phercyclidine (PCP, "angel dust"), and methylenedioxymethanphetamine (MDMA, or "ecstasy"), a drug that has gained popularity in recent years. Estimates suggest that about 10 percent of young people will have tried ecstasy by the time they complete high school (Feuer, 2000; Grimm, 2002). Although about 10 percent of the U.S. population has tried a hallucinogenic drug at some point, less than 0.5 percent of the U.S. population reports using one in the past year (U.S. Department of Health and Human Services, 2002).

Hallucinogens are nonaddictive but powerful, and they can sharply raise pulse rates and blood pressure and alter perceptions of time and distance. Indeed, their ability to produce vivid hallucinations is the main reason people use them. In some cases, people find taking hallucinogens very pleasurable; at best, people describe the experience as "consciousness-expanding." But these drugs can also trigger panic attacks; many people find the experience terrifying. Moreover, the experience varies from use to use; just because people have a "good trip" at one time does not mean they will not have a "bad trip" the next time. Perhaps most seriously, the effects are unpredictable. People who use hallucinogens may experience "flashbacks"—unexpected hallucinations—later on without taking the drug again. In short, hallucinogens are always dangerous; overdoses can cause psychosis and even death.

In the United States, the use of hallucinogens peaked in the 1960s. Even so, the government reports that use of these drugs rose in the 1990s among teens. White people are twice as likely as African Americans to use hallucinogens (U.S. Department of Health and Human Services, 2003).

Cannabis

Two drugs in this category, marijuana and hashish, gained widespread popularity in the 1960s. Even today, these two substances make up about 80 percent of all illegal drug use. Figure 9–1 puts the share of U.S. adults currently using marijuana or hashish at 6 percent, but almost half (some 90 million people) say they have used marijuana or hashish at some time in the past (Stein, 2002; U.S. Department of Health and Human Services, 2003).

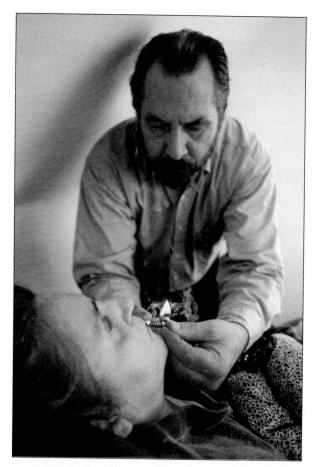

In a small number of U.S. communities, people can legally use marijuana for medical purposes. Do you think this practice will spread throughout the country in years to come? Why or why not?

People smoke marijuana and hashish or consume the drug after cooking it in food, such as "magic" brownies or cookies. Both drugs produce a sense of euphoria, help people relax, and increase appetite. However, as the dosages go up these drugs can produce fatigue, disorientation, paranoia, and even serious personality disorders (U.S. Department of Health and Human Services, 2002).

For decades, a social movement has tried to legalize marijuana, making the claim that this drug is not addictive and poses little danger to users. Opponents of legal marijuana counter that this drug does pose dangers, especially if users operate motor vehicles. At present, a handful of communities (mostly in Maine and California) permit the use of marijuana for medical purposes, under the supervision of a doctor. Many people undergoing chemotherapy for cancer or AIDS, for example, find that marijuana eases the nausea that often is a side effect of the treatment.

Whatever one's view on the legalization of marijuana, public opinion is against sending marijuana smokers to jail. One recent survey found that almost three-fourths of U.S. adults thought people convicted of possessing small amounts of marijuana should be fined rather than jailed (Stein, 2002).

Steroids

The full name for this class of drugs is quite a mouthful: *androgenic* (promoting masculine characteristics) *anabolic* (building) *steroids.* Many professional and amateur athletes use steroids, although athletic programs ban their use. Typically, to avoid detection, athletes use steroids in cycles: a few weeks or months on, followed by a similar period off before a drug test.

Government surveys suggest that about 10 percent of male high school athletes—but just 0.1 percent of female athletes—have used steroids at some time in their lives. Although some take steroids under a doctor's care to treat an injury, most (perhaps 1 million young people) have used steroids to gain a competitive edge (U.S. Department of Justice, 1999).

The use of steroids can improve athletic performance. But this drug also poses dangers, raising the risk of liver tumors, jaundice, fluid retention, high blood pressure, acne, and trembling. In addition, some men who take steroids experience infertility, baldness, and breast development. Women using steroids may stop menstruating, grow facial hair, and experience an enlargement of the clitoris and a deepening of the voice. Among young people, use of steroids sometimes causes the body to stop growing too soon. Moreover, because people typically inject steroids and some share needles, users increase their risk of contracting a range of diseases, including hepatitis and HIV (National Institute on Drug Abuse, 1999).

Prescription Drugs

In 2003, the statement by radio talk-show host Rush Limbaugh that he was addicted to pain killers reminded everyone that the use of prescription drugs can be hazardous. Physicians prescribe a wide range of drugs to patients, and almost everyone has taken drugs as part of treatment for a physical injury or illness or psychological condition. Especially with elderly patients, physicians sometimes overprescribe medications. More commonly, however, almost

15 million people in the United States use prescription drugs in a nonmedical way, taking a greater dosage, mixing drugs, or continuing to use a drug when the medical need no longer exists, and this number has tripled in the last decade (U.S. Department of Health and Human Services, 2003). Because prescription drugs are legal, and because most prescription drugs are used by relatively affluent people, the abuse of prescription drugs often is overlooked in the United States. For this reason, the abuse of prescription medications is sometimes called the invisible part of the drug problem (*ABC News*, 1997; Corliss, 2001).

Of all prescription drugs, the most often abused are pain killers (analgesics) such as codeine, diazepam (Valium), and, among college students, oxycodone (Percodan) and hydrocodone (Vicodin). One reason is that doctors often prescribe these drugs; another reason is that people build up tolerances to pain killers and gradually take higher and higher dosages. Prescriptions limit the number of pills available, of course, but many patients increase their supply by seeing several doctors at one time, obtaining prescriptions from each for the same drug.

This completes a brief survey of drugs, what they do to people, and some of their consequences for society as a whole. We now take a look at the role of drugs in various other social problems.

DRUGS AND OTHER SOCIAL PROBLEMS

There is little question that drugs play a part in many social problems, from crime to poverty. The government estimates that losses (in terms of medical costs and lost productivity) resulting from the use of illegal drugs—that is, excluding alcohol and tobacco—exceeds $150 billion (Office of National Drug Control Policy, 2003). But it is difficult to say how much drugs *cause* such problems and how much they are the *consequences* of the problems. We look first at the links between drugs and family life.

Problems of Family Life

Drugs play a part in many cases of child neglect and family violence. Although not usually the single cause of such problems, they often make the problems worse. Why? Drugs reduce inhibitions and affect judgment so that a person already inclined to abusive behavior is more likely to act in this way when "under the influence" (Gelles & Straus, 1988; Gelles, 1997). In extreme cases, such as the story of

Jennifer Smith's crank abuse, presented in the box on page 225, the craving for drugs can be so strong that parents abandon or otherwise harm their own children. In some cases, parents even force their children into prostitution or other criminal activity to earn money for drugs.

A drug problem rarely affects only a single person but typically involves parents, brothers and sisters, partners, and children. Many people addicted to alcohol or other drugs spend their whole paychecks on the substances they crave; others cannot keep a job at all. Such cases often create a pattern called **codependency,** *behavior on the part of others that helps a substance abuser continue.* In simple terms, others in the family change their behavior to make up for the shortcomings of the drug abuser. Family members may earn extra money, help keep house, hide evidence of accidents, cover for an abuser who misses work, or even provide drugs to the abuser in an effort to keep the peace and get through another day. Codependency draws others into a life distorted by drugs. In a study of the wives of alcoholics, for example, Jacqueline Wiseman (1991) found codependent women experienced a number of problems from uncertain income to outright violence. Children who live in a household with a substance abuser may lose their ability to trust others because the abuser has let them down so often. Such children often grow up too soon, taking over the tasks not performed by the older drug abuser and sacrificing their own needs and desires in the process. Not surprisingly, many of these young people end up in trouble with the law, dropping out of school, and abusing drugs later on. In short, drugs can begin a cycle of problems that spill over from one generation to another.

Homelessness

Many people link the use of drugs, especially alcohol, with homeless men. Research confirms that there is some truth to this belief: Half of homeless men and about 20 percent of homeless women have a serious drinking problem (Baum & Burnes, 1993). Moreover, one study at New York City homeless shelters found that 80 percent of single homeless men—but only 29 percent of adults in homeless families—tested positive for some drug (Cuomo, 1992).

Recall from Chapter 2 ("Poverty and Wealth") that much homelessness in the United States results from the recent increase in underemployment and a lack of affordable housing (Ratnesar, 1999). In short, although U.S. culture tends to define people

The use of drugs—especially alcohol—by people who are homeless is widespread. Do you think such drug use is more often the cause or the result of being desperately poor?

as responsible for their social position, many individuals and families become homeless through no fault of their own. Although some people may become homeless because they use drugs, the opposite is often true: People who do not have work, who lose the support of neighbors, family, and friends, and who are forced to live on the streets may turn to alcohol or other drugs as a coping mechanism (Wiseman, 1978; Snow & Anderson, 1993).

Drugs and homelessness interact in another way, too. The development of antipsychotic drugs in the 1960s helped many people suffering from mental illness. As a result, many mental institutions began releasing patients to live on their own, with periodic visits to community mental health centers. But less than half of the planned mental health centers were ever built; moreover, once patients were released, many did not take their medications and could not find jobs or affordable housing. As a result, a number of these mental patients became homeless, and some ended up abusing alcohol and other drugs (Weiss, Griffin, & Mirin, 1992; Baum & Burnes, 1993).

Health Problems

Although some drugs save lives, each year as many people die from the use of drugs (including cigarettes and alcohol) as die from gun violence, accidents, and infectious diseases combined. Some drugs (such as heroin, especially in high dosages) harm people right away, damaging the brain or other vital organs. But many drugs harm people over time: Long-term use of alcohol, for example, can lead to malnutrition and liver damage. Remember, too, that the distortion of judgment caused by drug use raises the risk of death or injury from accidents and from unsafe sex.

Learn more about drugs and health at the Web site of the Substance Abuse and Mental Health Services Administration: **http://www.samhsa.gov**

Prenatal Exposure to Drugs   Many people suffer from drug problems that began before they were born. Both physical and mental health problems can result from prenatal exposure to drugs, that is, the use of drugs by a pregnant woman. About one-third of all pregnant women drink alcohol at some time during pregnancy, putting their babies at risk; 5 to 10 percent of pregnant women use marijuana, cocaine, or some other drug (U.S. Centers for Disease Control and Prevention, 2002).

Of course, many of the women who use drugs in this way do not know they are pregnant. This is especially true of women whose drug use is so heavy that it causes irregular menstrual cycles. When they do learn of their pregnancies, most women stop taking drugs. But because an embryo's nervous system and major organs begin to develop within two months after conception, the damage may already be done. Others may find it all but impossible to stop their drug use without help (Abel, 1990; Gomby & Shiono, 1991; Gómez, 1997).

Drug exposure greatly increases the risk of premature delivery, low birth weight, and birth defects. Longer-term problems include developmental problems such as retarded growth, poor physical coordination, learning disabilities, and emotional problems. Each year, the cost of hospital care for children with prenatal exposure to drugs and alcohol exceeds $500 million (Inciardi, Lockwood, & Pottieger, 1993; Gómez, 1997; *Nation's Health*, 1998).

Given the personal harm and enormous costs that result when pregnant women use drugs, some people argue that society should hold these women responsible; others disagree. The Social Policy box takes a closer look.

Sharing Needles and HIV   Many users use syringes and hypodermic needles to take drugs intravenously, that is, to inject drugs directly into a vein. Introducing drugs to the body in this way produces the fastest and strongest effect. Like people who drink alcohol, intravenous (or IV) drug users usually "shoot up" in groups, and some engage in the dangerous practice of sharing needles.

Why is sharing needles dangerous? Because human immunodeficiency virus (HIV), the virus that causes AIDS, is found in blood and other bodily fluids, and a needle can easily transmit HIV from one person to another. To make matters worse, some women (who may or may not use needles themselves) trade sex for drugs, which risks further spread of HIV and other sexually transmitted diseases.

In 1994, officials at the U.S. National Centers for Disease Control and Prevention proposed a program of needle exchange: Local health centers would exchange used hypodermic needles for new ones to reduce the spread of HIV and other diseases. But this program never caught on because opponents view giving out needles as supporting drug use. As an alternative, many local health departments provide instructions on how to clean a used needle with a bleach solution to kill HIV and other dangerous agents.

Crime

The manufacture, distribution, and possession of illegal drugs is a crime. As we have already noted, many drugs (both illegal substances such as cocaine and legal substances such as alcohol) are linked to other criminal behavior also. Government officials report that about two-thirds of prison inmates convicted of violent offenses were under the influence of some drug considered in this chapter when they committed their crimes. Statistics such as these lead some people to conclude that drugs are a major cause of crime (Goldstein, 1995; Mendelson & Mello, 1995; U.S. Bureau of Justice Statistics, 2003).

But not everyone agrees. Some claim that drug policies in the United States actually make the crime problem worse. For one thing, drug laws drive up drug prices. High prices, in turn, lead users of cocaine, crack, or heroin to commit crimes, from prostitution to burglary to murder. Government research shows

Social Policy — "Pregnancy Police": Solution or Problem?

WHEN JENNIFER JOHNSON GAVE BIRTH TO HER daughter, the first three words she heard were not "It's a girl!" but "You're under arrest!" On July 13, 1989, moments after she delivered her baby, the Altamonte Springs, Florida, woman became the first to be arrested on a charge of furnishing drugs to a minor—in this case through the umbilical cord to her newborn infant.

For three years before the delivery, Johnson had used cocaine. When she learned she was pregnant, she sought treatment. But officials told her all programs were full; no one was able to help her.

Shortly before her delivery date, Johnson told her doctor about the cocaine. A urine test confirmed the presence of cocaine in her system, and—as required by law—hospital personnel notified the state's child protection agency. An investigator called the police, and a prosecutor brought the charges against Johnson soon after.

The court convicted Johnson of giving drugs to her child. Taking notice of the fact that Johnson's baby appeared healthy and that she had no prior criminal record, the court spared Johnson a jail term but sentenced her to one year of house arrest and fourteen years of supervised probation.

Each year, almost half a million drug-exposed infants are born in the United States. In response, some prosecutors have become aggressive, filing charges against mothers for child abuse and neglect, drug delivery, assault, and even manslaughter. As they see it, pregnant women who use drugs are endangering the lives of innocent children. Others view such cases as a public health issue. They point out that threatening pregnant women with criminal charges will scare away those who use drugs from prenatal care, increasing the risk to their children. In short, these women belong not in a courtroom but in a treatment facility where they and their children can get the help they need.

ISSUES AND EXERCISES

1. In the long run, do you think that punishing or treating pregnant drug users will be more effective in preventing injury to children? Why?

2. Conservatives (who oppose abortion rights) tend to support prosecuting pregnant women who use drugs; liberals (who support abortion rights) oppose the policy. Can you see why?

3. [Research Navigator.com] Use Research Navigator™ to learn more about pregnancy and drugs. (See instructions on page 25; keywords: "drugs," "drug abuse")

Sources: Adapted from Inciardi et al. (1993:142–43) and Siegel (1997).

---

that almost one in five federal prison inmates reports committing violent crime for money to buy drugs (Inciardi, 1996; U.S. Bureau of Justice Statistics, 1998).

Because the high price of drugs creates huge profits for drug dealers, the opportunity to earn a living from drugs may outweigh the risk of being sent to jail, especially among people with few other opportunities to get ahead. Moreover, there is little surprise in the fact that, to protect their profits, drug dealers may turn to violence, often harming not only each other but also innocent people caught in the crossfire (Goldstein, 1995; Bertram et al., 1996).

Currently, one-fourth of inmates in all state and local prisons and half of all federal prison inmates are there for drug offenses (U.S. Bureau of Justice Statistics, 2002; Anderson, 2003). To the extent that jail time stigmatizes people (as "convicts") and makes getting a good job upon release less likely, people who have "done time" may be more likely to commit later crimes.

If all of this is true, is legalization a way to bring the crime rate down? No one knows for sure. But it seems likely that doing so would reduce street crime, although perhaps it would add to other problems, such as accidents, child neglect, and drug addiction.

Global Poverty

In the United States, illegal drug use and poverty are linked, although it is difficult to sort out which is cause and which is effect. In fact, drugs are linked to poverty throughout the world.

To begin, drugs that are illegal in the United States represent a significant share of the global

The global trade in illegal drugs has much to do with widespread poverty in low-income nations. These Bolivians produce coca leaves, which are later refined into cocaine. Cocaine production represents a bigger part of the national economy in Bolivia than wheat production is to the economy of the United States.

economy. It is the millions of people in poor nations of the world without other economic opportunities who grow the plants and manufacture the drugs that are smuggled into rich nations such as the United States. For example, opiates from Afghanistan and other low-income countries in Asia are sold in the United States, Canada, the wealthy nations of Western Europe, and Australia. Hashish from the Middle East and western Africa moves readily to Western Europe, just as marijuana grown in Mexico, Cuba, and Central America is shipped to the United States. Finally, cocaine produced in mountainous regions of South America travels to both North America and Western Europe.

Each year, people in the United States spend more than $65 billion on heroin, cocaine, marijuana, hashish, and other illegal drugs. This sum exceeds the total economic output of dozens of the world's countries. On a local level, drugs can be a country's biggest export and the major source of economic opportunity. In Bolivia, for example, cocaine production represents three-fourths of all economic exports and one-fourth of all economic activity. Opium, also has great economic importance in Bolivia, as does cocaine in Peru, marijuana in Mexico,

and hashish in Afghanistan (Léons & Sanabria, 1997; Stares, 1996; Ramo, 2001).

Terrorism

In recent years, a mass media campaign in the United States by the Office of National Drug Control Policy has linked drug use and terrorism. Buying illegal drugs at home, the message goes, puts money in the hands of terrorists abroad. Worse still, terrorists may use this money to finance attacks on this country. In one television ad, a young man admits using cocaine and then says with regret, "I helped blow up buildings."

Since the September 11, 2001, attacks, the level of public concern about terrorism has remained high. But is the link between illegal drugs and terrorism real? There is no doubt that some organizations engaged in terrorism sell drugs to raise money. But critics point out that most of the illegal drug trade is not carried out by terrorists and that most terrorist funding does not come from drug sales. As these critics see it, the federal government is overstating the link between terrorism and drugs in an effort to discourage illegal drug use among young people (Grimm, 2002).

SOCIAL POLICY: RESPONDING TO THE DRUG PROBLEM

There is widespread agreement that the use of many drugs is a serious social problem. But there is far less agreement about what U.S. society should do to solve it.

Strategies to Control Drugs

Despite a sometimes fierce determination, reducing the amount of illegal drugs in the United States is extremely difficult. For one thing, the country has extensive political freedoms, which limit the power of police to conduct searches and make arrests. For another, there is a high demand for illegal drugs, which draws a huge supply. In the following sections, we take a closer look at several control strategies: interdiction, prosecution, education, and treatment.

Interdiction *Interdiction* means stopping the movement of drugs across this country's borders. Interdiction makes use of the Drug Enforcement Agency, U.S. Customs Service, Border Patrol, and U.S. military.

But consider what these agencies are up against: The United States has 12,000 miles of coastline and 7,500 miles of land borders. Each year, some 200,000 boats and ships, 600,000 aircraft, 200 million cars, and 500 million people cross this nation's borders, and each could be carrying drugs. Not surprisingly, agents manage to seize only a tiny share of the drugs that enter the United States. No one doubts that the problem would be greater without such efforts. But interdiction has had limited success in the war on drugs (Bertram et al., 1996).

Prosecution "Putting drug dealers where they belong: in jail" is a popular idea in the United States. But as we have explained, attempts to catch them are difficult and can threaten people's basic freedoms.

In addition, the policy of prosecuting drug dealers often punishes the poor and minorities unfairly. The war on crack is one example. Recall that in the 1980s, Congress passed tough mandatory sentencing laws for drug-related crimes. Conservatives support such laws to discourage people from using drugs; liberals, however, point out bias that harms minorities.

Why? The Federal Minimum Mandatory Sentencing Table, shown in Table 9–1, dictates prison sentences according to type of drug. Note that possessing 500 grams of cocaine—but only 5 grams of crack—leads to a five-year jail term. Because white people and middle-class people are more likely to use cocaine whereas black people and the poor are more likely to use crack, critics claim the sentencing difference reflects not the drug but the drug users (Tonry, 1995; Freedman, 1998).

Education A third strategy for controlling drug use is education. Unlike prosecution, which is aimed at current drug users, educational programs try to discourage people from trying drugs in the first place. Typically, such programs operate in schools and target young people.

The most widespread drug education program is Drug Abuse Resistance Education (DARE), begun in 1983, which brings police officers into schools to instruct children on the dangers of drugs. DARE boasts that programs operate in 75 percent of elementary schools across the United States.

Visit the DARE Web site at http://www.dare.org

Police, school administrators, and parents all agree on the need to instruct young people about drugs. Even so, research suggests that educational programs such as DARE do not make much of a difference in drug use among young people. In 2001, DARE officials acknowledged that their program is not having the effect they had hoped and began a new, more interactive program aimed at drawing older students, those in middle school and high school, into discussion about drug use (Glass, 1997; Zernike, 2001).

Treatment Another drug control strategy is to help users, especially people struggling with addiction, to kick their habits. Beginning in the early 1970s, the Nixon administration expanded drug treatment programs that offered methadone, a synthetic form of heroin, to treat heroin addicts. In practice, methadone programs simply replace one form of addiction with another. Even so, the government can ensure the purity of methadone, whereas street heroin is of unknown strength and is often mixed with other chemicals. Furthermore, by supplying methadone, the government reduces demand for heroin. Finally, programs offering methadone (and, more recently, a new drug called buprenorphine) have the added benefit of reducing a drug user's

---

TABLE 9–1 FEDERAL MINIMUM MANDATORY SENTENCING TABLE

TYPE OF DRUG	FIVE-YEAR SENTENCE WITHOUT PAROLE	TEN-YEAR SENTENCE WITHOUT PAROLE
LSD	1 gram	10 grams
Marijuana	100 plants or 100 kilograms	1,000 plants or 1,000 kilograms
Crack cocaine	5 grams	50 grams
Powder cocaine	500 grams	5 kilograms
Heroin	100 grams	1 kilogram
Methamphetamine ("crank")	5 grams	10 grams
PCP ("angel dust")	10 grams	100 grams

Source: 21 USC 841 (2003).

A DEFINING MOMENT

Bill Wilson: Alcoholics Can Learn to Be Sober

At thousands of AA meetings like this one, people throughout the United States learn to confront their alcoholism and to live a sober life.

BILL WILSON WAS WORKING AS A STOCKBROKER in New York City when he realized that he had a serious drinking problem. He reached a point where alcohol had made his life unmanageable, and he needed a way out. In 1935, he discovered that the solution to his own problem lay in support from others with similar problems and adoption of a new set of personal values.

Wilson built this idea into a program to help himself and others like him, and Alcoholics Anonymous (AA) was born. The organization quickly spread throughout the United States and abroad.

Today, AA is a global organization with some 2 million members. AA has changed the way people look at alcoholism. A century ago, most people regarded alcoholics as morally weak people who gave in to the temptation of drink and deserved little sympathy. AA redefined alcoholism as an illness—of the body but also of the mind and soul—that, like any other illness, can be treated successfully.

How does AA work? People who suffer from alcoholism join simply by coming to regular meetings. There they realize that they are not alone, that alcoholism has made the lives of others unmanageable, too. Recognizing that, alone, they are powerless over alcohol, they gain strength from one another and begin on the path toward a sober life.

Although AA believes alcoholics can learn to lead a sober life, it cautions that they will always remain alcoholics. Therefore, AA members never say they are "ex-alcoholics"; rather, they describe themselves as "recovering from" addiction.

The AA philosophy has been adapted by a number of similar organizations, including Al-Anon Family Groups (for friends and family members of addicts), Alateen (for teenagers whose parents are alcoholics), Adult Children of Alcoholics (for adults who grew up in an alcoholic home), Narcotics Anonymous (for people addicted to drugs other than alcohol), Gamblers Anonymous, and numerous programs aimed at helping people with eating disorders.

---

involvement in crime (Bowersox, 1995; Cloud, 1998; Hunt & Sun, 1998).

Treatment involves not only drugs but also counseling and group support (Cowley, 2001). No organization has done more to show the power of other people to help those addicted to drugs than Alcoholics Anonymous. The Defining Moment box provides a look at Bill Wilson and the organization he founded.

The success of programs such as Alcoholics Anonymous confirms the importance of treatment in the efforts to control drug abuse. But treatment also has its limitations. For one thing, there are not enough treatment programs to help all those who need them. Just as important, programs may help people stop using drugs, but they cannot change the environment that pushed the people toward drugs in the first place. The risk of relapse is why Alcoholics Anonymous teaches its members that they will always be alcoholics who must actively work to control their addiction for the rest of their lives. Finally, although there is public support for treatment of people who abuse drugs, public opinion has always favored prosecution over treatment for those who break the law.

The War on Drugs

All the strategies just noted—interdiction, prosecution, education, and treatment—play some part in U.S. drug policy. By and large, however, the main focus has always been on prosecution: targeting users and dealers with criminal penalties.

This emphasis emerged back in 1968, when President Richard Nixon declared that illegal drugs were "public enemy number one." He backed up those words by creating the Drug Enforcement Agency (DEA), a federal organization to oversee all government antidrug operations, including patrolling U.S. borders and working with the governments of countries where drugs are produced to reduce the flow to the United States. The Nixon administration also granted police broader powers to search private homes and seize illegal drugs (U.S. Department of Justice, 1999).

The next two presidents (Gerald Ford and Jimmy Carter) viewed illegal drugs as less of a problem. But the election of Ronald Reagan in 1980 brought renewed efforts to combat drugs. President Reagan declared drugs to be a major moral challenge, and he urged parents to teach their children the importance of resisting drugs, using the slogan "Just say no to drugs." During Reagan's two terms in the White House, the federal budget for fighting illegal drugs rose tenfold to almost $13 billion per year (U.S. Department of Justice, 1993). In addition, the federal government adopted a policy of mandatory prison sentences for convicted drug offenders. As shown in Figure 9–3, the result was a sharp increase in the number of people charged with federal crimes and sent to jail for drug offenses.

Finally, government officials knew that drug dealers were able to use their vast profits to avoid going to jail. In 1984, Congress enacted a law allowing police to seize drug dealers' property, *before* they were convicted of any crime (Eldredge, 1998). Supporters of this law claim that seizing property is one effective way to put drug dealers out of business. But critics argue that such a law allows government agents to harm innocent people. The Critical Thinking box on page 236 takes a closer look.

When George Bush became president in 1988, he created a new Office of National Drug Control Policy, headed by William Bennett, who became known as the "drug czar." Getting tough on drugs remained the order of the day. Public opinion surveys at that time showed that two-thirds of U.S. adults considered illegal drugs to be the most serious social problem facing the country (Bertram at al., 1996).

A change came when Bill Clinton was elected president in 1992. President Clinton pointed out that, once released from jail, most drug users simply go back to their old habits. Therefore, he urged a step back from mandatory sentencing policies and

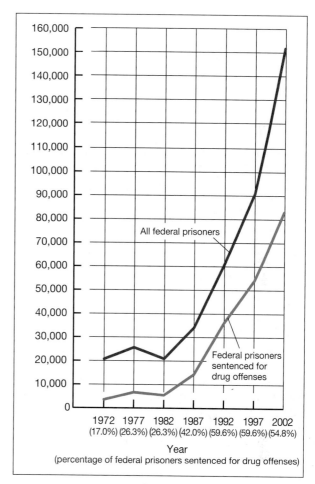

FIGURE 9–3 Total Federal Prison Population and Share of Drug Offenders, 1972–2002

The number of federal prisoners rose rapidly in the United States after 1982. (The total number of prisoners in federal, state, and local facilities is now about 2.2 million.) Increasing convictions for drug offenses has helped push up the total.

Source: U.S. Bureau of Justice Statistics (2003).

pushed for treatment as a strategy to deal with illegal drugs.

Conservatives charged that Clinton was soft on drugs, a charge reinforced in the public's mind by the president's admission that he had smoked but not inhaled marijuana. When a top official in the Clinton administration suggested that perhaps government should consider legalizing some drugs, public reaction was quick and negative. For the remainder of his presidency, Clinton adopted a tougher line on drugs. Soon, more than 1 million people a year were being arrested for drug offenses—almost twice as

Critical Thinking   The Drug Wars: Safer Streets or Police State?

FEDERAL AGENTS SEIZED THE HOME of seventy-five-year-old Mary Miller. She has never used illegal drugs; in fact, she doesn't know a thing about them. But Mary Miller has a grandson who came to stay with her for a while, and during that time he began selling drugs from the house. When federal agents were sure the young man was selling drugs, they turned to a law passed by Congress in 1984, which allowed them to seize the home where drugs had been sold.

Only by taking their money, cars, boats, and other property, say supporters of the 1984 seizure law, can police put drug dealers out of business. But critics counter that the law permits police to take property from people who may not have been convicted in a court of law and therefore should be presumed innocent until proven guilty.

Critics also point out that this law encourages police to investigate rich people for possible drug offenses, even if evidence of their guilt is weak. A case in point involved Donald Scott, a wealthy, sixty-one-year-old man living on a $5-million, 200-acre ranch in Malibu, California. In 1991, someone told the Los Angeles County Sheriff's Department that Scott was growing marijuana plants on his land. The tip was false; there were no illegal drugs anywhere at the ranch. But the sheriff's office sent a team to investigate. Early in the morning, thirty heavily armed officers surrounded the Scott ranch. They knocked and then forced open the door, rushing through the house. They confronted Scott, who, holding his wife, was armed with a gun. In the scuffle that followed, agents fired twice, killing Scott. Police found no drugs at the ranch. Later, an investigation of the tragic incident suggested that "the one purpose of this operation was to garner the proceeds expected from forfeiture of the $5 million ranch" (Blumenson, 1998:6).

ISSUES AND EXERCISES

1. List several ways in which the 1984 seizure law helps the public. List ways it may threaten basic freedoms.

2. Does this law seem likely to help people living in poor neighborhoods plagued by drug dealers? Why or why not?

3. Have a class discussion about this statement: "A society that provides extensive personal freedoms can never be drug free."

many as under the Reagan administration ten years before (U.S. Department of Justice, 2000).

In recent years, terrorism has taken public attention away from the war on drugs. Yet, as noted earlier, President George Bush argued that illegal drugs provided funding to terrorists. Therefore, the Bush administration stepped up efforts to reduce the supply of drugs, especially the growing of coca leaves (used to make cocaine) in Bolivia.

In general, the Bush administration looked to prosecution as the primary strategy to oppose illegal drug use. In recent years, the United States has spent more than $40 billion per year to prosecute and jail offenders and to seize illegal drugs at U.S. borders (Alter, 2001; Roosevelt, 2001; Padgett, 2002).

For current news on federal drug policy, go to
http://www.whitehousedrugpolicy.gov

Counterpoint: Decriminalization

Not everyone agrees with the idea that U.S. society should actively try to stamp out illegal drugs; some people believe that these substances should be legally available. These people favor a policy of **decriminalization**, *removing the current criminal penalties that punish the manufacturing, sale, and personal use of drugs.* In effect, this alternative to the current national policy argues that the way to end the drug problem is to define illegal drugs as no longer a problem.

Support for decriminalization varies according to the drug, of course. Although almost no one wants "hard" drugs such as heroin to be legally available, one-third of U.S. adults support making the "soft" drug marijuana legal. Making marijuana legal for medical purposes (prescribed by a physician) has the support of about 80 percent of U.S. adults (Stein, 2002; NORC, 2003:126).

In practice, providing legal access to a drug such as marijuana would mean treating it in much the same way we treat alcohol and tobacco, including banning sales to children. Doing so, supporters argue, would have three benefits. First, the government could regulate the quality of the drug (reducing the chance of injury or death from "bad" drugs). Second, legalization would bring down the cost of the drug, so that users would have less need to commit crimes to obtain drug money, and violence among drug dealers would end (because there would be no illegal sales). Third, the country as a whole would no longer bear the cost of locking up roughly 1 million people convicted of violating drug laws.

Most people oppose ending all criminal penalties for using even "soft" drugs, however. If drugs are widespread now, opponents point out, imagine how bad this problem would be if people were able to buy drugs the same way they buy, say, cigarettes at the corner store or even from vending machines. As the critics see it, legalizing drugs would send rates of poverty, homelessness, and family problems—not to mention automobile accidents—sky high (Inciardi, 1990; Inciardi & McBride, 1991; Goode, 1997).

Zurich: Decriminalization That Failed Would decriminalization make the drug problem in the United States better or worse? To get some idea, we can look to two countries that have experimented with such a policy, with very different results.

Switzerland is a high-income European nation. Beginning in the 1970s, people began gathering in the Swiss city of Zurich to use illegal drugs. By the mid-1980s, the drug activity had become centered in one of the city's public greens, which soon became known as "Needle Park."

As the AIDS epidemic began, Zurich officials feared that drug users sharing needles could create a health nightmare. A police crackdown on drug use would be counterproductive, they reasoned, serving only to spread drug users all over the city. By letting people use drugs in the park, health officials thought they would be able to monitor their behavior. An experiment at decriminalization began as police stopped making drug arrests and city health stations provided heroin and methadone along with clean needles and condoms to addicts in the hope of limiting the spread of AIDS.

But the program had an unexpected result, drawing more drug users and dealers to the park from all over Switzerland and beyond. By 1990, officials were handing out as many as 8,000 clean needles *each day*. It was becoming clear that the experiment was failing: The park had been completely overrun with drug users, vandalism was out of control, and everyone else in the community was afraid to go near the area. In February 1992,

Would legalization make the drug problem worse or better? When the Swiss permitted drug use in the city of Zurich, problems increased and officials reversed course. In the Netherlands, by contrast, legalization of soft drugs had a different result, and the policy continues to this day.

government officials gave up and closed the park. The city of Zurich continues to offer heroin to hard core addicts, but they must inject it at clinics rather than in public places (*Time*, 1992; Huber, 1994; Nadelmann, 1995).

The Netherlands: Decriminalization That Works   A second case of the Netherlands, another high-income European nation, has shown that decriminalization of some drugs can work. In 1976, Dutch officials enacted a drug policy that permits coffee shops ("cannabis cafes") to sell up to 5 grams of "soft" drugs such as marijuana or hashish (but not "hard" drugs such as heroin). Customers can legally buy and use these drugs as long as they do not sell drugs themselves or act in a disorderly manner. In 2003, based on clean-air concerns, the policy was amended so that beginning in 2004 customers can still buy marijuana or hashish, but they will have to smoke it outside (Ministry of Health, Welfare & Sport, 1998; van den Hurk, 1999; Henderson, 2003).

To date, the Dutch policy seems to be working. There has been no surge in crime rates; indeed, the crime rate in the Netherlands is well below that of the United States. Moreover, researchers report that marijuana use among Dutch teenagers is no higher (and may be a bit lower) than it is among teens in the United States. Perhaps most important, Dutch prisons are not filling with people convicted of drug offenses, as is the case in the United States (Common Sense for Drug Policy, 1999; MacCoun, 2001).

Does the Dutch case show that decriminalization works? Not exactly. What it does show is that legalizing "soft" drugs did not create a host of social problems *in the Netherlands*. Whether such a policy would work as well in this country remains an open question. But the Dutch experience does suggest that the worst fears about making "soft" drugs legally available may be exaggerated. In support of decriminalization, in 2002 Great Britain decided to leave criminal penalties on the books but to greatly reduce enforcement of drug laws involving private use of marijuana (Hoge, 2002).

THEORETICAL ANALYSIS: UNDERSTANDING DRUG-RELATED SOCIAL PROBLEMS

Each of sociology's major theoretical approaches offers insights into social problems involving drugs. As in earlier chapters, each approach highlights different facts and points toward a different conclusion.

Structural-Functional Analysis: Regulating Drug Use

The structural-functional approach focuses on the functions of drugs for the operation of society. Some drugs, such as alcohol, ease social interaction, as when new neighbors enjoy a drink together. Other drugs—including caffeine, diazepam (Valium), or methylphenidate hydrochloride (Ritalin)—help people cope with the day-to-day demands of modern life. Legal and illegal drugs also are a major source of economic activity, providing jobs and income for hundreds of thousands of people.

Because most drugs are harmful when used to excess, societies establish social controls to regulate their use. In general, the more disruptive a drug's effects, the stronger the measures society takes to regulate its use. Traditionally, the family, schools, and religion played a major part in regulating individual behavior. Indeed, it may be the case that a weakening in these social institutions, which leaves people with less certainty and meaning in their lives, explains some of the rise in drug use over the last century. In any case, as families and religion have lost some of their power over individuals, the task of regulating drug use has fallen more and more to health care professionals and, of course, the criminal justice system.

Critical evaluation.   The structural-functional approach suggests drugs can be both helpful and harmful to the orderly operation of society. Yet this approach is unclear about how one defines a particular drug as useful or not. Furthermore, the functional approach takes such a broad view that we learn little about the ways in which individuals understand drugs, which is the focus of the symbolic-interaction paradigm.

Symbolic-Interaction Analysis: The Meaning of Drug Use

The symbolic-interaction approach calls attention to the various meanings people attach to their surroundings and behavior. From this point of view, a drug that one society defines as a part of sacred, religious rituals another society may ban as dangerous. Even within any one society, a drug (say, cocaine in the United States) may be legal at one point in time and outlawed later on. Conversely, a drug once outlawed may become legal (as with cannabis in the Netherlands).

A second issue is how individuals make sense of drugs. People do not simply become drug users; they move gradually through a learning process. In the case of marijuana smoking, for example, a novice smoker usually "turns on" in the presence of more experienced people, who explain how to smoke the drug, the proper behavior expected when doing so, and how to enjoy the experience of being "high" (Becker, 1966).

Critical evaluation. Symbolic-interaction theory highlights the variable meanings people attach to all behavior, including drug use. Yet because of its situational focus, this approach runs the risk of missing broader patterns. One such pattern, which has to do with social power, is at the heart of the social-conflict approach.

Social-Conflict Analysis: Power and Drug Use

The social-conflict approach directs attention to the ways social power shapes the lives of everyone in a society. Earlier in this chapter we explained how, throughout the history of this nation, officials have acted to outlaw the drugs favored by powerless people, especially minorities and immigrants. In the mid-nineteenth century, whites on the West Coast outlawed the opium used mainly by Chinese immigrants; about 1900, southern whites who feared black violence pressed to outlaw cocaine. By 1920, the tide of European immigration led to Prohibition, which banned alcohol until 1933. On the other hand, powerful corporate interests sell highly profitable drugs—including tobacco and alcohol—with full protection of the law, even though these two drugs are linked to more deaths annually than all the illegal drugs combined.

Social conflict theory points out that the social standing of users also has much to do with how severely our society punishes illegal drug use. Earlier, we noted a case of power bias in the harsher sentences handed down for use of crack (a less expensive cocaine derivative favored by African Americans and the poor) compared with those for the use of cocaine (a middle-class drug favored by white people).

Critical evaluation. The social-conflict approach links drug problems to social inequality, suggesting that the poor bear the greatest burden. Yet it fails to account for the fact that many harmful drugs—such as nicotine and alcohol—are widely used by rich and poor alike. Moreover, the harm caused by alcohol—say, in contributing to automobile accidents—is not limited to any one class of people.

Conservatives claim that current drug laws are an effective tool to reduce the problem of illegal drugs. Liberals (and libertarians) argue that the main effect of our drug laws is putting people in jail. Do you favor enforcement or repeal of current drug laws? Why?

POLITICS AND DRUGS: CONSTRUCTING PROBLEMS AND DEFINING SOLUTIONS

Theory helps us understand social problems, but the position anyone takes on drug-related issues is a matter of values and politics. In the final section of this chapter, we explain how politics shapes views of drug-related problems and their solutions.

Conservatives: Just Say No

Conservatives emphasize the importance of moral values in their analysis of social problems. Historically, the family supported by the church was the main source of moral instruction. From a conservative point of view, young people who are raised by committed, caring parents and who are guided by religious beliefs usually are able to resist any temptation presented by drugs.

As noted in earlier chapters, however, conservatives argue that virtue has declined in U.S. society since the 1960s. They define the rise of drug use since then as one result of a society that has lost its way, replacing moral certainties with a culture of "permissiveness" and "relativism" in which anything goes.

The drug scene, as conservatives see it, amounts to a self-centered and pleasure-seeking way of life.

Conservatives define drug use as a serious social problem that encourages crime and weakens both individual character and society's families. In response, conservatives favor tough laws, aggressive enforcement, and severe penalties. In the end, however, conservatives warn that there is only so much that government can do to control drugs. The major responsibility will always lie with parents, who must raise their children to make good moral choices in a world full of temptation. Therefore, as Nancy Reagan, wife of President Ronald Reagan, concluded, the solution to the drug problem can be summed up in the simple phrase "Just say no."

Liberals: Reform Society

Liberals support personal freedoms in matters of lifestyle. They are uneasy with the moralistic tone of the conservative argument, which seems to force everyone into one traditional mold. Liberals support a different solution, claiming that increasing economic opportunity and decreasing poverty will make fewer people turn to drugs in the first place.

Because personal choice is important, liberals take a tolerant view of "soft" drugs, and some favor decriminalization, following the example of the Netherlands. Indeed, some liberals ask, why should marijuana be against the law when it causes much less harm than a legal drug such as tobacco?

Although they support law enforcement when it comes to "hard" drugs—especially for large-scale dealers—liberals argue that our current policies criminalize hundreds of thousands of people who pose little harm to anyone, perhaps not even to themselves. They call for less emphasis on police, courts, and prisons and more emphasis on programs of drug education for children and treatment programs for people struggling with drug addiction.

Radical Views: Right-Wing Libertarians and the Far Left

In political terms, **libertarians** are *people who favor the greatest individual freedom possible.* Although people who call themselves libertarians fall throughout the political spectrum, most libertarians see government as the biggest threat to personal freedom. Favoring the smallest government possible is generally consistent with the political far right.

Given this emphasis on personal freedom, libertarians oppose government efforts to regulate drugs (and almost anything else). As they see it, drug laws simply limit individual choice about how to live. Many libertarians believe the government's war on drugs has already reduced people's civil liberties, not only by limiting choice but by permitting widespread surveillance, searches, and seizure of property. In short, many libertarians see not a "drug problem" but a "government problem" that threatens everyone. Therefore, libertarians are at the forefront of the movement to legalize all drugs (Trebach & Inciardi, 1993).

Radicals on the far left of the political spectrum also oppose current drug laws, but for different reasons. From this point of view, drug laws (like all laws) simply reflect the interests of the rich and powerful members of society. Moreover, these laws criminalize the poor—especially people of color—who now fill U.S. prisons. But abolishing current drug laws is just one item on the radical left's agenda: Society itself needs to be completely restructured. If a new society were created on the principles of equality and opportunities for all people, radicals argue, there would be far less demand for drugs in the first place. The Left to Right table outlines the various political perspectives on drugs.

GOING ON FROM HERE

Ever since people discovered the powers of plants and learned to brew alcohol, they have taken drugs. Just as societies depend on the positive uses of drugs, they define other uses as problems that must be controlled.

There is little doubt that drugs—both illegal and legal—will remain controversial throughout the twenty-first century. Drugs such as heroin and cocaine will continue to claim victims; the death toll from alcohol abuse will almost certainly climb even higher.

People will continue to debate the causes of drug abuse, with the political right pointing to family breakdown and those on the left arguing the need to pursue economic equality. Radical voices will continue to be heard as well. Even so, the widespread support in the United States for aggressive use of the criminal justice system—including police, courts, and prisons—to combat drugs is likely to continue, although this policy finds little support from sociological research.

One hopeful sign: Research shows that illegal drug use declines with age (Wren, 1997). As the average age of people in the United States continues to rise in the decades to come, it seems reasonable to predict a trend toward less illegal drug use. But it is doubtful that aging alone will offer the solution to the drug problem in U.S. society.

LEFT TO RIGHT

THE POLITICS OF THE DRUG PROBLEM

	RADICAL LEFT VIEW	LIBERAL VIEW	CONSERVATIVE VIEW	RIGHT-WING LIBERTARIAN VIEW
WHAT IS THE PROBLEM?	Drug laws (like all laws) reflect the interests of the powerful and criminalize poor people and minorities.	Drug use is a symptom of the suffering of many people from various problems, such as poverty and powerlessness.	Drug use is a symptom of poor moral instruction to young people. Schools, churches, and especially families should raise children with the moral values that will give them the strength to resist the temptation to use drugs.	The government threatens civil liberties by using police power to make arrests, seize property, and monitor the lives of people suspected of using drugs.
WHAT IS THE SOLUTION?	A fundamental reorganization of society to spread wealth, power, and opportunity to all would go a long way toward reducing the conditions that lead people to sell and use drugs in the first place.	As economic opportunity and social equality increase, drug use should go down. Government should fund treatment programs for people with addictions.	Although enforcement of drug laws is important, active parenting is the first line of defense against the threat of drugs. Schools, houses of worship, and community organizations must play a part in educating children about the dangers of drugs.	Most drug laws—especially those regulating "soft" drugs—should be abolished as a step toward providing people with greater personal freedom.

Join the debate . . .

1. If you were put in charge of a national drug commission, what new policies would you enact to address this problem?
2. Where on the political spectrum do you find support for the various drug control strategies

discussed in this chapter: interdiction, prosecution, education, and treatment?
3. Which of the four political analyses of the drug problem included here do you find most convincing? Why?

CHAPTER SUMMARY

1. Drugs are substances other than food and water that affect the body or the mind. Throughout history, drugs have been a part of human society.

2. Which drugs people use, and which substances they define as helpful and harmful, varies from society to society. In addition, attitudes toward drugs in any one society change over time.

3. One factor shaping attitudes about drugs in the United States is controversy over immigration; in the past, government has outlawed drugs favored by various categories of immigrants.

4. Although about 6 percent of the U.S. population aged twelve and older currently uses at least one illegal drug, the trend in drug use in recent decades has been downward, with an upward trend in the last few years.

5. People use drugs for various reasons, including recreation, therapy, escape, spiritual or psychological stimulation, and social conformity.

6. Drugs fall into various categories according to their effect on the body. Stimulants produce alertness and speed up activity, whereas

depressants slow activity and dull pain; hallucinogens can distort sensory perceptions; steroids build muscle and strength.

7. Drug use—and especially addiction—causes codependency among family members and friends. Parental addiction harms children, who are more likely to use drugs themselves and to drop out of school and get in trouble with the law.

8. Drug and alcohol use is common among the homeless. But drug use is as likely to result from homelessness as it is to cause it.

9. Drug users can transmit HIV by sharing needles. Research has shown that needle exchange programs reduce HIV transmission, but critics claim that such programs support illegal drug use.

10. Drugs are linked to crime: Most violent offenders report being under the influence of alcohol or other drugs when they committed their crimes. Drug laws contribute to crime by driving prices up so that addicted users of crack, cocaine, and heroin turn to crime to support their habits.

11. People in poor nations produce drugs as a needed source of income.

12. Four strategies for controlling crime in the United States are interdiction, prosecution, education, and treatment.

13. The number of people jailed for drug offenses has gone up rapidly in recent decades. Although most people support criminal prosecution of users and dealers of illegal "hard" drugs, some people support legalization of "soft" drugs as a way to reduce the prison population.

14. The structural-functional approach explains that societies rely on some drugs to ease social interaction and help people cope with the demands of modern living; at the same time, societies control other drugs that have dangerous consequences.

15. The symbolic-interaction approach highlights the various meanings people attach to drug use; this approach explains that people learn to use drugs in the same way that they learn other forms of behavior.

16. The social-conflict approach focuses on how the issue of social power shapes our drug policies; one example is the pattern by which the United States has banned drugs favored by immigrants and other minorities.

17. Conservatives view illegal drug use as a serious social problem linked to the decline of traditional families and religion; they favor tough drugs laws and urge parents to provide moral instruction to children. Liberals are more tolerant of "soft" drug use; they support expanded education and drug treatment programs. Libertarians oppose drug laws in an effort to expand individual freedoms. Radicals on the left argue that current drug laws tend to criminalize the poor; they call for basic changes in U.S. social institutions leading to a more egalitarian society.

KEY CONCEPTS

drug (p. 219) any chemical substance other than food or water that affects the mind or body

addiction (p. 222) a physical or psychological craving for a drug

dependency (p. 223) a state in which a person's body has adjusted to regular use of a drug

stimulants (p. 223) drugs that elevate alertness, changing a person's mood by increasing energy

depressants (p. 225) drugs that slow the operation of the central nervous system

alcoholism (p. 226) an addiction to alcohol

codependency (p. 229) behavior on the part of others that helps a substance abuser continue

decriminalization (p. 236) removing the current criminal penalties that punish the manufacturing, sale, and personal use of drugs

libertarians (p. 240) people who favor the greatest individual freedom possible

THINKING CRITICALLY: QUESTIONS AND ISSUES

1. Common sense suggests that some drugs are illegal simply because they are dangerous. But can you note societal factors (such as who uses the drug) that play a part in how a society defines particular drugs as legal or illegal?

2. According to this chapter, what are some of the reasons people use illegal drugs? Do you think most people who try such drugs become "drug users"?

3. What evidence can you cite in support of the idea that drugs cause crime? What about the proposal that drug laws cause crime?

4. What are the four strategies to control drugs cited in this chapter? To what extent does the United States use each one? In your view, how effective is each?

GETTING INVOLVED: LEARNING ACTIVITIES

1. Take a walk around your campus with an eye toward drug use. What can you say about the places where people smoke cigarettes? Drink coffee? Drink alcohol? Do the social patterns surrounding the use of each drug differ? If so, how?

2. A fascinating and easy research project is to visit a library, obtain copies of U.S. magazines from the 1920s and 1930s, and look at cigarette advertising. What claims are made by cigarette companies regarding the benefits and dangers of smoking tobacco?

3. Most communities have Alcoholics Anonymous and Al-Anon Family Group meetings. Look up the number for AA in your local directory and ask about the time and location of a meeting open to the public. Attend a meeting and, afterward, talk to people about how AA helps them recover from alcoholism or helps them cope with a family member's addiction.

4. Go to your local library and see what you can learn about the extent of illegal drug use in your state. In what region of the state (for example, rural versus urban) is the arrest rate for drug offenses higher? Can you discover why?

GETTING CONNECTED: USEFUL WEB LINKS

http://www.prenhall.com/macionis
Visit the interactive Companion Website™ that accompanies this text. Begin by clicking on the cover of your book. You will find a chapter-by-chapter study guide, practice tests, suggested Web links, and links to other relevant material.

http://www.monitoringthefuture.org
The Institute for Social Research at the University of Michigan conducts an annual survey of high school students that includes data on drug use. Do any of the facts noted there surprise you?

http://www.usdoj.gov/dea/pubs/factsheet/fact0299.htm
Visit the Web site for the Drug Enforcement Agency, which provides information on current

trends in drug use and describes DEA programs. What is your view of this organization's work?

http://www.alcoholics-anonymous.org/
This Web site, operated by the most well-known self-help organization dealing with drug abuse, explains the AA program for alcoholics and for people living with an alcoholic.

http://www.health.org
Plenty of interesting data can be found at the Web site for the National Clearinghouse for Alcohol and Drug Information.

GETTING STARTED ON YOUR OWN: RESEARCH NAVIGATOR™

Follow the instructions found on page 25 of this text to access the features of Research Navigator™. Once at the Web site, enter your Login Name and Password. Then, to use the **Content Select** database, enter keywords such as "marijuana," "drug legalization," and "DARE," and

the search engine will supply relevant and recent scholarly and popular press publications. Use the *New York Times* **Search-by-Subject Archive** to find recent news articles related to sociology and the **Link Library** feature to find relevant Web links organized by the key terms associated with this chapter.

© Paul Marcus, *Look, Sweetie, Look!*, oil on panel, 24 × 30 in. Studio SPM, Inc.

PHYSICAL
AND MENTAL HEALTH

W HO ARE THE MOST STIGMATIZED PEOPLE in the United States? What kind of people are we most likely to avoid, to stereotype, and to fear? In the past, the answer might have been gays and lesbians, or perhaps members of various racial and ethnic minorities.

Today, while tolerance is building for many categories of people once widely shunned, there is still little acceptance of people with mental illness. Undoubtedly the mass media play a part; everyone remembers "crazy" and genuinely scary characters in films from Psycho to Friday the 13th to Silence of the Lambs. But such movies only frighten us because they play on fears that lie deep within U.S. culture. More than 100 million people—about half the adult population in the United States—suffer from a mental illness at some point in their lives. About one-third of adults claim that they have come close to a nervous breakdown (Ho, 2000). Given these very high numbers, it is surprising that most people know very little about what mental illness is and what its causes are.

This chapter explores problems related to both mental and physical health. We begin by looking at problems of physical health both in the United States and in low-income nations of the world, where illness caused by poverty kills half the population before they become adults. Then we survey health care systems with special attention to how people in various countries pay for care and why many people claim the U.S. health care system is in crisis. Finally, we turn to mental health, explaining what mental illnesses are, what causes them, and why there is so little understanding of this widespread problem. Although health is partly a matter of biology and medicine, society guides how we define people as "healthy" or "sick" and allows some categories of people to enjoy excellent health while stacking the odds against others from the day they are born.

GETTING THE PICTURE

✦ Does this country do enough to help people pay for medical care?

The United States remains the only high-income nation with no universal health care system.

✦ Can poverty kill?

In the world's poorest nations, half of all children die before they reach age ten.

✦ Is mental illness unusual?

About half of all adults in the United States have symptoms of mental disorders at some time in their lives.

245

A WORLD OF DIFFERENCES

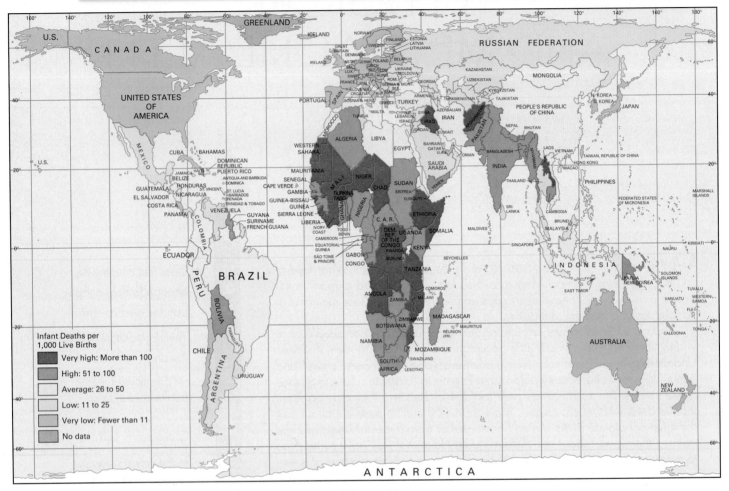

GLOBAL MAP 10–1   Infant Mortality around the World

A good measure of health for any nation is the rate of infant mortality: death in the first year of life. In rich nations, infant deaths are generally less than 10 per 1,000 live births. In poor nations, by contrast, infant mortality is high, with rates exceeding 100 across much of Africa and Asia.

Source: Population Reference Bureau (2003).

HEALTH AND ILLNESS: A GLOBAL PERSPECTIVE

Many of us think of being healthy simply in terms of not being sick. However, the World Health Organization (1946:3) defines **health** as *a state of complete physical, mental, and social well-being.* In other words, just as there are degrees of illness, there are degrees of health. To a significant degree, health depends on income. Looking around the world, we see a general pattern: "Health follows wealth."

High-Income Nations

On average, people living in rich nations—in North America and Western Europe—are far healthier than those living in poor countries. One general measure of a society's health is the **infant mortality rate,** *the number of babies who die in their first year of life per thousand live births.* In the world's rich nations, infant mortality rates are low, usually less than ten deaths for every 1,000 babies born. This means that infant deaths are quite rare (less than one in one hundred), and when they do occur, people view them as both unexpected and tragic. Global Map 10–1 shows that the infant mortality rates for rich countries of the world are quite low by world standards.

Another way to gauge global patterns of health is by how long, on average, people live. **Life expectancy at birth** is *the number of years, on average, people in a society can expect to live.* In the United States, boys born in 2001 can expect to life seventy-four years, and girls born that year can expect to live eighty years. By contrast, in the world's poorest nations, life expectancy is less than forty-five years (United Nations Development Programme, 2003).

For the Web site of the World Health Organization, go to **http://www.who.org**

The AIDS epidemic is among the most serious health problems facing the world today. Part of the solution is education: In this high school in Addis Ababa, Ethiopia, members of the Reproductive Health Club wrote and produced a play dramatizing the dangers of this deadly disease for their fellow students.

A society's average level of income also has a lot to do with the kinds of health problems its people face. People who live in rich societies typically consider health to be a larger problem as they get older. In most cases, they live long enough to die in old age (typically after age seventy-five) of some **chronic disease,** *an illness that has a long-term development* (Weitz, 1996). Chronic diseases include heart disease, cancer, and stroke.

Affluence is better for human health than poverty, but a higher standard of living does carry some health dangers of its own. For example, people in rich nations have high-fat diets; in addition, many do little physical work. Taken together, these factors help to explain the fact that many people (about two-thirds of the U.S. population) are overweight, which is a contributing factor to a host of health problems; half the population of rich nations eventually dies of heart disease (U.S. National Center for Health Statistics, 2002).

Low-Income Nations

Worldwide, according to the World Health Organization, 1 billion people—one in six—suffer from serious illness because they are poor. Inadequate nutrition is one important factor that leaves people—especially children—vulnerable to disease. The lack of safe drinking water is another; poor people are continuously exposed to germs and other disease-causing microorganisms. The consequences of such conditions for human health are easy to see. A glance back at Global Map 10–1 shows that infant mortality rates in poor countries are far higher than they are in rich countries such as the United States. For example, the poor African nation of Ethiopia has an infant mortality rate of 107, which means that more than one in ten children die before their first birthday (Population Reference Bureau, 2003).

Life expectancy in poor countries is also low by U.S. standards. In Ethiopia, as in other very poor nations, disease brought on by poor nutrition and unsafe water claims more than half of children before they reach age ten; overall life expectancy is less than fifty years (World Health Organization, 1998). In much of Asia, people can expect to live only to about age sixty. In rich nations, people typically die of chronic conditions (such as heart disease and cancer), people in poor nations die at any time in the life course from some **acute disease,** *an illness that strikes suddenly.* These illnesses include various infectious and parasitic diseases such as malaria, cholera, typhoid, measles, and diarrhea, the same diseases that were leading killers in the United States more than a century ago.

Rich and Poor Compared: The AIDS Epidemic

Investigating patterns of health is the work of **social epidemiology,** *the study of how health and disease are distributed throughout a society's population.* Epidemiologists study the origin and spread of diseases, noting how the social environment shapes people's health.

A Global Perspective

The Social Roots of AIDS: Poverty, Culture, and Gender

BRIGITTE SYAMALEUWE IS A FORTY-YEAR-OLD WOMAN living in the African nation of Zambia. Several years ago, her life changed when she learned that she was HIV positive. Brigitte had never had sex with anyone other than her husband, so she knew it was he who had infected her. Angrily, she confronted him. Shaken, he reacted by accusing *her* of infidelity. Only after several weeks was he willing to admit that he had been unfaithful, had become infected with HIV, and then infected his wife. Both of them decided to devote the remainder of their lives to educating others about the dangers of HIV.

As explained in Chapter 4 ("Gender Inequality"), low-income countries typically are very patriarchal. That is, in poor countries, women have little say in what their husbands or boyfriends do. Many men see little wrong with extramarital sex, often with prostitutes, which places them and their wives at high risk for infection with HIV. Another factor that contributes to the AIDS epidemic in Africa and elsewhere is that many men—sometimes even those who know they are infected with HIV—refuse to use condoms when they have sex. Some women may not insist that men use condoms, either because they don't know that their partners are being unfaithful or because the men threaten violence if they don't get their way.

To make matters worse, traditional laws make it easy for men to divorce their wives for being unfaithful, but women have a very hard time doing the same thing. Even women who can obtain a divorce will think twice because the law typically gives men control over family property; a divorce could leave a woman in poverty.

In poor countries, contracting HIV means death within several years. Well-off people with HIV in the United States now rely on new and expensive drugs to prolong their lives for a decade or more. But these drugs are out of reach for the world's poor. In Africa, perhaps 10 percent of HIV-positive people ever receive such drugs; most get little or no medical attention.

What strategies can be used to help the world's poor women protect themselves? One possible answer is the *female condom*, a plastic pouch that a woman inserts into her vagina before sexual intercourse and that offers protection from HIV and other sexually transmitted diseases. Although the female condom is gaining popularity in Africa, many men object to them, and, as noted before, the cost is often too high.

The larger answer to the problem of AIDS lies in research to discover a cure for this deadly disease and in raising the status of women in Africa and elsewhere. Greater political and economic power would give women the ability to say no to sex, to insist on condom use, and even to demand that their men be faithful.

ISSUES AND EXERCISES

1. How does the spread of AIDS in Africa confirm that health is a social rather than simply a medical problem?
2. If AIDS continues to spread unchecked, what do you see as the likely future for African societies? What are the likely effects on the United States?
3. [Research Navigator.com] Use Research Navigator™ to learn more about the AIDS epidemic in Africa. (See instructions on page 25; keywords: "AIDS," "Africa")

Sources: Based on Schoofs (1999) and Singer (2001).

The work of epidemiologists is especially important when people face an **epidemic,** *a disease that spreads rapidly through a population*. Epidemics—from the plagues in medieval Europe to the 2003 outbreak of severe acute respiratory syndrome (SARS)—threaten the health of millions of people. The most deadly epidemic—sometimes called a *pandemic* because it has spread around the world—is acquired immunodeficiency syndrome (AIDS). First identified in 1981,

AIDS is an incurable, deadly disease transmitted through bodily fluids, including blood, semen, vaginal secretions, and breast milk. We can illustrate the link between wealth and health by tracking the progression of AIDS, first in global perspective, and then within the population of the United States.

AIDS: The Global View Global Map 8–2 on page 208, mapping the global distribution of roughly

40 million cases of HIV infection, shows that they are concentrated in low-income nations. Africa, the world's poorest continent, is home to 70 percent of the world's HIV-positive people (although Africans are just 13 percent of the world's population). During a trip to Africa in 2003, President George W. Bush declared that AIDS is a threat to the political and economic future of many African nations. The AIDS epidemic has already killed more than 5 million people in Central African nations, dramatically dropping life expectancy there to about forty years. This epidemic has shattered these societies, overwhelming medical facilities, destroying families, and creating huge numbers of orphaned children (United Nations, 2001; Ashford, 2002; Whitelaw, 2003).

Why are many of the world's poorest nations so hard hit by AIDS? As already noted, poor people have weakened health, so they are less resistant to infection. In addition, poor countries have few resources for education and prevention programs (say, to provide condoms and teach people the importance of using them). But cultural patterns—especially those involving gender—also has an impact. The Global Perspective box takes a closer look at the problem of AIDS in Central Africa.

AIDS: The United States The AIDS epidemic is not nearly as serious in the United States as it is in the nations of Central Africa. This country accounts for less than 5 percent of the world's cases. In all, about 890,000 cases of HIV had been recorded in the United States as of 2002; of these, about 500,000 people have already died (U.S. Centers for Disease Control and Prevention, 2003).

AIDS is a serious social problem in the United States, but the infection rates are far lower than in many of the world's low-income nations. After AIDS education programs began back in 1987, people became less likely to engage in high-risk activities, such as having multiple sex partners, and were more likely to use condoms. Today, however, there is concern that a new generation of young people may not take this deadly threat seriously. The United States continues to spend more than $10 billion annually to fight AIDS (U.S. Department of Health and Human Services, 2002). Although researchers have yet to produce a cure for this deadly disease, they have developed drug treatments that delay the onset of full-blown AIDS among many people infected with HIV.

In the United States, as around the world, AIDS is primarily a disease of poor people. In 2002, official statistics show, there were 16,371 deaths from AIDS. This represents a major decline from an

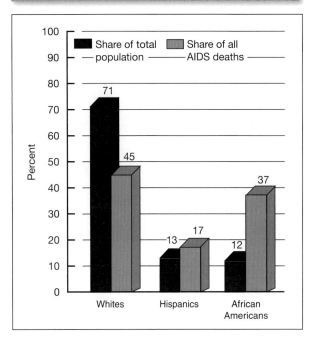

FIGURE 10–1 Deaths from AIDS in the United States, as of 2002

Death from AIDS among minorities is higher than population share would lead us to expect. Taken together, Hispanics and African Americans account for 25 percent of the U.S. population but 54 percent of all AIDS deaths.

Source: U.S. Centers for Disease Control and Prevention (2003).

annual high of 51,670 deaths in 1995. As Figure 10–1 shows, African Americans and Hispanic Americans, who represent one-fourth of the population, account for more than half of all AIDS deaths. From another angle, African Americans are five times more likely than whites to be infected; Hispanics are two times more likely. Moreover, among those who become infected, African Americans and Hispanics are more likely to be poor and to receive less treatment, which can cost up to $100,000 each year; as a result, they are more likely to die (U.S. Centers for Disease Control and Prevention, 2003).

HEALTH POLICY: PAYING FOR CARE

How should people pay the costs of health care? Should a person's ability to pay determine the quality of health care available? Every society faces such questions and provides varying answers according to political and economic systems.

Among children born to poor people, such as the Rom (Gypsies) in Eastern Europe, life expectancy is more than ten years lower than that typical of European nations and the United States.

Socialist Systems

In societies with mostly *socialist economies*, the government controls most economic activity. This means that government agencies provide medical services and operate hospitals and clinics; doctors and other medical professionals are state employees who receive salaries for their services. Examples of socialist systems are found in China and the Russian Federation.

The People's Republic of China   China is a middle-income country, in the process of industrializing, and is home to more than 1 billion people. In China, the government administers health care, operating hospitals and clinics in large population centers. In addition, China's famed "barefoot doctors" visit rural villages, providing basic health care to tens of millions of Chinese peasants.

The Chinese approach combines modern scientific medicine with traditional healing arts, including acupuncture and medicinal herbs. In most regions, China's traditional sexual norms remain strong, which is one reason that much of this vast country has so far escaped the AIDS epidemic that has ravaged other Asian nations to the south. On the other hand, two-thirds of Chinese men (but fewer than 10 percent of Chinese women) smoke, which takes its toll in high rates of cancer and heart disease (The World Bank, 2003).

The Russian Federation   Before the collapse of the Soviet Union in 1991, that nation had a government-controlled system of health care. Since then, the new Russian Federation has been changing its government-controlled, socialist economy in the direction of a market-based system. Yet health care is still mostly under government control so that, as in China, people go to government-run clinics for treatment. One consequence of state control is that physicians are paid much less for their work than their counterparts in the United States; many doctors in the Russian Federation earn little more than skilled factory workers. Also worth noting is the fact that about 70 percent of the Russian Federation's doctors are women, compared with about 30 percent in the United States.

In the 1990s, the Russian Federation suffered an economic decline. One result was a sharp drop in the health of the population. Despite a small rebound in the last few years, life expectancy for women has dropped by almost two years and, for men, almost eight years. This decline has further strained a bureaucratic system that has long provided standardized and impersonal care. Perhaps, as market reforms proceed, the quality of medical services will rise with living standards. For the moment, however, health and health care in the Russian Federation are serious problems (Specter, 1997; Bohlen, 1998; Gerber & Hout, 1998).

Capitalist Systems

Societies with mostly *capitalist economies* distribute health care—like other goods and services—through a market system. By and large, people purchase health care according to their individual needs and resources. But the high cost of health care can easily exceed the reach of even fairly well-off people, so capitalist nations such as Sweden, Great Britain, Canada, and Japan have additional strategies to help people cover the expense.

Sweden Although the Swedish economy is mostly market-based, for more than a century this country has taken the socialist approach that health care is a basic right for all citizens. The country raises money to fund its government-run health care system by taxation, making Swedish taxes among the highest in the world. Most physicians are government employees who receive salaries rather than collecting fees from patients; similarly, government officials manage most of the country's hospitals.

Because this system resembles that found in socialist countries, is often called **socialized medicine,** *a medical care system in which the government owns and operates most medical facilities and employs most physicians.* How well does this system perform? The United Nations calculates a life expectancy index for world nations, which is a good measure of the overall health of a population. As Figure 10–2 shows, the level of health in Sweden is high, and all Swedes receive much the same quality of care.

Great Britain Great Britain has had a system of socialized medicine since 1948. However, the British did not do away with private care; rather, they created a dual system of medical service. The National Health Service, funded by tax money, provides care to all British citizens and pays for a physician's services, hospital stays, and prescription drugs. At the same time, people who can afford to can also obtain the services of private doctors and hospitals. Indeed, many British doctors split their time between the National Health Service and private patients.

The British system does a fairly good job of providing basic care to that country's people. However, because only some people are able to purchase the best private care, the British system is marked by a measure of inequality.

Canada In Canada, the government does not control health care directly; rather, it operates rather like a large insurance company. In the Canadian "single-payer" system, the government pays physicians and hospitals, with the funding coming from taxes. Like Great Britain, however, Canada permits doctors to work outside the government-funded system, setting their own fees for those who can purchase care privately.

A glance at Figure 10–2 shows that health in Canada is very good. The Canadian system also

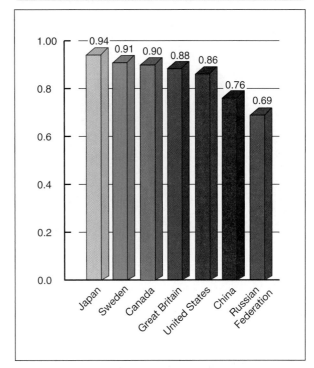

DIMENSIONS OF DIFFERENCE

FIGURE 10–2 Life Expectancy Index for Selected Countries

Although life expectancy is higher in the United States than in lower-income nations such as China and the Russian Federation, many high-income nations provide better health care for their people. The statistical index used here was developed by the United Nations to allow comparisons between countries.

Source: United Nations Development Programme (2003).

provides care at a lower cost than the U.S. system. Supporters point to success in holding the line on doctors' fees and hospital costs. Critics, however, note that the lower costs also reflect the fact that Canada uses less high-technology medicine, and the system is often slow to respond to people's needs, so they may wait months to receive major surgery. In short, Canada may not match the United States in providing advanced procedures to some people, but it seems to outperform the United States in providing basic care to the majority (Rosenthal, 1991; United Nations Development Programme, 2000; Macionis & Gerber, 2003).

Japan Physicians and hospitals in Japan operate privately in a market system. At the same time, a combination of government programs and private health insurance pays most medical costs. A glance

DIMENSIONS OF DIFFERENCE

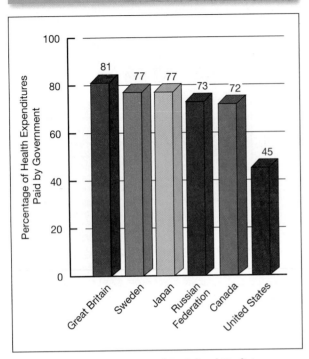

FIGURE 10–3   **Extent of Socialized Medicine in Selected Countries**

Compared with other high-income nations, government funding in the United States accounts for a far smaller share of health costs.

Sources: U.S. Census Bureau (2003) and The World Bank (2003).

back at Figure 10–2 shows that, based on the life expectancy index, the Japanese get the highest mark for health of all the world's nations.

As Figure 10–3 shows, in Japan and the other countries we have surveyed, government uses tax money to pay most of the cost of medical care. But one high-income nation stands out from the rest. As we now explain, the United States treats medical care not as a right but as a product to be purchased on the open market.

HEALTH CARE IN THE UNITED STATES: A SYSTEM IN CRISIS?

The United States ranks below most high-income nations when it comes to the health of the overall population. Although this country spends more money per person for health care than any other, the United States ranks only thirty-first in life expectancy (United Nations Development Programme, 2003).

This places the United States not only below Canada and almost every country in western Europe but also behind a number of less well-off nations, from Costa Rica in Latin America to Singapore in Asia. Likewise, despite its unmatched wealth, the United States does not even make it onto the top ten list of nations with the lowest infant mortality.

The government report Healthy People 2010 is found at
http://www.cdc.gov/nchs/hphome.htm

Although the U.S. health care system offers the best treatment in the world for those who can pay for it, it does far less for the poor. Why this mixed picture? The United States is the only high-income nation to rely on a **direct-fee system,** *a medical care system in which patients or their insurers pay directly for the services of physicians and hospitals.* In principle, people are free to shop for whatever health care they can afford, and hospitals and doctors compete with one another, offering various services and pricing.

According to some critics, the U.S. health care system is in a state of crisis. We now examine two of the most pressing issues: soaring costs and access to health care.

The Cost Problem

The cost of medical care in this country has soared in recent decades, from about $12 billion in 1950 to more than $1 trillion by 2002. Although the U.S. population has not even doubled in size since 1950, spending on health care has increased more than eighty times. Why has medical care become so expensive? There are six main reasons:

1. **The spread of private insurance.**   Before World War II, most people in the United States paid for medical care out of their own pockets, so they went to doctors and hospitals only when they had to. During World War II companies began to offer health insurance to employees, and the system of private insurance grew rapidly in the decades that followed. Although more insurance meant that people received more medical care, most people had little reason to question the bills they received for prescription drugs, office visits, and hospital stays. Under these conditions, doctors and hospitals could benefit by pushing prices upward, and that's exactly what they did (Starr, 1982).

2. **More doctors specialize.**   With the growth of medical knowledge and advances in scientific

technology, more doctors have chosen to specialize in limited areas of medicine, such as internal medicine or cancer treatment. Specialists also command higher fees, typically twice what a general practitioner receives. In a world of specialists, patients often end up paying several physicians to treat a single problem. Not surprisingly, the average income of physicians in the United States is now approaching $200,000 a year, more than twice the amount a decade ago (Kane & Loeblich, 2003).

3. **More high technology.** The United States is a technology-oriented society. We favor high-tech medical treatments, such as computed axial tomography (CAT) scans to create images of internal organs and angioplasty to open arteries. We often overlook the value of prevention—including changes in diet and exercise—that costs little and is highly effective in improving and maintaining health. Not surprisingly, advanced medical technologies account for most of the rise in health care spending since 1950 (Aaron, 1991; Blank, 1997).

4. **An aging population.** As Chapter 5 ("Aging and Inequality") explains, the average age in the United States is on the rise. As the baby boomers—those born between 1945 and 1960—have entered middle age, they have more income and are more concerned about their health. As baby boomers age, they will surely face more medical problems and push medical spending ever higher.

5. **A lack of preventive care.** Many people, especially those who cannot afford it, see doctors only during a medical crisis. People who go without preventive care (say for high blood pressure) often end up with a serious problem such as a stroke, which necessitates a lengthy and expensive hospital stay.

6. **More lawsuits.** People have come to expect that doctors and hospitals will always provide a cure. When treatment fails, patients or their families have been more inclined to sue, a practice that has driven up the cost of malpractice insurance, which is passed along to patients. The fear of lawsuits may drive doctors to order unnecessary tests and procedures just to protect themselves, a strategy of *defensive medicine* that pushes costs even higher (Birenbaum, 1995).

Controlling Costs In light of the rapidly rising spending on medical care, pressure to control costs

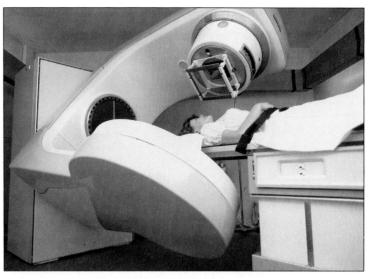

As a high-income country, the United States makes use of high-tech medical care that often seems almost miraculous in its effects. But, given the high costs of such care, what categories of the U.S. population do you think benefit most from it?

has grown on the part of both insurance companies (which pay much of the bills) and the public. But what can be done to keep the lid on medical costs? A number of policies have been developed to contain costs. One is *preadmission testing*; doctors order blood work, X-rays, and other tests before deciding whether to admit a patient to a hospital. A second policy is performing more procedures, including some surgery and cancer treatments, on an *outpatient* basis so that the patient enters and leaves the hospital on the same day. A third practice on the part of most insurance companies is *regulating the length of hospitalization* by limiting the hospital stay for a particular condition. Of course, both outpatient services and limited hospital stays put a greater burden on families to care for people in the home. Typically, this burden falls on women, who must juggle care of the sick and elderly with their careers and other family demands (Olesen, 1997). What effect have these cost-containment measures had? They have not reduced this country's spending on medical care, but they probably have slowed the increase.

Who Pays?

Every year, 32 million people in the United States enter the hospital, with an average stay of five days. The typical cost for this hospital care is about

Social Policy   The Price of Life: Sometimes Out of Reach

How would you feel about a government policy that says "People who are rich will be healthy; people who are poor will not." Few people would think such a policy fair. Yet as Elizabeth Hales sees it, this is how our medical system works.

Fifty-seven-year-old Elizabeth Hale has failing kidneys. As a result, three days a week, she must lie connected to a dialysis machine that cleans her blood, doing the work her kidneys no longer can. Because Hale has retired and has little money, she relies on both Medicare (based on her disability) and Medicaid (because she is poor) to pay most of her medical bills.

To become healthy, Hale needs a new kidney. But she will probably never get an organ transplant because she is too poor. Hospital officials explained that government assistance will pay for the surgery, but it covers just 80 percent of the cost of the antirejection drugs she would have to take for the rest of her life. According to hospital policy, Hale has to prove she can pay at least $1,500 toward the drugs before her name is even placed on the list to become an organ recipient. Hale shakes her head: "I have some money saved, but not that much. I am poor—who is going lend me the money?"

Should being poor prevent people from receiving a needed organ transplant? Existing policy says it should. With donated organs in such short supply, the argument goes, doctors and hospitals must restrict transplant surgery to "patients most likely to do well."

They do not want to risk wasting an organ by transplanting it into a patient who will not undergo follow-up treatment. In this case, that means someone who cannot afford the drugs needed after the operation.

But Elizabeth Hale disagrees. "It doesn't seem right," she concludes. "If I had the money to pay for the drugs, they would give me the transplant." In simple terms, if she cannot get the kidney she needs, she will die too soon, simply because she is poor.

ISSUES AND EXERCISES

1. Do you think people without the means to pay for treatment, such as Elizabeth Hale, should be kept off organ recipient lists? Why or why not?

2. Would you describe Elizabeth Hale's situation as discrimination against the poor or simply a hospital making the best decision about using a limited resource?

3. Should a society provide medical care on the basis of need or ability to pay? Develop arguments supporting both positions. If you think need is important, who should pay for treatments given to poor people?

Source: Adapted from Kaukas (1999).

$7,000, plus several thousand more in doctor's fees (U.S. Census Bureau, 2002). Clearly, this is a financial burden few families can easily afford. Who ends up paying the bills?

As we have already explained, in the United States people have to pay most of their own medical expenses. To do so, they rely on various types of health insurance.

Private Insurance Programs   Private insurance companies, such as Blue Cross and Blue Shield, sell policies to individuals and groups, usually through an employer. In 2002, 175 million people (61 percent of the population) were covered by a private health insurance policy. Of that number, 88 percent received

health insurance through an employer (their own or that of a family member); the remaining 12 percent bought policies on their own (U.S. Census Bureau, 2003).

Most employers require that people pay a share of the insurance premium. In addition, when people make claims, insurance companies rarely cover the entire bill. Thus, insurance greatly reduces but does not eliminate the financial burden caused by a serious accident or illness.

Health Maintenance Organizations   Health maintenance organizations (HMOs) are _private insurance organizations that provide medical care to subscribers for a fixed fee_. In an effort to hold the line on costs,

HMOs focus on disease prevention; they pay for weight loss classes, immunizations, and treatments to help people quit smoking. But HMOs also limit patients' choices. As a type of *managed care*, HMOs require patients to choose their medical care providers from a list of participating professionals, which often forces people to use doctors they do not know. In addition, nonemergency care must be preapproved by a *primary care physician*, who diagnoses the patient, provides some treatment, and makes referrals to specialists. In short, HMOs try to keep costs down by controlling the treatment process, sometimes even refusing to pay for a treatment altogether. For this reason, HMOs have become controversial.

Some 80 million individuals (28 percent of the U.S. population) are enrolled in HMOs (U.S. Census Bureau, 2003). Most have mixed feelings about their health plan, worrying they will be denied needed treatment, and many fear that their doctors will decide on a course of treatment based on what the HMO will cover rather than what they really need. Many physicians confirm that HMO rules sometimes deny patients needed treatment.

Thus, the success of HMOs comes at a price. But most employers favor HMOs because they typically cost less than traditional private insurance programs (Brink, 1998; Toner, 1999).

Government Insurance Programs In the United States, the federal government pays some of the health costs for some categories of the population. In 1965, Congress enacted Medicare and Medicaid, tax-funded programs that pay part of the medical costs for the elderly and poor and disabled people.

Medicare is part of the Social Security system and serves people aged 65 or older as well as people of all ages who are totally and permanently disabled. In 2002, more than 38 million people (13 percent of the population) were enrolled in Medicare, and nearly 90 percent of them were seniors over age 65.

Medicaid serves poor people who are pregnant, blind, permanently disabled, or aged or who live in families with dependent children. In 2002, 33 million people (12 percent of the population) were enrolled in Medicaid (U.S. Census Bureau, 2003). In addition, the nation's 25 million veterans (10 percent of the population) can obtain free care in government-operated hospitals.

In all, about 26 percent of U.S. citizens receive medical benefits from the government. Yet these programs provide only limited benefits, which is why many of those covered (especially by Medicare) purchase additional medical insurance from private

Medical care is beyond the reach of millions of people who are poor. A few may have the option of going to a free clinic; most, however, ignore health problems as long as possible. The result is that, by the time they show up at an emergency room, their illness may well be life-threatening.

companies. Those who rely totally on government programs may find that their coverage falls far short of their needs, as the Social Policy box explains.

The Coverage Problem

As we have explained, even most people with medical insurance may be unable to pay all the costs when they are faced with a serious condition. More serious still is the fact that some 43 million people—about 15 percent of the population—have no medical coverage at all.

One reason for the large population without insurance is changes in the workplace. Several decades ago, most jobs in the United States offered benefits, including vacation and sick leave, a retirement program, and health insurance. Today, fewer jobs offer these benefits, leaving more workers to fend for themselves.

The larger question is whether the United States should remain the only high-income country in the world without a universal health care program. In 1994, the Clinton administration proposed a sweeping program of health care reform by which

A NATION OF DIVERSITY

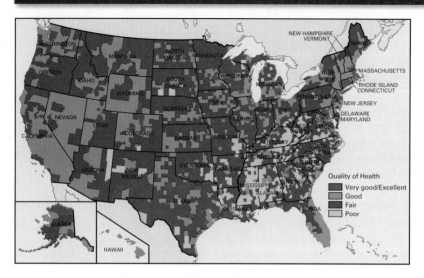

NATIONAL MAP 10–1

Patterns of Health across the United States

This map estimates the average health for people living in counties across the United States. People with good health eat wholesome foods (including lots of fruits and vegetables), do not smoke, and have enough income to pay for needed medical care. What patterns of health do you see in the map? Can you account for this pattern?

Source: American Demographics, October 2000. Copyright © 2000 by Primedia Business Magazines & Media, Inc. All rights reserved.

the government would ensure that everyone had medical insurance. The Clinton "managed competition" plan required employers to provide coverage to employees; employers could bargain with various providers to get the best plan. People not covered in this way (including those out of work) would be given insurance directly by the government.

Congress rejected the Clinton reforms, concluding that they would push medical spending far higher than it is now. In addition, critics objected to putting a new government bureaucracy—rather than doctors and patients—in charge of health care. Since then, there has been little movement toward universal coverage.

Health: Class, Ethnicity, and Race

The health of affluent people in the United States is without a doubt the best in the world. But many U.S. poor people fare little better than people who live in the world's low-income nations. For example, life expectancy among the Oglala Sioux Indians of South Dakota—among the poorest people in the United States—stands at just sixty-six years for women and fifty-six years for men. By contrast, life expectancy in the low-income Asian nation of Sri Lanka is seventy-four years for women and seventy years for men (Winslow, 1997; United Nations Development Programme, 2000).

As noted in Chapter 2 ("Poverty and Wealth"), roughly 40 million people in the United States—about 10 percent of the population—cannot afford

a healthful diet. Poor nutrition, in turn, leaves people (especially children) less able to fight off infectious diseases. But poverty harms health in other ways as well. Poor people are likely to live in a crowded and often unsafe environment marked by stress and violence. Other health hazards linked to being poor include inadequate heating and cooling, poisoning from lead-based paint, and higher rates of accidents. National Map 10–1 presents a health assessment for people across the United States.

The strong connection between class and health is evident in surveys carried out by the U.S. government. When researchers ask people living in families with adequate incomes (at least $35,000 annually) about their health, 78 percent report it as "excellent" or "good." By contrast, researchers find that only 53 percent of low-income people (family income under $20,000) say the same (U.S. National Center for Health Statistics, 2003).

This difference helps explain the fact that African Americans, who are three times as likely to be poor as white people, die an average of five years earlier than whites. Figure 10–4 provides life expectancy data for black and white men and women born in 2000. Black men fare the worst of all because poverty breeds not only poor health but violence. Indeed, the leading cause of death among African American men between the ages of fifteen and forty-four is homicide (U.S. National Center for Health Statistics, 2003). In 2002 alone, 2,802 African Americans were killed by others of their own race, 40 percent of the number of black soldiers killed in the entire Vietnam War (U.S. Federal Bureau of Investigation, 2002).

The health disadvantage linked to poverty begins early in life, often before birth. Because African Americans suffer from both higher poverty and higher unemployment, they have less access to health insurance. One result is that black women are twice as likely as white women to go without **prenatal care,** *health care for women during pregnancy,* and to have low-birthweight infants at high risk of dying soon after birth (U.S. National Center for Health Statistics, 2001).

Racial bias plays a part in patterns of health even for African Americans who are not poor. For example, research shows that people of color often receive less thorough medical care than whites. One study, which focused on men who complained to doctors about chest pain, found that doctors were 40 percent less likely to order advanced tests for African Americans than for white patients with the same symptoms, a racial bias that contributes to higher death rates (White, 1999).

Health: The Importance of Gender

On one level, women have a health advantage over men: Figure 10–4 shows that, on average, women outlive men by about six years. In fact, despite a much higher level of poverty, African American women actually have a higher life expectancy than white men. Such facts highlight the importance of gender to human health.

Gender affects the health of men and women in different ways. One important factor is the way U.S. culture defines masculinity. Because society encourages men to be more individualistic and aggressive, they are at higher risk for accidents, violence, and suicide. Taken together, these factors go a long way toward explaining men's lower life expectancy.

Despite their advantages, women's health is harmed by their subordinate standing to men. For one thing, women have traditionally been ignored by medical researchers. For years, most research on heart disease, smoking, and the effects of medications was conducted only on male subjects. The result is that doctors know far less about the needs of women and how women respond to many treatments. As a result, in 1990 the National Institutes for Health (NIH) created the Office of Research on Women's Health, a government agency that is working to direct more medical attention to women's health issues (Hafner-Eaton, 1994).

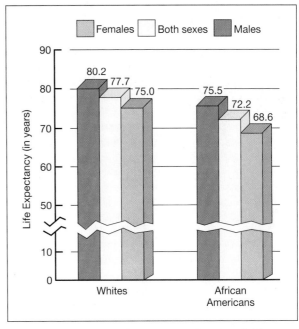

FIGURE 10–4 **Life Expectancy for U.S. Children Born in 2001**

On average, whites live about five years longer than African Americans. For both racial categories, however, women outlive men by an even greater margin.

Source: U.S. National Center for Health Statistics (2003).

Ideas about gender also distort medical treatment, further harming women's health. Some critics have long argued that doctors turn normal bodily functions, such as menopause, into medical "problems" that necessitate long-term medication. Moreover, they argue, many doctors and hospitals ignore the needs of pregnant women by doing things such as inducing labor so that an expected birth will not interfere with a doctor's vacation plans, using forceps to speed the delivery, and performing unnecessary *Caesarean sections,* the surgical delivery of an infant (Oakley, 1984). Now that about 30 percent of physicians are women, doctors and hospitals are responding to women's concerns. Still, critics maintain that many aspects of women's health continue to be overlooked and treated less aggressively than men's health. For example, heart disease is the second leading killer (behind cancer) of women age twenty-five and older. According to the American Heart Association. however, doctors are less aggressive in treating women with heart disease; they also

How does gender fuel eating disorders? The social roots of this disease lie in a culture that defines women in terms of physical attractiveness; girls learn to judge their looks and their self-worth against an unrealistic, media-based image of thinness and beauty. Because these beliefs are so deeply held, eating disorders are difficult to cure and often end up causing serious health problems, including kidney damage, brittle bones, life-threatening infections, heart disease, and, in extreme cases, death (Duffy, 1999; Lerner, 1999).

People with Disabilities

We have explained that people with lower social standing—women, minorities, and the poor—in the United States have greater health problems. Another category that struggles with the health care system is people with any **disability,** *a physical or mental condition that limits everyday activities.*

Medical professionals view a disability as some impairment to the functioning of the mind or body. Sociologists focus on how people construct the reality of a disability, that is, how people react to having a disability, and how others react to them. Thus, sociologists investigate how physical barriers, prejudice, and discrimination affect the everyday lives of people with disabilities. They note that physical disability often operates as a *master status*, meaning that other people may overlook a person's abilities and see only the disability. Thinking this way, people sometimes assume those with a physical disability have other problems, such as low intelligence, and treat them accordingly.

Because there is no simple definition of disability, there is no precise number of people with disabilities. One government tally estimates that about 6 percent of children, 20 percent of people aged six to sixty-four, and 40 percent of the elderly suffer from some disability (U.S. Census Bureau, 2003). This number is rising, partly because medical advances now save infants with birth defects who, several decades ago, would have died. Medical technology also helps people to survive accidents or severe illness that leave them with some permanent disability. More generally, people in the United States are living longer, so more people end up with a chronic and disabling condition, ranging from arthritis (inflammation of the joints) to Alzheimer's disease (a disease involving loss of brain function).

Several generations ago, most people considered those with disabilities to be incapable of living normal lives; therefore, most people with disabilities

A good example of how gender affects human health is the case of eating disorders. Research shows that 95 percent of those who suffer from anorexia nervosa and bulimia are young girls and women. What is it about U.S. culture that makes many women try to be much thinner than they should be?

offer women less counseling about proper nutrition, exercise, and weight loss (Key, 1999). Why? Perhaps because many doctors associate heart disease with men, they overlook potential problems in women.

An Illustration: The Case of Eating Disorders   A good illustration of the power of gender in shaping health involves eating disorders. Some 2 million people suffer from eating disorders, and more than 95 percent of them are girls and women. Experts estimate that about 2 percent of teenage girls in the United States suffer from *anorexia nervosa*, a form of compulsive dieting that leads people to eat too little to maintain a healthy body weight. Another 3 percent suffer from *bulimia*, a disease that involves binge–purge cycles, in which someone eats large amounts of food at one sitting and then purges by taking laxatives or inducing vomiting in order to avoid gaining weight (Duffy, 1999; American Psychiatric Association, 2002).

were housebound or even bedridden. Today's changed attitudes are reflected in barrier-free architecture—including wheelchair ramps, elevators, and bathrooms—that give everyone greater access to facilities including schools and the workplace. In addition, new technology ranging from motorized wheelchairs to computer-based communication systems permits people with disabilities greater movement and ease of expression.

Like all other dimensions of health, disability is linked to income. The disability rate for people in U.S. families earning less than $10,000 is three times higher than the rate for people in families earning $35,000 or more (Weitz, 1996; U.S. National Center for Health Statistics, 1999).

Disability Legislation In 1990, the disability rights movement, a political organization seeking to expand the rights and opportunities of people with disabilities, was successful in pressuring Congress to pass the Americans with Disabilities Act (ADA). This law outlawed discrimination against people with disabilities in employment and public accommodations, including hotels, theaters, restaurants, and stores.

Proponents call the ADA the most important civil rights legislation since the 1964 Civil Rights Act, which banned discrimination based on race and sex. When President George Bush signed the bill into law, he expressed his hope that the act would make most public places accessible to people with disabilities. But more than a decade later, there is still work to do, as many people with disabilities have trouble riding a bus, attending school, watching a sports events, or even eating in a restaurant.

In 1997, the federal government expanded the definition of "disability" beyond physical problems to include a host of conditions from mental illness to learning disabilities to fear of open places. As a result, schools, colleges, and employers are engaged in debates about diagnosis and proper accommodations. In 2000, the U.S. Supreme Court narrowed the definition of a disability to exclude impairments that can be corrected or do not substantially limit everyday activities (Fujiura, 2001).

The Nursing Shortage

A final problem facing the U.S. medical care system is a shortage of nurses. Although there were 2.3 million registered nurses in the United States in 2002, another 200,000 positions are currently unfilled, and the shortage is projected to double by 2020 (Schneider, 2003; U.S. Bureau of Labor Statistics, 2003).

Why the shortage? Part of the answer is that fewer people are choosing to become nurses. Since 1990, enrollments in nursing programs across the country have dropped by one-third. The range of jobs open to women has greatly increased in recent decades, leaving fewer people drawn to the traditionally female occupation of nursing. In addition, many of today's nurses are unhappy with their jobs: Many cite heavy patient loads, required overtime, a stressful working environment, and a lack of respect from supervisors, physicians, and hospital managers. Most working nurses say they would not recommend nursing to others, and many are leaving the field for other jobs.

Given the high demand, salaries are increasing. Currently, general duty nurses earn about $45,000, and many nurses with specialized skills (such as nurse anesthetists) are making $100,000 a year. Many hospitals and private practice physicians offer hiring bonuses to nurses. Finally, nursing programs are seeking to recruit more minorities as well as more men, who currently account for just 6 percent of registered nurses (DeFrancis, 2002a, 2002b; Dworkin, 2002; Yin, 2002).

MENTAL HEALTH AND ILLNESS

A **mental disorder** is *a change in thinking, mood, or behavior that causes distress and reduces a person's ability to function in everyday life* (U.S. Department of Health and Human Services, 1999:vii). According to the American Psychiatric Association, there are more than 300 different mental disorders, including anxiety disorders, mood disorders, eating disorders, sleep disorders, personality disorders, and mental retardation.

About 20 million adults suffer from a mental illness in any given year, and nearly half of U.S. adults (75 million people) do so at some point in their lives. Most of these disorders are of minor importance and do not threaten a person's long-term well-being. However, one-third of U.S. adults claim to have had serious mental problems (such as having felt close to a nervous breakdown), and 2 percent of the adult population (4 million people) experience mental illness serious enough to necessitate long-term hospitalization or other treatment. From another angle, the government estimates that the harm to society in terms of lost productivity from mental illness is greater than that caused by all forms of cancer (U.S. Department of Health and Human Services, 1999; U.S. National Institute on Mental Health, 2003).

We have all heard people call someone "crazy" for acting in a way that people find disturbing. Is such a label really an effort to discredit and control those who simply are different?

People experience various symptoms of mental illness, including extreme anxiety and fear, wild elation, mood swings, panic attacks, debilitating depression, or even hallucinations. Such symptoms, which can be troubling in themselves, often lead to other problems, ranging from family strain to child neglect to outright violence.

Why does mental illness provoke so much confusion and fear? Perhaps it is because some mental disorders prompt people to do the unexpected—to violate the norms that govern everyday life. Also, doctors know much less about mental illness than about physical ailments. For both these reasons, the public is quick to stigmatize those with mental disorders. Few people would label a person as "strange" for having the flu, but many will label someone who experiences severe mood swings or periodic hallucinations as "crazy." Of course, this kind of stigma only serves to socially isolate the person, which usually makes the problem worse.

Types of Mental Disorders

Effective treatment of any illness depends on accurate diagnosis. The most widely used classification of mental disorders, prepared by the American Psychiatric Association, is the *Diagnostic and Statistical Manual of Mental Disorders IV* (DSM-IV). The

DSM includes a wide range of disorders, as shown in Table 10–1.

As noted in the table, whereas some mental disorders have an immediate cause—such as those resulting from drug use—most have many causes, both biological and social. In other words, some people may be born with a higher risk of certain mental disorders, but social experiences beginning in childhood also play an important part in shaping mental health.

Mental Illness: A Myth?

Because mental disorders have many causes and are not well understood, it should be no surprise that some specialists in the field wonder whether they really exist. Psychiatrist Thomas Szasz charges that people apply the label of "insanity" to actions they find disturbing when, in reality, such behavior is only "different."

Consider a man who stands on a city street corner, shouting to anyone who will listen that God has told him that the end of the world is near. It may be that this action is unusual, and, if the man is agitated, it may even alarm passersby. But who is to say that the man is wrong? Even if he is, is he mentally ill or just expressing his deep religious convictions?

Szasz argues that people have long been too quick to condemn as "crazy" behavior that fails to conform to conventional norms. For that reason, he concludes, we should abandon the whole idea of mental illness (1961, 1970, 1994, 1995). As he sees it, illness is physical and afflicts only the body. In the absence of some physical abnormality, then, mental "illness" is simply a myth.

Szasz's thesis is controversial, and most of his colleagues reject the notion that mental illness is fiction. Still, many mental health professionals hail his work for pointing out the danger of using medicine to promote conformity. From time to time, just about everyone behaves in ways that disturb others. But does this give others the right to force us to change? Moreover, responding to "difference" with medical labels that stigmatize can do a great deal of harm—in the extreme, by defining those who are different as less than fully human.

Mental Illness: Class, Race, and Gender

The pattern found throughout this chapter—that disadvantaged categories of people suffer more from illness—applies to mental as well as physical health. We take a closer look at patterns of mental health linked to class, race, and gender.

TABLE 10–1 CATEGORIES OF MENTAL DISORDERS LISTED IN THE *DIAGNOSTIC AND STATISTICAL MANUAL OF MENTAL DISORDERS*, FOURTH EDITION

Disorders usually first diagnosed in infancy, childhood, or adolescence	Mental retardation, attention deficit hyperactivity disorder, dyslexia, stuttering, autism, Tourette's syndrome, and bed wetting
Cognitive disorders	Delirium and dementia: major changes in memory or the ability to think clearly, caused by brain damage or substance abuse
Mental disorders due to a medical condition, which are not included in other categories	Symptoms such as delirium, dementia, amnesia, and sexual dysfunction that are a direct result of another medical condition
Substance-related disorders	Disorders such as intoxication, addiction, and withdrawal resulting from the use of alcohol or other drugs, such as heroin, cocaine, and amphetamines
Schizophrenia and other psychotic disorders	Disorders characterized by extreme paranoia, delusions, and hallucinations
Mood disorders	Major depression and bipolar disorder (manic depression)
Anxiety disorders	Obsessive-compulsive disorder and disorders characterized by extreme anxiety, panic, or phobia
Somatoform disorders	Disorders that manifest themselves as symptoms of physical disease, such as pain of an unidentifiable origin or hypochondria
Dissociative disorders	Disorders that involve a splitting or dissociation of normal consciousness, such as amnesia or multiple personality
Eating or sleeping disorders	Anorexia, bulimia, and insomnia
Sexual and gender identity disorders	An absence of sexual desire, the inability to function sexually, masochism, sadism, and gender identity disorders such as transsexualism
Impulse control disorders	Disorders that manifest themselves in symptoms such as kleptomania (theft), pyromania (setting fires), and pathological gambling
Personality disorders	Chronic, inflexible, and maladaptive personality traits that are resistant to treatment, such as excessive dependence, paranoia, and narcissism (the need for constant admiration and a lack of empathy)

Mental Health and Class One of the earliest studies to document the link between class position and mental health was carried out by Robert E. Faris and H. Warren Dunham (1939). They traced 35,000 Chicago residents who had received psychiatric care from private and public mental institutions, and they found that most people with serious disorders lived in the worst slums. This link between poverty and mental illness has been confirmed by a great deal of later research both in the United States and elsewhere (Hollingshead & Redlich, 1958; Srole et al., 1962; Rushing, 1969; Levy & Rowitz, 1973; Srole, 1975; Eaton, 1980; Mirowsky & Ross, 1983; Ross, Mirowsky, & Cockerham, 1983; Wiersma et al., 1983).

But does mental illness cause poverty, or is it the other way around? Faris and Dunham concluded that poverty breeds both stress and social isolation, which, in turn, can cause mental disorders. Indeed, the isolation and stigma associated with being poor in the

United States is certainly capable of harming the mental health of many people (Cockerham, 1996).

Other researchers point to biological roots for mental illness, suggesting that genetics may place some people at higher risk for mental illness. For these people, mental problems can be triggered by a particularly stressful event. Such episodes can make it difficult for them to keep friendships and hold a job, resulting in social isolation and, of course, poverty (Shields, Heston, & Gottesman, 1975; Harkey, Miles, & Rushing, 1976; Snyder, 1980; Wiersma et al., 1983).

Mental Health and Race Sociologists have documented the lack of jobs that weakens many inner-city communities in the United States. Struggling economically and socially isolated by both racial prejudice and low income, many poor African Americans contend with high levels of stress and anxiety

(Wilson, 1987; Anderson, 1994; Feagin & Sikes, 1994; Feagin & Vera, 1995).

That said, research shows that race, by itself, does not seem to play a major part in patterns of mental health. African Americans and whites of roughly the same class position have comparable mental health (Williams, Takeuchi, & Adair, 1992; Kessler et al., 1994; Cockerham, 1996).

Research shows that people of Hispanic descent, who also are at higher risk of both prejudice and poverty, have an unexpectedly favorable pattern of mental health. Perhaps strong family ties common in many Hispanic communities help maintain mental health. Or because of cultural differences and language barriers, Hispanics may be less likely to seek treatment, so mental disorders may be underreported (Roberts, 1980; Mirowsky & Ross, 1984; Kessler et al., 1994).

Finally, Native Americans have higher than average levels of alcoholism, suicide, and mental illness. Numerous social factors probably explain this pattern, including very high rates of unemployment and poverty. Indeed, a sense of despair exists in many Native American communities (Cockerham, 1996).

Mental Health and Gender   Women and men have about the same overall incidence of mental illness. However, gender does seem to play a part in mental health. Because women are a less powerful category of the population, they are at higher risk of being labeled as deviant and even as mentally ill when they violate conventional gender norms (Chesler, 1989; Schur, 1984).

For their part, men are at risk because of the way U.S. culture defines "real men" as independent, tough, unemotional, and always in control. Trying to live this way ends up causing high levels of stress and social isolation for many men.

Given the way society defines the lives of women and men, we should not be surprised to learn that women—who constantly must worry about pleasing others—have higher rates of some mental disorders, notably anxiety and depression. Men, who try to contain their troubles, are more likely to experience personality disorders involving aggression and substance abuse (Ehrenreich, 1983; Rosenfield, 1989; Aneshensel, Rutter, & Lachenbruch, 1991; Gupta, 1993; Kessler et al., 1994).

Treatment Strategies

The idea of treating the mentally ill is fairly recent. In the Middle Ages, it was common to view people with mental illness as possessed by demons or suffering punishment by God. Therefore, some mentally ill people were tolerated as "village idiots," and others were burned as witches (Cockerham, 1996).

By about 1600, a new strategy arose for dealing with the mentally ill: locking them away with criminals and the poor. This era, sometimes called the Great Confinement, found people with mental disorders chained for years to walls or beds, often without clothing or blankets, in damp, rat-infested rooms (Foucault, 1965; Cockerham, 1996).

Reform came in the 1800s in large part because of the efforts of Dorothea Dix in the United States. The Defining Moment box takes a closer look at how Dix changed the way society viewed people with mental illness.

Dix made popular the idea that people with mental illnesses should be treated, not shut away in prisons, and it was her efforts that spread the concept of the asylum, or mental hospital, across the country. Unfortunately, the number of people who needed this kind of help was far greater than the number of facilities available. As a result, only a small share of people with mental illness received the humane care that Dix envisioned. Most were locked away in overcrowded buildings that were not all that different from the prisons in which they had been confined.

The twentieth century saw the development of several new treatment strategies. One important treatment is **psychotherapy,** *an approach to mental health in which patients talk with trained professionals to gain insight into the cause of their problems.* The famous psychologist Sigmund Freud played an important part in the rise of psychotherapy, and practitioners have developed this approach in various directions ever since.

Medical approaches also gained prominence during this time. One example is electric shock therapy, which was found to provide temporary relief for patients suffering from severe depression. But the most important medical treatment has been the creation of *psychoactive drugs,* substances that affect the mind and body in ways that control symptoms of mental illness. Once these drugs came on the scene in the 1950s, it was no longer necessary to confine people in institutions in order to control them. In 1963, Congress passed the Community Mental Health Centers Construction Act, a plan to move people out of big institutions and into communities where they could find outpatient treatment at local health centers. In practice, this law unleashed a wholesale **deinstitutionalization,** *the*

A DEFINING MOMENT

Dorothea Dix: Changing Society's View of People with Mental Illnesses

For centuries, people with mental illness were locked up in prisons with dangerous criminals. Dorothea Dix pioneered the building of asylums, where such people could find protection and treatment. Unfortunately, many asylums were no more than warehouses that did little to improve the condition of those locked within.

DOROTHEA DIX (1802–1887) WAS A WOMAN WHO made a difference. She began her career working at a girls' school. After she became head of the school, Dix's interest turned to prisons. She learned that the prison population included not only criminals but also people with mental illness—people who were sick and had broken no law. Dix was appalled at the uncaring treatment given to these innocent people. She pledged to change the way society viewed mental illness and devoted the remainder of her life to writing, speaking, and lobbying government officials.

In 1840, when Dix began her crusade, there were only thirteen facilities in the entire country that offered care to people with mental illness. Because of her efforts, twenty states passed laws creating what came to be known as asylums: places where troubled people could find shelter and peace. By 1885, near the end of Dix's life, she could boast that there were 125 asylums in the United States.

Dix is remembered today as the person who, probably more than anyone in history, changed the way society regards people with mental illness. Rather than locking people away, she showed society that people who are sick need help, whether their illness is of the body or the mind.

---

release of people from mental hospitals into local communities. Within several years, hundreds of thousands of men and women were released from mental hospitals in the belief that they could get by on their own as long as they took their drugs. But not nearly enough community health centers were built to monitor all the people who were released, so many of the former patients ended up back in hospitals, in prison, or living on the streets (Roche, 2000). The Personal Stories box on page 264 provides an all-too-typical case.

Read a recent government report urging the overhaul of our mental health system at **http://www.mentalhealthcommission.gov**

Today, just 30 percent of people suffering from mental disorders receive treatment (U.S. Substance Abuse and Mental Health Services Administration,

2003). Why the low percentage? There are too few community mental health centers; too many people lack health insurance, and many people are reluctant to admit that they have a mental health problem.

But efforts are growing to face up to mental illnesses. As noted earlier, in 1997 the federal government expanded the Americans with Disabilities Act to include mental disorders. The law now requires employers to make reasonable efforts to accommodate workers who suffer from depression, anxiety, or other mental disorders. Although doing this is not always easy, U.S. society is doing more to include people with mild mental illness in everyday activities.

Mental Illness on Campus It is no surprise to college faculty that the number of students who suffer from mental health problems is rising. According to the American College Health Association, about

Personal Stories

Deinstitutionalization: When Good Intentions Have Bad Results

MARY LEE LEANS FORWARD OVER THE SHOPPING CART that holds everything she owns. The fifty-nine-year-old woman pulls her coat tight against the cold, lowers her head, and pushes ahead into the icy wind. She is looking for a ventilation grate, where she can warm up without having to see anyone.

As a girl, Mary Lee lived in a poor Iowa farming family. Her parents worked hard and became impatient with their daughter, who often was disruptive in school. Unable to discipline her, the parents turned to a doctor for help. Mary recalls telling the doctor that, as long as she could remember, she had "heard voices." The doctor responded by declaring Mary mentally ill, suffering from paranoid schizophrenia, with symptoms including paranoia, anxiety, and hallucinations.

With her family's consent, the doctor sent Mary to a large state mental hospital, where she spent the next five years. Every day, she took chlorpromazine, a powerful psychoactive drug, to calm her. Mary recalls that the Chlorpromazine stopped her fears and ended the hallucinations, but at a price: As she puts it, "I felt like a zombie."

Then came the deinstitutionalization movement. Mary first learned about the new policy when a member of the hospital staff told all the patients that they would be released. Mary did not understand why, but she was glad when a social worker promised to help her find an apartment and apply for Food Stamps and government disability payments, and to visit her every week.

Mary left the asylum with a supply of her new drugs. For the next few years, things worked out pretty well. But then her social worker started missing visits, and Mary stopped taking her medication. Right away, the "voices" came back, filling Mary with panic. She left the apartment in fear, believing, in her words, that "government agents were coming to wire my brain."

This started a cycle that has now gone on for twenty years. Without medication, she is unable to keep track of her money, fights with her neighbors, and is evicted from her apartment. She ends up living on the streets, sleeping in abandoned buildings and cars. Within a few weeks, she ends up under arrest for stealing or breaking into a parked car. The court sends her back to the mental health care system, where she is assigned a new social worker, settles in another apartment, and receives a new supply of her medication. But eventually the system loses track of her again, she stops taking the drugs, and she ends up back on the street.

Mary Lee's story is the sad result of good intentions having bad consequences. Supporters of deinstitutionalization were hopeful that the new psychoactive drugs would bring an end to the use of restraints in mental hospitals, allowing people with mental illness to leave such settings and live a normal life in a local community. But budget cuts and bureaucratic indifference have left too many people to fend for themselves. Some people have been helped, but many others have become part of the problem of homelessness.

ISSUES AND EXERCISES

1. List several advantages and disadvantages of the policy of deinstitutionalization.
2. Do you think it is society's responsibility to care for people like Mary Lee? Why or why not?
3. Should people who are thought to be mentally ill but do not want help from others have the right to live as they wish, even if it is on the street? Why or why not?

Source: Based on Gagné (2001).

20 percent of students report having been so depressed they could not do their work; 75 percent claim to feel overwhelmed at times. Across the country, colleges are seeing a sharp rise in student demand for counseling.

Most serious is the problem of suicide. Experts estimate that about 10 percent of students have thought seriously about suicide, and 1.5 percent of students have attempted it (only a small share of these succeed) (U.S. Centers for Disease Control and Prevention, 1997; Shea, 2002).

Why the increase in mental health problems among college students? In most cases, colleges do not cause the problems. Analysts point to a number of factors, including high rates of children living in poverty, rising pressures on today's young people, and low levels of parental involvement in children's lives. In addition, drug therapies make it possible for more young people with mental health problems to attend college. However, once on campus, they may not take medications properly and may find the demands of college work to be too great. As a result, colleges are trying to define their proper role in providing health care for their students (Fujiura, 2001; Kelly, 2001; Fox, 2001; Shea, 2002).

THEORETICAL ANALYSIS: UNDERSTANDING HEALTH PROBLEMS

Each of sociology's major theoretical approaches offers insights into problems of physical and mental health. As we have seen in earlier chapters, each approach focuses on different aspects of the problems and points toward different conclusions.

Structural-Functional Analysis: Health and Social Roles

The structural-functional approach views society as a complex system of roles and responsibilities. It looks at how various patterns of behavior function to keep society running smoothly. Illness interferes with people's ability to fulfill their roles as workers and as members of families. Consequently, when people are sidelined by illness, society allows them to assume another role: **the sick role,** *patterns of behavior expected of people defined as ill.* As long as people are not to blame for their own illness, explains Talcott Parsons (1951), the sick role excuses them from most routine obligations. At the same time, the patient must try to get well by cooperating with medical personnel. This theory helps explain why some members of U.S. society feel little sympathy for people with mental disorders they see on the streets: It may seem that these people do not want treatment and therefore deserve no special concern. Of course, refusing to cooperate with medical personnel might be one symptom of a mental illness.

From a structural-functional point of view, problems of health often result from changes in other social institutions. For example, changes in the family have increased the number of people who live alone, the number of single parents, and the number of children growing up in poverty. Because people look less to family members when illness strikes, they depend more on health care professionals.

Critical evaluation. Some illness is to be expected, and the sick role allows people to recover while encouraging them to seek medical treatment. However, taking on the sick role depends on being able to afford to take time off work and to seek medical care.

Another limitation of the structural-functional approach is the implication that doctors hold the key to good health. The trend toward prevention highlights the fact that people can make choices to improve their own health by, for example, eating a balanced diet, exercising, and avoiding dangerous behavior such as smoking cigarettes.

Finally, health is not a simple matter of being "sick" or "well." On the contrary, health is highly variable, a fact that brings us to the symbolic-interaction approach.

Symbolic-Interaction Analysis: The Meaning of Health

The symbolic-interaction approach highlights how people construct reality in their everyday lives. In many parts of the world, for example, poor families consider poor nutrition and hunger to be a normal part of life, whereas people in rich countries define hunger and poor nutrition as illnesses that can be cured with more and better food. On the other end of the scale, people in rich nations have become much more accepting of obesity; two-thirds of U.S. adults weigh too much (U.S. Center for Health Statistics, 2003). Obviously, what is considered "normal"—with regard to both physical and mental health—depends not only on medical fact but also cultural standards that vary from place to place and from time to time.

The variable reality of health and illness is also evident in constantly changing medical definitions. For example, in the first half of the twentieth century, doctors and most others defined homosexuality not as an illness but as a moral wrong. In 1952, however, the publication of the first *Diagnostic and Statistical Manual of Mental Disorders* (DSM) defined homosexuality as a "personality disorder." By 1974, however, the definition changed again, when the DSM dropped homosexuality from the list of disorders. It is now considered simply a form of sexual behavior (Conrad & Schneider, 1980; Livingston, 1999).

Finally, how people define any health situation may actually affect how they feel. Doctors have long noted the existence of *psychosomatic* disorders, in which the mind appears to affect the body. When people believe they are sick (or destined to get well), their belief often comes true.

Critical evaluation. Because the symbolic-interaction approach highlights the variable meanings people attach to health and illness, it tends to ignore structural factors such as gender and wealth that play a major part in shaping the reality that people experience. For example, why do people stigmatize women more than men for having a sexually transmitted disease? Why do people blame those with low incomes for having poor health, rather than asking why the U.S. medical care system does not provide for all? Why are tens of millions of people in the United States poor in the first place? Such questions bring us to the social-conflict approach.

Social-Conflict Analysis: Health and Inequality

The social-conflict approach links health to inequality. A basic pattern, found in the United States and around the world, is that people with more wealth have better health. Social-conflict analysis points to various problems with health care in the United States.

Perhaps the most basic issue is access to care. If good health is necessary to be a productive member of society, then health care should be available to all. Yet as this chapter has explained, the United States stands alone among rich nations as having no system to provide care to everyone. In short, by linking care to ability to pay, this country undermines the health of millions of people.

A second issue is that in a capitalist economy, medical practice is based on the profit motive. This fact goes a long way to explain why the United States overlooks the health of the poor, who, by definition, have little money to pay for it. From this point of view, the profit motive ends up corrupting medical practice for everyone. Doctors are always keenly aware of their own interests when they make a diagnosis, decide on a treatment, or refer a patient to a hospital. Similarly, hospitals and insurance companies guide medical care with an eye on the bottom line, and pharmaceutical corporations strive to convince doctors and the public as a whole that health is less a matter of how we live than the pills we take (Pear & Eckholm, 1991; Cowley, 1995).

Critical evaluation. The social-conflict approach reveals that the health of some people is better than that of others because of social inequality. Thus, we can understand why people living in rich countries have relatively good health but also why the health of the poor in the United States is little better than

that of people in many of the world's low-income nations.

With its focus on the failings of the U.S. health care system, the social-conflict approach overlooks the fact that the overall health of the U.S. population has improved dramatically over the course of the twentieth century. Another criticism is that health care systems in countries with socialist economies—presumably with less social inequality—do not perform all that well, typically because they provide little incentive for people to develop new treatments and technology.

POLITICS AND HEALTH: CONSTRUCTING PROBLEMS AND DEFINING SOLUTIONS

What people see as right and wrong with the U.S. health care system is not just a matter of facts but of politics. We turn now to how politics shape what people across the political spectrum see as problems of health and the solutions they propose.

Conservatives: Free-Market Care

Whatever the issue—whether it is housing or health care—conservatives favor the policy of allowing companies to compete freely in a market system. Competition, they claim, improves value for consumers by encouraging doctors, hospitals, and other health care companies to keep quality high and prices low. Furthermore, would people be so eager to develop new drugs or so persistent in developing new technology were it not for the promise of substantial profits (Bartlett, 2000)? Conservatives boast that the U.S. free-market system offers the most advanced medical care in the world. Why else, they ask, do so many world leaders respond to illness by coming to the United States for treatment?

Another conservative value that applies to health is the importance of individual responsibility. As conservatives see it, our health reflects the choices we make about how to live. Personal choices are important because they can prevent disease before it happens: Having multiple sexual partners raises the risk of sexually transmitted diseases; pregnant women who use drugs or don't seek out prenatal care raise the risk of premature birth; people who smoke raise their risk of cancer; and people who overeat place themselves at risk for heart disease.

Given their support for free-market health care and personal responsibility for health, it is not surprising that conservatives endorse a limited role for government in this area. For the very poorest people—especially those who are elderly or disabled—and for veterans who have served their country, the government should (and does) provide health care programs. But, conservatives claim, to put government in charge of medical care for *everyone* is likely to do the same as it has for public schools: reduce quality and give people little choice about who provides the service.

Liberals: Government Care

Liberals believe that a fair and just society should strive to make everyone equal with regard to issues as basic as health care. As they see it, whereas the rich fare well in a free-market system, the poor are left out.

Many liberals accept the idea of doctors and hospitals operating for profit as long as government programs are expanded so that everyone receives care. One solution to this problem would be a national health care system similar to Great Britain's National Health Service or Canada's single-payer coverage.

Such a measure would certainly be expensive, at least in the short term. But the long-term benefit would be far better health for much of the population that is not well served now. If all mothers-to-be had prenatal care and all children had immunizations, regular checkups, and sound nutrition, this country's infant mortality rate would surely fall dramatically. Just as important, healthier people are more productive, leading to economic growth that would work to offset the cost of this kind of program.

Radicals: Capitalism Is Unhealthy

As we might expect, the strongest criticism of the U.S. health care system comes from radicals. Seen from the far left, the inequality in health care—both within the United States and among the nations of the world—is an injustice created by capitalism. When health is a commodity, those with wealth end up living longer and healthier lives than those without wealth. In effect, radicals charge, the profit motive turns physicians, hospitals, and the entire health care system into a multibillion-dollar industry up for sale to the highest bidders.

From a radical perspective, the solution to the world's health care needs is to eliminate the capitalist system in favor of an economic and political system that operates in the interests of the majority. The promise of such a socialist system lies in providing a

People who are poor not only endure more illness, they also "get old before their time." What do conservatives, liberals, and radicals support as solutions to the poor health of millions of people in the United States?

range of benefits—from safe drinking water to open heart surgery—on the basis of need.

The Left to Right table outlines the three political perspectives on health issues.

GOING ON FROM HERE

The central theme of this chapter is that health is not simply a medical matter; it is a reflection of society. Around the world, we see that most people living in rich nations now enjoy better health and longer lives than ever before. But billions of poor people have been left behind. Even in the United States—a rich nation—we might well wonder why anyone should suffer from poor health resulting from inadequate nutrition or too little income to afford medical care.

But the greatest health problems occur where the problem of poverty is greatest: in poor countries.

LEFT ⓉⓄ RIGHT

THE POLITICS OF HEALTH

	RADICAL LEFT VIEW	LIBERAL VIEW	CONSERVATIVE VIEW
WHAT IS THE PROBLEM?	The health of the rich is good, but the poor suffer. Not only is access to health care a problem, but the medical establishment itself is distorted by the profit motive.	The average health of the U.S. population is good, but disadvantaged people are less healthy; 43 million people lack health insurance.	The health of the U.S. population has steadily improved and is very good by global standards; individuals need to take greater responsibility for their own health.
WHAT IS THE SOLUTION?	High-quality health care should be the right of everyone. Only radical change toward an economic and political system that meets the needs of all will end the health inequalities in the U.S. population.	Government must extend access by putting in place a universal health care program so that prenatal care, nutrition, and appropriate medical treatment are available to all, regardless of their ability to pay.	Encouraging responsible behavior is key to illness prevention. Programs to extend health care coverage can help but should be provided by employers or paid for by individuals in a free-market system.

Join the debate . . .

1. How would you assess the overall health of the U.S. population? Provide support for your position.
2. Why do liberals favor a national program of health insurance? Why do conservatives oppose expanding government's role in health care?

3. Which of the three political analyses of health care included here do you find most convincing? Why?

Around the world, more than 1 billion people struggle to survive with too little income and almost no access to even basic medical care. In these nations—found in parts of Latin America, Africa, and Asia—illness and poverty form a vicious circle. Poverty breeds disease, which in turn reduces people's ability to work, so that they and their children remain poor.

The greatest health crisis is in central Africa, where many of the world's poorest countries are found. Adding to the long-time problem of hunger and unsafe drinking water in African nations including Burundi, Rwanda, Uganda, and Kenya is the AIDS epidemic, which in many villages and towns infects as many as 25 percent of young people (Scommegna, 1996; Singer, 2001). Worse still is the fact that 90 percent of the world's HIV-positive children live in countries with grossly inadequate health care systems, which makes the future of Africa's

poorest nations bleak. Moreover, unless Asian nations such as Thailand act quickly to stop the spread of HIV, their future will be no better.

Find a United Nations report on global AIDS at
http://www.unaids.org/wac/2002/index_en.html

Compared with the desperate struggle in poor countries, the outlook for the United States, home to the world's most advanced medical technology, is far brighter. The problem this country faces now is broadening access to the health care system. As we have explained, the United States falls behind many other nations—including those with much lower average incomes—in important health indicators. Where we stand a century from now probably will depend less on what happens in a high-tech laboratory than on the future extent of social inequality.

CHAPTER SUMMARY

1. Health is a state of complete mental, physical, and social well-being. Although health involves biological factors, the well-being of any population reflects the character of the society, including its level of technology and degree of social inequality.

2. Patterns of overall health are good in high-income nations of the world, which have low infant mortality and high life expectancy. Most people in these nations live at least seventy-five years and die of chronic conditions such as heart disease or cancer.

3. Patterns of health are poor in low-income nations, where infant mortality is high and life expectancy can be as low as forty years. Most people in these countries die of acute diseases such as malaria, cholera, or measles, and as many as half of all children die before reaching ten years of age.

4. Worldwide, some 40 million people are infected with HIV. The hardest-hit region is sub-Saharan Africa, with 70 percent of the world's AIDS cases. The United States accounts for less than 5 percent of global AIDS.

5. Socialist societies, in which governments own hospitals and employ doctors, treat health care as a basic right. Capitalist societies treat health care as a product to be purchased on the open market; some, such as Sweden and Great Britain, have socialized medicine, in which government-run care is available to all. Of all high-income nations, only the United States lacks a universal coverage program to help pay the costs of medical care.

6. The United States has a direct fee system in which doctors and hospitals operate on the open market. Health care spending in the United States has increased steadily and topped $1 trillion in 2002. Factors pushing up health care spending include the system of private insurance, the trend toward doctors specializing, increasing use of high-technology treatment, the aging U.S. population, a lack of preventive care, and a rising number of malpractice lawsuits.

7. Despite the fact that this country spends more on health care than any other, the United States lags behind other rich nations in key indicators of health, including life expectancy and infant mortality.

8. About 61 percent of the U.S. population have private health insurance, 28 percent have coverage from an HMO, and 26 percent have some coverage from the government (categories overlap). Still, 43 million people—15 percent of the population—lack health care coverage.

9. Poverty means a lack of adequate nutrition, medical care, and safe housing. Poverty is also associated with violence, especially among men. Certain categories of poor people—including Native Americans and African Americans—are at even greater risk of both physical and mental health problems.

10. On average, women outlive men by about six years. Even so, women's health concerns have often been treated less effectively and overlooked by researchers. Eating disorders, which are widespread among girls and women, illustrate the power of gender to harm health.

11. More than 50 million people in the United States suffer from some physical or mental disability. Changing laws, technology, and social attitudes enable people with disabilities to participate more widely in society.

12. Nearly half of all Americans have symptoms of a mental disorder at some time in their lives, and 2 percent of the population have serious mental disorders. Less than half of those with serious mental illness ever receive treatment.

13. The structural-functional approach views illness as a problem because it renders people unable to fulfill their social roles. People who become ill take on the sick role, which relieves them of most everyday social obligations as long as they make efforts to get well.

14. The symbolic-interactionist approach focuses on the meaning people attach to health and illness. For example, homosexuality has been viewed as a moral wrong, a mental illness, and, recently, simply as a sexual orientation.

15. The social-conflict approach focuses on how social inequality shapes patterns of health. Both in the United States and throughout the world, poor people suffer from the most health problems.

16. Conservatives favor placing health care services in the marketplace; they also emphasize individual responsibility for health. Liberals favor making government responsible for the health care system to ensure that it meets the needs of

everyone. Radicals reject relying on the profit motive to provide health care in favor of a system that would provide equal health care for all.

17. Looking ahead, the greatest challenge to human health will continue to be in the world's poorest nations.

KEY CONCEPTS

health   (p. 246) a state of complete physical, mental, and social well-being

infant mortality rate   (p. 246) the number of babies who die in their first year of life per thousand live births

life expectancy at birth   (p. 247) the number of years, on average, people in a society can expect to live

chronic disease   (p. 247) an illness that has a long-term development

acute disease   (p. 247) an illness that strikes suddenly

social epidemiology   (p. 247) the study of how health and disease are distributed throughout a society's population

epidemic   (p. 248) a disease that spreads rapidly through a population

socialized medicine   (p. 251) a medical care system in which the government owns and operates most medical facilities and employs most physicians

direct-fee system   (p. 252) a medical care system in which patients or their insurers pay directly for the services of physicians and hospitals

health maintenance organizations   (p. 254) private insurance organizations that provide medical care to subscribers for a fixed fee

prenatal care   (p. 257) health care for women during pregnancy

disability   (p. 258) a physical or mental condition that limits everyday activities

mental disorder   (p. 259) a change in thinking, mood, or behavior that causes distress and reduces a person's ability to function in everyday life

psychotherapy   (p. 262) an approach to mental health in which patients talk with trained professionals to gain insight into the cause of their problems

deinstitutionalization   (p. 262) the release of people from mental hospitals into local communities

the sick role   (p. 265) patterns of behavior expected of people defined as ill

THINKING CRITICALLY: QUESTIONS AND ISSUES

1. Physical and mental illnesses can have biological causes. But how do they also result from social factors?

2. What can you say about the distribution of good and poor health in the United States? In the world as a whole?

3. Why do you think the United States has not adopted a program of national health care? Do you favor or oppose such a program? Why?

4. Make the argument that mental illness is a myth—a label used to enforce conformity. Do you agree with this position? Why or why not?

GETTING INVOLVED: LEARNING ACTIVITIES

1. Most communities have public health clinics run by the county health department. Make an appointment to visit a clinic and speak to officials. See what you can learn about the extent of physical and mental health care in your own community and the programs available to treat illness. Try to profile the people likely to rely on the public health clinic.

2. Visit a local library that offers current copies of U.S. magazines. Look at the photographs of women in advertisements: What seems to be the ideal body shape for a woman? What effect do you think such images have on women? How might these images play a part in the problem of eating disorders?

3. Most communities have a shelter or soup kitchen for poor and homeless people. Visit such a facility in your area and ask the director about the role, if any, of mental disabilities among the people they serve. What programs does the facility offer to help clients cope with their problems?

4. Do research on the deinstitutionalization of people with mental illnesses that took place in the United States in the 1960s. See what you can learn about the causes of this movement and its consequences.

GETTING CONNECTED: USEFUL WEB LINKS

http://www.prenhall.com/macionis
Visit the interactive Companion Website™ that accompanies this text. Begin by clicking on the cover of your book. You will find a chapter-by-chapter study guide, practice tests, suggested Web links, and links to other relevant material.

http://drweilselfhealing.com
Dr. Andrew Weil explains how we can learn to improve our own health.

http://www.cdc.gov/
A good source for information about health in the United States is the Web site operated by the government's Centers for Disease Control and Prevention.

What are the goals of this organization? How does it go about doing its work?

http://www.who.int/en/
This site is operated by the World Health Organization. Here, you can find information and statistical data about health in the nations of the world.

http://www.mentalhealth.org
http://www.nimh.nih.gov
These U.S. government Web sites provide information on mental illness.

GETTING STARTED ON YOUR OWN: RESEARCH NAVIGATOR™

 Follow the instructions found on page 25 of this text to access the features of Research Navigator™. Once at the Web site, enter your Login Name and Password. Then, to use the **Content Select** database, enter keywords such as "mental illness," "AIDS," care," and "health care," and the search engine will supply relevant and recent scholarly and popular press publications. Use the *New York Times* **Search-by-Subject Archive** to find recent news articles related to sociology and the **Link Library** feature to find relevant Web links organized by the key terms associated with this chapter.

CHAPTER 11

© Paul Marcus, *Capital Dunking, oil on canvas, 50 × 50 in.* Studio SPM, Inc.

ECONOMY AND POLITICS

*J*UAN WILLIAMSON, A LIFELONG RESIDENT OF BROWARD COUNTY, FLORIDA, sat behind the large wooden table in his community's voting precinct station.
*Glancing at his watch, he saw it was time for the polls to open for the presi-
dential election of 2000. Williamson smiled as the first voter, an elderly woman
he remembered seeing on the street from time to time, walked up to him. After
she stated her name and address, he found her listing in the voter registration
book and gave her the ballot to complete.*

*As the day went on, Williamson repeated the process for perhaps a hun-
dred people. But by mid-afternoon, he was feeling disappointed. When his
brother Sebastián stopped by to vote, Williamson shared his feelings: "Today,
we are picking a president. What could be more important?" he asked. "But
where is everybody? I will bet you no more than one-third of the people in this
precinct will show up to vote." Sebastián listened and shook his head. "I know.
With so many people out of work, too much crime, and too many kids not learning to read, how can people not care? Well," he added with a smile, "at least I
am here. And don't you forget to vote!"*

We all learn in school that the United States is a democracy in which the
people rule. But how does the political system of this country really work?
In Florida, where the 2000 election was finally decided, George Bush de-
feated Al Gore by only 537 votes, and several million people never voted
at all. Can we really call this country a democracy when—across the country—half the people seem not to care who their leaders are?

This chapter explores the operation of **politics,** *the social institution that
guides a society's decision making about how to live.* As we shall explain, the political system has much to do with a country's **economy,** *the social institution
that organizes the production, distribution, and consumption of goods and services.*
By studying the operation of these two social institutions, beginning with the

GETTING THE PICTURE

✦ Who gets welfare?

*In the United States,
corporations receive
more government
assistance than poor
families.*

✦ In politics, does money
talk?

*U.S. corporations give
more money to political
campaigns than any
other type of
organization, including
labor unions, civil rights
groups, and women's
organizations.*

✦ Is the United States a
democracy?

*In recent national
elections, only about half
of eligible voters
bothered to vote.*

273

One way to "read" a nation's economic system is to examine housing in major cities. In the former East Berlin, socialist policies mandated similar, basic housing to almost everyone. In Brazil's capital city of São Paulo, a capitalist system provides luxurious housing for some, although others live in shanty settlements.

economy and then turning to politics, we will learn more about many familiar problems that affect the lives of people across the United States.

ECONOMIC SYSTEMS: DEFINING JUSTICE, DEFINING PROBLEMS

The economy is one expression of a society's concept of justice because its operation determines who gets what. In addition, as we shall see, the operation of the economy has a lot to do with what issues are likely to be defined as social problems. Therefore, we begin with a brief look at the basic economic models of capitalism and socialism.

The Capitalist Model

Capitalism is *an economic system in which natural resources and the means of producing goods and services are privately owned.* In a capitalist system, individuals own factories, machines, farms, and forests. The culture of capitalism teaches people to pursue not the common good but their own self-interest. According to Scottish economist Adam Smith (1723–1790), the pursuit of self-interest has widespread benefits by producing the greatest good for the greatest number of people (1937:508; orig. 1776).

How does all this work? In theory, capitalism operates as a system of market competition in which people buy and sell goods and services with prices set by economic forces of supply and demand. In a free-market environment—sometimes described as *laissez faire* (from French meaning "leave it alone")— sellers compete with one another for the business of buyers, who purchase goods and services that offer the most value. Businesses that offer products of high value prosper; those that offer products of little value fail. The overall result, explains Smith, is that the highest-quality goods are made available to consumers at the lowest possible prices.

According to Smith, a market economy is highly productive and such markets operate best without the interference of **government,** *a formal organization that directs the political life of a society.* Smith recognized that countries need government for some things, such as national defense, but warned that when government tells people what to produce or what to buy, it interferes with market forces, reducing value and shortchanging consumers.

In practice, mostly capitalist economies such as that of the United States have been highly productive and have generated a high overall standard of living. At the same time, capitalism does create problems, at least for some people, such as when companies lay off workers in hard times or when producers find machines that do a job more cheaply than human labor. In other words, a capitalist system benefits some people far more than others and, as noted in Chapter 2

("Poverty and Wealth"), it generates a high level of economic inequality. An additional problem linked to capitalism, discussed later in this chapter, is that concentrated wealth can also mean concentrated power, which weakens democracy.

The Socialist Model

In contrast to capitalism, **socialism** is *an economic system in which natural resources and the means of producing goods and services are collectively owned.* In a socialist economy, government limits the right of individuals to own productive property. Instead, the government owns and operates factories and offices, doing so in the interest of the people as a whole. Thus, in contrast to capitalism's individualistic orientation, socialism has a collective orientation: It teaches people to be motivated not by self-interest but by the common good.

The idea of socialism arose partly as a way to solve the problems of capitalism. According to Karl Marx (1964, orig. 1844; 1985, orig. 1847), capitalism's private ownership of productive property creates unequal social classes. By putting the *means of production* (such as factories and other productive property) in private hands, the economy benefits these owners. By contrast, socialism operates to meet the basic needs of everyone. The government, acting as an agent for the people as a whole, controls economic production. A socialist society expects everyone to work not out of self-interest but as a matter of social responsibility.

In practice, socialist nations such as the former Soviet Union and Cuba have far less economic inequality than a capitalist society such as the United States. At the same time, socialist systems create problems of their own, including a low standard of living. In addition, socialist societies have been criticized as highly regimented, with government limiting not only economic freedom (such as the freedom to start a new business) but also the freedom to speak out and to move about without restriction.

Mixed Systems

No nation in the world has an economy that is completely capitalist or completely socialist. As Global Map 11–1 on page 276 shows, most nations of the world are mostly capitalist; sixteen are mostly socialist, and about two dozen are a fairly even mix of capitalism and socialism. In Asian countries, including Japan, South Korea, and Singapore, as well as in Middle Eastern nations such as Saudi Arabia and Kuwait, a mixed system of *state capitalism* involves

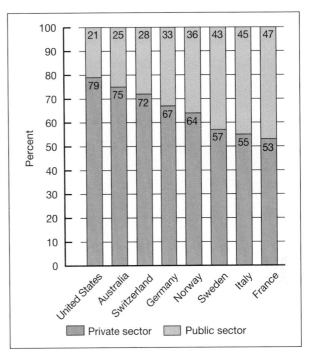

FIGURE 11–1 **Percentage of Gross Domestic Product (GDP) in Private Sector and Public Sector**

Compared with other high-income countries, the United States has a larger share of it's economic productivity in the private sector, making this country more capitalist.

Source: United Nations Development Programme (2000).

government working closely with large, privately owned companies. Although most property is privately owned, the government owns some large companies, such as automobile producers, telephone services, and airlines. In some cases (typically in Asia), this arrangement is intended to make big companies more efficient and more competitive in global markets. In others (such as Saudi Arabia), a small number of people own most of the country's productive wealth.

Another mixed system, common in Western Europe, including Italy, France, and Sweden, is *welfare capitalism.* Here, too, most production is carried out by privately owned companies; what distinguishes welfare capitalist societies is extensive government welfare programs, funded by high taxes, that provide child care, housing, and medical care for the entire population. The goal here is to keep productivity high while limiting economic inequality.

Although the U.S. economy is a mix of private and government activity, as Figure 11–1 shows, the United States is among the most capitalist of all

A WORLD OF DIFFERENCES

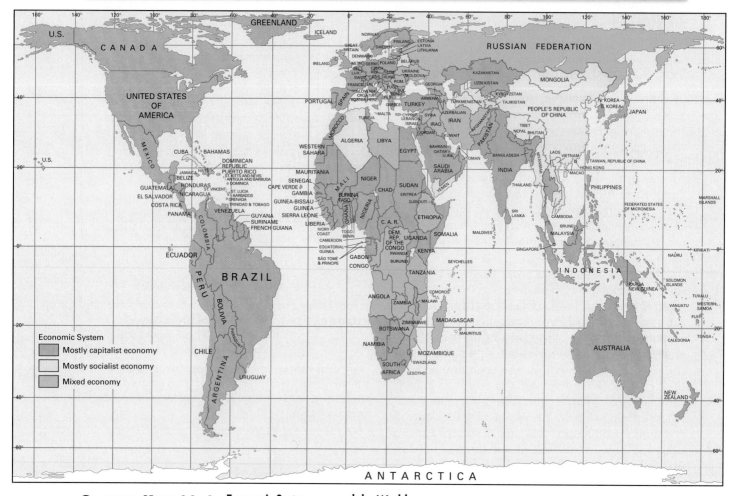

GLOBAL MAP 11–1　Economic Systems around the World

The map organizes the world's 192 nations into three general categories: countries with mostly capitalist economies, countries with mostly socialist economies, and countries with more evenly mixed economies. What can you say about the nations that fall in each of the three categories?

Source: Author's designations based on data from Freedom House (2000).

nations. The U.S. government carries out just 20 percent of the country's production, so that 80 percent of economic production is in the privately owned sector of the economy.

THE ECONOMY AND POLITICS

Analysts link the economy and politics in various ways. As some see it, the limited role of government in a capitalist society means that people enjoy extensive economic and political freedoms (Rueschemeyer, Stephens, & Stephens, 1992; Lipset, 1994). Peter Berger (1986) argues that capitalist societies typically give citizens the right to speak, travel, and work according to their individual desires.

But not everyone agrees with this argument. Those influenced by Karl Marx claim that capitalism actually reduces personal freedom, at least for most people (Domhoff, 1970; Bergsten, Horst, & Moran, 1978; Parenti, 1995). From this point of view, capitalism concentrates wealth and power to such an extent that a small share of the population (Marx's "capitalist elite") dominates the economic and political life of a society. In order for people to be free,

A Global Perspective

Why Capitalism Does Not Necessarily Mean Democracy: The Case of Saudi Arabia

IN TERMS OF ITS ECONOMY, SAUDI ARABIA is a global success story. The modern state of Saudi Arabia took form in 1932 when the late Abdul Aziz Bin Abdul Rahman Al-Saud replaced the local leaders of tribal clans (known as *Bedouin*), whose livelihood was based on herding camels, sheep, goats, and horses. At that time, Saudi Arabia had no airport, and the nation's few cities were linked by unpaved roads.

All this began to change with the discovery of oil and heavy investment from abroad beginning in 1936. Since then, Saudi Arabia has become a rich industrial nation that produces everything from petrochemicals to electronics. Today, with a population of just 22 million people (about the population of Texas), the country ranks twentieth in the world in economic output.

Saudi Arabia boasts of being a rich country with little of the crime, family breakdown, and other social problems that plague many industrial societies. In part, this orderliness results from the country's strict Islamic law. While respecting private property and economic freedom, the law demands that all citizens be Muslims. Moreover, Saudi culture places many restrictions on women, who cannot wear shorts or makeup or drive a car.

Ordinary citizens have no voice in Saudi politics. Politically, the country is a monarchy, with a royal family made up of several thousand people dominating economic and political life. Members of the royal family make "commissions" on deals they make, payments that many critics see as payoffs and other forms of corruption. But there is little public criticism in a country where the king rules by decree. Moreover, government severely restricts freedom of expression and severely punishes anyone who offends the ruling family, the government, or Islam. There are no elections, and no political parties are permitted. The government maintains strict control over the mass media, giving only one official version of the news.

In sum, the case of Saudi Arabia shows that capitalism does not necessarily mean democracy. Despite living in one of the most productive capitalist economies in the world, most people in Saudi Arabia have limited freedoms and no political voice at all.

ISSUES AND EXERCISES

1. Do you think the economic freedoms enjoyed by men in Saudi Arabia will eventually bring about political freedoms? Why or why not?

2. Do you think capitalism is a progressive force that will increase the rights and freedom of women? Why or why not?

3. Use Research Navigator™ to learn more about the economy and politics of Saudi Arabia. (See instructions on page 25; keyword "Saudi Arabia")

Sources: Saudi Arabia Embassy (1999), Freedom House (2000), Robinson & Cary (2002).

---

then, at least rough economic equality is needed, which is not the case in capitalist societies.

An important expression of political freedom is **democracy,** *a political system in which power is exercised by the people as a whole.* Most people in the United States claim that capitalist countries are democratic and socialist countries are not. But a quick look around the world today shows that this is not necessarily true. Many countries in Latin America, Africa, the Middle East, and Asia have mostly capitalist economies yet offer their people little voice in politics. Some such nations are **authoritarian,** with *a political system that denies popular participation in government.* Niger in northwestern Africa is run by the military; Iran is run by a religious elite; Malaysia and Singapore in the Southeast Asia have elections but are governed by a single political party. Others, such as Saudi Arabia in the Middle East, take the form of **monarchy,** *a political system in which a single family rules from generation to generation.* The Global Perspective box takes a closer look at the economy and politics in Saudi Arabia.

As the box explains, Saudi Arabia falls far short of the democratic ideal, in which all people have a political voice. But what about the United States? Is this country as democratic as many people like to think? We turn now to some of the economic and political problems in the "land of the free."

Social Policy — Corporate Welfare: Government Handouts for Big Business

Who benefits most from "welfare" in the United States? If you are like most people, you would answer that needy people benefit most. In reality, however, government programs provide more benefits to corporations than to poor people.

Why do companies get such special treatment? With all their wealth, corporations have great power. In addition, many states and cities are eager to increase the number of available jobs; all a large company has to do is announce a willingness to relocate, and then the offers—in the form of low-interest loans, tax relief, free utilities, and other benefits—from state and local governments come pouring in.

Some people call government aid to corporations "public-private partnerships." Such aid, they explain, creates jobs that can be vital to communities hard hit by business closings and the recent economic downturn. Critics counter that handouts for big business amount to corporate welfare. Furthermore, the amounts provided often are far greater than any promise of new jobs justifies. In 1991, for example, Indiana offered a $451-million incentive package to United Airlines to build an aircraft maintenance facility in that state. United Airlines built the facility and created 6,300 new jobs. Some simple math shows that the cost of these new jobs came out to a whopping $72,000 per person hired. In 1993, much the same happened when Alabama offered $253 million to lure Mercedes-Benz to

build an automobile assembly plant in Tuscaloosa. The corporation created 1,500 new jobs at an average cost of $169,000 each. In 1997, Pennsylvania gave a $307-million incentive package to a Norwegian company to reopen part of Philadelphia's naval shipyard. Soon after, 950 people were hired, at a cost of $323,000 per new job. In 2002, Georgia spent $67,000 per job to close a deal on a new auto plant. Across the United States, corporations benefit to the tune of about $15 billion per year—about twice the cost of welfare programs that benefit poor families.

ISSUES AND EXERCISES

1. If you were a public official in a state with high unemployment, would you support economic incentives to draw corporations to your state? Why or why not?

2. Why do you think welfare assistance to poor families has always been so controversial in the United States, when few people object to corporate welfare?

3. What effect, if any, do you think the recent corporate scandals will have on the corporate welfare described here?

Sources: Adapted from Barlett & Steele (1998); updated using various news reports.

PROBLEMS OF THE U.S. POLITICAL ECONOMY

Because the economic and political institutions influence one another, many analysts use the term **political economy** to refer to *the economic and political life of a nation or a region of the world.* The following sections investigate the political economy of the United States, looking first at the great power of large corporations and then exploring how well this nation lives up to its democratic ideals.

The Power of Corporations

In the United States, most goods and services are produced by **corporations,** *businesses with a legal existence, including rights and liabilities, apart from those of their members.* In the United States, some 5 million businesses (of 25 million total) are incorporated. Of these, the largest 100 corporations are giants, each with more than $35 billion in assets. Together, these 100 businesses are responsible for most corporate production in the United States, and this share has been increasing in recent decades (U.S. Census Bureau, 2002; Forbes, 2002).

The economic activity of corporations is far greater than that of government. Local, state, and federal governments in the United States do manage public resources, including highways, libraries, universities, parks, and beaches, and the federal government also operates the U.S. military. But, following the capitalist model, most production is in the private sector, which is dominated by huge corporations.

Government provides aid in the form of subsidies, price controls, and outright cash grants to businesses, especially when officials fear that a large industry might fail and cause damage to the overall economy. In the 1970s, for example, such fears led the federal government to provide financial assistance to bail out the Chrysler Corporation. Similarly, in the 1980s, the federal government provided $500 billion to head off collapse of the savings and loan industry (Calavita & Pontell, 1993).

Government help goes not only to companies in crisis but to almost all corporations. For one thing, federal, state, and local governments are some of U.S. corporations' biggest customers. In addition, corporations have come to expect favors from government, especially in recent decades. As the Social Policy box explains, handouts to corporations are common, with more taxpayer money in the United States going to wealthy corporations than to poor families.

Although the U.S. government does shape economic life by regulating the workplace, monitoring foreign trade, protecting consumers, and setting interest rates, it exercises no direct control over business. Given the fact that private corporations generate most of the economic output of the United States, are corporations more powerful than the government? If so, who really runs the country?

Monopoly and Oligopoly

One of the problems associated with large corporations is **monopoly,** *the domination of an entire market by a single company*. Monopolies arose in the final decades of the nineteenth century along with the Industrial Revolution. A small number of individuals—known as "robber barons" because most engaged in ruthless business tactics and lived like royalty—built enormous new corporations and dominated whole new industries. For example, Andrew Carnegie (1835–1919) took control of the nation's steel industry, John D. Rockefeller (1839–1937) dominated oil production, and J. P. Morgan (1837–1913) took a leading role in the country's banking. Not surprisingly, such men made enormous fortunes, earning of millions of dollars each year at a time when there was no income tax and the average worker earned about $600 annually.

In 1890, the federal government challenged the power of the giant monopolies by passing the Sherman Anti-Trust Act. One result was that Rockefeller's Standard Oil Company was broken up into

Toward the end of the nineteenth century, the ever-increasing power of corporations reached the point at which the largest businesses had more power and money than the federal government. The government responded in 1890 by passing the Sherman Anti-Trust Act, which forbids single companies from controlling an entire market. In this cartoon, drawn 100 years ago, President Theodore Roosevelt plays Jack (from the fable "Jack and the Beanstalk"), out to slay the Wall Street giants who dominate the U.S. economy. Can you think of recent cases in which the government has charged that a particular corporation has gained control of an entire market?

many smaller companies. Almost a century later, the government broke up AT&T's monopoly in long-distance telephone service, creating the "Baby Bells," making room for MCI, Sprint, and dozens of other long-distance companies and bringing down the price of long-distance calling. In 2002, federal and state governments settled action against the Microsoft Corporation based on alleged violations of antimonopoly laws.

Such actions have trimmed the power of giant corporations, but only to a point. The law forbids corporations from operating as outright monopolies because a single producer dominating a market eliminates competition and harms consumers. But the law does not prevent **oligopoly,** *the domination of the market by a few companies.* Today, for example, the manufacture of breakfast cereal is dominated by Kellogg, General Mills, and General Foods, which together control 90 percent of all sales (Folbre, 1995). Similarly, General Electric, Phillips, and Sylvania dominate the market for electric lights; Goodyear, Goodrich, and Michelin have a dominant position in the tire industry; Kodak, Polaroid, and Fuji are dominant producers of film; and General Motors, Ford, Toyota, and Honda dominate auto production.

Conglomerates and Other Linkages

Large corporations, by themselves, are powerful. Yet corporations join together to form even larger and more powerful businesses. A **conglomerate** is *a giant corporation composed of many smaller corporations.* Examples of conglomerates include Pepsico, the maker of Pepsi soft drinks, which also owns Taco Bell, KFC, Pizza Hut, Frito-Lay, and other snack and fast-food companies. Ford owns the British auto companies Jaguar and Aston Martin and also a share of Mazda, a Japanese corporation, Kia, a Korean corporation, and Volvo, a Swedish company. For their part, General Motors owns the German company Opel, the British company Vauxhall, and half of Saab in Sweden and has partnerships with Suzuki, Isuzu, and Toyota in Japan. Pearson, a large British corporation, operates around the world, running newspapers (including the London *Financial Times*) and overseeing a number of publishing companies (including Prentice Hall, the publisher of this textbook).

Another way corporations cooperate is by sharing members of their boards of directors. **Interlocking directorates** are *social networks of people who serve as directors of several corporations at the same time.* A member of Kodak's board of directors, for example, might also serve on the boards of other film companies such as Polaroid and Fuji. Indeed, the biggest corporations, such as General Electric, are linked to hundreds of other corporations through common board members (Scott & Griff, 1985; Weidenbaum, 1995; Kono et al., 1998).

Conglomerates and interlocking directorates are perfectly legal but can increase the power of large corporations and may encourage oligopoly and illegal activities such as price fixing, in which various companies share information on prices so they do not have to compete with one another. Price fixing harms the public because consumers end up paying more.

The Power of Money

The enormous wealth of corporations brings us to the question of how money influences the political process. Corporations are not the only organizations with a voice in the political system. On the contrary, people across the United States join together to form many kinds of organizations that seek to advance various political goals. A notable feature of the U.S. political system is **special-interest groups,** *political alliances of people interested in some economic or social issue.* We are all familiar with many special-interest groups such as the American Association of Retired Persons (AARP), the National Rifle Association (NRA), and the American Civil Liberties Union (ACLU).

Visit the ACLU Web site at
http://www.aclu.org

In general, the more money a person or organization has, the greater the political influence. One way in which money buys political power is **lobbying,** *the efforts of special-interest groups and their representatives to influence government officials.* The AARP, NRA, and ACLU all employ lobbyists in Washington, D.C., and elsewhere who work full-time pressuring members of Congress to pass legislation that advances their interests. In all, more than 12,000 lobbyists are registered with the U.S. Congress (Dodd, 2003).

Campaign Financing

Perhaps the biggest concern about the power of money centers on the financing of political campaigns. A reality of political life in the United States is that running for office is very expensive. Congressional candidates routinely spend more than $1 million in the course of their campaigns; in the 2000 presidential race, Al Gore spent $120 million and George W. Bush spent $186 million. It is likely that spending in the 2004 presidential election will be greater still.

Where does all the money come from? Corporations provide more campaign contributions than

A number of major donors have access to this country's political leaders. Is it also true that wealthy people and organizations shape the nation's political agenda?

all other types of groups, including labor unions, civil rights groups, and women's organizations. Political parties are another important source of money. In addition, candidates are free to spend as much of their own money as they wish. Although great wealth is no guarantee of success, very rich people have a huge advantage over "ordinary" people: For example, Steve Forbes spent $66 million of his own money to fund runs for the presidency in 1996 and 2000.

Most candidates raise the vast sums needed to run a political campaign by appealing to individuals and organizations to make contributions. Candidates at all levels of government receive money from **political action committees (PACs),** *organizations formed by special-interest groups to raise and spend money in support of political goals.* In 2003, there were 3,945 PACs in the United States, representing a wide range of special-interest groups, including the pharmaceutical and tobacco industries, defense industries, labor unions, agribusinesses, religious organizations, senior citizens, and gun owners (U.S. Federal Election Commission, 2003).

As recently as 2000, campaign finance laws limited any PAC's contribution to a candidate to $5,000 in a primary election and an additional $5,000 in the general election. But PACs could solicit donations for candidates directly from donors and just pass along the money to the candidate. Such *bundling* of checks, along with high-priced fund-raising dinners and other strategies that get around legal limits on campaign contributions, generated an unlimited amount of contributions called *soft money.*

In addition, there was no limit on how much a PAC could spend to assist candidates as long as the PAC did not operate under the control of the candidates or their campaign committees (Conway & Green, 1998). Therefore, many PACs focused their spending on particular issues that helped the candidates they favored. For example, raising money in support of abortion rights typically helps more liberal (usually Democratic) candidates, and raising money to oppose abortion typically helps more conservative (usually Republican) candidates.

Individuals, corporations, unions, and PACs were also able to donate larger sums of money to political parties. Although an individual could donate no more than $1,000 to any candidate in a specific political race, individuals were allowed to donate up to $20,000 per year to national parties and up to $5,000 to state parties (Herrnson, 1998). Federal law limited the amount an individual can contribute to all candidates for public office to $25,000 per year. Yet by combining the methods of support, many individuals easily spent much more. In fact, the available cash from contributors was so great that presidential candidates often refused the government's offer of campaign funding because it would impose additional limits on their spending.

As the 2000 presidential campaign got underway, one eighty-nine-year-old great-grandmother decided that she was fed up with the power of money in U.S. politics. The Defining Moment box on page 282 tells her story.

Visit the GrannyD home page at **http://www.grannyd.com**

A DEFINING MOMENT

Doris Haddock: Sparking a Movement for Campaign Finance Reform

ORIS HADDOCK IS LIVING PROOF THAT with enough determination, one person can make a difference in U.S. politics. Although she stands barely five feet tall and has emphysema and arthritis, this politically active woman knows how to talk up a storm and rally people to her cause.

In 1995, Doris Haddock—affectionately known as Granny D—became concerned about the state of campaign financing in the United States. She realized that campaigns depend on a vast supply of money, so that, above all else, most politicians have to worry about raising money. All too often, she concluded with great disappointment, our way of financing campaigns puts the U.S. political system up for sale.

By 1998, Haddock decided to sound a call for change by walking coast-to-coast across the United States. She spent much of the year getting into shape by walking around her hometown of Dublin, New Hampshire. Then, on January 1, 1999, she began her walk in Pasadena, California. She walked ten miles every day, six days a week, for fourteen months—tramping in the hot sun and pushing through blinding blizzards—and wore out four pairs of shoes before her 3,200-mile trek was done.

Along the way she gave speeches, spreading the message about the problem of campaign financing. Finally, on February 29, 2000, she arrived in Washington, D.C., walking the final few miles accompanied by many

Doris Haddock not only "talked the talk" about reducing the role of money in U.S. politics, she also "walked the walk," crossing the country on foot.

members of Congress to a waiting crowd of several thousand people on Capitol Hill.

Although Congress enacted campaign finance reform in 2002, Haddock and others see a need for further change in the years to come. Doris Haddock has shown that even small people can bring about change—in this case, generating widespread public support for campaign finance reform. The story has another happy ending: By the time she finished her nationwide walk, Haddock's emphysema and arthritis had gotten much better.

Source: Based, in part, on http://www.grannyd.com

The 2002 Reforms   Recently, Congress passed the Bipartisan Campaign Reform Act of 2002, popularly known as the McCain-Feingold bill. This act states that soft money can no longer flow to candidates or political parties. Individuals are limited to gifts of $2,000 each to political candidates in any primary or general election. Furthermore, individuals can give no more than $95,000 in total gifts (a ceiling of $37,500 to all candidates and $57,500 to all political parties). PACs can now give no more than $5,000 to any one candidate and $15,000 to any one political party, with no overall limit. Under the new system, PACs will change their strategy

from collecting money to pass along to candidates and parties to encouraging individuals to give money (under the limits noted earlier) directly to candidates and parties. Near the end of 2003, the U.S. Supreme Court (in a sharply divided 5-to-4 decision) upheld the key features of the campaign finance reform bill.

Why have so many people defined campaign financing as a serious problem? The simple answer is that the political contributions of $100 million and more made regularly by special-interest groups (such as organizations representing the real estate industry or lawyers) are given with the expectation that

A NATION OF DIVERSITY

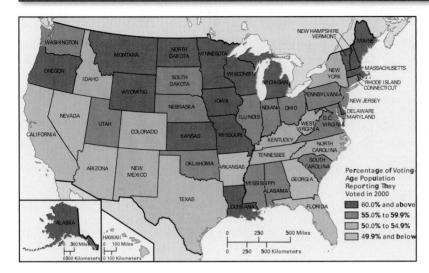

NATIONAL MAP 11–1

Voter Turnout across the United States

Overall, 55 percent of voting-age people went to the polls in the 2000 presidential election. By state, people in Wisconsin and Minnesota were most likely to vote (67.8 percent each) and people in Hawaii were least likely to do so (39.7 percent). What pattern do you see for the country as a whole? Can you explain the pattern?

Source: U.S. Census Bureau (2002).

Percentage of Voting-Age Population Reporting They Voted in 2000

- 60.0% and above
- 55.0% to 59.9%
- 50.0% to 54.9%
- 49.9% and below

candidates who receive this money will support certain political goals. In other words, few political officials write a law or even cast a vote without thinking about the effects on fund-raising for their next campaign. In practice, say critics, our system of campaign financing puts the U.S. political system up for sale (Allen & Broyles, 1991; Berry, 1989; Cook, 1993; Center for Responsive Politics, 1998; Cigler & Loomis, 1998; Starr, 2003).

Voter Apathy

If money plays such a big part in U.S. politics, allowing special interests to dominate political events, perhaps it is not surprising that many individuals do not bother to vote. The declining rate of voter turnout, that is, the share of eligible people who vote, is cause for concern. In 2000, just 55 percent of eligible voters went to the polls. In fact, the share of eligible voters going to the polls in presidential elections in the last seventy-five years has ranged from 45 percent to 58 percent (Casper & Bass, 1998; Ayers, 2001; U.S. Census Bureau, 2002).

This low rate of voter turnout is a dramatic contrast to the historical trend of expanding voting rights, which includes the Fifteenth Amendment, which extended the vote to African American men in 1870; the Nineteenth Amendment, which enfranchised women in 1920; and the Twenty-Sixth Amendment, which lowered the voting age from twenty-one years to eighteen in 1971. Today the

only adult citizens in the United States without the right to vote are convicted felons. National Map 11–1 shows where in the United States people are most likely and least likely to vote.

If almost everyone has the right to vote, why do many people lack the desire to do so? Conservatives suggest that the failure to vote is a sign of *indifference* on the part of people who are pretty much satisfied with the way things are. Liberals and radicals on the left take a different view, arguing that low voter turnout reflects widespread *alienation* from politics. As they see it, many people are dissatisfied with the way things are, but they doubt that voting will make any difference. Especially in recent decades, corporate fraud, negative campaign advertising, and outright political corruption have caused a decline in public confidence in "the system," with the results shown in Figure 11–2 on page 284. In sum, given the power of money in U.S. political life, many doubt that "the little guy" makes much of a difference (Greenburg, 1996; Dye, 1999; U.S. Census Bureau, 2000).

Perhaps the United States should follow the lead of Australia, Belgium, Italy, and other nations that have enacted laws requiring people to vote. Another approach is to offer more choices. The early attention given to Howard Dean, who strongly opposed Bush administration policies in the Democratic primary campaign for the presidency in 2004, suggests that a greater range of choices excites more voters. One important reason that U.S. voter turnout

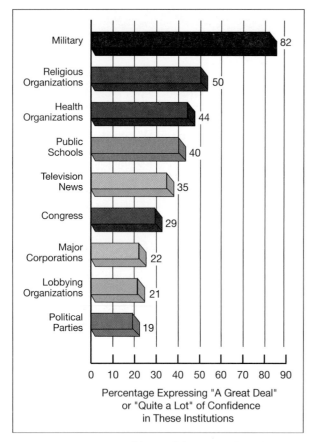

FIGURE 11–2   Public Confidence in Selected Institutions, 2003

Public confidence in important organizations has declined in recent decades. No organization listed here can claim the confidence of a clear majority of U.S. adults.

Source: U.S. Census Bureau (2003) and Lyons (2003).

is low—below that of many other high income nations—may be the fact that the major U.S. political parties have much in common. The political parties of other countries are farther apart on a wider political spectrum.

Who Votes? Class, Age, Race, Ethnicity, and Gender

Low voter turnout not only weakens this country's democratic ideal but also reflects the fact that certain categories of people are especially likely to be left out of the political process.

Income is one important factor. People with high incomes are more likely to vote than those with lower incomes. Figure 11–3 shows that 75 percent of people earning more than $75,000 per year reported

voting in the 2000 presidential election. By contrast, less than half of people earning under $20,000 said that they had cast a vote (U.S. Census Bureau, 2002).

Why this difference? Affluent people tend to be more highly educated, and college graduates are twice as likely to vote as high school dropouts. In addition, because income rises over the life course, affluent people, on average, are older. The older people are, the more likely they are to vote.

Historically, race has had much to do with voting. Until 1865, no person of color could vote in the United States. African American men gained the right to vote in 1870, as did all women in 1920. Today, white people (61 percent voted in 2000) are more likely to vote than black people (57 percent). African Americans provide strong support for Democratic candidates, with only a small share voting Republican (U.S. Census Bureau, 2002).

People of Hispanic descent are even less likely to vote (in 2000, just 30 percent did so). In part, this is because Hispanic Americans have a high rate of poverty. In addition, a sense of cultural marginality and less ability to speak English discourage many Hispanic women and men from voting. The Hispanic vote tends to favor Democratic candidates, but a rising share of Hispanics now support Republicans (Casper & Bass, 1998; Dye, 1999; U.S. Census Bureau, 2002).

Finally, what about gender? Are women as likely as men to vote? In recent national elections, women have turned out to vote at a slightly higher rate than men. In the 2000 presidential election, 56 percent of women cast a vote, compared with 53 percent of men. At the same time, women are more likely to support Democratic candidates, whereas men favor Republicans, as we now explain.

The Gender Gap: Seeing Problems Differently

In political terms, the **gender gap** is *a tendency for women and men to hold different opinions about certain issues and to support different candidates.* On average, women and men tend to define the problems the United States faces, as well as what should be done about them, in somewhat different ways. In general, women are more likely than men to support so-called compassion issues, those that address protecting vulnerable members of society (including the aged, children, and people with disabilities); women are also more likely to support gun control and to oppose the death penalty. Men, by contrast, are more likely to favor a strong military, the right to own a

Elderly people in the United States have enormous political clout, based not just on their relative wealth but also on their high voter turnout. Compared to young people in their late teens and twenties, people over the age of sixty-five are twice as likely to vote. How might the power of young people change if they, too, turned out to vote in large numbers?

gun, and a tough response to crime, including use of the death penalty.

This Web site explores women in U.S. politics:
http://www.gendergap.com

Such differences make women more likely to support Democrats, whereas men tend to favor Republicans. In the 2000 presidential election, 54 percent of women voted Democratic, and 54 percent of men voted Republican (U.S. Federal Election Commission, 2000; NORC, 2003).

Social Movements: How Much Change?

Donating money and voting are two important political activities. Other ways to be politically active range from signing petitions to engaging in violent protest. Over the course of the twentieth century, political activism on the part of women, African Americans, gay men and lesbians, poor people, and workers has led to important changes in social policy.

Early in the twentieth century, workers reacted to industrialization by demanding limited working hours and the rights to form unions and to bargain collectively with employers. In the Great Depression of the 1930s, and again in the 1960s, people successfully pressed for government programs to address problems such as poverty and homelessness.

In the 1950s and 1960s, African Americans joined together in the civil rights movement, demanding—

DIMENSIONS OF DIFFERENCE

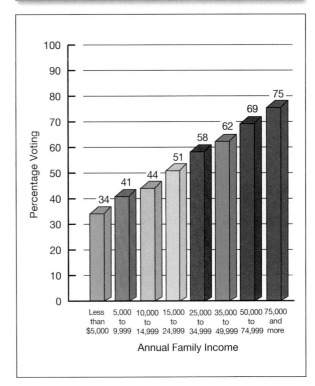

FIGURE 11–3 Voting by Income Level

Percentage of adults who reported voting in the 2000 presidential election. A clear pattern is present: As income goes up, so does the likelihood of voting.

Source: U.S. Census Bureau (2002).

Throughout this country's history, people have banded together in an effort to gain power and change the system. Forty years ago, African Americans tried to gain a greater political voice, marching from Selma to Montgomery, Alabama. In your view, how much real change do such movements create?

and winning—desegregation of schools and public facilities, the right to vote where it was still being denied to them, and protection from discrimination in employment, schooling, housing, and public accommodations. In the 1960s and 1970s, the women's movement gained similar protections from discrimination, guaranteeing women equal opportunities in schooling, athletics, employment, and obtaining credit and greater opportunities in the military. In some states and cities, the gay and lesbian movement has achieved protection from discrimination in the workplace and in access to housing; in certain places, homosexual partners have gained the right to form legal unions. Finally, throughout the twentieth century, senior citizens have steadily gained political power, which they have used to improve retirement and health care benefits.

No one can doubt that activism is a powerful political strategy in the United States, resulting in changes in the law and, over time, in public attitudes. But it is also true that none of the movements mentioned has altered the U.S. political economy in any fundamental way. Over the course of the last century there has been little change in the concentration of wealth; indeed, the last decade witnessed increasing economic polarization. Nor has there been any notable reduction in the power of corporations in this country; on the contrary, the largest corporations have become even bigger. Also keep in mind—as discussed in Chapter 2 ("Poverty and Wealth")—that during

the 1990s, welfare reforms reduced the social safety net for the poor.

In sum, the question of who controls the political economy of the United States remains as important today as ever. Analysts offer varying views on this important question, as we now explain.

THEORETICAL ANALYSIS: UNDERSTANDING ECONOMIC AND POLITICAL PROBLEMS

Sociology's two macro-level theoretical approaches offer insights into economic and political problems. Each approach highlights different facts and points to different conclusions.

Structural–Functional Analysis: Rule by the Many

A structural-functional approach views the economic system as operating to produce and distribute goods and services to the entire population. This approach has some resemblance to the laissez-faire model that underlies capitalism, arguing that individuals direct the economy through their decisions about what to produce and what to consume. As Adam Smith argued, from these individual decisions—guided from self-interest—comes the greatest good for the greatest number. The structural-functional approach takes much the same view of politics.

Robert Dahl: The Pluralist Model The **pluralist model** is *an analysis of the political system that sees power widely distributed among various groups and organizations in a society.* This model, based largely on the work of Robert Dahl (1961, 1982), suggests that individuals and organizations compete in the political "marketplace" in a democratic way. As Dahl sees it, all organizations have at least some political clout, and none is powerful enough to get its way all the time. In practice, organizations operate as *veto groups,* meaning that they can expect to realize some of their own goals but mostly they work to keep their opponents from achieving all of *their* goals. In the pluralist model, various political organizations—including parties, special-interest groups of all kinds, and government agencies—compete for public support and negotiate with one another, setting policy goals, forming alliances, and striking compromises. Through this process, public policy is created.

Overall, the pluralist model suggests that to a large degree, the United States is democratic. According to this model, U.S. political power is shared among many organizations, and voters also matter; candidates must campaign hard for public support. For this reason, the pluralist model concludes, all categories of people and all organizations have at least some political voice (Rothman & Black, 1998). Following this theoretical approach, competition between parties and special-interest groups serves the public interest, just as competition between businesses improves the economy.

Critical evaluation. Research by Robert Dahl and others (cf. Polsby, 1959) investigating how important decisions are made in large U.S. cities lends support to the pluralist position that power is distributed among many organizations. Dahl found that any group or organization typically has some control over only a narrow range of issues (for example, a school board has influence over school policy but little else). Indeed, the expansion of voting rights and the increase in the number of special-interest groups suggest that no single category of people has all the power.

But critics charge that this view of U.S. society as highly democratic does not reflect political reality. Why is it, critics ask, that so many people—especially the poor—see little reason to vote? Critics also point out that certain categories of people (for example, the rich in relation to the poor) and certain organizations (say, corporations compared with environmentalists) clearly have more political clout. Such criticism brings us to the social-conflict approach.

Each year, the political leaders of the United States assemble for the President's "State of the Union" speech. The pluralist approach claims that these leaders represent a wide range of interests and organizations. The power-elite model sees them as a ruling elite, representing mainly their own interests. The political-economy model claims that the political process is guided by the capitalist economy.

Social-Conflict Analysis: Rule by the Few

The social-conflict approach sees the economic system as operating under the control of an elite. From this perspective, a predominantly capitalist system such as the United States concentrates wealth in the hands of the few. The political system operates in much the same way, concentrating power and challenging the pluralist view that the United States is democratic. We briefly present two social-conflict theories: the power-elite model and the Marxist political economy model.

C. Wright Mills: The Power-Elite Model In 1961, as he prepared to leave office, President Dwight D. Eisenhower gave a farewell address in which he warned the country of the growing power of what he called the **military-industrial complex,** *a political alliance involving the federal government, the military, and the defense industries.*

In giving this warning, Eisenhower might well have been thinking of what sociologist C. Wright Mills (1956) called the **power-elite model,** *an analysis of the political system that sees power as concentrated among a small elite.* Who is this elite? According to Mills, the power elite is a small collection of individuals and their families: top military officials, the heads of major corporations, and top political leaders. In fact, many of the top military, corporate, and political officials end up being the same people because elites can move easily from one sector to another. For example, Eisenhower moved from a top spot in the military to a top spot in the world of politics. Likewise, many corporate leaders move into politics and return to corporate board rooms after leaving office. Dick Cheney left a cabinet position to become a corporate CEO and later moved back into government as vice president. Moreover, many power elite families are linked in various social ways: They live in the same expensive communities, belong to the same exclusive clubs, and send their children to the same private schools. Because they travel in the same social circles, Mills added, children of the power elite stand a good chance of marrying one another and passing along their privileges to another generation. Were he alive today, Mills might well have noted that both candidates in the 2000 presidential race were millionaires who grew up in politically powerful families: Al Gore is the son of a former U.S. senator, and George W. Bush is the son of a former U.S. president.

Based on such observations, the power elite model rejects the pluralist claim that power is widely dispersed throughout society, with organizations preventing each other from gaining too much power. On the contrary, this model leads to the conclusion that both wealth and power in U.S. society are highly concentrated so that the power elite can and do run the country as they wish.

Karl Marx: Capitalist Political Economy The **Marxist political-economy model** is *an analysis that sees the concentration of wealth and power in society as resulting from capitalism.* A Marxist approach accepts the power-elite model that U.S. society is far from democratic because it is dominated by an economic and political elite. But rather than focusing on the great power of certain individuals, the Marxist model focuses on the institutional system that creates this imbalance in the first place.

In Marx's view, the economy sets the foundation for any society's overall operation. Therefore, the concentration of wealth and power in the hands of a few results not from the ability and efforts of certain individuals but from the routine operation of the capitalist economy. From this point of view, as long as the United States has a mostly capitalist economy, the majority of people will be shut out of politics, just as they are exploited in the workplace.

Critical evaluation.   The social-conflict approach challenges the notion that U.S. society is democratic and highlights the extent of economic and political inequality. At the same time, this approach gives little attention to the progress U.S. society has made toward extending both economic and political opportunity over the course of its history. This greater opportunity is evident, in the rapidly increasing number of minorities and women who hold political office. Furthermore, although a few U.S. presidents were born into the upper class (George W. Bush is one example), many more rose from humble origins (for example, Bill Clinton was born into a working-class family) (Baltzell & Schneiderman, 1991). Another criticism comes from the observation, that elites also dominate the politics of nations with socialist economies such as China and Cuba (where leaders tolerate little opposition and many of the same people remain in power for decades).

ECONOMICS AND POLITICS: CONSTRUCTING PROBLEMS AND DEFINING SOLUTIONS

Theory provides helpful ways to think about the economy and politics, but what the problems are and how to go about solving them is a matter of political views. Here we present conservative, liberal, and radical left political positions on economic and political problems, and we define solutions from each of these points of view.

Conservatives: The System Is Working

Believing that free competition in the marketplace is good for society, conservatives favor limited government involvement in the economy. Likewise, they hold that competition between political candidates for voter support, as well as competition between special-interest groups, is good for democracy.

Conservatives point out that in the United States, every adult citizen is able to participate in the political process by voting, joining special-interest groups, contributing to candidates, working for political parties, and engaging in protests. Moreover, over the course of the last two centuries, the United States has steadily extended the right to vote to the entire adult population, and never have there been so many special-interest groups on the political scene. In short, individuals have many opportunities to express their view and to band together with others who share their positions.

Conservatives claim our economic and political systems serve the entire population. Liberals counter that the economy benefits the rich; therefore, a welfare state must protect the interests of the poor. Radicals claim that the capitalist political economy will always serve only the few. Which perspective is most convincing to you? Why?

As a result, conservatives maintain that the current economic and political systems work pretty well. As the old saying goes, if the economic and political systems in the United States are far from perfect, they are also better than any alternatives. In short, except for calling for smaller government in the interest of greater economic productivity, conservatives see few problems in the U.S. political economy.

Liberals: The Need for Reform

Liberals also favor a free market, but they support greater government regulation of the economy. As they see it, a laissez-faire economy concentrates wealth in the hands of the few. Those with the greatest wealth, in turn, are able to gain control of the political process so that government ends up benefiting the rich and powerful interest groups such as large corporations.

In order to reduce the economic inequality produced by a market economy, liberals support a **welfare state,** *a range of policies and programs that transfer wealth from the rich to the poor and provide benefits to needy members of society.* Part of the welfare state policy is progressive taxation, a policy that raises the tax rate as income goes up (take a glance back at Table 2–2 on page 31). In practice, those with higher incomes pay much of the tax money used to fund benefits for people with lower incomes. The result of such income transfers from rich to poor is that government is able to reduce economic inequality and assist those who are needy.

With regard to politics, liberals would like to see social policies that would reduce both the wealth and the political influence of the nation's richest citizens. For example, most liberals favor rolling back (or eliminating completely) the recent tax cuts championed by President Bush. In addition, liberals support a strong and activist government in the belief that only government, working for the interests of ordinary people, can effectively oppose the enormous power of special-interest groups such as large corporations.

Although it is true that liberals generally provide greater support for bigger government, both liberals and conservatives favor using government power as a solution to what they define as social problems. The Critical Thinking box takes a closer look.

Radicals: A Call for Basic Change

Generally speaking, the farther to the left one moves, the more one seeks to replace a market system with government control of the economy. Radicals (following Karl Marx) believe that the problem with a capitalist market system is that it concentrates wealth in the hands of the few. Government operates in support of the capitalist economy, protecting the wealth of the rich. The final result, then, is that the capitalist political economy makes some people very rich while most people have little financial security.

From a radical perspective, the problem is not that a power elite has managed to seize control of the government, as liberals are inclined to say. As long as a capitalist political economy exists in the United States, no small change—such as voters

Critical Thinking — Who's In Favor of "Big Government"? Everybody!

A COMMON ASSUMPTION IS THAT LIBERALS (typically people who vote Democratic) support a larger government than conservatives (typically those who vote Republican). There is some truth to this statement. But, more correctly, people on *both* sides of the political spectrum support the use of government power as long as it is in pursuit of the particular goals they consider important.

The figure below illustrates the politics of big government. Liberals typically define social problems in terms of social inequality. For example, liberals generally think that the rich have too much and the poor have too little. Therefore, liberals support progressive taxation, with the funds used to pay for extensive social welfare programs. In addition, liberals support government activism to end discrimination against women and other minorities. To help all poor people, liberals would like the country to adopt a universal health care program administered by the government. To reach these goals, government must get bigger.

But conservatives, too, support big government—except that they typically want government to do different things. Conservatives typically define social problems in moral terms. For example, conservatives see evil in the world that threatens the United States just as they oppose abortion and homosexual relationships as morally wrong here at home. Therefore, conservatives support a strong military, and increases in military spending mean that the government gets bigger. In addition, many conservatives support government action to restrict access to abortion and some also seek a constitutional ban on gay marriage.

In the end, liberals and conservatives do not differ drastically in their support for "big government." This is because government power is the only effective way to address many social problems. But identifying exactly what the problems are still depends on your point of view.

ISSUES AND EXERCISES

1. Make a list of three problems liberals want government to solve. Do the same for conservatives.

2. Can you find examples in the 2004 presidential campaign that illustrate patterns described here?

3. How would radicals on the left respond to both the liberal and conservative positions?

Are You in Favor of Big Government?

On issues of:	*Liberals would say . . .*	*Conservatives would say . . .*
Inequality	**YES!** Government should actively reduce social inequality by enlarging social welfare programs, opposing discrimination, and supporting affirmative action.	**NO!** Government should keep taxes low and should not seek to expand social welfare programs that discourage personal effort and threaten freedom.
Moral Issues	**NO!** Government should not try to legislate morality, because doing so weakens personal choice and threatens freedom.	**YES!** Government should actively promote national security (by enlarging military defense) and traditional morality (by opposing abortion and gay marriage).

Support for Government from the Liberal and Conservative Points of View

LEFT TO RIGHT

THE POLITICS OF THE POLITICAL ECONOMY

	RADICAL LEFT VIEW	LIBERAL VIEW	CONSERVATIVE VIEW
WHAT IS THE PROBLEM?	The capitalist economy concentrates wealth in the hands of the few; the government serves the interests of the capitalist elite. Overall, U.S. society is neither economically just nor politically democratic.	The economy is productive, but some people fare much better than others; those with greater wealth have the most influence in the political system.	Politics and economics are not a problem. The economy is highly productive and responds to consumer demand; the political system is based on elections in which individuals vote, and various organizations negotiate to form public policy.
WHAT IS THE SOLUTION?	Efforts to reform the capitalist political economy will have little effect. What is needed is fundamental change in the economic and political systems so that they reflect the interests and meet the needs of the majority.	Government social welfare programs should transfer wealth from rich to poor to lessen inequality. Political reforms are needed to reduce the role of corporate and individual wealth in the political process.	Market economics should be maintained because it provides the greatest good for the greatest number of people. The United States stands out among nations as a model of extensive rights and freedoms.

Join the debate . . .

1. What, in your opinion, are the strengths and weaknesses of the U.S. economy? Provide specific facts to support your position.
2. To what degree do you think the United States can be described as a political democracy? What

specific evidence can you present in support of your assessment?
3. Which of the three political analyses of political economy included here do you find most convincing? Why?

---

electing more liberal candidates or Congress passing campaign finance reform—will make much difference. For radicals, the only solution to capitalism's concentration of wealth and power is an end to capitalism itself. In order for a society to be truly democratic, all people must have an equal say in politics; for that to happen, there must be equity in wealth. The Left to Right table views issues of political economy from the various points of view.

GOING ON FROM HERE

A century ago, the rise of huge corporations prompted national concern about the power of "big money." Congress enacted various laws to combat corporate monopoly and to limit the power of big business to control the government. These laws had a modest effect, sharply reducing outright monopoly but

permitting widespread oligopoly. For much of the twentieth century, few doubted that corporations had enormous power in the halls of federal and state governments.

In the 1970s, Congress believed it was time to reduce corporate influence in U.S. politics. An important reform—the 1971 Federal Election Campaign Act—led to the creation of the political action committees (PACs) we have discussed in this chapter. This law tried to level the playing field by placing limits on the political contributions of both rich individuals and large corporations.

The practical results of this bill fell short of its promise. For one thing, the costs of campaigning—now conducted through thirty-second ads on television—have soared. Today's political candidates believe they need more money than ever to get into office and to stay there. Not surprisingly, in the last two decades the number and influence of PACs have grown steadily; PACs now provide more than four times as much money to members of Congress as they did in the 1970s. Although PACs represent a wide range of political interests, including labor unions, corporate PACs outnumber and give more money to candidates than any other type. This fact helps explain why many people continue to see special-interest groups as a serious political problem and why so much attention in recent years has been focused on campaign finance reform. What effect will the 2002 campaign finance reform law have? As in the past, the intention is to limit the power of big money on the political process. Even under the new law, however, candidates continue to rely on contributions to finance expensive campaigns. Of course, radicals on the left dismiss such a law as doing nothing to change the basic capitalist political economy of the United States.

There can be little doubt that the character of the U.S. economic and political systems will be debated in years to come. Most voices are calling for reform rather than revolution. Yet a troubling fact remains: About half of all U.S. citizens seem so turned off by the political process that they do not even bother to vote. Whether they really believe that the candidates and policy options presented offer no real choice (as radicals tend to say) or whether they are basically satisfied with their lives (as conservatives would have it) is hard to say. But the recent campaign finance reforms seem likely to have little effect on the low level of political participation in the United States.

In the end, perhaps we need to return to a basic question: What do we mean by the term "democracy"? Then we must face an even more difficult issue: how we as a nation will get there.

CHAPTER SUMMARY

1. The economy is the social institution that organizes the production, distribution, and consumption of goods and services. Politics is the social institution that guides a society's decision making about how to live. Government is the formal organization that directs the political life of a society.

2. Two major economic models are capitalism and socialism. Capitalism is based on the private ownership of productive property and a market system regulated by supply and demand. Socialism is based on collective ownership of productive property, with government control of the economy. Most nations have primarily capitalist economies, although the extent of government involvement in economic production varies.

3. Many people link capitalism to political democracy, yet some capitalist nations are authoritarian, giving people little voice in government. Moreover, although conservatives point out that capitalism provides personal freedom, liberals and radicals on the left counter that this system generates economic inequality, which threatens democracy.

4. Corporations stand at the center of the U.S. political economy. Government helps support corporations not only by buying corporate products but also with various incentives that critics call corporate welfare.

5. A century ago, some of the largest corporations operated as monopolies, completely dominating a segment of the market. Today, although government outlaws monopoly, many large corporations operate as oligopolies, in which a few giant corporations dominate a market.

6. Conglomerates are giant corporations formed of many smaller corporations. In addition, many corporations are linked through interlocking directorates, with common members of their boards of directors. Although such patterns are legal, they can encourage illegal activities such as price fixing, and they certainly increase corporate wealth and power.

7. Special-interest groups raise money for political candidates and lobby government officials to advance particular interests. Raising campaign funds is a major concern of public officials, who seek money from individual donors, political parties, and political action committees (PACs). The importance of fund-raising makes us ask whose interests government officials should serve.

8. Voter apathy is on the rise in the United States, with fewer than half of eligible people voting in presidential elections. Conservatives suggest low voter turnout means that most people are content with their lives, liberals and radicals counter that it means people are dissatisfied but

believe they have little power to bring about change. In general, voter apathy is greatest among the young, those with little education, and the poor.

9. A gender gap has emerged in U.S. politics, with women more likely than men to favor protections for society's most vulnerable members.

10. Guided by the structural-functional approach, the pluralist model states that power is widely dispersed throughout U.S. society. Organizations operate as veto groups so that no single organization can dominate the political system. Just as economic competition results in the greatest good for the greatest number, competition between organizations and between candidates for popular support results in sound policy.

11. Guided by the social-conflict approach, the power-elite model states that the U.S. political system is dominated by a power elite made up of the top leaders in this country's corporations, military, and government. The Marxist political-economy model shifts the focus from elites to the capitalist system, which concentrates wealth and power in the hands of a few.

12. Conservatives claim the U.S. economic and political systems work well. Competition in the marketplace and in the political arena serves the public interest. Conservatives look to government to advance some (typically moral) causes, such as national defense and restricting abortion and homosexual relationships.

13. Liberals favor more government regulation of the economy and political system (especially to lessen social inequality). They support social welfare programs funded by progressive taxation that redistribute income by providing various benefits to the poor.

14. Radicals on the left maintain that reform will not solve the political and economic problems of the United States. The root cause of these problems is capitalism's concentration of wealth and power; therefore, radicals call for elimination of the capitalist system.

KEY CONCEPTS

politics (p. 273) the social institution that guides a society's decision making about how to live

economy (p. 273) the social institution that organizes the production, distribution, and consumption of goods and services

capitalism (p. 274) an economic system in which natural resources and the means of producing goods and services are privately owned

government (p. 274) a formal organization that directs the political life of a society

socialism (p. 275) an economic system in which natural resources and the means of producing goods and services are collectively owned

democracy (p. 277) a political system in which power is exercised by the people as a whole

authoritarianism (p. 277) a political system that denies popular participation in government

monarchy (p. 277) a political system in which a single family rules from generation to generation

political economy (p. 278) the economic and political life of a nation or a region of the world

corporations (p. 278) businesses with a legal existence, including rights and liabilities, apart from those of their members

monopoly (p. 279) the domination of an entire market by a single company

oligopoly (p. 280) the domination of the market by a few companies

conglomerate (p. 280) a giant corporation composed of many smaller corporations

interlocking directorates (p. 280) social networks of people who serve as directors of several corporations at the same time

special-interest groups (p. 280) political alliances of people interested in some economic or social issue

lobbying (p. 280) the efforts of special-interest groups and their representatives to influence government officials

political action committees (PACs) (p. 281) organizations formed by special-interest groups to raise and spend money in support of political goals

gender gap (p. 284) a tendency for women and men to hold different opinions about certain issues and to support different candidates

pluralist model (p. 287) an analysis of the political system that sees power widely distributed among various groups and organizations in a society

military-industrial complex (p. 287) a political alliance involving the federal government, the military, and the defense industries

power-elite model   (p. 287) an analysis of the political system that sees power as concentrated among a small elite

Marxist political-economy model   (p. 288) an analysis that sees the concentration of wealth and power in society as resulting from capitalism

welfare state   (p. 289) a range of policies and programs that transfer wealth from the rich to the poor and provide benefits to needy members of society

THINKING CRITICALLY: QUESTIONS AND ISSUES

1. What exactly, is a society's economy supposed to do? How well do you think the U.S. economy meets its goals?

2. What are several similarities and differences between capitalism and socialism? What strengths and weaknesses do you see in each system?

3. Some people claim that capitalism supports political democracy because it affords personal freedom; others claim it opposes democracy because it concentrates wealth. Which position do you find more convincing? Why?

4. Considering the level of political apathy in the United States and the categories of people most and least likely to vote, do you think people who stay away from the polls are happy with the way things are? Or do you think that they are critical of the political system but feel powerless to change it? Why?

GETTING INVOLVED: LEARNING ACTIVITIES

1. Identify a small business in your area that is interesting to you; make an appointment for a brief interview with the owner or manager. Ask about the various laws and policies that regulate the business and the impact these policies have on workers and on the profitability of the business.

2. Go to a grocery store and make a list of the brand names you find for breakfast cereal, canned soup, frozen dinners, spaghetti sauce, and potato chips. How many manufacturers produce each item?

3. Do you know who your representative in Congress is? Find out and contact the person's office to see what you can learn about the costs of running campaigns and where this person's contributions come from. (By law, candidates must provide financial disclosure statements to all interested parties.)

4. Near your campus, find a local chapter of one of the following organizations: the National Organization for Women (NOW), the American Association of Retired Persons (AARP), the National Urban League, or the National Association for the Advancement of Colored People (NAACP). Explain your interest in the study of social problems and ask about the organization's agenda, challenges, and success.

GETTING CONNECTED: USEFUL WEB LINKS

http:www.prenhall.com/macionis
Visit the interactive Companion Website™ that accompanies this text. Begin by clicking on the cover of your book. You will find a chapter-by-chapter study guide, practice tests, suggested Web links, and links to other relevant material.

http://www.nber.org
This site, run by the National Bureau of Economic Research, offers a wide range of information and statistics on the operation of the U.S. economy.

http://www.fec.gov
The Web site operated by the Federal Election Commission provides up-to-date information on the issue of campaign financing, including data on PAC contributions to various parties and candidates.

http://www.pirg.org
The Public Interest Research Group is a politically active organization of interest to many college students. What are their goals? Where would you place them on the political spectrum?

http://thomas.loc.gov
At this site, you can read about current legislation pending in Congress.

http://www.govspot.com/features/youngvoterapathy.htm
This site examines voter apathy on the part of young people. Would you like to learn how you can register to vote on campus?

GETTING STARTED ON YOUR OWN: RESEARCH NAVIGATOR™

Follow the instructions found on page 25 of this text to access the features of Research Navigator™. Once at the Web site, enter your Login Name and Password. Then, to use the **Content Select** database, enter keywords such as "corporations," "politics," and "campaign finance reform," and the search engine will supply relevant and recent scholarly and popular press publications. Use the *New York Times* **Search-by-Subject Archive** to find recent news articles related to sociology and the **Link Library** feature to find relevant Web links organized by the key terms associated with this chapter.

CHAPTER 12

© Paul Marcus, *You Deserve a Smile, Studio SPM, Inc.*

WORK
AND THE WORKPLACE

STAN MARTON WAS DOING PRETTY WELL: His job as a software engineer for a large New Jersey insurance company paid him $77,000 a year and provided a good life for his family. Marton enjoyed his job, developing software that allows the insurance company to track the activities of its many agents.

But all that began to change one morning in 2001 when he walked into a meeting where company officials introduced him to a team of software developers from Tata Consultancy Services, the largest software company in India. Marton was told he was to train the new team, teaching them about the insurance company and its software needs. Marton did as he was told, but recalls having a bad feeling about it. His feelings only got worse several months later when one of the Tata staff was named manager of the software project Marton thought was his own. Then, only weeks after that, he and dozens of U.S. employees were notified that their whole division would lose their jobs because the company's software development was being transferred to India. There, a software engineer earns only about $10,000 per year, resulting in a huge savings to the insurance company.

Stan Marton went months with no job. Finally, he was able to find a temporary position at a one-third pay cut and fewer benefits. He is not happy about how his working life has changed, nor is he alone. Between now and 2015, analysts predict, U.S. companies will move more than 3 million jobs to other countries. These are not the industrial jobs that went abroad in decades past; most will be jobs in engineering, financial services, and computing—good jobs that were always considered "safe" (adapted from Thottam, 2003).

GETTING THE PICTURE

✦ Is your workplace a safe environment?

Every year 5 million U.S. workers suffer disabling accidents on the job; about 6,000 die as a result of their injuries.

✦ Are jobs secure?

About one-fifth of the U.S. labor force are temporary workers and part-timers.

✦ Are jobs open to everyone?

More than 98 percent of dental hygienists—but just 19 percent of dentists—in the United States—are women.

Work is more than a source of income: A job also provides prestige, identity, and—under favorable circumstances—a sense of satisfaction. With this in mind, how do you think most people feel about being unemployed?

A wide range of data about the U.S. economy can be found at the Web site of the U.S. Department of Labor: http://www.dol.gov

In sum, work is important because it provides not just income but also social identity, pride, and a sense of security and well-being. Therefore, problems in the workplace threaten people in many ways. Many workplace problems reflect broader economic trends beyond the control of ordinary people, as we now explain.

STRUCTURAL CHANGES IN THE U.S. ECONOMY

Many of the problems related to work in the United States have been brought on by changes in the economy. Over the history of this country, there have been two such major structural changes. The first change, which began about 200 years ago, was the Industrial Revolution; the second change, which began in the 1950s and continues today, is the Information Revolution. As we shall see, both revolutions transformed not only the economy but people's entire way of life.

The Industrial Revolution

In the nineteenth century, most people lived in rural areas and small towns and worked in the *primary sector* of the economy, producing raw materials by farming, fishing, ranching, mining, or clearing forests. The nature of work changed as factories sprang up, largely from New England to the new and rapidly growing cities of the Midwest. The Industrial Revolution pushed workers into the *secondary sector* of the economy, in which most transformed raw materials into finished products: For example, factory workers turned wood into furniture and steel into railroad tracks and, later, into automobiles.

Figure 12–1 shows that by 1900, industrial jobs were more numerous than farm work. Factories drew millions of people from farm towns to live in or near large cities. Many people, especially those who stayed behind in rural areas, saw this migration as a serious problem because it drained the population of small, rural communities, many of which became "ghost towns." From this point of view, the Industrial Revolution threatened a traditional, rural way of life that had existed in the United States since the colonial period.

The Industrial Revolution brought even more changes to the U.S. workplace by encouraging high levels of immigration. The new factories and rapidly growing cities attracted tens of millions of people

Across the United States, millions of people are in much the same situation as Stan Marton. Decades ago, millions of men and women lost their factory jobs as computers and robots replaced workers on assembly lines and old industrial plants shut down entirely. More recently, as corporations continue to "downsize," managers and other highly skilled people with office jobs have found that they, too, are at risk of unemployment. In short, the changes in the U.S. economy that have brought a windfall to some people have left others with low pay or no work at all. This chapter surveys social problems surrounding work and the workplace. We begin with a look at why work is important.

THE IMPORTANCE OF WORK

Most people in the United States see work as an important source of income. But work is more than that. A job gives many people a sense of pride and accomplishment, and for almost everyone what one does for a living is an important source of identity and self-esteem. Most people think of themselves as doctors, firefighters, or teachers, and they take pride in the work the perform every day. Even those who do not love their jobs can gain satisfaction from what they are able to do with the wages they earn.

from abroad—mostly from Europe, but thousands from other parts of the world as well. These men and women came to the United States in search of work and a better life, but they were not always welcomed. As explained in Chapter 3 ("Racial and Ethnic Inequality"), many people were critical of what they saw as a tide of foreign immigrants who threatened this country's established way of life.

Most of those who came to the new industrial cities to pursue their dreams found that life was far from easy. Many had no choice but to take poor housing, sometimes with little heat and no sanitation. Factories offered jobs, but the pay was low, the hours were long, and work was backbreaking and often dangerous. Many jobs involved rigid and monotonous routines amid smoke and deafening noise; moreover, supervisors closely monitored their workers and tolerated no complaint. In short, companies treated workers—especially the immigrants who spoke little English—as little more than muscle power. Because they needed wages to live and because they were not organized to demand better working conditions, workers had little choice but to take whatever work they could find.

The early decades of the twentieth century were a difficult time for working people in the United States. The struggle became worse in the 1930s when the Great Depression, a major economic collapse, put more than one-quarter of the labor force out of work. Hunger and other hardships became the norm across the country. Not until World War II, a decade later, did the U.S. economy rebound and living standards improve.

In the 1950s and 1960s, the economy boomed. Many—perhaps most—working people in the United States enjoyed rising wages and a better life. As Chapter 15 ("Urban Life") explains, many industrial workers found they earned enough to buy a modest house in a new subdivision outside the city limits, transforming the United States into a society centered in the suburbs.

The Information Revolution

Figure 12–1 shows that by 1950 the economy was changing again. By that time, the share of the labor force in industrial jobs was matched by the rising share of workers in the *tertiary (third) sector* of the economy. Today, most people in the labor force work not in factories but in offices, where they perform *service work* in sales, consulting, law, advertising, and other fields. One important reason for this economic transformation was the invention of the computer

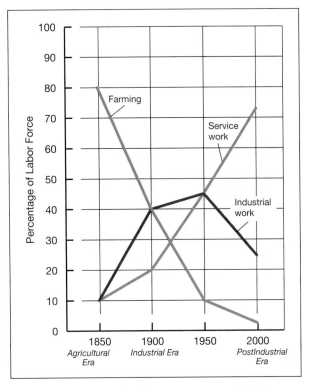

FIGURE 12–1 The Changing Nature of Work in the United States, 1850–2000

In 1850, 80 percent of U.S. workers were in the primary sector of the economy (farming); today, only a few percent of people in the labor force do such work. Industrial work in the secondary sector of the economy peaked about 1950 and has been in decline since then. Today, more than two-thirds of U.S. workers have service jobs in the tertiary sector of the economy.

Source: Author estimates based on U.S. Department of Labor (2003).

and the rapid spread of computer technology into almost every aspect of life by the end of the twentieth century.

The Information Revolution brought a shift from older, blue-collar industrial jobs toward newer, white-collar service work. Some people—the established professionals (including doctors, lawyers, and college professors) and the new professionals (in advertising, consulting, and computer programming)—were well paid and highly regarded and, until recently, enjoyed economic security. But the Information Revolution was not good news for all workers. Many of the new office jobs—especially those typically held by women who worked as secretaries or other office workers—were low paying and offered little chance for advancement. The high-paying industrial jobs were disappearing.

Policies such as the North American Free Trade Agreement (NAFTA) are intended to strengthen economic ties between the United States and other nations. Critics, however, point to a loss of jobs at home caused by more use of low-wage labor in poor countries.

Deindustrialization

The Information Revolution also signaled a process of **deindustrialization,** *the decline of industrial production that occurred in the United States after about 1950.* Many former assembly line workers and machine operators found their plants closing down, forcing them to take jobs as clerical workers, delivery personnel, maintenance workers, and fast-food employees. Almost all of these new jobs pay much less than industrial jobs do, and often they include fewer benefits. By the end of the twentieth century, as a glance back at Figure 12–1 shows, far more workers were employed in service jobs than in industrial jobs. For this reason, many workers—especially those with industrial skills but without college degrees—have found the last several decades to be tough economic times.

Globalization

The deindustrialization of the United States is tied up with the globalization of the economy. With regard to the economy, **globalization** is *the expansion of economic activity around the world with little regard for national borders.* Today, the largest corporations operate in many countries, and more and more products move from country to country.

Early in the twentieth century, the United States had higher industrial production than any other country in the world. By the end of the twentieth century, however, new information technology (including computers, modems, facsimile machines, and satellite communications) allowed corporations to operate production facilities all over the world.

In recent years, as the opening to this chapter illustrates, millions of highly skilled white-collar workers have seen their work exported to India and other lower-income countries (Thottam, 2003).

The main reason U.S. companies are moving both industrial and information work abroad involves wages. Whether the work involves factory assembly lines or computer programming in an office, workers in lower-income countries of the world earn far less than workers in the United States. As Figure 12–2 shows, industrial workers in South Korea, Taiwan, and Mexico make only a fraction of what industrial workers in the United States earn.

Not surprisingly, many industrial companies have closed production plants in the United States and opened plants abroad where labor costs are low. Similarly, many U.S. companies are sending work involving computers to companies abroad, paying roughly 20 cents for every dollar they would spend to keep the job at home. This global expansion of the economy has been good for corporations—lower wages and salaries for workers mean higher profits for stockholders—but bad for many workers in the United States.

OTHER PROBLEMS OF THE U.S. WORKPLACE

Going to work is a daily fact of life for many people in the United States. In addition to the job losses resulting from globalization of the economy, the workplace involves any number of problems, including low pay, alienation, unemployment, and various kinds of discrimination, and danger of physical injury and even death. Although work provides many benefits and great satisfaction to some, it offers far less to others. So great are differences in workplace experiences that sociologists have distinguished two broad categories of work.

The Dual Labor Market

Today's labor market involves two categories of jobs, divided in terms of what the jobs provide to the workers. The **primary labor market** includes *occupations that provide good pay and extensive benefits to workers.* Jobs in the primary labor market are challenging and rewarding, offer good pay, include extensive benefits such as pensions and health insurance, are secure, and provide a good chance to move ahead. They are the kinds of jobs people perform with satisfaction and think of as *careers.* At the top of the primary labor market are the *professions,* white-collar occupations—such as physician, lawyer, and professor—that require extensive schooling and offer high pay and prestige. Also included in the primary labor market are positions as business managers and executives, airline pilots, accountants, newspaper editors, and electrical engineers, and the remaining good jobs in factories.

Other work in the U.S. economy is in the **secondary labor market,** *jobs that provide low pay and few benefits to workers.* For example, restaurant work and jobs in retail sales, telemarketing, or building maintenance generally are low-paying, offer limited benefits, carry high risk of layoffs, and offer little opportunity for advancement. Workers with jobs in this segment of the labor market are economically insecure, aware of the limited income they have today, and never sure that they will have a job tomorrow. Typically, people who hold jobs in the secondary labor market are women and men with less schooling and fewer skills—in short, those who have fewer options. The Critical Thinking box on page 302 takes a closer look at work in the secondary labor market.

Danger to Workers

A century ago, at the height of the industrial era, it was common for people to labor in steel mills and deep in coal mines that exposed them to serious danger every day. Back then, employers and the government paid little attention to worker safety. Accidents also were common on the farm, where people used tractors, combines, and other powered machinery.

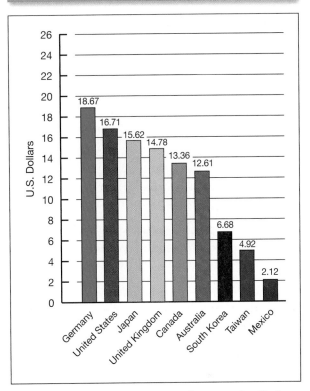

DIMENSIONS OF DIFFERENCE

FIGURE 12–2 Average Hourly Wages for Workers in Manufacturing, 2002

Workers in countries such as Taiwan and Mexico are paid far less than their counterparts in the United States. This disparity is a key reason that the United States has been losing industrial jobs to these nations.

Source: U.S. Department of Labor (2003).

In the decades since then, workplace accidents have become less common, mostly because of the changes in work—from industrial to service jobs—we have already described. But government has also played a role in today's better safety record. In 1970, the federal government created the Occupational Safety and Health Administration (OSHA) to regulate workplace health and safety. In addition, the government created the National Institute for Occupational Safety and Health (NIOSH) to conduct research on workplace hazards, ranging from toxic chemicals to ailments that result from repetitive motion or heavy lifting. In 1976, Congress passed the Toxic Substances Control Act, which set guidelines for handling dangerous substances in the workplace. With ever-increasing use of chemicals in the production of food, clothing, automobiles and other

Critical Thinking | Low-Wage Jobs: On (Not) Getting By in America

WHAT IS IT LIKE TO TAKE A JOB at Wal-Mart, clean rooms at a motel, or wait tables at a small diner, earning $7–8 an hour? Are low-pay jobs easy to do? Can you live on the pay they provide?

Barbara Ehrenreich, a Ph.D. and gifted writer, has made her living for years working behind a desk, writing about social issues including poverty. Sharing lunch in New York City with a magazine editor, she was kicking around the idea of writing about low-wage jobs and said, in passing, "Somebody ought to do the old-fashioned kind of [research]—you know, go out there and try it for themselves." Her editor paused, smiled, and came back with a simple reply: *"You!"*

And so, in the spring of 1998, Barbara Ehrenreich was on her way to a new life, joining the millions of people in the United States with low-income jobs. Her plan was simple but challenging: She would not fall back on her writing skills, she would take the best job she could find and do it as well as she could, and she would get the cheapest housing she could find, as long as it was safe.

Ehrenreich began her adventure in Key West, Florida, as she replied to twenty want-ads seeking workers for low-wage jobs. She soon landed a job waitressing at a small restaurant connected to a motel. The manager agreed that from 2 P.M. until 10 P.M. she was to wait tables; her pay was $2.43 per hour plus tips. When she reported for work the next day, she was given a shirt with the motel logo to wear. The first day's lesson was that working as a waitresses is much harder than most people think. Ehrenreich explains (2001:17), "As a server, I am beset by requests as if by bees: more iced tea here, catsup over there, a to-go box for table 14, and where are the high-chairs, anyway?" She also had to master a touch screen ordering system that does not work easily. And then there is the work she never

expected, including "sweeping, scrubbing, slicing, refilling, and restocking." All this while being constantly watched by the assistant manager for any signs of drug use, stealing, or simply slowing down.

When the tips were collected (and shared with the kitchen staff), Ehrenreich earned $6–$10 per hour, which totaled about $1,200 per month. The cheapest housing she could find was a half-size trailer home fifteen minutes from town that cost $675 per month, leaving her with $525, which was less than $20 a day for food, clothing, transportation, telephone, health needs, and everything else.

In the months that followed, Ehrenreich performed low-wage work in Florida, Maine, and Minnesota. She swept hotel rooms, cleaned private homes, worked as an aide in a nursing home, and signed on as a sales clerk at Wal-Mart. She found that all these jobs, like the waitressing, require many skills and demand long hours of hard labor. Everywhere she went, Ehrenreich learned a more important lesson: Low-wage jobs do not pay enough to live. To have any kind of life, you need to work two of these jobs, and that is no life at all.

ISSUES AND EXERCISES

1. Do you agree with Barbara Ehrenreich that low-wage work is much harder than most people think? Why or why not?
2. Should people who work full time have to live below the poverty line? Explain your position.
3. Would you support a higher minimum wage? Why or why not?

Source: Based on Ehrenreich (2001).

goods, federal agencies face the challenge of not only regulating the use of substances known to be dangerous but also testing new substances to see whether they may prove harmful.

Despite these efforts, on-the-job accidents and injuries are still a serious social problem in the United States. In 2002, about 3 million workers suffered disabling accidents that required time off from work.

More seriously, each year about 6,000 workers lose their lives in workplace accidents. As Figure 12–3 shows, mining and agriculture carry the greatest risks of death (U.S. Bureau of Labor Statistics, 2003).

Mining Mining has long been the most deadly kind of work because workers labor with heavy machinery underground, facing the ever-present dangers of cave-ins and poisonous fumes. But even more deadly in the long term is the coal dust that miners breathe every day. Over many years, coal dust causes a number of respiratory diseases, which eventually take their toll on retired miners. Working in the mines, as one man put it, "You die quick or you die slow but—either way—you're just as dead" (Gup, 1991:55).

Farming Although farm machinery is safer than it once was, farming still poses high risk to workers. Farmers now work with more toxic chemicals. Just as important, U.S. law that bans child labor does not apply to farming. Therefore, agricultural work places children at especially high risk of injury or death.

Toxic Substances and Radiation Human hazards are not limited to mines and farms. Toxic substances used in countless workplaces pose a hazard to workers. Nearly every production facility in operation today contains at least some chemicals known to cause cancer.

Radiation is another occupational hazard that places workers at risk of leukemia and other forms of cancer. A radiation hazard exists at the 110 nuclear power plants across the United States and dozens of factories that engage in the production of nuclear materials. Such hazards take time to document because the effects of human exposure to radiation are only evident years later. But workers do take action. In 1999, fourteen former employees of Kentucky's Paducah Gaseous Diffusion Plant filed a $10-billion lawsuit, alleging hazardous radiation at the plant that the firm concealed from workers and the general public. A government investigation documented that the workers had reason for concern: They found potential radiation leaks at the plant and some 37,000 uranium-containing cylinders stored outdoors (Carroll, 1999b, 1999c).

Workplace Violence Finally, not all job-related hazards involve accidents or illness; violence is another hazard in the workplace. Across the United States in 2002, workplace murder claimed the lives of 608 people, with some falling victim to robbers and others killed by fellow workers. Another 221 died from self-inflicted violence (U.S. Department of Labor, 2003). Although men predominate in hazardous occupations such as mining and farming, women hold most clerical and other service jobs dealing with the public. When violent people enter a business, the first people they see are women. For this reason, homicide trails only auto accidents as the leading cause of job-related death for women workers.

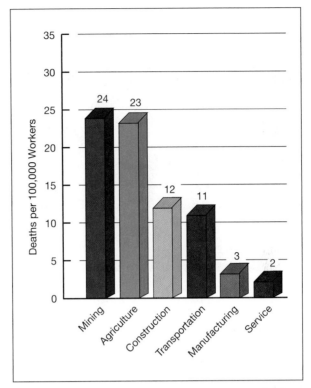

FIGURE 12–3 Workplace Deaths by Type of Job, 2002

Of all categories of work, mining and agriculture have the highest rates of on-the-job fatalities.

Source: U.S. Bureau of Labor Statistics (2003).

Workplace Alienation

Especially in the secondary labor market, workers have little control over what they do and how they do it. Therefore, a workplace problem for many workers is powerlessness.

Alienation: Marx's View More than a hundred years ago, Karl Marx (1818–1883) characterized this problem as **alienation,** *the experience of isolation and misery resulting from powerlessness in the workplace.* Marx saw the problem of alienation stemming not from work itself but from work in a capitalist economic system. He believed that work is a natural human act, an activity that should meet the needs of workers and develop their creative potential.

To illustrate the problem of worker alienation, consider the job of making a coat. Traditionally, coats were made by highly skilled people who were responsible for the entire production of the garment, could sell the final product, and could keep whatever profit was earned. Under the capitalist system, however, coat making falls under the control of mill

A long-established workplace trend is the increasing use of automation. This trend leaves fewer and fewer human workers involved in the production process. What are the good consequences of this pattern? What about the bad consequences?

owners, who pay wages for various tasks; some workers spin wool into yarn, others weave the yarn into cloth, still others cut different pieces of cloth, which they pass along to be assembled into a coat. Notice that under this system work becomes a series of simple, repetitive tasks that require little skill. Furthermore, the coat is sold by the mill owner, who keeps whatever profit it brings. Obviously, then, workers have no say in the production process and can take little pride in the finished product.

Because they have few skills, workers are easily replaced and have little job security. As a result, they end up competing with one another for work. In the end, Marx concluded, capitalism alienates workers from their jobs, from the products they make, from each other, and from their human potential. No wonder, Marx observed, that workers in a capitalist economy find so little satisfaction in their jobs and look for pleasure only in their leisure time. The Personal Stories box takes a closer look at the experience of Marxist alienation.

Alienation: Weber's View Max Weber (1864–1920) agreed with Marx that alienation is widespread in the modern workplace, but he described this concept a bit differently. To Weber, **alienation** is *the depersonalization of the workplace, and of society in general, caused by modern society's rational focus on efficiency.* For Weber, then, the cause of alienation is not capitalism as it was

for Marx, but the rationality—the impersonal focus on efficiency—that is a trait of modern social life.

Weber understood the Industrial Revolution as the **rationalization of society,** *the historical change from tradition to rationality and efficiency as the typical way people think about the world.* In the Middle Ages, tradition guided people's lives, so that the "right" way to do something was simply the way it had been done in the past. Such an emphasis on tradition made for strong families and tightly knit communities but not for efficient production.

In the modern world, by contrast, rationality leads people to approach a goal by weighing the consequences of different courses of action. Doing this, they decide what works best with little regard for what people did long ago. In this way, efficiency becomes the most important aspect of the workplace, but often at the cost of the more human side of our lives. Bank tellers, like Janice Moran in the Personal Stories box, are instructed simply to process transactions without taking time to get to know the people they serve. For their part, customers want to get the job done and move on. The result of such rationality may well be higher productivity; however, Weber feared that such work strips us of our basic humanity.

McDonaldization and "McJobs"

Marx and Weber agreed that much of the work people do in today's society is unsatisfying. Marx defined the problem as exploitation of workers by capitalist owners of production. However, Weber claimed that the problem is modern rationality, which makes production highly efficient at the expense of the worker's humanity. Both points of view help us to understand the spread of the low-paying yet productive workplace system typical of McDonald's fast-food restaurants.

According to George Ritzer (1993, 1998), **McDonaldization** is *defining work in terms of four principles:*

- **Efficiency.** McDonald's tries to serve food quickly and easily.
- **Predictability.** McDonald's prepares all food using set formulas.
- **Uniformity.** McDonald's serves meals that are exactly the same in all of its restaurants.
- **Automation.** By automating all tasks, McDonald's is able to precisely control the production process, minimizing human decision making.

Ritzer points out that that these principles are used not only by fast-food companies; they guide

Personal Stories   "You Can't Take Pride in Your Job Anymore"

IF YOU WERE TO TRAVEL ACROSS THE COUNTRY asking people about their work, the results might surprise you. Many people have a lot to say, and much of it is not good.

Take the case of Mark Grannis, a thirty-seven-year-old steel worker. Grannis describes the experience of workplace alienation in these words:

> There aren't many like me left. I work—I mean *really* work. I am a laborer. A steel puller. All day long, I pick up steel, move it from here to there, there to here. You know how much I move in a day? Maybe forty or fifty thousand pounds. Real work. I am one of the last to do this kind of thing.
>
> The pay is not that bad. So what's my biggest complaint? You can't take pride in your job. It used to be that a man could point to a house he'd built with his own hands. Me? I move steel, load it on a truck going who knows where? I never see what other guys build with that steel. Just once I would like to see a building or something made with the steel I moved. Somebody should put a plaque on the side of all the big skyscrapers in Chicago and Los Angeles with the names of all the people whose sweat made the building in the first place—every electrician, every engineer, every stone cutter, every plumber, every guy like me. That way a worker could say to his kids, "See, that's me, I helped build this building." Everyone should have something to point to. Otherwise you work all day and no one ever knows.

Janice Moran is a twenty-eight-year-old bank teller, a job she has had for eight years. Like Mark Grannis, she finds little satisfaction in her work.

> My job? I'm a teller in the local bank. What do I do? Well, people walk up to my window, and I have to say, "Good morning, may I help you?" Then I transact their business: I take money from them and put it into their account, or I give them money out of their account. Take it out, put it in. Put it in, take it out. It's pretty simple, really, as long as you make sure the right amount goes to the right

place. Then I have to say "Thank you. Have a nice day," or something like that. That's what my work is. I think they call it a service job.

> The bank has a time clock, and every day you punch in and punch out. I have to be there at 8:45. If I am even a few minutes late, the supervisor yells and screams about it. After punching in, I go to my vault, take out my cash, set up my booth, get my stamps and ink pad set up, and turn on my computer. Then I talk to the other tellers for a few minutes until the bank opens at nine. I get to talk to people on my breaks and at lunch—that's the best part of my job.

> I would really like to be able to strike up a conversation with customers, you know, to make my job more interesting. But don't let the supervisor find out—he says my job is to get people in and out of the bank as quickly as possible. The bank tracks our work on their computers. The people downtown know who's the fastest and who is slow. The know if you make a mistake. If you're too slow or you screw up, they'll fire you. It's as simple as that.

ISSUES AND EXERCISES

1. In what ways are these two workers powerless over their jobs? What changes to the workplace would give them more power and satisfaction?

2. Why is Mark Grannis so concerned with seeing the buildings that are made using the steel he moves? Can you offer a similar personal experience based on your own work?

3. Based on these two accounts, list several differences and several similarities between older industrial work and newer service work. On balance, do you think the two types of jobs are more different or more alike? Why?

Source: Written by the author, inspired by characters found in Terkel (1974).

---

people's work throughout the low-skill service sector of the U.S. economy. The result is that work has become "McJobs," a series of simple tasks (often involving pushing buttons on a computer or other machine) that the worker repeats over

and over. Not surprisingly, workers find little satisfaction in such jobs, which are marked by high rates of worker turnover.

McDonald's is a highly successful multinational corporation serving meals to hundreds of millions of people around the world. Furthermore, McDonald's (and similar companies) offer entry-level work experience to countless people. Indeed, Ritzer estimates, one of every fifteen U.S. workers first worked at McDonald's, and one of every eight U.S. adults has worked at McDonald's at some time. But McJobs do not teach employees to think, nor do they encourage creativity and imagination. On the contrary, such jobs almost turn workers into robots for eight hours a day.

The Temping of the Workplace

After World War II, the U.S. economy was booming. Factories in Europe and Japan had been devastated by the war, and many people in these countries had lost their homes and all of their possessions. The United States was one of the few countries that could supply the goods demanded by people in these war-torn nations. In the strong postwar economy, employers and employees alike assumed that hard-working people could count on having a job for life.

Today, as the story of software engineer Stan Marton in the chapter opening illustrates, this rule no longer applies. The deindustrialization of the United States—the closing of factories and, more recently, the loss of white-collar jobs to foreign companies—means that more and more workers have temporary jobs. As temps, workers typically earn less money, have less say about their work, and have little certainty that they will be working in the future.

Every day, temp agencies such as Manpower and Kelly Services send 3 million people to work in temporary jobs. If we add in all part-timers and people contracted from outside agencies, 30 percent of the U.S. labor force works without at least some of the benefits other workers count on, including retirement plans, sick leave, health insurance, and, especially, job security.

Where can temps be found? Almost everywhere. Even universities use adjunct faculty—who work year to year or even semester to semester—to fill about one-third of all teaching positions (Will, 1999). Although all categories of the population are included in the ranks of temporary workers, women and other minorities are most likely to have such work, and they are over represented in the least desirable jobs (Hudson, 1999).

Some workers are glad to move from job to job. They may be looking for short-term employment–say, over the summer while they are out of school or to help with unexpected expenses. Others may be seeking experience, trying out a line of work, and still others do not want the commitment of a permanent position. But overall the use of temporary

workers provides the greatest benefits to employers. By relying on temps, employers save the costs of training, health and retirement benefits, sick leave, and vacation time (Hudson, 1999).

Unemployment

If many people have little security at work, others have no work at all. Officially, the unemployment rate in 2004 stood just below 6 percent (about 9 million people), rising during the recent economic recession. But the real unemployment rate is higher. To be counted among the ranks of the unemployed, a person must register with an unemployment office and actively seek work. Yet many people who are looking for jobs never register. Others become *discouraged workers*, who initially look for work but give up without finding a job, so that they are dropped from the official unemployment statistics.

Read a report on employment among African American men at
http://www.brookings.edu/dybdocroot/es/urban/
publications/offnerexsum.htm

Reasons for Unemployment   Some unemployment occurs in every society because people new to the labor force are looking for jobs and others are between jobs as they move from one position to another. This is why some analysts consider a 4 or 5 percent unemployment rate to be normal and describe this situation as "full employment."

Others claim that a capitalist economy benefits from a reserve labor pool of unemployed people. How? Having too few jobs for everyone ensures that there is always someone willing to do even the least desirable work. A reserve labor pool also increases the chance that there is someone out there willing to do a job for less money; in this way, unemployment pushes wage levels down.

When the economy has a downturn, as in the last few years, many more people are laid off. Some out-of-work people are eligible for unemployment benefits; others are forced to go on welfare. Frances Fox Piven and Richard Cloward (1971) argue that when the economy is weak, the government expands welfare assistance to keep people from rising up against the system. On the other hand, when the economy is strong and demand for workers is high, the government cuts welfare programs to push more people into the labor force. Support for the Piven and Cloward theory is found by looking back at the 1990s: Government reacted to a strong economy in 1996 by making cuts in welfare programs that are detailed in Chapter 2 ("Poverty and Wealth").

Unemployment can be a very challenging experience. As noted at the beginning of this chapter, work is important not only as a source of income but also as a basic element of social identity and self-esteem. To be out of work robs people of all these things. In addition, in the individualistic and competitive culture of the United States, an out-of-work person often carries the stigma of personal failure, called the "hidden injury" of unemployment.

Who Is at Risk for Unemployment? In the U.S. population, some categories of people are at higher risk of unemployment than others. Figure 12–4 shows that, in 2002, the unemployment rates were about the same for women and men. Race and ethnicity are important: The unemployment rates for African Americans (10.2 percent) and Hispanic Americans (7.5 percent) were well above the rate for non-Hispanic whites (5.1 percent). Education also plays an important part for people in all racial and ethnic categories: High school dropouts had an unemployment rate three times higher than that of college graduates (U.S. Department of Labor, 2003).

Race, Ethnicity, and Gender

In earlier chapters (Chapter 3, "Racial and Ethnic Inequality" and Chapter 4, "Gender Inequality"), we explained that racial and ethnic minorities and women were legally barred from most good jobs throughout most of U.S. history. Indeed, it was only in the 1950s and 1960s that social movements opened the way for fuller participation for all categories of people in the labor force.

However, even though many formal barriers have fallen, women and other minorities have only recently been well represented in many better jobs. Moreover, as the last ones hired, they are often the first fired; that is, with the least seniority women and other minorities are at higher risk for layoffs than white men, who, on average, have been in the labor force longer. In addition, we noted earlier that women and minorities are more likely to work as temps or part-timers and in low-skill "McJobs."

Women do have one advantage over men, however: Women are less likely to work in dangerous occupations. This means that women are less likely than men to die on the job. Racial and ethnic minorities also have one advantage over white workers: Minorities are more likely to be represented by a union (U.S. Bureau of Labor Statistics, 2003). The reason for this is the fact that minorities are more likely to work in jobs where unionization is more common.

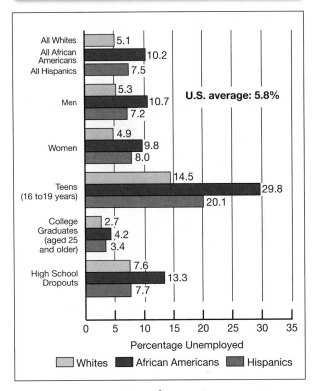

DIMENSIONS OF DIFFERENCE

FIGURE 12–4 Unemployment Rates for Various Categories of the U.S. Population

Many factors affect the unemployment rate; among all categories of people, however, unemployment affects African Americans most, followed by Hispanic Americans, and (non-Hispanic) white people.

Source: U.S. Department of Labor (2003).

Institutional Discrimination Although lower than it was in the past, the share of women and other minorities in the secondary labor market remains high. Some analysts see this pattern as evidence of *institutional discrimination*, discussed in Chapter 3 ("Racial and Ethnic Inequality") and Chapter 4 ("Gender Inequality"). Institutional discrimination is bias built into the operation of the economy, education, and other social institutions.

To see how institutional discrimination places certain categories of the U.S. population at a disadvantage, consider the fact that through most of the twentieth century, women were underrepresented in college and university campuses—as administrators, faculty, and, most importantly, students. Today, most colleges and universities select presidents with

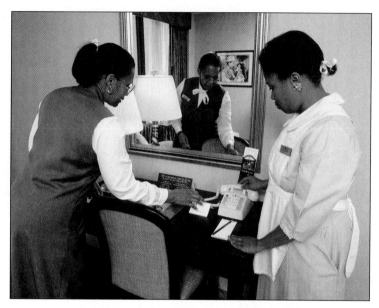

In most workplace settings across the United States, minorities are disproportionately found in the jobs that provide the lowest pay and prestige. Based on your own observations in hospitals, hotels, or office buildings, do you think this pattern holds?

distinguished records of scholarly publications and academic leadership. Given women's disadvantage in higher education for so long, it is any wonder that 79 percent of college and university presidents are men? Much the same can be said about people of color, who today account for only 13 percent of college and university presidents (American Council on Education, 2002). In short, the fact that some categories of the U.S. population are less likely to rise to the highest positions in the workplace reflects long-term patterns of institutional discrimination.

The Glass Ceiling   In the past, women and other minorities were often banned outright from some work settings. Today, such blatant discrimination is rare because it is against the law. But more subtle forms of discrimination persist.

For example, most employers have ideas about what kind of person is most suitable for various types of work. When hiring a secretary, a company almost always selects a woman. When hiring an executive, by contrast, a company almost most always hires a white person, who is usually male. Of course, few universities, corporations, or other organizations would admit to blatant prejudice and discrimination against women or other minorities. Even so, most

workplaces have a *glass ceiling*, as noted in Chapter 4 ("Gender Inequality"); this refers to barriers—often invisible—that prevent women and other minorities from moving upward in the workplace (Benokraitis & Feagin, 1995).

Workplace Segregation

Consider the following jobs, which people in the United States rank at the bottom of the occupational ladder: shoe shiner, janitor, bellhop, and home health aide. What race and ethnicity do you imagine most people who perform these jobs are? Or consider positions near the very top rung of the job ladder: physician, lawyer, judge, architect, and university professor. What color do you think most people who hold these jobs are? Are most of these people women or men? (NORC, 2003)

It is easy to link gender and race to various occupations because the workplace is, indeed, highly segregated. Minorities are concentrated in the least desirable jobs, and white men predominate in the most desirable jobs. Figure 12–5 shows the racial and ethnic composition of various occupations in the United States. These data show that African Americans and Hispanic Americans are overrepresented in lower-paying jobs (such as private child care) and underrepresented in higher-paying jobs (such as physicians and dentists). Such differences in work are a major reason for disparities in income between the different racial and ethnic categories of the U.S. population. Among full-time workers in 2001, median income for whites ($43,194 for men and $31,794 for women) was well above that for African Americans ($31,921 and $27,297) and Hispanic Americans ($25,271 and $21,973) (U.S. Census Bureau, 2002).

Compared with African Americans and Hispanic Americans, women make out somewhat better in the U.S. labor market, with better representation in many more desirable jobs. This is because women come from all social classes, whereas minorities are overrepresented among the poor and among families just one generation removed from being poor.

However, men dominate in leadership positions (such as business executives, clergy, and judges), whereas women dominate in low-status positions in the business world (such as secretaries and other office workers) and in caring for the young (child care and teaching). Other notable examples involve health care: 81 percent of dentists are men, whereas 98 percent of dental hygienists are women; 69 percent of physicians are men, whereas 93 percent of nurses are

DIMENSIONS OF DIFFERENCE

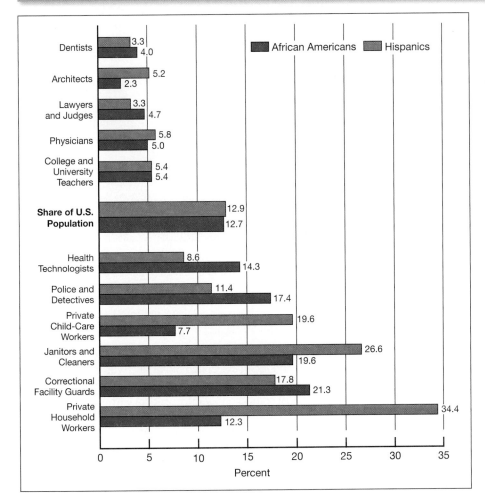

FIGURE 12–5

Percentage of Various U.S. Occupations Held by African Americans and by Hispanics, 2002

Minorities, including Hispanic Americans and African Americans, are underrepresented in jobs that provide high income and prestige and overrepresented in jobs that offer lower income and prestige.

Source: U.S. Department of Labor (2003).

women. Again, such differences in work result in differences in income. Among full-time workers in 2002, median income for men was $39,429, compared with $30,203 (77 percent as much) for women (U.S. Census Bureau, 2003).

Finally, women are less likely than men to be in the paid labor force in any position at all. Women make up about 51 percent of the U.S. adult population but only 42 percent of the full-time labor force (47 percent if we count part-timers) (U.S. Department of Labor, 2003).

Union Decline

Faced with many problems in the workplace, can workers improve their situation? One of the most effective strategies for working people has been to join together to form **labor unions,** *worker organizations*

that seek to improve wages and working conditions through various strategies, including negotiations and strikes.

Labor unions are a fairly recent development in the United States. As already noted, in the early twentieth century, workers in the new industrial economy labored for long hours under dangerous conditions for very low wages, with few benefits and almost no job security. After all, there was a steady stream of immigrants entering the United States who were eager to work. Factory owners had little reason to offer workers more, and they readily replaced anyone who did not play by the company's rules. Under the law, company officials also could fire workers who tried to organize a union and, if workers did go out on strike, they could ask a court to force striking workers back to the job. In short, in the early twentieth century, employers held all the high cards. Even so, a number of people devoted

A DEFINING MOMENT

Eugene Debs: Standing Up for the Union

A CENTURY AGO, AT THE HEIGHT of the Industrial Revolution, working conditions in the United States were unimaginable to most people today. People worked ten, twelve, or more hours per day, usually six days a week, earning 15 to 20 cents an hour. Work was dangerous; with many people eager to take any available job, employers gave little thought to worker safety.

Eugene Debs (1855–1926) was born into this world. Raised in Indiana, Debs attended school until age fourteen, when he went to work for the railroad as a painter. The longer Debs worked, the more he saw that workers were barely able to survive. But how could he bring about change? The company had the power, and there were no laws protecting workers. Standing alone, Debs realized, workers had no voice. But standing together, they could meet the bosses head on.

And so it was that Debs took a new job, working for the Brotherhood of Locomotive Firemen, an early union. By the late 1880s, Debs had become the editor of the union's national magazine; he also played a part in the creation of a number of other railroad unions. He was a skillful writer and a powerful speaker; coupled with his passion for building the union, these skills soon earned Debs a national reputation.

But opposition to unions was strong, and as an agent of change Debs lived a life of controversy. He led strikes against the railroad companies and spent years in jail. The controversy grew more intense in the final decades of

Eugene Debs was a dynamic speaker who stirred the workers of his time to organize in pursuit of better lives.

his life, when Debs spoke openly about the need for radical change in the United States and was a five-time presidential candidate representing the Socialist party (he ran his last campaign for the presidency from inside the federal prison in Atlanta, Georgia). Debs did not succeed in bringing about socialism. But he did change U.S. society; as a result of his efforts, people accepted the idea that workers were entitled to a living wage, safe working conditions, and, above all, the right to organize into unions. Today, Debs's home in Terre Haute, Indiana, is a museum documenting the struggle of early industrial workers and a state and federal landmark.

---

their lives to promoting unions as a way to improve the lives of working people. The Defining Moment box explains how Eugene Debs advanced the cause of unions in the United States.

Learn more about labor pioneer Eugene Debs at **http://www.eugenevdebs.com**

By the time of the Great Depression in the 1930s, workers' organizations were making gains. The Great Depression put one-fourth of the labor force out of work, which made the government take notice of the plight of working people. Congress passed several new laws (the Railway Labor Act, the Norris–La Guardia Act, and National Labor Relations Act) that guaranteed the right of workers to organize and form labor unions.

Millions of working people responded to the union call and found greater strength in numbers. Throughout the 1930s, union membership increased sharply. By 1950, unions claimed one-third of the entire U.S. nonfarm labor force. Union membership peaked in the 1970s at some 25 million people.

But this strength was not to last. One reason was falling support for unions at the highest level of government. In 1981, air traffic controllers, who are federal employees, went on strike and President Ronald Reagan ordered them back to work. When they refused, President Reagan fired them all and replaced them. This one incident was a major symbolic defeat for labor.

The larger problem facing labor unions was structural change in the U.S. economy. As noted earlier in this chapter, the number of factory jobs—the type of work that is heavily unionized—has declined since 1950. Since then, most new jobs have been in the service sector and are not likely to be unionized. Therefore, in 2003 just 13 percent of nonfarm workers were members of labor unions—a dramatic drop from 33 percent in 1950. Another way to gauge the declining strength of the labor movement is the falling number of strikes in the United States in recent decades, as shown in Figure 12–6.

In the last few years, however, unions have been rallying. Workers in the public sector of the economy—government employees—are now highly unionized. In addition, because many of today's service jobs provide low pay and few benefits (just as most industrial jobs did a century ago), more workers in the service sector are looking to unions as a means to increase their bargaining power and improve working conditions and rewards (Goldfield, 2000; Greenhouse, 2000; U.S. Census Bureau, 2002).

NEW INFORMATION TECHNOLOGY: THE BRAVE NEW WORKPLACE

Just as the Industrial Revolution brought sweeping changes to the workplace a century ago, the Information Revolution is transforming the workplace today. As Global Map 12–1 on page 312 shows, the United States and other high-income nations use most of the world's personal computers.

Perhaps the biggest difference is the type of skills the workplace demands. A century ago, workers had to develop the industrial skills needed for making *things*; today, workers in the postindustrial economy must develop literacy skills needed to create and manipulate *symbols* (words, ideas, music, and computer code): Of course, the Information Revolution has affected some parts of the United States more than others. National Map 12–1 on page 313 shows the availability of Internet service across the country.

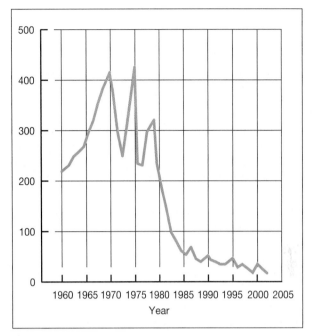

FIGURE 12–6 **Number of Labor Strikes in the United States, 1960–2002**

One indication of the declining power of unions in the U.S. workplace is the small number of labor strikes in recent decades.

Source: U.S. Bureau of Labor Statistics (2003).

In the workplace, the Information Revolution is changing not only the character of work but also how and where we do it. As the following sections explain, new information technology is changing the location of work, providing employees with more options and giving companies new ways to monitor their employees. As we shall see, although many see these changes as positive, others point out that tomorrow's workers will face new challenges every bit as serious as those faced by workers a century ago (Zuboff, 1982; Rule & Brantley, 1992; Vallas & Beck, 1996; Gottlieb, Kelloway, & Barham, 1998).

Telecommuting

Before the Industrial Revolution, most people worked in or near their homes. The development of industrial machinery changed this pattern, so that workers left home in the morning and traveled to factories. In this way, the Industrial Revolution *centralized* work. Today, however, the trend is in the opposite direction. With computers, fax machines, and other information technology at hand, offices can be located just about anywhere. In addition, this new technology has made it

A WORLD OF DIFFERENCES

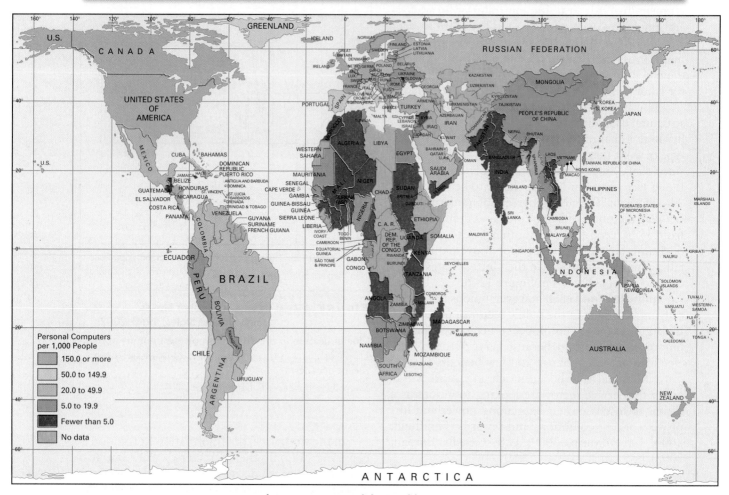

GLOBAL MAP 12-1   Personal Computers around the World

Personal computers are becoming common in high-income countries such as the United States, the nations of Western Europe, Japan, and Australia. By contrast, personal computers are rare in the world's poorest countries, which are in Africa and Asia. What does this suggest about who benefits most from the new information economy?

Source: The World Bank (2000).

possible for more people to work from home, in some cases not going to the office at all.

Telecommuting refers to *linking employees to the office using information technology, including telephones, fax machines, and e-mail.* Only a small share of the U.S. labor force works exclusively in the home, but as many as one in three workers spends at least some work time at home each week. Telecommuting has some obvious benefits, such as the time workers save not having to commute to and from the office. Telecommuting also has special appeal to workers

who want to hold a job but need to care for small children or aging parents. For many people, in short, telecommuting offers the flexibility they need to balance career goals and family obligations.

Telecommuting solves some problems, but it creates others. This pattern blurs the line between home and work, so that the pressures of work—which used to stay in the office—now pervade the home. In addition, workers who stay at home risk becoming isolated, left out of key decisions, and overlooked for promotion. In addition, because

A NATION OF DIVERSITY

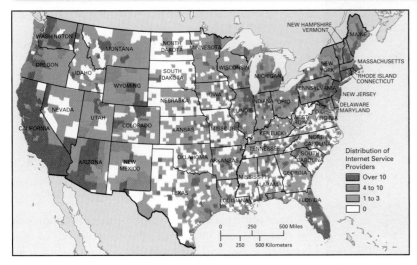

Source: *Time*, March 22, 1999. Copyright © 1999, *Time*, Inc. Reprinted by permission.

NATIONAL MAP 12–1
Internet Access across the United States

In 2000, about half of U.S. households had at least one personal computer and this share is rising each year. Even so, access to the Internet is not equally distributed across the country. In general, Internet service is best in densely populated counties, where a provider's market is larger and, on average, people have higher incomes. People living in poor, rural counties across the South and through the mid-section of the country are not yet able to take part in the new information economy (or must use toll calls to connect). What would you guess is the average age of the population in these areas?

telecommuting is more popular with women (who have greater family responsibilities), this pattern has the potential to perpetuate gender inequality in the workplace. In short, telecommuting gives working people the opportunity to care for their families, possibly at the cost of career advancement (Macionis, 2001).

Workplace Isolation

Even people who travel to the office the old-fashioned way find that the Information Revolution is changing life in the workplace. By connecting people in information networks, computer technology has greatly reduced the need for face-to-face interaction. Many workers connect using e-mail, which has greatly reduced the need for meetings and even for telephone calls. The result, for many workers, is a growing problem of workplace isolation.

A quick look at today's office setting is enough to see the pattern: Many of today's office employees perform most of their work in small cubicles facing computer screens, having little contact with anyone else. Much the same is true at the corner gas station: The days when a service station attendant pumped your gas, checked the oil, and washed the windshield while chatting about the weather are gone. Now, a motorist inserts a credit card into a computer terminal at the pump, fills the car, and rarely sees the attendant, who sits inside to wait on those who come in to buy

coffee or cigarettes. Similarly, today's bank officials receive loan applications online, use computer programs to review the information and make a decision, and approve or reject customers they may never meet.

Controlling Employees

It is easy to see that computer technology makes processing information easier than ever. But computer technology also gives employers new tools that they can use to keep an eye on employee behavior and productivity. For example, telemarketing companies use computers to monitor the work of their employees who sell products and services over the phone. Especially after the creation of the "Do Not Call" list in 2003, these companies have tried to control their costs by tracking how many calls their workers make, how long each call lasts, and the outcome of every call. In many cases, high-tech equipment records the actual conversation "for quality assurance purposes," which means the company is able to listen in on each employee. Never before have organizations had more ability to control the working lives of their employees.

"Deskilling" Workers

When it comes to monitoring workers, computer technology makes managers' jobs easier. But in other respects information technology threatens managers'

Computer technology makes workers more efficient, but it also has the effect of reducing the skill level needed to do many jobs. Checkout workers in discount stores and supermarkets are an illustration of this: With scanners, it is no longer necessary to identify a product and a price; the worker simply scans a barcode on the product and the computer does the rest. Would you expect that technology like this will someday eliminate the need for checkout workers entirely?

job security. How? Many of the decisions once made by experienced managers are now made automatically by computers programmed to take account of every important consideration. Which car models should the assembly line build? Simply input data on current sales, projected interest rates, and profitability and let the computer decide. When should a movie theater chain replenish supplies of popcorn and candy? Computers monitor sales and automatically process orders for additional products. Given the proper input, computers are able to make more and more decisions without human assistance, which has the effect of *deskilling* managers. The final result is a decline in job security even for those in the primary labor market.

Lower-level employees have long been aware that companies can use new technology to make them obsolete. Robots replaced humans in many jobs on auto assembly lines decades ago. What is new is the trend toward using new information technology to replace the work of managers and executives.

THEORETICAL ANALYSIS: UNDERSTANDING WORK-RELATED PROBLEMS

Each of sociology's major theoretical approaches offers insights into work-related problems. Each approach highlights different facts and points to different conclusions.

Structural-Functional Analysis: Finding a New Equilibrium

A basic principle of the structural-functional approach is that all social institutions are interrelated, so that change in one institution leads to adjustments in all the others. In this chapter (and Chapter 11), we have noted numerous changes in the economy and the workforce, many of which have caused hardship. But the structural-functional approach suggests that disruption of past economic patterns eventually brings a new social order. Therefore, although the decline of industry has eliminated millions of factory jobs, other institutions—especially education—will respond by preparing workers for other types of work.

The structural-functional approach helps us understand the ability of technological change to reshape the economy, as the Industrial Revolution did centuries ago and the Information Revolution is doing today. The new technology that signals progress and greater profits to some threatens the jobs of others. The various social institutions will respond to these short-term problems and help people to redirect their lives. In the longer term, society is likely to become more productive, making everyone better off.

Critical evaluation.   The structural-functional paradigm takes an optimistic view of society and its ability to rebound from the disruptions caused by structural changes in the workplace. It downplays the human suffering caused by characterizing these disruptions as temporary and likely to strengthen society in the long run.

In addition, by treating society as a broad system, this macro-level approach provides little understanding about how real people who face workplace problems feel about their jobs and themselves. To better understand how workplace issues are experienced by individuals, we turn to the symbolic-interaction approach.

Symbolic-Interaction Analysis: The Meaning of Work

The symbolic-interaction approach highlights the ways in which people construct the reality they experience. In the case of work, this paradigm leads us to focus on the meaning people attach to the jobs they hold and the work they perform. Many people, especially professionals and others in the primary labor market, generally look forward to going to work every day and are motivated to advance, a desire that lies at the heart of the term *career*. In short, people attach positive meaning to work that, in turn, reflects well on them. Indeed, even after retiring from active work, people who have had careers may still cling to the positive identity their work has provided, which helps explain why, for example, those who retire from teaching at universities enjoy their new status as professor *emeritus* (Latin, meaning "fully earned").

At the same time, people doing unskilled, repetitive jobs—whether in factories or office buildings—usually find little positive meaning in their work. These people are likely to go to work each day only because they have no choice, and they may watch the clock as the day goes on, looking forward to quitting time when they can do something else. Such work rarely provides a chance for advancement and positive identity. People with secondary labor market jobs talk little about their work to others, and the value of their job lies only in the paycheck it provides.

Critical evaluation. Symbolic interaction theory highlights the different meanings people attach to their work, helping us to better understand why some people look forward to going to work while others only look forward to "punching out."

Although the meanings people attach to work vary with the individual, they are not random. Rather, the reality of work has much to do with people's social standing, a fact the symbolic-interaction approach does not address. The U.S. economy provides advantages to some categories of people that it denies to others, which brings us to the social-conflict approach.

Social-Conflict Analysis: Work and Inequality

The distinguishing feature of the social-conflict approach is its emphasis on social inequality. In the case of work, this approach highlights how the experience of earning a living is very different for advantaged and disadvantaged categories of people.

Following the lead of Karl Marx, the operation of a capitalist economy serves to concentrate wealth and power in the hands of a small elite. From this point of view, a small share of the labor force does not actually work; they *own* everything. This capitalist elite benefits from the economic system for the simple reason that they control it. By contrast, the majority of workers suffer from low wages and have little control over the production process. For most people, therefore, work is far from satisfying and produces only alienation—from the act of working, from the products of work, from each other, and from our human potential.

As noted earlier, Max Weber took a different tack, arguing that capitalism was only one dimension of the larger rationality that pervades modern society. This matter-of-fact worldview that stresses efficiency at the expense of human individuality and dignity has transformed the workplace into a highly regulated setting in which people have come to resemble machines. Such observations led Weber to the same conclusion as Marx: To most people, work is alienating rather than satisfying.

Both Marx and Weber agreed that such workplace problems result not from temporary disruptions in the economy (as structural-functional analysis maintains) but from business as usual. The trend over past decades has been a decline in jobs in the primary labor market and an increase in jobs in the secondary market. Ever-present concerns for maximizing profit and efficiency encourage employers to exert rigid control over workers and, when possible, to replace them with machines. It is no surprise, then, that an ever-increasing number of workers are forced to settle for "McJobs" and worry at the same time whether in the future they will have any work at all.

Critical evaluation. The social-conflict approach helps us to see how the operation of the economy and major economic changes (such as the Information Revolution) do not affect all members of society equally. A limitation of this approach, however, is that it downplays the real gains in living standards realized by average people over the course of the twentieth century. In 2000, rank-and-file workers earned about five times as much as they did back in 1900 (controlling for inflation). This means that, today, the typical U.S. family owns a house with air conditioning, cable television, and at least one automobile parked in a garage. Inequality does persist, but in an absolute sense, just about everyone lives much better than people did in the past.

POLITICS AND THE WORKPLACE: CONSTRUCTING PROBLEMS AND DEFINING SOLUTIONS

Theory provides helpful ways to think about work, but the position anyone takes on exactly what the problems are and what is the best way to go about improving them is largely a matter of values and politics. Here, we apply the conservative, liberal, and radical perspectives to topics involving work and the workplace.

Conservatives: Look to the Market

As noted in Chapter 11 ("The Economy and Politics"), conservatives favor limited government regulation of the economy, believing that free competition is best for society. The conservative claim is that free-market economics—with minimal regulation from government—generates the greatest good for the greatest number of people.

Like everyone else, conservatives recognize that economic downturns occur, and they also agree that the technological change (including the Industrial and Information Revolutions) causes problems for some people as new jobs are created and old jobs disappear. But from this point of view, such dislocations are temporary problems because market forces will gradually redirect people's efforts from old to new types of work. When factories close, for example, workers are temporarily thrown out of work, but this makes them available for retraining. Eventually, they will find work in newer, more technologically advanced companies. In the end, as the economy grows stronger, everyone in the society benefits.

Another important conservative principle is individual responsibility. From this point of view, every able-bodied person should work, even at the lowest paying jobs if that is all that is available. In general, conservatives see that the market offers lots of opportunity so that it is up to individuals to prepare themselves to take advantage of it. For workers with limited skills, this means starting out at an entry-level job (perhaps even at McDonald's) with the expectation that, over time, ability and hard work will lead to advancement. Government may be able to help people in the short term, providing training and locating new employment, but people should never expect government to do for them what they should do for themselves.

Such thinking helps explain conservative support for the 1996 welfare reforms, discussed in Chapter 2 ("Poverty and Wealth"), which moved millions of people capable of working from depending on government handouts to receiving paychecks. Similarly, most conservatives oppose raising the legal minimum wage, in part because it is a form of government regulation but also because artificially setting wages above what some workers are really worth ends up increasing unemployment. In short, conservatives see the free market not as a problem but as a solution.

Liberals: Look to Government

Liberals also support a market-based economy as highly productive, but they believe that the market creates a number of workplace problems. Therefore, liberals believe that there is also a need for government regulation to protect the interests of everyone.

Liberals claim that without regulation, a market system would leave less powerful people at the mercy of the rich, resulting in problems such as low wages, few benefits, and a host of workplace dangers. After all, liberals continue, these problems were epidemic in the United States before the 1930s, when government took a larger hand in regulating the economy.

There is an old saying that the market provides "rough justice," meaning that a free market allocates greater rewards to those who work harder and especially to those with rare talents and highly creative minds. But liberals look to the government to smooth the rough edges of such economic justice to ensure that workers are treated fairly. Thus, liberals support a wide range of government policies, including minimum wage laws (most liberals consider the current minimum wage too low), laws protecting people from workplace hazards (so that workers are not harmed by, say, hazardous chemicals), and laws protecting workers' right to join unions (so that they can bargain for higher wages). In short, liberals see an important role for both the marketplace and the government in the operation of an economy that truly serves the interest of all.

It is on the role of government, then, that conservatives and liberals have their sharpest disagreement. In the 2004 presidential campaign, for example, Republican George W. Bush claimed that it is the people rather than government that make the U.S. economy strong. In response, Democrat John Kerry claimed that most people—especially those in need—look to government to ensure their economic well-being, and they support expanded government programs for both education and health care.

Conservatives believe that the capitalist market system benefits everyone by directing investment toward the companies that are most productive. Liberals, by contrast, maintain that, because the market system favors some more than others, government regulation is needed to ensure that everyone is treated fairly and honestly. Radicals claim that the market system can only serve the rich and the powerful; as they see it, we must devise a more egalitarian economic and political system before the interests of all will be served.

Radicals: Basic Change Is Needed

The farther left people move on the political spectrum, the greater they believe the role of government should be in the operation of the economy. Radicals on the far left, therefore, seek to eliminate private enterprise by placing the entire economic system under the control of government.

As radicals see it, the free market causes many serious problems. How? For one thing, because it places the economy in private hands—so that individuals own factories and other businesses as their personal property—the purpose of the economy will always be owner profits. Such an economy will pay the lowest possible wages and have little concern for worker well-being or basic safety in the workplace. Thus, low wages, workplace hazards, and unemployment are predictable results of the operation of a privately owned, capitalist economy.

Given this view of the market, radicals reject conservative claims that the market provides "the greatest good for the greatest number," and do not think that liberals' demand for government regulation of the market will provide a solution. Radicals call for the replacement of the capitalist economy with a political and economic system that makes people rather than profits its highest priority.

How will such a change occur? Karl Marx claimed that, in their misery, working people would join together in opposition to the capitalists who oppress them and eventually overthrow the capitalist system itself. In short, Marx believed that because

capitalism fails to meet the needs of the majority of people, it sows the seeds of its own destruction. Only when workers own and direct the workplace will they derive the rewards they should from a day's labor. The Left to Right table outlines the three political perspectives on work and the workplace.

GOING ON FROM HERE

In the early twentieth century, the black smoke that streamed from factory chimneys in the large cities of the Northeast and Midwest signaled that the United States was becoming the world's most economically powerful nation. Indeed, the captains of this new industrial empire lived in mansions that rivaled the great castles of European monarchs.

But all was not well with the majority of working people. Wages were low, thousands of workers were injured and killed in factories and mines each year, and there was no opportunity for workers to organize to better their working conditions.

In the 1930s, as the Great Depression forced factories to close and farmers unable to pay their mortgages lost their land, it must have seemed as if the problems of unemployment and poverty could not get any worse. Indeed, driven by such serious suffering, political support for radically changing the capitalist system was on the rise.

Yet with the start of World War II in 1939, the nation's attention turned to international problems. At the same time, the war effort provided a huge

LEFT ⓣⓞ RIGHT

THE POLITICS OF WORK AND THE WORKPLACE

	RADICAL LEFT VIEW	LIBERAL VIEW	CONSERVATIVE VIEW
WHAT IS THE PROBLEM?	The capitalist market system gives rise to a host of related problems, including low wages, workplace hazards, and unemployment. Capitalism fails to meet most people's economic needs by placing profits ahead of people.	The market system is productive but does not ensure the welfare of all. Low wages, unemployment, and discrimination based on gender, race, and ethnicity are all problems in the U.S. workplace.	The market system operates efficiently and is highly productive. Government regulation reduces the productivity of the market. Therefore, government should regulate the economy as little as possible.
WHAT IS THE SOLUTION?	Workers should own and control the means of economic production. Government acting in the interest of the population as a whole should be responsible for economic policy.	While allowing market forces to operate, government agencies must regulate the economy to ensure that workers receive a living wage and that the workplace is safe and free from discrimination.	The greatest number of people will benefit most if market forces are allowed to operate freely. The economy does a good job of regulating itself and moving workers from older industries to newer kinds of work.

Join the debate . . .

1. What do you consider to be the most serious problems involving work in the United States today? What is being done to address these problems?

2. Do you think that, on balance, the state of work in the United States improved over the course of the twentieth century? Why or why not? What new problems do workers face in the twenty-first century?

3. Which of the three political analyses of work and the workplace included here do you find most convincing? Why?

boost to the struggling economy so that with the return to peace in 1945, the United States entered a period of great economic prosperity.

Despite some ups and downs in the economy since then, the overall record has been impressive. The economic productivity of this nation has never been so great, nor have so many ever lived so well. But whereas many have prospered, many others have been left behind. As noted in Chapter 2 ("Poverty and Wealth"), the incomes of those already doing well have increased substantially in recent years, but tens of millions of working families have made little or no gains. Furthermore, millions of jobs—both blue-collar jobs in factories and white-collar jobs in offices—have been lost. Most of the new service jobs being created provide low pay, few benefits, and no union representation. Most families now depend on the incomes of at least two people, and economic insecurity remains widespread in the United States (Sennett, 1998).

In the foreseeable future, it seems highly likely that the United States will continue to rely on a market economy because this system has generated so much new wealth. The challenge will be whether the U.S. political and economic systems can be made to operate so that not just some but all of the population can achieve economic security.

Finally, the problems of want extend far beyond the United States. Indeed, as Chapter 16 ("Population and World Hunger") explains, the plight of a billion people around the world is so desperate that they struggle day to day simply to survive. In the long run, the stability and security of the entire planet—including the United States—may well depend on humanity's ability to provide for the needs of everyone.

CHAPTER SUMMARY

1. Work is a source of not only income but also personal pride and social identity.

2. About 200 years ago, the Industrial Revolution changed the nature of work, moving people from the primary sector jobs (producing raw materials) to secondary sector jobs (turning raw materials into finished products). By 1950, the Information Revolution began moving people once again, this time into service jobs in the tertiary sector of the economy.

3. The process of deindustrialization took place as the United States moved toward a service-based economy. This transformation put many people out of work; many of those whose factory jobs disappeared ended up with service jobs offering lower pay and fewer benefits.

4. Deindustrialization is linked to the rise of a global economy. Many U.S. corporations moved manufacturing plants abroad, where they could pay lower wages; in the process, many U.S. workers lost their jobs. In recent years, white-collar jobs have also moved from the United States to lower-income countries.

5. Work in the primary labor market offers good pay and many benefits, but jobs in the secondary labor market do not. Most of the new jobs created by today's service economy are in the secondary labor market.

6. Dangers to health and well-being exist in the workplace, especially in mining, agriculture, and construction work. Although the rate of U.S. workplace fatalities fell over the last century, 6,000 workers die on the job each year.

7. Alienation is a common workplace experience. Marx linked alienation to the powerlessness of workers in a capitalist economy. Weber linked alienation to modern rationality, which makes the workplace impersonal by emphasizing efficiency above all else.

8. McDonaldization defines work in terms of efficiency, predictability, uniformity, and control of workers through automation. The simplified, repetitive occupations that result can be described as "McJobs," which resemble the low-skill factory jobs common a century ago.

9. Counting temporary workers, contract employees, and part-timers, 30 percent of the U.S. labor force lacks job security and has few benefits, such as employer-sponsored health insurance. Although some workers enjoy the freedom that temp work provides, this pattern benefits employers by reducing what they pay for wages and benefits.

10. Some unemployment is normal as people enter the labor force or change jobs. Yet unemployment is also produced by the economy itself. The official U.S. unemployment rate in 2004 was just below 6 percent of the labor force (about 9 million people).

11. Although a wider range of jobs are open to women and other minorities, minorities remain concentrated in lower-paying work. Institutional prejudice and discrimination generate workplace segregation and limit the advancement of minorities; informal barriers of this kind are called the "glass ceiling."

12. Labor unions gained strength along with the industrial economy in the twentieth century and, by 1950, claimed one-third of all nonfarm workers. However, union membership has fallen since then with deindustrialization and the expansion of service work. Today, just 13 percent of workers are union members.

13. Computers and other new information technology is redefining work in the United States. One effect is an increase in telecommuting as more people work away from the office. But at home or at the office, computer technology can isolate workers and offer employers greater ability to control worker activity. New technology also contributes to the "deskilling" of many jobs, including the work of managers.

14. The structural-functional approach suggests that changes (especially those brought on by new technology) can disrupt established patterns of work, causing problems such as unemployment. But other institutions, such as education, help retrain workers for new kind of jobs, thereby restabilizing society.

15. The symbolic-interaction approach highlights the meaning people attach to work. In general, people in the primary labor market attach positive meaning to their work; their jobs are an important part of their social identity. People in the secondary labor market find less positive meaning in their work and value a job only for the income it provides.

16. The social-conflict approach focuses on how wealth and power shape the workplace. A Marxist analysis argues that because factories and other productive property are privately owned, most people are powerless and find work alienating. Max Weber adds that modern rationality makes efficiency an all-important goal so that the workplace becomes impersonal, with workers coming to resemble machines.

17. Conservatives hold that a free-market economy, with minimal government regulation, produces the greatest good for the greatest number of people. New technology and downturns in the economy cause temporary disruptions, but the market solves these problems over time, in the end creating a stronger economy.

18. Liberals concede that a free-market economy is productive but point out that it does not meet the needs of everyone. Rather, market systems cause problems, including dangerous working conditions, unemployment, and low wages. Therefore, liberals support government regulation of the economy and the workplace to enhance the well-being of all.

19. Radicals see the free-market system as a source of problems. From this point of view, capitalism is concerned only with profits rather than the welfare of people. Mere reform will not solve this problem; the capitalist system must be replaced with a economic system that operates in the interests of all workers.

KEY CONCEPTS

deindustrialization (p. 300) the decline of industrial production that occurred in the United States after about 1950

globalization (p. 300) the expansion of economic activity around the world with little regard for national borders

primary labor market (p. 301) occupations that provide good pay and extensive benefits to workers

secondary labor market (p. 301) jobs that provide low pay and few benefits to workers

alienation (Marx) (p. 303) the experience of isolation and misery resulting from powerlessness in the workplace

alienation (Weber) (p. 304) the depersonalization of the workplace, and of society in general, caused by modern society's rational focus on efficiency

rationalization of society (Weber) (p. 304) the historical change from tradition to rationality and efficiency as the typical way people think about the world

McDonaldization (p. 304) defining work in terms of four principles: efficiency, predictability, uniformity, and automation

labor unions (p. 309) worker organizations that seek to improve wages and working conditions through various strategies, including negotiations and strikes

telecommuting (p. 312) linking employees to the office using information technology, including telephones, fax machines, and e-mail

THINKING CRITICALLY: QUESTIONS AND ISSUES

1. Both Karl Marx and Max Weber were concerned about worker alienation. Can you identify similarities and differences in their theories?

2. What principles underlie the operation of McDonald's restaurants? Can you identify areas of the economy other than the fast-food industry where these principles have transformed work into "McJobs?"

3. What long-standing problems faced by workers in the United States have improved along

with the decline of industrial work and the rise of service jobs? What new problems have been created?

4. How would you assess the likely impact of new information technology on work and the work force in the United States? In what ways is this technology beneficial? In what ways is it likely to be harmful? On balance, does new technology benefit workers, employers, or both? Why?

GETTING INVOLVED: LEARNING ACTIVITIES

1. Identify a factory in your community. Contact the human resources department at your college or university and ask about faculty pay and benefits such as health insurance, retirement pension, vacation time, and sick leave. Compare these with the pay and benefits offered to low-skill service workers, such as those in the campus food service.

2. Using your college catalogue, Web page, or information available from college officials, try to calculate the share of campus faculty who have adjunct or visiting positions. Ask several administrators and several visiting faculty why universities hire so many short-term teachers. How do visitors compare with regular faculty in terms of pay and benefits?

3. Observe the race and gender of faculty, secretarial staff, grounds workers, janitors, and cleaners on your campus. What patterns can you uncover?

4. Do some fieldwork at a local discount store such as Wal-Mart or KMart. Look at various products—electronics, cameras, housewares, and clothing—and note in which countries various products are made. Does your research support the idea that the United States has deindustrialized?

GETTING CONNECTED: USEFUL WEB LINKS

http://www.prenhall.com/macionis
Visit the interactive Companion Website™ that accompanies this text. Begin by clicking on the cover of your book. You will find a chapter-by-chapter study guide, practice tests, suggested Web links, and links to other relevant material.

http://stats.bls.gov/home.htm
Interested in learning more about the U.S. labor force? A wide range of interesting data and informative reports can be found at the Web site operated by the federal government's Bureau of Labor Statistics.

http://www.campaignforlabor rights.org/
Interested in sweatshops? This site, operated by the Campaign for Labor Rights, provides information on this and other controversial labor issues.

http://www.epinet.org
Visit the site for the Economic Policy Institute. What is the goal of this organization?

http://www.bls.gov/opub/rylf/rylfhome.htm
What role do young people play in the U.S. economy? Visit this government Web site to find out.

GETTING STARTED ON YOUR OWN: RESEARCH NAVIGATOR™

Follow the instructions found on page 25 of this text to access the features of Research Navigator™. Once at the Web site, enter your Login Name and Password. Then, to use the **Content Select** database, enter keywords such as "work," "unemployment," and "globalization," and the search engine will supply relevant and recent scholarly and popular press publications. Use the *New York Times* **Search-by-Subject Archive** to find recent news articles related to sociology and the **Link Library** feature to find relevant Web links organized by the key terms associated with this chapter.

CHAPTER 13

© Paul Marcus, *Picnic in the Bronx*, *Studio SPM, Inc.*

FAMILY LIFE

WHEN ADAM NASH WAS BORN IN 2000 he made the news even before he came home from the hospital. The Colorado infant was special because he was the first test-tube baby resulting from a genetic screening process. The story began when Adam's older sister, Molly, developed a blood disorder. Her only hope was a bone marrow transplant from a genetically matching donor. With no such donor available, Molly's parents decided to have another child using in vitro fertilization, and doctors carefully selected a matching embryo that would become the child who could provide Molly with the exact tissue she needed.

The story has a happy ending—Molly's treatment was successful—and Adam is growing up as a healthy boy. In several hundred cases of this kind since Adam's birth, genetic screening has been performed for medical reasons, typically to be sure children did not have serious genetic defects. But in the brave new world of genetic technology, parents can also "order" a baby that is, say, tall, blond, and right-handed, with all that it takes to become a great tennis player. Should parents be able to use genetic screening to select the traits of their child in the same way they would check off the options when ordering a new minivan? (Park, 2000)

The story of Adam Nash illustrates how new medical technology is creating ethical questions about the creation of families. But the controversy goes far beyond the use of genetic screening. Families are changing: More people are living alone, divorce rates are high, and more children are living with a single parent. This chapter explores the problems of family life in the United States. We begin by defining some basic terms.

A wide range of family forms is now shown in the mass media. In the television show, Reba, a divorced mother raises her young son and late-teen daughter, who became pregnant and married the father-to-be, so that now they all share one household.

WHAT IS A FAMILY?

The **family** is *a social institution that unites individuals into cooperative groups that care for members, regulate sexual relations, and oversee the bearing and raising of children.* **Kinship,** a related concept, is *a social bond, typically based on blood, marriage, or adoption, that joins individuals into families.*

The forms families take have varied over time and from place to place. In modern, high-income societies such as the United States, most people focus on the **nuclear family,** *one or two parents and their children.* In low-income nations around the world, however, people typically recognize the **extended family,** *parents and children and also grandparents, aunts, uncles, and cousins who often live close to one another and operate as a family unit.*

Everywhere, families form around **marriage,** *a lawful relationship—expected to be lasting—involving economic cooperation, sexual activity, and, usually, childbearing.* In the United States and throughout the world, people link marriage to having children, which explains why the word *matrimony* come from the Latin word meaning "the state of motherhood." This link is the reason a child born to an unwed mother may be defined as "illegitimate," although as single parenting becomes more common in the United States and other countries, this definition is far less common.

Debate over Definitions

With so much change surrounding the family, we should not be surprised to find disagreement over what the term *family* ought to mean. In the United States, the traditional view of a family is a married couple and their children. Fifty years ago, most U.S. families fit this form. Today, however, less than one-fourth do. More people now favor recognizing a wide range of **families of affinity,** that is, *people with or without legal or blood ties who feel they belong together and want to define themselves as a family.*

For a survey of family change shown in the 2000 census, go to the Web site for the Council on Contemporary Families:
http://www.contemporaryfamilies.org/public/families.php

Does it matter how we define families? The answer is "yes" because this question involves moral concerns (Are some kinds of relationships morally right or wrong?) and practical concerns (Is one kind of relationship better or worse for children?). The remainder of this chapter explores these questions.

A Sociological Approach to Family Problems

When most people speak about "family problems" or "problems at home," they usually have in mind conflicts between individuals or, perhaps, a situation involving a family member who is struggling with alcohol or some other drug.

The sociological perspective looks beyond the behavior of individuals to how the organization of society creates certain challenges for families. As the opening to this chapter illustrates, advancing genetic technology is forcing people to confront the question of whether parents should select their children's physical traits. Similarly, the fact that most women as well as men now work for income helps explain why so many families struggle to balance work and family responsibilities and to find good, affordable child care.

CONTROVERSIES OVER FAMILY LIFE

Families in the United States are changing. The trends include a rising number of people living together without being married, an increase in the share of children born to single mothers, more mothers joining fathers in the labor force so that more young children spend the day in care programs, a divorce rate much higher than it was fifty years ago, an increase in the number of blended families, gains by gay men and lesbians in the movement to win the right to legally marry, and new medical technology that has made miraculous new possibilities for reproduction. All these trends have sparked both praise and criticism. In the following sections, we examine the trends in turn.

Living Together: Do We Need to Marry?

Fifty years ago, most people took it for granted that couples married before moving in together. But a recent trend favors **cohabitation**, *the sharing of a household by an unmarried couple.* The number of cohabiting couples in the United States has risen from about 500,000 couples in 1970 to about 5.6 million (about 5 million heterosexual couples and 600,000 gay or lesbian couples). In all, cohabiting people represent 9 percent of all couples (Miller, 1997; U.S. Census Bureau, 2003).

For research reports on cohabitation and other intimate relationships, visit the Web site of the Marriage Project at Rutgers University: http://marriage.rutgers.edu

---

In some countries, especially Sweden and other Scandinavian nations, cohabitation is very common, even for couples with children. This practice is rare in more traditional (and Roman Catholic) nations such as Italy. In the United States, almost half of people between twenty-five and forty-four years of age cohabit at some point in their lives. About one-third of these couples include at least one child under eighteen (Popenoe, 1991, 1992; Bumpass & Sweet, 1995; Raley, 1996).

Critics of cohabiting, typically political conservatives, contend that marriage rather than cohabitation provides the more stable setting to raise children. As

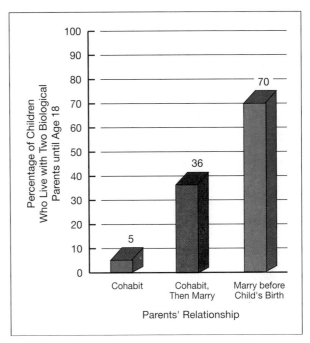

FIGURE 13–1 Chances of a Child Living with Both Biological Parents to Age Eighteen, by Type of Parental Relationship

Seventy percent of children born to married parents live with them until age 18, compared with just 5 percent of children born to cohabiting parents.

Source: Phillips (2001).

shown in Figure 13–1, just 5 percent of children born to cohabiting parents go on to live with both parents until age eighteen, compared with 70 percent of children born to married parents. One reason for this difference, say the critics, is that unmarried men more easily walk out on women and children. But cohabitation carries risks for men, too: When informal unions break up, men run the risk of losing legal rights to children. Research shows that 60 percent of cohabiting couples eventually split up. In addition, researchers caution that living together often discourages marriage because partners get used to relationships with less commitment (Popenoe & Whitehead, 1999; Smock, 2000; Phillips, 2001; Zimmer, 2001; Scommegna, 2002).

Supporters of cohabitation, typically liberals, argue that decisions about sexual relationships are private matters that should be left to individuals. Moreover, there is little reason to expect that one relational form—monogamous marriage—will meet the needs of everyone in a large and diverse population. On the contrary, some argue that cohabitation better reflects U.S. cultural values of choice and freedom and

The proportion of young people who cohabit—that is, who live together without being married—is rising. What are some of the benefits of this type of relationship? What are some of the dangers?

typically encourages a more equal relationship between a woman and a man. What about the well-being of children? Supporters of cohabiting argue that all parents who separate, whether married or not, must take responsibility for the support and care of their children (Brines & Joyner, 1999; Scommegna, 2002).

Postponing Marriage

The trend toward cohabitation is one reason that more people in the United States are delaying marriage than ever before. In 1950, the median age at first marriage in the United States was 20.3 years for women and 22.8 years for men. By 2002, these figures had jumped about five years to 25.3 years for women and 26.9 years for men (U.S. Census Bureau, 2003).

Why are people putting off marriage? One important reason is that a larger share of young people are attending college and graduate school; another is that, after graduation, a rising share of women are entering the labor force. In addition, recent economic insecurity has discouraged young people from living on their own; most of today's young people between eighteen and twenty-four are still living with parents. Finally, improvements in birth control technology and the availability of legal abortion also

play a part because an unexpected pregnancy no longer forces a couple to marry the way it often did in the 1950s.

Is this delay in marriage itself a problem? Not necessarily, but it does have some important consequences. For one thing, couples who marry later are also likely to have children later in life. For example, the share of women who have children in their forties jumped dramatically in the decades after 1950. Older parents may not be able to match the energy level of parents who are ten to twenty years younger, but they typically have more time to offer their children and earn much more money (Chandler, Kamo, & Werbel, 1994). Delayed marriage is also linked to a drop in overall childbearing: A U.S. woman's average number of children has dropped from 3.0 in 1976 to 1.9 in 2000. Other patterns linked to delayed marriage include a rising share of couples who have no children (up from 9 percent in 1970 to 19 percent in 2000) and a rising share of the population that remains single (up from 11 percent in 1950 to 28 percent in 2002) (U.S. Census Bureau, 2001, 2003). In later life, remaining single is more likely for women than for men because U.S. culture encourages men (but not women) to marry a younger partner.

Parenting: Is One Enough?

In 2003, about one in three families with children under eighteen years of age had just one parent in the household, a share that has doubled since 1970. Half of U.S. children will live with a single parent at some point before reaching age eighteen.

For articles on various family forms, visit http://www.urban.org

There is no doubt that many children raised by a single parent turn out just fine; similarly, having two parents in the home is no guarantee of a child's well-being. Still, evidence is mounting that growing up in a one-parent family puts children at a disadvantage in various ways. Some studies indicate that a father and a mother each make a distinctive contribution to a child's social development, so either parent alone cannot do as complete a job as two working together. But the biggest problem confronting one-parent families—especially if the parent is a woman, which is true in 80 percent of all cases—is poverty. Children in one-parent families begin with a one in three chance of being poor and, on average, end up with less education and lower incomes. Such disadvantages often form a vicious cycle as boys and girls raised by single parents become single parents themselves (Astone &

McLanahan, 1991; Li & Wojtkiewicz, 1992; Biblarz & Raferty, 1993; Popenoe, 1993; Shapiro & Schrof, 1995; Webster, Orbuch, & House, 1995; Kantrowitz & Wingert, 2001; McLanahan, 2002; U.S. Census Bureau, 2003).

Families, Race, and Poverty

There are many reasons that children live with a single parent. Among white families, divorce is the most common reason; among African American families, most single women who have children have never married. Although the risk of poverty is great for all children living with a single parent, it is especially high for African American children. In the United States, about 23 percent of families headed by white women are poor, but 36 percent of families headed by African American women are poor, which contributes to the fact that one-third of all African American youngsters grow up in poverty (U.S. Census Bureau, 2003).

The Moynihan Report   In 1965, U.S. Senator Daniel Patrick Moynihan sounded an alarm that the African American family was in crisis because of the growing number of absent fathers who leave single mothers to raise children on their own. In Moynihan's view, single motherhood threatened the African American community with a cycle of poverty spilling from mothers to children.

When Moynihan issued his warning, 20 percent of African American children were born to single mothers; today the figure is 68 percent (U.S. National Center for Health Statistics, 2003). But critics claim that Moynihan's concern was based on using one traditional type of family as the ideal, rejecting anything different as "dysfunctional." From this point of view, there is no problem with a female-headed household, at least nothing that adequate income cannot solve (Norton, 1985; Angelo, 1989). In other words, for African Americans, single-parent families and poverty are not so much *family* problems as they are *economic* problems. Eleanor Holmes Norton (1985) argues that the "breakdown" of the African American family is the result of long-term racism, which results in discrimination in education, jobs, and housing. Sociologist William Julius Wilson (1987, 1996) adds that African Americans who fall within a disadvantaged urban "underclass" find that there are simply not enough jobs to allow men and women to support a family. To claim that African Americans choose their family patterns (much less choose to be poor) amounts to blaming the victim (Hewlett & West, 1998).

One of the strengths of African American families is the tendency to form multigenerational households. Why do you think this pattern is more common among African Americans than among whites?

African American Families: A Closer Look   Stereotypes abound about African American families. A widespread attitude in the United States describes the average "welfare mother" as an unmarried African American woman. As Chapter 2 ("Poverty and Wealth") explained, however, most people who receive public assistance are white. The Critical Thinking box on page 328 presents five common but wrong stereotypes about African American families.

African American families take many forms, and no single description accurately portrays them. Indeed, U.S. families—black families, white families, rich families, and poor families alike—are much more diverse than most people realize.

Strengths of African American Families   There is little doubt that African American families struggle with more problems—including low income, racial prejudice, and discrimination—than white families do. Research shows that African American families, especially those struggling with poverty, have real strengths. These families adapt to their situation in a number of ways, building strong kinship bonds, drawing strength from traditional religious beliefs, and using the resources of grandparents (especially grandmothers) to form three-generation households. In addition, many poor households band together in networks of mutual assistance that help everyone

Critical Thinking   Five Stereotypes about African American Families

IN THE UNITED STATES, MANY PEOPLE HOLD incorrect, stereotypical views of African American families. Here we evaluate five widespread stereotypes about African American families.

Stereotype 1. African Americans do not form strong families.   Historical studies show that, even under slavery, most African Americans lived in families with a father and a mother. This pattern continued well into the twentieth century. After about 1960, a combination of racial segregation (which trapped many African Americans in inner cities) and industrial decline (which meant many inner city communities lacked jobs) resulted in a declining rate of marriage among African Americans and a rising rate of children born to single mothers. Even under such adverse conditions, half of African American families still have both husband and wife in the home.

Stereotype 2. African American men do not make good husbands and fathers.   This stereotype is based on the fact that a larger share of African American families (43 percent) have no husband present than is the case with Hispanic families (23 percent), white families (14 percent), or Asian families (7 percent). This stereotype assumes that the lack of a husband in the home reflects people's choices rather than the fact that many African American communities do not provide the jobs men need to support a family (Wilson, 1996).

Stereotype 3. The African American family is a matriarchy: Women dominate family life.   History shows that African American men have played vital leadership roles both in individual families and in larger communities. It is also important to recognize that men or men and women together head a majority (55 percent) of African American families.

Stereotype 4. African American women have more children, often in order to increase welfare benefits.   Regardless of race, poor women receiving income assistance have the same number of children as women who are not poor. The overall birth rates for white and black women are almost identical.

Stereotype 5. Today, African Americans have the same opportunities as everyone else.   Many white people believe (or want to believe) that racial prejudice and discrimination are things of the past in the United States. However, the evidence suggests that African American men and women—whether poor, middle class, or rich—continue to face barriers based on race (Benjamin, 1991).

_____

Source: The idea for this box is taken from Benokraitis (1999); data from U.S. Census Bureau (2003).

ISSUES AND EXERCISES

1. Why do you think stereotypes about African American families are widespread?
2. How does sociology play a part in responding to stereotypes such as these?
3. [Research Navigator.com] Use Research Navigator™ to learn more about African American families. (See instructions on page 25; keyword: "African American family")

get by (Stack, 1975; Littlejohn-Blake & Darling, 1993; Clemetson, 2000).

Conflict between Work and Family Life

For much of U.S. history, work and family life occurred together because families lived and labored together on farms. With the Industrial Revolution, people (primarily men) went off to work in factories, which separated the home from the workplace.

With the rapid entry of women in the labor force after 1950, people began to feel greater tension between work and family life. A majority of U.S. families, even those with young children, now have two parents working for income. These families, and women more than men, still perform almost another full-time job in the form of housework (Hochschild, 1989; Stapinski, 1998; Lewin, 2000; England, 2001). As a result, marriage and family life often turns out to be the interaction of tired, overworked people who are trying to juggle their many responsibilities.

As Chapter 12 ("Work and the Workplace") explains, the Information Revolution has again changed the nature of work; about one-third of people in the labor force now spend some time each week working at home. For many of them, doing so helps to reduce work–family tensions. At the same time, however, as more people work at home or maintain home offices, workplace activities and concerns are likely to further intrude into family life (Macionis, 2001).

Child Care

A century ago, most families considered child care the job of the mother, who worked in the home. Today, 60 percent of U.S. women are in the labor force working for income. A majority of women with children (50 percent of women with infants, 59 percent of women with preschoolers, and 75 percent of women with school-age children) are employed outside the home (U.S. Bureau of Labor Statistics, 2003).

With so many women and men working, child care is a major concern across the United States. Who cares for the children of mothers in the labor force? Figure 13–2 answers this question. Most children (54 percent) receive care from a parent (27 percent) or a grandparent or other relative (27 percent). An additional 18 percent receive care from a nonrelative, in either the caregiver's home (14 percent) or the child's home (4 percent). The remaining 28 percent of youngsters receive care in a child-care facility (Sonenstein et al., 2002).

The option a family chooses has a lot to do with income. Parents with higher incomes can afford to send their children to care programs that emphasize learning and early childhood development. By contrast, those with lower incomes turn to relatives or friends, piece together a patchwork of babysitters, or send their children to less costly care centers whose staff may lack necessary training and provide minimal attention to children.

Older children spend most of the day at school. But after school, as many as 2 million youngsters (about 13 percent of the total) are "latchkey" kids who fend for themselves until a parent returns from work (Capizano, Taut, & Adams, 2001; Sonenstein et al., 2002). Some children adapt well to being alone after school, becoming more self-reliant. But especially in poor neighborhoods, unsupervised children are at high risk for problems involving drugs, crime, and sexual exploitation.

In short, caring for children is not a problem for some families, but it is a problem for millions of others. What role, if any, should the government should play in ensuring that child care needs are met? In most other high-income nations, the government uses tax money to operate child-care centers. In the United States, working parents can deduct child-care costs on their income tax returns; in addition, states provide some financial assistance to poor families who need child care. But with its strong culture of self-reliance, the United States has yet to offer child-care programs on a large scale.

Those who favor expanded government child-care programs point out that many low-income families would welcome the assistance; in this way, the government could do more to ensure that children receive high-quality care. Most child-care centers operate only during business hours from Monday to Friday, which is of little help to parents who work night shifts or "swing" shifts that change from week to week.

Because workers who worry about their children are not very productive, more employers now offer on-site child-care programs. In most cases, employees pay for this care, but some employers provide this service as a workplace benefit. Such programs usually are of good quality and have two added advantages:

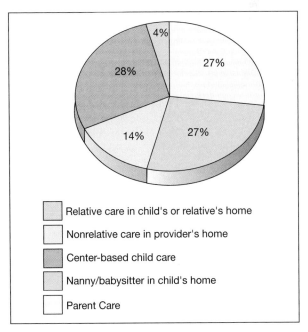

FIGURE 13–2 Child-Care Arrangements for Working Mothers

Just over half of the young children of working mothers receive care from a parent, grandparent, or other relative.

Source: U.S. Census Bureau (2002).

Personal Stories   Dying for Foster Care

TERRELL PETERSON WAS BORN INTO A WORLD that he never made, a world that ended his life six years later. Born to a mother addicted to crack, Terrell lived a turbulent life with two other children, each of whom had a different father. Soon after his birth, the state of Georgia began tracking Terrell, fearing that he was being neglected. After five years, state child welfare officials had gathered enough evidence to conclude that Terrell was in danger in his present home, and they placed him in foster care. There was no blood relative available to provide care, so he ended up in the home of the grandmother of one of his half-siblings.

Pharina Peterson was the last person who should have been given a child to care for. Looking back, it is clear she did not want the child; apparently she took him in order to get the monthly child support. As Georgia officials now know, Terrell was abused horribly. His ordeal included being beaten, starved, and tied to a stairway. By the time he died he weighed only twenty-nine pounds; his body showed so many injuries that the medical examiner did not document them all.

Pharina Peterson was charged with murder, but many wonder whether the real fault lies with our system of foster care. The idea of foster care is to protect children, but it clearly failed Terrell Peterson. He is not the only one to fall through the cracks of a system some claim is in crisis. One recent count found that 513 foster care children died over a three-year period in Georgia alone. Reports of abuse can be found in all other states as well. In 2003, four foster children—including a nineteen-year-old boy weighing just forty-five pounds—were found starving in a New Jersey home, despite the fact that records showed caseworkers had visited the home thirty-eight times in the last two years.

Across the country, more than 500,000 children are in foster care, twice the number a decade ago. The cost of foster care is about $9 billion a year, or roughly $18,000 per child. In a majority of cases, children are better off in foster care than they were before. But the foster care system cannot guarantee their safety. Most analysts agree that the rate of neglect and abuse among foster children is far higher than among children living with biological parents. The exact number of abused foster children is a matter of guesswork: There are roughly 5,000 reported cases, but the actual total could easily be twice this high. This may be the heart of the problem: Too often government agencies place children only to lose track of them. "These systems should be a national scandal," claims Marcia Robinson Lowry, head of Children's Rights, Inc., a children's advocacy group. "In virtually every state there is no accountability" (2000:75).

ISSUES AND EXERCISES

1. Why do you think foster care fails many children? What do you think should be done about this problem?

2. Do you think the public considers foster care to be a problem or a solution? Why?

3. [Research Navigator.com] Use Research Navigator™ to learn more about foster care. (See instructions on page 25; keyword: "foster care")

Sources: Based on Roche (2000b) and Polgreen & Worth (2003).

Parents have a chance to visit their children during breaks throughout the day, and companies that provide workplace child care have the edge in attracting and retaining the best employees.

A final issue involving child care involves children whose parents cannot or will not care for them. Such children are likely to come under the supervision of the foster care system; as the Personal Stories box explains, in too many cases this system fails the children it was created to serve.

Divorce

Many people recite marriage vows that say they will stay together "til death us do part." But the reality today is that divorce, not death, ends many marriages. In the United States, more than four in ten of today's marriages will end in divorce (among African Americans, the rate is six in ten).

The divorce rate today is ten times what it was a century ago. Then, family members (almost half of whom worked on farms) depended on one another to get by; there was strong economic pressure to remain married. In addition, women had yet to enter the labor force in large numbers, so unless a woman could turn to relatives for support, divorce often meant poverty. In addition, many people viewed divorce as sinful, so moral pressure also kept couples together, even those who were not happily married.

During the twentieth century, the share of women working for income rose steadily, while the average number of children a woman bore declined steadily. These trends made divorce a more realistic option, and public attitudes toward divorce became more accepting (Weitzman, 1985; Furstenberg & Cherlin, 1991; Etzioni, 1993).

As Figure 13–3 shows, the divorce rate soared for a time after World War II (a war that forced millions of couples to live apart for years), and the divorce rate began a steady climb from about 1965 to 1980. Since then, the divorce rate has eased downward. National Map 13–1 on page 332 shows the percentage of the population that is divorced throughout the United States.

No-Fault Divorce In addition to the increasing economic independence of women, which gave women the resources to leave an unhappy marriage (Schoen et al., 2002), changes in law also helped make divorces easier to get. In 1969, California became the first state to implement a policy of no-fault divorce, and every state had done the same by 1985.

What is no-fault divorce? Before this policy was enacted, a couple could divorce only if one or both partners claimed in court that the other was at fault for ruining the marriage, typically through abandonment, adultery, or physical or emotional injury. More than just blame was at stake because courts took fault into account when dividing a couple's property and assigning custody of children.

No-fault divorce laws did away with the idea that one or both partners were to blame for the collapse of a marriage. Instead, couples simply declare their marriage is over and cannot be resumed because of "irreconcilable differences." The court then tries to divide property fairly and places children where they seem best off. In addition, the court assigns child support according to the need of the custodial parent, the ability to pay of the noncustodial parent, and the ability of both parents to work. Rarely does no-fault divorce involve *alimony*, regular payments from one ex-spouse to the other.

By greatly reducing payment of alimony, no-fault divorce ended the historical idea that men

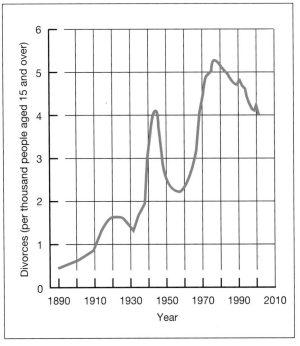

FIGURE 13–3 The U.S. Divorce Rate, 1890–2001

After 1890, the U.S. divorce rate climbed rapidly, especially during World War II (1939–1945). After falling in the 1950s, the rate rose again through the late 1970s, and has since been on the decline.

Source: U.S. National Center for Health Statistics (2002).

ought to take care of women. But this does not mean that women are better off. Lenore Weitzman (1985) found that after divorce the living standard of men went up, while the living standard of women and their children went down, a pattern confirmed by other researchers (Faludi, 1991; Holden & Smock, 1991; Weitzman, 1996). Why the difference? Allen Parkman (1992) explains that no-fault divorce harms women because it ignores *cultural capital*, which includes skills and schooling that increase a person's earning power. In traditional marriages, a wife puts little or no time into paid work, instead devoting herself to helping her husband develop his career. In doing so, she assumes she will stay married and that her husband's success will benefit her as well. After divorce, the husband still has his job while, in most cases, the stay-at-home wife faces the expense of caring for the children.

Many support no-fault divorce as a solution to the problem of unhappy marriages. In addition, supporters claim this policy treats men and women as equals, reflecting the fact that a majority of both sexes now work for income. But some see no-fault

A NATION OF DIVERSITY

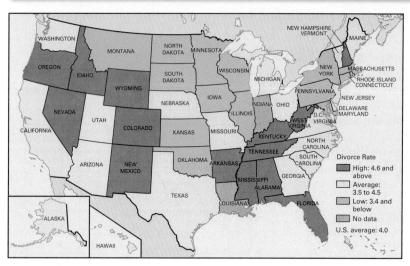

NATIONAL MAP 13–1

Divorce across the United States

The map shows the divorce rate (that is, the number of divorces per 1,000 population), by state, for 2001. Overall, about 12 percent of U.S. adults over age fifteen are divorced. But divorce is far more common near the West Coast (and especially in Nevada, a state with very liberal divorce laws), somewhat less common in the East, and much less common in the middle of the country. Research suggests that divorce is more likely among people who are younger, who have weaker religious ties, and who move away from their parents' hometown. Can you apply these facts to make sense of this map?

Source: U.S. Census Bureau (2003).

divorce as a problem because it is harmful to women. Pointing to the fact that men still earn more money than women, they claim that we should bring back the system of alimony so that the person with the greater earning power (usually the man) helps support the ex-partner who stayed at home (usually the woman).

Finally, many couples try to spell out the terms of any future divorce by writing a premarital agreement. Is this a good idea? The Social Policy box takes a closer look.

Too Much Divorce?   Just about everyone recognizes that divorce can be preferable to remaining in an unhappy relationship. But is today's divorce rate too high? Liberals, especially, favor easy divorce as a means by which women can free themselves from abusive relationships. Conservatives are more critical of a high divorce rate, suggesting that it signifies a "me-first" attitude that places individual needs and desires over obligations to others (Whitehead, 1997; Popenoe, 1999). In addition, there is evidence that many divorces end up being difficult for the children involved (Amato & Sobolewski, 2001). When asked in a national survey whether divorce is too easy to get these days, 22 percent of U.S. adults say they are satisfied with the system as it is, 26 percent think divorce is still too hard to get, and 49 percent say that divorce is too easy to get (NORC, 2003:232).

In global perspective, as shown in Figure 13–4 on page 334 most high-income nations have a higher divorce rate than most low-income countries. The United States has one of the highest divorce rates in the world, surpassed only by Sweden (United Nations, 2000).

In recent years, a few states—notably Louisiana and Arizona—have responded to high divorce rates by enacting "covenant marriage" laws. These laws allow couples, when they marry, to choose a conventional marriage or a covenant marriage, which is harder to dissolve. Couples who choose a covenant marriage agree, first, to seek marital counseling if problems develop during the marriage. They agree to seek divorce only for very limited reasons, including adultery, conviction of a felony resulting in a long prison sentence or the death penalty, abandonment for at least one year or living separately for at least two years, habitual drug or alcohol abuse, or physical or sexual abuse of the spouse or a child. Couples who enter a covenant marriage reject the idea of divorcing simply because one spouse no longer wants to stay married (Nock, Wright, & Sanchez, 1999). Some twenty other states are considering covenant marriage laws. But to date only a small share of people in states that permit covenant marriages are choosing them. In short, this policy may have more symbolic importance than practical significance.

Social Policy — Should You Prepare a Premarital Agreement?

FOR A COUPLE CONSIDERING MARRIAGE TODAY, a sobering fact is that there are almost even odds that the marriage will end in divorce. Therefore, lawyers and others suggest that it makes good sense to prepare a premarital or prenuptial agreement.

What should be included in such an agreement? The answer depends on the individuals involved and on how much property each has going into the marriage.

1. **Property.** Start by making a list of each person's assets and liabilities. Will individuals keep separate existing property—including homes, furniture, jewelry, cash, cars, and investments—or combine it as joint property? Will partners keep their own savings and checking accounts or create new joint accounts? Will they be responsible for each other's existing debts (such as loans for college tuition or purchase of a car)? What about property that will accumulate during the marriage? In the event of divorce or death of one partner, what will happen to all property? If either partner enters the marriage with children, what property rights do the children have?

2. **Income.** Do partners know each other's income? How will these incomes be applied to household expenses, savings and investments, and future purchases such as a new home? Who will be responsible for paying bills? For supporting children?

3. **Children.** Do both partners want (more) children? How will responsibility for child care be divided? What are each partner's attitudes about disciplining children? Is giving children a religious upbringing important? Will children from a previous marriage have inheritance rights equal to those of any children born to the couple?

4. **Housework.** Consider the likely scope of housework, which reflects the size of a family and the size of a home. How will responsibility for housework be divided?

5. **In case of divorce.** Should the partners desire to end the marriage, how will property be divided? What marital property will be sold? What about appreciation in assets (such as a house or investments) that occurs during the marriage? What about custody and care of any children? What share of either individual's income would be reasonable as child support? Will one or both parents take responsibility for paying for college? Does either party expect to receive alimony? If so, how much and for how long?

Raising questions such as these may seem too businesslike when people are deeply in love. Indeed, some people wonder whether, by preparing a premarital agreement, a couple isn't inviting conflict. Perhaps. But discussion and perhaps written statements of expectations for the marriage will reduce the chances for conflict later on and may even raise the chances of a happy marriage.

ISSUES AND EXERCISES

1. Have you ever prepared a prenuptial agreement? How well did it work?
2. On balance do you think prenuptial agreements are a good or bad idea? Why?
3. Use Research Navigator™ to learn more about prenuptial agreements. (See instructions on page 25; keyword: "prenuptial agreement")

Child Support

After divorce, many children do not receive adequate financial support from parents. Indeed, the failure of noncustodial parents to provide financial support is one cause of high poverty rates among U.S. children.

After a separation or divorce, many noncustodial parents fail to make court-ordered payments. The government reports that courts order support for about 59 percent of children. Yet of the children who should receive support, 55 percent receive partial payments or no payments at all (U.S. Census Bureau, 2002).

After divorce, courts usually award custody of children to mothers. For this reason, most parents who fail to support their children are men, which explains the national attention given to the problem of "deadbeat dads." However, noncustodial mothers are actually less likely than fathers to make child

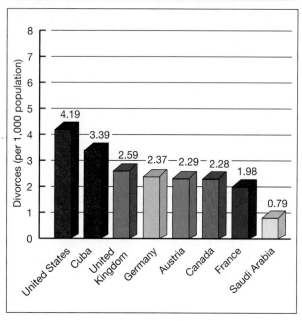

DIMENSIONS OF DIFFERENCE

FIGURE 13–4   Divorce in Selected Countries

The odds of a marriage ending due to divorce are higher in the United States than in other countries.

Source: United Nations Human Development Programme (2003).

support payments, probably because single women have lower incomes (U.S. Census Bureau, 2002).

What can be done about parents who do not support their children? The law requires an employer to withhold money from the earnings of a parent who fails to pay up. Of course, many parents have managed to duck their responsibilities by moving or switching jobs (Weitzman, 1985; Waldman, 1992). In 1998, therefore, Congress passed the "Deadbeat Parents Punishment Act," making it a felony to refuse to provide support payments to a child residing in another state or to move to another state in order to avoid making such payments. In addition, many states have adopted the strategy of publishing "Wanted" posters of delinquent parents on billboards or in newspapers in the hope that such publicity will shame them into paying up.

Remarriage: Problems of Blended Families

Just as divorce is common in the United States, so is remarriage. In fact, four out of five people who divorce remarry, and most do so within five years.

Nationwide, about half of all marriages are *remarriages* for at least one partner.

For women and men with children from a previous relationship, remarriage creates **blended families,** *families in which children have some combination of biological parents and step-parents.* In the United States, one-fifth of all white and one-third of all African American married couple households are blended families, which bring with them a number of special challenges. For one thing, children who become part of a new family must learn new household rules and routines and build relationships with new siblings. Step-parents must make adjustments, establishing new relationships with children as well as a spouse. Most couples also have to maintain a relationship with a child's other biological parent and, perhaps, that person's new partner.

Most blended families manage to cope with these challenges. But research shows that members of blended families carry some special risks. For children, step-parent families have a high rate of physical and sexual abuse. For spouses, the likelihood of divorce (especially those who remarry at a younger age) is higher than for those in first marriages (Holden & Smock, 1991; Ahlburg & De Vita, 1992; Fleming, Mullen, & Bammer, 1997; McLanahan, 2002).

Gay and Lesbian Families

Not all couples even have the choice of marrying. Throughout the United States, gay men and lesbians are banned by law from marrying a same-sex partner. Nonetheless, between 600,000 and 1 million gay couples have formed committed partnerships, and about 25 percent of these couples have children. Typically, these children are offspring from a previously heterosexual relationship, although many gay couples adopt children of their own (U.S. Census Bureau, 2002).

Many gay men and lesbians view the right to legally marry someone of the same sex as an important measure of society's acceptance of their sexual orientation. Beyond symbolic importance, gay marriage has practical value because marriage extends benefits to legal spouses, ranging from hospital visitation rights to health insurance.

The first nation to extend legal marriage to gay couples was Denmark. The Defining Moment box takes a closer look at how this new law changed the definition of marriage.

At present, five nations—Denmark (1989), Norway (1993), Sweden (1995), The Netherlands (2001),

A DEFINING MOMENT

Axil and Eigil Axgil: Changing the Marriage Rules

OCTOBER 1, 1989, WAS A DAY WHEN marriage changed. It was that day, in the small European nation of Denmark, that Axil and Eigil Axgil became the world's first gay couple to be legally married.

Their relationship, however, was hardly new. At that time, the two men had already been together for forty years (Axil was seventy-four, Eigil sixty-seven). Eight years into their relationship, they had decided to merge their first names into a common last name.

Axil was a pioneer gay rights advocate in a country where homosexuality had been illegal until 1933. In 1948, as one of the few openly gay men in Denmark, he organized the first group committed to gay rights. Doing this cost him his job as an auto worker; in addition, he was evicted from his apartment. He moved to Copenhagen, where he met Eigil. They agreed to make their relationship as "public" as possible by dressing in identical clothing, and continued their work as gay activists. During the 1950s, after being arrested for publishing a gay rights magazine containing photographs declared to be obscene, they both spent time in jail.

When Denmark passed the new law in 1989 allowing gay couples to marry, the gay community asked the Axgils to be the first to wed, in recognition of their lifelong efforts to broaden people's understanding of marriage. Ten other gay couples followed them into

In 1989, Axil and Eigil Axgil became the world's first same-sex couple to legally marry. In light of the recent efforts by the Massachusetts Supreme Court and the city of San Francisco to extend marriage to all people, will the United States join the growing list of nations permitting same-sex marriage?

marriage that day. At their wedding, the Axgils were easy to recognize—they were again dressed in different colors of the same clothing.

Asked if he had a message for other gay people, Axil said at the end of his wedding ceremony: "Be open. Come out. Keep fighting. This is the only way to move anything. If everyone comes out of the closet, then this will happen everywhere."

Source: Based, in part, on Wockner (2003).

and Canada (2003)—legally sanction gay marriage. Interestingly, none of these countries allows homosexual couples to adopt children, a practice that is legal in the United States. In 2000, Vermont became the first state to recognize lawful "civil unions," which is close to marriage by a different name. In 2003, the Massachusetts Supreme Court ruled that the state had to extend legal marriage to all people; in 2004, San Francisco and several other cities and towns performed thousands of marriages for same-sex couples. The state of Hawaii and a number of cities across the country already permit gay and lesbian couples to register "domestic partnerships," which confer some, but not all, the legal benefits of marriage. In addition, hundreds

of employers now include partners of gay and lesbian employees in their benefits programs.

The significance of any state's decision to enact a gay marriage law is great because according to the "full faith and credit" clause of the U.S. Constitution, a contract (including marriage) performed in one state must be recognized in *all* states. For this reason, in 1996 congressional opponents of gay marriage passed the "Defense of Marriage Act," which states that marriage must involve one man and one woman and that no state or other jurisdiction has to recognize a same-sex marriage law enacted by any other state or jurisdiction.

The gay marriage debate brings us again to the question of how to define a "family." In general,

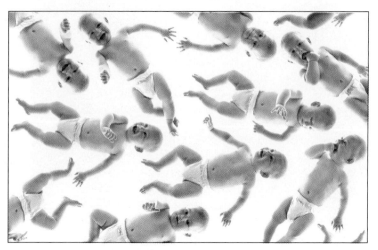

In 2004, news reports indicated that a team of Korean scientists had cloned a human embryo. What advantages do you see to new reproduction technology? What are some of the reasons many people oppose such efforts?

conservatives argue that gay marriage undermines the traditional definition of families and does not offer the best setting in which to raise children (Knight, 1998). Most liberals think of families as people—straight or gay—who share one another's lives and want that relationship to be recognized, leading them to support gay marriage. However, the lines are not clearly drawn in this debate: Some conservatives who believe in the importance of "family values" also support gay marriage, claiming that all people, whatever their sexual orientation, benefit from being married.

What about Gay Parenting?   As many as 250,000 gay couples in the United States are raising young children. Therefore, the diversity of families in this country includes not only one-parent and two-parent families but also families in which children have two "moms" or two "dads." Gay parenting is a controversial issue: Although no federal or state laws ban this practice, in many custody disputes courts decide that children are better off with heterosexual parents.

Public opinion is divided on whether gay parenting is in the best interest of children. Some people fear that children living with homosexual parents are at higher risk of sexual abuse; however, research does not support such fears. On the contrary, research shows that gay and lesbian parents are capable of the same supportive and effective parenting as heterosexual couples. Nor is there any evidence that children raised by homosexual parents are any

more likely to be gay themselves. In short, gay and lesbian families face problems, but they come more from the stigma society attaches to homosexuality than from the family form itself (Barret & Robinson, 1990; Peterson, 1992).

Brave New Families: High-Tech Reproduction

In 1978, Louise Brown became the world's first "test-tube baby." She was conceived not in the usual way but in a laboratory in England, where doctors fertilized a human ovum with a sperm cell in a glass dish and implanted the embryo in a woman's womb. As noted in the opening to this chapter, in 2000 Adam Nash became the first test-tube baby in the United States to be created with medical screening to "design" his genetic makeup. Such births illustrate how advancing reproductive technology has created new choices for families and sparked new controversies as well.

In Vitro Fertilization   So-called "test-tube babies" result from the process of in **vitro** (that is, "in glass") **fertilization,** which means *uniting eggs and sperm in a laboratory.* Once a fertilized embryo is produced, doctors may implant it in a woman's body, or they can freeze it for later use.

In vitro fertilization offers the 3 million couples in the United States who are unable to conceive children in the normal way an exciting new opportunity to become parents. However, the procedure is very expensive, so fewer than 100,000 couples a year actually undertake it, resulting in about 35,000 births annually (U.S. Centers for Disease Control and Prevention, 2003). Those who are finally able to have the child they want view this procedure as nothing short of miraculous. But critics point out that the cost places this procedure out of reach of most people. As the case of Adam Nash illustrates, new reproductive technology also permits parents to select the physical and perhaps even mental traits of their children, raising the troubling possibility of the creation of a "super-race" of genetically designed children.

Surrogate Motherhood   One of the controversies arising from new reproductive technology is the issue of **surrogate motherhood,** *an arrangement by which a woman carries and bears a child for another.*

In 1986, the case known as "Baby M" brought surrogate motherhood to the nation's attention. In that case, William Stern, whose wife was unable to bear children, agreed to pay Mary Beth Whitehead to bear a child conceived with his sperm via artificial insemination. Although Whitehead would be the baby's biological mother, she agreed to give up all claims to the child. All went according to plan, and Whitehead gave birth to a healthy child. But by that time Whitehead had changed her mind and wanted to keep her baby. The Sterns reacted by filing a court case seeking custody of the baby and pointing to the signed agreement. In 1988, the New Jersey Supreme Court declared surrogacy contracts of this kind illegal in that state; furthermore, the court declared that the natural mother (in this case, Whitehead) should have custody of a child born from such an arrangement. However, other states have honored such contracts, so there is no consistent policy across the United States.

Cases of surrogate parenthood also raise questions about responsibility for child support. In California, John and Luanne Buzzanca, a married couple unable to have children, enlisted a woman to serve as a surrogate mother. In this case, both the egg and sperm came from unknown donors. In 1995, the surrogate mother gave birth a baby who had no biological ties to either her or the Buzzancas. However, a month before the child's birth John Buzzanca filed for divorce from his wife. His wife, Luanne, took custody of the child and sought child support from her ex-husband. But John refused, claiming he was not the child's father.

In the court suit that followed, a California judge ruled that although they were not the child's biological parents, both John and Luanne Buzzanca were the child's "intended parents." Thus, the court ruled that both parties who engage a surrogate mother are responsible for a child born in this way. In the end, Luanne Buzzanca received custody of the baby, and her ex-husband was ordered to pay monthly child support.

Cases such as these show that although new reproductive technology has obvious benefits to some couples, we have yet to devise clear laws to guide its application. This fact illustrates a pattern sociologists call *cultural lag*, when scientific discoveries occur faster than our ideas about the right ways to use them. The result is scientifically possible procedures that may or may not be considered to be morally right.

THEORETICAL ANALYSIS: UNDERSTANDING FAMILY PROBLEMS

We can sharpen our understanding of issues surrounding the family by applying sociology's three theoretical approaches: structural-functional analysis, symbolic-interaction analysis, and social-conflict analysis.

Structural-Functional Analysis: Family as Foundation

The structural-functionalist paradigm views the family as the most important unit of social organization. George Murdock (1949) claims that families exists everywhere in the world because they perform four major tasks essential for the operation of society.

First, as explained in Chapter 8 ("Sexuality"), families regulate reproduction, encouraging the birth of children to parents who have made a public commitment to one another. Second, families create a stable and caring environment for their children. Third, families are units of economic cooperation between husband and wife as well as other kin. Fourth, and finally, family members look to one another for emotional support in a world that can be cold and even dangerous.

Because these functions are vital to any society, structural-functional analysis claims that families are the foundation of a healthy society. Therefore, any threat to family life is defined as a social problem. Thus, a structural-functional approach views many of the trends discussed in this chapter—including living together, single parenting, and high divorce rates—as threats to the stability of U.S. society.

Critical evaluation. There is evidence that families do matter: For example, children living in single-parent households grow up completing less schooling and are at higher risk of poverty than those from two-parent households. Furthermore, it is difficult to see how other social institutions could step in to perform the various functions that families perform now.

At the same time, the structural-functional approach is criticized for overlooking the extent of conflict and violence in families (discussed in Chapter 7, "Violence"). In addition, critics point out that today's families also contribute to social inequality, typically supporting the dominance of men over women and perpetuating class inequality as parents pass along wealth and privileges to children. Then, too, the structural-functional approach takes a macro-level view of the family as a system, saying little about how individuals experience it as part of everyday life. This concern brings us to the symbolic-interaction approach.

Symbolic-Interaction Analysis: Family and Learning

The symbolic-interaction approach views the family less as an institution and more as the ongoing interaction of individuals. Following this approach, we see that family life has a great deal to do with the ways children learn to think about themselves. Parents who raise children with love and steady guidance help them to develop a positive self-image and to make decisions confidently as they move through life. By contrast, parents who continuously call their children's behavior into question end up fostering self-doubt.

A symbolic-interaction approach also highlights how the experience of family life varies from one family to another. Ideally, marriage helps a couple build a relationship that is *intimate* (a word with Latin roots meaning "free from fear"), one in which each partner finds comfort and support in the presence of the other. But the same marital ties that offer the promise of intimacy can work in the opposite direction to script the behavior of men (who, thus, act "just like men") and women (who feel constrained to act in "feminine" ways), with the result that the two sexes can have trouble opening up to one another (Macionis, 1978). This fact helps explain why women and men often have very different perceptions of the same marriage (Bernard, 1982).

Critical evaluation.   The symbolic-interaction approach shows the varied ways in which individuals experience family life. A husband, wife, and child typically perceive the same family quite differently, and all these experiences change over time.

Critics of this approach point out that although family life is variable, a number of patterns are common. Gender stratification, for example, is built into almost all families. The social-conflict approach offers a look at how the family is linked to this and other dimensions of social inequality.

Social-Conflict Analysis: Family and Inequality

As a macro-level approach, social-conflict analysis shares with structural-functional analysis the idea that the family plays an important part in the operation of society. But rather than highlighting ways in which family life benefits everyone, social-conflict analysis points to how the family operates to benefit some and disadvantage others. In simple terms, families *reproduce* social inequality in each new generation.

An early social-conflict theory of family life comes from Friedrich Engels (1902; orig. 1884). As Engels saw it, the family actually came into being among the wealthy mostly so men could be reasonably sure who their offspring were and could be sure they were passing their property from father to son.

In this way, the family (along with the legal system that protects inheritance) ensures that the class structure stays much the same from one generation to another.

Perpetuating classes is only one way in which the family supports inequality. In addition, Engels explained, by making men the heads of households, the family gives men power over women. Furthermore, for men to know who their heirs are, they must control female sexuality. To Engels, this fact went a long way toward explaining the concern that women be virgins before they marry and faithful wives afterward. In short, the family transforms women into the sexual and economic property of men.

Critical evaluation.   From a social-conflict point of view, the path toward making a society more egalitarian is to eliminate the family, at least in its current form (Mare, 1991). However, this approach overlooks the fact that a large majority of people in the United States claim a great deal of satisfaction from family life (NORC, 2003:182). If society were to eliminate the family for the reasons Engels suggests, it is far from clear how important tasks such as raising children would be accomplished.

POLITICS AND FAMILY LIFE: CONSTRUCTING PROBLEMS AND DEFINING SOLUTIONS

Theory provides helpful ways to think about families, but exactly what people define as family problems and what they think we ought to do about them depends on their values and politics. We conclude this chapter by applying the conservative, liberal, and radical perspectives to issues surrounding families and family life.

Conservatives: Traditional "Family Values"

Conservatives see the family as the core of a society—the social institution that does the most to instill basic values that bind people together and define a way of life. For this reason, conservatives advance a position they call "family values," which emphasizes the importance of committed marriages and a low divorce rate and defends the two-parent family as the best setting in which to raise children.

From a conservative point of view, the rise in cohabitation spells trouble for U.S. society. Indeed, many conservatives do not approve of living together because such a relationship carries less commitment than legal marriage. According to conservatives, the popularity of cohabitation signals the rise of a "me-first" culture in which people favor individualism over commitment. The greatest losers in such a trend are children, who have a higher chance of ending up in a single-parent family, which, in turn, raises their immediate risk of poverty right away and future risk of divorce (Popenoe & Whitehead, 1999).

In addition, conservatives point to evidence that marriage is good for people. Compared with unmarried people, married spouses are better off financially, claim to be happier, and report having more sex (Waite & Gallagher, 2000; Simon, 2002).

Conservatives see the high rate of divorce after the 1960s as a serious problem. Claiming that no-fault divorce laws make divorces too easy to get, conservatives oppose them, and they urge a change from an individualistic culture favoring cohabitation and easy divorce to a pro-commitment "culture of marriage." Favoring commitment over independence would give both men and women better mental and financial health and would provide children with more stability. Commitment to families also means spending more time with children. Conservatives criticize the popular tendency to stake out "quality time" with children as an excuse for not spending enough time with the kids. Conservatives recognize that many households depend on the earnings of both mothers and fathers but suggest that couples with young children should consider limiting their total work week to, say, sixty hours so that they may be sure to meet the needs of their children (Broude, 1996; Whitehead, 1997; Popenoe, 1988, 1993, 1999).

Liberals: Many Kinds of Families

Because liberals celebrate individual freedoms, their take on today's families and family problems is very different from that of the conservatives. Liberals claim that conservatives recognize only one type of "real" family as best for everyone. But as liberals see it, this is not the case; different people favor different kinds of families (or no families at all). A wide range of families has existed throughout U.S. history, and this diversity continues today (Kain, 1990; Koontz, 1992).

Liberals support the right of people to choose from a wide range of family forms, including cohabitation, single-parent families, blended families, same-sex marriage, and singlehood. For liberals, such family patterns are not the problems they are to

Conservatives think that U.S. society should support the traditional family because families headed by both a father and a mother are good for individuals and good for society as a whole. Liberals support the expanding range of family forms, recognizing that no single family form is likely to be right for everyone. Radicals condemn traditional families for perpetuating social inequality, and favor collective living arrangements that promote social equality.

conservatives. On the contrary, locking people in "traditional families" is likely to limit the opportunities of women and trap some women in abusive relationships. Therefore, liberal family problems are poverty and domestic violence.

From a liberal perspective, then, the greater diversity in family forms is a solution to the historical problem of women remaining in the home under the control of men (Stacey, 1990, 1993). But what do liberals say about the fact that single-mother families have a higher risk of poverty? The liberal solution to this problem is to increase child-care programs so that more women can work and to combat gender discrimination so that working women are paid as much as working men. For similar reasons, liberals support raising the minimum wage and perhaps even setting a guaranteed minimum income as sound policies that are likely to promote the strength of U.S. families.

Radicals: Replace the Family

The radical view begins with the close link between the family and social inequality. From a radical

LEFT TO RIGHT

THE POLITICS OF FAMILY LIFE

	RADICAL LEFT VIEW	LIBERAL VIEW	CONSERVATIVE VIEW
WHAT IS THE PROBLEM?	Family life is bound up with inequality: Families support inequality based on class, gender, and sexual orientation, all of which is unjust.	There is not enough tolerance for the broad range of family life in today's society; efforts to impose any model of an "ideal family" limit people's choices; poverty among women and children is a serious problem.	Conventional families are breaking down: Divorce, single parenting, and living together without marriage are symptoms of a "me-first" culture that weakens society and places children at risk.
WHAT IS THE SOLUTION?	Increasing social equality is possible only by radically restructuring the family as it exists today; society should consider collective arrangements for performing housework and child care.	Encourage tolerance for various kinds of families, including gay marriage. Increasing women's economic opportunities will benefit children. Enforce all antidiscrimination laws and expand affordable child-care programs.	Encourage the spread of a "culture of marriage": Make covenant marriage more widely available, abolish no-fault divorce laws; and discourage couples from living together in low-commitment relationships.

Join the debate . . .

1. In the case of families, one person's "problem" is often another person's "solution." Can you illustrate this idea using issues examined in this chapter?

2. How do people who favor each of the three political perspectives define a "family"? Highlight areas of agreement and disagreement.

3. Which of the three political analyses of U.S. families included here do you find most convincing? Why?

---

perspective, the family (at least in its current form) perpetuates inequality in at least three ways.

First, following the analysis of Friedrich Engels, noted earlier, the family helps perpetuate class stratification. Through the family individuals pass private property from one generation to another, reproducing the class system.

Second, Engels also explained that the family helps perpetuate gender stratification. Men must control the sexuality of women in order to know who their heirs are. Furthermore, so that men can leave home for the workplace, women must perform unpaid work as homemakers.

Third, because legal marriage is restricted to partners of the opposite sex, the current family system does not accept homosexual couples, instead pushing them to the margins of society. Therefore, the family also perpetuates stratification based on sexual orientation.

Taken together, these arguments give radicals who advocate an egalitarian society good reason to support an end to the family as we know it. But what is their solution to the "problem" of the family? To eliminate class inequality, society would have to treat all children in the same manner, probably by making child care a collective enterprise. Similarly, to eliminate gender inequality, society would have to redefine marriage as a partnership with shared responsibility for housework and child care as well as earning income. Collective living arrangements might enable people to share housework and child care even more efficiently. Finally, as noted in Chapter 4 ("Gender Inequality"), radical feminists envision a future in which new reproductive technology allows women to break the bonds of biology that now require them to carry children.

The Left to Right table views family problems and solutions from the three political perspectives.

GOING ON FROM HERE

The twentieth century was a time of remarkable change for families in the United States. That century opened with women having, on average, five children, no jobs, and no right to vote. The last century closed with women having, on average, two children, the availability of an ever-wider range of jobs, and growing political power.

In the decades ahead, families will continue to change. For one thing, the share of women working for income continues to rise steadily while the birth rate is falling. As the lives of women and men become more alike, conventional ideas about marriage and family life are giving way to a greater diversity in relationships. It seems likely that even if the divorce rate continues to decrease marriage for many people will not be a lifetime commitment. On the contrary, many family patterns—conventional marriage, living together, living alone, blended families, and raising children outside marriage—will all remain a part of U.S. society.

One issue that is likely to remain a topic of controversy is the rising share of children living in poverty. As conservatives see it, the solution to this problem is a return to a more traditional two-parent family; as liberals see it, the solution lies in policies that increase women's economic opportunities.

A second important question is whether—or when—gay men and lesbians will have access to legal marriage. In a 2003 decision striking down a Texas sodomy law, the U.S. Supreme Court stated that adults (whether gay or straight) have a right to privacy and respect in their sexual relationships. Gay rights activists applauded this decision as a step closer to allowing gay marriage. Although there remains strong opposition to gay marriage in the United States, there can be no question that the tide of public opinion is turning in favor of permitting all people, whether homosexual or heterosexual, to marry.

Third, and finally, the possibilities raised by new reproductive technology are sure to expand. However, it is essential that ethics keep pace with scientific ability.

For all these reasons, the debate over problems of family life is sure to continue. Indeed, a century from now, people may still be lining up on different sides as they try to answer the question, "What is a family?"

CHAPTER SUMMARY

1. The family is a social institution that unites individuals into cooperative groups that care for members, regulate sexual relations, and oversee the bearing and raising of children. Kinship is a social bond, typically based on blood, marriage, or adoption, that joins individuals into families.

2. In high-income countries including the United States, people attach importance to nuclear families; in the world's low-income nations, most people live in extended families. Around the world, families are based on marriage.

3. A traditional definition of family is a married couple with children; in recent decades, however, more people have taken a broader definition of families, even including families of affinity made up of individuals who simply think of themselves as a family.

4. A sociological view of family problems highlights the way in which society organizes family life and creates challenges for family members.

5. Some 5.6 million U.S. couples (9 percent of the total) cohabit. Given the high rate of divorce in the United States, many young people see cohabiting as a sensible way to try out a relationship. Evidence suggests that cohabitation discourages marriage and raises the rate of single parenting.

6. A trend since 1950 has been for first marriages to occur later in life; currently, the age at first marriage is about twenty-five years for women and twenty-seven for men.

7. About one-third of U.S. youngsters under eighteen live with only one parent in the home, a share that has doubled since 1970. About half of children live with one parent at some point before age they reach eighteen. Children raised in single-parent homes are at high risk for being poor and for being single parents themselves.

8. Among white families, single-parent families typically result from divorce; among African American families, two-thirds of children are born to unmarried mothers. Research suggests that a lack of jobs is the major reason for the high proportion of single-parent households in poor African American communities. African American families have a number of distinctive

strengths: building strong kinship bonds, drawing on religious faith, and having grandparents help in child rearing.

9. Because most women and men work for income, the demands of work and family life often collide, especially for women, who bear more responsibility for housework and child care.

10. Securing affordable child care is a serious problem for millions of families, especially those with low income.

11. More than 40 percent of today's marriages will end in divorce, ten times the rate of a century ago. Women's increasing independence from men, as well as no-fault divorce laws, have made divorce easier.

12. Courts order a parent to provide financial support to 59 percent of young children after parental divorce. Yet in 55 percent of all such cases, these children receive only partial payments or no payments at all.

13. Because four of five people who divorce remarry, half of all of today's marriages are remarriages for at least one partner. Remarriage creates blended families, which present some special challenges, such as forming new relationships with step-parents and step-siblings.

14. In the United States and in all but five nations of the world, the law prohibits gay couples from legally marrying. Still, there are as many as 1 million committed partnerships among gay men and lesbians, and these couples are steadily winning greater legal rights and social acceptance.

15. In vitro fertilization and other reproductive technologies help many infertile couples have children. But new reproductive technology also raises ethical questions about creating "designer" children.

16. The structural-functional approach claims that families make a vital contribution to the operation of society by regulating sexual activity, overseeing the socialization of the young, fostering economic cooperation, and generating emotional support among kin. From this perspective, threats to family stability are defined as social problems.

17. The symbolic-interaction approach views family life as the interaction of individuals. The self-image of children and the degree of intimacy shared by couples are not fixed but variable outcomes of ongoing interactions.

18. The social-conflict approach highlights the link between families and social inequality. Friedrich Engels charted the rise of families as a strategy by which men could pass property from one generation to another.

19. Conservatives define the traditional family as the foundation of a healthy society and therefore define cohabitation, a high divorce rate, and single parenting as social problems. Liberals define family diversity as positive and therefore support personal choice of family form. Radicals claim that conventional families support inequality based on class, gender, and sexual orientation and therefore support the abolition of the family as we know it.

KEY CONCEPTS

family (p. 324) a social institution that unites individuals into cooperative groups that care for members, regulate sexual relations, and oversee the bearing and raising of children

kinship (p. 324) a social bond, typically based on blood, marriage, or adoption, that joins individuals into families

nuclear family (p. 324) one or two parents and their children

extended family (p. 324) parents and children and also grandparents, aunts, uncles, and cousins who often live close to one another and operate as a family unit

marriage (p. 324) a lawful relationship—expected to be lasting—involving economic cooperation, sexual activity, and, usually, childbearing

families of affinity (p. 324) people with or without legal or blood ties who feel they belong together and want to define themselves as a family

cohabitation (p. 325) the sharing of a household by an unmarried couple

blended families (p. 334) families in which children have some combination of biological parents and step-parents

in vitro (that is, "in glass") **fertilization** (p. 336) uniting eggs and sperm in a laboratory

surrogate motherhood (p. 336) an arrangement by which a woman carries and bears a child for another

THINKING CRITICALLY: QUESTIONS AND ISSUES

1. On balance, do you think families are an "endangered species" in the United States? Why or why not?

2. Of the issues discussed in this chapter—living together, single parenting, child care, conflicts between work and family life, divorce, child support, gay marriage, and new reproductive technology—which do you view as the most serious problem? State your reasons.

3. Arlie Hochschild (1989:258) writes that changes in men's and women's lives are mostly *caused* by changes in the economy, but people *feel* these changes in their marriages. Apply this insight to various problems raised in this chapter.

4. Looking ahead to 2050, what changes in family life do you expect? Why?

GETTING INVOLVED: LEARNING ACTIVITIES

1. Call a nearby office of the Department of Health and Human Services or another local social services agency and set up an appointment to talk about the range of services the organization offers to assist families. Are there ways you can become involved in helping local families?

2. Just about everyone has friends who live in blended families. Ask several people about the rewards and challenges of living with step-parents and step-siblings.

3. Family life plays a part in almost every political campaign. Pay attention to the speeches and statements from candidates for national office and note their views on family issues. What do Democrats see as family problems? What about Republicans? How are their solutions different?

4. Every community has a good deal of ethnic diversity: Can you identify people whose culture differs from your own and learn how they see many of the issues raised in this chapter?

GETTING CONNECTED: USEFUL WEB LINKS

http://www.prenhall.com/macionis
Visit the interactive Companion Website™ that accompanies this text. Begin by clicking on the cover of your book. You will find a chapter-by-chapter study guide, practice tests, suggested Web links, and links to other relevant material.

http://www.cc.org
http://www.frc.org
Here are the Web sites for two conservative organizations: the Christian Coalition and the Family Research Council. What are their goals? What policies do they support in pursuit of what they call "family values"?

http://www.ngltf.org
This is the home page of the National Gay and Lesbian Task Force. What are this liberal organization's goals? What family policies does it advocate?

http://www.savethechildren.org
This site explains how families and, especially, children around the world are affected by war, poverty, and AIDS. Would you like to know how you can help?

http://www.slowlane.com
This site bills itself as an online resource for stay-at-home dads. What are the challenges and pleasures of this lifestyle?

GETTING STARTED ON YOUR OWN: RESEARCH NAVIGATOR™

Follow the instructions found on page 25 of this text to access the features of Research Navigator™. Once at the Web site, enter your Login Name and Password. Then, to use the **Content Select** database, enter keywords such as "family," "cohabitation," and "gay marriage,"
and the search engine will supply relevant and recent scholarly and popular press publications. Use the *New York Times* **Search-by-Subject Archive** to find recent news articles related to sociology and the **Link Library** feature to find relevant Web links organized by the key terms associated with this chapter.

CHAPTER 14

© Paul Marcus, There's Public, Then There's Public, Studio SPM, Inc.

EDUCATION

I T IS TOUGH GOING TO SCHOOL IN *Victoria Flores's neighborhood in the flatlands of Oakland, California. The fourteen-year-old recalls the time a couple of months ago when one of her girlfriends was recruited by a pimp as she walked along the street on her way to school. When she refused to talk to the man, he beat her and left her bloody on the sidewalk. "She was lucky," Victoria adds, "She's pregnant but her baby is okay."*

Growing up in such a community, Victoria has learned how to take care of herself. But her confidence was shaken when she recently entered high school. She says, "It was like hell." The room was so crowded that she and a number of other students sat in the hallway, pushing against each other as they tried to listen to the teacher through the open door. The school, originally designed for 500 students, now enrolls about 1,400. Overcrowding is not the only problem; there are not enough lockers or water fountains, there is little space for play, and the school cannot even think about buying the new computers and other scientific instruments found in high schools in wealthier parts of the Los Angeles area. It is no surprise that the school is labeled "underperforming," with more than two-thirds of the students reading below grade level (Mulrine, 2002).

―――――

Students throughout the United States pass through a school system that many people claim is in crisis. Some of the problems that contribute to this crisis include low funding, poor teaching, high dropout rates, and even outright violence. All of these problems relate to **education**, *the social institution by which society transmits knowledge—including basic facts and job skills, as well as cultural norms and values—to its members.* This chapter begins with a brief survey of schooling around the world and then assesses how well schools in the United States meet their goals of preparing young people for productive lives as adults.

GETTING THE PICTURE

✦ Can you imagine getting through the day without knowing how to read and write?

Around the world, some 850 million women and men are illiterate.

✦ Does the United States provide equal opportunity for schooling?

The poorest public school districts spend about $2,000 per year on each student; the richest spend nearly $17,500.

✦ Does schooling help youngsters from poor families raise their social standing?

Children from the poorest 20 percent of U.S. families are eight times more likely to drop out of school than those from the richest 20 percent of families.

PROBLEMS OF EDUCATION: A GLOBAL PERSPECTIVE

Everywhere in the world, parents and other community members join together to teach young people important knowledge and skills. However, **schooling,** *the formal instruction carried out by specially trained teachers,* is far more available to people in some parts of the world than in others.

Low-Income Countries: Too Little Schooling

All of the world's nations provide primary education for most children. However, in the poorest nations of central Africa and western Asia, most youngsters never set foot in a classroom. Secondary education is less common. Across Latin America, Africa, and

This young girl working in a clothing factory in Thailand is evidence of a pattern common in low-income nations: Parents are more likely to send boys to school while girls go to work to earn income. Can you explain this double standard?

Asia, about two-thirds of children do not receive secondary education.

Why is schooling so limited in poor regions of the world? Low-income countries have largely agrarian, or farming, economies; roughly half the population lives in rural communities. In such an environment, parents take primary responsibility for passing along the knowledge and skills needed for everyday life. Many families in the poorest countries of the world need their children to work rather than attend school.

To encourage economic growth, governments in poor nations are trying to expand **literacy,** *the ability to read, write, and do basic arithmetic.* Workers need literacy skills in order to work with machinery or to work in offices; a literate work force also helps attract foreign investment, which in turn creates more jobs. Literate people are more likely to take advantage of new technology that increases productivity.

But the job is not easy. Countries struggling to feed their people have few resources to expand schooling. As a result, more than 850 million of the world's adults (about one in three) are still illiterate (United Nations Development Programme, 2003). Global Map 14–1 shows that literacy rates are low—often below 50 percent—in poor regions of the world.

Gender also plays an important part in patterns of global literacy. In the poorest countries, girls and women are far less likely than boys and men to be literate. In Nepal, a poor Asian nation, only 22 percent of women can read, compared with 57 percent of men. This disparity reflects the fact that in patriarchal societies, parents are more likely to send boys to school. In poor countries, a new bride leaves her parents to live with her husband's family, so parents view investing in a daughter's future as wasteful. Parents get what they can from a daughter while she is young, typically pressuring her to take a job for wages, which explains why most child labor in the world is performed by girls. Sons remain close to home after they grow up, so parents are more willing to invest in their schooling (United Nations Development Programme, 1999; Women's International Network News, 1999b).

Obviously, low literacy rates mean a low quality of life for hundreds of millions of the world's women. But a lack of schooling also contributes to other problems. Without the ability to read, mothers have difficulty providing nutrition and health care to their young children and have few opportunities to work for income. This pattern slows economic development for the entire country. Women

A WORLD OF DIFFERENCES

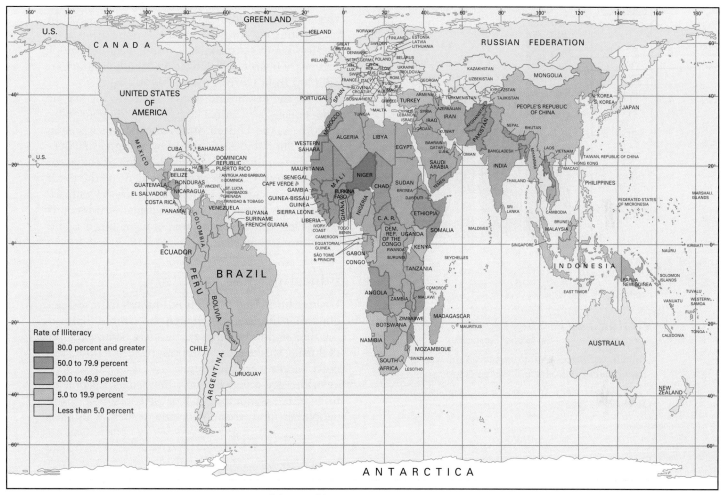

GLOBAL MAP 14–1 Literacy around the World

Illiteracy is a problem in the United States and other high-income nations, typically among the very poor. But in many of the world's lower-income countries, half or more of the people cannot read and write.

Source: United Nations Development Programme (2003) and The World Bank (2003); map projection from *Peters Atlas of the World* (1990).

who lack economic opportunity also end up having more children, adding to the burden of a poor nation already struggling to feed its people. In sum, schooling, the social standing of women, and economic development are all closely related.

High-Income Countries: Unequal Schooling

In high-income countries, where most jobs require literacy and specialized skills, people regard schooling as necessary to help young people become productive adults. This is why most people living in rich nations complete both primary and secondary schooling. In the United States, it was almost a century ago that the last of the states passed laws requiring young people to attend school until age sixteen or completion of the eighth grade.

For more on how income affects schooling, go to
http://www.census.gov/population/www/socdemo/fld-of-trn.html

DIMENSIONS OF DIFFERENCE

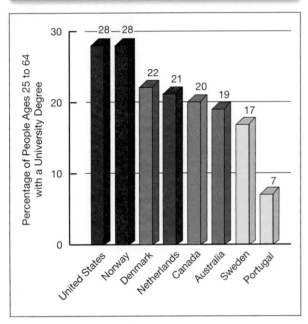

FIGURE 14–1   College Degrees in Global Perspective

The United States and Norway lead the world in the share of adults who have a college degree.

Source: Organization for Economic Cooperation and Development (2003).

High-income nations also provide postsecondary schooling for a significant share of their people. Figure 14–1 shows that the United States and Norway lead the world in sending people to college: In both countries, 28 percent of the population aged twenty-five to sixty-four has a four-year college or university degree (Organization for Economic Co-operation and Development, 2003).

But the extent and quality of schooling are far from equal. Even with a large share of people going to college, the United States also has a surprising level of illiteracy, estimated to be as high as 20 percent. This compares with 17 percent of the adult population in Canada and 10 percent of the adult population in Scandinavian nations such as Denmark and Sweden. As the next section explains, this country has fallen short of the goal of providing a sound education to everyone.

Education in U.S. History

Early political leaders, such as Thomas Jefferson, argued that literacy was vital to the United States if the new nation was to be a political democracy. At that time, this country was both rural and poor, and most people were illiterate.

Illiteracy was not widely defined as a problem, though, at least not for much of the population. Many people saw no reason to educate women, who, they

Over the course of U.S. history, the doors of schools have opened wider for white people than for African Americans. The school pictured here might seem to be from the nineteenth century, but the photograph was taken in Georgia in 1941.

thought, belonged in the home. African Americans, most of whom lived as slaves, received no schooling at all for fear that literacy would encourage rebellion. Only after the Civil War, with the abolition of slavery, did school doors opened to African Americans. In almost all cases, the schools were both separate from and unequal to those enrolling white people.

Not until the Industrial Revolution was well underway in the late 1800s was illiteracy widely defined as a problem, leading states to extend schooling. To operate the ever–more complex machinery, workers needed basic skills in reading, writing, and arithmetic. In addition, about 1 million immigrants were entering the country each year. The public expected schools to give these newcomers not only the skills they needed to work but also the cultural lessons (especially mastering the English language) they needed to become "Americanized." Many immigrants resisted such changes and did not want to send their children to public schools. Catholic immigrants, in particular, responded by forming church-sponsored *parochial schools*, which still exist throughout the country (Gutek, 1993).

By 1918, every state had enacted a mandatory education law requiring children to attend school until age sixteen or the completion of the eighth grade. Since then, as shown in Figure 14–2, the extent of schooling for the U.S. population has increased steadily. In 1920, just 16.4 percent of people aged twenty-five or older had completed high school; a college degree was even more rare, held by only 3.3 percent of adults. By 2002, however, 84 percent of adults were high school graduates, and 28 percent had earned a college degree (U.S. Census Bureau, 2003).

The twentieth century, then, was a era of dramatic change in terms of schooling in the United States. We now *expect* young people to attend school. But, as we shall now explain, today's schools face a number of serious problems. Indeed, many people think that public education in the United States is in a state of crisis.

PROBLEMS WITH U.S. EDUCATION

To understand what schools are up against, consider the scope of their task. Across the country, more than 50 million students, who speak more than 100 different languages, are enrolled in more than 100,000 public, parochial, and private schools. The budget for the country's public schools, which enroll 90 percent of all students, is almost $375 billion (U.S. National Center for Education Statistics, 2003).

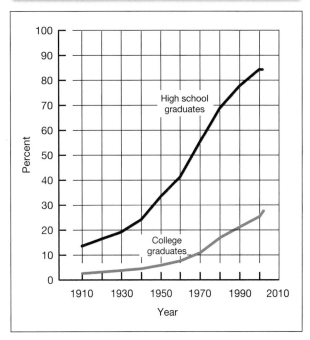

DIMENSIONS OF DIFFERENCE

FIGURE 14–2 **Schooling in the United States, 1910–2002**

Today, the share of U.S. adults who complete college is more than twice as high as the share finishing high school back in 1910.

Source: U.S. Census Bureau (2003).

Yet many are unsatisfied with the public schools. One annual survey asks a representative sample of U.S. adults to grade their local public schools. In the 2003 survey, half gave the grade of "A" or "B," but an equal share gave a grade of "C" or below (Rose & Gallup, 2003). In the following sections, we survey the performance of U.S. schools and then consider a number of other problems and controversies surrounding schooling in the United States.

Find a national survey on the quality of public schools at
http://www.pdkintl.org/kappan/k0309pol.pdf

The Academic Performance of U.S. Schools

As already noted, in no nation of the world does a larger share of the population earn a college degree than in the United States. But as shown in Table 14–1 on page 350, this country lags behind many other high-income countries in basic literacy

TABLE 14-1   BASIC LITERACY SCORES FOR THIRTY-ONE COUNTRIES

	READING	MATHEMATICS	SCIENCE	TOTAL SCORE
Japan	522	557	550	1,629
South Korea	525	547	552	1,624
Finland	546	536	538	1,620
Canada	534	533	529	1,596
New Zealand	529	537	528	1,594
Australia	528	533	528	1,589
United Kingdom	523	529	532	1,584
Ireland	527	503	513	1,543
Austria	507	515	519	1,541
Sweden	516	510	512	1,538
Belgium	507	520	496	1,523
France	505	517	500	1,522
Switzerland	494	529	496	1,519
Iceland	507	514	496	1,517
Liechtenstein	483	514	510	1,507
Norway	505	499	500	1,504
Czech Republic	492	498	511	1,501
United States	504	493	499	1,496
Denmark	497	514	481	1,492
Hungary	480	488	496	1,464
Germany	484	490	487	1,461
Spain	493	476	491	1,460
Poland	479	470	483	1,432
Italy	487	457	478	1,422
Russian Federation	462	478	460	1,400
Portugal	470	454	459	1,383
Greece	474	447	461	1,382
Latvia	458	463	460	1,381
Luxembourg	441	446	443	1,330
Mexico	422	387	422	1,231
Brazil	396	334	375	1,105

Source: U.S. National Center for Education Statistics (2003).

in reading, mathematics, and science. Of the thirty-one countries in the table, the United States ranks eighteenth in total literacy scores.

Another well-known measure of academic performance is the college entrance examination taken by U.S. high school students. The Scholastic Assessment Test (SAT), which measures both verbal and mathematical achievement, shows mixed performance over the last half century. As shown in Figure 14–3, the average test scores for both parts of the test fell dramatically after 1967 for both women and men, with some improvement after 1980. In 2003, average scores on the mathematics test (537 for men and 503 for women) stood above the 1967 averages, but average scores in the verbal test (512 for men and 503 for women), although the highest in sixteen years, remained below the 1967 averages.

The Effects of Race, Ethnicity, and Class on Academic Performance If the *average* performance of U.S. students raises concerns, the achievement of socially disadvantaged students is an even more serious problem. Indeed, the evidence suggests that our schools have failed whole segments of the population.

Although Asian American students, on average, score about the same as white students on the SAT, Hispanics trail non-Hispanic whites by an average of 120 points, and African Americans score about 180 points below the average for white students (College Board, 2003). Why such differences? A number of factors are at work. African American youngsters are more likely to live with a single parent and also more likely to have to deal with racial stereotypes that call into question their academic ability, sometimes to the point that they begin to doubt themselves. Many Hispanic youngsters begin school with little ability to speak English. If your only language is English, imagine how you might perform if you attended a school where Spanish was spoken and almost everyone was a native Spanish speaker. Although most Native Americans enter school speaking English, many view schools as representing an alien culture. Hispanics and Native Americans are the categories of the population least likely to complete a college education (about 10 percent do) (U.S. Census Bureau, 2003).

In addition, the poverty rates for Hispanic children (29 percent), African American children (32 percent), and Native American children (about 40 percent) are far greater than that for white children (14 percent) (U.S. Census Bureau, 2003). As you might expect, income is closely linked to how much schooling people receive. Moreover, the schools enrolling well-off students also have much higher per-student funding, which gives them access to better teachers, smaller classes, and better educational materials, which raises student performance on achievement tests. This is one reason high school students from families earning more than $100,000 per year average about 260 points higher on the SAT than those from families with incomes below $10,000 per year (Zernike, 2000; College Board, 2003).

Dropping Out

Beyond the question of how good schools are in the United States is the fact that many young people are not in school at all. *Dropping out*, that is, quitting school before earning a high school diploma, is a serious problem in this country.

How widespread is dropping out? Overall, 10.9 percent of the U.S. population aged sixteen to

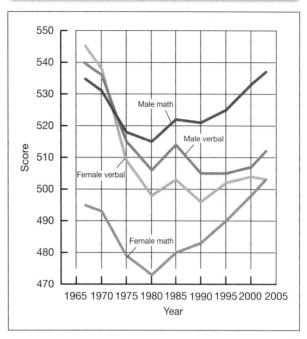

DIMENSIONS OF DIFFERENCE

FIGURE 14-3 Performance on the Scholastic Assessment Test (SAT), 1967–2003

Average scores on the mathematics part of the SAT have rebounded over the last twenty years. Scores on the verbal test, however, remain below the 1967 level.

Source: College Board (2003b).

twenty-four (3.8 million people) have left school without graduating. Over time, dropping out of school has become less common: In 1960, the rate was even higher: 14 percent. But it is still high among certain segments of the U.S. population. Figure 14–4 on page 352 shows that the dropout rate is 7 percent for non-Hispanic whites, 13 percent among African Americans, 28 percent among Hispanics, and 33 percent among Native Americans (U.S. National Center for Education Statistics, 2002).

Differences in income underlie much of this pattern. The dropout rate for young people from families with incomes in the top fifth (roughly $90,000 and above) is about 3 percent; for those from families with incomes in the bottom fifth (roughly $24,000 and below), the dropout rate is 24 percent (U.S. National Center for Education Statistics, 2002). But culture also plays a part in dropping out. For people whose native language is not English, including many Hispanics, dropout rates are especially high. The same is true for people—including

DIMENSIONS OF DIFFERENCE

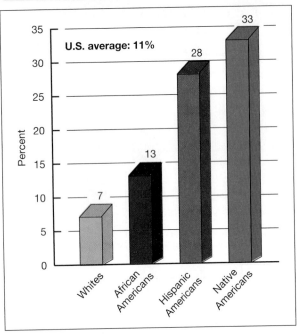

FIGURE 14-4   **Percentage of Dropouts among Categories of the U.S. Population, Ages 16 to 24**

Dropping out of school is a problem for all categories of people. But the rates are especially high among Hispanics and Native Americans.

Source: U.S. Center for Education Statistics (2002).

many Native Americans—with a historical suspicion of schools run by "outsiders."

There are many specific reasons for leaving school, including the need to work, attractive career opportunities, pregnancy, a lack of ability to speak English, and sometimes outright boredom. The decision to leave school is always complex and may or may not be seen by the person involved as an indication of failure (Hodkinson & Bloomer, 2001). But the problem of dropping out is greatest among minorities, the poor, and those whose parents have little schooling (Roscigno & Crowley, 2001). The Critical Thinking box takes a closer look at one struggling school in Nebraska.

Dropping out of school is not simply a choice made by students themselves. Take the case of Cleveland, Ohio. In that city, of all children who begin high school, only 38 percent graduate four years later (Catalyst, 2003). If most students do not graduate, it seems reasonable to wonder whether the school system itself is the problem. In Cleveland and a number of other large U.S. cities, it is quite possible that the schools are failing the students.

Whatever its causes, failing to finish school raises the risk of future problems for young people, including unemployment, drug abuse, arrest, and poverty as adults (U.S. National Center for Education Statistics, 2003). Schooling plays a part in a multigenerational cycle: Children who grow up in a disadvantaged setting are likely to become disadvantaged as adults.

Functional Illiteracy

The poor performance of many schools helps to explain the fact that roughly 20 percent of the U.S. adult population (about 35 million men and women) lacks literacy skills. This is the problem of **functional illiteracy,** *the inability to read and write or do basic arithmetic well enough to carry out daily responsibilities.* Almost half the U.S. adult population has some difficulty drawing conclusions from written material, reading an airline schedule posted on the Internet, or understanding tables and graphs such as those found in this text (National Center for Education Statistics, 2003).

Functional illiteracy is a source of embarrassment and shame. More importantly, in a world that demands increasing literacy skills with each passing year, functional illiteracy stands as a barrier to job opportunities, locking people into low-wage jobs or unemployment and, often, poverty. The fact that a sizable share of the work force cannot read or write well reduces this nation's competitiveness in a global marketplace and wastes a vital resource: human talent and ability.

School Segregation and Busing

Before the Civil War, few African Americans ever got to attend school. After the abolition of slavery in 1865, African Americans took their place in a new system of racially segregated schools. In 1896, the U.S. Supreme Court (*Plessy v. Ferguson*) affirmed the principle of racial segregation as long as the facilities for blacks and whites could be described as "separate but equal." In reality, however, black and white schools were anything but equal. Most white children attended schools with modern buildings, well-trained teachers, and up-to-date textbooks; by contrast, most African American children attended run-down schools, with poorly trained teachers and outdated, hand-me-down books.

Critical Thinking

Dropping Out: Sometimes an Epidemic

TODD CHESSMORE KNEW WHAT HE WAS GETTING INTO when he took the job as superintendent of schools in Macy, Nebraska. Part of his job is to oversee the Omaha Nation Public School, where almost all of the students are Native Americans.

The problem is that many of the students are not in school. Truancy is an issue throughout the school year, but once spring warms the cold Nebraska plains, with sunshine and rising temperatures, most of the students simply stop coming. One predictable result is that the Omaha Nation Public School ranks at the bottom of the state in student academic performance. Chessmore shakes his head and points out that in any given year, half the students do not even take the achievement test because they skip school; only a handful ever make it to college; and, worst of all, half the students who enter the school never graduate. Nationwide, the rate of dropping out among Native Americans—one in three—is only slightly better.

Chessmore has worked hard to improve attendance at the Omaha Nation Public School. He started by improving the building, washing floors, painting walls, and replacing hundreds of burned-out light bulbs. He has hired more Native American teachers and provides cultural sensitivity classes to non-Native teachers to help them understand the students' heritage and current problems. Finally, Chessmore hired several truancy officers to track down students who are not in school and, if necessary to threaten legal action against their families.

But all his efforts have had little effect. With the numbers of students in school remaining low, Chessmore decided to cancel Christmas vacation and spring break so that there are more school days before the weather turns warm and inviting. This plan may reduce truancy. But it remains highly doubtful that it will do much for the dropout rate.

ISSUES AND EXERCISES

1. Why, in your opinion, is the dropout rate so high among Native Americans?
2. Can you suggest ways to address this problem?
3. Is the situation described in this box a matter of students failing the school or the school failing the students? Why? Explain your answer.

Source: Based on Belluck (2000).

Formal segregation was the norm throughout the post–Civil War South. The North also had racially segregated schools, due not so much to law as to the fact that almost all African Americans were forced to live in mostly black neighborhoods with underfunded schools (Morgan, 1995).

As the civil rights movement gained momentum in the 1950s, activists challenged the system of segregated schools. They rallied around the case of Linda Brown, a nine-year-old girl living in Topeka, Kansas. The Defining Moment box on page 354 tells her story.

Some local governments tried to overcome the segregation that persisted long after the Supreme Court ruled, in the case of *Brown v. Board of Education of Topeka*, that separate schooling for blacks and whites was unconstitutional. But how could they achieve racial balance in schools when most black people and white people lived in separate neighborhoods? One answer was the policy of busing students from one neighborhood to a school in another neighborhood where most students were a different race. Most white parents opposed the policy, objecting to the time their children had to spend on buses and claiming that "neighborhood schools" were best for children. Black parents had a mixed reaction to busing: Some hoped the policy would improve their children's educational opportunities, but others objected to the time spent traveling to another part of the city.

As the debate continued, it became clear that busing would not succeed in integrating urban schools. In the 1960s, many white families moved from the central cities to suburbs—a pattern commonly called *white flight*—beyond the reach of busing plans (Taylor, 1998). As described in Chapter 15 ("Urban Life"), the loss of population meant a decline in tax revenues, so schools in central cities actually became worse than before.

A DEFINING MOMENT

Linda Brown: Fighting to Desegregate the Schools

It has been fifty years since Linda Brown lent her name to a landmark legal effort intended to desegregate U.S. public schools. How much has changed in that half century?

FIFTY YEARS AGO, IN THE CITY OF TOPEKA, KANSAS, a minister and his nine-year-old daughter walked hand in hand to the public elementary school four blocks from their home. The young girl, named Linda Brown, wanted to enroll in the fourth grade. But school officials refused, directing Rev. Brown to take his daughter to another school two miles away. The reason? Topeka's public schools, like those in most of the United States, were segregated by race. Because she was African American, the rules stated, Linda Brown had to go to the school for "colored" children.

Linda Brown's parents considered this policy unjust. They were not alone. A civil rights movement was developing across the United States, and the Browns became the focus of what turned out to be a defining moment in U.S. schooling. They filed a lawsuit on behalf of Linda and other African Americans challenging laws that mandated "separate but equal" schools for black and white children. In 1954, the Supreme Court of the United States considered the case, and on May 17 of that year the justices handed down a historic ruling. In *Brown v. the Board of Education of Topeka,* the Supreme Court decided that racially segregated schools provide African Americans with inferior schooling and declared the practice unlawful, overturning the doctrine of "separate but equal" schooling by race, which had been created in 1896 in the case of *Plessy v. Ferguson.*

Despite the ruling, the reality of racially segregated schools continued in the United States because black and white people typically live in different neighborhoods. Because children attend schools near their homes, many schools—even today—are filled almost entirely with children of one race. But the name Linda Brown will long stand out in the ongoing drive for racial justice in U.S. schooling.

In the 1990s, the courts finally called an end to school busing. Because most neighborhoods are still home to mostly people of the same race, schools today remain just about as racially segregated as they were in the 1960s (Bernstein, 1998).

School Funding

Schools throughout the United States differ not only in terms of their racial composition but also in the resources they can offer students. Why? Typically, a school system is controlled by the people in the local community, whose taxes (combined with money from the state) pay the cost of operating the schools.

But differences in tax revenues produce striking inequality of school budgets. Jonathan Kozol (1991) reported that affluent Great Neck, New York was spending about $15,500 per student each year, whereas less than 200 miles to the south, Camden, New Jersey, was spending just $3,500 per student each year. On a national scale, per student funding differs even more, from about $17,500 per student each year in Long Island, New York, down to only $2,000 in many poor areas of Texas (McUsic, 1999).

Such differences in funding produce great differences in schooling. The school in a poor neighborhood may be run down, lack library and science facilities, have large class sizes, and be staffed with poorly trained teachers. The Social Policy box takes

Social Policy   The "Savage Inequalities" of Schooling in the United States

"EXCUSE ME," CALLS SOCIOLOGIST JONATHAN KOZOL out his car window, "Can you tell me where P.S. 261 is?" "Sure," replies one of the two women drawing shopping baskets behind them, "Just keep going straight ahead another two blocks and look for the mortician's office."

"Mortician's office, indeed," thinks Kozol to himself as he looks for a parking spot across from the school. There seems to be something deadly about this whole neighborhood: run-down buildings, trash on empty lots, graffiti on walls, and the deafening sound of an elevated train thundering overhead.

Across the street stands New York's Public School 261, although one may not realize it because the school has no sign. As Kozol introduces himself and steps through the door, a teacher mentions that the building used to be a roller skating rink.

Kozol makes his way to the principal's office. She explains that P.S. 261 is in a minority area of the North Bronx, which means that 90 percent of the school's students are African American or Hispanic. Officially, she continues, the school is supposed to have 900 students, but actual enrollment is about 1,300. City education guidelines state that class size should not exceed 32 students, but Kozol soon observes classes with as many as 40. The cafeteria is small, forcing the school to feed the children in three shifts. There is no playground, so, after lunch, teachers try to keep children in their seats until it is time to return to the classrooms. In the entire school, Kozol finds only one classroom with a window.

An interview with a teacher sums up the state of this school. "I had an awful room last year," she explains shaking her head. "In the winter, it was 56 degrees. In the summer, it was up to 90." Kozol asks, "Do the children ever comment on the building?" "They don't say much," she responds, "but they know. All these kids see TV. They know what suburban schools are like. Then they look around them at their school. They don't comment on it, but you see it in their eyes. They understand."

Kozol visits a second school a few months later. Public School 24 is in New York's affluent Riverdale section (also in the Bronx). Like the other buildings in this upscale neighborhood, the school stands in good repair and is set back from the road by a green lawn with flowering trees. To the left, Kozol notes a playground for the youngest children; farther behind the school are playing fields where the older kids engage in team sports.

"It is no surprise," explains the principal, "that many people are willing to pay the high prices of Riverdale homes to be able to send their children to a school like this." "What is the enrollment?" asks Kozol. "Eight hundred and twenty-five children," comes the reply, "almost all in classes under thirty." Looking up and down the halls reveals that most students are white, with a handful of Asian, Hispanic, and black children. The building is a wonderful learning facility, featuring attractive, bright classrooms, a large library, and even a planetarium.

During his visit, Kozol joins a group of children in one of the many classes for gifted students. "What are you learning today?" he asks. A well-dressed young girl answers, "My name is Laurie; today, we're doing problem solving." A tall, good-natured boy continues, "I'm David. The point is to develop our ability to do logical thinking. Some problems, we find, have more than one good answer." "Let me ask your opinion," says Kozol. "Do you think this kind of reasoning is innate or is it something a child learns?" Susan smiles, revealing shiny braces, and responds: "You know some things to start with when you enter school. But we learn some things that other children don't. We learn certain things that other children don't know because we're *taught* them."

ISSUES AND EXERCISES

1. Some people argue that local communities have the right to spend whatever they want to educate their children, even though some school systems will be better funded than others. How do you respond to this argument?

2. If you were in a position to create an education funding policy, what would you do?

3. Use Research Navigator™ to learn more about U.S. schools. (See instructions on page 25; keywords: "schools," "school funding")

Source: Written by the author, based on Kozol (1992:85–88, 92–96).

The quality of any child's learning experience reflects not only the local school but the involvement of parents. Parents can increase the "cultural capital" of their children by reading to them regularly.

a closer look at Jonathan Kozol's account of what he calls the "savage inequalities" in U.S. education.

Is it possible to level the educational playing field? Doing so would require equalizing the school funding in rich and poor communities. In 1998, Vermont tried to do exactly that, enacting a law (Act 60) that pools all school taxes across the state and redistributes funding on an equal, per student basis. This means that students in affluent communities, with higher than average property taxes, get the same amount as those in poorer communities. Such "Robin Hood" laws, which take from the rich and give to the poor, do work. But they are controversial, finding favor in poor school districts and criticism in wealthier communities (Edwards, 1998; Shlaes, 1998; Goodman, 1999).

Cultural Capital Funding is not the only way schools differ. Even if all schools received the same amount of money per child, the educational experiences of richer and poorer children would still be unequal. This is because children's learning also reflects the quality of their home life. Parents with higher incomes are able to give their children greater **cultural capital,** that is, *experiences and opportunities that enhance a student's ability to learn and to succeed.* High-income parents are more likely to have a home that is spacious, quiet, and equipped with a personal computer. Having more education themselves, these parents are more likely to teach children language

skills by, say, reading with them regularly. Low-income parents are more likely to have a smaller, more crowded home and are less likely to own a computer. With less education (and a higher likelihood of speaking a language other than English in the home), they can provide less help to children doing schoolwork; with lower earnings, poor parents have less money to buy books and other learning materials (Coleman, 1966, 1988; McNeal, 1999).

Tracking

Unequal education is found not only from school to school but even within a single school as a result of **tracking,** *the policy of assigning students to different educational programs.* Supporters claim that, by tracking students based on their performance on achievement tests, schools can better address the abilities and interests of each child. They argue that if all students were to take the same curriculum, the brightest and most motivated would succeed and less intelligent and less motivated students would quickly fall behind (Brantlinger, 1993; Loveless, 1999).

Critics counter that tracking amounts to a form of institutional discrimination: Affluent children receive the best a school has to offer, leaving children from lower-income families with a second-class education. Any testing used to assign tracks is likely to be culturally biased, asking for information that well-off children are more likely to have. Because family background affects how well a child performs in school, tracking transforms a *social* advantage into an *educational* advantage (Jencks et al., 1972; Bowles & Gintis, 1976; Oakes, 1985; Cloud, 2003).

Typically, students in higher tracks attend classes that move them along quickly, with emphasis on critical thinking and creativity. Those in lower tracks are likely to progress more slowly, with a focus on basic skills and the importance of following directions. Imagine that children in two different tracks were studying the civil rights movement. Teachers in the advanced track might ask students to identify the strategies used by activists to bring about change and to assess the strengths and weaknesses of each one. Based on this discussion, they might move on to considering ways people today might improve the status of African Americans. Teachers in a lower track might ask children only to identify the movement's leaders and highlight key events.

Read a recent report on school tracking in Canada at
http://www.peopleforeducation.com/tracking/
summrpts/second/03/summary.pdf

In light of the controversy over tracking, schools across the country are now more careful about assigning children to different programs and allow more mobility from one track to another. The goal of schooling is to help all students learn as much as they can, but tracking can affect the ability and desire of students to learn. Children in higher tracks tend to think of themselves as bright and able; children in lower tracks have lower self-esteem and come to question their own abilities (Kozol, 1991; Gamoran, 1992; Loveless, 1999; Olin, 2003).

Gender Inequality

Gender also shapes the quality of education in the United States. For generations, the two sexes followed different programs of study. Schools steered boys into courses such as woodworking and mechanical shop that would prepare them for industrial jobs. Girls were tracked into courses such as home economics, typing, and shorthand that prepared them to be homemakers or to perform clerical work. College men were encouraged to study the sciences (including physics, chemistry, biology, and mathematics), whereas college women studied English, foreign languages, and the social sciences.

School text books also reflected the two sexes in stereotypical roles. They portrayed women working in the home and men in the paid work force (Spender, 1989; Basow, 1992; Wood, 1994). Even the organization of the school itself provided lessons concerning gender. Generations of students observed that most teachers (especially in lower grades) were women, whereas most of the people in charge—principals and senior administrators—were men (Richardson, 1988; U.S. Census Bureau, 2002).

Over the course of the twentieth century, girls and women gradually gained more equal standing in schools. One important step occurred in 1972 when Congress passed Title IX of the Education Amendments to the Civil Rights Act. Title IX bans sex discrimination in education and mandates schools receiving federal funding to provide equal programs for male and female students. Since then, change has accelerated. In the elementary grades, girls are as likely as boys to be placed in classes for gifted students. In the higher grades today, more young women than young men qualify for advanced placement courses, which provide better preparation for college. For more than a decade, women have outnumbered men on this country's college and university campuses; nationwide, women now represent

This nation's high rate of immigration creates challenges for schools. In this ESL (English as a Second Language) classroom, students who speak a wide range of languages at home come together to learn English.

56 percent of all undergraduates (U.S. National Center for Education Statistics, 2003).

Even so, women still predominate in many traditionally feminine majors, such as the allied health professions (including nursing and physical therapy), teaching, graphic arts, and office technology, as well as languages, drama, and dance (Sadker, 1999).

At all levels of the educational system, researchers point to differences in the ways in which teachers relate to female and male students. Typically, teachers call on males more often than females, ask males more challenging questions, and encourage males more. Some analysts claim that as a result, the educational and career aspirations of many girls decline over time, which may play a part in the fact that men still dominate almost all high-prestige areas of graduate study, including law and medicine (Sadker & Sadker, 1986, 1994; Spender, 1989; Sadker, 1999; U.S. National Center for Health Statistics, 2000).

Immigration: Increasing Diversity

Another challenge facing U.S. schools involves the more than 1 million immigrants who enter this country every year. As Chapter 3 ("Race and Ethnic Inequality") describes in detail, these immigrants represent more than 100 cultures and languages. Most of these newcomers look to public schools to provide their children with the knowledge and skills needed to get good jobs.

Social Policy   It's More than Talk: The Politics of Bilingual Education

ONE TASK OF SCHOOLING HAS ALWAYS BEEN to socialize children—including those from diverse social backgrounds—to U.S. culture. As immigration to the United States intensified a century ago, people looked to schools to help newcomers learn the ways of their new land and, most important, to teach them the English language. To ensure that everyone learned English, Nebraska passed a law in 1919 stating that all public school teachers were prohibited from teaching in any language other than English until at least the ninth grade. Many other states followed suit. Such laws were popular because people feared that immigrants who kept their native language might be disloyal to the United States in times of war. In 1923, however, the U.S. Supreme Court (*Meyer v. State of Nebraska*) declared the Nebraska law and similar laws in other states to be unconstitutional.

Fast-forward to 1971, when the 2,800 Chinese students enrolled in the San Francisco school system found no classes in Chinese and not enough classes to teach them English. A group of parents sued the school district, claiming that the lack of language classes violated the Civil Rights Act of 1964, which bans any program receiving federal funds from discriminating on the basis of race, color, or national origin. This case went to the U.S. Supreme Court (*Lau v. Nichols*, 1974), which ruled that all students have a right to be taught in a language they can understand. School administrators took this decision to mean that public schools had to create programs to give all children instruction in their native language, whether it is English or some other tongue.

Opposition to bilingual education remains strong. Critics of bilingualism claim that teaching in a language other than English may have short-term benefits but harms the long-term career prospects of students. Furthermore, critics continue, bilingual education encourages cultural division instead of emphasizing the cultural patterns most people share.

In 1998, Californians passed Proposition 227, which bans bilingual programs in favor of the English immersion approach. Supporters claim that this law helps minority students. Opponents challenge this claim. Recent studies suggest that the effects of the new law have been minimal, ensuring that the debate will continue.

ISSUES AND EXERCISES

1. Have any members of your sociology class had experience with either English immersion or bilingual education? If so, discuss advantages and disadvantages of each policy.

2. In your opinion, is the debate surrounding language instruction in schools really about what's good for students or more about whether people favor cultural unity or cultural diversity?

3. [Research Navigator.com] Use Research Navigator™ to learn more about bilingual education. (See instructions on page 25; keywords: "bilingual education," "Proposition 227")

Sources: Chavez (1998), Mitchell et al. (1999), Mora (1999), Ochoa (1999), Parrish et al. (2002).

English Immersion versus Bilingualism   Many young immigrants and children of immigrants do well in school. But almost one in five people under the age of eighteen speaks a language other than English at home. How should schools respond to the challenge of teaching students who know little English? Two opposing policies are being hotly debated. The first policy is **English immersion.** Under this policy, non–English speakers in classes are taught in English, except perhaps for one class (known as English as a Second Language, or ESL) in which they learn English with a native language teacher.

The second approach is **bilingual education,** *a policy of offering most classes in students' native language while also teaching them English.* In this case, schools must hire many teachers skilled not only in a particular subject matter but also in a non-English language. In California, where students speak more than 100 languages, bilingual education is a tremendous challenge (Mitchell et al., 1999).

Almost everyone agrees that young people from diverse cultural backgrounds should finish school knowing how to speak English. But people disagree over the emphasis on English versus a native language. The issue is controversial because English immersion and bilingual education are grounded in different political objectives: to "Americanize" students by teaching them the dominant culture (English immersion) or to teach respect for the cultural backgrounds of all students (bilingual education). The Social Policy box takes a closer look at the politics underlying this debate.

Click on the bilingual resources link at
http://www.edb.utexas.edu/coe/depts/ci/bilingue/index.html

Whatever its long-term effects, bilingualism has certainly sparked debate over the best way to teach students whose first language is not English. The projected increase in Hispanic American and Asian American students, shown in Figure 14–5, means that this issue will only grow in importance in the years to come (Wellner, 2000; U.S. Census Bureau, 2003).

Schooling People with Disabilities

The debate over whether schools meet the needs of students extends to people of all classes, colors, and cultures with mental or physical disabilities. In 2001, more than 6 million students with disabilities were enrolled in special education programs in public schools, at a cost exceeding $20 billion (Lipsky & Gartner, 1997; U.S. Department of Education, 2002).

Throughout most of U.S. history, few children with disabilities received any schooling at all. This changed in 1975, when Congress passed the Education for All Handicapped Children Act, which requires states to educate all children with disabilities. Furthermore, this law directs schools to place students with disabilities in the "least restrictive environment," meaning that, as much as possible, schools should treat them like anyone else while meeting their special needs (Winzer, 1993). This mandate to include students with disabilities in regular school programs led to the policy of **mainstreaming,** *integrating special students into the overall educational program.* Supporters of mainstreaming argue that taking part in regular classes affords students with disabilities a better, more challenging education. In addition, students without disabilities learn to interact with people who differ from themselves.

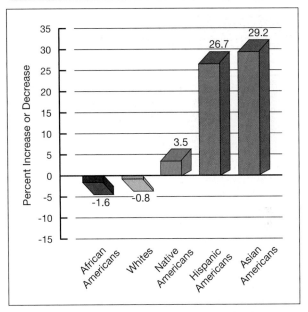

DIMENSIONS OF DIFFERENCE

FIGURE 14–5 **Projected Change in School-Age* U.S. Population, 2003 to 2013**

The challenge of schooling a multicultural population will increase in years to come, with large projected increases in the number of Hispanic- and Asian-American children.

*Children ages five to eighteen.

Source: U.S. Census Bureau (2003).

Critics of mainstreaming point out that there is little solid research showing that it improves academic performance. Furthermore, they argue that many students with disabilities find it difficult or even impossible to participate in regular classes. The alternative to mainstreaming is special classes, with teachers specially trained to meet the particular needs of people with physical or mental disabilities. This approach generally is more costly than mainstreaming.

How widely is each approach used? In the United States, about half of students with disabilities are mainstreamed, remaining in their regular classroom or leaving for no more than 20 percent of the day, another one-fifth attend mostly special classes, and the remaining one-third split their time between general classes and special classes. In general, students with physical or mental disabilities that do not greatly restrict their activities are mainstreamed; those who are more severely challenged attend special classes (Lipsky & Gartner, 1997; Winzer, 1993; U.S. Department of Education, 2002).

A NATION OF DIVERSITY

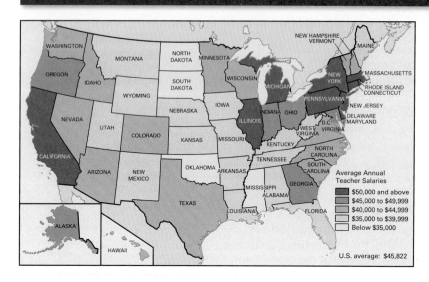

NATIONAL MAP 14–1
Public School Teachers' Pay across the United States

Over the last decade, teachers' salaries have increased only about 0.3 percent per year, not keeping up with the rate of inflation. Average pay in some states is far higher than in others. Looking at the state-by-state averages, what pattern can you see?

Source: National Education Association (2003).

The Teacher Shortage

Yet another problem for U.S. public schools is hiring enough teachers to fill the classrooms. Across the country, roughly 200,000 jobs remain unfilled each year. Looking ahead, more than 2 million new teachers will be needed over the coming decade (NEA, 2003). A shortage of teachers means larger class sizes and a greater burden on existing staff. Low salaries are one factor: Many districts simply pay too little to attract many well-qualified teachers. National Map 14–1 shows teacher salaries across the United States.

But more than money is involved. Many people have left teaching, frustrated by extensive bureaucracy and frightened by high levels of school violence. In addition, large urban school systems typically are very slow to screen candidates, so applicants grow tired of waiting and take other jobs.

How will these slots be filled? About the same number of people graduate with education degrees each year, but except for their education courses, most lack a degree in a specific field (such as mathematics, biology, or English), and many have trouble passing state certification tests in the areas they want to teach.

As a result, schools have adopted new recruitment strategies. Some analysts suggest that community colleges could provide more programs to prepare people to become teachers. Others support using incentives such as higher salaries and signing bonuses to draw people who have already established successful careers into teaching. Finally, many school districts are going global, actively recruiting in countries such as Spain, India, and the Philippines to bring talented women and men to U.S. classrooms (Dervarics, 1999; Lord, 2001; Philadelphia, 2001; Evelyn, 2002).

School Violence

The 1990s was a decade of deadly violence at schools in several U.S. cities and towns. Shootings took place in schools in Paducah, Kentucky; Jonesboro, Arkansas; and, most seriously, Littleton, Colorado, where two students went on an armed rampage that left twelve students and one teacher dead (Elliott, Hamburg, & Williams, 1998; Gibbs, 1999).

Homicide is the most serious form of school violence; other serious violence, including aggravated assault, rape, and armed robbery are far more common. According to the federal government, one in five public middle schools and high schools reported at least one of these serious violent crimes in 2002 (U.S. Departments of Education and Justice, 2002).

What kinds of schools experience the most violence? In general, the larger the school, the higher the risk of violence, a fact that helps explain why most serious incidents take place in large urban or suburban schools rather than in small, rural schools. School violence is a greater problem in poor areas of cities, in schools with mostly minority students. Research shows that the greatest fear of school violence is reported by African American and Hispanic students (Elliott,

Hamburg, & Williams, 1998; Thernstrom, 1999; U.S. Departments of Education and Justice, 2002).

What can schools do to fight back? One recent approach is for school officials to take a *zero-tolerance policy* not only toward violence but also toward possession of a weapon, alcohol, or other drugs. Students who violate these rules are severely punished, even to the point of being permanently expelled from school. Across the United States, 95 percent of schools have adopted zero-tolerance policies for firearms, and many also use metal detectors and security guards. In addition, many schools have enacted dress codes to prevent students from wearing gang colors and insignia, and others have turned to school uniforms to prevent students from being attacked for their shoes, jackets, or other apparel. Finally, some schools now offer conflict resolution programs to teach students how to avoid violence by resolving conflict peacefully (Samples & Abner, 1998; Ballantine, 2001; U.S. Departments of Education and Justice, 2002).

Are these policies working? Government data show the level of violence by 2000 had fallen by 10 percent compared with 1990 (U.S. Departments of Education and Justice, 2002). But critics claim that the "get-tough" zero-tolerance policy often is racially biased, subjecting minority students to more frequent searches and more severe penalties than whites. Critics also point out that kicking students out of school does them little good because, on the street, the likelihood of further crime and violence is even higher (Bowditch, 1993; Skiba, 2000; Ballantine, 2001).

THEORETICAL ANALYSIS: UNDERSTANDING EDUCATIONAL PROBLEMS

Each of the sociology's major theoretical perspectives offers insights into the purposes and the problems of schooling. We begin with the structural-functional approach.

Structural-Functional Analysis: The Functions of Schooling

Structural-functional analysis points out that the smooth operation of modern societies depends on schooling. A wide range of knowledge and skills enables young people to take their place as productive adults. As the U.S. economy has expanded, responsibility for training the young has moved from parents to specially trained teachers.

Schooling also functions as an important system of social placement. Our society looks to schools to help people develop their talents and abilities so they can find an appropriate job. Over the course of this nation's history, schooling has proven to be a major avenue of upward social mobility for generations of people (including millions of immigrants) who want a better life.

Given the cultural diversity of the U.S. population, schools also have an important task in helping to teach widely shared cultural beliefs and values. For example, U.S. schools teach young people about the importance of achievement and the rules of fair play. More specifically, U.S. society relies on schools to teach people how they can participate in this country's political and economic systems. In short, schools help to integrate individuals from many different cultural traditions into a single national community (Washburn, 1986; Fine, 1993; Ballantine, 2001).

Schooling also performs many latent, or less widely recognized, functions. For example, schools provide child care for working parents and, in many cases, offer before- and after-hours child care. They also occupy young people who might otherwise have trouble finding jobs or engage in crime. In sum, given the central part schooling plays in the organization of modern societies, it is easy to understand why many people view issues such as poor teaching, dropping out, and classroom violence as serious social problems (Fuller, Elmore, & Orfield, 1996; Stone, 1998).

Critical evaluation. The structural-functional approach points out how schools make important contributions to the operation of society. In this analysis, schooling is good for everyone. But critics of this approach point out that schools do not serve the interests of all. On the contrary, not everyone finds the experience of going to school a positive one. To better understanding how people experience schools, we turn to second theoretical approach, which highlights the interaction between students and school personnel.

Symbolic-Interaction Analysis: Labels in the Schools

The symbolic-interaction approach provides a micro-level look at how individuals might experience the school system. At this level, we see how school officials define the academic ability of each student.

As students move through each school year, they receive grades for their work. In addition, based on their performance on standardized tests, school officials label them as, say, "gifted," "average," or "deficient." To some extent, of course, these labels are a reflection of the work students have done in the past. At the same time, as already noted in the earlier discussion of tracking, other factors—including social class and race—play a part in the label attached to each child's performance.

Just as important, labels have importance for the future. When school officials label students as exceptionally bright or as slow learners, the students, over time, are likely to come to think of themselves in this way and perform accordingly. Thus, symbolic-interaction analysis shows us how tracking and other forms of labeling can create a **self-fulfilling prophecy,** *a situation in which people who are defined in one way eventually think and act as if the definition were true.* In practice, therefore, students labeled as slow learners are likely to perform poorly. It is not surprising that they are at higher risk for leaving school altogether (Bowles & Gintis, 1976; Ballantine, 2001).

The way in which teachers and counselors react to female and male students can also shape the future. For example, to the extent that school personnel consider some areas of study suitable for girls and others suitable for boys, we can understand why, by the time students reach college, many end up segregated into different areas of study (Sadker & Sadker, 1986, 1994; Spender, 1989; Sadker, 1999).

Critical evaluation.   The strength of the symbolic-interaction approach lies in providing a "street-level" view of how interacting individuals generate reality. At the same time, however, the participants in any social situation are not all equal. For example, teachers have more power to shape the reality of the classroom than students do. In the same way, larger social forces—such as social class—influence what different students may experience in the same school and generate different realities from school to school. These disparities bring us to the social-conflict approach.

Social-Conflict Analysis: Schooling and Inequality

The social-conflict approach highlights how schooling is linked to social inequality in U.S. society. Following this approach, we see that schooling in this country is very unequal because some categories of students benefit and others are left behind. Behind this inequality is the fact that the U.S. educational system simply fails to teach some categories of students, through no fault of their own.

As explained earlier in this chapter, some schools receive far higher levels of funding than others. The predictable result, according to a social-conflict analysis, is that some schools are well-maintained and richly equipped, with well-trained and highly motivated teachers. Others are run down and lacking in basic facilities, with teachers who are poorly trained and unenthusiastic about teaching.

In addition, within any single school, the policy of tracking mandates that the best the school has to offer goes to the students who already have a lot going for them: those from higher class backgrounds. As a result, children who are socially disadvantaged at the outset find that school only

One example of tracking is placing "gifted" students together in "enriched" classes. What effect might the label "gifted" have on the way teachers treat students?

reaffirms their second-class standing (Oakes, 1982, 1985; Kozol, 1991).

More broadly, social-conflict theory maintains that schooling in the United States amounts to a system of social control. Not only does the system perpetuate social inequality based on class, race, and gender, but it socializes all students to be docile, obedient workers and patriotic citizens. In this way, schooling incorporates a **hidden curriculum,** *explicit and subtle presentations of political or cultural ideas in the classroom that support the status quo.* Students are taught to view social problems as the personal failings of individuals, to support the existing economic and political system, and to believe that the United States is a better nation than any other. In short, rather than learning to think critically and creatively—especially about social justice—most students learn only to follow directions, to respect authority figures, and to fit into the system (Bowles & Gintis, 1976; Kozol, 1991; McLaren & Giarelli, 1995).

Critical evaluation. A strength of the social-conflict approach is that it shows the many ways in which schooling reflects and perpetuates social inequality. But this approach, too, has its critics. One issue is that a social-conflict approach overlooks the great strides that U.S. society has made in educating its people over the course of the last century. Moreover, schooling has provided the opportunity for upward social mobility for generations of people of all social backgrounds. Finally, although schools teach beliefs and values that support the status quo, the fact that schools mix people of different cultures and class positions suggests that schooling also is a force for change.

POLITICS AND EDUCATION: CONSTRUCTING PROBLEMS AND DEFINING SOLUTIONS

As we found in earlier chapters, politics plays an important part in what people define as social problems and what policies they support as solutions. Here, we present conservative, liberal, and radical perspectives on the state of education in the United States.

Conservatives: Increase Competition

Schooling is one area in which conservatives do not support the status quo; on the contrary, they are outspoken in their criticism of public education in the United States. As they see it, the poor performance of many public schools has become a scandal, and they point to the failure of many big-city public school systems (including, as noted earlier, Cleveland, Ohio) to graduate even half their students. Moreover, throughout the United States, educational standards haven fallen. The reason for the crisis, as conservatives see it, is that the government has an educational monopoly—controlling the system of public education—so that public schools across the country do not have to compete for students. Schools receive tax money regardless of how schools perform, and parents living in districts with poor schools have few choices.

No business operating as a monopoly has any incentive to provide consumers with high value; therefore, conservatives argue, we must make schools more competitive. If public schools had to compete for students, they would have to do a good job or they would go out of business.

Increased competition is the heart of the strategy of school choice. One policy designed to increase choice is the creation of **charter schools,** *public schools that are given more freedom to try out new policies and programs.* Charter schools are subject to less regulation as long as their students perform above the average. Almost 2,500 charter schools in thirty-six states now enroll 1.5 percent of public school students.

Adopting a similar strategy, some districts have developed **magnet schools,** *public schools that offer special facilities and programs in pursuit of educational excellence.* There are more than 1,700 magnet schools in the United States offering special instruction in areas including the sciences and foreign languages. Magnet schools, which enroll less than 1 percent of public school students, have been able to improve education for a limited number of children (U.S. National Center for Educational Statistics, 2003).

Conservatives also support increased competition by allowing private companies to engage in *schooling for profit.* Private schools are nothing new, of course: More than 25,000 private schools now operate in the United States. The point here is to let for-profit companies take over the operation of inefficient public schools, with the expectation that they can operate the school system more efficiently than government bureaucrats, who have shown little inclination to make needed changes. A number of U.S. cities, including Baltimore, Miami, Hartford, Boston, and Philadelphia, have experimented with for-profit schooling, with mixed results: Some companies have succeeded in improving learning, others have not (Caruso, 2002; McGurn, 2002; Winters, 2002).

A final conservative policy is the **school voucher program,** *a program that provides parents with funds*

Most people agree that inner-city schools have problems. Conservatives blame the government monopoly and teachers' unions that resist competition. Liberals call for greater spending on schools and more equal funding from district to district. Radicals claim that, as long as striking inequality exists in society, schools will serve some and fail to teach others.

they can use at a public school or private school of their choice. A voucher program says, in effect, "You are entitled to use your tax money to school your children wherever you want." Vouchers are especially popular among low-income families, who seek alternatives to the poor public schools in their neighborhoods. Many who have this option choose to send their children to parochial schools—that is, schools run by a church (most are operated by the Roman Catholic Church)—where there is greater discipline, less disruption, more learning, and fewer students dropping out. Many U.S. cities, including Cleveland, Indianapolis, Minneapolis, Milwaukee, Chicago, and Washington, D.C., have experimented with choice plans in recent years, and in 2002 the U.S. Supreme Court upheld Cleveland's voucher program as lawful (McUsic, 1999; Lord, 2002; Morse, 2002). The Personal Stories box takes a closer look at one family's experiences with vouchers.

Conservatives support school choice and the certification or testing of teachers as means to force all schools, both public and private, to show greater *accountability*. In 2002, President Bush signed an education bill calling for the testing of all public school students in grades 3 through 8 in language arts, mathematics, and science, a law that received wide support from conservatives. Schools in which students perform poorly are required to show improvement in coming years; if they do not, parents will get the option of moving their children to another school. However, the 2002 bill did not call for expanded voucher programs (Espo, 2001; Lindlaw, 2002).

Liberals: Increase Special Programs

Liberals consider public schools to be a vital part of U.S. society. Although they concede that some schools are not doing their job very well, they view struggling schools as a symptom of broader social problems including racial discrimination and economic inequality. Recall the great differences in school funding, for example: With some schools receiving only a fraction of what others get each year, should we be surprised that some students are left behind? In addition, given the striking class differences in U.S. society, some students benefit from greater cultural capital, just as others have the odds stacked against them long before they reach their first year in school. In addition, as we have already noted, millions of young people face the challenge of speaking a first language other than English.

Liberals support some forms of school choice (particularly magnet schools), but their policy for improving schools is to call for greater investment in all schools so that they can better meet the needs of all students. For preschoolers, liberals support expanded funding for Head Start, a government program that helps prepare disadvantaged children for school. Head Start helps children from low-income families catch up to more privileged children in the critical early years (Zigler & Styfco, 1994; Eskenazi, 2000).

Liberals also voice strong support for bilingual programs, which conservatives oppose. Liberals claim that bilingual education not only allows students to progress in other subjects at the same time that they are learning English but also helps everyone recognize and value the full range of cultural diversity found in the United States (Ochoa, 1999).

Finally, liberals argue in favor of programs, both during and after school, that help involve students more deeply with their school and, in the process, decrease the likelihood of problems such as drug use and violence (Hawkins, Farrington, & Catalano, 1998; Samples & Abner, 1998).

Liberals support expanding the national budget for education to fund all these strategies. They

Personal Stories   Choosing a Better School: "The Best Feeling"

EVERY MORNING DELVOLAND SHAKESPEARE WALKS from his home in Cleveland, Ohio, buckles his two sons into the back seat of his gray Ford Taurus, and drives them to a Catholic school called Our Lady of Peace. Mr. Shakespeare thinks the school is the best opportunity his sons have ever had. Eight-year-old Landel has learned to use a computer; five-year-old Isaiah is learning to read. After dropping off the boys, Mr. Shakespeare parks the car and watches his sons line up to enter the building. "That," he says with a wide grin, "gives me the best feeling."

When Landel was ready to begin kindergarten, Mr. Shakespeare and his wife, Charlynn, decided to do some investigating. They knew that Cleveland's public schools, like other inner-city schools across the United States, have their share of problems, and that more than half the students who reach high school never graduate. So they planned a visit to the public school in their neighborhood. On several corners around the school, they noticed drug dealers and prostitutes. Inside, they found the books to be in terrible shape—some without covers, many replaced by photocopies. Mr. Shakespeare's worst fears were confirmed when he entered the boys' restroom and a young man offered to sell him marijuana.

One visit was enough to convince the Shakespeares that they had to do whatever it took to find a better school for their children. They cut back on their expenses, trying to save enough to afford a private school. But the cost of private schooling is high, and the tuition for two children was simply out of their reach. Then they heard about a new, experimental "choice" program: Low-income families could enter a lottery in the hope of winning a voucher worth $2,500 that could be used for tuition at any school. They signed up and

were delighted when Landel won a school voucher. Three years later, when Isaiah was ready to start kindergarten, he also won a voucher.

Like most low-income families in the inner city, the Shakespeares are strong supporters of school choice, which they believe has greatly benefited their children. But not everyone agrees that a voucher program is a good idea. Some people object to giving tax dollars to any religious school on the grounds that doing so violates the Constitutional separation of church and state. Others claim that voucher programs are drawing the best students from public schools, leaving the weakest students behind. Finally, some oppose vouchers simply because, as they see it, the real problem is fixing public schools, not abandoning them.

ISSUES AND EXERCISES

1. Older students have long used government grants and loans to attend colleges and universities affiliated with religious organizations. Do you think younger people should be able to use vouchers to attend parochial schools? Why or why not?

2. Do you think families such as the Shakespeares who apply for vouchers differ, on balance, from those families who don't? How? Might a voucher system penalize children of less involved parents?

3. Research Navigator.com — Use Research Navigator™ to learn more about school choice. (See instructions on page 25; keywords: "school choice," "school vouchers")

Source: Shlaes (1998).

---

contend that it is far less costly to pay for good schools today than to pay the costs of dealing with the problems that result from poor schools—including crime, drug abuse, and functional illiteracy—later on.

Radicals: Attack Structural Inequality

Radicals on the left argue that many social problems, including problems of our schools, arise from basic

flaws in the economic and political structure of society. As long as wealth and power are highly concentrated, this nation can never provide good schooling to all. Indeed, as they exist now, schools make the problem worse by defining the problem of poor academic performance as the shortcoming of *individuals* rather than as the result of *structural inequality*.

Radicals agree with liberals that public schools deserve more funding. At the very least, they argue,

LEFT ⊚ RIGHT

THE POLITICS OF EDUCATION

	RADICAL LEFT VIEW	LIBERAL VIEW	CONSERVATIVE VIEW
WHAT IS THE PROBLEM?	Because schools operate within a social system marked by striking inequality of wealth and power, they fail much of the U.S. population and perpetuate class differences.	Although schools are educating more young people than ever before, they lack the funds and programs to meet the needs of some categories of the population.	Schools are a government monopoly that does not operate efficiently and is not accountable. Schools fail to educate a significant share of young people.
WHAT IS THE SOLUTION?	Equalize funding for all schools; ultimately, the solution lies in making radical changes in the economic and political systems to create a more egalitarian society.	Increase government funding for schools, especially in disadvantaged areas; expand Head Start and bilingual programs to improve schooling for minorities and low-income children.	Various strategies such as schooling for profit and the use of school vouchers will force public schools to become more competitive; all schools must be made accountable for their performance.

Join the debate . . .

1. All political perspectives agree on one thing: schools in the United States are not doing the job they should be. In light of this fact, why do you think there has been little change in schools over recent decades?

2. Using each of the three political perspectives, respond to the following assertion: "Schooling in

the United States advances the goal of equal opportunity by providing a learning program that matches a student's abilities and interests."

3. Which of the three political analyses of U.S. schooling included here do you find most convincing? Why?

---

we need to eliminate the disparity of funding between wealthy schools and those in less affluent districts. A step in that direction is the action taken by the state of Vermont in 1998 to equalize funding to school districts statewide on an even, per student basis. The Vermont program should raise the quality of schools in poor communities without harming the quality of schools in rich neighborhoods (although taxes in wealthy communities will have to go up in order to maintain existing standards).

Yet such a program goes only so far. Even if schools were all exactly the same, some students would still have great advantages over others based on their social background. Radicals conclude that the only way to make good education available to everyone is to eliminate the striking inequality found throughout society as a whole. This revolutionary idea would require basic changes to both the capitalist economy and the existing political system. The Left to Right table summarizes the conservative, liberal, and radical perspectives on the state of U.S. schools.

GOING ON FROM HERE

Most people in the United States believe that schooling is the key to economic opportunity: A high school diploma and college degree (perhaps also a graduate degree) open doors to better jobs and higher income (NORC, 2003). For this reason, we like to say that our schools provide every child not only with basic learning but with the chance to develop personal abilities and interests.

In recent decades, as the Information Revolution has raised the importance of literacy skills, schooling has become more important than ever. Yet, as this chapter has shown, U.S. public schools are plagued by shortcomings: Measures of student performance have fallen in recent decades, and almost 20 percent of young people (more than 50 percent in some large cities) drop out before finishing high school.

What are the prospects for change? People across the political spectrum agree that changes must be made. But there is far less agreement as to exactly what the problems and solutions are. Conservatives argue that public school systems as we know them may have to change before student performance will improve. Indeed, school choice policies and school accountability have become hotly debated issues in dozens of cities across the country and were played out again in the 2004 presidential campaign. Liberals, who offer strong support for the idea that government should run high-quality schools, counter that school choice policies are likely to help some students (especially those with involved parents) but will leave others behind. Liberals push for greater funding for all schools, with the belief that greater investment in public education will raise student performance. They also note that in decades to come, this country's schoolchildren will become ever more culturally diverse,

highlighting the importance of bilingual and multicultural programs.

Radical ideas are also likely to shape the future of schooling. Vermont already has enacted a bold (and controversial) program to ensure that all school systems receive equal per student funding. Will governments elsewhere enact similar legislation? Because the idea of equal funding challenges the long-established practice of local control of schools, change in this direction is likely to be slow and hotly contested. Yet given the extent of funding inequality noted in this chapter, public support for a more equal policy may well grow.

In sum, when it comes to schools in the United States, almost everyone is in favor of change. But precisely what changes are to come is a political decision that will be made as today's students take their places as adults.

CHAPTER SUMMARY

1. Education is the social institution by which society transmits knowledge—including basic facts, job skills, and cultural norms and values—to its members. As societies industrialize, they require young people to attend schools, where students receive instruction by specially trained teachers.

2. In low-income countries of the world, many young people, especially girls, receive little or no schooling; about one-third of adults in the world are illiterate. In high-income countries, most people complete secondary school, and a significant share complete a college degree.

3. Only after the abolition of slavery did large numbers of African Americans attend school; with industrialization and the rise in immigration, all states passed mandatory education laws by 1918. As women moved into the labor force over the course of the twentieth century, they also joined men at colleges and universities.

4. Of all industrialized nations, the United States has the highest percentage of people (about 28 percent) with college degrees. But on tests of literacy and science skills, U.S. students lag behind their counterparts in many other high-income nations.

5. In 2001, 10.9 percent of young people (3.8 million) had dropped out before completing a high school diploma. Compared with whites (7 percent), African Americans (13 percent), Hispanics (28 percent), and Native Americans (33 percent) have higher dropout rates.

6. Functional illiteracy is a serious problem in the United States, where about 20 percent of adults cannot read or write well enough to carry out their daily tasks.

7. The concept of "separate but equal" schools was established by the Supreme Court in 1896 (*Plessy v. Ferguson*). In 1954, the U.S. Supreme Court declared laws that racially segregate schools to be unconstitutional. When busing was used to integrate schools, "white flight" took many white families to the suburbs. As a result, public schools today remain about as racially segregated as they were in the 1960s.

8. Because U.S. public schools are funded by state and local taxes, the richest school districts spend eight to nine times as much per student as the poorest school districts. In addition to attending better schools, children from affluent families also benefit from greater cultural capital: experiences and opportunities at home that enhance learning.

9. Tracking is a school policy that assigns children to various academic programs. Supporters claim that tracking provides students with schooling

consistent with their interests and abilities. Critics claim that tracking assignments often are made according to social background, so that affluent students benefit and disadvantaged students are harmed.

10. Today, a majority (56 percent) of college students are women. However, gender still operates as a form of tracking that guides women and men into different majors.

11. Cultural diversity is another challenge to U.S. schools. A debate centers on whether it is better to place non–English speakers in English immersion courses or to use a policy of bilingual education.

12. Some 6 million people with disabilities are enrolled in U.S. schools. Whether it is better to mainstream these students or to provide them with separate specialized programs is an ongoing issue.

13. Violent crime is a serious problem in U.S. schools. In response, most schools have adopted a zero-tolerance policy toward both violence and bringing weapons to school.

14. A structural-functional analysis of schooling highlights the importance of schools to the operation of society as a whole, including the tasks of preparing young people for the work force and teaching dominant cultural values.

15. The symbolic-interaction approach highlights how the interaction of students and school personnel constructs reality, including how students come to see themselves. The ways schools label students as gifted or deficient can be a self-fulfilling prophecy with important consequences for what students expect of themselves.

16. The social-conflict approach highlights the links between schooling and social inequality. Unequal funding from school to school and tracking within any single school perpetuate class differences from one generation to another.

17. Conservatives criticize U.S. public schools as inefficient and not accountable to the people. To solve this problem, they propose making education competitive by giving parents choices about where to send their children through the use of charter schools, magnet schools, for-profit schools, and voucher programs.

18. To liberals, the problems of schools have their roots in the larger society. Liberals support greater investment in schools, especially in programs such as Head Start and bilingual education to enhance the cultural capital of disadvantaged students.

19. Radicals argue that the shortcomings of U.S. schools are symptoms of the structural inequalities of U.S. society. A first step toward solving this problem is to equalize per student funding in all schools. Ultimately, the radical goal is to bring about basic change in the direction of economic and political equality in the United States.

KEY CONCEPTS

education (p. 345) the social institution by which society transmits knowledge—including basic facts and job skills, as well as cultural norms and values—to its members

schooling (p. 346) formal instruction carried out by specially trained teachers

literacy (p. 346) the ability to read, write, and do basic arithmetic

functional illiteracy (p. 352) the inability to read and write or do basic arithmetic well enough to carry out daily responsibilities

cultural capital (p. 356) social experiences and opportunities that enhance a student's ability to learn

tracking (p. 356) the policy of assigning students to different educational programs

bilingual education (p. 358) a policy of offering most classes in students' native language while also teaching them English

mainstreaming (p. 359) integrating special students into the overall educational program

self-fulfilling prophecy (p. 362) a situation in which people who are defined in one way eventually think and act as if the definition were true

hidden curriculum (p. 363) explicit and subtle presentations of political or cultural ideas in the classroom that support the status quo

charter schools (p. 363) public schools that are given more freedom to try out new policies and programs

magnet schools (p. 363) public schools that offer special facilities and programs in pursuit of educational excellence

school voucher program (p. 363) a program that provides parents with funds they can use at a public school or private school of their choice

THINKING CRITICALLY: QUESTIONS AND ISSUES

1. What should be the goals of the U.S. system of schooling? To educate children? Advance equal opportunity? Promote social equality? Explain.

2. What, in your opinion, are the most serious problems that confront U.S. public schools? Propose solutions.

3. Do you think that, over the last fifty years, public schools in the United States have become better or worse? Why?

4. Explain how political attitudes affect what someone defines as a problem of U.S. schools and as solutions to these problems.

GETTING INVOLVED: LEARNING ACTIVITIES

1. Most communities offer programs that train volunteers to teach adults to read. To find one in your area, ask about literacy programs at a local school or library, or call a social services agency. See how you can help others learn to read.

2. Head Start is a government program that helps disadvantaged children succeed in school. Contact your county government and ask about volunteer opportunities with a Head Start program in your area.

3. How does your campus deal with students with learning disabilities? What about access for people with physical disabilities? You can learn about programs and policies by speaking with a college officer responsible for assisting students with special needs.

4. On your campus or one nearby you probably can find a education department with faculty who are preparing tomorrow's teachers. Arrange to visit several such faculty and ask what they see as the prospects for U.S. public schools in the decade ahead.

GETTING CONNECTED: USEFUL WEB LINKS

http://www.prenhall.com/macionis
Visit the interactive Companion Website™ that accompanies this text. Begin by clicking on the cover of your book. You will find a chapter-by-chapter study guide, practice tests, suggested Web links, and links to other relevant material.

http://www.proliteracy.org
Would you like to help people learn to read? Find out how at the Web site for Adult Literacy Volunteers of America.

http://www.nces.ed.gov
Interested in finding statistics about U.S. schooling? This is the main page for the National Center for Education Statistics, where you can find a wide range of information and data.

http://www.publicagenda.org/specials/rc2001/reality.htm
Here is a site that presents the results of surveys investigating public opinion about the state of public schooling in the United States.

GETTING STARTED ON YOUR OWN: RESEARCH NAVIGATOR™

Follow the instructions found on page 25 of this text to access the features of Research Navigator™. Once at the Web site, enter your Login Name and Password. Then, to use the **Content Select** database, enter keywords such as "illiteracy," "bilingual education," and "school choice," and the search engine will supply relevant and recent scholarly and popular press publications. Use the *New York Times* **Search-by-Subject Archive** to find recent news articles related to sociology and the **Link Library** feature to find relevant Web links organized by the key terms associated with this chapter.

CHAPTER 15

© Paul Marcus, Flying, oil on panel, 21$\frac{1}{2}$ × 21$\frac{1}{2}$ in. Studio SPM, Inc.

URBAN LIFE

FROST CHOKED OFF THE LIGHT COMING THROUGH THE WINDOWS of Verna Berryman's apartment on this cold February morning. Berryman had been up since before dawn, packing so that she and her four children could leave the apartment that had been their home for six years. As they carried the last of the boxes out the door and down the stairs, they didn't look back.

The family was escaping Chicago's Cabrini-Green housing project, a high-rise housing complex that has been home to thousands of that city's poor for forty years. City officials and residents alike have known for decades that Cabrini-Green was a failure. From the outset, there were complaints that Cabrini-Green isolated the poor from much of the city. In addition, drug sales were common, crime rates were sky-high, and many of the complex's walls were marked with bullet holes. Chicago is now moving people from Cabrini-Green and similar housing into newer low-rise housing and private apartments in mixed-income neighborhoods. Whatever the future may bring, it has to be better than what Verna Berryman and her children have known at Cabrini-Green. Chicago will close the book on this ill-starred housing project by demolishing the buildings (Thigpen, 2002).

The story of Cabrini-Green is evidence that not all is well in the cities of the United States. U.S. cities are home to beautiful architecture, brightly lit shopping districts, and universities, museums, and other cultural centers. But cities also are centers of much of this country's poverty, poor housing, homelessness, and crime.

This chapter examines a number of urban problems in the United States and offers a brief look at the state of cities around the world. To begin, we offer a short historical account of how U.S. cities have fared.

GETTING THE PICTURE

✦ What is urban sprawl?

Atlanta, probably the fastest growing urban area in the United States, is sprawling outward, gobbling up 500 acres of open ground each week.

✦ Are cities centers of work?

In the inner-city neighborhoods of many large U.S. cities, a majority of adults have no jobs.

✦ How big a problem is homelessness in the United States?

More than 1 million people are homeless for at least some time during the course of a year.

City life was widely defined as a social problem by rural people in the nineteenth century. This drawing—painting city streets as chaotic and dangerous—appeared in several rural newspapers in 1858.

CITIES IN THE PAST

Today, the United States is a nation of cities; three-fourths of the U.S. population lives in an urban area. It is not easy to imagine this country without great cities such as New York, Atlanta, Chicago, or Los Angeles. Four centuries ago—before we became the United States—this continent was home to several million native people who made few permanent settlements. From coast to coast, there was not a single tall structure or even a paved road.

Colonial Villages: 1565–1800

The first cities were created by Europeans who colonized the "new world." The Spanish settled St. Augustine, Florida, in 1565. In 1607, the English founded Jamestown, Virginia. In 1624, the Dutch founded New Amsterdam—later called New York—at the southern tip of Manhattan Island. In 1630, the English settled in Boston.

These tiny villages, with narrow streets, small houses, and just a few hundred residents, provided shelter for settlers in a new world. People living in these settlements worked hard and barely managed to survive. By the time the United States declared independence in 1776, five percent of the population lived in cities. The largest city in the new nation was Philadelphia, a small town with just 42,000 people (and a far cry from the more than 6 million in today's Philadelphia metropolitan area).

Westward Expansion: 1800–1860

After 1800, people began pushing westward, following new transportation routes, including the National Road (1818), the Baltimore & Ohio Railroad (1825), and the Erie Canal (1825). Along these routes, migrants settled the cities of the Midwest, including Buffalo, Cleveland, Detroit, and Chicago. During this time, *urbanization*, the share of the population living in cities, continued to increase. By the time of the Civil War in 1860, 20 percent of the nation's people were urbanites.

The Industrial Metropolis: 1860–1950

The outbreak of the Civil War encouraged the building of factories, which drew even more people from rural counties to the cities. By this time, about a million immigrants (mostly from Europe) were entering the United States each year, and they, too, settled in cities. Together, the expanding factories and surging population created the industrial *metropolis* (from Greek words meaning "mother city"). By 1900, Chicago boasted of 2 million residents, and New York City, with 4 million, surpassed the entire colonial population in 1790.

Cities also grew upward and outward. New train and trolley routes allowed city boundaries to move outward, and steel beams and elevators ushered in the age of skyscrapers. By 1930, New York's Empire State Building towered 102 stories above the streets.

Social Problems in Cities By 1900, most people in the United States were coming to think of cities in terms of social problems. One reason was the flood of immigrants. At that time, one-third of the people living in the ten largest cities had been born abroad, and another one-third had parents who were born elsewhere (Glaab, 1963). Ethnic prejudice fueled an anti-urban bias; in rural communities, city people were defined as "different," and not "real Americans." By the 1920s, Congress passed laws restricting the number of foreigners entering this country.

To make matters worse, in 1900, more than one-third of New Yorkers lived in *tenements*, small apartments, many with few or no windows, and shared bathrooms. All were filled with immigrants who were very poor. In most industrial cities of this time, the air was fouled by factory smoke, and sewage flowed freely into the streets, eventually reaching the same rivers and lakes used for drinking water. Children ran around dirty and unsupervised, epidemics raged in poor neighborhoods, and violence and other crime were rampant. Worst off were the thousands of people—including children—who had no place to live at all, except under a bridge or a stairway.

In the early twentieth century, cities offered plenty of jobs, but most demanded hard labor for low wages. When the Depression began in 1929, more than one-fourth of workers were thrown out of work and lost all their income. World War II (1939–1945) gradually lifted the United States out of the Depression, and soon a new prosperity was at hand. But this was a mixed blessing for cities.

Postindustrial Cities and Suburbs: 1950–Present

The industrial metropolis reached its peak population in the 1940s. With the end of World War II in 1945, soldiers returned, and many couples wasted little time before they began having children. The postwar baby boom sent the U.S. birth rate soaring and pushed many families to look for new housing. Economic prosperity allowed many households to own at least one car, and the federal government rapidly expanded the national highway system, including beltways around central cities. The search for new housing, prosperity, and greater physical mobility combined to propel more and more people outward from the cities into **suburbs,** *urban areas beyond the political boundaries of cities.*

Almost all new construction took place in the suburbs. Federal loan programs helped families buy new homes with just a small down payment, and

some new developments offered single-family homes at unheard-of prices. On New York's Long Island, a development called Levittown priced new houses lower than ever before (about $8,000 in 1948, or $40,000 in today's dollars). Many people made fun of Levittown's small (720 square feet), identical "cookie-cutter" houses. But Abraham Levitt sold 17,447 homes in the first Levittown; he went on to build two more large developments in suburban Philadelphia (Wattel, 1958). Across the country, developers had little trouble selling new homes to families eager to own their own piece of leafy suburban real estate.

In the decades that followed, the suburbs grew even more as a result of economic change. The industrial production that had built the great metropolis *centralized* the population in cities where factories and transportation links were found. The postindustrial economy that emerged in the final decades of the twentieth century, marked by service work and computer technology, *decentralized* the population. By 1970, most of the *urban* population of the United States lived not in central cities but in suburban communities; by 2000, a majority of the *entire* population were suburbanites (U.S. Census Bureau, 2003).

PROBLEMS OF TODAY'S CITIES

The population shift away from central cities toward the suburbs created a number of urban problems, including bankruptcy, sprawl, and high rates of inner-city poverty.

Fiscal Problems

Is it possible for a city to go bankrupt? In 1950, New York, this country's largest city, had a population of 8 million. But it stood at the center of an expanding urban region, which was drawing population from the central city to outlying suburbs. Between 1970 and 1980, New York lost 860,000 people (more than the entire population of Boston). The movement of industry from old factory districts downtown to suburban industrial parks cost the city jobs and people. Corporate mergers and downsizing further reduced the demand for both industrial and office workers. By 1980, New York lost more than half a million jobs.

These trends brought on a fiscal crisis. Fewer people and fewer businesses in the city meant a smaller tax base. To make matters worse, those who moved from the city were, on average, more affluent. Those who remained behind, by contrast, were more likely to be poor and unemployed and to rely on social service programs. By the mid-1970s, New York could no longer meet the costs of social service programs on top of the payroll for city employees and was on the brink of bankruptcy. The picture was much the same in many other cities in the industrial regions of the Northeast and Midwest (Johnson & Lueck, 1996; U.S. Bureau of the Census, 2003).

The Postindustrial Revival New York and other industrial metropolises such as Cleveland and Detroit have managed to survive and thrive once again. Cities have replaced many of the jobs lost when factories closed with new types of work, especially in the service sector: entertainment, sales, financial services, law, consulting, publishing, and other computer-based businesses. New York's midtown and downtown thrive today not as industrial regions but as business centers.

A second factor that has helped cities recover is rising immigration. After 1980, New York once again began gaining population as immigrants, many from Latin America and Asia, arrived in search of the same economic opportunities that drew people from Europe a century before. Most of these immigrants hold service jobs in restaurants, hotels, and hospitals, working long hours for low wages and adding billions of dollars to U.S. economic output (Martin & Midgley, 2003). Although the economies of almost all cities have improved, problems remain for millions of urban residents.

Urban Sprawl

Cities have expanded outward, forming vast urban regions. French geographer Jean Gottman (1961) coined the term **megalopolis** to refer to *a vast urban region containing a number of cities and their surrounding suburbs.*

The megalopolis is the result of specific government policies. After World War II, the federal government began building the interstate highway system. This policy, coupled with the increasing popularity of personal automobiles, drew traffic out of downtowns to outlying areas served by urban "outerbelts." In addition, federal programs providing low-cost home loans encouraged movement away from central cities.

Flying south from Boston on a clear night, you can look down on an unbroken carpet of lights all the way to northern Virginia, some 700 miles away. The same super-city pattern extends from Cleveland to Chicago, down the east coast of Florida, and up and down most of the west coast.

The decentralization of the urban population has led to **urban sprawl,** *rapid, unplanned, and low-density development at the edge of urban areas.* Urban sprawl is composed of new homes, schools, and shopping areas. There is no doubt that people are eager to buy into these developments. But most analysts consider urban sprawl a serious problem. Why? One reason is the numbing sameness of much of this cityscape (Kunstler, 1996). Across North America, mass-produced strip malls and housing developments have no regional distinctiveness and often provide little that is pleasing to the eye. Driving through the urban sprawl around Atlanta, for example, one sees many of the same stores and housing that one would see outside of Columbus, Ohio; Portland, Oregon; Denver, Colorado, or any other large city.

Urban sprawl is sure to remain a matter of controversy for decades to come. Should we define a suburban development like this one in Las Vegas as a problem, or is it a solution for people who seek affordable housing in a residential area? Explain your position.

Find out more about the problem of urban sprawl at
http://www.sierraclub.org/sprawl/

Another, more serious, problem is the fact that sprawling urban development is consuming land at a dizzying rate. The population of the New York metropolitan area grew by just 5 percent between 1980 and 2000; in the same twenty years, people there ended up using 60 percent more land. Atlanta, which is probably the fasting-growing urban area in the United States, has reached 130 square miles, twice its size just twenty years ago. The Atlanta sprawl gobbles up 500 acres of fields and farmland every week. Over the next fifty years, California is expected to lose 3.5 million acres of its Great Central Valley, its agricultural heartland, to development. Nationwide, development engulfs about 1 million acres of open land annually (Lacayo, 1999; Pederson, Smith, & Adler, 1999; Purdum, 1999).

About the only way to get around those vast urban regions is by automobile. This means that most suburban households need several cars and that today's suburbanites spend a great deal of time on the road. The typical worker in the Los Angeles metropolitan area drives twenty-one miles round-trip to the job, those in the Dallas area drive thirty miles, and those in Atlanta travel thirty-seven miles (Florian, 1999:25). Because much of this driving is in stop-and-go traffic, travel time to and from work can exceed two hours a day. The consequences of sprawl, then, include loss of personal time in stressful circumstances and the high cost of cars (buying them, fueling them, maintaining them, insuring them, and garaging them), traffic congestion, and air pollution. Many say what is needed now is more and bigger highways. But is that likely to solve the problem or make it worse? The more roads we build, the more we encourage people to rely on their cars (Carty, 1999).

Edge Cities The movement of businesses from the central city has created *edge cities,* business centers some distance from the old downtowns. Unlike suburbs, which contain mostly homes, edge cities are mostly commercial developments, with corporate office buildings, shopping malls, hotels, and entertainment complexes. Whereas the population of suburbs peaks at night, the population of edge cities peaks during the working day.

Most major urban areas in the United States now contain one or more edge cities. Examples include Tyson's Corner (in Virginia, near Washington, D.C.), King of Prussia (northwest of Philadelphia), and Las Colinas (near Dallas–Fort Worth airport). Many edge cities do not have clear boundaries, and in some cases they even lack names and are known by the major highways that flow through them. Examples include Route 1 near Princeton, New Jersey, and Route 128 near Boston (Garreau, 1991; Macionis & Parrillo, 2004).

Poverty

The high costs of suburban, automobile-based living screen out most of the poor. With urban decentralization, then, the well-to-do move away from the central cities, leaving the poor behind. As more jobs relocate to outlying areas, economic opportunities for inner-city residents decrease. This is one reason that the highest concentrations of poverty are found in central cities (U.S. Census Bureau, 2003).

After the 1950s, businesses in downtown Camden, New Jersey, began to move out to the suburbs. Some people—particularly those who were younger, more educated, and better off financially—followed suit. Camden saw its population fall from 125,000 in 1950 to about 85,000 today. Two-thirds of the remaining households are poor. The future is bleak for Camden's children, who are half the population, as once busy streets stand empty, with houses torn down or boarded up.

Camden is not alone. Across the United States, every large city contains such neighborhoods. Typically, the residents of these so-called ghetto communities are African Americans, Latinos, or other disadvantaged minorities. Many of these communities were once thriving industrial areas, with many retail stores and professionals and working-class residents. Today, people living in poor, inner-city communities are cut off from economic opportunity, as the Social Policy box on page 376 explains.

In 2002, the poverty rate for central cities in the United States stood at 16.7 percent. In the suburbs, the rate was 8.9 percent. For the entire urban region, this yields an overall poverty rate of 11.6 percent. The poverty rate is even higher—14.2 percent—in rural areas, which have even fewer jobs (U.S. Census Bureau, 2003). On balance, then, although cities contain high concentrations of poverty, urban areas generally provide more economic opportunity than rural areas do.

Housing Problems

Like work, housing is a basic human need. Because housing is bought and sold, a family's income determines their housing. The economic inequality of

When Work Disappears: Can We Rescue the Inner City?

WILLIAM JULIUS WILSON, ONE OF THE MOST influential social scientists today, points out that the problems of the inner city can be traced to one major factor: a lack of jobs. As jobs have disappeared from the inner city over recent decades, few of our national political leaders have paid much attention. In the 1990s, when Congress enacted welfare reform intended to move poor people from welfare to work, little was said about where to find jobs (Wilson, 1996b:27)

By the mid-1990s, Wilson claims, most of the adults in poor, inner-city communities from New York to Los Angeles were not working. Wilson found that in 1950, when industrial cities were at their peak populations, most adults in the African American community of Washington Park in Chicago were working and supporting their families. By the 1990s, however, two-thirds were unemployed. One elderly woman, who moved to the neighborhood in 1953, explains:

When I moved in, the neighborhood was intact. It was intact with homes, beautiful homes, mini-mansions, with stores, Laundromats, with Chinese cleaners. We had drugstores. We had hotels. We had doctors over on 39th street. We had doctor's offices in the neighborhood. We had the middle class and the upper-middle class. It has gone from affluent to where it is today. (1996b:28)

Why has this neighborhood declined? Based on eight years of research in the area, Wilson points to a stark reality: There is almost no work to be found. The loss of jobs pushed people into desperate poverty, weakened families, and forced people to turn to welfare. In Woodlawn, another Chicago community near Washington Park, more than 800 businesses operated in 1950; today, there are just 100. A number of big employers, including Western Electric and International Harvester, closed their plants in the late 1960s. The inner cities

U.S. society creates enormous disparities in the quality of housing.

Tenement Housing   Most people today can only imagine the housing problems in the early industrial metropolis. In the final decades of the nineteenth century, developers built tenements to house the greatest number of families in the smallest amount of space. Not only were tenement apartments small, but most had few windows and little ventilation; as many as six families commonly shared a single bathroom. Insulation was poor, and in the winter, heat was uncertain.

Although tenement residents were far from comfortable, others were even worse off. Historian James D. McCabe describes the conditions in the cellars of the tenement buildings:

If the people [in the tenements] suffered, at least they lived upon the surface of the earth. But what shall we say about those who pass their lives in the cellars of these wretched buildings?

Most have but one entrance and that furnishes the only means of ventilation . . . and . . . the filth of the streets comes washing down the walls of the

rooms within. The air is always foul. The drains of the houses above pass within a few feet of the floor, and as they are generally in bad condition, the filth frequently comes oozing up and poisons the air with foul odors. . . .The poor wretches who seek shelter here are half stupefied by it. (1970:405, 406, 409)

Because the vast majority of the 1 million immigrants entering the United States each year were poor, most of the public accepted the tenements as a necessary evil. But some had the courage to speak out against the horror. The leading opponent of tenement housing a century ago was Jacob Riis, who managed single-handedly to sway public opinion. The Defining Moment box on page 378 tells his story.

As millions of people lived out their lives in tenements and cellars, the few who owned the industries and controlled the financial life of our nation enjoyed lives of luxury. These families, with names most people still recognize today, including Vanderbilt (railroads), Morgan (finance), and Rockefeller (oil) in New York, Ford (automobiles) in Detroit, and Armour and Swift (meat packing) in Chicago, lived in spacious mansions staffed by dozens of servants.

collapsed as companies closed, downsized, or moved industrial jobs abroad.

Wilson believes we can rescue the inner cities by creating jobs. But how? As a first step, the government can hire people to do all kinds of needed work, including clearing slums and building low-income housing. This strategy, modeled on the Works Progress Administration (WPA) enacted in 1935 during the Great Depression, can move people from welfare to work and, in the process, create much-needed hope. A second step is to improve city schools. Doing so will mean raising the necessary financing, attracting good teachers, and expecting students to meet challenging academic standards. Of special importance is teaching children the language and computer skills needed to succeed in today's postindustrial economy. A third step involves improved regional public transportation to connect workers with companies in suburban areas. Finally, affordable child-care programs must be made available to help parents balance the responsibilities of parenting and work.

Why have these steps not been taken already? Wilson explains that many people believe cities have plenty of jobs and conclude, therefore, that poor people simply don't want to work. Another concern is that Wilson's proposals, at least in the short term, are more expensive than continuing to funnel welfare assistance to jobless communities. In the long term, what are the costs of letting parts of our cities decay? Of letting generation after generation of children grow up in hopeless and often violent surroundings so that they join the ranks of the restless and often angry people without work?

ISSUES AND EXERCISES

1. Do you support Wilson's proposals for change? Why or why not?
2. Why is there little official concern about the state of our inner cities?
3. If the United States is willing to spend almost $100 billion to redevelop Iraq, should we not spend what it takes to redevelop our own cities? Explain your opinion.

_____

Source: Based on Wilson (1996).

This pattern of mansions for the few and inadequate housing for the many continued for decades even as public opposition to tenements grew. Not until the 1930s did housing problems begin to improve. As part of Roosevelt's New Deal, the federal government raised taxes to fund the construction of new housing and began to provide loans to help people buy homes. In addition, cities across the United States enacted housing codes with the goal of eliminating the worst conditions of the tenements. Despite these efforts, in 1940 the government reported that 40 percent of houses in urban areas had some serious defect, such as inadequate plumbing or even a lack of running water.

Urban Renewal After World War II, as people migrated from the 'old neighborhoods' in central cities toward suburbs, housing in many central city neighborhoods became worse. In response, the federal government passed the Urban Housing Act of 1949, which marked the beginning of *urban renewal*. Urban renewal gave local city governments the right to seize a decaying neighborhood, forcing the families who lived there to move and paying them nominal compensation for their homes. The city then sold the properties to a developer, who tore down the remaining houses and rebuilt the area. Because developers were interested in profits, they built townhouses and apartments for people with higher incomes. Rarely was the housing produced by urban renewal within reach of the people who had lived there before. As this policy went into effect in cities across the United States, many so-called slum areas were rebuilt. But urban renewal failed to provide housing for those who needed it the most. In practice, urban renewal has operated as a form of "urban cleansing," pushing out poor people without providing housing alternatives. Many of the poor who were evicted by urban renewal crowded into the remaining low-cost housing, creating more slums in the process (Macionis & Parrillo, 2004).

Public Housing With urban renewal clearing away block after block, city officials gradually realized that some poor people displaced from their homes had nowhere to go. The need for low-income housing led to the creation of **public housing**, *high-density apartment buildings constructed to house poor people.*

A DEFINING MOMENT

Jacob Riis: Revealing the Horror of the Tenements

I N 1870, AT AGE TWENTY-ONE, Jacob Riis (1849–1914) left his native Denmark for the United States hoping to find a better life. He settled in the Richmond Hill district of New York City, a neighborhood of tenements filled with immigrants.

Riis made his career as one of the earliest photojournalists. On countless evenings, Riis walked around the poorest neighborhoods of New York collecting stories, which became the basis for his writing, and photographing scenes of urban life. He used his writing—and especially his photos—to call public attention to the suffering of families in New York's tenements and other slum housing. To those who never ventured into these areas, the photographs were eye-opening. Riis wrote many books featuring thousands of photographs and gave hundreds of public lectures. Riis made a lifetime effort that helped define tenement housing as a serious social problem.

Jacob A. Riis, *Family in Poverty.* Courtesy of the Museum of the City of New York.

From the outset, public housing was met with criticism from all sides. Liberals viewed it as a Band-Aid approach to the problem of a lack of affordable housing. As they saw it, public housing often was worse than the neighborhoods that had been knocked down by the urban renewal bulldozers. Conservatives objected to government getting into the housing business at all. Most important, however, poor people themselves didn't like public housing. It is not hard to see why. Given how important owning a home is to our society's definition of success, few people are proud to live in a government-owned apartment, and many find they are stigmatized by living in "the projects." But the bottom line was that, for people such as Verna Berryman who lived in Chicago's Cabrini-Green (described in the opening of this chapter), public housing was bad housing. Public housing projects in almost every major city suffered from all the social problems that accompany poverty: buildings in disrepair, illegal drug use, crime, and outright violence.

A final concern was the physical design of public housing. At the outset, because city officials wanted to house poor people in as little space as possible, they favored public housing projects in the form of high-rise towers. Soon, however, the problem of rampant crime in these high-rise structures could not be ignored. Could such problems result from the design of the buildings? In 1972, Oscar Newman provided some answers. In a study of New York housing projects, Newman compared buildings that had the same tenant profile but different architectural designs. Newman reported that crime rates in high-rise buildings (those with more than six stories) were much greater than in low-rise buildings (with six or fewer stories). In general, the taller the building, the higher the crime rate. Newman also discovered that most crimes took place not in people's apartments but in public parts of the buildings, including parking lots, entrances, hallways, stairways, and elevators.

The reason that high-rise buildings have higher crime rates, Newman reasoned, is that they breed anonymity. Placed far above the ground, residents are likely to feel detached from their surroundings. Lower buildings, by contrast, encourage a greater sense of community and allow people to know their neighbors and to keep an eye on public spaces.

In light of such findings and the generally dismal record of early public housing projects, change began in the 1970s. In 1972, the city of St. Louis dynamited several high-rise towers of the Pruitt-Igoe public housing complex, a stark indication that this type of public housing was failing to address the residents' needs. As noted earlier, Chicago has been destroying the Cabrini-Green apartments as well.

"Projects" still exist in many cities. But the policy in recent decades has shifted from large-scale developments to financial assistance that helps pay the rent for families in private housing. Created in 1974, the federal Section 8 Program directs subsidies to developers who rehabilitate existing rental housing or build new apartments. In exchange for this subsidy, developers agree to allocate a share of the housing to low-income families. When low-income families move in, they pay 30 to 40 percent of their adjusted gross income for rent, with the government paying the rest. The advantages of this program include giving low-income families some choice about where to live and avoiding the past practice of creating housing in which all the residents are poor. The Section 8 Program has increased the availability of low-income housing, but funding has not been sufficient to meet the demand. In 2003, New Orleans had almost 20,000 people on the waiting list for Section 8 vouchers, and Chicago had almost 40,000 people on a waiting list for its housing voucher program (Housing Authority of New Orleans, 2002; Thigpen, 2002).

Highrise "superblocks" can be hazardous to your health. This claim became widespread by the 1970s, leading many cities to dynamite huge public housing projects. This demolition took place in 1996 in Newark, New Jersey. What were some of the reasons cities took such drastic action?

Learn more about the Housing Authority of New Orleans at
http://www.hano.org

Racial Segregation

In cities across the United States, the poor—especially poor people of color—are isolated from the mainstream of society. Douglas Massey and Nancy Denton (1988, 1989) examined large cities across the United States and documented the existence of what they called *hypersegregation:* entire districts of cities (commonly called ghettos) contain only poor African Americans, and these people are cut off from the larger society in several ways. Most obviously, poor minority urbanites are isolated *spatially,* meaning that they are highly concentrated in certain neighborhoods, typically near the city's central business district. In addition, they are isolated *socially;* they live almost entirely in these neighborhoods, rarely venturing out into the larger city. In affluent sections of the city, residents or police sometimes question the very presence of poor-looking African Americans. Similarly, affluent people rarely enter their communities.

How prevalent is hypersegregation? Massey and Denton estimate that about one in five African Americans lives cut off from the larger society; by contrast, hypersegregation characterizes just a few percent of Hispanics and whites with the same income levels (Jagarowsky & Bane, 1990).

The fact that a large share of the African American population but few people of other categories experiences hypersegregation shows that race is a key element in the problems of U.S. cities. Our cities remain racially divided; the urban decentralization of the last fifty years was prompted, to a significant extent, by a desire by whites to distance themselves from nonwhites. The trend continues: The white share of the population of the one hundred largest U.S. cities fell from 52 percent in 1990 to 44 percent in 2000 (U.S. Census Bureau, 2003). The pattern of largely white suburbs and largely African American inner cities exists throughout the United States.

Homelessness

A century ago, every large city in the United States had tens of thousands of homeless people. In fact, the homeless were so much a part of the urban landscape that many people at that time considered homelessness a normal part of city life rather than a serious social problem.

Although the number of homeless people is lower than it was a century ago, homelessness remains a social problem in the United States. One might also say that homelessness is a greater tragedy today because our nation is now much more affluent than it was 100 years ago. There is no precise tally, but estimates suggest that about 500,000 people are homeless on any given night, and three times that number—or about 1.5 million—are homeless at some time during the course of a year (Wickham, 2000; Marks, 2001).

Homelessness is primarily an urban problem. A Housing and Urban Development (HUD, 1999) study of more than 4,000 poor people across the country—most of them homeless at the time they were interviewed—concluded that 92 percent are urban: 71 percent reside in central cities and 21 percent live in suburbs. Just 8 percent live in rural areas.

Learn more about homelessness at **http://www.nlchp.org**

This HUD report documented that homeless people are the poorest of the poor. In the survey, homeless people reported income averaging $348 per month (barely ten dollars a day); for homeless families, the figure was $475. With such low income, it is easy to understand why people cannot afford housing. Moreover, 40 percent of homeless people said they went without food for at least one day in the previous month.

The homeless in our urban areas suffer from more than hunger and lack of housing. The problems of many homeless people began in childhood. Of homeless people interviewed in the HUD study, 25 percent say they were physically or sexually abused as children, one-third report running away from home, and 27 percent claim to have lived for some time in foster care. Half of the adult homeless report significant problems of physical health, 40 percent have mental health problems, 40 percent

TABLE 15–1   THE TEN LARGEST CITIES IN THE UNITED STATES, 1950 AND 2000

	1950			2000	
RANK	**CITY**	**POPULATION**	**RANK**	**CITY**	**POPULATION**
1	New York	7,892,000	1	New York	8,008,278
2	Chicago	3,621,000	2	Los Angeles	3,694,820
3	Philadelphia	2,072,000	3	Chicago	2,896,016
4	Los Angeles	1,970,000	4	Houston	1,953,631
5	Detroit	1,850,000	5	Philadelphia	1,517,550
6	Baltimore	950,000	6	Phoenix	1,321,045
7	Cleveland	915,000	7	San Diego	1,223,400
8	St. Louis	857,000	8	Dallas	1,188,580
9	Boston	801,000	9	San Antonio	1,144,646
10	San Francisco	775,000	10	Detroit	951,270

Note: Cities shaded in blue are located in the Snowbelt; those shaded in yellow are Sunbelt cities.
Source: U.S. Census Bureau (2003).

A NATION OF DIVERSITY

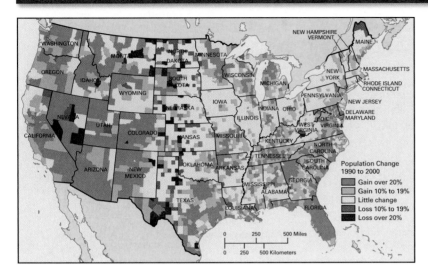

NATIONAL MAP 15–1

**Population Change
across the United States, 1990–2000**

The map shows areas of the country where population density went up or down in the 1990s. What is the general pattern to this change? What problems does rapid population increase bring to a county? What about rapid population loss?

Source: Map constructed for *U.S. News & World Report* by Kevin Neimond, ESRI, Inc.

abuse alcohol, and 25 percent have some other drug problem.

The homeless, then, suffer many kinds of disadvantages. Yet the HUD study also shows that social programs are successful in improving the problems associated with homelessness. After receiving physical and mental health care services and substance abuse treatment, 75 percent of those living in families and 60 percent of individuals living alone were able to move to what the report called "an improved living situation."

In some cases, the key to a more secure life is **supportive housing,** *a program that combines low-income housing with on-site social services.* People with substance abuse problems, mental disabilities, or simply the scars of living poor and alone on the streets find they can live independently and hold a job with the help of such programs.

The HUD study concludes that increasing funding for such programs may end up saving money. In New York, the cost of supporting one person with affordable housing and social services comes to $12,500 per year. By contrast, supporting a prison inmate costs $40,000 or more per year (HUD, 1999).

In the 1980s, the federal government allocated billions of dollars to house and treat homeless people. In the 1990s, however, public opinion became more critical of the homeless. Social service programs were cut back at all levels, and many cities adopted a "get tough" approach. Three dozen cities across the United States began using antivagrancy laws to ticket homeless people for a range of behaviors,

including sleeping in doorways, asking for money in public, or carrying open containers of alcohol. Moreover, many cities conduct nightly "police sweeps" to get homeless people off the streets. Even as the numbers of homeless people increased during the recent economic recession, there have been few efforts—such as increasing the stock of low-income housing and providing more social support services—to reduce the extent of this problem (Morse, 1999).

Snowbelt and Sunbelt Cities

Every city contends with poverty and homelessness. But the way these problems play out across the United States is part of a definite trend: Take a look at the changing list of the ten largest cities in the United States, shown in Table 15–1. In 1950, eight of the ten top cities were in the Northeast and Midwest, often called the Snowbelt; by 2000, however, six of ten were in the South and West, often called the Sunbelt (U.S. Census Bureau, 2003).

Snowbelt cities have lost population in the postindustrial era as people and businesses have decentralized across the city limits to suburbs. By contrast, cities in the Sunbelt are rapidly gaining population. In part this is because our national population is shifting south and west. In 1940, the Snowbelt was home to 60 percent of the U.S. population; today, the Sunbelt holds 60 percent of the people. National Map 15–1 shows the population shifts that occurred in the United States in the 1990s.

A Global Perspective

World-Class Poverty: A Visit to Manila's Smokey Mountain

IN THIS PAGE FROM HIS TRAVEL JOURNAL, the author provides his firsthand observations of life in Smokey Mountain, a section of Manila, the capital city of the Philippines.

What caught my eye was how clean she was—a girl no more than seven or eight years old, hair carefully combed and wearing a freshly laundered dress. Her eyes followed us as we walked past; camera-toting Americans stand out here, in one of the poorest neighborhoods in the entire world.

Fed by methane from the decomposing garbage, the fires never go out on Smokey Mountain, Manila's vast garbage dump. The smoke envelops the hills of refuse like a thick fog. But Smokey Mountain is more than a dump, it is a neighborhood that is home to thousands of people. The residents of Smokey Mountain are the poorest of the poor, and one is hard pressed to imagine a setting more hostile to human life. Amidst the smoke and the squalor, men and women do what they can to survive, picking plastic bags from the city's garbage and washing them in the river, salvaging cardboard boxes that pile up alongside a family's plywood shack. All over Smokey Mountain are children—kids who must already sense the enormous odds against them. The girls and boys we see are the lucky ones, of course. But what chance do they have, living in families that earn scarcely a few hundred dollars a year? With barely any opportunity for schooling? Year after year, breathing this air? Against this backdrop of human tragedy, one lovely little girl has put on a fresh dress and gone out to play. . . .

With Smokey Mountain behind us, our taxi driver threads his way through heavy traffic as we head for the other side of Manila. The change is amazing: the forbidding smoke and smells of the dump have given way to polished neighborhoods one might find in Miami or Los Angeles. On the bay, a cluster of yachts is visible in the distance. No more rutted streets; now we glide quietly along wide boulevards lined with trees and filled with expensive Japanese cars. On each side, we pass shopping plazas, upscale hotels, and high-rise office buildings. Every block or so stands the entrance to an exclusive residential enclave set off by gates and protected by armed guards. Here, in large, air-conditioned homes, the rich of Manila live—and many of the poor work.

ISSUES AND EXERCISES

1. Are any members of your class from countries with similar low-income populations? If so, invite them to share their experiences.

2. How would you feel witnessing such intense poverty? Why?

3. See photographs of Smokey Mountain at http://www.jkfoto.nl/manilla/manilla.html

Source: Based on the author's visit to Manila, the Philippines, October, 1994.

Another difference between Snowbelt and Sunbelt cities relates to political geography. A century ago, Snowbelt cities were surrounded by politically independent suburbs. Therefore, decentralization has meant central cities losing population. In the Sunbelt, however, cities have simply sprawled outward as population has grown. By annexing new land, Sunbelt cities have become much larger physically than the older, industrial metropolises. (Jacksonville, Florida, for example, now covers more than 750 square miles, more than three times Columbus, Ohio's 210 square miles, although both cities have about 725,000 people). Sunbelt cities have increased rather than reduced their tax base as people and jobs move outward while remaining within the city limits (Rybczynski & Linneman, 1999).

Cities and Terrorism

The terrorist attacks of September 11, 2001, were directed against the entire United States. Yet they were experienced most intensely where the death toll was greatest: in Washington, D.C., and in New York City, where the collapse of the World Trade Centers claimed almost 3,000 lives.

The risk of terrorism is greater in large population centers, particularly in high-profile areas containing major business activity, political centers, and

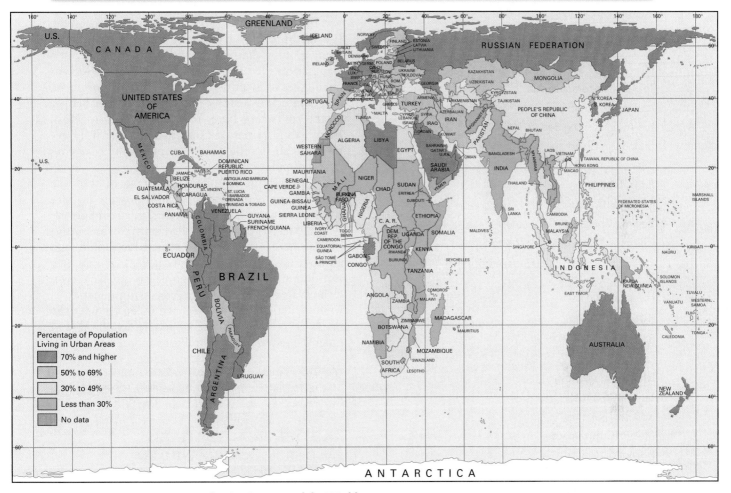

GLOBAL MAP 15–1 **Urbanization around the World**

In the next few years, for the first time, half the world's people will live in cities. Looking around the world, a nation's share of city-dwellers depends on its level of economic development. In high-income nations such as the United States and Canada, more than three-fourths of the people live in urban places. By contrast, in low-income nations in Africa and Asia, only one-fourth of the population lives in cities. Even so, the largest cities in these countries are growing very rapidly.

Source: Population Reference Bureau (2003).

national monuments. This fact has led some analysts to wonder whether U.S. cities will lose some of their attractiveness. Certainly, some people will shun large central cities out of fear. Some also predict that cities such as New York will see businesses spread out from the clusters of high-rises in downtown Manhattan to less congested areas of the city, such as Brooklyn and Harlem (Kotkin, 2001). But many will continue to seek out the social mix and high energy of downtown living, just as many businesses will continue to benefit from an easily accessible central location.

Cities in Poor Countries

As we have noted in a number of earlier chapters, the social problems we face at home often are far worse in poor nations around the world. The same is true of urban problems such as poverty, inadequate housing, and poor sanitation. The Global Perspective box offers a look at the striking poverty in one of the world's capital cities.

Global Map 15–1 shows the level of urbanization for all regions of the world. More than 75 percent of

TABLE 15–2 THE WORLD'S TEN LARGEST URBAN AREAS, 1980 AND 2015

1980

URBAN AREA	POPULATION (IN MILLIONS)
New York, U.S.A.	16.5
Tokyo–Yokohama, Japan	14.4
Mexico City, Mexico	14.0
Los Angeles–Long Beach, U.S.A.	10.6
Shanghai, China	10.0
Buenos Aires, Argentina	9.7
Paris, France	8.5
Moscow, U.S.S.R.	8.0
Beijing, China	8.0
Chicago, U.S.A.	7.7

2015 (PROJECTED)

URBAN AREA	POPULATION (IN MILLIONS)
Tokyo–Yokohama, Japan	26.4
Bombay, India	26.1
Lagos, Nigeria	23.2
Dhaka, Bangladesh	21.1
São Paulo, Brazil	20.4
Karachi, Pakistan	19.2
Mexico City, Mexico	19.2
Shanghai, China	18.0
New York, U.S.A.	17.4
Calcutta, India	17.3

Source: United Nations (2001).

the populations of rich nations live in and around cities; in the poorest countries, by contrast, just one-fourth are urbanites. But everywhere the number of city dwellers is increasing. Within a few years, analysts predict that for the first time most of the world's people will be living in urban places. As explained in Chapter 16, "Population and Global Inequality," world population was about 6.3 billion in 2003 and is increasing by about 80 million people each year. The urban population of the world is increasing twice as fast; in Latin America, Africa, and Asia, people are migrating from rural areas to cities in search of economic opportunity, more schooling, and a better quality of life. By 2015, as Table 15–2 shows, eight of the ten largest cities in the world will be in

economically developing nations. Note that only one of these cities (New York) will be in the United States.

Bombay, Lagos, Mexico City, and others on the list are becoming true mega-cities, with populations greater than at any time in history. Even a rich nation such as the United States faces serious challenges in meeting the housing, transportation, and sanitation needs of some 17 million people in the sprawling New York urban region. How, then, will poor nations such as Bangladesh, Nigeria, and Mexico be able to support their soaring urban populations?

Throughout history, cities have offered the promise of a better life. But cities provide no sure solution to many social problems, including poverty. This fact is evident in the shantytowns: settlements where people have constructed makeshift (and typically unsafe) homes from whatever materials they can find and where most people do not have even clean water and sewerage. A pressing question is whether cities that, so far, have failed to meet the needs of so many millions of people will, be able to meet the needs of many millions more.

Read about squatter settlements in the cities of low-income countries at **http://www.gdrc.org/uem/squatters/squatter.html**

THEORETICAL ANALYSIS: UNDERSTANDING URBAN PROBLEMS

We now apply sociological theory to the problems of cities. Each of the major theoretical approaches provides insights into how urbanization is changing people's lives.

Structural-Functional Analysis: A Theory of Urbanism

The main contribution of structural-functional analysis to our understanding of cities is the theory of urbanism. The theory emerged in the writings of two European sociologists, Ferdinand Tönnies and Emile Durkheim, and U.S. sociologist Louis Wirth.

Ferdinand Tönnies: *Gemeinschaft* and *Gesellschaft*

Tönnies (1855–1937), who lived during the Industrial Revolution, sought to understand how social life changed as rural living gave way to life in the industrial metropolis. His answer centered on the two terms *gemeinschaft* and *gesellschaft*.

Gemeinschaft is the German word (roughly translated as "community") meaning *a type of social organization in which people are closely bound by kinship and tradition.* Living in small rural villages, people have a strong sense of community based on kinship and shared traditions. Ideally, explained Tönnies, rural living is guided by a concern for the needs of all rather than the pursuit of individual self-interest.

In the industrial city, however, traditional community is lost and life approximates *Gesellschaft* (roughly translated as "association"), *a type of social organization in which people interact on the basis of self-interest.* In the city, Tönnies explained, the typical person pays only passing attention to the welfare of the community but rather "looks out for number one."

Emile Durkheim: Mechanical and Organic Solidarity

French sociologist Emile Durkheim (1858–1917) agreed with Tönnies that the rise of cities brought changes to the organization of society. Durkheim characterized social ties in rural areas as **mechanical solidarity,** *social bonds based on common sentiments and shared moral values.* Durkheim's concept of mechanical solidarity is similar to Tönnies's concept of *Gemeinschaft.*

Durkheim agreed that the rise of industrial cities weakened mechanical solidarity. But urban life also creates new connections between people. **Organic solidarity** consists of *social bonds based on specialization and mutual interdependence.* In the city, people tend to work at different types of jobs and have less in common. At the same time, increasing specialization makes urban people need each other more and more. As city dwellers, we look to others to meet just about all out daily needs, from driving the bus to policing the streets to teaching our children in school. In short, whereas rural society holds together because of *likeness,* urban society holds together because of *difference.*

Durkheim's view of urban life is more positive than that of Tönnies. Although something may be lost in the process of urbanization, Durkheim concluded, people gain more individual choice, moral tolerance, and personal privacy.

Louis Wirth: Urbanism as a Way of Life

From the ideas of Tönnies and Durkheim, Louis Wirth (1938) developed a formal theory of urban life. Wirth began by defining the city as a settlement with a large, dense, socially diverse population. These traits confer a particular character on social ties within the city, which he described as fleeting and impersonal.

Because urbanites live with millions of others around them, they never get to know most of those with whom they interact on a daily basis. Indeed, when urbanites can identify others, it is usually not in terms of *who they are* in any personal sense but *what they do.* In other words, we recognize but know little about the bus driver, the school principal, the police officer on the beat, or the grocery store owner. This limited knowledge of others, coupled to the social diversity of the city, encourages urbanites to become more tolerant than rural villagers.

Critical evaluation. The major structural-functional argument about cities is that they generate urbanism, a distinctive form of social life. We can understand the popular conception of the city as a cold and heartless place and appreciate why at least some city dwellers seem to lack any sense of community. From this point of view, one reason that social problems are pronounced in urban areas is that cities encourage people to take an "I just don't care" attitude about their surroundings.

But is the urbanism thesis correct? Herbert Gans (1968) argues that cities contain much more social diversity than Wirth's theory suggests. Gans agrees that some people do have the detached, cosmopolitan attitude that Wirth describes. But what about "ethnic villagers" who live in traditional neighborhoods where almost everyone else is like them? The Italian and Polish communities that existed in New York's Lower East Side early in the twentieth century—and Korean and Vietnamese neighborhoods in Philadelphia and Los Angeles today—have many of the traditions we link to rural living. Gans's research reminds us that class, race, ethnicity, and age create an urban mix far more complex than any single profile of "urbanites" will allow.

Claude Fischer (1975) points out that cities also create new social groups because their size allows a critical mass of individuals of almost every kind. Although every small town has some gay men and lesbians, for example, only large cities such as New York and San Francisco have gay communities, with thousands of residents and a distinctive subculture supported by gay newspapers and gay theater and other entertainment.

Symbolic-Interaction Analysis: Experiencing the City

On a micro-level, the reality of city living is a matter of personal experiences. How do people construct reality in the city?

A common theme in the writings of Tönnies, Durkheim, and Simmel is the impersonality of cities. Urban living, it seems, makes people indifferent to those around them. Do you agree with this assessment? What evidence can you point to in support of your position?

Georg Simmel: Urban Stimulation and Selectivity

The German sociologist Georg Simmel (1858–1918) explained that people experience intense stimulation in cities. The sights, sounds, and smells of the city—not to mention the vast number of people—all combine to overwhelm the senses. The result, claimed Simmel, is that urbanites develop a *blasé attitude;* they "tune out" much of what is around them. In other words, urbanites couldn't respond to most of what takes place around them, even if they wanted to.

Simmel stressed that a blasé attitude is a strategy for survival in the midst of urban overstimulation. It does not mean that people do not care about others. On the contrary, by being selective in their responses to others, urban people focus their time and energy on those who really matter.

Leo Srole: Mental Health in the Metropolis

If people have to tune out most of what goes on around them to survive in the city, are cities an unhealthy environment? Over the years, a number of researchers have tackled this issue, and their general conclusion is that cities pose no harm to people's mental health. In one of the largest studies, Leo Srole (1972) monitored the mental health of New Yorkers in the 1950s and again in the early 1970s. Srole found that, overall, mental health in the "Big Apple" (especially for women) was actually a little better than in rural areas.

Later research confirmed these results (Fischer, 1973; Hackler, 1979; Weisner, 1981; Kadushin, 1983). City living may involve more stimulation, but this does not contribute to problems of mental illness. On the contrary, many people thrive in an environment where they have access to so many other people and activities and so much choice about with whom they interact.

Critical evaluation.   On a micro-level, we find that cities do differ from rural areas in the level of stimulation that people commonly experience. Yet, contrary to the impression we get from Simmel's theory (and also that of Tönnies), cities turn out to be fairly healthful places.

But this upbeat conclusion has a major limitation: Some urbanites live far better than others. Any general conclusions about the quality of life in the city must take into account social inequality, which brings us to the social-conflict approach.

Social-Conflict Analysis: Cities and Inequality

As in earlier chapters, the social-conflict approach focuses on social inequality. In this case, the issue is how pronounced social stratification in the United States shapes the city and urban life.

Urban Political Economy   The application of social-conflict theory to cities—urban political economy—differs from the approaches of Tönnies and Wirth, who treated the city as defined simply by its size, density, and social diversity. Rather than treating the city as self-defining, this approach asks how the economic and political structures of the larger society shape the city and its problems. Following the lead of Karl Marx, this approach asserts that social class plays an important part in defining urbanism. Consider, in any city, how much the lives of the rich differ dramatically from those of the working class and, even more, from those of the poor and the homeless. On another level, this approach seeks to explain how the physical development of the city reflects the private property and profit seeking central to a capitalist economy.

David Harvey: A Study of Baltimore David Harvey's (1973) study of Baltimore shows that the growth and decline of an urban area have much to do with the process of capital investment. Harvey found that banks had little interest in lending money to people in inner-city Baltimore for housing or other development. As a result, poor people had to finance their housing through their own funds, through private loans, or through government programs. Under such conditions, this section of the city remained poor and run-down.

On the other hand, banks favored the affluent sections of Baltimore. Middle-class and upper-middle-class people had little trouble obtaining home mortgages; banks saw these as good investments.

Harvey reports that even government programs end up serving the interests of investors. In Baltimore and elsewhere, urban renewal turned out to be "slum clearance" programs that forced out the poor, who often ended up in "projects" that were worse than the housing they had lived in before. The city turned over their old neighborhoods to profit-seeking developers who built housing and shopping centers aimed at those with more money. In short, the investment of investment capital—who makes money available to whom—goes a long way toward explaining the differing fortunes of people across the urban area.

Critical evaluation. Whereas older structural-functional theories point to factors such as population size and density as defining cities and urban life, the newer political-economy approach considers the most overriding factor to be the capitalist drive to make profits. The power of money is at work not only in the rise and fall of neighborhoods in the central city but also in the decentralization of population as investment shifts from older industrial production to newer information companies.

However, social patterns do differ in cities and in rural areas. Moreover, the effects of capital investment are not always clear. Too little investment may well cause a community to decline. But too much investment often results in overbuilt areas and urban sprawl. In the final sections of this chapter, we turn to how politics guides the ways in which people construct urban problems and define solutions.

POLITICS AND URBAN LIFE: CONSTRUCTING PROBLEMS AND DEFINING SOLUTIONS

To hear some people tell it, our large cities are enjoying a rebirth; others, see our cities in crisis. To better understand how people define urban problems—and what they see as solutions—we must look at today's urban issues from different political viewpoints.

Conservatives: The Market and Morality

Before deciding the state of our cities, conservatives often suggest that we look at where we have been and how far we have come. A century ago, when Jacob Riis walked the streets and alleyways of New York's Lower East Side, one-third of New Yorkers lived in desperate circumstances, with many families crowded together into dark tenement rooms. Sanitation was minimal, to put it mildly. In the tenements, infant mortality rates (death rates for children in their first year) often reached 200 or more, which means that 200 of every one thousand (two in ten) children born did not live even one year. This level of infant mortality is four times higher than the rate today across Africa, the poorest region of the world (Population Reference Bureau, 2003).

In historical perspective, then, urban life has improved. Today's urbanites live far longer, and most take for granted warm housing, safe water, and dependable plumbing. Why this improvement? Conservatives would say "economic forces." As the United States became a wealthy, industrial society, generating more products and services than ever before, cities grew and living standards rose for everyone.

More recently, changes in cities have also reflected economic forces. The rise of a service economy helped push population outward from the old central cities to the expanding suburbs. These same trends caused economic decline in the central cities, especially in the Snowbelt, which is sometimes called the "Rustbelt," a term reflecting all the obsolete factories that now stand empty and rusting.

Because conservatives accept the operation of the market economy, they view the decline of the inner cities as unfortunate but not permanent. Indeed, as we have seen, the expansion of the postindustrial economy has already transformed many old industrial areas into business centers or arts and entertainment districts. Examples of this inner-city comeback can be found in the lakefront of Cleveland, the Baltimore harbor area, and the riverfront of New Orleans.

If economic forces shape cities, what about the role of government? Conservatives have supported the creation of **enterprise zones,** *areas in the inner city that attract new businesses with the promise of tax relief.* Under such programs, government reduces or eliminates taxes on businesses that relocate to an economically depressed area where jobs are needed (Kemp, 1994).

Beyond such limited policies, conservatives oppose the growth of government social welfare programs that expanded in the 1960s. Consider, for example, this account by the late Senator Daniel P. Moynihan (1993) of New York City in 1943, the year he graduated from one of the city's high schools:

> By 1943, [the number of New Yorkers on welfare] was down to 73,000 persons, of which the city reported that only 93 were employable. . . . In 1943, there were exactly forty-four homicides by gunshot in all of the City of New York. . . . In 1943, the illegitimacy rate was 3 percent. Last year, it was 45 percent. Ours was a much poorer city fifty years ago, but a much more stable one.

Fifty years later, when Moynihan wrote his account, New York's population had actually declined, but many urban problems had become much worse. Almost 1 million people (one in seven New Yorkers) were on welfare, and the number of murders had risen to almost 2,000 a year. (By 2002, the number of people receiving public assistance was 425,000, the number of murders was 590, and 45 percent of babies were born to unwed mothers.)

As conservatives see it, the expansion of the welfare state caused the long-term rise in public assistance and violence. Everyone agrees that the intention of expanding government social programs is to help people. But as Charles Krauthammer (1995:15) puts it, "The growth in the size and power of the welfare state is the primary cause of the decline of society's . . . institutions—voluntary associations, local government, church, and, above all, the family." Conservatives link problems such as street violence and poverty to family breakdown; they blame the breakdown of the family on welfare policies that support people who do not work and that

provide child support for mothers without jobs or husbands. In short, the strength of a city lies not just in its economic prosperity but also in the character of its people. From a conservative point of view, the economic indicators are way up, but the moral indicators are way down (Myers, 2000).

Liberals: Government Reform

From a liberal point of view, U.S. cities are beset with a number of serious social problems. Some people are becoming richer, but a large share of the urban population remains in poverty. In large cities—from New York to Los Angeles, and from Chicago to Houston—we find tens of millions of poor people, many neighborhoods in which housing falls short of basic health and safety standards, and urban schools that can barely teach students.

Liberals believe that all of these problems stem from social inequality and cannot be fixed until government takes action. Vigorous enforcement of antidiscrimination laws, for example, is one part of the liberal solution to urban problems. The law must ensure that racial prejudice does not prevent people of any color or ethnicity from living where they may choose, within the limits of their housing budget.

But minorities are disadvantaged economically. A second part of the liberal political agenda, then, looks to government to reduce the income and wealth gaps between different categories of people. At the top, this involves raising taxes (in opposition to the recent Bush administration tax cuts) especially on the rich, who derive the greatest benefit from our cities. At the bottom, reform involves a host of social supports and programs. As William Julius Wilson (1996) argues, we must face up to the lack of available work in many inner-city areas. With the private sector abandoning many of our inner cities, government must step in to create needed jobs and provide transportation to outlying areas (often in the suburbs) where jobs are more readily available.

As explained in Chapter 2 ("Poverty and Wealth"), economic inequality in the United States is greater than it has been in at least fifty years; the gap continues to grow with the phasing in of recent tax cuts. Cutbacks in social services, a stalled minimum wage, and a loss of jobs have combined to make problems worse for millions of urban families. Liberals believe our country is on the wrong track and seek a turnaround in our national political agenda in the 2004 national elections.

Clearly, liberals are not content to allow our cities to rise and fall as the result of changing economic

A generation ago this downtown area of Cleveland was little more than abandoned factories—a place to avoid. Today, it is a thriving entertainment district, home to the Rock and Roll Hall of Fame. Conservatives claim that market forces are the key to reviving inner cities; liberals look to government intervention; radicals claim that capitalism can never save our cities. Which view do you find most convincing? Why?

forces, the way conservatives are. Whereas conservatives see government programs as likely to make matters worse, liberals believe government has an essential role in creating a greater level of social justice.

Radicals: The Need for Basic Change

Like liberals, radicals see the cities of the United States as being in crisis. So great is the economic inequality, so persistent is the racism, and so limited are government efforts to improve matters that radicals argue only a basic change in our economic and political systems will solve urban problems. Radicals flatly reject the conservative reliance on the market system to guide the development of our cities and claim that, by giving free rein to market forces, the United States is simply creating urban problems such as urban sprawl, crime, and poverty. For this reason, radicals believe that the reforms proposed by liberals cannot be effective because they rest on the same capitalist economic foundation.

To illustrate their approach, radicals might point to the history of urban renewal in the United States. Government enacted urban renewal with the goal of reversing the physical decline of the central cities. But rather than providing better housing for the poor (who, by definition, have the greatest need), the program turned poor neighborhoods over to private developers who used the land for their own profit by building shopping centers and housing for more affluent people. This process points to the conclusion that, under a capitalist system, the government

has little control over the private sector. Furthermore, because the private sector is concerned not with people but with profits, it will not meet the need for low-income housing.

Following Marxist theory, the capitalist economy operates in the interest of the capitalist class, not the majority. Today, as a century ago, it operates to the benefit of those who own productive property (most of whom now live in suburbs and work there or in edge cities), leaving urban officials struggling to control the anger among those left behind in the central cities. Districts of striking poverty remain in New York, Chicago, St. Louis, Houston, Los Angeles, and just about every other major city in the country. As multinational corporations export industrial jobs to poor countries, the urban poor are left with less and less. As John Logan and Harvey Molotch (1987) conclude, the new global economy benefits major corporations and their stockholders, but ordinary people in U.S. cities face declining prospects. Social welfare programs may have grown over the course of the last century, but they have not altered the basic patterns of inequality. On the contrary, as Manuel Castells (1977, 1983, 1989) argues, they only "extend" capitalism—that is, they keep the system from collapsing entirely.

Thus, radicals conclude, solutions are not a matter of time. The radical perspective seeks more basic change in the economic foundation of U.S. society. Until the basic institutions of the United States operate to the benefit of the many rather than the few, urban problems will remain with us. The Left to

LEFT TO RIGHT

THE POLITICS OF URBAN LIFE

	RADICAL LEFT VIEW	LIBERAL VIEW	CONSERVATIVE VIEW
WHAT IS THE PROBLEM?	Cities are in crisis: Under capitalism, cities have evolved to support and benefit the few who own productive property, ignoring the needs of the majority; without a national urban policy, urban sprawl is out of control.	Cities suffer from the effects of social inequality; poor people and minorities fare the worst with regard to housing, schools, and other resources.	Urban life is far better than it was a century ago because living standards have risen. Inner cities declined as economic forces relocated and replaced industry after 1950, but the postindustrial economy is reviving them.
WHAT IS THE SOLUTION?	Neither the economy operating on its own nor government programs can bring about needed changes; capitalism itself must be transformed into a system that meets the needs of the many rather than the few.	Government must attack racial segregation by enforcing antidiscrimination laws and by reducing income inequality and differences in opportunity between inner cities and suburbs.	The improvements in urban life result from this nation's productive, market economy. Where needed, government can stimulate economic development with enterprise zones.

Join the debate . . .

1. To what degree, from each of the political perspectives, are cities in the United States in serious trouble?
2. From the point of view of each of the political perspectives, what is the proper role of the

    marketplace in meeting the needs of urbanites? What about the proper role of the government?
3. Which of the three political analyses of urban life included here do you find most convincing? Why?

Right table sums up the state of U.S. cities from each of the three political perspectives.

GOING ON FROM HERE

Cities seem to generate controversy. In part, this is because a great deal of social change involves the growth or decline of cities. More than a century ago, the Industrial Revolution occurred mostly in cities; in addition, for several centuries most immigrants to the United States have settled in cities. Even more important, cities have a way of intensifying both the good and the bad in any society. For example, the best hospitals and universities, the most celebrated museums, and the most popular newspapers and other mass media all city-based. Finally, cities have long offered the most of what people in the United States want: economic opportunity.

But cities also reveal the failings of U.S. society. Poverty exists almost everywhere, but the greatest concentration of poor people is found in central cities. Similarly, concern over terrorism exists everywhere in the United States, but the targets of terror typically are in large cities.

For almost a century, the United States has been an urban nation, and no one doubts that cities will stand at the center of our way of life far into the future. From a conservative point of view, the major force shaping future cities should be the economy: In this chapter, we have described the sprawling postindustrial cities now taking shape across the United States. A liberal perspective suggests that the market-based economy alone will not solve many of the problems—such as increasing inequality and racial and ethnic conflict—that continue to plague us. Indeed, as radicals point out, the capitalist economy lies at the heart of the problem; letting the economy shape cities rules out any meaningful solution.

The main question for the future, then, is this: Should government take a larger role in shaping cities and urban life? With ever-increasing sprawl, mounting problems of pollution, and social inequality on the rise, perhaps the time is at hand to consider what kind of cities we want our children and grandchildren to inherit. The debate will place those (typically conservatives) who want to limit government power in favor of letting market forces shape urban life against those (typically liberals and radicals) who favor giving government more power to define the urban landscape. How this debate is resolved will greatly affect the cities of tomorrow.

CHAPTER SUMMARY

1. U.S. cities evolved from small villages along the eastern seaboard. New cities sprang up as the nation pushed westward after 1800. The Civil War marked the rise of the industrial metropolis.

2. Not until 1920 did a majority of the U.S. population live in cities. An anti-urban bias grew stronger in the late nineteenth century as industrial cities swelled with immigrants.

3. After 1950, urban decentralization rapidly expanded suburbs, which now contain more than half the U.S. population. One consequence of the outward flow of people was fiscal crisis for central cities, especially in the Snowbelt. A declining tax base, coupled to rising need for social services, led some cities to the brink of bankruptcy in the 1970s.

4. Cities have rebounded since the 1970s, along with the growth of the new postindustrial economy. But millions of urbanites—especially recent immigrants from Latin America and Asia—work in low-paying service jobs.

5. The decentralization of cities has led to urban sprawl. This rapid, unplanned development has caused three problems: a boring sameness in the urban landscape, a rapid decline in our nation's open spaces, and increasing reliance on personal automobiles which consumes resources and causes personal stress.

6. Many businesses fleeing the old downtowns have helped expand edge cities. As more business moves outward in the urban region, the urban poor who remain in central cities find their communities have fewer jobs.

7. This loss of jobs is the key reason the poverty rate is twice as high in the central cities as it is in the suburbs.

8. Inadequate housing has always been a problem for some people in U.S. cities. At least one-third of people in the early industrial metropolis lived in overcrowded tenements. Not until the New Deal of the 1930s did the federal government act to improve urban housing.

9. Urban renewal began in 1949 to improve declining central city neighborhoods. In practice, cities claimed poor and working-class neighborhoods and sold the land to developers, who built profitable commercial districts and housing for more well-to-do people.

10. Urban public housing—often called "projects"—were constructed to house poor people displaced by urban renewal. Many of these communities housed only poor people, and problems with drugs and crime were widespread. The most serious problems were found in high-rise buildings that discouraged neighborhood ties.

11. Hypersegregation affects one in five African Americans, who live in urban ghettos socially isolated from the larger society.

12. Estimates suggest that about 500,000 people are homeless on any given night; 1.5 million people in the United States are homeless for at least some time during any year. Research shows that homelessness is an urban problem, with 71 percent of homeless people living in central cities and another 21 percent residing in suburbs.

13. The U.S. population is now less concentrated in the Snowbelt (the North and Midwest) and more concentrated in the Sunbelt (the South and West). Whereas Snowbelt cities have fixed borders where they meet politically independent suburbs, Sunbelt cities have annexed surrounding territory to grow larger.

14. Within a few years, half the planet's people will live in urban areas. Most of the world's largest cities are in poor nations, and their populations are soaring. These cities cannot meet the needs of this surging population.

15. Structural-functional analysis contrasts rural and urban living. In Europe, Tönnies devised

the concepts of *Gemeinschaft* and *Gesellschaft*, and Durkheim developed similar concepts of mechanical solidarity and organic solidarity. In the United States, Louis Wirth set out a theory of urbanism that stressed impersonality and tolerance.

16. At a micro-level, Georg Simmel explained that the overstimulation found in cities generates a blasé attitude in urban people. Even so, despite the widespread idea that cities threaten mental health, research documents that urbanites have better mental health than people living in rural areas.

17. Social-conflict analysis explores how our society's economic and political institutions shape urban life. Economic inequality generates very different neighborhoods in U.S. cities; in addition, profit-seeking investors favor affluent areas while being reluctant to lend money in low-income areas they see as "bad investments."

18. Conservatives point to market forces as shaping cities. They claim that most government programs to improve city life are ineffective or counterproductive. Liberals praise government efforts to improve city life by reducing income inequality and combating discrimination. Radicals claim that only basic change in the capitalist economy is likely to result in a better life for the majority.

KEY CONCEPTS

suburbs (p. 373) urban areas beyond the political boundaries of cities

megalopolis (p. 374) a vast urban region containing a number of cities and their surrounding suburbs

urban sprawl (p. 374) rapid, unplanned, and low-density development at the edge of urban areas

public housing (p. 377) high-density apartment buildings constructed to house poor people

supportive housing (p. 381) a program that combines low-income housing with on-site social services

Gemeinschaft (p. 385) a type of social organization in which people are closely bound by kinship and tradition

Gesellschaft (p. 385) a type of social organization in which people interact on the basis of self-interest

mechanical solidarity (p. 385) social bonds based on common sentiments and shared moral values

organic solidarity (p. 385) social bonds based on specialization and mutual interdependence

enterprise zones (p. 388) areas in the inner city that attract new businesses with the promise of tax relief

THINKING CRITICALLY: QUESTIONS AND ISSUES

1. Over the course of U.S. history, how have cities been shaped by economic development? By immigration? By new technology?

2. There is an old saying, "One half of the world does not know how the other half lives." Assess the truth of this statement with regard to life in U.S. cities, past and present.

3. Do you think urban life has improved over the last century? For the rich? The poor? If so, how and why?

4. Contrast the views of urbanism developed by Tönnies, Durkheim, Wirth, and Simmel. How does the urban political economy perspective understand cities and city life differently?

GETTING INVOLVED: LEARNING ACTIVITIES

1. What is the extent of the homeless problem in your city? Contact a local social services agency or office of the city government and ask for available information or an interview. What programs are in place to assist homeless people? What can others do to help?

2. To appreciate the plight of millions of New Yorkers a century ago, go to the local library and obtain a copy of *Jacob A. Riis: Photographer and Citizen*, by Alexander Alland, Sr. (New York: Aperture Books, 1974). Not only does this book provide instructive text, but you can see hundreds of Riis's own photographs, taken in the tenements of that time.

3. A tour on foot or by bicycle or car in your local area can be enlightening when you bring along

a sociological perspective. Travel around your community, making a sociological map as you go. Note the commercial, industrial, and residential areas. From the size and quality of housing, note the rich and poor neighborhoods. Where do people of different class positions live in relation to commercial and industrial areas? Do rich people live on high ground or low ground? How far from the rich do poor people live?

4. Is there a homeless shelter or food pantry in your community? If so, get in touch with someone there and offer your assistance. This is an excellent way to learn about problems of housing and hunger as you help others.

GETTING CONNECTED: USEFUL WEB LINKS

http://www.prenhall.com/macionis
Visit the interactive Companion Website™ that accompanies this text. Begin by clicking on the cover of your book. You will find a chapter-by-chapter study guide, practice tests, suggested Web links, and links to other relevant material.

http://urban.nyu.edu/research/index.html
This Web site at New York University's Taub Urban Research Center describes recent research on urban problems.

http://www.riotmanhattan.com/old_riot_site/webcam.html
Sometimes we can learn just by careful observation of everyday life. At this Web site, you can see images from a cyber-view camera at the corner of New York City's Fifth Avenue and Forty-Fifth Street. What can you learn from people-watching in this way? What can you *not* appreciate?

http://www.hud.gov
This is the main Web site for the government's Department of Housing and Urban Development, and it provides information on many urban issues.

GETTING STARTED ON YOUR OWN: RESEARCH NAVIGATOR™

Follow the instructions found on page 25 of this text to access the features of Research Navigator™. Once at the Web site, enter your Login Name and Password. Then, to use the **Content Select** database, enter keywords such as "urban poverty," "homelessness," and "urban sprawl," and the search engine will supply relevant and recent scholarly and popular press publications. Use the *New York Times* **Search-by-Subject Archive** to find recent news articles related to sociology and the **Link Library** feature to find relevant Web links organized by the key terms associated with this chapter.

© Paul Marcus, Crossing the Rio Grande, 1999, oil painting on canvas, 63 × 72 in.,
Studio SPM, Inc.

POPULATION AND GLOBAL INEQUALITY

"WE DON'T WANT TO HAVE CHILDREN," DECLARES Naomi Matsui, a twenty-eight-year-old Tokyo housewife. "My husband just doesn't like annoying things. And, since he won't help out raising them, I don't want kids, either."

To hear his wife tell it, Mr. Matsui sounds like something of a grouch. But in today's Japan, he has a lot of company. Why? A look around Tokyo provides some clues. Apartments in Japan are small by U.S. standards, and housing costs are among the highest in the world. Outside, the streets are highly congested, and parks for children to play—where they exist at all—are barely bigger than the family's living room at home (Kristof, 1996; Kent, 1999).

———

Japan's population is expected to start falling within a few years, a trend that has many people worried. But Japan's situation is exceptional: Most nations have increasing populations. Overall, the world is gaining population rapidly. In 2003, the global population was 6.3 billion, twice the level in 1960. Although the rate of population increase has been coming down, humanity continues to add about 80 million people to the planet each year, a number equal to the population of Great Britain, Norway, Sweden, and Finland combined (Population Reference Bureau, 2003). One important reason for concern is that population increase is greatest in the world's poorest countries. Some 1 billion of the world's people—about one in six—are desperately poor.

We begin this chapter by surveying the state of world population, highlighting the reasons population is increasing, and suggesting strategies to slow this trend. Then we turn to the problems of global poverty and hunger, presenting explanations of the striking inequalities found around the world and possible solutions to these problems.

✦ How fast is population increasing?

In 2003, the Earth's population was 6.3 billion people, four times what it was a century ago.

✦ How many of the world's people are hungry?

Around the world, 1 billion people—about one in six—experience daily hunger.

✦ How does gender figure into the issue of global poverty?

Around the world, 70 percent of adults facing life-threatening poverty are women.

GLOBAL POPULATION INCREASE

Global population has not always been cause for concern. For most of human history, population was low and fairly steady. Only after the Industrial Revolution did the world's population begin to rise. But when it did, it skyrocketed.

Population by the Numbers

Some 12,000 years ago, when our distant ancestors were first forming permanent settlements and beginning to develop a way of life we came to call civilization, the population of the entire world was just 5 million, less than the population of New York City today. Around the time of Christ 2000 years ago, the Earth had a population of about 300 million people, about the number of people living in the United States today (Haub, 2002).

The world's population began to rise sharply around 1750, as the Industrial Revolution began in Europe, shortly before the American colonies fought a war for independence from Great Britain; Figure 16–1 shows that the world's population jumped to 1 billion by 1800. By 1930, not much more than one

century later, it was 2 billion. At this point, not only was the population rising, but it was rising faster and faster. The world passed the 3 billion mark in 1962, just thirty-two years later, and 4 billion people crowded the planet by 1974, after only another twelve years. No wonder that, about this time, people began to talk about "overpopulation" as a serious problem.

Although the rate of increase began to slow by about 1970, global population kept pushing upward. The world passed the 5 billion mark in 1987 and the 6 billion mark in 1999. Over the twentieth century, global population quadrupled.

Most of the 80 million people being added to the world every year live in poor countries where the problem of poverty is already serious. Looking ahead, the United Nations projects that global population will surpass 8 billion by 2050 (O'Neill & Balk, 2001; United Nations, 2003). Whether the Earth can support 8 billion people or more—and at what standard of living—is one of the most serious questions we face today (Smail, 2004).

Causes of Population Increase

Tracking these trends is the focus of **demography,** *the study of human population.* Demography (from the Greek words meaning "the study of people") is one branch of sociology that not only keeps track of population levels but also seeks to explain why they rise and fall. Demographers point to two basic reasons for the current population increase: high fertility and falling mortality.

High Fertility   **Fertility** is *the incidence of childbearing in a country's population.* Demographers measure a society's fertility using the **crude birth rate,** *the number of live births in a given year for every thousand people in a population.* The crude birth rate is calculated by dividing the number of live births in a year by the society's total population and multiplying the result by 1,000. In the United States in 2003, there were 4.1 million live births in a population of 292 million (Population Reference Bureau, 2003). That yields a crude birth rate of 14.0.

To learn more about U.S. population patterns, visit
http://www.census.gov

Demographers describe this measure as "crude" because it is based on the entire population, not just women in their childbearing years. But the crude birth rate is a good, easy-to-figure measure of a society's fertility. Figure 16–2 shows the crude birth rate for the major regions of the world.

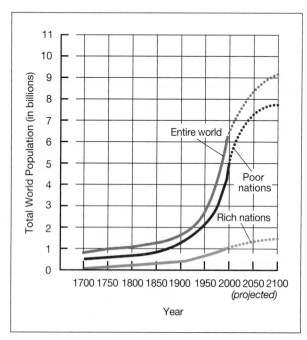

FIGURE 16–1   **The Increase in World Population, 1700–2100**

Global population began to increase rapidly after about 1800. Although the rate of increase is now declining, the world is likely to have more than 8 billion people by 2050.

DIMENSIONS OF DIFFERENCE

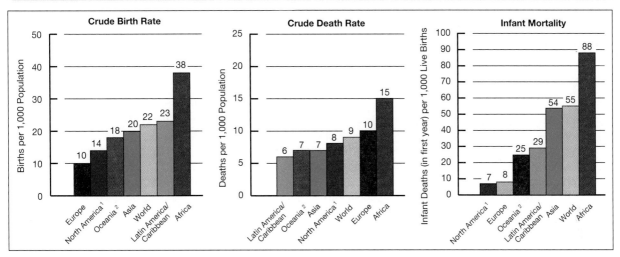

FIGURE 16-2 **Three Population Statistics for World Regions**

These figures provide a comparative look at the birth rates, death rates, and infant mortality rates for major regions of the world.

[1]United States and Canada

[2]Australia, New Zealand, and South Pacific islands.

Source: Population Reference Bureau (2003).

If other factors are equal, the higher a nation's fertility, the faster its population increases. For the world as a whole, the crude birth rate is 22. Against this global average, the birth rate in the United States (14) is low. Birth rates are higher in poor countries such as the Philippines (28) and higher still in many of the world's poorest nations, including Afghanistan (42) in Asia, Angola (48) in central Africa, the Palestinian Territory of the Middle East (38), and Nicaragua (32) in Latin America (Population Reference Bureau, 2003). The Social Policy box on page 398 explains how the lack of effective birth control contributes to high birth rates in poor countries.

Falling Mortality An even more important factor in the upward surge in global population is falling **mortality,** *the incidence of death in a country's population.* Demographers track mortality using a **crude death rate,** *the number of deaths in a given year for every thousand people in a population.* The number of deaths in a year is divided by the total population, and the result is multiplied by 1,000. In 2003, there were 2.6 million deaths in the U.S. population of 292 million, yielding a crude death rate of 8.9 (Population Reference Bureau, 2003).

When all other factors are equal, the lower a nation's mortality, the faster its population increases. For the world as a whole, the crude death rate is 9, which makes the U.S. rate about average. The global pattern of death rates is not as simple as that for birth rates, however. At first glance, it may seem that the lower the crude death rate, the heathier the society. This is true to a point. Some very poor nations such as Laos (13) and Mali (19) have high crude death rates. But poor nations also have populations that are, on average, very young (resulting from the high birth rates we have already discussed). Rich nations such as the United States have populations that are, on average, much older. These facts explain why the death rate for the United States is higher than one might initially expect and why the death rates in some poor countries, such as Vietnam (6) and Nicaragua (5), are lower than expected (Population Reference Bureau, 2003). The middle graph in Figure 16–2 shows the crude death rates for all the major world regions.

A better measure of a nation's quality of life is the **infant mortality rate,** *the number of deaths among infants under one year of age for every thousand live births in a given year.* In this case, the number of deaths of children under one year of age is divided

Social Policy   Contraception: One Key to Controlling Population

As recently as 1960, family planning was almost unknown in poor societies around the world and not all that common even in the United States. Today, about three-fourths of U.S. couples in their childbearing years use some form of contraception. Worldwide, however, less than half of all couples make effective use of contraception.

There are many reasons for not using contraception, including religious beliefs and women's lack of social power in many poor societies. But the most important factor is poverty: When people are poor, it is unlikely that they will pay for—or even know about—contraception.

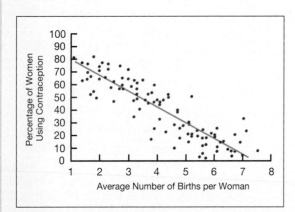

Contraceptive Use and Fertility in 100 Countries

This pattern shows a negative correlation represented by the regression line: As the share of women using contraception goes up, a woman's average number of children goes down.

The figure clearly shows the difference contraception makes in lowering fertility. The vertical axis shows the percentage of women using contraception; the horizontal axis shows the average number of children a women bears during her lifetime. The dots represent about 100 countries in the world. The dots show a strong *correlation*, or association, between the two variables; the *regression line* is a statistical way of summarizing this linear relationship. In countries where contraception is widespread, women have about two children; in countries where it is not, women have five or more children. It is easy to imagine the consequences of each pattern for population increase.

Issues and Exercises

1. In 1900, the average woman in the United States had about five children. What factors do you think brought that number down to less than two today?

2. Generally, contraception use is common where women have more choices about their lives. What does this suggest about the need to raise the social standing of women?

3. ![Research Navigator.com] Use Research Navigator™ to learn more about contraception. (See instructions on page 25; keywords: "contraception," "global population")

Source: Data from the Population Reference Bureau (1999).

by the number of live births during a year; the result is multiplied by 1,000. In 2003, there were 28,300 infant deaths and 4.1 million live births in the United States. Dividing the first number by the second and multiplying the result by 1,000 yields an infant mortality rate of 6.9. For the world as a whole, the infant mortality is 55, so quality of life in the United States must be quite good. However, the U.S. rate is still somewhat higher than that of most other rich countries, including Great Britain (5), Sweden (4), Japan (3), and Australia (5) (Population Reference Bureau,

2003). What explains the weaker standing of the United States? For one thing, social inequality is greater here than in other industrial nations; for another, ours is the only high-income country without universal access to health care.

In poor countries, infant mortality is dramatically higher. The rates for Nicaragua (31), Angola (145), Cambodia (95), and Laos (104) reflect the fact that the people of these nations lack adequate nutrition and safe water and have little or no access to high-quality medical care (Population Reference Bureau, 2003).

Measuring Population Increase

Demographers can calculate a society's *natural growth rate* (or rate of natural increase) by combining fertility and mortality rates. To do this, simply subtract the crude death rate from the crude birth rate. In the case of the United States, a crude birth rate of 14.0 minus the crude death rate of 8.9 yields a natural growth rate of 5.1 per thousand, or .51 percent annual growth.

For the world as a whole, population is increasing at the rate of 1.3 percent each year. Global Map 16–1 on page 400 shows that population growth is slow in the United States and Canada (0.5 percent annually), Europe (−0.2 percent), and Oceania (0.7 percent), rich regions of the planet.

To calculate the *doubling time* for a nation's population, simply divide the number 70 by the growth rate. The population of Central America, with an annual growth rate of 2.4 percent, will double in about thirty years. The population of Central Africa, with a 3 percent growth rate, will double in about twenty-three years. Clearly, a country that has trouble feeding the population it has now can hardly afford to let population double within little more than one generation.

One other factor, that plays a part in nations' overall population growth—but which is not included in measures of natural growth rate—is immigration. As explained in Chapter 3 ("Racial and Ethnic Inequality"), about 800,000 people enter the United States each year. Today, high-income nations such as the United States grow as much or more from immigration as they do from natural increase; low-income nations such as Afghanistan, on the other hand, grow almost entirely from natural increase (births exceeding deaths).

We turn now to a survey of population around the world. Generally speaking, population growth is slowest in the Northern Hemisphere, where most high-income countries are found. It is in the Southern Hemisphere, which contains most of the world's low-income countries, that population increase is the greatest problem today.

The Low-Growth North When the Industrial Revolution began, population growth in Western Europe spiked upward to about 3 percent annually. Since then, the growth rate has fallen steadily. Now the birth rate in Europe, the United States, and Canada is below the replacement level of 2.1 children per woman; demographers call this point **zero population growth,** *the level of reproduction that maintains population at a steady state.* More than fifty nations, almost all high-income, have dropped below the point of zero population growth (Population Reference Bureau, 2003).

Why the great decline in population increase? Important factors include the high cost of raising children, widespread use of contraceptives and abortion, the trend toward later marriage and singlehood, and the fact that the typical family now has both husband and wife in the labor force.

The birth rate in Cambodia, a low-income nation, is three times that of the United States. Because agrarian societies depend on human labor, large families make economic sense. This explains why almost all of the world's population increase is taking place in poorer countries.

A WORLD OF DIFFERENCES

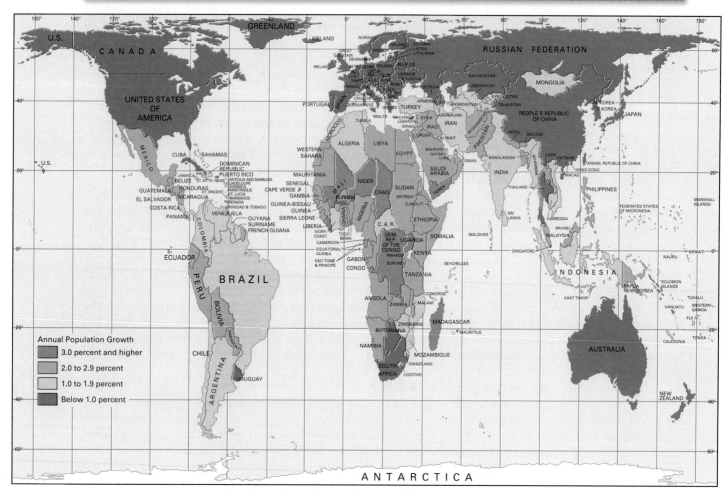

GLOBAL MAP 16–1   Population Growth around the World

The richest countries in the world—including the United States, Canada, and the nations of Europe—have low rates of population growth, which are generally below 1 percent annually. In more than one dozen high- and middle-income nations (including Sweden, Germany, Italy, and Russia), populations are declining. In Asia, population increase is greater—currently about 1.4 percent annually, which will double the population in fifty years. In Latin America, population increase is greater still—1.8 percent annually, which will double the population in thirty-nine years. The population of Africa is currently increasing at 2.4 percent, which will double the population there in twenty-nine years. In general, population is increasing fastest in the poorest regions of the world. China, with a rigid "one-child policy," is an exception to this pattern.

Source: Population Reference Bureau (2003); map projection from *Peters Atlas of the World* (1990).

In sum, in high-income nations such as the United States population increase is not a serious problem. In fact, sixteen European nations are *losing* population. Some analysts suggest that these nations (and possibly others) may face the problem of underpopulation in the future because the rising number of elderly people will have fewer and fewer young people to care for them and support them financially (Chesnais, 1997; Population Reference Bureau, 2003). In the United States, high immigration rates probably will ensure that population continues to increase (McDonald, 2001; Kent & Mather,

A Global Perspective

Can Too Few People Be a Problem? The Case of Japan

As the opening to this chapter suggested, more and more people in Japan are deciding not to have children. This fact has government officials worried. The Japanese birth rate now stands at just 1.4 children per woman, less than the level necessary to replace the people alive today. Japan's rate of annual population increase has fallen to just 0.1 percent. If people keep putting the brakes on childbirth, experts predict that by 2007 the population of Japan will start to decline. By 2100, the nation could have half the people it has today.

In this way, Japan stands out from many other nations in Asia, as well as Africa and Latin America, where population is rising rapidly. In Japan, people are now discussing the possibility of a future with too few people.

Japan's population would become older and older on average. A larger share of elderly people means greater and greater demands for care and medical attention with fewer young people to care for them. An aging population also means that there are fewer workers paying taxes to fund government care for the elderly. Most seriously of all, some are concerned that a falling population could cause the Japanese to disappear completely.

To reverse the falling birth rate, some government officials are proposing new policies, including cash incentives to couples who have large families, maternity leave from work, and expansion of workplace child care. Other, more extreme proposals have already caused a firestorm of controversy. These include restricting women's access to college and careers and even encouraging Japanese men to import "mail-order" brides from the Philippines, where the culture favors larger families.

ISSUES AND EXERCISES

1. If population increase is a global problem, should we worry about the population of any nation going down?

2. Would you support or oppose the solutions to the declining population problem noted at the end of the box? Why?

3. Some people in the United States are concerned that our declining birth rate and rising immigration rate will threaten the future of "American culture." Do you agree or disagree? Why?

Source: Kristof (1996), Kent (1999), and Population Reference Bureau (2003).

2002). In Japan, however, population is expected to start declining within a few years. The Global Perspective box takes a closer look.

The High-Growth South Rising population is a serious problem for poor nations, most of which lie in the Southern Hemisphere. Programs to limit births have been successful in many low-income countries. As a result, the number of children born to the average woman in the world has fallen from six children in 1950 to about four children today.

But bringing down the birth rate goes only so far in controlling rising population. In the twentieth century, advances in medical technology sharply reduced death rates. In fact, most of the population increase in recent decades has resulted not from high fertility but from falling mortality. Most poor nations today have high birth rates coupled with declining death rates. Although it is certainly good news that fewer children and adults are dying, the result is rising populations that threaten everyone's ability to survive. Worldwide, 96 percent of population increase is taking place in the low-income nations of the Southern Hemisphere.

Most population experts agree that a key element in controlling world population growth is raising the status of women. Making birth control technology more widely available is important, but the population will continue to increase as long as a culture defines women's primary responsibility as raising children.

A DEFINING MOMENT

Thomas Robert Malthus: Claiming Population Is a Problem

PROBABLY NO ONE IN HISTORY HAS HAD more of an effect on how people look at the issue of population increase than Thomas Robert Malthus. Born in 1766 to a prosperous and highly educated family, Malthus was the second of eight children, a number not uncommon for his time. He became a priest and, later, a university professor. But he is remembered for the treatise on population that he published in 1798 under the full title "An Essay on the Principle of Population as It Affects the Future Improvement of Society, with Remarks on the Speculations of Mr. Godwin, M. Condorcet and Other Writers."

Perhaps sensing the controversy he would cause, Malthus originally published the work anonymously. Five years later, he republished his work under his name in a much expanded form. The essential statement of his treatise is this: "Population increases in a geometric ratio, while the means of subsistence increases in an arithmetic ratio." Malthus believed that human beings had two powerful needs—for sex and for food. Living at a time when families were very large and there was no reliable form of birth control, he reasoned that "the number of mouths to be fed will have no limit" so that "the food that is to supply them cannot keep pace."

Was there any hope? Malthus pointed out that "crime, disease, war, and vice" might well slow population increase. But he rejected birth control on religious grounds and thought it highly unlikely that people would give up sex (Malthus, himself, had just three children). In the end, Malthus could imagine no escape from a future of "famine, distress, havoc, and dismay."

Read the original 1798 treatise by Malthus at
http://www.ac.wwu.edu/~stephan/malthus/malthus.0.html

Thomas Robert Malthus (1766–1834) lived in England at a time when population was beginning to soar. His prediction that population would increase far more quickly than food and other resources prompted one artist to imagine this future for his native country.

More than two centuries later, we can be thankful that Malthus was at least partly wrong. Especially in high-income nations, birth rates have fallen dramatically in recent decades, and, thanks to advancements in technology, food production is far greater than Malthus imagined. But the fact remains that global population continues to increase. Is it possible that the Malthusian nightmare will not happen? Or has it just been delayed?

Dr. Nafis Sadik, an Egyptian woman who heads the United Nations' efforts at population control, sums up the new approach: Give a woman more choices about how to live, and she will have fewer children. A woman who has access to schooling and jobs can decide when and whether she wants to marry, and she will bear children as a matter of choice, not because it is the only option open to her. Under these conditions, evidence shows, women have fewer children (Linden, 1994; Ashford, 1995; Axinn & Barber, 2001; Population Reference Bureau, 2002).

Explaining the Population Problem: Malthusian Theory

Thomas Robert Malthus (1766–1834) was an English economist, priest, and pioneering demographer who lived at just the time when global population was turning sharply upward. Malthus (1926; orig. 1798) offered a simple mathematical analysis of population increase that led to a troubling prediction. Population, he explained, would increase according to what mathematicians call a *geometric progression*, illustrated by the series of numbers 2, 4, 8, 16, 32, and so on. At such a rate, Malthus concluded, world population would soon soar out of control.

Food production would also increase, Malthus added, but only in *arithmetic progression* (as in the series 2, 3, 4, 5, 6) because, no matter what new technology people invent, there is only so much farmland. Thus, Malthus concluded that people would soon reproduce beyond what the planet could feed, leading to starvation and social chaos. The Defining Moment box takes a closer look at the warning sounded by Malthus.

Critical evaluation. If Malthus had been right, life as we know it might well have ended by now. But he failed to realize that as the Industrial Revolution took hold, birth rates would drop; children were no longer needed to farm the land, and they became more costly to raise. In addition, most people began using artificial birth control. Finally, Malthus underestimated how much food people would eventually produce: Irrigation, fertilizers, and pesticides have increased farm output far beyond what he imagined.

But was Malthus entirely wrong? Habitable land, clean water, and fresh air are all limited resources, so population cannot continue to expand indefinitely. In short, no level of population growth can go on forever. To avoid Malthus's dire prediction, humanity must work out ways to control its own numbers.

A More Recent Approach: Demographic Transition Theory

A more recent analysis of population change is **demographic transition theory,** *a thesis linking demographic changes to a society's level of technological development.* Figure 16–3 shows how population is affected by four levels of technological development. Preindustrial, agrarian societies—that is, almost the entire world before 1750—fall into Stage 1. These

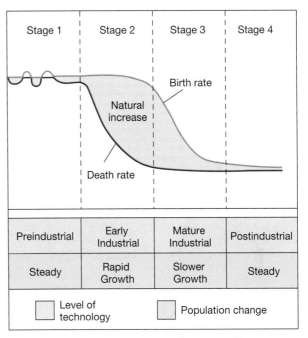

FIGURE 16–3 The Stages of Demographic Transition
Demographic transition theory shows the process by which societies move from high birth rates and high death rates (Stage 1) to low birth rates and low death rates (Stage 4).

societies have high birth rates because families depend on the labor of children and because there is little effective birth control. But death rates are also high because poor people understand little about health and disease. Periodic outbreaks of plague and other infectious diseases balance out any rise in births, so population remains steady over long periods of time.

Stage 2, the onset of industrialization, begins the demographic transition. Death rates fall because of higher living standards, including better nutrition and the benefits of scientific medicine. Because birth rates remain high, population begins increasing rapidly. Malthus lived during Europe's Stage 2, which helps to explain his pessimistic view of the world's future. The poorest countries on the planet are in this high-growth stage today.

In Stage 3, a mature industrial economy, the birth rate falls into line with the death rate, and population growth slows down. Fertility falls partly because families no longer have to bear several children to ensure that a few will survive to adulthood. Moreover, mature industrial societies transform children from economic assets (who, by working, contributed to their families' income) to economic liabilities (instead, children's schooling and other expenses now

DIMENSIONS OF DIFFERENCE

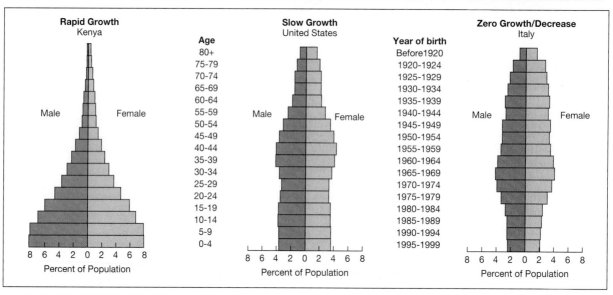

FIGURE 16–4 Population Pyramids: Kenya, United States, and Italy, 2000

Population pyramids are graphic representations of the population according to sex (male and female) and age (from birth to 80 + years). In a very poor nation such as Kenya, the youngest people make up the largest share of the society, guaranteeing that population increase will continue as children enter their childbearing years. The United States has a more box-like shape because we are, on average a much older population. (The average age in the United States is about thirty-six, compared with about sixteen in Kenya.) Italy is one of the nations that is recording a slight population decrease. There are proportionately fewer young people in Italy, and a larger share are elderly. There, the average age is forty and rising.

Source: U.S. Census Bureau (2003).

put a strain on family finances). Effective birth control becomes widely available, and limiting family size is important to women who want to work outside the home.

Stage 4 corresponds to a postindustrial economy, which promotes stable population size once again. Both the birth rate and the death rate are low, so there is little or no natural increase in population size. As noted earlier, this is now the case in much of Western Europe and Japan (Population Reference Bureau, 2003).

Critical evaluation.   Compared with Malthus's dire prediction, demographic transition theory offers a more hopeful view of our demographic future. In this analysis, advancing technology first sparks population increase but then brings it under control, all the while providing a world of material plenty.

But will poor societies develop economically to the point that their birth rates drop? If they remain poor, there is little chance that the world will ever bring rising population under control. Moreover, as shown in Figure 16–4, even if birth rates fall, the very young population of poor nations (such as Kenya) means that most people have yet to bear children. So at least some population increase is inevitable, at least for decades to come.

GLOBAL INEQUALITY

We have seen that population problems are far greater in some parts of the world than others. The same is true in terms of poverty and hunger. Indeed, the problems of rapid population increase and hunger typically are found in the same parts of the world.

Chapter 2 ("Poverty and Wealth") explained that people in the United States are divided into classes, with some having far more wealth, income, prestige, and power than others. Such inequality is even greater if we consider people not just in the United

States but all around the world. Figure 16–5 divides the world's total income by fifths of humanity. For comparison, recall (from Figure 2–1 on page 29) that the richest 20 percent of the U.S. population earns about 48 percent of the national income. The richest 20 percent of the world's people, however, receive fully 80 percent of all income. In the United States, the poorest 20 percent of the population earns 4 percent of all income; globally, the same proportion struggles to survive on just 1 percent of all income.

With the world's income so unevenly distributed, even people who are counted among the poor in the United States live much better than most people around the world. Well-off people in rich countries such as ours live so well that they may have trouble understanding just how serious the plight of others in the world really is. Then there are the super-rich: Bill Gates, the world's richest person, is worth $47 billion, which exceeds the wealth of the world's twenty poorest *nations* (World Bank, 2003; *Forbes*, 2004).

High-Income Nations

Just as a single society places individuals at various class levels, the global system of inequality contains high-income, middle-income, and low-income nations. Global Map 16–2 on page 406 shows which of the world's 191 nations fall in each category. There are about forty high-income nations in the world, including United States and Canada, Argentina, the countries of Western Europe, Israel, Saudi Arabia, Japan, Australia, and New Zealand.

The world's rich nations benefit from the productivity of advanced technology; it was in these nations that the Industrial Revolution steadily boosted productivity beginning more than two centuries ago. How much of a difference does advanced technology make? The tiny high-income nation of Holland produces more than the mostly agrarian continent of Africa below the Sahara Desert. Tiny Belgium outproduces all of India (United Nations Development Programme, 2003).

In 2003, high-income nations were home to about 1.2 billion people, or 18 percent of the Earth's population. Even at the bottom of this favored category (for instance, in South Korea), annual income is at least $10,000; the figure is more than twice that much in the world's richest countries such as the United States and Switzerland. Overall, people in the forty high-income countries earn 79 percent of the world's total income.

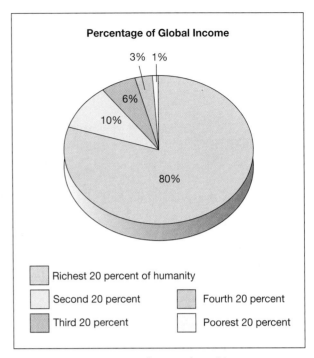

FIGURE 16–5 Distribution of World Income

The total income earned by all the people of the world is distributed very unevenly, with the richest 20 percent of people receiving 80 percent of all income.

Sources: Calculated by the author based on United Nations Development Programme (2003) and The World Bank (2003).

Middle-Income Nations

People living in *middle-income countries* have incomes ranging from $2,500 (in, say, Ecuador in Latin America, Albania in Europe, Swaziland in Africa, and Russia in Europe and Asia) to almost $10,000 (in Chile, South Africa, and Malaysia). These nations—ninety in all—have significant industrialization, but almost half the people still live in rural areas and work in agriculture. In general, people in rural areas have less access to schooling, medical care, good housing, and safe water than those who live in cities.

By 2003, both India and China had entered the ranks of middle-income nations. In all, this category includes some 4.5 billion people, or about 70 percent of humanity. Overall, they earned about 20 percent of the world's income.

Low-Income Nations

The world's sixty low-income nations have populations that are, on average, agrarian and very poor.

A WORLD OF DIFFERENCES

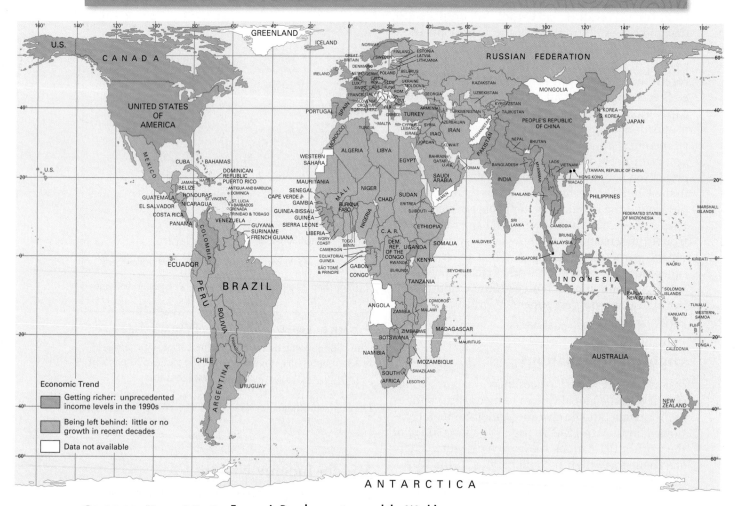

GLOBAL MAP 16–2   Economic Development around the World

Living standards vary dramatically around the world. At one end of the scale, high-income nations—which include the United States, Canada, Argentina, the nations of Western Europe, Israel, Saudi Arabia, Australia, New Zealand, and Japan—are very rich. Their people consume a large share of global resources. Middle-income nations—which include most of the countries of Latin America, Eastern Europe, and Asia, as well as a number of African nations—have a more modest standard of living. At the other end of the scale, in low-income nations—including most of Africa and some of Asia—poverty is both severe and widespread. Although these countries contain much of the world's natural resources, their people consume only a small share of them.

Sources: Prepared by the author using data from United Nations Development Programme (2003). Map projection from *Peters Atlas of the World* (1990).

Most of these sixty nations are found in Central and East Africa or in Asia. In poor countries, about 75 percent of the people live in rural areas and farm as their ancestors have done for centuries. The remainder live in or near cities, where many work in factories. With limited industrial technology, low-income nations are not very productive, which is one reason that hunger, disease, poor schooling, and unsafe housing are so common.

In 2003, 28 percent of the planet's population, or 1.8 billion people, lived in low-income nations earning only 3 percent of the world's income. For every dollar earned by people living in a rich nation, these people earn just pennies. We now turn to a closer look at the problems of global poverty and hunger.

The World's Poverty Problem

Poverty is far more widespread in the world as a whole than it is in the United States. Around the world, about 1 billion people do not have enough to eat; hunger makes it hard to work and raises the risk of disease (United Nations Development Programme, 2003).

In more scientific terms, the typical adult in a rich nation, such as the United States, consumes about 3,500 calories a day, which is too much for optimal health. The result is that about two-thirds of the people in this country are overweight. The typical adult in a low-income country, who performs a great deal of physical labor, consumes just 2,000 calories a day. This is too little, and the result is hunger and undernourishment.

Learn more about world hunger from this Web site:
http://www.worldhunger.org

The long-term effects of poverty are deadly. In the ten minutes it takes to read through this section of the chapter, about 300 people in the world, sick and weakened from hunger, will die. This amounts to about 40,000 people each day, or 15 million people each year. Global hunger is among the most serious social problems facing the world today.

Relative versus Absolute Poverty Poverty exists in rich countries such as the United States. But most of what we call poverty is *relative poverty*, referring to a lack of the resources that most people take for granted. In global perspective, however, we face the problem of *absolute poverty*, a lack of resources that is life threatening. Human beings in absolute poverty lack the nutrition necessary for health and long-term survival. There is no denying that some absolute poverty exists in the United States. But such immediately life-threatening poverty strikes only a small percentage of the U.S. population; by contrast, one-third or more of people in low-income countries are in desperate need. When absolute poverty becomes widespread, death comes early. Whereas death typically occurs after age seventy-five in rich countries, in the poorest regions of Central Africa, half of all children do not live to age ten.

For every dollar earned by the average person in the United States, people in India earn about six cents. Widespread poverty is evident on the streets of Madras and other Indian cities as families beg for money. If you were a visitor from the United States, what degree of responsibility would you feel for the welfare of a family like this one?

Poverty and Children

Poverty warps the lives of young people, even those lucky enough to survive. Perhaps 100 million children in the cities of poor countries beg, steal, sell sex, or work for drug gangs to provide needed income for their families. Such children miss out on schooling and are likely to fall victim to disease and violence. Many young girls become pregnant, truly a case of children having children.

Read more about the plight of street children at
http://www.hrw.org/children/street.htm

Another 100 million of the world's children have left their families and are living on the streets doing

A general rule is that the poorer a nation is, the greater the domination of women by men. In a country like Afghanistan, how is this fact reflected in the number of children a woman has, as well as her opportunities for schooling and for paid work?

whatever they must to get by. Latin America faces the greatest problem of poor, homeless children: Brazil reports that millions of children are living on their own, underfed and unschooled, often sniffing glue or using other cheap drugs to numb their suffering (Ross, 1996; One World, 1998; Collymore, 2002).

Poverty and Women

As Chapter 4 ("Gender Inequality") explains, rich societies treat women in many ways as inferior to men. One consequence is that, compared with men, women are at much higher risk of poverty.

In poor countries, however, gender stratification is even more pronounced. Because traditional societies often are strongly patriarchal, women have few choices, limited schooling, and little economic opportunity. As a result, 70 percent of the adults facing absolute poverty are women (Hymowitz, 1995; Bearak, 2001).

Slavery

Surely the greatest horror linked to global poverty is slavery. Many people assume slavery to be an evil of the past. The British Empire banned slavery in 1833; the United States did so in 1865. But according to Anti-Slavery International (ASI), some 400 million men, women, and children (almost 7 percent of the world's people) are currently living in conditions that amount to slavery (Janus, 1996).

One form of bondage is *child slavery*, in which desperately poor families send their children out

to hustle on the streets to bring in income. Perhaps 100 million children, many in poor countries of Latin America, fall into this category.

A second kind of bondage is *debt slavery*, in which employers enslave workers of all ages by paying them too little to cover the costs of their debts. In sweatshops throughout the world, workers do receive a wage, but not enough to pay for the food and housing their employers provide. For practical purposes, then, they are slaves who are not free to leave.

Third, *servile forms of marriage* can amount to slavery. In India, Thailand, and some African nations, families marry off women against their will. Many end up as slaves performing work for their husband's family; in other cases, women are forced into prostitution.

Fourth, ASI reports that *chattel slavery*, in which one person owns another, still flourishes in parts of the world. No one knows exactly how many chattel slaves exist because the practice of buying and selling human beings is against the law throughout the world. But the practice has been documented in many countries in Asia, the Middle East, and, especially, Africa and involves hundreds of thousands of people. Trading in people is one of the most profitable forms of crime (next to dealing in guns and drugs) to organized crime syndicates around the world (Orhant, 2002).

In 1948, the United Nations issued a Universal Declaration of Human Rights, which states, "No one shall be held in slavery or servitude; slavery and the slave trade shall be prohibited in all their forms."

Even though slavery remains morally wrong and against the law, it persists as part of the sad story of global poverty.

Read the United Nations Declaration of Human Rights at
http://www.un.org/rights/50/decla.htm

THEORETICAL ANALYSIS: UNDERSTANDING GLOBAL INEQUALITY

Both macro-level paradigms provide explanations for global poverty and insights into the problem of population increase.

Structural-Functional Analysis: The Process of Modernization

Modernization theory is *a model of economic and social development that explains global inequality in terms of technological and cultural differences between societies.* Modernization theory begins by pointing out that as recently as two centuries ago, every nation in the world was very poor. As the Industrial Revolution took hold in Europe and later in North America and elsewhere, an increasing number of societies gradually became affluent. At first, new industrial wealth benefited just a few. But industrial technology was so productive that gradually the living standard of even the poorest people began to rise.

In the last century, living standards in high-income countries, including the United States, have jumped fivefold. Most of today's middle-income nations in Asia and Latin America are also industrializing and thereby becoming richer. But in low-income countries, where there is less industrial technology, people remain poor.

At this point, one might ask why every society hasn't adopted industrial technology. Modernization theory's answer is this: Not every society is eager to sacrifice tradition in favor of change toward higher living standards. In this analysis, then, tradition (sometimes in the form of fundamentalist religious beliefs) is the greatest barrier to economic development. In societies that have strong families and whose people are taught to respect the past, culture acts as an anchor that prevents people from exploring new ways of life and adopting technologies, even those that might improve their lives. In today's world, there are many examples of societies that reject modernization, including the Amish of North America, the Semai of Malaysia, and fundamentalist Islamic people in Iran, Afghanistan, and elsewhere.

Typically, these societies reject industrial technology as a threat to their family relationships, customs, and religious beliefs.

Near the end of the Middle Ages, as sociologist Max Weber (1958; orig. 1904–5) explained, the cultural environment of Western Europe favored change. As Protestant religious beliefs (especially those of John Calvin) took hold in parts of Europe, a progress-oriented way of life emerged. People came to view getting rich—which the Catholic tradition regarded with suspicion—as a sign of personal virtue and ultimate salvation. A new ethic of individualism gradually replaced the traditional emphasis on kinship and community. Such cultural beliefs led people to adopt new technology and helped bring about the Industrial Revolution. Before long, culture and technology had succeeded in lifting Western Europeans from poverty and creating widespread prosperity.

W. W. Rostow: The Stages of Modernization

Modernization theory draws on the work of Max Weber, as well as that of Ferdinand Tönnies and Emile Durkheim, whose ideas were discussed in Chapter 15 ("Urban Life"). But it was Walt Whitman Rostow (1960, 1978) who expressed modernization theory as an easy-to-understand series of stages.

1. **Traditional stage.** People living in traditional, agrarian societies raise their children to look to the past, respecting old ways. Such people do not easily imagine how life can be very different. Therefore, they build their lives around their families and local communities, following the ways of their ancestors with little personal choice or individual freedom. Such societies provide a life that is spiritually rich but poor in a material sense.

   Several centuries ago, most of the world was in this first stage of economic development. Today, nations such as Bangladesh, Niger, and Somalia are still stuck in the traditional stage and remain just as poor as they were then.

2. **Take-off stage.** As societies begin to break free of cultural tradition, they allow people to use their talents and imagination, and the economy begins to grow. As people produce goods not just for their own consumption but to trade with others for profit, a market takes form. Greater individualism, a willingness to take risks, and a desire for material goods all are forces for positive change, although they also

Modernization theory claims that, as rich nations colonized much of the world, they spread progressive culture and new technology. World system theory challenges this claim, charging that colonization did little more than make some nations rich while making others poor. Which approach do you find more convincing? Why?

weaken family ties and time-honored norms and values.

Great Britain and the United States reached take-off in the early 1800s. Thailand, a middle-income country in eastern Asia, is now in this stage. Reaching take-off sometimes depends on progressive influences from richer nations, which provide foreign aid, export advanced technology and investment capital, and invite foreign students to take advantage of advanced schooling.

3. **Drive to technological maturity.** As this stage begins, people come to define poverty as a problem that can be solved by "progress" and "economic growth." Industrialization is well underway; the economy grows and diversifies as new products are invented. People realize that their new way of life is weakening traditional family and local community life, but the ways of the past are left behind as "old fashioned." Great Britain reached this point by about 1840, the United States by 1860. Today, Mexico, the U.S. territory of Puerto Rico, and South Korea are among the nations driving toward technological maturity.

Once a society reaches Stage 3, there is much less absolute poverty. Cities swell with people who leave rural villages in search of better jobs and schooling; occupational specialization makes relationships less personal; and the rising importance of individual freedom and social equality sparks social movements demanding greater political rights for all, including women. Governments pass laws requiring everyone to attend school, and a large share of people go on to college or other advanced training.

4. **High mass consumption.** At this point, industrial technology is widespread, and the economy is growing rapidly with steadily rising living standards. Mass production of an endless assortment of new goods and services fuels mass consumption. People take affluence for granted and learn to "need" things their ancestors never imagined.

The United States, Japan, and other rich nations moved into this stage of development by about 1900. Recently entering this level of economic development are two former British colonies that are now prosperous small societies of east Asia: Hong Kong (part of the People's Republic of China) and Singapore (independent since 1965).

Rostow explains that rich nations play an important part in helping poor countries move through the four stages. Rich nations can export high-tech farming methods to poor nations to help raise agricultural yields. Such techniques—part of what is commonly called the "Green Revolution"—include hybrid seeds, modern irrigation methods, chemical fertilizers, and pesticides for insect control. Of course, poor countries also look to rich nations for industrial technology, and computers and other new information technology.

Even an expanding economy will not lift living standards if poor societies do not control their population growth. Rich nations can help poor nations limit population growth by giving them birth control technology and educational programs to promote its use. Also, according to modernization theory, once economic development is underway, birth rates should decline as they have in industrialized nations because children are no longer an economic asset but become an economic liability (Lino, 2003).

Critical evaluation.   Since it first emerged in the 1950s, modernization theory has shaped the foreign policy of the United States and other rich nations. Supporters point to rapid economic development in much of the world—especially the Asian nations of South Korea, Taiwan, Singapore, and Hong Kong—as evidence that the affluence created in Western Europe and North America is within reach of all countries (Parsons, 1966; W. Moore, 1977, 1979; Bauer, 1981; Berger, 1986; Firebaugh & Beck, 1994; Firebaugh, 1996; Firebaugh & Sandu, 1998).

But critics see modernization theory as a flawed defense of capitalism. If modernization theory is correct, they ask, why is there still so much poverty in much of the world? Moreover, why are living standards in a number of nations, including Haiti and Nicaragua in Latin America and Sudan, Ghana, and Rwanda in Africa, actually *lower* than in 1960? (United Nations Development Programme, 1996)

Second, critics point out that modernization theory says little about how rich nations often seek to prevent poor countries from developing. Centuries ago, European nations began a system of colonial control over much of the world that benefited the European conquerors at the expense of most of the world's people. As we explain presently, such exploitation continues to the present day.

Third, modernization theory sets up the world's most developed countries as the standard for the rest of the world, as if we have nothing to learn from others. This ethnocentric (culturally self-serving) bias can have harmful consequences. The Western idea of progress encourages the exploitation of other nations and also fuels wasteful consumption, causing harm to the physical environment of the planet, the focus of Chapter 17 ("Technology and the Environment").

Fourth, and finally, critics reject modernization theory's implication that poor societies are responsible for their own poverty. Instead of blaming the victims, critics suggest shifting the focus to the behavior of rich nations (Wiarda, 1987).

Such concerns point to a second major approach to understanding global inequality, called world system theory.

Social-Conflict Analysis: The Global Economic System

World system theory is *a model of economic development that explains global inequality in terms of the historical exploitation of poor societies by rich ones.* In other words, the global economic system produces affluence for some and poverty for others. For centuries, this global economic system has exploited poor nations for the benefit of rich countries.

This approach rejects the idea that poor nations are simply "behind" in their economic development. On the contrary, some nations have become rich only because others have become poor.

The origins of the capitalist world economy go back five centuries to the time at which Europeans began establishing colonies, which eventually included the Americas to the west, Africa to the south, and Asia to the east. **Colonialism** is *the process by which some nations enrich themselves through political and economic control of other nations.* Great Britain established so many colonies around the world that in 1900 it controlled about one-fourth of the world's land and could boast, "The sun never sets on the British Empire." The United States, which was itself one of the early British colonies, eventually pushed west across the continent, purchased Alaska, and gained control of Haiti, Puerto Rico, Guam, the Philippines, the Hawaiian Islands, and parts of Panama and Cuba.

Formal colonialism began to decline in the mid-nineteenth century. Today, colonialism has almost disappeared from the world. However, exploitation continues in the form of **neocolonialism** (*neo* means "new"), *a new form of economic exploitation that involves the operation of multinational corporations rather than direct control by foreign governments.* In the past, colonial powers directly ruled their colonies. Today, rich nations continue to exploit poor nations as multinational corporations operate throughout the world (Bonanno, Constance, & Lorenz, 2000).

Immanuel Wallerstein: The Capitalist World Economy
Immanuel Wallerstein (1974, 1979, 1983, 1984) explains that the "capitalist world economy," in operation for more than five hundred years, is centered in today's rich nations. These high-income

countries (see Global Map 16–2) are the core of the world economy. These nations became rich as they established colonies and drew gold, silver, and other raw materials from countries around the world. This wealth helped them begin the Industrial Revolution. Today, multinational corporations dominate the global economy by drawing wealth from around the world to North America, Western Europe, Australia, and Japan.

Low-income countries form the periphery of the world economy. Brought into the world economy by colonial exploitation, poor nations continue to support rich ones in two ways. First, they provide inexpensive labor; recall from earlier chapters that multinational corporations have "exported" jobs from the United States to the Philippines, Taiwan, and China. Second, lower-income nations provide a vast market for industrial products.

The remaining countries are considered the semiperiphery of the world economy. They include middle-income countries such as Mexico, South Africa, and South Korea that have close ties to the global economic core.

According to Wallerstein and others who use this approach (Frank, 1980, 1981; Delacroix & Ragin, 1981; Bergesen, 1983; Dixon & Boswell, 1996; Kentor, 1998, 2001) the world economy not only exploits poor nations but also places them in a position of dependency on rich nations which is why this approach to also called *dependency theory*. This dependency occurs in three ways:

1. **Poor countries have only narrow, export-oriented economies.** Poor nations produce only a few crops to meet the needs of rich countries. For example, coffee and fruits from Latin American nations, petroleum from Nigeria, hardwoods from the Philippines, and palm oil from Malaysia are all consumed by affluent people in rich nations. With production under the control of multinational corporations, low-income countries develop little of their own industrial production.

2. **Poor countries lack industrial production.** Having little industrial base, poor nations depend on rich nations to buy their inexpensive raw materials. At the same time, they turn to rich countries for more expensive manufactured goods. For example, British colonialists encouraged the people of India to raise cotton but prevented them from weaving their own cloth. The British shipped Indian cotton to English textile mills in Birmingham and Manchester,

where they made cloth; the finished goods were then shipped back to India for sale.

The same pattern applies today to agricultural products. What modernization theorists call the Green Revolution involves poor countries selling cheap raw materials to rich nations and in turn buying expensive fertilizers, pesticides, and mechanical equipment from those same rich nations. Rich countries gain much more than poor nations from such trading.

3. **Poor countries are deeply in debt.** Given such unequal trade patterns, it is little wonder that poor countries have fallen into debt to rich nations. All together, the poor nations of the world owe rich countries more than $2.5 trillion. Such staggering debt leaves poor countries with little money to build economically; the result is high unemployment and high inflation (Walton & Ragin, 1990; World Bank, 2002).

As Wallerstein and other social-conflict theorists see it, the policies of rich nations are the cause of global poverty. It is here that they differ sharply from modernization theorists, as summarized in Table 16–1. Modernization theorists claim that rich nations produce wealth through capital investment and technological innovation. As poor nations do business with rich nations and adopt progrowth policies and more productive technology, they, too, will produce more wealth and prosper. World system theorists, by contrast, highlight how the global economy distributes wealth. They argue that the world's economic system only makes rich countries richer, so that poor nations have little or no chance to improve their living standards. In short, the global economy has *overdeveloped* rich nations and *underdeveloped* the rest of the world.

From this point of view, the problem of global population increase is likely to continue. As long as many of the world's nations remain poor, their fertility rates will remain high. Not until the world moves toward a more equal distribution of wealth and resources will there be a real chance for controlling population and ensuring the economic security of all.

Critical evaluation. The central point of world system theory (or dependency theory) is that no nation develops or fails to develop in isolation: The global economic system shapes the destiny of all nations. Citing Latin America, Africa, and other poor regions of the world, dependency theorists claim that there can be no development under the current market

TABLE 16–1 EXPLAINING GLOBAL INEQUALITY FROM TWO PERSPECTIVES: WORLD SYSTEM THEORY AND MODERNIZATION THEORY

	WORLD SYSTEM THEORY	MODERNIZATION THEORY
How has the world changed over past centuries?	People around the world were roughly equal until the beginning of colonialism, which made some nations rich and other nations poor.	People everywhere were very poor until industrial technology started to raise living standards; although some nations are more productive than others, all nations today are better off compared to centuries ago.
Why is there global inequality?	Colonialism created inequality, and the world capitalist system dominated by multinational corporations continues to enrich some nations at the expense of others.	Differences in culture and technology are the major reasons: While some countries have shown eagerness to change, others remain more traditional.
What part do rich nations such as the United States play?	The United States and other rich countries are part of the problem because they benefit from the capitalist world economy while other nations become poor.	The United States and other rich countries are part of the solution because they help lower-income countries develop economically.
What is the political character of the approach?	This approach is favored by Marxists and others on the political left: It calls for radical change to the world capitalist system in favor of a more egalitarian economic system.	Although liberals support the way modernization theory attacks traditions, this approach finds greatest support among conservatives who support the capitalist economy.

system dominated by rich countries and their multinational corporations.

But critics claim that this approach is incorrect in implying that no one gets richer without someone else getting poorer. They point out that corporations, small business owners, and farmers can and do create new wealth through their hard work, imagination, and use of new technology. This is precisely why the wealth of the world has increased six fold over the last fifty years.

Second, critics challenge the argument that rich nations are to blame for global poverty by pointing to many of the world's poorest countries (such as Ethiopia) that have had little contact with rich countries. On the positive side, many nations with long histories as colonies, including Sri Lanka, Singapore, Hong Kong, and, more recently, India, have prospered (Vogel, 1991; Firebaugh, 1992; Zakeria, 2004).

Third, critics say that by citing a single factor—world capitalism—as the cause of global inequality, world system theory treats poor societies as victims with no responsibility for their own situation (Worsley, 1990). They note that while the Taliban enforced fundamentalist Islam in Afghanistan, that nation had few economic ties with other countries. Similarly,

many nations, including Panama, Haiti, Zaire, the Philippines, and Iraq, have suffered as dictators looted their wealth. Capitalist societies, then, cannot be blamed for economic stagnation in these nations.

POLITICS AND GLOBAL INEQUALITY: CONSTRUCTING PROBLEMS AND DEFINING SOLUTIONS

Politics guides what people see as problems and solutions. We conclude this chapter with three political perspectives on global poverty and the solutions each of these perspectives offers.

Conservatives: The Power of the Market

In his study of the beginnings of industrial capitalism, Peter Berger (1986:36) concludes, "Industrial capitalism has generated the greatest productive power in human history. To date, no other socioeconomic system has been able to generate comparable productive power." This statement provides a strong foundation for the conservative view of global inequality.

Conservatives praise the power of the marketplace and see world trade as benefiting all nations, rich and poor alike. Liberals argue that markets alone cannot ensure the well-being of a billion desperately poor people around the world—world governments, too, must take action. Radicals contend that global capitalism is incapable of lifting the living standards of the world as a whole; they call for a new, more equitable economic and political system. In your opinion, which viewpoint offers the greatest promise to people like these women, who work for a few dollars a day in sweatshops?

Conservatives believe that poverty is a serious problem throughout the world. Yet they are quick to point out that the problem is much smaller today than in centuries past. For tens of thousands of generations, most people were poorly nourished, had minimal shelter, received little schooling, and had almost no medical care. Today, on average, people live better than ever before. Some 3 billion—about half—of the world's people enjoy long, healthy, and comfortable lives beyond the imagination of their ancestors. Another 2 billion, though not as well off, still live better than the average person centuries before the Industrial Revolution.

But that still leaves 1 billion people whose lives are in serious danger. Consistent with modernization theory, conservatives believe the solution to global poverty lies in allowing the productive power of industrial capitalism to spread. They point to United Nations Studies (1994, 1996, 1998, 2003) that show progress is being made toward a better life: Daily calorie intake and average life expectancy are both up, and access to safe water and adult literacy are more widespread than ever before. Worldwide, infant mortality is half of what it was in 1960. Considering many formerly poor nations of the world that have made great progress in recent years, including South Korea, Taiwan, Hong Kong, and Singapore, Peter Berger (1986:138–39) credits their "all-out growth strategies" as responsible for their prosperity. Berger adds that the greatest gains in these countries are among the poor.

Liberals: Governments Must Act

Liberals accept the fact that the capitalist market system is highly productive. Yet they reject the position that the capitalist market *by itself* is the solution to global poverty. In addition, they claim, governments must act to help the poor.

One reason government help is needed is that modernizing influences, such as the use of high technology, have yet to reach many nations, especially the rural areas. Liberals claim that governments of rich nations—the countries that benefit most from global economic production—have a moral obligation to provide foreign aid, especially in the areas of health care and education, to poor nations.

A second issue is that businesses can make high profits by paying low wages to people, especially those who work in sweatshop factories. Thus, governments in both rich and poor countries must cooperate to eliminate the exploitation that occurs in such businesses. Some sweatshops exist in the United States, but most are in low-income nations; many are owned and operated by multinational corporations. Whereas the typical U.S. worker in manufacturing earns about $15 per hour, across our southern border in Mexico, the comparable figure is about $2 (U.S. Department of Labor, 2002). Sweatshops pay workers very little, and many are extremely dangerous workplaces. The Global Perspective box describes one deadly example.

A Global Perspective

Sweatshop Safety: How Much Is a Life Worth?

POOR PEOPLE HAVE FEW CHOICES ABOUT WHAT to eat, where to live, or where to work. Sweatshops exist because millions of poor people in the world have little choice but to take whatever jobs they can find. The worst sweatshops pay workers only ten to twenty cents an hour. Yet they have little trouble finding people willing to work ten hours a day, seven days a week, all year long, to earn perhaps $750 a year. Sweatshops provide workers with no benefits. As the following incident suggests, they may not even provide basic safety protections.

On April 12, 2002, more than one thousand people were at their jobs in a garment factory in Narsingdi, a small town near Dhaka, the capital city of Bangladesh. Crowded together on the fourth floor of the large building, the women and men worked at sewing machines making T-shirts, creating a steady roar that went on for ten hours a day, every day of the week.

But April 12 ended in tragedy. A worker who was shooting spot remover on stained fabric suddenly noticed a spark fly from her machine into an open can of flammable cleaning fluid. In a flash, the entire table burst into flames. A dozen of her fellow workers rushed to the scene, trying to smother the fire with shirts, but it was too late. The room, filled with highly combustible materials, was engulfed in flames in only a matter of minutes.

Trying to escape the smoke and fire, workers poured down the steep, narrow staircase that led to the street. But as the human wave reached the bottom, it crashed up against a folding metal gate that was kept locked during working hours to keep workers from leaving. The first people to reach the gate turned in panic, only to be crushed by hundreds behind them. In less than a minute, fifty-two people were trampled to death.

Sweatshop factories such as this one are big business in Bangladesh, where garment making represents 75 percent of the country's total economic exports. Approximately half of the garments shipped from Bangladesh end up in clothing stores across the United States. People who look for bargains on store clothing racks rarely stop to think that the reason for the low price may well be that the workers halfway around the world who made the garments are paid only pennies a day.

Learn more about sweatshops by visiting
http://www.sweatshops.org

This particular factory is owned by the family of Tanveer Chowdhury, who complained bitterly to reporters after the fire. "This fire has cost me $586,373, and that does not include $70,000 for machinery and $20,000 for furniture. I made commitments to meet deadlines and I still have the deadlines. I am now paying for air freight at $10 a dozen when I should be shipping by sea at 87 cents a dozen."

Mr. Chowdhury had one other expense as a result of the fire. To settle claims by families for the loss of their loved ones, he eventually agreed to pay $1,952 per person. In Bangladesh, life—like labor—is cheap.

ISSUES AND EXERCISES

1. Some people view the wages paid by textile factories abroad as the "going rate" in low-income nations. Others see them as exploitation of poor people. Which is closer to your view? Why?

2. Are consumers in high-income nations such as the United States partly responsible for situations such as that described in this box? Why or why not?

3. **Research Navigator.com** Use Research Navigator™ to learn more about sweatshops. (See instructions on page 25; keyword: "sweatshops")

Source: Bearak (2001).

A WORLD OF DIFFERENCES

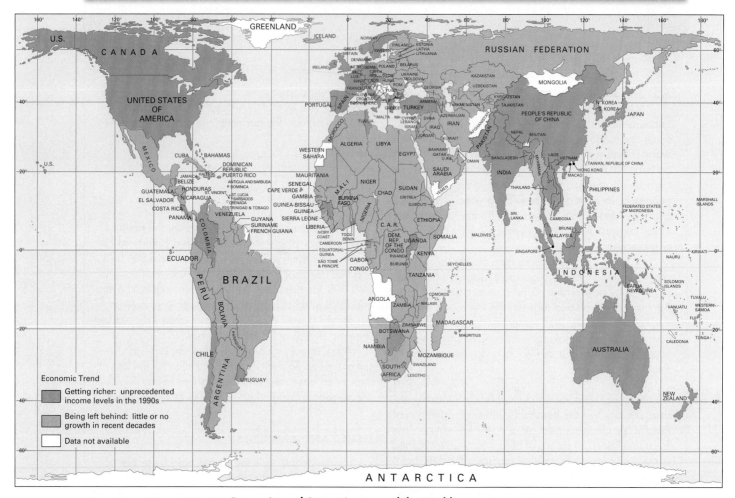

GLOBAL MAP 16–3   Prosperity and Stagnation around the World

For the world as a whole, many indicators of how well people live are up. But some regions are doing much better than others. In about sixty nations of the world (about one-third of all nations), people are living notably better than ever. These nations include most of the high-income countries but also dozens of middle- and low-income countries, especially in Asia. For most countries, however, living standards have remained stable or have declined in recent decades. Especially in Eastern Europe and the Middle East, nations have reported declines since 1980. And in much of sub-Saharan Africa, nations are no better off than they were in 1960. The evidence points to an increasing gap between rich and poor countries.

Source: United Nations Development Programme (1996), updated by the author.

Lastly, around the world, most peasants do not own the land they work. In Brazil, for example, half of all farmland is owned by wealthy landowners who are less than 1 percent of the population (Bergamo & Camarotti, 1996). Thus, another important government reform that liberals support as a step toward reducing global poverty is giving working families the opportunity to own land.

Radicals: End Global Capitalism

The radical position on global poverty is consistent with world system theory. Hunger activists Frances Moore Lappé and Joseph Collins (Lappé, Collins, & Kinley, 1981; Lappé & Collins, 1986) claim that many in the United States have been raised to think of global poverty as the inevitable result of "natural"

LEFT to RIGHT

THE POLITICS OF GLOBAL INEQUALITY

	RADICAL LEFT VIEW	LIBERAL VIEW	CONSERVATIVE VIEW
WHAT IS THE PROBLEM?	Some of the world is overdeveloped, and much of the world is underdeveloped. The world's wealth is concentrated in a handful of very rich nations.	Whereas most people in rich nations have more than they need, more than 1 billion people around the world contend with a poor diet, inadequate housing, and little education.	Although 5 billion people in the world live far better than our ancestors several centuries ago, 1 billion of the world's people remain poor.
WHAT IS THE SOLUTION?	Replace the capitalist world economy with a system that values people above profits, eliminate multinational corporations, use land to grow food for local consumption, and cancel foreign debt.	The rich of the world must share their wealth in the form of foreign aid that will improve health, schooling, and housing; oppose sweatshops and support land reform.	Allow the productive power of the market to raise the living standards of poor nations today as it has done in the past; encourage capital investment and technology transfers to poor nations.

What do you think?

1. From each of the three political perspectives, what role do rich nations such as the United States have in addressing global poverty and hunger?

2. What importance does each perspective assign to government? To a free market?

3. Which of the three political analyses of global inequality included here do you find most convincing? Why?

events: periodic natural disasters such as droughts and floods and lack of population control on the part of "backward" societies.

From the radical point of view, however, global poverty is tragic because it is *not* inevitable. Lappé and Collins point out that the world already produces plenty of food for everyone. In fact, if all the world's food were distributed equally, every person on the planet would soon grow quite fat. Moreover, even poor regions of the world such as India and most of Africa actually *export* food, even though many people in these regions go hungry.

How, then, can we explain the existence of poverty amid plenty? Lappé and Collins see the problem as policies by which rich nations direct the production of food for profits, not people. Corporations in poor nations prefer to produce "export crops" such as coffee, which bring high profits when sold in the United States and other rich nations. But this means land is not used for staples such as beans and corn that would feed local families. Government officials in poor countries also favor growing for export because they need the money to pay foreign debt. At the core of this vicious cycle, according to Lappé and Collins, is the capitalist global economy.

From this point of view, the problem of global poverty is likely to get worse. Global Map 16–3 shows that many poor nations are not developing at all. On the contrary, many of the world's poorest nations are sinking ever deeper in debt to rich nations. The solution, from the radical perspective, is the transformation of global capitalism toward a more socially conscious economic system. At the very least, poor nations should demand a cancellation of existing debt and end economic relations with multinational corporations; in addition they should nationalize (that is, take control of) foreign-owned industries within their borders. Doing this strikes at the very root of our global power structure. But from this point of view, nothing less is likely to work. The Left to Right table summarizes the three approaches to global poverty.

What is the likely future of humanity? While most people living in high-income countries have all they need, hundreds of millions of people remain desperately poor. To make matters worse, population increase is greatest in the poorest nations. If you were one of these people living in Haiti, what might you have to say about global inequality?

GOING ON FROM HERE

The increasing world population remains one of the most serious problems facing humanity. As we have explained, population soared in the twentieth century, and projections call for continued increases—although the *rate* of increase will slow—in the twenty-first century. Indeed, because half of the people in high-growth nations have yet to reach child-bearing age, there is little doubt that global population will continue to rise for decades to come. This increase will place greater demands on the limited resources in low-income nations, making the task of raising living standards more difficult. For this reason, the United Nations and other organizations are working to bring a halt to global population increase. A few analysts even argue that we need to *reduce* global population to perhaps half of what we have now if everyone in the world is to have a safe and secure life (Smail, 2004).

An even larger problem is global inequality. Currently, the world's wealth is very unequally distributed, with a small share of humanity (including people in the United States and Canada) producing most of the goods and services and consuming most of the planet's resources. As this chapter has explained, although almost everyone considers this situation to be serious, there is disagreement about what to do about it. The official policy of the United States has been fairly close to modernization theory; government leaders long have claimed that poor nations can develop economically as rich nations did in the past. To help poor nations make economic progress, the United States provides roughly $20 billion in foreign aid annually (not counting money for rebuilding Iraq or Afghanistan) to nations in every region of the world.

Yet according to the United Nations and other international organizations, the problem of global inequality is getting worse. The gap between the richest 20 percent and the poorest 20 percent of the world's people doubled in the twentieth century (*Population Today*, 2000). Whereas the United States, Canada, Western Europe, Australia, and much of Asia are prospering, Latin America shows only slight improvement, Africa is being left behind, and much of Eastern Europe has been losing ground (United Nations, 1996; Population Reference Bureau, 2003).

The plight of the 1 billion people struggling to survive is reason enough for the world to take action. But something even bigger is at stake: Unless the world changes so that all people have a secure existence, can any of us expect the nations of the world to find peace?

CHAPTER SUMMARY

1. Fertility and mortality, measured as crude birth rates and crude death rates, are major factors affecting population size. In global terms, U.S. population growth is low.

2. Historically, world population grew slowly because high birth rates were mostly offset by high death rates. About 1750, a demographic transition began as world population rose sharply, mostly because of falling death rates.

3. Thomas Robert Malthus warned that population growth would outpace food production, resulting in starvation and social chaos. However, demographic transition theory holds that technological advances gradually slow population increase.

4. World population is expected to reach between 8 and 9 billion by 2050. Such an increase threatens to overwhelm many poor societies, where 96 percent of the increase will take place.

5. Social inequality in the world as a whole is greater than in the United States. About 18 percent of the world's people live in high-income countries such as the United States and receive 79 percent of all income. Another 70 percent live in middle-income countries, receiving about 20 percent of all income. Twelve percent of the world's population live in low-income countries that have yet to industrialize and earn only 1 percent of global income.

6. Relative poverty is found everywhere, but poor nations contain widespread absolute poverty. Worldwide, the lives of some 1 billion people are at risk because of poor nutrition. About 15 million people, most of them children, die annually from various causes brought on by hunger and lack of adequate nourishment.

7. Nearly everywhere in the world, women are more likely than men to be poor. About 70 percent of adults facing absolute poverty are women.

8. Modernization theory maintains that economic development hinges on breaking free of traditional cultural patterns to seek prosperity and adopt advanced technology.

9. Modernization theorist W. W. Rostow identifies four stages of development: traditional, take-off, drive to technological maturity, and high mass consumption.

10. Critics of modernization theory say that rich nations do not encourage but actually prevent economic development around the world. Therefore, they claim, poor nations cannot follow the path to development taken by rich nations centuries ago.

11. World system theory (dependency theory) claims that global wealth and poverty are the historical products of the capitalist world economy beginning with colonialism and continuing, more recently, with the operation of multinational corporations.

12. Immanuel Wallerstein views the high-income countries as the advantaged core of the capitalist world economy, middle-income nations as the semiperiphery, and poor societies as the global periphery. Economic relations make poor nations dependent on rich ones.

13. Critics of world system theory argue that this approach overlooks the sixfold increase in the world's wealth since 1950. Furthermore, the world's poorest societies are not those with the strongest ties to rich countries.

KEY CONCEPTS

demography (p. 396) the study of human population

fertility (p. 396) the incidence of childbearing in a country's population

crude birth rate (p. 396) the number of live births in a given year for every thousand people in a population

mortality (p. 397) the incidence of death in a country's population

crude death rate (p. 397) the number of deaths in a given year for every thousand people in a population

infant mortality rate (p. 397) the number of deaths among infants under one year of age for every thousand live births in a given year

zero population growth (p. 399) the level of reproduction that maintains population at a steady state

demographic transition theory   (p. 403) a thesis linking demographic changes to a society's level of technological development

modernization theory   (p. 409) a model of economic and social development that explains global inequality in terms of technological and cultural differences between societies

world system theory (also called **dependency theory**)   (p. 411) a model of economic development that explains global inequality in terms of the historical exploitation of poor societies by rich ones

colonialism   (p. 411) the process by which some nations enrich themselves through political and economic control of other nations

neocolonialism   (p. 411) a new form of economic exploitation that involves the operation of multinational corporations rather than direct political control by foreign governments

THINKING CRITICALLY: QUESTIONS AND ISSUES

1. Define fertility and mortality rates. Which one has been more important in increasing global population?

2. Evaluate the environmental prediction of Thomas Robert Malthus. On balance, do you think he was more wrong or more right? How does demographic transition theory help explain Malthus's prediction?

3. Do you place more responsibility for solving the problems of global hunger on poor countries or rich ones? Why? What is your prediction about the extent of global hunger fifty years from now? Will the problem be more or less serious? Explain your answer.

4. Why do many analysts argue that economic development and population control in low-income countries depend on raising the social standing of women?

GETTING INVOLVED: LEARNING ACTIVITIES

1. Keep a log book of mass media advertising mentioning low-income countries (ads selling, say, coffee from Colombia or exotic vacations to India). What images of life in low-income countries does the advertising present? In light of the facts presented in this chapter, do you think these images are accurate?

2. Millions of students from abroad study on U.S. campuses. Identify a woman and a man on your campus raised in a poor country. Approach them, explain that you have been studying global inequality, and ask whether they would be willing to talk with you about what life is like in their country. Also ask them about their impressions of inequality in the United States.

3. Looking over the various global maps in this text, identify social traits associated with the world's richest and poorest nations. Make use of both modernization theory and dependency theory to explain the patterns you find.

4. Do some research in the library and on the Internet to explore the status of women in a number of low-income nations. One good source is the *Human Development Report*, published annually by the United Nations (**http://www. undp.org**). In poor countries, are women and men more unequal than they are in high-income nations such as the United States? If so, why?

GETTING CONNECTED: USEFUL WEB LINKS

http://www.prenhall.com/macionis
Visit the interactive Companion Website™ that accompanies this text. Begin by clicking on the cover of your book. You will find a chapter-by-chapter study guide, practice tests, suggested Web links, and links to other relevant material.

http://members.aol.com/casmasalc/
Is slavery a reality in today's world? Find out more by visiting the Web site of the Coalition against Slavery in Mauritania and Sudan.

www.oneworld.net
Want to learn more about global poverty and hunger? Here you can find information about a variety of issues related to global inequality.

http://www.fh.org
http://www.worldconcern.org
http://www.worldvision.org
http://www.care.org
http://www.savethechildren.org
All these sites address the problems of global poverty and hunger. Can you see differences in how they define the problem of global poverty? What about their proposed solutions?

http://www.census.gov/ipc/www/idbnew.html
To learn more about the inequality of nations, visit the Census Bureau's International Data Base.

GETTING STARTED ON YOUR OWN: RESEARCH NAVIGATOR™

Follow the instructions found on page 25 of this text to access the features of Research Navigator™. Once at the Web site, enter your Login Name and Password. Then, to use the **Content Select** database, enter keywords such as "population," "world hunger," and "global poverty," and the search engine will supply relevant and recent scholarly and popular press publications. Use the *New York Times* **Search-by-Subject Archive** to find recent news articles related to sociology and the **Link Library** feature to find relevant Web links organized by the key terms associated with this chapter.

CHAPTER 17

© Paul Marcus, *Day Dreaming, oil on canvas, 50 in. × 50 in., Studio SPM, Inc.*

TECHNOLOGY
AND THE ENVIRONMENT

GRANDMA MACIONIS, WE ALWAYS USED TO SAY, never threw anything away. Born in Lithuania—the "old country"—she grew up in a poor village, an experience that shaped her life even after she came to the United States as a young woman.

Her birthday was an amusing occasion for the rest of the family. After opening a present, she would carefully put aside the box, refold the wrapping paper, and roll up the ribbon; all this meant as much to her as the gift itself. Probably more, because Grandma never wore the new clothes given to her, and she was never known to go shopping for herself. Her kitchen knives were worn down from decades of sharpening, and every piece of furniture she ever bought stayed with her to the end of her life (I still eat at the same table she had in her kitchen seventy-five years ago).

As curious as Grandma Macionis was to her grandchildren, she was a product of her culture. A century ago, there was little "trash." If a pair of socks wore thin, people mended them, probably more than once. When they became worn beyond repair, they used them as rags for cleaning or sewed them (with other old clothing) into a quilt. For people like Grandma, everything had value, if not in one way, then in another (Recollections of the author).

Grandma Macionis never thought of herself as an environmentalist. But she was: She lived simply, using few resources and creating almost no solid waste. This way of life seems hopelessly old fashioned to most people in the United States today; we measure social standing by how much people consume, and the value we place on "convenience" begins with instant breakfast foods and ends with dinner at the drive-through. As this chapter explains, this materialistic, fast-paced way of life places a great strain on our natural environment.

423

ECOLOGY: STUDYING THE NATURAL ENVIRONMENT

Ecology, *the study of how living organisms interact with the natural environment,* is a field that connects the social and natural sciences. In this text, we focus on the aspects of ecology related to sociological concepts and issues.

The term **natural environment** refers to *the earth's surface and atmosphere, including air, water, soil, and other resources necessary to sustain living organisms.* Like every other living species, humans depend on the natural environment. Yet humans stand apart from other species in our capacity for culture; we alone take deliberate action to remake the world according to our interests and desires. To do this, we rely on **technology,** *knowledge that people apply to the task of living in a physical environment.* As technology becomes more complex and powerful, people gain the ability to transform the world, for better or for worse.

The Role of Sociology

Problems related to the environment include solid waste, pollution, acid rain, global warming, and the declining number of living species. None of these problems is a product of the natural world operating on its own. They all result from the way humans organize social life and are therefore *social* problems.

The most important lesson sociology offers about environmental issues is that the state of our planet reflects how societies operate. What facts about U.S. society can you "read" in this photograph?

Sociologists examine how people waste or try to conserve natural resources. They study what categories of people support one side or the other of environmental issues. They report what the public thinks about global warming or toxic waste dumps. But the most important contribution sociologists make is in demonstrating how particular cultural patterns and specific political and economic arrangements affect the natural environment (Cylke, 1993; Roberts, 1993; Crenshaw & Jenkins, 1996).

The Global Dimension

Like the problems of rising population and world hunger (discussed in Chapter 16), environmental problems are necessarily global in scope. Why? Because, regardless of national divisions, our planet is a single **ecosystem,** a *system composed of the interaction of all living organisms and their natural environment.*

The Greek meaning of *eco* is "house," which reminds us that our planet is our home, a place where living things and their natural environment are interconnected. Changes to any part of the natural environment ripple throughout the entire global ecosystem.

Chlorofluorocarbons (CFCs, marketed under the brand name "Freon"), widely used as propellents in aerosol spray cans and gas in refrigerators and air conditioners, illustrate these connections. CFCs are cheap, easy to use, nontoxic, and effective. But once released into the environment, they accumulate in the upper atmosphere, where they react with sunlight to form chlorine atoms. Chlorine destroys ozone, the layer in the atmosphere that filters out harmful ultraviolet radiation. This has caused a huge hole to open in the atmospheric ozone layer over Antarctica that is increasing the incidence of human skin cancers and otherwise harming plants and animals. To protect the ozone layer, the United States and many other nations have banned the use of CFCs in favor of environmentally safer alternatives.

The Rising Power of Technology

Our earliest ancestors—hunters and gatherers—had only simple technology, so they had a very little effect on the environment. Nature ruled much of their way of life: They lived according to the migration of animals, the changing of the seasons, and natural events such as fires, floods, and droughts.

Societies that make use of horticulture (small-scale farming), pastoralism (the herding of animals), or agriculture (with animal-drawn plows) have a

A WORLD OF DIFFERENCES

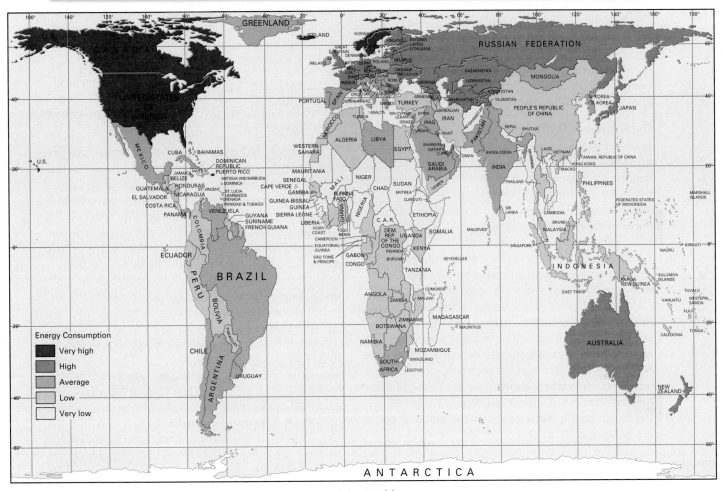

GLOBAL MAP 17–1   Energy Consumption around the World

People in high-income nations consume far more energy than those living in poor countries. The typical U.S. resident uses the same amount of energy in a year as 100 people in Ethiopia or the Central African Republic. This means that the most economically productive nations also put the greatest burden on the natural environment. In fact, in recent years the demand for energy in the United States has exceeded the available supply.

Source: Peters Atlas of the World (1990), updated by the author

somewhat greater capacity to affect the environment. But the environmental impact of these technologies is limited because people using them still rely on muscle power.

When the Industrial Revolution replaced muscle power with combustion engines that burn fossil fuels (coal and, later, oil), societies began changing the environment much more, by consuming energy resources and by releasing pollutants into the atmosphere. Armed with industrial technology, humans can bend nature to their will, tunneling through

mountains, damming rivers, irrigating deserts, and drilling for oil on the ocean floor. As a result of technological power, humans have brought more change to this planet in the last two centuries than over the last billion years (Milbrath, 1989).

Global Map 17–1 shows that high-income, industrialized societies consume a great deal of the world's energy. Although high-income nations account for just 15 percent of humanity, they use fully 80 percent of all energy. The typical adult in the United States consumes about one hundred times more energy each year than the average person in the world's poorest nations (Connett, 1991; Miller, 1992; York, Rosa, & Deitz, 2002).

Equally important, members of industrial societies produce one hundred times more goods than agrarian societies. Thus, raising living standards greatly increases the problem of solid waste because people end up throwing away most of what their society produces.

The Environmental Deficit This short look at human history teaches an important lesson: By using more powerful technology to improve living standards, people put the lives of future generations at risk. The evidence is mounting that we are running up an **environmental deficit,** *profound and long-term harm to the environment caused by humanity's focus on short-term material affluence* (Bormann, 1990).

Recognizing the existence of an environmental deficit is important for three reasons. First, it reminds us that environmental quality is a *social issue*, reflecting choices people make about how to live. Second, it suggests that environmental damage often is *unintended*. By focusing on the short-term benefits of, say, cutting down forests or using throwaway packaging, we fail to see that such behavior has long-term, harmful environmental effects. Third, in some respects the environmental deficit is *reversible*. Societies can undo many of the environmental problems they have created.

Population Increase

The development of more powerful technology is not the only threat to the natural environment. As Chapter 16 ("Population and Global Inequality") explained, 2,000 years ago the entire world's population was about 300 million—about the population of the United States today (Haub, 2002).

Once humans developed industrial technology, higher living standards and improved medical treatments sharply decreased the death rates in Western Europe. The predictable result was a sharp upward spike in world population. By 1800, global population had soared to 1 billion.

In the decades that followed, growth became even faster, with global population reaching 2 billion by 1930, 3 billion by 1962, 4 billion by 1974, 5 billion by 1987, and 6 billion by 1999. In 2003, the world's population was about 6.3 billion. Although the rate of increase is slowing, we are adding 80 million people to the world's total each year (218,000 every day) (Population Reference Bureau, 2003).

Visit Population Connection, an educational and activist organization, at **http://www.populationconnection.org**

A classic riddle illustrates how runaway growth can wreak havoc with the natural environment (Milbrath, 1989:10):

A pond has a single water lily growing on it. The lily doubles in size each day. In thirty days, it covers the entire pond. On which day did the lily cover half the pond?

The answer that comes readily to mind—the fifteenth day—is wrong. The lily was not increasing in size by the same amount every day; it was doubling. The correct answer is that the lily covered half the pond on the twenty-ninth day. The point of the riddle is that for a long time, the size of the growing lily seems manageable. Only on the twenty-ninth day, when the lily covers half the pond, do people finally see the problem, but it is too late to do anything about it because in a day, the lily chokes the life out of the entire pond.

Most experts predict that the world population will reach 8 to 9 billion people by 2050 (O'Neill & Balk, 2001; United Nations, 2003). The most rapid population growth is occurring in the poorest regions of the world. A glance back at Global Map 16–1 on page 400 shows the growth rates for nations around the world. Taken together, the nations of Africa are adding to their population at an annual rate of 2.6 percent, which will double Africa's population by 2030 (Population Reference Bureau, 2003).

Rapid population growth makes the problem of poverty worse. This is because a surging population offsets any increase in productivity so that living standards stay the same. If a society's population doubles, doubling its productivity amounts to no gain at all. But poverty also makes environmental problems worse. Because they are preoccupied with survival, poor people have little choice but to consume whatever resources are at hand, without thinking about long-term environmental consequences.

Now imagine the consequences of rising population and advancing technology *together*. That is, what would happen if poor societies suddenly industrialized? An affluent India, for example, would suddenly be a nation with more than 1 billion additional cars on its streets. What effect would that have on the world's oil reserves and global air quality?

Simply put, if people around the world lived at the level of material abundance that people in the United States take for granted, the natural environment would soon collapse even if birth rates were to drop. From an environmentalist point of view, our planet suffers from economic underdevelopment in some regions and economic overdevelopment in others.

Cultural Patterns: Growth and Limits

Our cultural outlook, especially how we envision "the good life," has serious environmental consequences. Along with technology and population growth, culture has a dramatic effect on the environment.

The Logic of Growth Why does our society designate specific areas as parks or wildlife preserves? The unspoken message is that except for these special areas, people may freely use the Earth and its resources for their own purposes (Myers, 1991). Where does such an aggressive approach to the natural environment come from?

Our way of life in the United States is based on the value of *material comfort*. Most people believe that money and the things it buys enrich our lives. Most people also believe in *progress*, thinking that the future will be better than the present, and *science*, looking to experts and new technology to improve our lives. Taken together, these cultural values form an outlook that environmentalists call *the logic of growth*.

The logic of growth is an optimistic view of the world. In simple terms, the logic of growth amounts to the beliefs that "people are clever," "having things is good," and "life will improve."

Even optimists realize that progress can lead to unexpected problems. For example, the rising number of motor vehicles in the world may be good in many ways, but it also threatens to drain the planet's oil reserves. The logic of growth argues that people (especially scientists and other experts) are inventive and will find a way around any problems. By the time oil supplies run short (which is likely by the end of this century), scientists will have come up with electric, solar, hydrogen, nuclear, or some as-yet-unknown type of engine to free us from oil dependence.

The logic of growth is deeply rooted in U.S. culture. However, environmentalists point to several flaws in this line of thinking (Milbrath, 1989). First, this approach wrongly assumes that natural resources such as oil, clean air, fresh water, and the earth's topsoil will always be plentiful. On the contrary, these are *finite* resources (that is, they can be used up) that people will exhaust by pursuing growth at any cost.

Second, environmentalists do not share the belief that human ingenuity can solve any problems of

The "logic of growth" is an optimistic view of environmental issues that places a high reliance on science and human ingenuity. Within a century, for example, the world will be running out of oil. But, by that time, we will have new transportation technology, such as high efficiency cars like this one that run on stored electric power. How much confidence do you have in advancing technology to solve environmental problems?

scarcity. It would be arrogant and dangerous to assume that human resourcefulness has no limits. Moreover, the more powerful and complex the technology (using nuclear reactors, say, instead of gasoline engines), the greater the dangers posed by miscalculation and the more significant the unintended consequences. Thus, environmentalists argue that we cannot call on the earth to support the increasing burden of higher living standards without using up finite resources, destroying the environment, and harming ourselves in the process.

The Limits to Growth Believing we cannot invent our way out of the problems created by the logic of growth, environmentalists say that we need another way of thinking about the world. They claim that growth must have limits. Simply stated, the *limits to growth thesis* is that humanity must limit the growth of population and our use of finite resources to avoid eventual environmental collapse.

A book called *The Limits to Growth*, published in 1972, had a large hand in launching the environmentalism movement. In the book, Donella Meadows

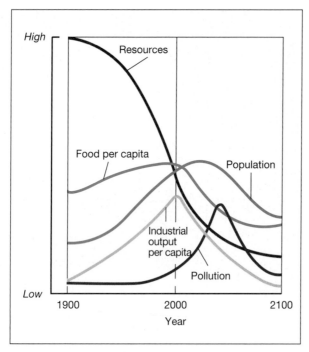

FIGURE 17–1   The Limits to Growth: Projections

This computer model predicts that humanity will deplete most of the earth's resources within a century. Although people disagree over the specifics of such predictions, most agree that significant change is needed to avoid environmental catastrophe.

Source: Based on Meadows et al. (1972).

and her colleagues (1972) devised a computer model that calculated the planet's available resources, rates of population growth, amount of land available for cultivation, levels of industrial and food production, and amount of pollutants released into the atmosphere. Based on historical trends, the model made projections to the end of the twenty-first century. The authors admit that such long-range predictions are, to some extent, guess work, and some critics think they are plain wrong (Simon, 1981). But right or wrong, Meadows's conclusions, shown in Figure 17–1, deserve serious consideration.

According to the limits to growth thesis, humans (especially those using industrial technology) are quickly consuming Earth's finite resources. Supplies of oil, natural gas, and other sources of energy are already falling sharply and will continue to drop, a little faster or more slowly depending on policies in rich nations and the speed at which other nations industrialize. Global population is likely to rise for several decades during this century, with a gradual

decline after that. At this point, world hunger—caused by too many people and unequal distribution of food—may well reach a crisis level. And before long, the world will begin running out of vital resources, reducing industrial output.

For a recent analysis of *The Limits to Growth,* visit
http://www.abc.net.au/science/slab/rome/default.htm

Environmentalists who support the limits to growth thesis are sometimes called neo-Mathusians because, like Thomas Robert Malthus (discussed in Chapter 16, "Population and Global Inequality"), they are pessimistic about the future of humanity. Believing that current patterns of life are not sustainable through this century, they conclude that we face a basic choice: Either we make deliberate changes in how we live, or calamity will force change on us.

ENVIRONMENTAL PROBLEMS

Environmentalists express serious worries about our future. A majority of U.S. adults say they, too, are concerned about the environment; most characterize pollution and other related problems as "dangerous" (Kluger, 2001; NORC, 2003:1168–71). This represents a shift in public opinion from fifty years ago, when only a handful of people spoke about environmental problems. The Defining Moment box takes a closer look at one person who did.

What, then, is the state of the natural environment today? The following sections briefly examine several environmental issues, with particular attention to problems in the United States.

Solid Waste: The Disposable Society

One environmental problem is waste—or, more precisely, too much of it. The average person in the United States discards about five pounds of paper, metal, plastic, and other disposable materials daily; over a lifetime, that comes to 50 tons. The country as a whole generates 1 billion pounds of solid waste *each and every day.* Figure 17–2 on page 430 shows the composition of our national trash.

The problem of solid waste stems from a simple fact: The United States is a *disposable society.* Not only is this country materially rich, but its people value convenience. As a result, we consume more products than any nation on Earth, and many of these products come with excessive packaging. The most familiar case is the cardboard, plastic, and Styrofoam containers that we buy with our fast food and throw

A DEFINING MOMENT

Rachel Carson: Sounding an Environmental Wake-Up Call

I N THE 1950S, FEW PEOPLE CONSIDERED the environment to be a problem. Rachel Carson saw things differently. Carson (1907–1964) grew up in a western Pennsylvania farm community, where she developed a lifelong passion for nature. After finishing college, she earned a master's degree in zoology and went to work for the U.S. Bureau of Fisheries, where she wrote pamphlets on conservation. Carson went on to write books about nature, gaining a national reputation as a naturalist, and in 1952 she left her government post to write full time.

Soon, Carson's attention turned to the rapidly increasing use of pesticides. After World War II, pesticide use in the United States skyrocketed, and no one was showing much concern for the harm they posed to the environment. In 1962, Carson published the book *Silent Spring,* which was truly a wake-up call. The book explained how the use of pesticides such as DDT was poisoning the streams, rivers, and lakes of the United States. It was immediately controversial (chemical companies tried to have the book banned), but it went a long way to defining the state of the environment as a problem. Carson (1995:409; orig. 1962) pulled no punches, asking, "Can anyone believe it is possible to lay down such a barrage of poisons on the surface of the earth without

Rachel Carson is credited with turning public attention to the environment. Her 1962 book, Silent Spring, *documented the health and environmental hazards of pesticides (such as DDT) that were being widely used on farms and almost everywhere else. Rather than seeing chemicals as a solution, Carson defined them as a problem, and helped spark the modern environmental movement.*

making it unfit for all life?" In making such statements, she challenged the common view that science was always a force for good; in the process, she helped to launch the modern environmentalist movement.

---

away within minutes. But countless other products—from film to fishhooks, cosmetics to CD-ROMs—are elaborately packaged to appeal to the customer (and to discourage tampering and theft).

Manufacturers market soft drinks, beer, and fruit juices in aluminum cans, glass jars, and plastic containers, which not only use up finite resources but also generate mountains of solid waste. Finally, our society produces countless items intentionally designed to be disposable: pens, razors, flashlights, batteries, and even cameras. Other products, from computers to automobiles, are designed to have a short useful life and then become unwanted junk.

In the United States, the average person consumes 50 times more steel, 170 times more newspaper, 250 times more gasoline, and 300 times more plastic each year than the typical person in India (Miller, 1992). This high level of consumption means

that we in the United States not only use a large share of the planet's natural resources but also generate most of the world's solid waste.

We like to say that we "throw things away." But the two-thirds of our solid waste that is not burned or recycled never really "goes away." Rather, it ends up in landfills. These dumping grounds are a threat to the natural environment for several reasons.

First, the sheer volume of discarded material is filling up landfills all across the country. Already the United States is shipping trash to other countries to be discarded. Second, the material in landfills contributes to water pollution. Although the laws in most localities now regulate what can go in a landfill, the Environmental Protection Agency has identified 30,000 dump sites across the United States containing hazardous materials that are polluting water both above and below the ground. Third, what

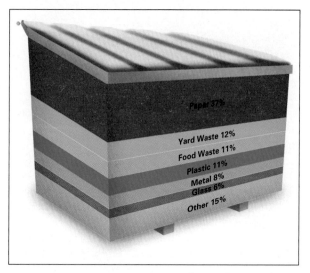

FIGURE 17–2   Composition of Household Trash

Here is a rough breakdown of the trash that U.S. society generates—a total of 1 billion pounds each day.
Source: U.S. Environmental Protection Agency (2002).

goes into landfills all too often stays there, sometimes for centuries. Tens of millions of tires, diapers, and plastic utensils do not readily decompose and will be an unwelcome environmental burden for generations to come.

Environmentalists argue that we should address the problem of solid waste by doing what Grandma Macionis and many of our ancestors did: turn "waste" into a resource. This is the basic idea behind *recycling*, reusing resources we would otherwise throw away. Recycling is a common practice in Japan and many other nations, and it is becoming more widespread in the United States, where we now recycle about 30 percent of waste materials. The share is increasing as laws mandate reuse of certain materials such as glass bottles and aluminum cans. Because of our market-based economy, recycling will increase if and when it becomes more profitable. The Global Perspective box provides a look at one recycling success story in Egypt.

Learn more about recycling at **http://www.nrc-recycle.org/**

Preserving Clean Water

Oceans, lakes, and streams are the lifeblood of the global ecosystem. Humans depend on water for drinking, bathing, cooling, cooking, recreation, and a host of other activities.

According to what scientists call the *hydrological cycle*, the Earth naturally recycles water and refreshes the land. The process begins as heat from the sun causes water, 97 percent of which is in the oceans, to evaporate and form clouds. Next, water returns to Earth as rain, which drains into streams and rivers and rushes toward the seas. The hydrological cycle not only renews the supply of water but also cleans it. Because water evaporates at lower temperatures than most pollutants, the water vapor that rises from the seas is pure, leaving contaminants behind. Although the hydrological cycle generates clean water in the form of rain, pollutants steadily build up in the oceans.

There are two major problems associated with water: inadequate water supply and water pollution.

Inadequate Water Supply   As early as the ancient civilizations of China, Egypt, and Rome, water rights have figured prominently in codes of law, reflecting the importance of water to society. As Global Map 17–2 on page 432 shows, some regions of the world, especially the tropics, enjoy a plentiful supply of water. However, in much of North America and Asia, people look to rivers rather than rainfall for their water, making supply a problem. In some U.S. regions, the main source is groundwater, water underground that supplies wells and springs. In many regions, the supply is running low. For example, the Ogallala aquifer runs below ground across seven states from South Dakota to Texas; it is now being pumped so rapidly that some experts fear it could run dry within several decades.

Nowhere is water supply a bigger problem than in the Middle East. In Egypt, an arid region of the world, people depend on the Nile River for most of their water. But because of population increases, Egyptians make do with one-sixth as much water per person as they did in 1900. Experts project that the supply may shrink by half again by 2015. Throughout the Middle East and Africa, where populations are rising rapidly, experts predict that as many as 1 billion people may lack necessary water by 2030 (Postel, 1993; *Popline*, 2001; World Health Organization, 2001).

Soaring populations are only part of the problem. Complex technology, especially in manufacturing and power-generating facilities, has made the water problem worse. Why? Such technology itself uses water, especially for cooling, which greatly increases the need for water. The global use of water (estimated at 2 billion cubic meters per year) is rising much faster than the world's population (Rosegrant, Cai, & Cline, 2002).

A Global Perspective

Turning the Tide: Reclaiming Solid Waste in Egypt

Half an hour from the center of Cairo, Egypt's capital city, the bus loaded with students from the United States bumped along a dirt road and then jerked to a stop. It was not quite dawn, that November morning in 1988, and the Mo'edhdhins were soon to climb the minarets of Cairo's many mosques to call the Islamic faithful to morning prayers. The driver turned, genuinely bewildered, to face us. "Why," he asked, mixing in a few Arabic words, "do you want to be here? And in the middle of the night?"

Why, indeed? No sooner had we left the bus than smoke and stench, the likes of which we had never before encountered, swirled around us. Eyes squinting, handkerchiefs pressed against noses and mouths, we slowly moved up the mountain of trash that extended for miles. This is the Cairo dump, the final resting place for the trash generated by 20 million people in one of the world's largest cities. Bent over and walking with great care, we were guided by flickers of light from small fires that burned around us. Up ahead, through clouds of smoke, we saw blazing piles of trash where local people were warming themselves and talking.

As we approached, the fires cast a strange light on the local people's faces. We stopped some distance from them, separated by a vast chasm of culture and circumstances. But smiles pulled the two groups closer, and soon we all shared the comfort of the fire. At that moment, the call to prayer sounded across the city.

The people of the Cairo dump, called the Zebaleen ("rubbish people"), number about 25,000 and are a religious minority—Coptic Christians—in a mostly Muslim society. Barred by religious discrimination from many jobs, the Zebaleen use donkey carts and small trucks to pick up Cairo's refuse and haul it here. At dawn, hundreds of Zebaleen gather at the dump, swarming over the new piles in search of anything of value.

During this visit in 1988, our group observed men, women, and children picking through Cairo's refuse and filling baskets with anything of value: bits of metal,

strips of ribbon, even scraps of food. Every now and then, someone gleefully displayed a precious find that would bring the equivalent of a few dollars in the city. Watching in silence, we became keenly aware of our sturdy shoes and warm clothing and self-conscious that our watches and cameras represented more money than most of the Zebaleen earn in a whole year.

In 2003, the Cairo Zebaleen still work the city's streets collecting trash. But much has changed, and they are now one of the world's environmental success stories. The Zebaleen have a legal contract to perform their work and they have built a large recycling center near the dump. Dozens of the workers operate huge shredders that turn discarded cloth into stuffing to fill furniture, car seats, and pillows. Other workers separate plastic and metal into large bins for cleaning and sale. In short, using startup loans from the World Bank, the Zebaleen have become businesspeople.

The Zebaleen are still poor by U.S. standards. But they are prospering and now own the land on which they live and work. They have even built an apartment complex with electricity and running water. Many international environmental organizations hope their example will inspire others elsewhere.

ISSUES AND EXERCISES

1. Why do you think recycling takes place at the margins in most societies?
2. Do you think recycling will ever become big business in the United States? Why or why not?
3. [Research Navigator.com] Use Research Navigator™ to learn more about recycling. (See instructions on page 25; keywords: "recycling," "Zebaleen")

Source: Based on the author's trips with students to Egypt (1988 and 1994), Garwood (2003), and news updates.

In light of such developments, we must face the reality that water is a finite resource. Greater conservation of water by individuals (the average person consumes 10 million gallons in a lifetime) is part of the answer. However, individuals in households around the world account for just 10 percent of all water use. We need to curb consumption by industry, which is responsible for 25 percent of global water use, and by farming, which consumes nearly two-thirds of the total for irrigation.

A WORLD OF DIFFERENCES

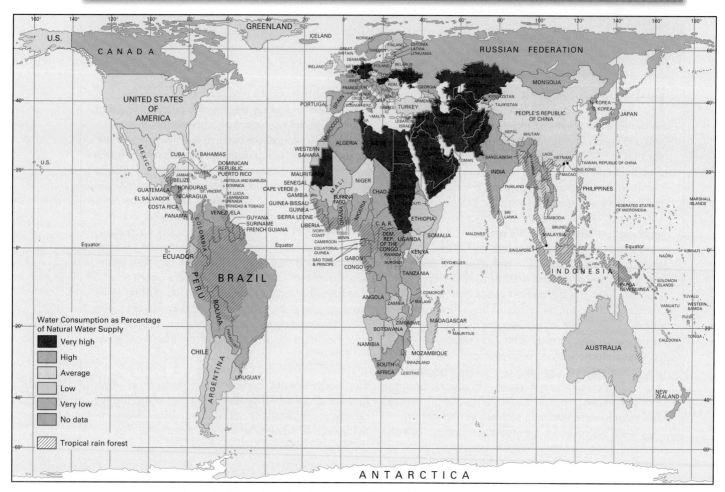

GLOBAL MAP 17–2   Water Consumption around the World

This map shows each country's water consumption in relation to available resources. Nations near the equator consume only a tiny share of their available resources and do not face fresh water shortages. Northern Africa and the Middle East are a different story, however, with dense populations drawing on very limited water resources. As a result, in Libya, Egypt, Saudi Arabia, and other countries there is a serious problem of too little fresh water, especially for the poor.

Source: United Nations Development Programme (1995).

More efficient irrigation technology may reduce this demand in the future. But, here again, we see how population increase, advancing technology, and economic expansion combine to strain the Earth's resources (Goldfarb, 1991; Falkenmark & Widstrand, 1992; Postel, 1993; World Health Organization, 2001).

Water Pollution   In large cities, from Mexico City to Cairo to Shanghai, many people routinely drink contaminated water. As a result, infectious diseases caused by waterborne microorganisms—including diarrhea, intestinal worms, typhoid, cholera, and dysentery—spread rapidly through these populations and result in millions of deaths each year (World Health Organization, 2001). Thus, water *quality* is as serious a problem as *supply*.

By global standards, water quality in the United States is generally good. However, even here the problem of water pollution is growing steadily. According to the Sierra Club (1999), an environmental

A NATION OF DIVERSITY

NATIONAL MAP 17–1

Air Pollution across the United States

The Environmental Protection Agency monitors air quality throughout the United States. This map of the continental United States shows the level of carbon monoxide pollution in the air of all counties. Carbon monoxide pollution is commonly generated by cars and trucks as well as factories. In general, what is the national pattern of air pollution? Can you explain this pattern?

Source: Environmental Protection Agency (2004).

activist organization, 1 million different chemicals are handled in large quantities throughout the country, and rivers and streams across the United States absorb some 500 million pounds of toxic chemicals and waste each year from intentional dumping and from runoff carrying agricultural fertilizers, lawn treatments, and other chemicals.

Air Pollution

One result of the spread of industrial technology—especially the factory and the motor vehicle—has been a decline in air quality. A century ago, the thick, black smoke belching from factory smokestacks, often twenty-four hours a day, alarmed residents of industrial cities. By 1950, exhaust fumes from automobiles hung over cities such as Los Angeles that had escaped the earlier rush of industrial development.

In London, factory discharge, automobile emissions, and smoke from coal fires used to heat homes combined to create what some British jokingly called "pea soup." But during five days in 1952, an especially thick haze covered London and killed 4,000 people (Clarke, 1984a).

Fortunately, great strides have been made in combating air pollution. Laws now forbid high-pollution heating methods, including the coal fires that literally choked some Londoners to death. Smokestack "scrubbers" have decreased the noxious output of factories. The switch to unleaded gasoline in the early 1970s coupled with changes in engine design and exhaust systems have greatly reduced the automobile's

harmful emissions. Still, with some 211 million vehicles in the United States alone, keeping the air clean remains a challenge. National Map 17–1 shows the level of carbon monoxide pollution for counties throughout the continental United States.

As Chapter 12 ("Work and the Workplace") explained, the rich societies of the world have entered a postindustrial era in which computer technology is replacing industrial technology. For this reason, air quality has been improving. But the problem of air pollution in poor societies is getting worse. One reason is that people in low-income countries still rely on wood, coal, peat, or other "dirty" fuels for heat. Moreover, many nations are so eager for short-term industrial development that they ignore the longer-term dangers of air pollution. As a result, many cities in Latin America, Eastern Europe, and Asia have air pollution as bad as London's was fifty years ago.

Learn more about air pollution at **http://www.epa.gov/airnow/**

Acid Rain

Across the 6 million acres of the Adirondack Park in upstate New York, 400 lakes and ponds have been declared "dead" because they are too acidic to support fish or plant life. If this trend continues, another 1,000 lakes and ponds may die by 2050.

The cause of this problem is **acid rain**, *precipitation, made acidic by air pollution, that destroys plant and animal life.* The complex reaction that creates acid rain (or acid snow) begins with power plants

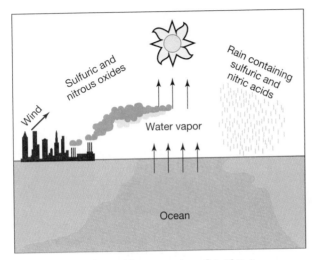

FIGURE 17–3   The Formation of Acid Rain

This figure illustrates the process of creating acid rain, which threatens plant and animal life in many parts of the world.

burning fossil fuels (oil and coal) to generate electricity; this burning releases sulfur and nitrogen oxides into the air. Swept into the atmosphere by winds, these gases react with the air to form sulfuric and nitric acid, which makes atmospheric water acidic. Figure 17–3 illustrates this process.

Acid rain is an example of how one type of pollution can cause another. In this case, air pollution (from smokestacks) ends up contaminating water (in lakes and streams that collect acid rain). Acid rain is a global phenomenon; many of the regions that suffer the harmful effects are thousands of miles from the original pollution. Thus, power-generating facilities in the South and Midwest threaten all of New England. Likewise, tall chimneys of British power plants produce acid rain that has devastated forests and fish as far away as Norway and Sweden.

The Disappearing Rain Forests

Rain forests are *regions of dense forestation, most of which circle the globe close to the equator*. A look back at Global Map 17–2 on page 432 shows that the largest rain forests are in South America, west central Africa, and southeast Asia. In all, the world's rain forests cover some 2 billion acres, or 7 percent of the Earth's total land surface.

Like other global resources, the rain forests are falling victim to the increasing needs and appetites of the human population. For example, to meet the demand for beef in North America, ranchers in

Latin America burn down forests to increase grazing land for cattle. Timber companies are also cutting forests to produce hardwood that ends up being used in high-income countries for furniture, wood floors and paneling, yachts, and even high-grade coffins. Under such pressure, the world's rain forests are now just half their original size, and they continue to shrink by about 1 percent (65,000 square miles) annually. If this rate of destruction remains unchecked, these forests will vanish by about 2100 and, with them, much of the plant and animal biodiversity of this planet.

Global Warming

Scientists document the fact that average temperatures throughout the world are rising, a trend called *global warming*. Over the last two centuries, as societies have developed industrial technology, the amount of carbon dioxide (CO_2) released by factories and automobiles into the atmosphere has soared. Experts estimate that the current atmospheric concentration of carbon dioxide is 20 to 30 percent higher than it was 150 years ago (Revkin, 2002).

The oceans absorb much of this CO_2. Plants also play a vital role because they remove carbon dioxide from the air and expel oxygen. This is one reason the rain forests are so important to our planet's future.

Because the production of carbon dioxide has gone up while the amount of plant life on the earth has gone down, the concentration of CO_2 in the atmosphere is rising. To make matters worse, many rain forests are being destroyed by burning, which releases even more carbon dioxide into the atmosphere.

As carbon dioxide builds up in the atmosphere, it behaves much like the glass roof of a greenhouse, letting heat from the sun pass to the Earth while preventing much of it from radiating back away from the planet. This *greenhouse effect* is the major mechanism by which global warming occurs.

Scientists report that, over the last century, the Earth's average temperature rose 1.0 degree to an average of 58 degrees Fahrenheit. It is likely that the planet's average temperature will rise several more degrees over the course of this century. Such a warming trend would melt much of the polar ice caps and raise the sea level, flooding low-lying land around the world. Low-lying nations such as Bangladesh would be completely covered with water; much of the coastal United States would be flooded, with the Atlantic Ocean rising right up to the steps of the White House in Washington, D.C. Weather patterns would also change. The Great Plains, in the midwestern United States, currently one of the most productive agricultural regions in the world, probably would lose enough rain so that little would grow there.

Global warming melts polar ice, causing oceans to rise; to learn more go to http://www.heinzcenter.org/ecosystems/coastal/coast_ero.shtml

---

Not all scientists share this vision of global warming. Some point out that global temperature changes have been taking place throughout history, with no link to the status of the rain forests. Moreover, higher concentrations of carbon dioxide in the atmosphere might actually accelerate plant growth (because plants thrive on this gas), which would correct the imbalance and nudge the Earth's temperature downward once again. But most now agree that global warming is a real threat to the planet (Silverberg, 1991; Begley, 1997).

Declining Biodiversity

Another reason to worry about the planet's loss of rain forests is loss of the earth's *biodiversity*. There are about 30 million different living species on the planet, counting all forms of bacteria, plants, and animals. Several dozen species of plants and animals cease to exist each day. But given such a vast number of living species, why is declining biodiversity a problem? There are three reasons.

First, the Earth's biodiversity plays a major role in feeding the world's people. By cross-breeding familiar crops with more exotic plant life, agricultural scientists make crops more plentiful and increase their resistance to insects and disease.

Second, the Earth's biodiversity is a vital genetic resource. Medical and pharmaceutical researchers investigate the entire range of animal and plant life, seeking compounds that will cure disease and improve our lives. As examples, the oral birth control pill is a product of plant research involving the Mexican forest yam, and the Pacific yew tree produces a drug that is widely used to treat breast cancer.

Third, with the loss of any species of life—from a tiny ant to the magnificent California condor to the adorable Chinese panda—we lose part of the beauty and complexity of our natural environment. The warning signs are already posted: Three-fourths of the world's 10,000 bird species are declining in number, and more than 1,000 will disappear during this century (Youth, 2003). Protecting the rain forests is vital to maintaining the

More and more scientists are now convinced that global warming is a real threat to the environment. They note, for example, that polar ice is melting, which will raise the levels of the oceans. If the average temperature of the planet rises just a few degrees during this century, much of the coastal United States will be under water. What are strategies to limit global warming?

© Daniel Beltra/Greenpeace.

planet's biodiversity because they are home to half the Earth's living species.

Finally, the extinction of species is irreversible and final. Do we have the right to impoverish the world for those who live tomorrow (Myers, 1991; Wilson, 1991; Brown et al., 1993; Stevens, 2003)?

THEORETICAL ANALYSIS: UNDERSTANDING ENVIRONMENTAL PROBLEMS

We turn now to sociology's two macro-level approaches to help us gain a deeper understanding of environmental issues.

Structural-Functional Analysis: Highlighting Connections

The structural-functional approach links environmental issues to the overall operation of society. This approach offers three important lessons. First, environmental problems are linked to technology. As noted earlier, the more powerful a society's technology, the greater the society's capacity to alter the natural environment.

Second, environmental problems are linked to culture. A structural-functional analysis points out how values and beliefs guide human actions. Thus, the state of the environment reflects our attitudes about the natural world. Members of industrial societies generally view nature as a resource to serve our needs (a point of view described earlier as "the logic of growth"). It was this vision that pushed our ancestors to clear forests for farmland, dam rivers for irrigation and water power, cover vast areas with asphalt and concrete, and erect buildings to make cities. Moreover, our culture is materialistic, so that we look to *things* (often more than, say, kinship or spirituality) as a source of comfort and happiness. Our tendency toward what sociologists call "conspicuous consumption" leads us to purchase and display things not because we really need them but simply as a way of indicating our social position to others (Veblen, 1953; orig. 1899). Such values set the stage for environmental stress.

Third, structural-functionalist theory points up the interconnectedness of all social patterns. Our ideas about efficient and private travel, for example, go a long way to explain the U.S. fascination with automobiles. Building and operating hundreds of millions of vehicles, in turn, has put great stress on resources (such as oil) and the environment (especially the air). Given the connection between the natural environment and the operation of society, the solutions to environmental problems are complex. Is it possible to control the rate at which humanity consumes the earth's resources, for example, while we add about 200,000 people to the global population each day? Limiting population growth, in turn, depends partly on expanding the range of occupational and educational opportunities open to women so they have alternatives to staying home and having more children.

Solving environmental problems is surely a difficult task. But structural-functional analysis provides grounds for optimism because of its view that systems adapt to changing conditions. Take the case of air pollution. Air quality declined sharply as nations developed industrial technology. But, gradually, societies in Europe and North America recognized the problem, enacted new laws, and developed more new technology to clean the air. In short, as long as we are vigilant and creative, we can make the changes needed to ensure a livable environment.

Critical evaluation.   Structural-functional analysis shows that problems of the natural environment are products of the operation of society itself. But, as we have noted before, critics charge that structural functional analysis pays little attention to social inequality. Thus, we may recognize environmental problems but fail to see that burdens of pollution and scarcity fall disproportionately on people with less social power: the poor and minorities. Critics also question structural-functionalism's optimistic view that society can resolve most environmental problems. For one thing, many people—particularly those operating large corporations—have vested interests in continuing past ways, even if they threaten the well-being of the general public. For another, many environmental problems, especially rapid population growth, are simply too far out of control to justify an optimistic outlook.

Social-Conflict Analysis: Highlighting Inequality

Social-conflict theory highlights the issues that structural-functionalism tends to overlook: power and inequality. Far from being inevitable, conflict theorists maintain, problems of the natural environment result from social stratification. In other words, elites directly or indirectly make environmental problems worse as they advance their self-interest.

From a social-conflict point of view, the hierarchical organization of U.S. society gives a small number of people control over our society. As Chapter 11 ("Economy and Politics") describes, a bias in our economic and political systems generates a power elite who set the national agenda.

As the Industrial Revolution began, early capitalists eagerly consumed the Earth's resources and turned out manufactured goods in pursuit of profits, with little regard for environmental consequences. Even today, capitalists and their managers are protected by laws that treat corporate pollution as a white-collar crime (as discussed in Chapter 6, "Crime and Criminal Justice"), so that any legal action usually results in fines paid by the company rather than jail time served by individuals. Thus, corporate executives who order the dumping of toxic waste may never be held personally accountable for their actions.

Conflict theorists taking a Marxist view of society see capitalism itself as a threat to the environment. For one thing, capitalism demands the pursuit of profit, which, in practice, means continuous economic growth at the expense of environmental concerns. For another, strategies to maximize profits may include designing products with only a limited useful life (the concept of *planned obsolescence*). Such policies may increase profits in the short term, but they use up natural resources and produce mountains of solid waste.

A second issue raised by social-conflict theory is inequality. It is the people in rich countries who consume most of the Earth's resources and who generate most air, water, and land pollution. In other words, not only do we maintain our affluent way of life by exploiting the poor in low-income countries, but we poison the world's air and water in the process.

In sum, rich nations are actually *overdeveloped* and consume too much. As Chapter 16 ("Population and Global Inequality") explains, conflict theorists doubt that the majority of the Earth's people, who live in poor societies, will ever raise their living standards under the current capitalist world economy. But from an environmental point of view, this would not even be desirable. What is needed is a more equitable distribution of resources among all people of the world, which would achieve greater social justice and better preserve the natural environment (Schnaiberg & Gould, 1994; Szasz, 1994).

Environmental Racism One important issue that emerges from social-conflict theory is **environmental racism,** *a pattern of discrimination in which environmental hazards are greatest for poor people, especially minorities.* Historically, factories that spew pollution have been located in or near neighborhoods of the poor and people of color. Why? In part because factories draw the poor, who are in search of work. Then, once hired, people with low incomes often find that the only housing they can afford stands in the very shadow of the plants and the mills.

Nobody wants a factory or a dump nearby, of course, but what choice do people have? Through the years, the most serious environmental hazards have been found near Newark, New Jersey (not upscale Bergen County), in southside Chicago (not wealthy Lake Forest), or on Native American reservations in the West (not in affluent suburbs of Denver or Phoenix) (Commission for Racial Justice, United Church of Christ, 1994; Szasz, 1994; Pollock & Vittas, 1995; Bohon & Humphrey, 2000).

Critical evaluation. The social-conflict perspective raises important questions about who sets a society's agenda and who benefits—and who suffers—from decisions that are made. From this point of view, environmental problems result from the class structure within a society and, globally, from the world's hierarchy of nations.

Critics of this approach point out that the record shows a steady trend toward legal protection of the natural environment. Over the last half century, this country has achieved significant improvements in

No one wants to live near a toxic dump. But, because poor people have less power, they are the ones who usually end up living in hazardous areas. What effects has living near dangerous chemicals had on people in the past?

air and water quality. Moreover, some analysts have concluded that the evidence of a systematic pattern of environmental racism is far from convincing (Boerner & Lambert, 1995; Yandle & Burton, 1996).

What of the charge that capitalism itself is particularly hostile to the natural world? There is no doubt that capitalism does support the logic of growth, and, as we have already discussed, this way of thinking does place stress on the environment. At the same time, however, capitalist societies in North America and Europe have shown that they are able to make strides toward environmental protection. Just as important, the environmental record of socialist societies has been strikingly poor. Surveys confirm that the strongest complaints about the poor quality of the local environment come not from capitalist countries but from the socialist nations of Eastern Europe, such as Poland and Russia (Dunlap, Gallup, & Gallup, 1992).

What is our environmental future? Conservatives base their optimism on the power of technology. Liberals, by contract, look to government to mandate reforms. Radicals doubt anything short of fundamental change will turn the tide. Which viewpoint do you support? Why?

POLITICS AND THE ENVIRONMENT: CONSTRUCTING PROBLEMS AND DEFINING SOLUTIONS

How do politics shape the way people see environmental problems and define solutions? The conservative approach offers grounds for optimism that environmental problems are improving. The liberal approach emphasizes the need for greater government action to protect the environment. Radicals argue that the only way to head off environmental collapse is to make fundamental changes to the capitalist system.

Conservatives: Grounds for Optimism

Like just about everyone else, conservatives are concerned about environmental issues. However, they take an optimistic view that society is able to recognize and willing to respond to and solve environmental problems.

Conservatives point out that increasing environmental awareness is one mark of life in a postindustrial society (Pakulski, 1993; Jenkins & Wallace, 1996). Especially as production shifts from smoky factories to clean information technology, society awakes to environmental problems and takes action to address them. Julian Simon (1995) asks, "Why the doom and gloom?" Simon argues that ever since Thomas Robert Malthus (1766–1834) predicted social chaos, based on his belief that a rising population would consume all the world's resources, people have forecast society's collapse. But the planet supports six times as many people as in Malthus's time, and on average they have longer, more affluent lives than ever before. As Simon sees it, these facts should be cause not for gloom but for celebration.

Why has the world done as well as it has? Simon points to human ingenuity. In effect, he says, people keep rewriting the rules for living by developing new forms of energy and new productive technologies. This can be good news for the environment; today's information technology is far cleaner than the industrial production it is replacing. Looking ahead, there is every reason to be confident that the future will be brighter still.

Because this position opposes the view of Malthus, it is often described as *anti-Malthusian*. This viewpoint, which is similar to the logic of growth viewpoint described earlier, is conservative—not because it assumes steady progress toward a better life—but because it expresses support for the current system, believing that problems people create are problems people can solve.

Liberals: Grounds for Concern

Not everyone shares the optimism of people such as Julian Simon. Most environmentalists are deeply concerned about problems such as population increase, resource consumption, and various types of pollution. Many predict a catastrophe if humanity does not change its ways (Brown et al., 1993; Brown, 1995; Bright, 2003). Given this prediction, it is easy to see why such activists are sometimes called *neo-Malthusians* (present-day analysts who agree with the warnings given two centuries ago by Malthus and who support the limits to growth position described earlier in the chapter).

Neo-Malthusians realize that humans have been able to devise new, more productive technologies,

LEFT (TO) RIGHT

THE POLITICS OF THE ENVIRONMENT

	RADICAL LEFT VIEW	LIBERAL VIEW	CONSERVATIVE VIEW
WHAT IS THE PROBLEM?	The natural environment is in serious danger: Given capitalism's appetite for ever-increasing growth and profits, U.S. society is unlikely even to face up to the extent of the problem.	The natural environment is in danger: Both pollution and the rapid use of natural resources including fresh water threaten people now and will threaten future generations even more.	There is no serious problem: Although humanity has created problems of pollution and has taxed natural resource humanity has shown itself capable of devising "clean" technologies and alternative forms of energy.
WHAT IS THE SOLUTION?	A sound environment requires a socially conscious economic system that will ensure the well-being of today's and tomorrow's people; overconsumption in high-income nations must end, and global wealth must be distributed more equally.	Government must enact and enforce laws to prevent further environmental damage in the United States; global organizations must work to protect the remaining rain forests.	Allow the market system to develop new technology; doing so will extend the human record of living longer and healthier lives.

Join the debate . . .

1. Looking over the three political perspectives on the environment, do you see any areas of agreement? If so, what are they?
2. From the point of view of each of the three political perspectives, what changes should take place in the United States to protect the future of the planet?

3. Which of the three political analyses of the natural environment included here do you find most convincing? Why?

even those that Malthus himself could not have imagined. With these technologies, the world now produces more food and other goods. But the unequal distribution of these resources means that some people benefit far more than others, and as both production and population rise, we are steadily consuming the planet's finite resources. In many poor countries, there is little firewood for cooking or heating. Water supplies are already inadequate in much of the Middle East. Rich nations are rapidly consuming the Earth's supplies of oil and natural gas. *When* these supplies will give out is open to debate; *whether* they will give out is not.

In the same way, there is a limit to the Earth's ability to absorb pollution. As both population and production rise, environmental quality will necessarily decline. Many analysts suggest that we have already passed the planet's carrying capacity, or the

number of people than it can support in the long term. Indeed, some argue that our natural environment may only be able to support half of the world's present population, that is, about 3 billion people (Smail, 2004).

In the face of such predictions, liberals call for reform on a number of fronts. Important steps include conservation efforts—including mandatory recycling programs—that limit consumption of natural resources, including clean water. Such programs are especially important in rich countries because this is where most consumption takes place. In practice, this means that people in rich nations may need to make some sacrifices in their living standards for the interest of a better natural environment. The final piece of the solution lies in expanded efforts to reduce pollution. These include development of cleaner-burning fuels and engines (for cars, power

Social Policy   The Environmental Movement: How Far Will You Go?

T HE ENVIRONMENTAL MOVEMENT BEGAN IN THE LATE 1800s with a focus on conservation. The goal was to protect natural wilderness, especially in the western United States, in the face of rapid settlement as more and more people migrated westward. Conservationists succeeded in their efforts as Congress created national parks and established the U.S. Forest Service to oversee them. Early activists also founded the Sierra Club and the National Audubon Society, both of which continue to work for environmental causes today.

It was in the 1960s that the second wave of environmentalism arose, a movement much more critical of the status quo. Many were rallied by Rachel Carson's 1962 book *Silent Spring,* which exposed the danger of spraying pesticides across the land. The new message was that drastic changes had to be made, because proceeding with "business as usual" would lead to eventual disaster.

By 1970, with the celebration of the first Earth Day, the environmental movement had gone mainstream. Awareness of finite resources, the problem of pollution, and the need to limit population increase had become widespread. Most people accepted the idea that reforms were necessary; some called for more radical changes in our way of life. During the pro-business era of the 1980s, the Reagan administration battled the environmental movement, trying to paint environmentalists as a special interest group who were outside the political mainstream. Nevertheless, public support for environmental protection remained strong.

Today, surveys show that a large share of the U.S. public expresses support for environmentalism. At the same time, most people are not willing to give up very much to improve the environment. As the figure shows, 58.4 percent support higher government spending on environmental issues. Yet only 40.6 percent say they are willing to pay higher prices to protect the environment. Just 28.9 percent claim to be willing to pay much higher taxes, and 27.0 percent will accept a lower standard of living in exchange for greater environmental protection. In sum, people express concern about the environment, but what are they willing to do about it?

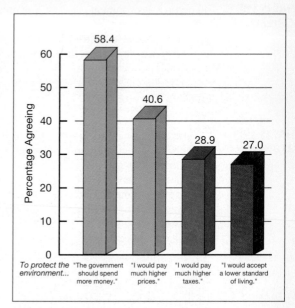

Concern for the Environment: A Survey

Public support for protecting the environment falls if the cost is higher taxes or a lower standard of living.

Source: NORC (2003).

ISSUES AND EXERCISES

1. Do you think limiting economic growth is necessary to protect the environment? Would you be willing to accept higher taxes in order to protect the natural environment? What about a lower standard of living?

2. What action (signing a petition, participating in a demonstration, changing your household consumption patterns) have you ever taken to safeguard the environment?

3. ![Research Navigator.com] Use Research Navigator™ to learn more about environmentalism. (See instructions on page 25; keywords: "environment," "environmental movement")

Source: Data from NORC (2003).

plants, and factories), lighter and more efficient motor vehicles, and the development of strategies to reduce solid waste. In short, liberals look to government to enact and enforce laws to protect the environment.

Radicals: Grounds for Fundamental Change

Radicals do not share conservatives' optimism about humanity's present course on this planet. Although radicals support the liberal agenda, they doubt that liberal reforms will solve the problem. Those who follow a Marxist approach charge that significant environmental change is impossible under a capitalist system that places profits above all other concerns. Then, too, a number of Marxist and non-Marxist critics consider the real issue to be the sharp and increasing degree of global stratification. That is, rich nations are simply too overdeveloped already; in the interests of social justice and environmental safety, wealth must be redistributed more equitably around the world. The Left to Right table on page 439 outlines these three political positions.

None of the political positions argues that things should stay the way they are right now. Everyone recognizes environmental problems; the differences lie mainly in the degree of change people think is necessary to solve these problems. The Social Policy box explains that although most people in the United States agree that the government should do more to improve the natural environment, most people are not willing to pay a very high price for change.

GOING ON FROM HERE

India's great leader Mahatma Gandhi once declared that societies must provide "for people's need but not for their greed." From an environmental point of view, this means that the Earth will be able to sustain future generations only if people today slow their consumption of finite resources such as oil, hardwoods, and water. Nor can we go on polluting the air, water, and soil at anything close to current levels. We must stop cutting down our rain forests if we are to preserve the global climate. Finally, we cannot risk the future of the planet by adding people to the world at the rate of 80 million each year (Population Reference Bureau, 2003).

Sociologists sum up a society's ability to have an environmental impact (I) using a simple formula: $I = PAT$, where P refers to total population, A its

level of affluence, and T its level of technology. Worldwide, population is increasing, living standards are rising, and technology is advancing. The predictable result: a larger environmental impact. The planet's environmental deficit is growing. In effect, our present way of life is borrowing against the future well-being of our children and their children. From a global perspective, members of rich societies who currently consume so much of the Earth's resources are endangering the entire planet.

However the politics play out, the solution to the entire range of environmental problems described in this chapter must be for humanity to live in a way that does not enlarge the environmental deficit. We need to develop an **ecologically sustainable culture,** *a way of life that meets the needs of*

The main lesson of this chapter has been that the state of the natural environment reflects the policies and cultural priorities of society. What aspects of our current way of life do you think represent the greatest threat to the natural environment? What specific changes would you like to see over the next century in the interest of protecting the environment for generations to come?

the present generation without threatening the environmental legacy of future generations.

The future prospect of sustainable living depends on the implementation of three basic strategies. First, the world must *conserve finite resources* by satisfying present needs with a responsible eye toward the future. Conservation involves using resources more efficiently, seeking alternative resources, and, in some cases, learning to live with less. The second basic strategy is to *reduce waste*. The best way to reduce waste is to use less in the first place. In addition, societies around the world need to expand recycling programs through education and legislation. The third key element in any plan for a sustainable ecosystem is to *bring world population growth under control*. Our current population of 6.3 billion (2003) is already straining the natural environment. Clearly, the higher world population climbs, the greater environmental problems will become. Controlling population growth requires immediate action in poor regions of the world where growth rates are highest.

In the end, perhaps, solving environmental problems depends on developing a new outlook. An *egocentric* outlook, common in rich nations today, seeks to meet an ever-expanding set of personal needs. However, a sustainable environment demands an *ecocentric* outlook, one that highlights the environmental consequences of our actions. Such a way of thinking reminds us that today's actions shape tomorrow's world and encourages us to make choices

mindful of their long-range consequences for the natural environment.

In addition, instead of viewing humans as superior to other life forms and assuming that we have the right to dominate the planet, we must remember that all forms of life are interdependent. Ignoring this truth not only threatens the diversity of animal and plant life on the planet but will eventually harm our own well-being.

Finally, achieving a sustainable ecosystem will certainly require global cooperation. The planet's rich and poor nations differ greatly in terms of interests, cultures, and living standards. Policies such as conservation and reducing waste mean little to people who are desperately poor. The most difficult part of any effort to solve the world's environmental problems will be coming to terms with global inequality. Most environmentalists argue that the high-income countries of the world are already overdeveloped, using more resources than the Earth can sustain over the long term. At the same time, low-income nations are underdeveloped, unable to meet the basic needs of many of their people. Establishing a sustainable ecosystem will certainly depend on bold new programs of global cooperation. Although the challenge is enormous, it is nothing compared with the eventual consequences of not responding to the growing environmental deficit. One certainty is that the state of tomorrow's world depends on choices we make today (Kellert & Bormann, 1991; Brown et al., 1993; Bright, 2003).

CHAPTER SUMMARY

1. The state of the natural environment reflects how human beings organize social life. Thus, ecologists study how living organisms interact with their environment.

2. Analyzing environmental problems demands a global perspective. All parts of the ecosystem, including the air, soil, and water, are linked. Actions in one part of the world affect the natural environment elsewhere.

3. As the only species that relies on culture, humans have developed technology that is ever more powerful. The more powerful human

technology, the greater our capacity to alter the natural environment.

4. By focusing on short-term benefits and ignoring the long-term consequences brought on by their way of life, societies build up an environmental deficit.

5. Population increase affects the natural environment. Even though the rate of growth is slowing, world population threatens to overwhelm available resources.

6. Cultural patterns are also involved in environmental problems. The "logic of growth" view of

the world supports economic development and asserts that people can solve whatever environmental problems may arise. Countering this view, the "limits to growth" thesis states that societies have little choice but to curb development in order to avoid environmental collapse.

7. As a "disposable society," the United States generates 1 billion pounds of solid waste each day, 80 percent of which ends up in landfills.

8. Water consumption is rapidly increasing everywhere. Much of the world, notably Africa and the Middle East, is reaching a water supply crisis.

9. Since 1950, high-income countries have made significant progress in reducing air pollution. In poor nations, especially in cities, air pollution remains a serious problem because homes and factories burn "dirty" fuels.

10. Acid rain, the product of pollutants entering the atmosphere mostly from industrial smokestacks, contaminates land and water thousands of miles away.

11. Rain forests serve the planet by removing carbon dioxide from the atmosphere and maintaining the earth's biodiversity. With millions of trees being cut down each year by logging companies and ranchers in search of grazing land for their livestock, global rain forests are now half their original size and are shrinking by about 1 percent annually.

12. Global warming is the rise in the average temperature of the earth, caused by increasing levels of carbon dioxide released into the atmosphere by factories and automobile engines. Destroying the rain forests makes the problem worse because plant life consumes carbon dioxide.

13. Structural-functional theory highlights the importance of both technology and cultural values to a society's impact on the natural environment.

14. Social-conflict analysis highlights the role of inequality in environmental problems, blaming environmental decay on the self-interest of elites. It also points to a pattern of environmental racism in which the poor, especially minorities, suffer most from environmental hazards.

15. Although conservatives acknowledge the reality of environmental problems, they argue that human beings will use their ingenuity and technology to solve them. Because conservatives take an optimistic view of the future, their position is described as anti-Malthusian.

16. Liberals and radicals, sometimes called neo-Malthusians, argue that change is necessary to avoid eventual environmental collapse. Whereas liberals say reforms are sufficient, radicals contend that basic change must occur.

17. A sustainable environment is one that does not threaten the well-being of future generations. Achieving this goal entails conserving finite resources, reducing waste, and controlling the size of the world's population. The most difficult task may well turn out to be dealing with the overdevelopment of some nations of the world and the underdevelopment of the rest.

KEY CONCEPTS

ecology (p. 424) the study of how living organisms interact with the natural environment

natural environment (p. 424) the Earth's surface and atmosphere, including air, water, soil, and other resources necessary to sustain living organisms

technology (p. 424) knowledge that people apply to the task of living in a physical environment

ecosystem (p. 424) a system composed of the interaction of all living organisms and their natural environment

environmental deficit (p. 426) profound and long-term harm to the environment caused by humanity's focus on short-term material affluence

acid rain (p. 433) precipitation, made acidic by air pollution, that destroys plant and animal life

rain forests (p. 434) regions of dense forestation, most of which circle the globe close to the equator

environmental racism (p. 437) a pattern of discrimination in which environmental hazards are greatest for poor people, especially minorities

ecologically sustainable culture (p. 441) a way of life that meets the needs of the present generation without threatening the environmental legacy of future generations

THINKING CRITICALLY: QUESTIONS AND ISSUES

1. Explain how advancing technology allows human beings to manipulate the natural environment. What role do cultural values play in creating environmental problems?

2. What role does sociology play in understanding and addressing problems of the natural environment?

3. What is the environmental deficit? In what ways are environmental problems getting worse? In what ways are they getting better?

4. Suggest a number of specific ways in which people's lives might have to change in order to establish an environmentally sustainable society.

GETTING INVOLVED: LEARNING ACTIVITIES

1. Carry a plastic trash bag around for an entire day and fill it with everything you throw away. What is the weight of one day's trash? Are you surprised by how much you discard?

2. In Genesis, chapter 1, verses 28–29, God instructs humanity to "fill the earth and subdue it; rule over the fish of the sea and the birds of the air and over every living creature that moves on the ground. . . . I give you every seed-bearing plant on the face of the whole earth and every tree that has fruit with seed in it. They will be yours for food." Do you think this statement gives humans the right to exploit the environment as they see fit or the responsibility to care for it? Why?

3. Do some research on the price of gasoline in the United States compared with other countries. In light of the dangers of depleting the world's oil reserves, should oil (and other energy sources) be priced so cheaply?

4. On your campus there are sure to be a number of faculty in the social sciences and the natural sciences who are concerned about the natural environment. Identify several, visit them during office hours, and ask what they think are the most critical environmental issues. What do they propose as solutions to environmental problems?

GETTING CONNECTED: USEFUL WEB LINKS

http://www.prenhall.com/macionis
Visit the interactive Companion Website™ that accompanies this text. Begin by clicking on the cover of your book. You will find a chapter-by-chapter study guide, practice tests, suggested Web links, and links to other relevant material.

http://www.worldwatch.org
The Worldwatch Institute is an organization that monitors the state of the natural environment. Their Web page provides information on a number of environmental problems.

http://www.ran.org
This is the Web site of the Rainforest Action Network, an organization seeking to end the destruction of rain forests around the world. What are their strategies to end the destruction?

http://www.sierraclub.org
http://www.greenpeace.org
Here are two environmental sites maintained by the Sierra Club and Greenpeace. How are these two organizations similar? How do they differ?

http://www.members.aol.com/casmasalc/
To learn more about human slavery, visit this site operated by the Coalition against Slavery in Mauritania and Sudan.

http://www.prb.org
Interested in social indicators for world nations? Find data at the Population Reference Bureau Web site.

http://www.worldvision.org
http://www.worldconcern.org
Wondering what you might be able to do to help in the battle against world hunger? Visit these sites for some answers.

GETTING STARTED ON YOUR OWN: RESEARCH NAVIGATOR™

Follow the instructions found on page 25 of this text to access the features of Research Navigator™. Once at the Web site, enter your Login Name and Password. Then, to use the **Content Select** database, enter keywords such as "environment," "pollution," and "environmental racism," and the search engine will supply relevant and recent scholarly and popular press publications. Use the *New York Times* **Search-by-Subject Archive** to find recent news articles related to sociology and the **Link Library** feature to find relevant Web links organized by the key terms associated with this chapter.

Francisco de Goya, *Los fusilamientos del 3 de mayo, 1808,* 1814. Oil on canvas, 8'6" × 11'4". © Museo Nacional del Prado, Madrid.

WAR AND TERRORISM

"EVERYBODY KNOWS ABOUT 'EM, EXCEPT US," SAYS Lt. Julio Tirado, a member of the 124th Infantry Regiment, shaking his head. He and others in his regiment are talking to reporters about the roadside bombs that have taken a high toll among the U.S. armed forces stationed in Iraq. The bombs are planted by the side of the road, usually with a few Arabic words written nearby to warn local people. Sooner or later, a truckload of U.S. soldiers drives past, the bomb is detonated, and the list of casualties gets longer (Thomas, Barry, & Caryl, 2003).

The War in Iraq is the latest in the long history of military engagements that have cost the lives of our men and women in uniform. Many people in the United States believe that war serves the interest of freedom. But given the tremendous human cost, people in the United States also commonly identify war as one of our most serious social problems.

Then why do people go to war in the first place? Some analysts have suggested that humans, especially men, are naturally aggressive (Chagnon, 1997). If this is so, there seems to be little that we can do to prevent war. But social scientists have made a careful study of war, investigating both its causes and its costs. What we have learned is that war and terrorism, a closely linked form of violent conflict, have their origins in society itself. By focusing on the causes of war, society should be able to work out effective strategies for peace.

WAR AND PEACE: BASIC DEFINITIONS

War is *violent conflict between nations or organized groups.* **Peace,** an opposing concept, is *the absence of violent conflict.* Many people think of peace as the normal state of affairs. Yet wars have always been a part of human history. The United States has been involved in many large-scale wars, shown

447

TABLE 18–1	**MAJOR WARS INVOLVING THE UNITED STATES**	
	DATES	**U.S. DEATH TOLL**
American Revolutionary War	1775–83	25,324
War of 1812	1812–15	6,780
Mexican War	1846–48	13,271
Civil War	1861–65	618,222
Spanish-American War	1898	5,807
World War I	1914–18	116,516
World War II	1939–45	405,399
Korean War	1950–53	54,246
Vietnam War	1965–75	57,777
Persian Gulf War	1991–92	148
War in Iraq	2003–	701*

Sources: Compiled from various sources by Maris A. Vinovskis (1989) and various news reports.

*As of April 2004.

in Table 18–1, and a larger number of minor conflicts played out in Grenada, Panama, Haiti, Somalia, and Bosnia. In the twentieth century, there was no time at which there was not a conflict occurring somewhere around the world. Global Map 18–1 shows the nineteen countries that experienced at least one armed conflict in 2002 (SIPRI, 2003).

The Increasing Destruction of War

Over time, the level of war-related violence has increased sharply. A thousand years ago, the most a human could do in battle was to kill one other person at a time by swinging a sword, throwing a spear, or launching an arrow. About the twelfth century, the development of guns using black powder made killing far more efficient. By the early sixteenth century, large cannons were able to knock down stone walls and kill many people at one time. The U.S. Civil War, fought between 1861 and 1865, was this country's bloodiest, in part because soldiers confronted each other with guns and cannons that were far more deadly than ever before.

In the twentieth century, weapons became even more lethal. Machine guns replaced single-shot rifles, armies used new kinds of chemical weapons and explosive bombs, and aircraft (and, later, missiles) were able to rain death and destruction on entire cities from miles above. Such **weapons of mass destruction,** *weapons with the capacity to kill many thousands of people at one time,* increase the destruction of war not only because of their greater power but also because they target civilian populations. As the deadly potential of weapons increases, the problem of war becomes an ever-greater concern.

The Causes of War

Sociologists have identified seven factors that promote the outbreak of war (Wright, 1987; Kaldor, 1999; Van Evera, 1999):

1. **Perceived threats.**   Societies mobilize their military resources in response to perceived threats. In 1962, the United States prepared for war against the Soviet Union after learning that Soviet nuclear missiles were operational on the island of Cuba, a nation ninety miles south of Florida that had recently experienced a communist revolution. Only after the Soviets agreed to remove the missiles did the two nations step back from the brink of war. In 2003, the United States invaded Iraq because it suspected that nation had stockpiles of weapons of mass destruction. Yet by the end of the year, no such weapons were found (Dworkin, 2003).

2. **Cultural and religious differences.**   Another cause of war is cultural or religious differences. Members of various nations or ethnic groups are taught to "demonize" those in some other country or group—that is, to see them as evil. At the extreme, one group may try to rid an entire geographic area of people who differ from themselves. In the Balkan conflict of the 1990s, ethnic Serbs rounded up hundreds of thousands of Croats, Muslims, and ethnic Albanians, deported them, placed them in prison camps, or simply killed them, in a process called ethnic cleansing.

3. **Political objectives.**   Political objectives can be an underlying factor in war. A periodic show of force can be one way for a nation to assert a leadership position in the world. Examples include the United States invasion of Grenada in 1982, its deployment of troops in the Persian Gulf War in 1991–92, its bombing of Serbia in 1999, and its invasion of Iraq in 2003.

4. **Moral objectives.**   Nations may go to war to achieve a moral objective. Leaders in the United States justified the Korean War and the war in Vietnam as efforts to make the world safe

A WORLD OF DIFFERENCES

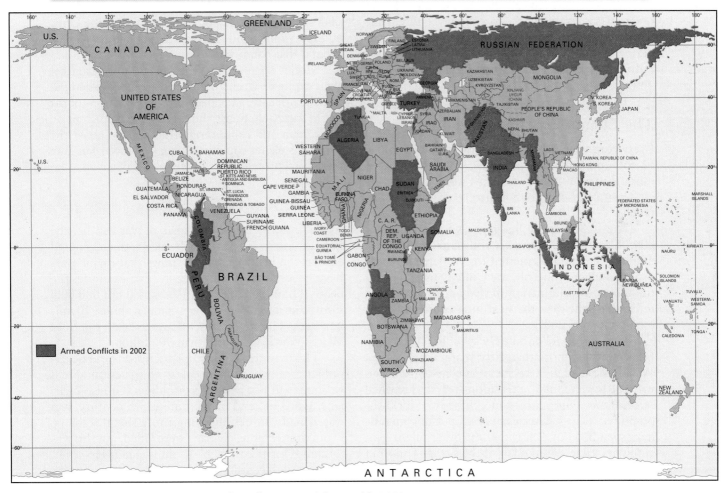

GLOBAL MAP 18–1   Armed Conflicts around the World, 2002

In 2002, there were armed conflicts in nineteen nations, most of them in Africa and Asia. The most serious conflict of the year involved India and Pakistan, both of which are nuclear powers. The United States was involved in a military conflict in Afghanistan, but the War in Iraq did not begin until 2003.

Source: Based on data from Stockholm International Peace Research Institute (2003).

from communism. The War in Iraq was justified, in part, by the moral goal of ending the rule of Iraq's brutal dictator, Saddam Hussein, and encouraging the development of democracy in the Islamic world.

5. **Wealth and power.**   Nations may go to war to increase their wealth and power. This was why Iraqi leader Saddam Hussein invaded the oil-rich nation of Kuwait in 1990, sparking the Persian Gulf War.

6. **Social problems.**   Leaders sometimes use armed conflicts to divert attention from social

problems. For example, the People's Republic of China managed to turn attention away from great economic hardship by supporting military conflict in Korea, Vietnam, and Tibet. Focusing national attention on an external threat encourages people to unify against a common enemy rather than blame the government for their problems.

7. **Absence of alternatives.**   Finally, nations go to war because of an absence of alternatives. A nation may simply have no diplomatic means to accomplish its political or moral objective.

Leaders may draw on many of these factors in making claims about the need for military action. Moreover, leaders typically define military action in one way (say, as a response to a perceived threat and in pursuit of a moral objective), whereas critics may define the military action quite differently (say, as a political strategy or an effort to gain wealth and power).

The Economic Costs of Militarism

Every year, the nations of the world spend more than $1 trillion for military purposes, which amounts to more than $160 for every many, woman, and child on a planet where a billion people are desperately poor.

The U.S. defense budget was $376 billion in 2003, about $1,300 for each of its citizens. Overall, military spending accounted for 16 percent of the federal budget. Militarily, the United States is by far the most powerful nation in the world, with more military might than the next nine countries combined (Gergen, 2002).

This high level of military spending has been a fact of life for more than fifty years. After World War II, the United States maintained tense relations with the Soviet Union, a situation analysts described as a *cold war*. During this time, these two world superpowers engaged in an *arms race*, pushing up military spending out of fear that the other might gain a military edge. Yet the fall of the Soviet Union in 1991 brought only a slight decline in military spending. The war on terrorism that began with the attacks on September 11, 2001, will ensure that military spending will remain high for years to come.

Some analysts claim that the United States—or, more specifically, powerful interests in this country—benefits from high levels of military spending. They see the United States as dominated by a **military-industrial complex,** *a political alliance involving the federal government, the military, and the defense industries* (Marullo, 1987). From this point of view, militarism in the United States is less a matter of defense and national security than a matter of profit and power for the country's power elite (see Chapter 11, "Economy and Politics").

The Economic Costs of War

The economic costs of war involve more than military spending. War also destroys the *infrastructure* of a society: its homes and workplaces, water systems, electrical and communication networks, roads,

bridges, railways, harbors, and airports. By the end of World War II, much of Europe lay in ruins and had to be rebuilt at the cost of hundreds of billions of dollars. In the wake of the War in Iraq, the United States will spend more than $100 billion to help rebuild that country.

Money spent on war takes economic resources away from programs that improve people's nutrition, health care, and education. If the nations of the world were able to use the funds currently spent on militarism and rebuilding after wars to assist the poor, this planet could go a long way toward ending the global problems of hunger and disease.

The Human Costs of War

As huge as the economic costs of war can be, the greatest loss is measured in human terms. As noted earlier, the historical trend shows that major wars have become ever more deadly. For example, the death toll in the U.S. Civil War was about 600,000. Fifty years later, World War I claimed almost 10 million lives. Thirty years after that, the death toll from World War II was more than 50 million.

The main reason for this increase is the development of weapons of mass destruction. Such weapons kill not only more soldiers but also civilians. Until the end of the nineteenth century, war was armed conflict involving professional soldiers. From time to time, civilians were killed, but this was rare and, for the most part, unintended. However, the twentieth century saw the development of a new strategy of **total war,** *deadly conflict that targets both population centers and military targets.* With airplanes and bombs at their command, military leaders had the power not just to kill enemy soldiers but to level entire cities. In efforts to reduce the enemy's production of weapons they demolished factories, also killing the civilians who worked in the factories and those who lived nearby. During World War II, for example, both the Germans and the Allied forces repeatedly bombed one another's cities in attacks that weakened the enemy's ability and will to fight. Most of the people who died in World War II in fact, were civilians. In effect, the strategy of total war blurs the lines between soldiers and civilians, greatly raising the death toll (Renner, 1993; Ehrenreich, 1997).

Also during World War II, some nations set up **concentration camps,** *centers where prisoners are confined for purposes of state security, exploitation, punishment, or execution.* The United States imprisoned about 100,000 people of Japanese ancestry between 1942 and 1944. These camps, set up within a year of

The most dramatic example of total war was the use of two atomic bombs by the United States against Japan at the end of World War II. The first bomb almost completely destroyed the industrial city of Hiroshima. The second, wiped out Nagasaki (shown here). In each case, the death toll exceeded 100,000 people.

the Japanese attack on Pearl Harbor, were an effort to control a segment of the U.S. population thought to represent a threat to national security. In Europe, concentration camps took on a deadly mission. Both Soviet leader Josef Stalin and German leader Adolf Hitler operated camps that forced prisoners to work so hard, with so little food, that many eventually died of exhaustion, starvation, and disease. During World War II, the Nazis exterminated some 6 million Jews, along with millions of political prisoners, Catholics, Gypsies, homosexuals, and anyone else defined as undesirable, in many death camps, including those at Auschwitz and Buchenwald. The death toll under Stalin was greater still, reaching as high as 30 million.

War Crimes Strangely enough, there are rules of war. These include individual nations' own standards for fighting a war and also a series of formal agreements negotiated in Geneva, Switzerland, between 1864 and 1949, called the *Geneva Conventions.*

Learn more about war crimes at http://www.crimesofwar.org

Violation of these standards is a **war crime,** *an offense against the law of war as established by international agreements and international law.* In the wake of World War II, the Geneva Conventions recognized three categories of war crimes. First, *crimes against peace* include preparing for or starting a war against another nation. Second, *conventional war crimes* include the murder, rape, torture, deportation, or other ill treatment of a population in any occupied territory. Third, *crimes against humanity* include political,

racial, or religious persecution—including systematic killing—of any civilian population during war.

After World War II, an International War Crimes Tribunal tried twenty-four Nazi leaders at Nuremberg, Germany, convicting nineteen. A separate tribunal tried and convicted twenty-five Japanese leaders, their sentences ranged from lengthy prison terms to execution. More recently, the United Nations International Criminal Tribunal has prosecuted a few officers for war crimes in Rwanda and the former Yugoslavia. However, because this tribunal's power depends on the political cooperation of individual nations and their willingness to aid in apprehending alleged criminals, many manage to escape prosecution (Newman, 2002).

War-Related Disabilities Many of those who survive a war suffer from mental and physical disabilities. Soldiers have long talked about "battle fatigue" or "shell-shock." After the Vietnam War, about 15 percent of soldiers experienced *post-traumatic stress disorder* (PTSD), a war-related disability resulting from trauma or stress in battle. Symptoms of PTSD include nightmares, difficulty with concentration and sleeping, flashbacks to traumatic events, jumpiness and hyperalertness, guilt about surviving, and feelings of detachment from other people (American Psychiatric Association, 1994). An everyday event such as hearing a car backfiring or seeing a helicopter flying overhead can trigger a PTSD episode, causing the person to relive the terror of combat.

In all, some 2.7 million U.S. veterans have some disability resulting from an injury during active duty

Personal Stories   Children in Combat: Not Too Young to Kill

A BOY CALLED "TS" IS A SOLDIER WITH MORE than six years of combat experience. He fights on the front lines of Sierra Leone, a war-torn nation in western Africa. In raids of villages along the border of his country, TS has killed many people. He has seen so much violence that he finds it difficult to sleep and often wets his bed. TS is twelve years old.

The story of this boy-soldier begins in 1993, when rebels invaded TS's village. Soldiers killed his parents and kidnaped the six-year-old boy, telling him he would be a freedom fighter. TS joined the ranks of thousands of child-soldiers in Sierra Leone.

Military units that abduct children often turn them against their own relatives and neighbors, a strategy that leaves the children no home to which they can return and no identity other than soldier. Children are easily molded into unquestioning fighters, and many develop an intense loyalty to the military that comes from knowing no other way of life. Many children think they are invincible, and they readily obey orders to spy on the enemy, clear mine fields, and even serve as suicide bombers.

According to the Coalition to Stop the Use of Child Soldiers, a Swiss organization, some 300,000 children in more than thirty countries work as soldiers. This organization reports that in recent years about 8,000 have been abducted and forced to fight by rebels in Uganda. In Colombia, 15,000 children serve in various military organizations. The British navy recruits sixteen-year-olds, and its army takes people as young as seventeen. Finally, this organization estimates that about 3,000 seventeen-year-olds are serving in active military duty in the United States.

Learn more about child soldiers at
http://www.child-soldiers.org

Should children be in uniform? In many lower-income societies, adulthood begins much earlier than is typical in the United States. As early as age six or seven many young people are working; by thirteen or fourteen, many marry and assume other adult roles. Critics point out that most children enter military service after abduction or because they think they have few other options. After very young people spend a year or more as soldiers, they become socialized to accept violence as a way of life and may find it difficult to live any other way.

ISSUES AND EXERCISES

1. In poor countries, most young children work for income. In light of this fact, is joining the military so different? Explain your position.

2. Whereas most high-income countries have laws that prohibit children serving as soldiers, many low income countries either do not have such laws or do not enforce them. What can other nations do to help children pressed into military service by rebel groups?

3. U.S. soldiers currently serving in Iraq are as young as eighteen. Is that too young to be asked to perform such service? Why or why not?

Sources: The Economist (1999), Schlumpf (1999), and Coalition to Stop the Use of Child Soldiers (2001).

---

in the military; of these, about 170,000 are totally disabled. As medical technology available to seriously wounded soldiers has advanced, more men and women who would have died from their injuries are now surviving, but many are left with serious disabilities. To provide care for disabled veterans, the Department of Veterans Affairs (VA) operates 163 hospitals, 137 nursing homes, and 850 outpatient clinics across the country. Care is provided free of charge to ex–prisoners of war, those with service-related

injuries or disabilities, and veterans with income below the poverty line. Thousands of other veterans are treated on a space-available basis (Findlay, 1992; Konigsberg, 1992; Matthews, 1995; Gardner, 1998; Moakley, 1999; U.S. Veterans Administration, 2003).

A problem related to illness and disability among veterans is difficulty finding and keeping jobs. This is one reason that 1.5 million veterans live with incomes below the poverty line; one veterans' organization claims that 275,000 are homeless at any given time, and about 500,000 are homeless for some time during any give year (National Coalition for Homeless Veterans, 2000).

War and Children Finally, the human toll of war falls heavily on children. All of the major wars of the last century left vast numbers of orphans; hundreds of thousands of children also died in bombings and other attacks. More recently, increasing numbers of children are taking an active part in military operations. The Personal Stories box takes a closer look.

War in the Nuclear Age

Warfare became much more deadly with the development of **nuclear weapons,** *bombs that use nuclear reactions to generate enormous destructive force.* Only twice have nuclear weapons been used in war. In 1945, the United States dropped two atomic bombs on Japan at the conclusion of World War II: the first on the city of Hiroshima, the second, three days later, on Nagasaki. Each bomb instantly killed 100,000 people and leveled the city.

Today, there are about 17,500 nuclear weapons worldwide, and most of these weapons are thousands of times more powerful than the bombs used against Japan. Indeed, today's nuclear weapons are capable of destroying most of the life on the planet (Institute for Stategic Studies, 2003; SIPRI, 2003).

The Increase and Spread of Nuclear Weapons The arms race that followed World War II led the United States and the Soviet Union to build large arsenals of nuclear weapons. At their peak in the 1960s, the two superpowers had about 60,000 nuclear weapons—far more than needed to end all life on the planet.

After the collapse of the Soviet Union in 1991, the Russian Federation and the United States gradually reduced their nuclear arsenals, cutting them back by 75 percent as of 2003. But these superpowers are not the only nations with nuclear weapons. Global Map 18–2 identifies the United States, Great Britain, France, India, Pakistan, and the People's Republic of China as nations with a substantial nuclear capability. Moreover, recent decades have witnessed a pattern of **nuclear proliferation,** *the acquisition of nuclear weapon technology by more and more nations.* Nuclear proliferation increases the likelihood that regional conflicts, such as the tensions between India and Pakistan in 2002, could trigger the use of nuclear weapons. The use of such weapons not only would cause a huge number of casualties but also could very well draw other nations into the conflict.

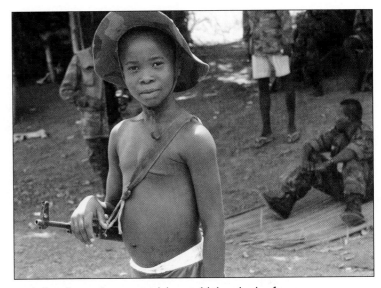

A chilling fact is that, around the world, hundreds of thousands of children work as soldiers. This eleven-year-old boy is on duty defending an army checkpoint near the capital of Sierra Leone. What factors, especially in poor societies, lead children to become involved in war?

Today, Israel and North Korea are believed to possess nuclear weapons. Other nations, including Iran, may well be developing them. A few nations—Argentina, Brazil, South Africa, and Libya—have decided to stop their development of nuclear weapons. Even so, it is likely that within several decades as many as fifty of the world's nations may have at least some nuclear weapons, a fact that places the entire world in increasing danger (Molander & Wilson, 1994; Hilsman, 1999; SIPRI, 2003).

The Effects of Nuclear War The power of nuclear weapons is almost beyond comprehension. The bomb that the United States dropped on Hiroshima was a "primitive" 15-kiloton device, with an explosive power of 15,000 tons of TNT. Many of the warheads in the world's nuclear arsenals are rated at 50 megatons, equivalent to 50 million tons of TNT.

Even a small nuclear weapon rated at a single megaton can produce temperatures that exceed the heat on the surface of the sun. Instantly, such heat will vaporize anything close to the bomb and unleash a firestorm that will consume everything for ten miles in every direction. The bomb also generates a shockwave that extends outward, destroying everything in its path and drawing debris upward into a giant mushroom cloud. In the days that follow, radioactive debris rains down over a vast area (Sagan & Turco, 1990).

A WORLD OF DIFFERENCES

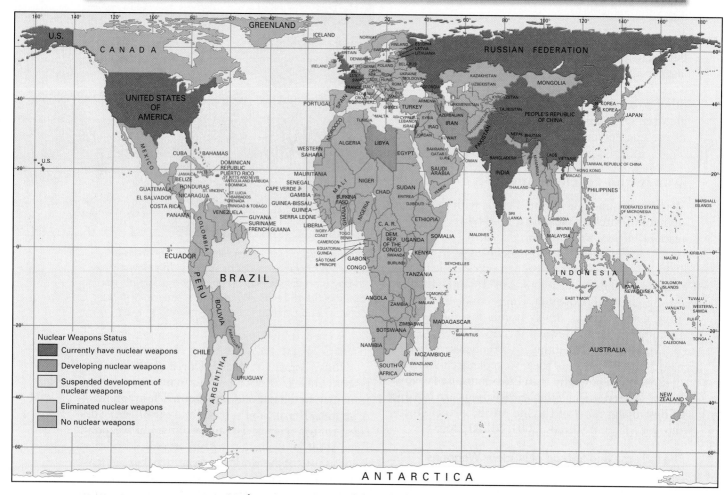

GLOBAL MAP 18–2   Nuclear Weapons around the World

In 2003, eight countries possessed nuclear weapons. Many more, especially high-income nations, could build these weapons but have chosen not to. How many countries do you think will have nuclear weapons in the year 2050?

Source: Stockholm International Peace Research Institute (2003).

Some scientists claim that exploding even a few nuclear bombs at one time would draw enough debris and dust into the atmosphere to block the sun's rays from reaching the planet's surface. This blockage, they believe, would remain for months or even years, triggering a *nuclear winter*, a cooling of the earth's atmosphere by as much as 50 degrees Fahrenheit. The resulting semidarkness and subfreezing temperatures, together with radiation from nuclear fallout, would be sufficient to kill most of the Earth's vegetation and wipe out animal life. Should hundreds of nuclear bombs ever be used in war, life on earth might end entirely (Sagan & Turco, 1990).

Strategies for Peace

Given the unimaginable horrors of war in a nuclear age, the nations of the world must seek to live in peace. But how can peace be achieved? There are several strategies to keep peace, including deterrence, high-technology defense, arms control, and resolving underlying conflicts.

Deterrence   Deterrence is *a strategy to keep peace based on the threat of retaliation.* The strategy of deterrence, also known as *mutual assured destruction (MAD),* has helped prevent all-out war for more than

In 2004, Dr. Abdul Qadeer Kahn (left), founder of Pakistan's nuclear program, admitted to his president, Pervez Musharraf, that he had sold information about building atomic bombs to agents of several other countries. Do you think it is possible to limit the spread of nuclear weapons in the decades to come? Why?

fifty years. Despite this success, deterrence as a strategy for peace has three drawbacks. First, the cost of the nuclear arms race has been extremely high, taking money away from education, housing, nutrition, and medical care. Second, today's submarine-based missiles are capable of delivering nuclear warheads in a matter of minutes. If one country believed it was under attack, leaders—or computers—would have little time to decide whether to launch a retaliatory strike. With so little time to react, the risk of error—and of entering an unintended war—goes up. Third, deterrence cannot control nuclear proliferation. As more nations develop nuclear weapons, the risk that they will be used in war increases (Kugler & Organski, 1989).

High-Technology Defense A second strategy to keep the peace is the use of new technology, including satellites, to defend against a nuclear attack. The Strategic Defense Initiative (SDI) first proposed by the Reagan administration in 1981, is just such a program. In principle, such a system would detect enemy missiles soon after launch and destroy them with lasers and particle beams before they reenter the atmosphere.

But there are problems with this approach. First, preliminary tests of SDI have not shown much success. Second, more than $100 billion has already been spent on this technology, and the cost will rise far higher (Hsin, 2003). Third, having such weaponry puts international relations on shaky ground because other nations might take developing such a system as a sign of preparation for war.

Arms Control A third strategy to keep the peace is **arms control,** *international agreements on the development, testing, production, and deployment of weapons.* Since World War II, the focus of arms control efforts has been on limiting the nuclear stockpiles held by the United States and the Soviet Union. In the 1970s the two nations entered into the Strategic Arms Limitation Talks (SALT), which resulted in agreements freezing the number of nuclear weapons held by each side and limiting the development of antimissile defense systems. In the 1980s and 1990s, the United States and the Soviet Union (after 1991, the Russian Federation) entered into the Strategic Arms Reduction Talks (START), which led both nations to reduce the number of their nuclear weapons. As of 2003, the world's stockpile of nuclear weapons had declined from a peak of about 60,000 bombs to about 20,000 (DefenceIndia, 2003).

Arms control has limitations. First, such treaties focus on existing weapons and do little to slow the development of newer weapons. Second, it is difficult to verify whether nations are living up to arms control agreements. Third, despite recent progress toward arms control, enough nuclear weapons still remain to destroy the entire planet. The more important issue, therefore, is resolving the underlying conflicts that might end up causing their use.

Resolving Underlying Conflict The most effective path to peace is to resolve conflicts, the strategy of *diplomacy.* Peace depends on the efforts of ambassadors posted in various countries and international

A DEFINING MOMENT

Mohandas Gandhi: Spreading a Message of Peace

MOHANDAS K. GANDHI WAS A SMALL MAN who carried a mighty message. He built his life around the idea that the most effective path to peace and justice is to practice nonviolence rather than war.

Gandhi's primary goal was the liberation of his native India from the colonial control of the British. Rather than attacking the British militarily or resorting to suicide bombers or other forms of terror common in today's world, he advocated a strategy of *nonviolent resistance,* the refusal to cooperate with a system they believe to be wrong. In one of his most effective tactics, Gandhi urged his people to make their own clothes rather than buy garments manufactured in England as part of the colonial economic system.

Gandhi was arrested many times during his life. But he succeeded in ending British colonial rule in 1947. Ironically, one year later, this man of peace was murdered by a crazed opponent. But his message lives

Mohandas Gandhi (1869–1948) taught the world that it is possible to pursue justice using nonviolent means rather than war. In the half-century since Gandhi's death, how well has this lesson been learned?

on, and it has been embraced by many others, including U.S. civil rights leader Martin Luther King.

---

agencies such as the United Nations. In recent years, diplomats have used the term *peace process* to refer to the back-and-forth negotiations between parties in conflict, including the steps each side will take to end hostilities in exchange for a desired objective. Negotiating peace is always difficult: Although the Middle East peace process has been going on for decades, violent confrontations between Israelis and Palestinians continue.

Throughout the world today, there are hundreds of conflicts between nations and groups based on territorial disputes, ethnicity, religion, ideology, and inequality. To suppose that humankind can resolve all these conflicts may seem far-fetched. But the fact remains that the world spends far more money on weapons of war than on strategies for peace (Sivard, 1988; Dedrick & Yinger, 1990; Kaplan & Schaffer, 2001).

At the same time, many people have devoted their lives to peace, and some outstanding leaders have helped show the way. Perhaps the most influential is Indian leader Mohandas K. Gandhi (1869–1948), whose lessons are described in the Defining Moment box.

TERRORISM

Terrorism involves *unlawful, typically random acts of violence or the threat of such violence used by an individual, group, or government to achieve a political goal.* Whereas war involves systematic, ongoing conflict and follows international law and conventions, terrorism involves sporadic and random acts of violence that cause widespread fear. Acts of terror, which include bombings, hijackings, and assassinations, typically are used by individuals or groups against a more powerful enemy.

We also see **state-sponsored terrorism,** *the practice by one government of providing money, weapons, and training to terrorists who engage in violence in another nation.* For example, the Taliban regime in Afghanistan provided military training and other support to members of al-Qaeda, who later engaged in terrorist attacks against the United States and other countries. After the terror attacks of September 11, 2001, the United States militarily attacked Afghanistan to drive the Taliban from power and weaken the al-Qaeda network. The claim that Iraq was supporting terrorism was also one justification for the U.S. invasion of Iraq in 2003, although the U.S. government later stated there was no evidence of any direct link between Iraq and al-Qaeda.

Terrorist organizations seek to focus world attention on their issues and demands. They define violent acts as a legitimate political response to some injustice. For this reason, whether people celebrate or condemn an act of violence, or whether they label a participant a "freedom fighter" or "terrorist," depends on their own support or opposition to the cause (Marchak, 1999; Sheehan, 2000 Jenkins, 2003).

Governments also use terrorism against their own people. **Repressive state terrorism** is *government use of ruthless violence within its own borders to repress political opposition.* Many governments have used kidnaping, torture, rape, and systematic killing to stay in power. Soviet dictator Josef Stalin used secret police and a system of concentration camps to control or eliminate anyone he considered a threat. Adolf Hitler used similar methods to rule Germany during the Nazi era. In the 1970s, Pol Pot conducted a campaign of repressive state terrorism against the people of Cambodia. Until his overthrow by U.S. forces, Saddam Hussein used a brutal campaign of terror to maintain an iron grip on the nation of Iraq.

The Extent of Terrorism

In 2002, there were 199 terrorist attacks worldwide, which claimed 725 lives and injured 2,013 people. Although most people in the United States began paying close attention to terrorism only after the attacks of September 11, 2001, Figure 18–1 shows that the number of terror attacks in the world has been high for more than twenty years and has actually declined slightly. Most terrorist attacks target the United States (U.S. Department of State, 2003).

Terrorism: A Global Perspective For at least a century, terrorism has played a part in efforts to end colonial rule in many nations of the world. In 1916, for example, Irish people opposed to British rule formed the Irish Republican Army (IRA) to force the British from Ireland. In 1922, the British gave up claim to most of Ireland but kept control of Northern Ireland; since then, the IRA has used terrorism as part of its efforts to end British control there as well. After World War II, a militant faction of the Zionist movement sought to establish a Jewish state in the Middle East and used terrorism to drive the British from Palestine. In 1954, a group called the Mau-Mau used terror in its efforts to force British colonialists from the African nation of Kenya. That same year,

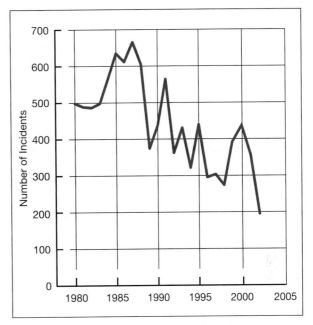

FIGURE 18–1 **International Terrorist Attacks, 1980–2002**

Although terrorism has been on people's minds in recent years, the trend in terrorism over the last two decades has been downward.

Source: U.S. Department of State (2003).

Algerian terrorists began a campaign of violence against French citizens in their country, which played a part in ending French colonial rule of Algeria in 1962. In recent decades, Palestinian organizations committed to establishing a Palestinian state on land controlled by Israel have made Israelis the targets of terrorism (U.S. Department of State, 2000, 2003).

Much world terrorism has been directed against the United States. In 1993, al-Qaeda members exploded a truck full of dynamite at the World Trade Center in New York's downtown business district, killing six people and injuring more than a thousand. In 1998, the same organization exploded bombs at the U.S. embassies in Tanzania and Kenya, killing 257 people and injuring more than 5,000. In 2001, the most deadly attack on the United States in history took almost 3,000 lives when al-Qaeda terrorists seized and crashed airliners loaded with passengers and fuel into the World Trade Center and the Pentagon. Another plane, in which passengers fought with terrorists, crashed in rural Pennsylvania. The targeting of the United States reflects this nation's substantial military, economic, and political presence around the world. In addition, Osama bin Laden's al-Qaeda organization defines the U.S. as an evil

One part of the costs of terrorism is economic. Even months after the attacks on September 11, 2001, the streets around the site of the World Trade Center remained largely empty.

influence in the world (McGeary, 1998; Reeve, 1999; Stern, 1999; Thomas & Harsh, 2000).

Read the U.S. State Department's annual report on global terrorism at **http://www.usemb.se/terror/rpt2002/index.html**

Terrorism in U.S. History   Although many people think of terrorists as people from other countries, the United States has a long history of home-grown terrorism. After the abolition of slavery, the Ku Klux Klan and other organizations resorted to cross burnings, beatings, lynchings, and bombings to prevent African Americans from exercising their new political rights. Historians estimate that more than 5,000 black men were lynched in the century after the Civil War (Williams, 2000).

Early in the twentieth century, many businesses used violence to prevent union organizing, and some labor groups fought back. The Industrial Workers of the World (IWW), a radical labor union, began a war against capitalism that included violent strikes, bombings, and assassinations (Lukas, 1997). In the 1960s, some radical students formed the Weather Underground, a group committed to forming a classless society and destroying the nation's economic and military institutions. This group carried out a number of violent attacks, including a bombing of the Pentagon in 1975 (Finlayson, 1998).

On April 19, 1995, Gulf War veteran Timothy McVeigh parked a truck full of explosives in front of the Murrah Federal Building, seeking revenge on the federal government for actions taken against Randy Weaver at Ruby Ridge, Idaho, and against the Branch Davidian Compound in Waco, Texas (events discussed in Chapter 7, "Violence"). The explosion killed 169 people—many of them children—and injured hundreds more (Hughes, 1998; Perlstein, 1998).

The Costs of Terrorism

One great cost of terrorism is loss of life and physical injury: Some 20,000 people a year worldwide are directly harmed by terrorism (U.S. Department of State, 2000). Like soldiers who suffer from battlefield trauma, hostages and other victims of terrorist acts often experience posttraumatic stress disorder. But perhaps an even greater toll is the widespread fear caused by such acts. Everyone living in the United States at the time of the attacks on September 11, 2001, can recall the fear and anxiety caused by the events of that day.

The economic costs of the September 11 attacks are impossible to measure, but they reach into the billions of dollars. Beyond the immediate loss of property, the entire economy was shaken, and businesses near New York's "ground zero" endured hard times for several years. In addition, the costs of this country's "war on terrorism" will reach the hundreds of billions of dollars. Such vast sums could easily end poverty and provide everyone with universal health insurance.

Terrorism as a Type of War

In recent years, U.S. government officials have described terrorism as a new type of war. Terrorism is certainly a form of armed conflict, but it differs from conventional war in three major ways.

1. **The warring parties are not clearly known.** Typically, war is fought between nations known to one another. Terrorism is carried out by organized groups whose identity, leadership, membership, and location may be unknown. Several years after the beginning of the U.S. "war on terrorism," there is still much to learn about the al-Qaeda organization.

2. **The objectives of the terrorist groups are not clearly stated.**   Wars usually are fought with clear objectives, such as gaining territory. The goals of terrorist groups, by contrast, may be far from clear. Although al-Qaeda clearly has the

intention of harming the United States, the precise goals of the September 11 attacks and other terrorist acts have never been clearly stated.

3. **Terrorism is asymmetrical.** Conventional warfare is symmetrical, with opposing powers sending their armies into battle. By contrast, terrorism is an asymmetrical (uneven) conflict in which a small number of attackers use terror and their own willingness to die in order to take on a far more powerful enemy (Ratnesar, 2003).

Strategies for Dealing with Terrorism

The following five strategies for dealing with terrorism are part of official U.S. policy and have widespread support elsewhere in the world: Make no concessions, prosecute terrorists, apply economic sanctions, use military force if necessary, and help friendly nations defend against terrorism. In addition to these responses, nations must address the root causes in order to counter terrorism (Tucker, 1998).

Make No Concessions   Many nations state that they will never give in to terrorist groups. This policy is based on the logic that giving terrorists what they want (by, say, paying ransom, surrendering land, or freeing prisoners) only encourages further terrorism. Some nations say they will not even negotiate with terrorists.

Critics charge that a no-concessions policy has little impact on terrorism. They point out that terrorists, such as those led by Osama bin Laden, are not looking for concessions but simply want to inflict as much damage as possible. In addition, research suggests that the number of terrorist attacks following a refusal to make concessions is about the same as that after concessions took place.

Prosecute Terrorists   A second strategy to deal with terrorists is criminal prosecution. The federal government successfully prosecuted Timothy McVeigh for the Oklahoma City bombing; he was executed in 1999. In 2003, prosecution of Zacarias Moussaoui, the alleged "twentieth hijacker" in the September 11, 2001, attacks, was underway. Prosecuting people engaged in terrorism abroad is far more difficult than in the United States. Thirteen years after the 1988 bombing of Pan Am Flight 103 over Lockerbie, Scotland, only one Libyan intelligence operative was convicted and sentenced to life in prison (Katz, 2003).

Apply Economic Sanctions   The United States has applied *economic sanctions* (trade restrictions) against a number of nations believed to be supporting terrorism, including Libya (1973) and Syria (1986); before the U.S. military intervention, the United Nations applied economic sanctions against Iraq.

Economic sanctions may have a real effect, but bringing about the desired effect may take years. In addition, economic sanctions may harm the civilian population of a country while having little effect on leaders. Sanctions against Iraq were said to cause great hardship to the Iraqi people although they had little effect on the nation's leader, Saddam Hussein.

Use Military Force   A fourth strategy to punish terrorists and their supporters is direct use of military force. In 1986, the United States bombed Libya following terrorist attacks on United States citizens in Europe. After the Gulf War, the United States bombed Iraq for attacking its own Kurdish population; after the September 11, 2001, attacks, the United States went to war in Afghanistan. In 2003, the United States ousted the leadership of Iraq, claiming they were or soon would be engaged in terrorism against this country.

Of course, the use of military force carries great risks because it may provoke further terrorist attacks. In addition, going to war is almost always controversial, as the mixed response (both among the U.S. public and among world leaders) to the use of force by the United States in Iraq clearly showed.

High security, including the presence of armed soldiers, has long been a fact of life in airports around the world. The same is now true of the United States. How has today's heightened security affected you or members of your family?

After winning the military campaign in Iraq, the United States faced a much tougher job—winning the hearts and minds of the Iraqi people. How might you react to a foreign army occupying your country?

Defend against Terrorism   A fifth strategy is to make terrorism harder to accomplish. For more than twenty-five years, the U.S. government has used security measures to protect airports, buildings, and personnel. In addition, the government gathers intelligence data in an effort to identify terrorist groups, monitor their activities, and prevent their attacks. After the September 11, 2001, attacks, the U.S. Congress passed the USA PATRIOT Act, which greatly expanded the power of government officials to monitor the behavior of people in the United States.

Government leaders claim the USA PATRIOT Act has worked, helping to prevent new attacks. Critics reply that giving broad new powers to government threatens people's civil liberties, an effect that may be more harmful to the country than terrorism itself. The Social Policy box takes a closer look at this controversy.

Address the Root Causes of Terrorism   A final issue, which often gets little attention, may be the most important of all. It points to the need to examine the underlying conflicts and conditions that cause people to engage in terrorism in the first place.

This approach does not assume the claims made by terrorists are valid, nor does it excuse terrorists' use of violence against innocent people. But terrorism is a symptom of the passionate belief on the part of less powerful people that they are being treated unfairly. If there were greater opportunity for such people to express their grievances, and if the powerful nations of the world took greater interest in patterns of global inequality and showed greater respect for the cultures of less powerful nations, it seems reasonable to expect that fewer terrorist acts would occur in the first place.

THEORETICAL ANALYSIS: UNDERSTANDING WAR AND TERRORISM

Theory involves organizing facts to gain understanding. In the sections that follow, we apply various theoretical perspectives to the issues of war and terrorism.

Biological Theories of Conflict

We began this chapter noting that some people wonder whether a tendency toward war and violence is part of being human. Some biological scientists claim that it is. Konrad Lorenz (1966, 1981) claims that just as some animals will defend a nest, den, or burrow, humans turn to war to defend their homeland.

Edward O. Wilson (1975) claims that certain types of human behavior, including war and aggression, result from competition for reproductive success. In the case of most animals, males fight with each other for sexual access to females; in the case of humans, however, the process is more complex. Wilson argues that more aggressive men typically achieve higher social standing, which, in turn, is attractive to females. Thus, Wilson continues, more aggressive men are more likely than less aggressive men to reproduce. Over hundreds of generations, this fact means that genetic traits favoring aggression are likely to become more common in the human species.

Critical evaluation.   Most sociologists are highly skeptical of claims of natural aggressiveness in humans. They point out that humans make choices about their behavior and are not guided by biological instincts the way other animals are. According to sociologists, culture and social structure have the greatest influence on human behavior. These factors, rather than biology, explain why some societies are more warlike than others. If war is natural to humans, why do nations have to go to such great lengths to convince their people to go to war (Montagu, 1976)?

Social Policy — The USA PATRIOT Act: Are We More Secure? Less Free?

THE USA PATRIOT ACT (Uniting and Strengthening America by Providing Appropriate Tools Required to Intercept and Obstruct Terrorism) was passed by Congress and signed into law by President George W. Bush at the end of October 2001, less than two months after the September 11 terrorist attacks.

The complex law was born out of fear that the United States was likely to be the target of future terrorist attacks and needed to better defend itself. In practice, the new law gives expanded powers to law enforcement officials here and intelligence agencies working abroad so that they can more effectively battle terrorists.

Under the new law, law enforcement can track suspected terrorists by monitoring e-mail, checking visits to suspicious Web sites, tapping phone lines, more closely inspecting bank accounts, and even keeping track of the books people check out of libraries. Supporters of the PATRIOT Act—and polls show a majority of U.S. adults are behind the measure—believe that it will make the country more secure.

Critics disagree. First, they doubt that these new powers are necessary to fight terrorism. Second, they claim that expanding government powers has a serious consequence: reducing freedom. "We all want to fight and win the war against terrorism," says one former Republican congressman, "but there is absolutely no need to sacrifice civil liberties." The thought of the government monitoring the telephone calls, e-mails, Web surfing, and reading habits of people across the country raises great concern among liberals and a number of conservatives. Many fear that the law allows the government to silence legitimate dissent.

Both supporters and opponents of the PATRIOT Act may be partly right. The new law probably does empower officials to better defend the country against terrorism, but the law is just as likely to reduce personal freedoms.

ISSUES AND EXERCISES

1. Do you think that defending national security means having to give up some personal freedoms? Why or why not?

2. Would you mind if government officials read your e-mail or listened in on your telephone conversations to be sure you were not planning to engage in terrorism? Explain your position.

3. Use Research Navigator™ to learn more about the USA PATRIOT Act. (See instructions on page 25; keyword: "PATRIOT Act")

Sources: Doyle (2002), American Library Association (2003), Center for Constitutional Rights (2003), and Electronic Frontier Foundation (2003).

Structural-Functional Analysis: The Functions of Conflict

The structural-functional approach highlights the functions that war and other conflict have for society. Although war has obvious costs in terms of the loss of lives and property, it may accomplish important goals.

Two centuries ago, Prussian military theorist Carl von Clausewitz (1780–1831) studied the functions of warfare. War, he stated, is simply politics carried on by other means. Nations go to war to achieve political goals, such as gaining land or increasing their international prestige. Therefore, von Clausewitz (1968, orig. 1832) cautioned, nations should go to war only when the expected gains outweighed the likely costs of fighting and when the nation could be sure of winning.

Sociologists point out that war continues to have important political consequences. Most of the world's territorial boundaries have been established by wars. Similarly, war and even terrorism have played a major part in creating new nations, including the United States. Throughout the twentieth century, war and terrorism have been strategies used by ethnic and religious minorities seeking their own nation states (Kaldor, 1999; United Nations, 2003).

Other functions of military conflict include uniting the population of a nation, creating tens of thousands of jobs, and greatly expanding the economy. In addition, many of the technological developments

Critical Thinking   Women in the Military: An Equal Right to Kill?

ALTHOUGH MOST PEOPLE THINK OF THE MILITARY as a man's world, women have served in the U.S. military since colonial times. At the beginning of World War II, women represented 2 percent of the U.S. military forces. By the time of the Persian Gulf War in 1991, women were almost 7 percent of the U.S. military. In this war, five of the 148 U.S. deaths were women; in the War in Iraq, of 510 casualties (as of January 2004) four were women (Roy, 2003).

The share of women in uniform has continued to rise. Today, women represent 15 percent of U.S. armed forces personnel. Even so, the Coast Guard is the only branch of the service to make every assignment available to both women and men; at the other extreme, the U.S. Marine Corps makes just one-third of assignments available to women and limits women's role in combat.

Those who favor denying women full access to military jobs argue that, on average, women have less physical strength than men. But in today's high-technology wars, physical strength plays a smaller and smaller role in combat. Mental strength may be more important to today's soldiers, and data show that women in uniform are better educated and more intelligent than their male counterparts. Moreover, in the age of high technology, it is hard to draw a line between combat and noncombat personnel. For example, a (combat) soldier may safely fire a missile at an enemy position miles away, whereas a (noncombatant) team operating a helicopter may come under fire as they carry the wounded from a battlefield.

In the end, the greatest resistance to opening more combat assignments to women is the traditional view of women as *nurturers,* that is, as people who give life and help others. As long as U.S. culture defines women in this way (and as long as we engage in wars), it is likely that the military will resist putting women in harm's way.

ISSUES AND EXERCISES

1. Do you think the fact that, on average, women have less physical strength than men is important in today's military?

2. How much of the media attention directed at private Jessica Lynch's capture and rescue during the War in Iraq resulted from the fact that she was a woman?

3. What about the fact that women in combat will be taken as prisoners of war? Do you think enemy soldiers view women POWs differently from men who are POWs? Why? What about U.S. soldiers?

Sources: Based on Segal & Hansen (1992), Wilcox (1992), and Kaminer (1997).

---

we take for granted today, including the interstate highways, high-speed jet travel, cellular telephones, and the Internet, were the products of military research. Finally, war has played a part in improving the social standing of women and other minorities. It was during World War II, for example, that African Americans and women of all colors first gained access to good jobs in factories turning out war equipment (Flexner, 1975; Chafe, 1977; Galbraith, 1985). The Critical Thinking box takes a look at the place of women in today's armed forces.

Critical evaluation. Critics of the structural-functional approach point out that the von Clausewitz thesis makes far less sense today, because modern warfare has the power to destroy whole nations, and even the entire planet. In addition, by pointing out the positive functions of war and other violent conflict, this approach downplays the tremendous costs of war, including loss of life and property and damage to the environment.

Symbolic-Interaction Analysis: The Meanings of Conflict

The symbolic-interaction approach focuses attention on the meanings people attach to engaging in war and other violent conflict. We already noted the importance of meanings in the contrasting definitions of one side's "terrorists" as the other side's "freedom fighters."

In general, nations use symbols and meanings to convince a population that war is in their best interest. Societies use symbols to define their own cause as just, making claims that their soldiers march "with God on their side." In addition, societies demonize the enemy. A generation ago, President Ronald Reagan justified greater military spending by painting the Soviet Union as an "evil empire" that was a danger to the entire world; recently, President George W. Bush characterized Iran, Iraq, and North Korea as an "axis of evil."

On the individual level, the military trains recruits to view the enemy as less than human. In the Vietnam War, for example, many U.S. soldiers learned to regard their Vietnamese counterparts as "gooks." Killing a dehumanized enemy is, of course, much easier (Said, 1981; Aditjondro, 2000).

Critical evaluation. The symbolic-interaction approach shows us that war is a battle not only of armies but of symbols as competing sides try to define themselves as just and their opponents as unjust. But this approach says little about the role of power in international conflict. The side that turns out to be "right" typically is the side that is stronger. And, within a population, which categories of people declare wars? Which categories benefit from war? These questions turn our attention to the social-conflict approach.

Social-Conflict Analysis: Inequality and Conflict

Social-conflict theory highlights the link between war and social inequality. Karl Marx, one of the architects of the social-conflict approach, explained that political leaders are servants of the capitalist class, those who own the means of production. Capitalists demand ever-increasing profits, which they get from new sources of raw materials, new products, and new markets. Thus, in Marx's day capitalists supported colonial expansion abroad, which led rich nations in Europe to conquer and control most of the world.

Today, although formal colonialism is largely gone from the world, the pattern of foreign control remains. Rich nations, including the United States, use their military power to ensure the success of the global capitalist economy (Wallerstein, 1979; Hudson, 1992; Tabb, 1992). From this point of view, the War in Iraq is less about helping that country (and Muslim nations around the world) secure freedom and justice than it is about opening more of the world to multinational corporations. Furthermore, the rich are the primary beneficiaries of war, and ordinary people make up most of the soldiers and sailors who do the fighting (Halbfinger & Holmes, 2003).

As noted earlier in this chapter, the military industry contributes to the capitalist economy. The U.S. military budget goes a long way to push up corporate profits. An arms race may or may not make the nation safer, but there is no doubt that developing and producing new weapons and military technology is highly profitable for those who control the U.S. economy (Mills, 1956).

And what of terrorism? Historically, poor nations have been no match for the military might of the colonial powers. For that reason, groups opposing colonial rule must act outside the established political system. As noted earlier, terrorism can be an effective way for less powerful people to focus the world's attention on what they consider to be injustice. In short, war is the means by which powerful nations dominate the globe; terrorism is the means by which the powerless fight back (Hoffman, 1998; Kaldor, 1999; Lesser et al., 1999; Reeve, 1999; Stern, 1999; Zanini, 1999).

Critical evaluation. By linking war or terrorism to social inequality, social-conflict analysis helps to explain ongoing support for militarism in the United States even during times of peace. One limitation of the claim that capitalism is the major cause of war is that socialist nations have also engaged in war. For example, the Soviet Union used military force to gain and maintain control of Eastern Europe at the end of World War II, just as China has directed its military power against Vietnam, Cambodia, and Tibet. A broad view of history shows that wars break out not only because of economic concerns but also as the result of religious beliefs and ethnic pride.

POLITICS AND WAR: CONSTRUCTING PROBLEMS AND DEFINING SOLUTIONS

Theory provides useful insights about war and terrorism, but the positions people take on problems and their solutions reflect their values and politics. In the following sections we present conservative, liberal, and radical views of war and terrorism.

Conservatives: Strength Means Security

Believing that this country represents good in the world and that the United States has enemies abroad, conservatives generally favor military strength. Similar to their "law and order" view that a strong police

Conservatives regard the United States as a force for good in the world; from this perspective, the War in Iraq is an effort to spread democracy. Liberals are more cautious in this regard; they voice greater support for multinational efforts led by the United Nations. Radicals see militarism as a strategy to extend capitalism; they typically oppose the use of U.S. military power.

force is needed to fight crime at home, conservatives believe that a strong military protects the national interest against hostile forces abroad.

During the cold war, which lasted from the end of World War II until the collapse of the Soviet Union in 1991, conservatives supported increased military expenditures in the belief that nothing less than the freedom of the United States was at stake. In 2003, as the war in Iraq continued to unfold, President George Bush pushed military expenditures higher, claiming that a strong U.S. military presence in the world is as vital for extending freedom to people living in countries that lack democracy as it is for ensuring the security of the United States.

Conservatives also take a hard line against terrorism. In general, they paint those who use violence against innocent people as criminals who are opposed to freedom and economic development in the world, and they think the United States should do whatever is necessary to identify those responsible and bring them to justice. President Bush made the "war on terrorism" the defining goal of his administration. He and other conservatives believe that the most effective path to peace is using military strength to prevent terrorism and to encourage the spread of democracy abroad.

Liberals: The Dangers of Militarism

Liberals agree with conservatives that the United States needs to be able to defend itself from attack. For this reason, liberals also support a strong military. However, liberals typically do not support the same degree of miliary spending as conservatives do. One reason is that, as liberals see it, the United States has not always used its military wisely. In the 2004 presidential campaign, John Kerry and other Democratic candidates spoke out in opposition to the War in Iraq, claiming that this invasion has turned world opinion against the United States and encouraged even greater terrorism.

A second disagreement centers on how a society should use its limited resources. Whereas conservatives tend to make military spending a top priority, liberals are keenly aware that military spending takes money away from education, health care, and other important programs. In short, liberals see militarism as draining away resources that could be used to provide universal health insurance, reduce poverty, and improve rundown schools. Therefore, liberals typically offer strong support for arms reduction.

When it comes to international tensions as well as terrorism, liberals believe that the first response should be diplomacy and negotiations rather than the deployment of troops. For this reason, liberals emphasize the importance of international efforts at building peace, such as the work of the United Nations.

Radicals: The Need for Justice

Radicals on the political left believe that the root cause of war, terrorism, and militarism is inequality. Given the enormous gulf between the rich and the poor around the world, they ask, why should we expect people to live in peace? Radicals claim that the United States pours money into militarism not so much for national defense but so that it can

LEFT TO RIGHT

THE POLITICS OF WAR AND TERRORISM

	RADICAL LEFT VIEW	LIBERAL VIEW	CONSERVATIVE VIEW
WHAT IS THE PROBLEM?	The basic problem is capitalism, which encourages militarism in order to fuel corporate profits at home and to defend the capitalist economy around the world.	There is a need for defense, but militarism itself can be a problem because an arms buildup provokes conflict; nuclear proliferation raises the risk of nuclear war; terrorism poses dangers to the United States.	The problem is that some nations and groups are hostile to the United States; nuclear arms development by these nations threatens the security of the United States; terrorists engage in periodic attacks against the United States.
WHAT IS THE SOLUTION?	The solution to militarism is ending the domination of the world by rich nations; eliminating capitalism will end the need for ongoing militarism as well as terrorism.	Reasonable military strength is necessary, but the United States should seek arms reductions and rely on diplomacy as much as possible. Addressing the grievances of less powerful people will reduce terrorism.	Maintaining military strength and strong counterterrorism measures will encourage peace and ensure the security of the United States.

Join the debate . . .

1. Looking over the three political perspectives on war and terrorism, do you see any areas of agreement? If so, what are they?
2. From the point of view of each of the three political perspectives, what would be the proper role of the U.S. military around the world?
3. Which of the three political analyses of war and terrorism included here do you find most convincing? Why?

operate as a global police force to protect U.S. interests around the world. This high level of spending on militarism also keeps corporate profits high.

In practice, then, the United States engages in military action when any other nation threatens the operation of the world's capitalist economy. Radicals point to the economic boycott of Cuba after that country's socialist revolution in 1959; hostility toward the socialist Sandinistas in Nicaragua; the 1991 Gulf War, declared when the Iraqi army threatened this nation's oil supply in Kuwait; and the 2003 War in Iraq and the larger "war on terrorism," both seen as efforts to stabilize the world and allow expansion of corporate influence. U.S. leaders may justify wars on moral grounds, but radicals claim that the real motive is little more than greed.

Given this critical view of U.S. intentions, it is not surprising that radicals tend to be sympathetic toward the efforts of those around the world who seek change. From this point of view, terrorism is a response to powerlessness; as long as a handful of

powerful nations rule the world, we should expect some groups to strike back.

In sum, radicals believe that war and terrorism will continue until the world moves toward greater social equality. Thus, radicals call for a national and international redistribution of wealth in favor of the poor majority. The Left to Right table summarizes the conservative, liberal, and radical views of war and terrorism.

GOING ON FROM HERE

Albert Einstein, whose discoveries in physics led to the development of nuclear weapons, once observed, "The unleashed power of the atom has changed everything save our modes of thinking, and we thus drift toward unparalleled catastrophe." Given humanity's history of warfare and the stockpiles of nuclear weapons on the planet, what are the odds that the twenty-first century will pass without a nuclear war? No one can say for sure, but this chapter points out that the world has learned a great deal more about making war than making peace. As we look to the future, the fact that more and more nations will have nuclear weapons and other weapons of mass destruction means that even local conflicts could threaten the entire planet.

As we move ahead, winning peace may well depend on implementing three strategies. First, the nations of the world must make significant efforts at arms control, with the goal of greatly reducing the number of weapons of mass destruction. The United States and the Russian Federation have made good progress already. A challenge to this goal is that some nations (North Korea, for example) currently do not permit any inspections of their arms production. Second, controlling nuclear proliferation is equally important. No nation can be secure as long as nuclear weapons continue to spread around the world. The third and final strategy—clearly the most difficult of all—is to address the underlying causes of war and terrorism. In part, this requires the leaders of all nations, rich and poor alike, to demonstrate genuine concern for the well-being of people everywhere, especially the poor. In addition, all world nations must support a forum (whether it be the United Nations or some other organization) in which nations can gather to present and discuss their grievances, with the goal of replacing violence with negotiation and diplomacy.

In the end, the planet's prospects for peace may hinge on real change that reduces the exploitation of poor people by elites. The greatest challenge on the road to peace may be confronting the tremendous problem of poverty and hunger (the focus of Chapter 16, "Population and Global Inequality"). The goal must be to bring about economic development in regions of the world where, at present, widespread suffering prevents political stability. There is every reason to think that, given the will to succeed, world leaders can accomplish this goal. How the world responds to this challenge will shape the lives of us all.

CHAPTER SUMMARY

1. War has occurred throughout human history. During the twentieth century, the development of weapons of mass destruction made war far more deadly.

2. The causes of war include perceived threats, cultural or religious differences, political objectives, moral objectives, the desire to gain wealth and power, the desire to turn a population's attention away from domestic social problems, and the absence of alternatives for resolving disputes.

3. Each year the world spends more than $1 trillion on militarism; the U.S. military budget was $376 billion in 2003. The arms race and, more recently, the "war on terrorism" have pushed U.S. military spending upward.

4. The economic costs of war go beyond military spending to include damage to a society's entire infrastructure. Money used for war is taken away from other areas that benefit a population. The human toll in war has gone up because of more deadly weapons and the strategy of total war, which greatly increases the number of civilian casualties.

5. Suffering from war continues after the end of hostilities in the form of post-traumatic stress disorder. In all, 2.7 million U.S. veterans suffer from war-related disabilities; of these, 170,000 are totally disabled.

6. The danger of war rose dramatically with the development of nuclear weapons at the end of World War II. A single nuclear bomb can destroy an entire city. Even with recent arms reductions, there are still some 17,000 nuclear weapons, which is enough destructive power to end life on the planet.

7. Given the horrors of all-out war, humanity must use strategies for peace. These include deterrence, high-technology defense, arms control, and resolving underlying conflicts.

8. Terrorism involves unlawful and typically random acts of violence in the pursuit of political goals. State-sponsored terrorism refers to training and support given by one country to terrorists who operate in another country. Repressive state terrorism is the use of terror and violence to repress political opposition within a country.

9. In 2002, there were 199 terrorist attacks worldwide, killing 725 people; most terrorist attacks target the United States.

10. The costs of terrorism include injury to some 20,000 people a year worldwide, as well as the expense of antiterrorism measures. However, the greatest costs of terrorism may lie in making peace harder to achieve.

11. Strategies for dealing with terrorism include prosecution, a policy of making no concessions, the application of economic sanctions to nations that support terrorism, the use of military force, defense against terrorism, and addressing the underlying causes of terrorism.

12. Although some biological theories argue that aggression is natural in human beings, most sociologists are skeptical of such claims, pointing to the greater importance of culture and social structure.

13. A structural-functional approach views war as a strategy for pursuing political goals, which typically unifies a population and encourages economic growth and technological innovation.

14. The symbolic-interaction approach highlights the use of symbols and meanings to mobilize a population toward war. Typically, both sides describe their enemy as evil to justify hostilities. Similarly, soldiers learn to dehumanize the enemy, which makes killing easier.

15. The social-conflict approach highlights how both war and terrorism are linked to social inequality. Karl Marx saw militarism as fueling the capitalist economy at home and expanding the reach of capitalism abroad.

16. Pointing to forces in the world hostile to the United States, conservatives favor a strong defense. Conservatives supported the arms race and favor achieving peace through strength. From this point of view, terrorism amounts to criminal acts opposing freedom.

17. Liberals support military defense of the United States but caution that a military buildup can provoke the very conflict it is intended to prevent. In addition, liberals point out that spending on militarism takes money away from various social programs that benefit the population. Liberals generally support diplomacy as a way to address the problems that lead to terrorism.

18. Radicals on the political left link war and militarism to social inequality. The United States and other rich nations use their military power to defend their economic interests and to support the global capitalist economy. From this point of view, terrorism is a form of rebellion, one way poor and powerless people can make their suffering known.

KEY CONCEPTS

war (p. 447) violent conflict between nations or organized groups

peace (p. 447) the absence of violent conflict

weapons of mass destruction (p. 448) weapons with the capacity to kill many thousands of people at one time

military-industrial complex (p. 450) a political alliance involving the federal government, the military, and the defense industries

total war (p. 450) deadly conflict that targets both population centers and military targets

concentration camps (p. 450) centers where prisoners are confined for purposes of state security, exploitation, punishment, or execution

war crime (p. 451) an offense against the law of war as established by international agreements and international law

nuclear weapons (p. 453) bombs that use nuclear reactions to generate enormous destructive force

nuclear proliferation (p. 453) the acquisition of nuclear weapon technology by more and more nations

deterrence (p. 454) a strategy to keep peace based on the threat of retaliation (also known as *mutual assured destruction* [*MAD*])

arms control (p. 455) international agreements on the development, testing, production, and deployment of weapons

terrorism (p. 456) unlawful, typically random acts of violence or the threat of such violence used by an individual, group, or government to achieve a political goal

state-sponsored terrorism (p. 456) the practice by one government of providing money, weapons, and training to terrorists who engage in violence in another nation

repressive state terrorism (p. 457) government use of ruthless violence within its own borders to repress political opposition

THINKING CRITICALLY: QUESTIONS AND ISSUES

1. Consider this statement: "Several centuries ago, war involved soldiers; today, those most affected by war are civilians." Do you agree or disagree? Why? Use material from this chapter to develop your response.

2. In your opinion, why has military spending in the United States risen rapidly since 1950? Do you support a high level of military spending? Why or why not?

3. What factors do you think are the major causes of war? Based on your list, what are the most promising paths to world peace?

4. This chapter has described terrorism as a form of warfare used by less powerful groups against those they perceive as oppressing them. Do you agree with this characterization? Based on your understanding of terrorism, what steps would you suggest to eliminate terrorism in the world?

GETTING INVOLVED: LEARNING EXERCISES

1. Speak to several people you know about their military experiences. For those who were in combat, ask whether the experience changed them and changed their attitudes toward war.

2. Contact a military recruiter in your area. See what you can learn about the categories of people (consider gender, age, race, ethnicity, and social class) who are most likely to join the military.

3. Two older films—*Fail-Safe* and *On the Beach*—were made at the height of the arms race between the United States and the Soviet Union. Try to find a copy of one or both films and watch to see the results of runaway militarism. For a humorous look at the arms race and dangers of nuclear war, watch *Dr. Strangelove*.

4. What student or community organizations on or near campus oppose war? Identify one or two and try to learn what these organizations do. What are their positions regarding terrorism?

GETTING CONNECTED: USEFUL WEB LINKS

http://www.prenhall.com/macionis
Visit the interactive Companion Website™ that accompanies this text. Begin by clicking on the cover of your book. You will find a chapter-by-chapter study guide, practice tests, suggested Web links, and links to other relevant material.

http://www.amnesty.org
Amnesty International is a human rights organization that offers information about political repression and war crimes. What are some of its objectives?

http://www.didyouknow.com/conflicts.htm
This Web site provides a current overview of armed conflicts throughout the world.

http://www.state.gov/www/coalition
http://www.usis.usemb.se/terror/index.html
These two Web sites operated by the U.S. government provide information about national and international terrorism. What trends can you identify?

http://www.coara.or.jp/~ryoji/abomb/e-index.html
At this Japanese site, you can read an eyewitness account of the dropping of a nuclear bomb on the city of Hiroshima in 1945.

http://www.sipri.se/
The Stockholm International Peace Research Institute studies both war and peace.

GETTING STARTED ON YOUR OWN: RESEARCH NAVIGATOR™

Follow the instructions found on page 25 of this text to access the features of Research Navigator™. Once at the Web site, enter your Login Name and Password. Then, to use the **Content Select** database, enter keywords such as "war," "arms race," and "terrorism," and the search engine will supply relevant and recent scholarly and popular press publications. Use the *New York Times* **Search-by-Subject Archive** to find recent news articles related to sociology and the **Link Library** feature to find relevant Web links organized by the key terms associated with this chapter.

GLOSSARY

abortion (p. 206)   the deliberate termination of a pregnancy

acid rain (p. 433)   precipitation, made acidic by air pollution, that destroys plant and animal life

activity theory (p. 128)   the idea that people enhance personal satisfaction in old age by keeping a high level of social activity

acute disease (p. 247)   an illness that strikes suddenly

addiction (p. 222)   a physical or psychological craving for a drug

affirmative action (p. 75)   policies intended to improve the social standing of minorities subject to historical prejudice and discrimination

ageism (p. 117)   prejudice and discrimination directed against the elderly

age stratification (p. 121)   social inequality among various age categories within a society

alcoholism (p. 226)   an addiction to alcohol

alienation (Marx) (p. 303)   the experience of isolation and misery resulting from powerlessness in the workplace

alienation (Weber) (p. 304)   the depersonalization of the workplace, and of society in general, caused by modern society's rational focus on efficiency

anti-institutional violence (p. 166)   violence directed against the government in violation of the law

arms control (p. 455)   international agreements on the development, testing, production, and deployment of weapons

asexuality (p. 195)   the absence of sexual attraction to people of either sex

assimilation (p. 62)   the process by which minorities gradually adopt cultural patterns from the majority population

authoritarianism (p. 277)   a political system that denies popular participation in government

battered child syndrome (p. 172)   a pattern of physical and psychological injury to a child caused by the action (or neglect) of another person

bilingual education (p. 358)   a policy of offering most classes in the students' native language while also teaching them English

bisexuality (p. 195)   sexual attraction to people of both sexes

blaming the victim (p. 44)   finding the cause of a social problem in the behavior of people who suffer from it

blended families (p. 334)   families in which children have some combination of biological parents and step-parents

capitalism (p. 274)   an economic system in which natural resources and the means of producing goods and services are privately owned

caregiving (p. 120)   informal and unpaid care provided to a dependent person by family members, other relatives, or friends

charter schools (p. 363)   public schools that are given more freedom to try out new policies and programs

chronic disease (p. 247)   an illness that has a long-term development

claims making (p. 5)   the process of trying to convince the public (and important public officials) that a particular issue or situation should be defined as a social problem

codependency (p. 229)   behavior on the part of others that helps a substance abuser continue

cohabitation (p. 325)   the sharing of a household by an unmarried couple

colonialism (p. 411)   the process by which some nations enrich themselves through political and economic control of other nations

community-based corrections (p. 152)   correctional programs located in society at large rather than behind prison walls

concentration camps (p. 450)   centers where prisoners are confined for purposes of state security, exploitation, punishment, or execution

conglomerate (p. 280)   a giant corporation composed of many smaller corporations

corporate crime (p. 146)   an illegal act committed by a corporation or others acting on its behalf

corporations (p. 278)   businesses with a legal existence, including rights and liabilities, apart from those of their members

crime (p. 136)   the violation of the criminal laws enacted by federal, state, or local governments

crime against persons (p. 136)   crime that involves violence or the threat of violence against others

crime against property (p. 136)   crime that involves theft of property belonging to others

criminal justice system (p. 148)   society's organized means to enforce the law through the use of police, courts, and prisons

criminal recidivism (p. 151)   subsequent offenses by people previously convicted of crimes

crude birth rate (p. 396)   the number of live births in a given year for every thousand people in a population

crude death rate (p. 397)   the number of deaths in a given year for every thousand people in a population

cultural capital (p. 46)   skills, values, attitudes, and schooling that increase a person's chances of success

culture (p. 2)   a way of life including widespread values (about what is good and bad), beliefs (about what is true), and behavior (what people do every day)

culture of poverty (p. 43)   cultural patterns that make poverty a way of life

decriminalization (p. 236)   removing the current criminal penalties that punish the manufacturing, sale, and personal use of drugs

deindustrialization (p. 300)   the decline of industrial production that occurred in the United States after about 1950

deinstitutionalization (p. 262)   the release of people from mental hospitals into local communities

democracy (p. 277)   a political system in which power is exercised by the people as a whole

demographic transition theory (p. 403)   a thesis linking demographic changes to a society's level of technological development

demography (p. 396)   the study of human population

dependency (p. 223)   a state in which a person's body has adjusted to regular use of a drug

depressants (p. 225)   drugs that slow the operation of the central nervous system

deterrence (p. 150)   using punishment to discourage further crime

deterrence (p. 454)   a strategy to keep peace based on the threat of retaliation (also known as *mutual assured destruction [MAD]*)

direct-fee system (p. 252)   a medical care system in which patients or their insurers pay directly for the services of physicians and hospitals

disability (p. 258)   a physical or mental condition that limits everyday activities

discrimination (p. 74)   unequal treatment of various categories of people

disengagement theory (p. 127)   the idea that modern societies operate more smoothly by removing people from positions of responsibility as they enter old age

drug (p. 219)   any chemical substance other than food or water that affects the mind or body

ecologically sustainable culture (p. 441)   a way of life that meets the needs of the present generation without threatening the environmental legacy of future generations

ecology (p. 424)   the study of how living organisms interact with the natural environment

economic issues (p. 22)   political debates about how society should distribute material resources

economy (p. 273)   the social institution that organizes the production, distribution, and consumption of goods and services

ecosystem (p. 424)   a system composed of the interaction of all living organisms and their natural environment

education (p. 345)   the social institution by which society transmits knowledge—including basic facts and job skills, as well as cultural norms and values—to its members

enterprise zones (p. 388)   areas in the inner city that attract new businesses with the promise of tax relief

environmental deficit (p. 426)   profound and long-term harm to the environment caused by humanity's focus on short-term material affluence

environmental racism (p. 437)   a pattern of discrimination in which environmental hazards are greatest for poor people, especially minorities

epidemic (p. 248)   a disease that spreads rapidly through a population

ethnicity (p. 58)   a shared cultural heritage, which typically involves common ancestors, language, and religion

Eurocentrism (p. 74)   the practice of using European (particularly English) cultural standards to judge everyone

euthanasia (p. 124)   assisting in the death of a person suffering from an incurable disease

experiment (p. 16)   a method by which a researcher investigates cause-and-effect relationships under highly controlled conditions

extended family (p. 324)   parents and children and also grandparents, aunts, uncles, and cousins who often live close to one another and operate as a family unit

families of affinity (p. 324)   people with or without legal or blood ties who feel they belong together and want to define themselves as a family

family (p. 324)   a social institution that unites individuals into cooperative groups that care for members, regulate sexual relations, and oversee the bearing and raising of children

family violence (p. 171)   emotional, physical, or sexual abuse of one family member by another

felony (p. 136)   a more serious crime punishable by at least one year in prison

feminism (p. 13)   a political movement that seeks the social equality of women and men

feminism (p. 101)   the study of gender with the goal of changing society to make women and men equal

feminization of poverty (p. 34)   the fact that women represent an increasing share of the poor

fertility (p. 396)   the incidence of childbearing in a country's population

field research (participant observation) (p. 16) a method by which researchers observe people while joining them in their everyday activities

forcible rape (p. 170)   the carnal knowledge of a female forcibly and against her will

functional illiteracy (p. 352)   the inability to read and write or do basic arithmetic well enough to carry out daily responsibilities

Gemeinschaft (p. 385)   a type of social organization in which people are closely bound by kinship and tradition

gender (p. 86)   the personal traits and life chances a society attaches to being female or male

gender gap (p. 284)   a tendency for women and men to hold different opinions about certain issues and to support different candidates

gender stratification (p. 93)   the unequal distribution of wealth, power, and privilege between men and women

genocide (p. 60)   the systematic killing of one category of people by another

gerontocracy (p. 112)   a social system that gives a society's oldest members the most wealth, power, and prestige

gerontology (p. 112)   a branch of the social sciences dealing with aging and the elderly

Gesellschaft (p. 385)   a type of social organization in which people interact on the basis of self-interest

glass ceiling (p. 94)   subtle discrimination that effectively blocks the movement of women into the highest positions in organizations

globalization (p. 300)   the expansion of economic activity around the world with little regard for national borders

government (p. 274)   a formal organization that directs the political life of a society

hate crime (p. 145)   a criminal offense against a person, property, or society motivated by the offender's bias against a race, religion, disability, sexual orientation, or ethnicity or national origin

health (p. 246)   a state of complete physical, mental, and social well-being

health maintenance organizations (HMOs) (p. 254)   private insurance organizations that provide medical care to subscribers for a fixed fee

heterosexism (p. 212)   bias that treats heterosexuality as the norm while stigmatizing anyone who differs from this norm as "queer"

heterosexuality (p. 195)   sexual attraction to someone of the other sex

hidden curriculum (p. 363)   explicit and subtle presentations of political or cultural ideas in the classroom that support the status quo

homelessness (p. 38)   the plight of poor people who lack shelter and live primarily on the streets

homophobia (p. 198)   an aversion or hostility to people thought to be gay, lesbian, or bisexual

homosexuality (p. 195)   sexual attraction to someone of the same sex

hospice (p. 126)   homelike care that provides physical and emotional comfort to dying people and their families

in vitro (that is, "in glass") **fertilization** (p. 336) uniting eggs and sperm in a laboratory

income (p. 28)   salary or wages from a job plus earnings from investments or any other source

infant mortality rate (pp. 246, 397)   the number of babies who die in their first year of life per thousand live births

institutional discrimination (p. 74)   discrimination that is built into the operation of social institutions, including the economy, schools, and the legal system

institutional racism (p. 73)   racism at work in the operation of social institutions, including the economy, schools, hospitals, the military, and the criminal justice system

institutional violence (p. 166)   violence carried out by government representatives under the law

interlocking directorates (p. 280)   social networks of people who serve as directors of several corporations at the same time

intersection theory (p. 46)   the investigation of the interplay of race, class, and gender, often resulting in multiple dimensions of disadvantage

juvenile delinquency (p. 144)   the violation of the law by young people

kinship (p. 324)   a social bond, typically based on blood, marriage, or adoption, that joins individuals into families

labeling theory (p. 157)   the assertion that crime and all forms of rule-breaking result not so much from what people do as from how others respond to those actions

labor unions (p. 309)   worker organizations that seek to improve wages and working conditions through various strategies, including negotiations and strikes

law (p. 136)   norms formally created through a society's political system

libertarians (p. 240)   people who favor the greatest individual freedom possible

life course (p. 112)   the socially constructed stages that people pass through as they live out their lives

life expectancy (pp. 133, 247)   the number of years, on average, people in a society can expect to live

literacy (p. 346)   the ability to read, write, and do basic arithmetic

lobbying (p. 280)   the efforts of special-interest groups and their representatives to influence government officials

McDonaldization (p. 304)   defining work in terms of four principles: efficiency, predictability, uniformity, and automation

magnet schools (p. 363)   public schools that offer special facilities and programs in pursuit of educational excellence

mainstreaming (p. 359)   integrating special students into the overall educational program

manslaughter (p. 167)   the unlawful, unintentional killing of one person by another

marriage (p. 324)   a lawful relationship—expected to be lasting—involving economic cooperation, sexual activity, and, usually, child-bearing

Marxist political-economy model (p. 288)   an analysis that sees the concentration of wealth and power in society as resulting from capitalism

mass murder (p. 168)   the intentional, unlawful killing of more than four people at one time and place

matriarchy (p. 86)   a social pattern in which females dominate males

mechanical solidarity (p. 385)   social bonds based on common sentiments and shared moral values

megalopolis (p. 374)   a vast urban region containing a number of cities and their surrounding suburbs

mental disorder (p. 259)   a change in thinking, mood, or behavior that causes distress and reduces a person's ability to function in everyday life

meritocracy (p. 43)   a system of social inequality in which social standing corresponds to personal ability and effort

military-industrial complex (pp. 287, 450)   a political alliance involving the federal government, the military, and the defense industries

minority (p. 59)   any category of people, distinguished by physical or cultural traits, that a society subjects to disadvantages

misdemeanor (p. 136)   a less serious crime punishable by less than one year in prison

modernization theory (p. 409)   a model of economic and social development that explains global inequality in terms of technological and cultural differences between societies

monarchy (p. 277)   a political system in which a single family rules from generation to generation

monopoly (p. 279)   the domination of an entire market by a single company

mortality (p. 397)   the incidence of death in a country's population

multiculturalism (p. 73)   educational programs designed to recognize cultural diversity in the United States and to promote respect for all cultural traditions

murder (p. 167)   the unlawful, intentional killing of one person by another

natural environment (p. 424)   the Earth's surface and atmosphere, including air, water, soil, and other resources necessary to sustain living organisms

neocolonialism (p. 411)   a new form of economic exploitation that involves the operation of multinational corporations rather than direct political control by foreign governments

norms (p. 136)   rules and expectations by which a society guides the behavior of its members

nuclear family (p. 324)   one or two parents and their children

nuclear proliferation (p. 453)   the acquisition of nuclear weapon technology by more and more nations

nuclear weapons (p. 453)   bombs that use nuclear reactions to generate enormous destructive force

oligopoly (p. 280)   the domination of the market by a few companies

organic solidarity (p. 385)   social bonds based on specialization and mutual interdependence

organized crime (p. 146)   a business operation that supplies illegal goods and services

patriarchy (p. 86)   a social pattern in which males dominate females

peace (p. 447)   the absence of violent conflict

plea bargaining (p. 149)   a negotiation in which the state reduces a defendant's charge in exchange for a guilty plea

pluralism (p. 62)   a state in which people of all racial and ethnic categories have roughly equal social standing

pluralist model (p. 287)   an analysis of the political system that sees power widely distributed among various groups and organizations in a society

political action committees (PACs) (p. 281)   organizations formed by special-interest groups to raise and spend money in support of political goals

political economy (p. 278)   the economic and political life of a nation or a region of the world

political spectrum (p. 21)   a continuum representing a range of political attitudes

politics (p. 273)   the social institution that guides a society's decision making about how to live

pornography (p. 198)   words or images intended to cause sexual arousal

poverty gap (p. 32) the difference between the actual income of the typical poor household and the official poverty line

poverty line (p. 32) a standard set by the U.S. government for the purpose of counting the poor

power-elite model (p. 287) an analysis of the political system that sees power as concentrated among a small elite

prejudice (p. 69) any rigid and irrational generalization about an entire category of people

prenatal care (p. 257) health care for women during pregnancy

primary labor market (p. 301) occupations that provide good pay and extensive benefits to workers

progressive taxation (p. 29) a policy that raises tax rates as income increases

prostitution (p. 203) the selling of sexual services

psychotherapy (p. 262) an approach to mental health in which patients talk with trained professionals to gain insight into the cause of their problems

public housing (p. 377) high-density apartment buildings constructed to house poor people

queer theory (p. 212) a body of theory and research that challenges the heterosexual bias in U.S. society

race (p. 56) a socially constructed category of people who share biologically transmitted traits that a society defines as important

racism (p. 70) the assertion that people of one race are less worthy than or even biologically inferior to others

rain forests (p. 434) regions of dense forestation, most of which circle the globe close to the equator

rationalization of society (Weber) (p. 304) the historical change from tradition to rationality and efficiency as the typical way people think about the world

rehabilitation (p. 150) reforming the offender to prevent future offenses

repressive state terrorism (p. 457) government use of ruthless violence within its own borders to repress political opposition

retribution (p. 150) moral vengeance by which society inflicts suffering on an offender comparable to that caused by the offense

schooling (p. 346) formal instruction carried out by specially trained teachers

school voucher program (p. 363) a program that provides parents with funds they can use at a public school or private school of their choice

secondary analysis (p. 16) a method by which a researcher uses data originally collected by others

secondary labor market (p. 301) jobs that provide low pay and few benefits to workers

segregation (p. 60) the physical and social separation of categories of people

self-fulfilling prophecy (p. 362) a situation in which people who are defined in one way eventually think and act as if the definition were true

serial murder (p. 169) the killing of several people by one offender over a period of time

sex (pp. 86, 192) the biological distinctions between females and males; also, sexual activity that leads to physical gratification and possibly reproduction

sexism (p. 88) the assertion that one sex is less worthy than or even innately inferior to the other

sexual harassment (pp. 96, 200) unwanted comments, gestures, or physical contact of a sexual nature

sexual orientation (p. 195) a person's romantic, emotional, and sexual attraction to another person

sexually transmitted diseases (STDs) (p. 207) diseases spread by sexual contact

the sick role (p. 265) patterns of behavior expected of people defined as ill

social classes (p. 28) categories of people who have similar access to resources and opportunities

social-conflict approach (p. 12) a theoretical framework that sees society as divided by inequality and conflict

social-constructionist approach (p. 4) the assertion that social problems arise as people define conditions as undesirable and in need of change

social disorganization (p. 43) a breakdown in social order caused by rapid social change

social epidemiology (p. 247) the study of how health and disease are distributed throughout a society's population

social institution (p. 11) a major sphere of social life, or societal subsystem, organized to meet a basic human need

socialism (p. 275) an economic system in which natural resources and the means of producing goods and services are collectively owned

social issues (p. 21) political debates involving moral judgments about how people should live

socialized medicine (p. 251) a medical care system in which the government owns and operates most medical facilities and employs most physicians

social movement (p. 6) an organized effort to shape the way people think about an issue, thereby encouraging or discouraging social change

social policy (p. 18) formal strategies to shape some dimension of social life

social problem (p. 2) a condition that undermines the well-being of some or all members of a society and that is usually a matter of public controversy

social stratification (p. 28) society's system of ranking categories of people in a hierarchy

social welfare program (p. 39)   organized effort by government, private organizations, or individuals to assist needy people defined as worthy of assistance

societal protection (p. 150)   protecting the public by rendering an offender incapable of further offenses through incarceration or by execution

society (p. 2)   people who live within some territory and share many patterns of behavior

sociological perspective (p. 2)   a point of view that highlights how society affects the experiences of individuals

sociology (p. 2)   the systematic study of human societies

special-interest groups (p. 280)   political alliances of people interested in some economic or social issue

stalking (p. 139)   persistent efforts by someone to establish or reestablish a relationship against the will of the victim

state-sponsored terrorism (p. 456)   the practice by one government of providing money, weapons, and training to terrorists who engage in violence in another nation

stereotype (p. 69)   an exaggerated description applied to every person in some category

stigma (p. 157)   a powerful negative social label that radically changes a person's self-concept and social identity

stimulants (p. 223)   drugs that elevate alertness, changing a person's mood by increasing energy

structural-functional approach (p. 10)   a theoretical framework that sees society as a system of many interrelated parts

structural violence (p. 182)   the use of violence by elites to protect their power and privileges

suburbs (p. 373)   urban areas beyond the political boundaries of cities

supportive housing (p. 381)   a program that combines low-income housing with on-site social services

surrogate motherhood (p. 336)   an arrangement by which a woman carries and bears a child for another

survey (p. 15)   a research method by which a researcher asks subjects to respond to items in a questionnaire or an interview

symbolic-interaction approach (p. 13)   a theoretical framework that sees society as the product of individuals interacting with one another

technology (p. 424)   knowledge that people apply to the task of living in a physical environment

telecommuting (p. 312)   linking employees to the office using information technology, including telephones, fax machines, and e-mail

terrorism (p. 456)   unlawful, typically random acts of violence or the threat of such violence used by an individual, group, or government to achieve a political goal

theoretical approach (p. 10)   a paradigm or basic image of one's subject matter that guides theory and research

theory (p. 10)   a statement of how and why specific facts are related

total war (p. 450)   deadly conflict that targets both population centers and military targets

tracking (p. 356)   the policy of assigning students to different educational programs

underclass (p. 37)   poor people who live in areas with high concentrations of poverty and limited opportunities for schooling or work

urban sprawl (p. 374)   rapid, unplanned, and low-density development at the edge of urban areas

victimless crimes (p. 147)   offenses that directly harm no one but the person who commits them

violence (p. 165)   behavior that causes damage to property or injury to people

violent crime (p. 167)   crime that involves violence or the threat of violence against others

war (p. 447)   violent conflict between nations or organized groups

war crime (p. 451)   an offense against the law of war as established by international agreements and international law

wealth (p. 29)   the total economic assets owned by a person or family

weapons of mass destruction (p. 448) weapons with the capacity to kill many thousands of people at one time

welfare state (p. 289)   a range of policies and programs that transfer wealth from the rich to the poor and provide benefits to needy members of society

white-collar crime (p. 145)   illegal activities committed by people during the course of their employment or regular business activities

world system theory (also called **dependency theory**) (p. 411)   a model of economic development that explains global inequality in terms of the historical exploitation of poor societies by rich ones

youth gangs (p. 177)   groups of young people who identify with one another and with a particular territory

zero population growth (p. 399)   the level of reproduction that maintains population at a steady state

REFERENCES

AARON, HENRY J. 1991. *Serious and Unstable Conditions: Financing America's Health Care.* Washington, D.C.: The Brookings Institution.

ABADINSKY, HOWARD. 1989. *Drug Abuse: An Introduction.* Chicago: Nelson Hall.

ABC NEWS. 1997. *World News Tonight.* (March 15).

ABEL, E. L. 1990. *Fetal Alcohol Syndrome.* Oradell, N.J.: Medical Economics.

ADITJONDRO, GEORGE J. 2000. "Ninjas, Nanggalas, Monuments, and Mossad Manuals: An Anthropology of Indonesian State Terror in East Timor." In Jeffrey A. Sluka, ed., *Death Squad: The Anthropology of State Terror* (pp. 158–88). Philadelphia: University of Pennsylvania Press.

ADLER, JERRY, and MAGGIE MALONE. 1996. "Toppling Towers." *Newsweek.* (November 4): 70–72.

ADORNO, T. W., et al. 1950. *The Authoritarian Personality.* New York: Harper & Brothers.

AGNEW, ROBERT. 1992. "Foundation for a General Strain Theory of Crime and Delinquency." *Criminology.* Vol. 30, No. 1: 47–87.

———. 1994. "The Contribution of Social-Psychological Strain Theory to the Explanation of Crime and Delinquency." In F. Adler and W. Laufer, eds., *Advances in Criminological Theory.* Vol. 6. New York: Transaction Publishers.

AHLBURG, D. A., and C. J. DeVITA. 1992. "New Realities of the American Family." *Population Bulletin.* Vol. 47, No. 2. Washington, D.C.: Population Reference Bureau.

AKERS, RONALD L., MARVIN D. KROHN, LONN LANZA-KADUCE, and MARCIA RADOSEVICH. 1979. "Social Learning and Deviant Behavior." *American Sociological Review.* Vol. 44, No. 4 (August): 636–55.

THE ALAN GUTTMACHER INSTITUTE. 1999. [Online] http://www.agi-usa.org Accessed September 19, 1999.

———. 2002. "Teen Pregnancy: Trends and Lessons Learned." *Issues in Brief.* 2002 Series, No. 1. [Online] http://www.agi-usa.org/pubs/ib_1-02.pdf Accessed August 14, 2002.

———. 2003. *U.S. Teenage Pregnancy Statistics with Comparative Statistics for Women Aged 20–24.* [Online] http://www.agi-usa.org/pubs/teen_stats.pdf Accessed September 30, 2003.

ALBON, JOAN. 1971. "Retention of Cultural Values and Differential Urban Adaptation: Samoans and American Indians in a West Coast City." *Social Forces.* Vol. 49, No. 3 (March): 385–93.

ALLEN, MICHAEL PATRICK, and PHILIP BROYLES. 1991. "Campaign Finance Reforms and the Presidential Campaign Contributions of Wealthy Capitalist Families." *Social Science Quarterly.* Vol. 72, No. 4 (December): 738–50.

ALONSO-ZALDIVAR, RICHARD. 2002. "Cellphone-Related Car Crashes Increasing." *Columbus Dispatch.* (December 2): 3.

ALTER, JONATHAN. 2001. "The War on Addiction." *Newsweek.* (February 12): 36–9.

ALTHEIDE, DAVID L. 2002. *Inciting Fear: News and the Construction of Crisis.* Hawthorne, N.Y.: Aldine de Gruyter.

AMATO, PAUL R., and JULIANA M. SOBOLEWSKI. 2001. "The Effects of Divorce and Marital Discord on Adult Children's Psychological Well-Being." *American Sociological Review.* Vol. 66, No. 6 (December): 900–21.

AMERICAN COUNCIL ON EDUCATION. 2002. *The American College President: 2002 Edition.* Washington, D.C.: The Council.

AMERICAN LIBRARY ASSOCIATION. 2003. [Online] http://www.ala.org Accessed November 19, 2003.

AMERICAN MEDICAL ASSOCIATION. 1997. [Online] http://www.ama-assn.org Accessed March 4, 1997.

AMERICAN PSYCHIATRIC ASSOCIATION. 2002. "Practice Guideline for the Treatment of Patients with Eating Disorders. In *Facts about Eating Disorders and the Search for Solutions.* Bethesda, Md.: APA.

ANDERSON, CURT. 2003. "States Face Growing Prison Population." *Yahoo News.* [Online] http://www.Yahoonews.com Accessed July 27, 2003.

ANDERSON, ELIJAH. 1994. "The Code of the Streets." *Atlantic Monthly.* Vol. 273 (May): 81–94.

———. 1999. *Code of the Street: Decency, Violence, and the Moral Life of the Inner City.* New York: W. W. Norton.

———. 2002. "The Ideologically Driven Critique." *American Journal of Sociology.* Vol. 197, No. 6 (May): 1533–50.

ANDERSON, JOHN WARD, and MOLLY MOORE. 1993. "World's Poorest Women Suffer in Common." *Columbus Dispatch.* (April 11): 4G.

ANESHENSEL, CAROL S., CAROLYN M. RUTTER, and PETER A. LACHENBRUCH. 1991. "Social Structure, Stress, and Mental Health: Competing Conceptual and Analytic Models." *American Sociological Review.* Vol. 56, No. 1 (July): 166–78.

ANETZBERGER, GEORGIA J. 1987. *The Etiology of Elder Abuse by Adult Offspring.* Springfield, Ill.: Charles C. Thomas.

ANGELO, BONNIE. 1989. "The Pain of Being Black" (an interview with Toni Morrison). *Time.* Vol. 133, No. 21 (May 22): 120–22.

ANGIER, NATALIE. 1992. "Scientists, Finding Idiosyncrasy in Homosexuals' Brains, Suggest That Orientation Is Physiological." *The New York Times.* (August 1): A7.

ANNAN, KOFI. 1998. "Astonishing Facts." *The New York Times* (September 27): 16.

ARIÈS, PHILIPPE. 1974. *Western Attitudes toward Death: From the Middle Ages to the Present.* Baltimore, Md.: Johns Hopkins University Press.

ARMSTRONG, ELISABETH. 2002. *The Retreat from Organization: U.S. Feminism Reconceptualized.* Albany: State University of New York Press.

ARRIGHI, BARBARA A., ed. 2001. *Understanding Inequality: The Intersection of Race/Ethnicity, Class, and Gender.* New York: Roman & Littlefield.

ASHFORD, LORI S. 1995. "New Perspectives on Population: Lessons from Cairo." *Population Bulletin.* Vol. 50, No. 1 (March).

ASTONE, NAN MARIE, and SARA S. McLANAHAN. 1991. "Family Structure, Parental Practices and High School Completion." *American Sociological Review.* Vol. 56, No. 3 (June): 309–20.

ATCHLEY, ROBERT C. 1982. "Retirement as a Social Institution." *Annual Review of Sociology.* Vol. 8. Palo Alto, Calif.: Annual Reviews: 263–87.

AVRIL, TOM, DOUGLAS A. CAMPBELL, and THOMAS GINSBURG. 1999. "N.J. Admits That Race Played Role in Some Police Stops on Turnpike." *Philadelphia Inquirer.* (April 21): A1, A14.

AXINN, WILLIAM G., and JENNIFER S. BARBER. 2001. "Mass Education and Fertility Transition." *American Sociological Review.* Vol. 66, No. 4 (August): 481–505.

AYERS, B. DRUMMOND, JR. 2001. "Political Briefing: Some New Thoughts on Raising Turnout." *The New York Times.* (January 14): Sec. 1, p. 20.

BABWIN, DOHN. 2003. "Illinois Governor to Commute Death-Row Sentences." *Yahoo! News.* [Online] http://dailynews.yahoo.com Accessed January 11, 2003.

BAKER, MARY ANNE, CATHERINE WHITE BERHEIDE, FAY ROSS GRECKEL, LINDA CARSTARPHEN GUGIN, MARCIA J. LIPETZ, and MARCIA TEXLER SEGAL. 1980. *Women Today: A Multidisciplinary Approach to Women's Studies.* Monterey, Calif.: Brooks/Cole.

BALLANTINE, JEANNE H. 2001. *The Sociology of Education: A Systematic Analysis.* 5th ed. Upper Saddle River, N.J.: Prentice Hall.

BALTZELL, E. DIGBY, and HOWARD G. SCHNEIDERMAN. 1991. "Social Class in the Oval Office." In E. Digby Baltzell, *The Protestant Establishment Revisited* (pp. 241–59). New Brunswick, N.J.: Transaction.

BANDURA, ALBERT. 1983. "Psychological Mechanisms of Aggression. In R. G. Green and E. I. Donnerstein, eds., *Aggression: Theoretical and Empirical Reviews.* Vol. 1. New York: Academic Press.

BARNES, EDWARD. 1995. "A Rare Visit with the Rebel of Ruby Ridge." *Time.* Vol. 145, No. 22 (May 29): 24.

BARNETT, OLA W., CINDY L. MILLER-PERRIN, and ROBIN D. PERRIN. 1997. *Family Violence across the Lifespan: An Introduction.* Thousand Oaks, Calif.: Sage.

BARONE, MICHAEL, and GRANT UJIFUSA. 1981. *The Almanac of American Politics.* Washington, D.C.: Barone and Co.

BARRET, R. L., and B. E. ROBINSON. 1990. *Gay Fathers.* Lexington, Mass.: Lexington Books.

BARRY, D. S. 1993. "Growing Up Violent: Decades of Research Link Screen Mayhem with Increase in Aggressive Behavior." *Media and Values.* Vol. 6, No. 1: 8–11.

BARRY, KATHLEEN. 1983. "Feminist Theory: The Meaning of Women's Liberation." In Barbara Haber, ed., *The Women's Annual 1982–1983* (pp. 35–78). Boston: G. K. Hall.

BARTLETT, BRUCE. 2000. "Death, Wealth, and Taxes." *The Public Interest.* Vol. 141 (Fall): 55–67.

BARTLETT, DONALD L., and JAMES B. STEELE. 1998. "Corporate Welfare." *Time.* Vol. 152, No. 19 (November 9): 36–54.

———. 2002. "Wheel of Misfortune." *Time.* Vol. 160, No. 25 (December 16): 44–58.

BASOW, SUSAN A. 1992. *Gender Stereotypes and Roles*, 3rd ed. Pacific Grove, Calif.: Brooks/Cole.

BAUER, P. T. 1981. *Equality, the Third World, and Economic Delusion.* Cambridge, Mass.: Harvard University Press.

BAUM, ALICE S., and DONALD W. BURNES. 1993. *A Nation in Denial: The Truth about Homelessness.* San Francisco: Westview Press.

BAYDAR, NAZLI, and JEANNE BROOKS-GUNN. 1991. "Effect of Maternal Employment and Child-Care Arrangements on Preschoolers' Cognitive and Behavioral Outcomes: Evidence from Children from the National Longitudinal Survey of Youth." *Developmental Psychology.* Vol. 27: 932–35.

BEARAK, BARRY. 2001. "Lives Held Cheap in Bangladesh Sweatshops." *New York Times* (April 15): A1, A12.

BEARMAN, PETER S., and HANNAH BRÜCKNER. 2002. "Opposite-Sex Twins and Adolescent Same-Sex Attraction." *American Journal of Sociology.* Vol. 107, No. 5 (March): 1179–1205.

BECKER, HOWARD S. 1966. *Outside: Studies in the Sociology of Deviance.* New York: Free Press.

BEGLEY, SHARON. 1997. "How to Beat the Heat." *Newsweek* (December 8): 34–38.

———. 2001. "How It All Starts Inside Your Brain." *Newsweek.* (February 12): 40–2.

BELLANDI, DEANNA. 2003. "Study Finds Meal Portion Sizes Growing." *Yahoo! News* [Online] http://www.yahoo.com Accessed January 3, 2003.

BELLAS, MARCIA L. 1994. "Comparable Worth in Academia: The Effects on Faculty Salaries of the Sex Composition and Labor-Market Conditions of Academic Disciplines." *American Sociological Review.* Vol. 59, No. 6 (December): 807–21.

BELLAS, MARCIA L., and BARBARA THOMAS COVENTRY. 2001. "Salesmen, Saleswomen, or Sales Workers? Determinants of the Sex Composition of Sales Occupations." *Sociological Forum.* Vol. 16, No. 1 (March): 73–98.

BELLUCK, PAM. 2000. "Indian Schools, Long Failing, Press for Money and Quality." *The New York Times.* (May 18): A1.

BENDICK, M. F. 1992. "Reaching the Breaking Point: Dangers of Mistreatment in Elder Caregiving Situations." *Journal of Elder Abuse & Neglect.* Vol. 4, No. 3: 39–59.

BENJAMIN, BERNARD, and CHRIS WALLIS. 1963. "The Mortality of Widowers." *The Lancet.* Vol. 2 (August): 454–56.

BENJAMIN, LOIS. 1991. *The Black Elite: Facing the Color Line in the Twilight of the Twentieth Century.* Chicago: Nelson-Hall.

BENNETT, WILLIAM J. 1995. "Redeeming Our Time." *Imprimis.* Vol. 24, No. 11 (November). Hillsdale, Mich.: Hillsdale College.

BENOKRAITIS, NIJOLE V. 1997. *Subtle Sexism: Current Practices and Prospects for Change.* Thousand Oaks, Calif.: Sage.

BENOKRAITIS, NIJOLE, and JOE FEAGIN. 1995. *Modern Sexism: Blatant, Subtle, and Overt Discrimination*, 2nd ed. Englewood Cliffs, N.J.: Prentice Hall.

BERGAMO, MONICA, and GERSON CAMAROTTI. 1996. "Brazil's Landless Millions." *World Press Review.* Vol. 43, No. 7 (July): 46–47.

BERGER, PETER L. 1986. *The Capitalist Revolution: Fifty Propositions about Prosperity, Equality, and Liberty.* New York: Basic Books.

BERGESEN, ALBERT, ed. 1983. *Crises in the World-System.* Beverly Hills, Calif.: Sage.

BERGSTEN, C. FRED, THOMAS HORST, and THEODORE MORAN. 1978. *American Multinationals and American Interests.* Washington, D.C.: Brookings Institute.

BERKOWITZ, LEONARD. 1993. *Aggression: Its Causes, Consequences, and Control.* New York: McGraw-Hill.

BERKOWITZ, LEONARD, and A. LePAGE. 1994. "Weapons as Aggression-Eliciting Stimuli." *Journal of Personality and Social Psychology.* Vol. 7: 202–7.

BERNARD, JESSIE. 1982 (orig., 1973). *The Future of Marriage.* New Haven, Conn.: Yale University Press.

BERNARD, LARRY CRAIG. 1980. "Multivariate Analysis of New Sex Role Formulations and Personality." *Journal of Personality and Social Psychology.* Vol. 38, No. 2 (February): 323–36.

BERRY, JEFFREY M. 1989. *The Interest Group Society*, 2nd ed. Boston: Scott, Foresman/Little, Brown Series in Political Science.

BERTRAM, EVA, MORRIS BLACHMAN, KENNETH SHARPE, and PETER ANDREAS. 1996. *Drug War Politics: The Price of Denial.* Berkeley: University of California Press.

BEST, JOEL, ed. 1995. *Images of Issues: Typifying Contemporary Social Problems*, 2nd ed. New York: Aldine de Gruyter.

———, ed. 2001. *How Claims Spread: Cross-National Diffusion of Social Problems.* New York: Aldine de Gruyter.

BIBLARZ, TIMOTHY J., and ADRIAN E. RAFERTY. 1993. "The Effects of Family Disruption on Social Mobility." *American Sociological Review.* Vol. 58, No. 1 (February): 97–109.

BINSTOCK, ROBERT H. 1996. "Shelter and Care for the Elderly Population: Reasons for Cynicism." *The Gerontologist.* Vol. 36, No. 3: 410–13.

BIRENBAUM, A. 1995. *Putting Health Care on the National Agenda.* Westport, Conn.: Praeger.

BLACK, DONALD W., WITH C. LINDON LARSON. 2000. *Bad Boys, Bad Men*. New York: Oxford University Press.

BLACKWOOD, EVELYN, and SASKIA WIERINGA, EDS. 1999. *Female Desires: Same-Sex Relations and Transgender Practices across Cultures*. New York: Columbia University Press.

BLANK, ROBERT H. 1997. *The Price of Life: The Future of American Health Care*. New York: Columbia University Press.

BLANKENHORN, DAVID. 1995. *Fatherless America: Confronting Our Most Urgent Social Problem*. New York: HarperCollins.

BLUM, LINDA M. 1991. *Between Feminism and Labor: The Significance of the Comparable Worth Movement*. Berkeley: University of California Press.

BLUMENSON, ERIC D. 1998. "The Drug War's Hidden Economic Agenda: Corrupting Effects of Financing Police Departments by Asset Forfeitures in Drug Cases." *The Nation*. Vol. 266 (March 9): 1–12.

BLUMENTHAL, SUSAN J. 2002. "Prescriptions for a New Year." *U.S. News & World Report*. Vol. 132, No. 1 (January 14): 52.

BLUMER, HERBERT G. 1969. "Collective Behavior." In Alfred McClung Lee, ed., *Principles of Sociology*, 3rd ed. (pp. 65–121). New York: Barnes & Noble Books.

BLUMSTEIN, ALFRED, and RICHARD ROSENFELD. 1998. "Assessing the Recent Ups and Downs in U.S. Homicide Rates." *National Institute of Justice Journal*. Vol. 237 (October): 9–11.

BOERNER, CHRISTOPHER, and THOMAS LAMBERT. 1995. "Environmental Injustice." *The Public Interest*. Vol. 118 (Winter): 61–82.

BOGARDUS, EMORY S. 1925. "Social Distance and Its Origins." *Sociology and Social Research*. Vol. 9 (July–August): 216–25.

———. 1967. *A Forty-Year Racial Distance Study*. Los Angeles: University of Southern California Press.

BOGGESS, SCOTT, and JOHN BOUND. 1997. "Did Criminal Activity Increase during the 1980s? Comparisons across Data Sources." *Social Science Quarterly*. Vol. 78, No. 3 (September): 725–39.

BOHANNAN, CECIL. 1991. "The Economic Correlates of Homelessness in Sixty Cities." *Social Science Quarterly*. Vol. 72, No. 4 (December): 817–25.

BOHLEN, CELESTINE. 1998. "Facing Oblivion, Rust-Belt Giants Top Russian List of Vexing Crises." *New York Times* (November 8): 1, 6.

BOHON, STEPHANIE A., and CRAIG R. HUMPHREY. 2000. "Courting LULUs: Characteristics of Suitor and Objector Communities." *Rural Sociology*. Vol. 65, No. 3 (September): 376–95.

BONILLA-SANTIAGO, GLORIA. 1990. "A Portrait of Hispanic Women in the United States." In Sara E. Rix, ed., *The American Woman 1990–91: A Status Report*. New York: Norton, pp. 249–57.

BONILLA-SILVA, EDUARDO. 1999. "The Essential Social Fact of Race." *American Sociological Review*. Vol. 64, No. 6 (December): 899–906.

BORDREAU, F. A. 1993. "Elder Abuse." In R. L. Hampton, T. P. Gullotta, G. R. Adams, E. H. Potter, III, and R. P. Weissberg, eds., *Family Violence: Prevention and Treatment* (pp. 142–58). Thousand Oaks, Calif.: Sage.

BORMANN, F. HERBERT. 1990. "The Global Environmental Deficit." *BioScience*. Vol. 40: 74.

BOSWORTH, BARRY, and GARY BURTLESS. 1998. "Population Aging and American Economic Performance." In Barry Bosworth and Gary Burtless, eds., *Aging Societies: The Global Dimension* (pp. 267–310). Washington, D.C.: Brookings Institution Press.

BOURDIEU, PIERRE, and JEAN-CLAUDE PASSERON. 1977. *Reproduction in Society, Education, and Culture*. Newbury Park, Calif.: Sage.

BOVARD, JAMES. 1995. "Not So Wacko." *New Republic*. Vol. 212, No. 20 (May 15): 18.

BOWDITCH, CHRISTINE. 1993. "Getting Rid of Troublemakers: High School Disciplinary Procedures and the Production of Dropouts." *Social Problems*. Vol. 40, No. 6 (November): 493–509.

BOWERSOX, JOHN A. 1995. "Buprenorphine May Soon Be Heroin Treatment Option." *NIDA Notes* (January–February). [Online] http://www.nih.gov/NIDANotes/NNVol10N1/Bupren.html Accessed May 3, 1999.

BOWLES, SAMUEL, and HERBERT GINTIS. 1976. *Schooling in Capitalist America: Educational Reform and the Contradictions of Economic Life*. New York: Basic Books.

BOYER, DEBRA. 1989. "Male Prostitution and Homosexual Identity." *Journal of Homosexuality*. Vol. 17, Nos. 1–2: 151–84.

BOYLE, ELIZABETH HEGER, FORTUNATA SONGORA, and GAIL FOSS. 2001. "International Discourse and Local Politics: Anti–Female-Genital-Cutting Laws in Egypt, Tanzania, and the United States." *Social Problems*. Vol. 48, No. 4 (November): 524–44.

BOZA, TANYA GOLASH. 2002. Proposed American Sociological Association Statement on "Race." [Online] http://www.unc.edu/~tatiana/ Accessed October 24, 2002.

BRAITHWAITE, JOHN. 1981. "The Myth of Social Class and Criminality Reconsidered." *American Sociological Review*. Vol. 46, No. 1 (February): 36–57.

BRANTLINGER, ELLEN A. 1993. *The Politics of Social Class in Secondary School: Views of Affluent and Impoverished Youth*. New York: Teachers College Press.

BRENNAN, PATRICIA, SARNOFF MEDNICK, and JAN VOLAVKA. 1995. "Biomedical Factors in Crime." In J. Q. Wilson and J. Petersilia, eds., *Crime*. San Francisco: Institute for Contemporary Studies.

BRIGHT, CHRIS. 2003. "A History of Our Future." In *State of the World 2003*. The Worldwatch Institute. New York: W. W. Norton, pp. 3–13.

BRINDIS, CLAIRE, and LAURA DAVIS. 1998. *Mobilizing for Action*. Washington, D.C.: Advocates for Youth.

BRINES, JULIE, and KARA JOYNER. 1999. "The Ties That Bind: Principles of Cohesion in Cohabitation and Marriage." *American Sociological Review*. Vol. 64, No. 3 (June): 333–55.

BRINK, SUSAN. 1998. "HMOs Were the Right RX." *U.S. News & World Report*. Vol. 124, No. 9 (March 9): 47–50.

BRODKIN, KAREN. 2001. "How Jews Became White Folks." In Paula S. Rothenberg, ed., *White Privilege*. New York: Worth.

BROUDE, GWEN J. 1996. "The Realities of Day Care." *The Public Interest*. No. 125 (Fall): 95–105.

BROWN, LESTER R. 1995. "Reassessing the Earth's Population." *Society*. Vol. 32, No. 4 (May–June): 7–10.

BROWN, LESTER R., ET AL., EDS. 1993. *State of the World 1993: A Worldwatch Institute Report on Progress toward a Sustainable Society*. New York: Norton.

BROWNMILLER, SUSAN. 1975. *Against Our Will: Men, Women, and Rape*. New York: Simon & Schuster.

BUMPASS, LARRY, and JAMES A. SWEET. 1995. "1992–1994 National Survey of Families and Households." Reported in "Report from PPA." *Population Today*. Vol. 23, No. 6 (June): 3.

BURKETT, ELINOR. 1997. "God Created Me to Be a Slave." *New York Times* Sunday Magazine (October 12): 56–60.

BURNS, PETER F., PETER L. FRANCIA, and PAUL S. HERRNSON. 2000. "Labor at Work: Union Campaign Activities and Legislative Payoffs in the U.S. House of Representatives." *Social Science Quarterly*. Vol. 81, No. 2 (June): 507–22.

BUTLER, ROBERT N. 1975. *Why Survive: Being Old in America*. New York: Harper & Row, 1975.

———. 1994. "Dispelling Ageism: The Cross-Cutting Intervention." In Dena Shenk and W. Andrew Achenbaum, eds., *Changing Perceptions of Aging and the Aged*. New York: Springer.

BUZAWA, EVE S., and CARL G. BUZAWA. 1996. *Domestic Violence: The Criminal Justice Response*, 2nd ed. Thousand Oaks, Calif.: Sage.

CAIN, BRAD. 2001. "Ashcroft Overturns Assisted Suicide." *Yahoo! News*. [Online] http://dailynews.yahoo.com Accessed November 7, 2001.

CALAVITA, KITTY, and HENRY N. PONTELL. 1993. "'Heads I Win, Tails You Lose': Deregulation, Crime, and Crisis in the Savings and Loan Industry." In Henry N. Pontell, ed., *Social Deviance: Readings in Theory and Research* (pp. 341–63). Upper Saddle River, N.J.: Prentice Hall.

CALHOUN, KAREN S., and BEVERLY M. ATKESON. 1991. *Treatment of Rape Victims: Facilitating Social Adjustment*. New York: Pergamon.

CAMARA, EVANDRO. Personal communication, 2000.

CAPIZANO, JEFFREY, KATHRYN TOUT, and GINA ADAMS. 2001. "Child-Care Patterns of School-Age Children with Employed Mothers." Report of the Urban Institute. [Online] http://www.newfederalism.urban.org/html/op41/occa41.html#childcare

CAPRON, ALEXANDER MORGAN. 1997. "Death and the Court." *Hastings Center Report* (September–October): 25–29.

CARMICHAEL, STOKELY, and CHARLES V. HAMILTON. 1967. *Black Power: The Politics of Liberation in America*. New York: Vintage Books.

CARROLL, JAMES R. 1999a. "Congress Is Told of Coal-Dust Fraud UMW; Senator from Minnesota Rebukes Industry." *Louisville Courier Journal* (Thursday, May 27): 1A.

———. 1999b. "Three Congressional Panels Probe Uranium Plant." *Louisville Courier-Journal* (September 14): 4B.

———. 1999c. "U.S. Warns of Uranium, Officials Cite Problems Linked to Waste Storage." *Louisville Courier-Journal* (September 15): 1A.

CARSON, RACHEL. 1995 (orig., 1962). "Silent Spring." In John J. Macionis and Nijole V. Benokraitis, eds., *Seeing Ourselves: Classic, Contemporary, and Cross-Cultural Readings in Sociology* (pp. 407–10). 3rd ed. Upper Saddle River, N.J.: Prentice Hall.

CARTER, STEPHEN. 1991. *Reflections of an Affirmative Action Baby*. New York: Basic Books.

———. 1998. *Civility: Manners, Morals, and the Etiquette of Democracy*. New York: Harper Perennial.

CARTY, WIN. 1999. "Greater Dependence on Cars Leads to More Pollution in World's Cities." *Population Today*. Vol. 27, No. 12 (December): 1–2.

CARUSO, DAVID B. 2002. "42 Philadelphia Schools Privatized." *Yahoo! News*. [Online] http://www.yahoo.com Accessed April 18, 2002.

CASPER, LYNN M., and LORETTA E. BASS. 1998. "Voting and Registration in the Election of November 1996." *Current Population Reports* (July). U.S. Census Bureau. Washington, D.C.: U.S. Department of Commerce.

CASTELLS, MANUEL. 1977. *The Urban Question*. Cambridge, Mass.: MIT Press.

———. 1983. *The City and the Grass Roots*. Berkeley: University of California Press.

———. 1989. *The Informational City*. Oxford, UK: Blackwell.

CATALYST. 2003. *2001 Catalyst Census of Women Board of Directors of the Fortune 1000*. [Online] http://www.catalystwomen.org/research/censuses.htm Accessed November 1, 2003.

———. 2003. *Women Corporate Officers and Top Earners*. [Online] http://www.catalystwomen.org/press_room/factsheets/factcote98.htm Accessed December 26, 2003.

CENTER FOR AMERICAN WOMEN AND POLITICS. 2003. "Women in Statewide Elective Executive Office 2003. Eagleton Institute of Politics, Rutgers University." [Online] http://www.cawp.rutgers.edu/facts/stwide-03.html Accessed February 11, 2003.

CENTER FOR CONSTITUTIONAL RIGHTS. 2003. [Online] http://www.ccr-ny.org Accessed November 19, 2003.

CENTER ON HUNGER AND POVERTY. 2000. "Paradox of Our Times: Hunger in a Strong Economy." Medford, Mass: Tufts University.

CENTER FOR MEDIA AND PUBLIC AFFAIRS. 2002. [Online] http://www.cmpa.org Accessed January 24, 2002.

CENTER FOR RESPONSIVE POLITICS. 1998. "The Big Picture." [Online] http://www.crp.org/crpdocs/bigpicture/default.htm Accessed February 12, 1998.

CHAFE, WILLIAM. 1977. *Women and Equality: Changing Patterns in American Culture*. New York: Oxford University Press.

CHAGNON, NAPOLEON A. 1997. *Yanamamo*. Fort Worth, Tex.: Harcourt Brace College Publishers.

CHAMBLISS, WILLIAM J. 1995. "Crime Control and Ethnic Minorities: Legitimizing Racial Oppression by Creating Moral Panics." In Darnell F. Hawkins, ed., *Ethnicity, Race, and Crime: Perspectives across Time and Place*. Albany: State University of New York Press.

CHANDLER, TIMOTHY D., YOSHINORI KAMO, and JAMES D. WERBEL. 1994. "Do Delays in Marriage and Childbirth Affect Earnings?" *Social Science Quarterly*. Vol. 75, No. 4 (December): 838–53.

CHAUNCEY, GEORGE. 1994. *Gay New York: Gender, Urban Culture, and the Making of the Gay Male World 1890–1940*. New York: Basic Books.

CHAVEZ, LINDA. 1998. "Bilingual Activists Try to Nullify Election." *Human Events*. Vol. 54, No. 45 (November 27): 23.

CHESLER, PHYLLIS. 1989. *Women and Madness*. New York: Harcourt Brace Jovanovich.

CHESNAIS, JEAN-CLAUDE. 1997. "The Demographic Sunset of the West?" *Population Today*. Vol. 25, No. 1 (January): 4–5.

CHILDREN'S DEFENSE FUND. 1995. *The State of America's Children Yearbook, 1995*. Washington, D.C.: Children's Defense Fund.

CHIRICOS, TED, RANEE MCENTIRE, and MARC GERTZ. 2001. "Perceived Racial and Ethnic Composition of Neighborhood and Perceived Risk of Crime." *Social Problems*. Vol. 48, No. 3 (August): 322–40. *Chronicle of Higher Education. Almanac 2002–3*. [Online] http://chronicle.com/weekly/almanac/2002/nation/0103201.htm Accessed October 23, 2002.

CHUA-EOAN, HOWARD. 2000. "Profiles in Outrage." *Time*. Vol. 156, No. 13 (September 25): 38–39.

CIGLER, ALLAN J., and BURDETT A. LOOMIS, EDS. 1998. *Interest Group Politics*, 5th ed. Washington, D.C.: CQ Press.

CLARKE, ROBIN. 1984a. "Atmospheric Pollution." In Sir Edmund Hillary, ed., *Ecology 2000: The Changing Face of the Earth* (pp. 130–48). New York: Beaufort.

CLAUSEWITZ, CARL VON. 1968 (orig., 1832). *On War*. Edited with an introduction by Anatol Rapaport. Baltimore: Penguin.

CLEMETSON, LYNETTE. 2000. "Grandma Knows Best." *Newsweek* (June 12): 60–61.

CLOUD, JOHN. 1998. "Harassed or Hazed?: Why the Supreme Court Ruled That Men Can Sue Men for Sex Harassment." *Time*. Vol. 151, No. 10 (March 16): 55.

———. 2003. "Inside the New SAT." *Time*. Vol. 162, No. 17 (October 27): 48–56.

CLOWARD, RICHARD A., and LLOYD E. OHLIN. 1966. *Delinquency and Opportunity: A Theory of Delinquent Gangs*. New York: Free Press.

COALITION TO STOP THE USE OF CHILD SOLDIERS. 2001. *The Child Soldiers Global Report*. [Online] http://www.child-soldiers.org Accessed November 19, 2003.

COCKERHAM, WILLIAM C. 1996. *Sociology of Mental Disorder*, 4th ed. Upper Saddle River, N.J.: Prentice Hall.

COHEN, ALBERT K. 1971 (orig., 1955). *Delinquent Boys: The Culture of the Gang*. New York: Free Press.

COHEN, ELIAS. 2001. "The Complex Nature of Ageism: What Is It? Who Does It? Who Perceives It?" *The Gerontologist*. Vol. 41, No. 5 (October): 576–78.

COHEN, LLOYD R. 1991. "Sexual Harassment and the Law." *Society*. Vol. 28, No. 4 (May–June): 8–13.

COLE, GEORGE F., and CHRISTOPHER E. SMITH. 2002. *Criminal Justice in America*, 3rd ed. Belmont, Calif.: Wadsworth.

COLEMAN, JAMES S. 1966. *Equality of Educational Opportunity*. Washington, D.C.: U.S. Government Printing Office.

———. 1988. "Social Capital in the Creation of Human Capital." *American Journal of Sociology*. Vol. 94, No. 1 (July): 95–120.

COLLEGE BOARD. 2003. 2003 College Bound Seniors: A Profile of SAT Program Test Takers. (n.p.) College Board.

———. 2003b. "SAT Verbal and Math Scores Up Significantly as a Record-Breaking Number of Students Take the Test." Press release.

COLLYMORE, YVETTE. 2002. "Migrant Street Children on the Rise in Central America." *Population Today*. Vol. 30, No. 2 (February–March): 1, 4.

COMMISSION FOR RACIAL JUSTICE, UNITED CHURCH OF CHRIST. 1994. *CRJ Reporter*. New York: Commission for Racial Justice, United Church of Christ.

COMMON SENSE FOR DRUG POLICY. 1999. "Factbook—The Netherlands and the United States, Drug War Facts: Common Sense for Drug Policy." [Online] http://www.csdp.org/factbook/thenethe.htm Accessed May 10, 1999.

CONNERLY, WARD. 2000. "The Content of Our Children's Character." *Imprimis*. Vol. 29, No. 2 (February): 1–3, 5.

CONNETT, PAUL H. 1991. "The Disposable Society." In F. Herbert Bormann and Stephen R. Kellert, eds., *Ecology, Economics, and Ethics: The Broken Circle* (pp. 99–122). New Haven, Conn.: Yale University Press.

CONRAD, PETER, and JOSEPH W. SCHNEIDER. 1980. *Deviance and Medicalization: From Badness to Sickness*. St. Louis: Mosby.

CONWAY, M. MARGARET, and JOANNE CONNOR GREEN. 1998. "Political Action Committees and Campaign Finance." In Allan J. Cigler and Burdett A. Loomis, eds., *Interest Group Politics*, 5th ed. (pp. 193–214). Washington, D.C.: CQ Press.

COOK, RHODES. 1993. "House Republicans Scored a Quiet Victory in '92." *Congressional Quarterly Weekly Report*. Vol. 51, No. 16 (April 17): 965–68.

CORLEY, ROBERT N., O. LEE REED, PETER J. SHEDD, and JERE W. MOREHEAD. 1993. *The Legal and Regulatory Environment of Business*, 9th ed. New York: McGraw-Hill.

CORLISS, RICHARD. 2001. "Who's Feeling No Pain?" *Time*. Vol. 157, No. 11 (March 19): 69.

CORRELL, SHELLEY J. 2001. "Gender and the Career Choice Process: The Role of Biased Self-Assessment." *American Journal of Sociology*. Vol. 106, No. 6 (May): 1691–1730.

CORTESE, ANTHONY J. 1999. *Provocateur: Images of Women and Minorities in Advertising*. Lanham, Md.: Roman & Littlefield.

COSTA, DORA L. 1998. *The Evolution of Retirement: An American Economic History, 1889–1990*. Chicago: University of Chicago Press.

COURTNEY, ALICE E., and THOMAS W. WHIPPLE. 1983. *Sex Stereotyping in Advertising*. Lexington, Mass.: D. C. Heath.

COVINGTON, JEANETTE. 1995. "Racial Classification in Criminology: The Reproduction of Racialized Crime." *Sociological Forum*. Vol. 10, No. 4 (December): 547–68.

COWLEY, GEOFFREY. 1995. "The Prescription That Kills." *Newsweek* (July 17): 54.

———. 1998. "Why Children Turn Violent." *Newsweek*. Vol. 131, No. 14 (April 6): 24–25.

———. 2001. "New Ways to Stay Clean." *Newsweek*. (February 12): 44–7.

COYOTE. [Online] http://www.freedomusa.org/coyotela/ Accessed April 2, 2000.

CRENSHAW, EDWARD M., and J. CRAIG JENKINS. 1996. "Social Structure and Global Climate Change: Sociological Propositions Concerning the Greenhouse Effect." *Sociological Focus*. Vol. 29, No. 4 (October): 341–58.

CROSSETTE, BARBARA. 1995. "Female Genital Mutilation by Immigrants Is Becoming Cause for Concern in the U.S." *New York Times International* (December 10): 11.

CUMMING, ELAINE, and WILLIAM E. HENRY. 1961. *Growing Old: The Process of Disengagement*. New York: Basic Books.

CUNNINGHAM, WILLIAM C., JOHN J. STRAUCHS, and CLIFFORD W. VAN METER. 1990. *The Hallcrest Report II*. Stoneham, Mass.: Butterworth-Heinemann.

CUOMO, ANDREW M. 1992. *The Way Home: A New Direction in Social Policy*. New York: New York City Commission on the Homeless.

CURRIE, ELLIOTT. 1985. *Confronting Crime: An American Challenge*. New York: Pantheon.

CYLKE, F. KURT, JR. 1993. *The Environment*. New York: HarperCollins.

DAHL, ROBERT. 1961. *Who Governs?* New Haven, Conn.: Yale University Press.

———. 1982. *Dilemmas of Pluralist Democracy*. New Haven, Conn.: Yale University Press.

DALY, KATHLEEN, and MEDA CHESNEY-LIND. 1988. "Feminism and Criminology." *Justice Quarterly*. Vol. 5 (December): 497–583.

DALY, MARTIN, and MARGO I. WILSON. 1996. "Violence against Stepchildren." *Current Directions in Psychological Science*. Vol. 5, No. 3 (June): 77–81.

DARROCH, JACQUELINE E., JENNIFER J. FROST, SUSHEELA SINGH, and THE STUDY TEAM. 2001. "Teenage Sexual and Reproductive Behavior in Developed Countries: Can More Progress Be Made?" New York: The Alan Guttmacher Institute (November). [Online] http://www.agi-usa Accessed August 14, 2002.

DAVIS, DONALD M. 1993. Cited in "T.V. Is a Blonde, Blonde World." *American Demographics*, special issue: *Women Change Places*. Ithaca, N.Y.

DAVIS, KAREN, PAULA GRANT, and DIANE ROWLAND. 1992. "Alone and Poor: The Plight of Elderly Women." In Lou Glasse and Jon Hendicks, eds., *Gender & Aging* (pp. 79–90). Amityville, N.Y.: Baywood.

DAVIS, KINGSLEY. 1971. "Sexual Behavior." In Robert K. Merton and Robert Nisbet, eds., *Contemporary Social Problems*, 3rd ed. (pp. 313–60). New York: Harcourt Brace Jovanovich.

DAVIS, KINGSLEY, and WILBERT MOORE. 1945. "Some Principles of Stratification." *American Sociological Review*. Vol. 10, No. 2 (April): 242–49.

DAVIS, NANETTE J. 1980. *Sociological Constructions of Deviance: Perspectives and Issues in the Field*, 2nd ed. Dubuque, Iowa: William C. Brown.

———. 2000. "From Victims to Survivors: Working with Recovering Street Prostitutes." In Ronald Weitzer, ed., *Sex for Sale: Prostitution, Pornography, and the Sex Industry* (pp. 139–55). New York: Routledge.

DECKARD, BARBARA SINCLAIR. 1979. *The Women's Movement: Political, Socioeconomic, and Psychological Issues*, 2nd ed. New York: Harper & Row.

DEDRICK, DENNIS K., and RICHARD E. YINGER. 1990. "MAD, SDI, and the Nuclear Arms Race." Unpublished manuscript. Georgetown, Ky.: Georgetown College.

DEFENCEINDIA. 2003. "The World's Nuclear Arsenals." [Online] http://www.defenceindia.com/def_common/world_nuclear-arsenals.html Accessed December 2, 2003.

DEFINA, ROBERT H., and THOMAS M. ARVANITES. 2002. "The Weak Effect of Imprisonment on Crime: 1971–1998." *Social Science Quarterly*. Vol. 83, No. 3 (September): 635–53.

DEFRANCIS, MARC. 2002a. "U.S. Elder Care Is in a Fragile State." *Population Today*. Vol. 30, No. 1 (January): 1–3.

———. 2002b. "A Spiraling Shortage of Nurses." *Population Today*. Vol. 30, No. 2 (February–March): 8–9.

DELACROIX, JACQUES, and CHARLES C. RAGIN. 1981. "Structural Blockage: A Crossnational Study of Economic Dependency, State Efficacy, and Underdevelopment." *American Journal of Sociology*. Vol. 86, No. 6 (May): 1311–47.

DELLA CAVA, MARCO R. 1997. "For Dutch, It's as Easy as Asking a Doctor." *USA Today* (January 7): 4A.

D'EMILIO, JOHN. 1984. *Sexual Politics, Sexual Communities: The Making of a Homosexual Minority, 1940–1970*. Chicago: University of Chicago Press.

DERVARICS, CHARLES. 1998. "Is Welfare Reform Reforming Welfare?" *Population Today*. Vol. 26, No. 10 (October): 1–2.

———. 1999a. "Is There a Teacher Shortage?" *Population Today*. Vol. 27, No. 11 (November): 1–2.

———. 1999b. "The Coming Age of Older Women." *Population Today*. Vol. 27, No. 2 (February): 2–3.

DESLATTE, MELINDA. 2003. "Serial Killing Suspect Returns to Louisiana." *The Examiner* (San Francisco), July 3. [Online] http://www.examiner.com Accessed July 3, 2003.

DIAZ, JOHNNY. 2001. "Ritalin Is Big on Campus." *The Philadelphia Inquirer*. (November 22): A38.

DIETZ, P. 1986. "Mass, Serial, and Sensational Homicides." *Bulletin of the New York Academy of Medicine*. Vol. 62: 477–91.

DINITZ, SIMON, F. R. SCARPITTI, and WALTER C. RECKLESS. 1962. "Delinquency and Vulnerability: A Cross Group and Longitudinal Analysis." *American Sociological Review*. Vol. 25, No. 4 (August): 555–58.

DIXON, WILLIAM J., and TERRY BOSWELL. 1996. "Dependency, Disarticulation, and Denominator Effects: Another Look at Foreign Capital Penetration." *American Journal of Sociology*. Vol. 102, No. 2 (September): 543–62.

DIZARD, JAN E., and HOWARD GADLIN. 1990. *The Minimal Family*. Amherst: The University of Massachusetts Press.

DOBYNS, HENRY F. 1966. "An Appraisal of Techniques with a New Hemispheric Estimate." *Current Anthropology*. Vol. 7, No. 4 (October): 395–446.

DODD, MIKE. 2003. "USOC Ethics Committee Leader Wields Power, Influence in DC." *USA Today*. (January 31): 7C.

DOLLARD, JOHN, et al. 1939. *Frustration and Aggression*. New Haven, Conn.: Yale University Press.

DOMHOFF, G. WILLIAM. 1970. *Higher Circles: The Governing Class in America*. New York: Random House.

DONNERSTEIN, E., R. SLABY, and L. ERON. 1994. "The Mass Media and Youth Violence." In J. Murray, E. Rubinstein, and G. Comstock, eds., *Violence and Youth: Vol. 2. Psychology's Response* (pp. 219–50). Washington, D.C.: American Psychological Association.

DORESS-WORTERS, PAULA B., and DIANA LASKIN SIEGAL. 1994. *Ourselves, Growing Older: Women Aging with Knowledge and Power*. New York: Touchstone.

DOYLE, CHARLES. 2002. "The USA Patriot Act: A Sketch." [Online] http://www.fas.org/irp/crs/RS21203.pdf Accessed November 9, 2003.

DOYLE, RICHARD F. 1980. *A Manifesto of Men's Liberation*, 2nd ed. Forest Lake, Minn.: Men's Rights Association.

DU BOIS, W. E. B. 2001 (orig., 1903). "The Souls of Black Folk." In John J. Macionis and Nijole V. Benokraitis, eds., *Seeing Ourselves: Classic, Contemporary, and Cross-Cultural Readings in Sociology*, 5th ed. (pp. 226–30). Upper Saddle River, N.J.: Prentice Hall.

DUFFY, TOM. 1999. "Campus Crusader: Dartmouth College Nutritionist Gives Students Food for Thought." *People*. Vol. 51, No. 13 (April 12): 71–72.

DUNCAN, CYNTHIA M. 1999. *Worlds Apart: Why Poverty Persists in Rural America*. New Haven, Conn.: Yale University Press.

DUNLAP, RILEY E., GEORGE H. GALLUP, JR., and ALEC M. GALLUP. 1992. *The Health of the Planet Survey*. Princeton, N.J.: The George H. Gallup International Institute.

DURKHEIM, EMILE. 1964a (orig., 1895). *The Division of Labor in Society*. New York: Free Press.

———. 1964b (orig., 1893). *The Rules of Sociological Method*. New York: Free Press.

DWORKIN, ANDREA. 1987. *Intercourse*. New York: Free Press.

———. 1991. "Against the Male Flood: Censorship, Pornography, and Equality." In Robert M. Baird and Stuart E. Rosenbaum, eds., *Pornography: Private Right or Public Menace?* (pp. 56–61). Buffalo, N.Y.: Prometheus.

DWORKIN, ANTHONY. 2003. "The Iraq War in Retrospect." *Crimes of War Project*. (September 14). [Online] http://www.crimesofwar.org/onnews/news-iraq3.html Accessed November 20, 2003.

DWORKIN, RONALD W. 2002. "Where Have All the Nurses Gone?" *Public Interest*. Vol. 148 (Summer): 23–36.

DYE, THOMAS R. 1999. *Politics in America*, 3rd ed. Upper Saddle River, N.J.: Prentice Hall.

EATON, WILLIAM W., JR. 1980. "A Formal Theory of Selection for Schizophrenia." *American Journal of Sociology*. Vol. 86, No. 1 (July): 149–58.

The Economist. 1999. "Kalashnikov Kids." Vol. 352, No. 8127 (July 10): 19–21.

EDIN, KATHRYN, and LAURA LEIN. 1996. "Work, Welfare, and Single Mothers' Economic Survival Strategies." *American Sociological Review*. Vol. 62, No. 2 (April): 253–66.

EDWARDS, TAMALA M. 1998. "Revolt of the Gentry." *Time*. Vol. 151, No. 23 (June 15): 34–35.

EGAN, TIMOTHY. 2002. "Pastoral Poverty: The Seeds of Decline." *Sunday Week in Review*. (December 8).

EHRENREICH, BARBARA. 1983. *The Hearts of Men: American Dreams and the Flight from Commitment*. Garden City, N.Y.: Anchor.

———. 1997. *Blood Rites: Origins and History of the Passions of War.* New York: Henry Holt.

———. 1999. "The Real Truth about the Female Body." *Time.* Vol. 153, No. 9 (March 15): 56–65.

———. 2001. *Nickel and Dimed: On How (Not) to Get By in America.* New York: Henry Holt.

EISENSTEIN, ZILLAH R., ed. 1979. *Capitalist Patriarchy and the Case for Socialist Feminism.* New York: Monthly Review Press.

ELASH, ANITA. 1997. "Older and Needier." *Maclean's.* Vol. 110, No. 44 (November): 66.

ELDREDGE, DIRK CHASE. 1998. *Ending the War on Drugs: A Solution for America.* Lanham, Md.: National Book Network.

ELECTRONIC FRONTIER FOUNDATION. 2003. [Online] http://www.eff.org Accessed November 19, 2003.

ELIAS, ROBERT. 1997. "A Culture of Violent Solutions." In Jennifer Turpin and Lester R. Kurtz, eds., *The Web of Violence: From Interpersonal to Global* (pp. 117–47). Chicago: University of Illinois Press.

ELLIOT, DELBERT S., and SUZANNE S. AGETON. 1980. "Reconciling Race and Class Differences in Self-Reported and Official Estimates of Delinquency." *American Sociological Review.* Vol. 45, No. 1 (February): 95–110.

ELLIOTT, DELBERT S., BEATRIX A. HAMBURG, and KIRK R. WILLIAMS. 1998. "Violence in American Schools: An Overview." In Delbert S. Elliott, Beatrix A. Hamburg, and Kirk R. Williams, eds., *Violence in American Schools: A New Perspective* (pp. 3–28). New York: Cambridge University Press.

EMERSON, MICHAEL O., GEORGE YANCEY, and KAREN J. CHAI. 2001. "Does Race Matter in Residential Segregation? Exploring the Preferences of White Americans." *American Sociological Review.* Vol. 66, No. 6 (December): 922–35.

ENGELS, FRIEDRICH. 1902 (orig., 1884). *The Origin of the Family.* Chicago: Charles H. Kerr & Company.

ENGLAND, PAULA. 1992. *Comparable Worth: Theories and Evidence.* Hawthorne, N.Y.: Aldine de Grutyer.

———. 2001. "Three Reviews on Marriage." *Contemporary Sociology.* Vol. 30, No. 6 (November): 564–5.

ENGLAND, PAULA, JOAN M. HERMSEN, and DAVID A. COTTER. 2000. "The Devaluation of Women's Work: A Comment on Tam." *American Journal of Sociology.* Vol. 105, No. 6 (May): 1741–60.

EQUAL EMPLOYMENT OPPORTUNITIES COMMISSION. 2003. [Online] http://www.eeoc.gov/stats/harass.html Accessed August 18, 2003.

ESKENAZI, MICHAEL. 2000. "Fighting Chance." *Washington Monthly.* Vol. 32, No. 4 (April): 9–15.

ESPO, DAVID. 2001. "Bush's School Voucher Plan Is Nixed." Associated Press (May 2). Accessed May 7, 2001.

———. 2003. "Drug Benefit Bill Gets Bipartisan Support." *Yahoo! News.* [Online] http://www.Yahoonews.com Accessed June 12, 2003.

ESTES, RICHARD J. 2001. "The Commercial Sexual Exploitation of Children in the U.S., Canada, and Mexico." Reported in "Study Explores Sexual Exploitation." *Yahoo! News.* [Online] http://dailynews.yahoo.com Accessed September 10, 2001.

ETZIONI, AMITAI. 1993. "How to Make Marriage Matter." *Time.* Vol. 142, No. 10 (September 6): 76.

EVELYN, JAMILAH. 2002. "Community Colleges Play Too Small a Role in Teacher Education, Report Concludes." *Chronicle of Higher Education Online.* [Online] http://chronicle.com/daily/2002/10/2002102403n.htm Accessed October 24, 2002.

FAGAN, JEFFREY, FRANKLIN E. ZIMRING, and JUNE KIM. 1998. "Declining Homicide in New York City: A Tale of Two Trends." *National Institute of Justice Journal.* Vol. 237 (October): 12–13.

FALKENMARK, MALIN, and CARL WIDSTRAND. 1992. "Population and Water Resources: A Delicate Balance." *Population Bulletin.* Vol. 47, No. 3 (November). Washington, D.C.: Population Reference Bureau.

FALUDI, SUSAN. 1991. *Backlash: The Undeclared War against American Women.* New York: Crown.

FARIS, ROBERT E. L. 1967. *Chicago Sociology 1920–1932.* Chicago: University of Chicago Press.

FARLEY, CHRISTOPHER JOHN, and LISA MCLAUGHLIN. 1997. "A Beating in Brooklyn." *Time.* Vol. 150, No. 8 (August 25): 38.

FEAGIN, JOE. 1991. "The Continuing Significance of Race: Antiblack Discrimination in Public Places." *American Sociological Review.* Vol. 56, No. 1 (February): 101–16.

FEAGIN, JOE R., and CLAIRECE BOOHER FEAGIN. 1986. *Discrimination American Style: Institutional Racism and Sexism,* 2nd ed. Malabar, Fla.: R. E. Krieger.

FEAGIN, JOE R., and MELVIN P. SIKES. 1994. *Living with Racism: The Black Middle-Class Experience.* Boston: Beacon Press.

FEAGIN, JOE R., and HERNÁN VERA. 1995. *White Racism: The Basics.* New York: Routledge.

FELSON, RICHARD B. 2000. "The Normative Protection of Women from Violence." *Sociological Forum.* Vol. 15, No. 1 (March): 91–116.

FETTO, JOHN. 2002. "Gay Friendly?" *American Demographics.* Vol. 24, No. 5 (May): 16.

———. 2002. "A View from the Top?" *American Demographics.* Vol. 24, No. 7 (July–August): 14.

———. 2003. "Drug Money." *American Demographics.* Vol. 25, No. 2 (March): 48.

FEUER, ALAN. 2000. "Distilling the Truth in the Ecstasy Buzz." *The New York Times.* (August 6): Sec. 1: 25, 28.

FINDLAY, S. 1992. "Military Medicine." *U.S. News & World Report.* Vol. 112, No. 23 (June 15): 72–74.

FINE, MELINDA. 1993. "'You Can't Just Say That the Only Ones Who Can Speak Are Those Who Agree with Your Position': Political Discourse in the Classroom." *Harvard Educational Review.* Vol. 63, No. 4 (Winter): 421–33.

FINEMAN, HOWARD, and TAMARA LIPPER. 2003. "Spinning Race." *Newsweek* (January 27): 26–9.

FINLAYSON, JOHN. 1998. "Student Terror: The Weathermen." In *Encyclopedia of World Terrorism.* Vol. 3 (pp. 534–35). Armonk, N.Y.: M. E. Sharpe.

FIREBAUGH, GLENN. 1992. "Growth Effects of Foreign and Domestic Investment." *American Journal of Sociology.* Vol. 98, No. 1 (July): 105–30.

———. 1996. "Does Foreign Capital Harm Poor Nations? New Estimates Based on Dixon and Boswell's Measures of Capital Penetration." *American Journal of Sociology.* Vol. 102, No. 2 (September): 563–75.

FIREBAUGH, GLENN, and FRANK D. BECK. 1994. "Does Economic Growth Benefit the Masses? Growth, Dependence, and Welfare in the Third World." *American Sociological Review.* Vol. 59, No. 5 (October): 631–53.

FIREBAUGH, GLENN, and DUMITRU SANDU. 1998. "Who Supports Marketization and Democratization in Post-Communist Romania?" *Sociological Forum.* Vol. 13, No. 3 (September): 521–41.

FISCHER, CLAUDE. 1973. "Urban Malaise." *Social Problems.* Vol. 52, No. 2 (May): 221–35.

———. 1975. "Toward a Subcultural Theory of Urbanism." *American Journal of Sociology.* Vol. 80, No. 6 (May): 1319–41.

FLEMING, JILLIAN, PAUL MULLEN, and GABRIELE BAMMER. 1997. "A Study of Potential Risk Factors for Sexual Abuse in Childhood." *Child Abuse & Neglect.* Vol. 21, No. 1: 49–58.

FLEXNER, ELEANOR. 1975. *Century of Struggle: The Women's Rights Movement in the United States*, rev. ed. Cambridge, Mass.: The Belknap Press of Harvard University Press.

FLORIAN, ELLEN. 1999. "Oh, No: It's Spreading." *Newsweek.* (July 19): 24–25.

Forbes. "Billionaires: The World's Richest People." Special issue. March 15, 2004.

FORDHAM, SIGNITHIA, and JOHN U. OGBU. 1992 (orig., 1986). "Black Students' School Success: Coping with the Burden of 'Acting White'." In John J. Macionis and Nijole V. Benokraitis, eds., *Seeing Ourselves: Classic, Contemporary, and Cross-Cultural Readings in Sociology*, 2nd ed. (pp. 287–303). Englewood Cliffs, N.J.: Prentice Hall.

FOST, DAN. 1991. "American Indians in the 1990s." *American Demographics.* Vol. 13, No. 12 (December): 26–34.

FOUCAULT, MICHEL. 1965. *Madness and Civilization: A History of Insanity in the Age of Reason.* New York: Pantheon.

———. 1990. *A History of Sexuality, Part I.* New York: Vintage.

FOX, MAGGIE. 2001. "Report: Children's Mental Health 'Crisis' in U.S." *Yahoo! News.* [Online] http://www.yahoonews.com Accessed January 4, 2001.

FRANK, ANDRÉ GUNDER. 1980. *Crisis: In the World Economy.* New York: Holmes & Meier.

———. 1981. *Reflections on the World Economic Crisis.* New York: Monthly Review Press.

FRANKLIN, JOHN HOPE. 1967. *From Slavery to Freedom: A History of Negro Americans*, 3rd ed. New York: Vintage Books.

FRANKLIN ASSOCIATES. 1986. *Characterization of Municipal Solid Waste in the United States, 1960–2000.* Prairie Village, Kans.: Franklin Associates.

FREEDMAN, ESTELLE B. 2002. *No Turning Back: The History of Feminism and the Future of Women.* New York: Ballantine.

FREEDMAN, SAMUEL G. 1998. "Is the Drug Racist?" *Rolling Stone.* Vol. 786 (May 14): 35.

FREEDOM HOUSE. 2000. *Freedom in the World 1999–2000.* New York: Freedom House.

FRENCH, HOWARD W. 2002. "Teaching Japan's Salarymen to Be Their Own Men." *New York Times* (November 27): A4.

FUCHS, VICTOR R. 1986. "Sex Differences in Economic Well-Being." *Science.* Vol. 232 (April 25): 459–64.

FUJIURA, GLENN T. 2001. "Emerging Trends in Disability." *Population Today.* Vol. 29, No. 6 (August–September): 10–11.

FULLER, BRUCE, RICHARD F. ELMORE, and GARY ORFIELD. 1996. "Policy-Making in the Dark: Illuminating the School Choice Debate." In Bruce Fuller, Richard F. Elmore, and Gary Orfield, eds., *Who Chooses? Who Loses? Culture, Institutions, and the Unequal Effects of School Choice* (pp. 1–24). New York: Teachers College Press.

FULMER, T. T., and T. A. O'MALLEY. 1987. *Inadequate Care of the Elderly.* New York: Springer.

FURSTENBERG, FRANK F., JR., and ANDREW CHERLIN. 1991. *Divided Families: What Happens to Children When Parents Part.* Cambridge, Mass.: Harvard University Press.

GAGNÉ, PATRICIA. 1998. *Battered Women's Justice: The Movement for Clemency and the Politics of Self-Defense.* New York: Twayne.

GALBRAITH, JOHN KENNETH. 1985. *The New Industrial State*, 4th ed. Boston: Houghton Mifflin.

GALL, TERRY L., DAVID R. EVANS, and JOHN HOWARD. 1997. "The Retirement Adjustment Process: Changes in the Well-Being of Male Retirees across Time." *Journal of Gerontology: Psychological Sciences.* Vol. 52B, No. 3: 110–17.

GALLAGHER, MAGGIE. 1999. "Does Bradley Know What Poverty Is?" *New York Post* (October 28): 37.

GAMBOA, SUZANNE. 2003. "INS: 7 Million Illegal Immigrants in U.S." *Yahoo! News.* [Online] http://www.yahoonews.com Accessed January 31, 2003.

GAMORAN, ADAM. 1992. "The Variable Effects of High-School Tracking." *American Sociological Review.* Vol. 57, No. 6 (December): 812–28.

GANS, HERBERT J. 1968. *People and Plans: Essays on Urban Problems and Solutions.* New York: Basic Books.

———. 1971. "The Uses of Poverty: The Poor Pay All." *Social Policy.* Vol. 2 (July–August): 20–24.

GARDNER, JONATHAN. 1998. "The VA on the Firing Line." *Modern Healthcare.* Vol. 28, No. 47 (November 23): 48–50.

GARFINKEL, HAROLD. 1956. "Conditions of Successful Degradation Ceremonies." *American Journal of Sociology.* Vol. 61, No. 2 (March): 420–24.

GARREAU, JOEL. 1991. *Edge City.* New York: Doubleday.

GARWOOD, PAUL. 2003. "Garbage Collectors Trash Governor's Plan." *Middle Eastern Times.* [Online] http://www.metimes.com/2K1/issue2001-20/eq/garbage_collectors_trash.htm Accessed November 29, 2003.

GELLES, RICHARD J. 1997. *Intimate Violence in Families.* Newbury Park, Calif.: Sage.

GELLES, RICHARD J., and CLAIRE PEDRICK CORNELL. 1990. *Intimate Violence in Families*, 2nd ed. Newbury Park, Calif.: Sage.

GELLES, RICHARD J., and MURRAY A. STRAUS. 1988. *Intimate Violence: The Causes and Consequences of Abuse in the American Family.* New York: Touchstone.

GELMAN, DAVID. 1992. "Born or Bred?" *Newsweek* (February 24): 46–53.

GENDELL, MURRAY. 2002. "Boomers' Retirement Wave Likely to Begin in Just Six Years." *Population Today.* Vol. 30, No. 3 (April): 1–2.

GERBER, THEODORE P., and MICHAEL HOUT. 1998. "More Shock than Therapy: Market Transition, Employment, and Income in Russia, 1991–1995." *American Journal of Sociology.* Vol. 104, No. 1 (July): 1–50.

GERGEN, DAVID. 2002. "King of the World." *U.S. News & World Report.* Vol. 132, No. 6 (February 25–March 4): 84.

GERNER, D. L., M. MORGAN GROSS, and N. SIGNORELLI. 1994. "Growing Up on Television: The Cultivation Perspective." In J. Bryant and D. Zilmann, eds., *Media Effects* (pp. 17–41). Hillsdale, N.J.: Erlbaum.

GIBBS, NANCY. 1999. "In Sorrow and Disbelief, Special Report: The Littleton Massacre." *Time.* Vol. 153, No. 17 (May 3): 20.

GIBBS, NANCY, and TIMOTHY ROCHE. 1999. "The Columbine Tapes." *Time.* Vol. 154, No. 25 (December 20): 40–51.

GIBEAUT, JOHN. 1997. "Deadly Inspiration." *ABA Journal.* Vol. 83 (June): 62–67.

GIELE, JANET Z. 1988. "Gender and Sex Roles." In Neil J. Smelser, ed., *Handbook of Sociology* (pp. 291–323). Newbury Park, Calif.: Sage.

GILBERTSON, GRETA A., and DOUGLAS T. GURAK. 1993. "Broadening the Enclave Debate: The Dual Labor Market Experiences of Dominican and Colombian Men in New York City." *Sociological Forum.* Vol. 8, No. 2 (June): 205–20.

GILDER, GEORGE. 1980. "The Myths of Racial and Sexual Discrimination." *National Review*. Vol. 32, No. 23 (November 14): 1381–90.

GILDERBLOOM, JOHN I., and JOHN P. MARKHAM. 1996. "Housing Modification Needs of the Disabled Elderly: What Really Matters?" *Environment & Behavior*. Vol. 28, No. 4 (July): 512–36.

GILENS, MARTIN. 1999. *Why Americans Hate Welfare: Race, Media and the Politics of Antipoverty Policy*. Chicago: University of Chicago Press.

GILLIGAN, JAMES. 1996. *Violence: Our Deadly Epidemic and Its Causes*. New York: Putnam.

GILLON, RAANAN. 1999. "Euthanasia in the Netherlands: Down the Slippery Slope?" *Journal of Medical Ethics*. Vol. 25, No. 1 (February): 3–4.

GLAAB, CHARLES N. 1963. *The American City: A Documentary History*. Homewood, Ill.: Dorsey.

GLAAB, CHARLES N. and A. THEODORE BROWN. 1967. *A History of Urban America*. New York: Macmillan.

GLASS, STEPHEN. 1997. "Don't You D.A.R.E." *New Republic*. Vol. 216, No. 9 (March 3): 18–25.

GLUECK, SHELDON, and ELEANOR GLUECK. 1950. *Unraveling Juvenile Delinquency*. New York: Commonwealth Fund.

GODKIN, M. A., R. S. WOLF, and K. A. PILLEMER. 1989. "A Case-Comparison Analysis of Elder Abuse and Neglect." *International Journal of Aging and Human Development*. Vol. 28, No. 1: 207–25.

GOETTING, ANN. 1999. *Getting Out: Life Stories of Women Who Left Abusive Men*. New York: Columbia University Press.

GOFFMAN, ERVING. 1963. *Stigma: Notes on the Management of Spoiled Identity*. Englewood Cliffs, N.J.: Prentice Hall.

———. 1979. *Gender Advertisements*. New York: Harper Colophon.

GOLDBERG, STEVEN. 1974. *The Inevitability of Patriarchy*. New York: William Morrow.

———. Personal communication, 1987.

GOLDFARB, WILLIAM. 1991. "Groundwater: The Buried Life." In F. Herbert Bormann and Stephen R. Kellert, eds., *Ecology, Economics, and Ethics: The Broken Circle* (pp. 123–35). New Haven, Conn.: Yale University Press.

GOLDFIELD, MICHAEL. 2000. "Rebounding Unions Target Service Sector." *Population Today*. Vol. 28, No. 7 (October): 3, 10.

GOLDMAN, HENRY. 1991. "The Plight of the Black Child." *Philadelphia Inquirer*. (February 10): 5E.

GOLDSTEIN, AVRAM. 1994. *Addiction: From Biology to Drug Policy*. New York: W. H. Freeman.

GOLDSTEIN, PAUL J. 1995. "The Drugs/Violence Nexus: A Tripartite Conceptual Framework." In James A. Inciardi and Karen McElrath, eds., *The American Drug Scene: An Anthology* (pp. 255–64). Los Angeles: Roxbury.

GOMBY, DEANNA S., and PATRICIA H. SHIONO. 1991. "Estimating the Number of Substance-Exposed Infants." *Future of Children*. Vol. 1, No. 1: 17–25.

GÓMEZ, LAURA E. 1997. *Misconceiving Mothers: Legislators, Prosecutors, and the Politics of Prenatal Drug Exposure*. Philadelphia: Temple University Press.

GOODE, ERICH. 1993. *Drugs in American Society*, 4th ed. New York: McGraw-Hill.

———. 1997. *Between Politics and Reason: The Drug Legalization Debate*. New York: St. Martin's Press.

GOODMAN, DAVID. 1999. "America's Newest Class War." *Mother Jones*. Vol. 24, No. 5 (September–October): 68–75.

GORDON, SOL, and CRAIG W. SNYDER. 1989. *Personal Issues in Human Sexuality: A Guidebook for Better Sexual Health*, 2nd ed. Boston: Allyn & Bacon.

GOTTLIEB, BENJAMIN H., E. KEVIN KELLOWAY, and ELIZABETH BARHAM. 1998. *Flexible Work Arrangements: Managing the Work-Family Boundary*. New York: Wiley.

GOTTMANN, JEAN. 1961. *Megalopolis*. New York: Twentieth Century Fund.

GRADY, DENISE. 1992. "The Brains of Gay Men." *Discover*. (January): 29.

GREENBERG, J. R., M. McKIBBEN, and J. A. RAYMOND. 1990. "Dependent Adult Children and Elder Abuse." *Journal of Elder Abuse & Neglect*. Vol. 2: 73–86.

GREENBURG, STANLEY B. 1996. *Middle Class Dreams: The Politics and Power of the New American Majority*, rev. and updated ed. New Haven, Conn.: Yale University Press.

GREENHOUSE, STEVEN. 2000. "Despite Defeat on China Bill, Labor Is on the Rise." *The New York Times*. (May 20): A1, A18.

GRIFFIN, SUSAN. 1979. *Rape: The Power of Consciousness*. San Francisco: Harper & Row.

GRIMM, MATTHEW. 2002. "A Dubious Pitch." *American Demographics*. Vol. 24, No. 5 (May): 44–6.

GROVES, BETSY McALISTER. 1997. "Growing Up in a Violent World: The Impact of Family and Community Violence on Young Children and Their Families." *Topics in Early Childhood Special Education*. Vol. 17, No. 1 (Spring): 74–101.

GUP, TED. 1991. "The Curse of Coal." *Time*. Vol. 138, No. 18 (November 4): 54–64.

GUPTA, GIRI RAJ. 1993. *Sociology of Mental Health*. Boston: Allyn & Bacon.

GUTEK, GERALD L. 1993. *American Education in a Global Society: Internationalizing Teacher Education*. White Plains, N.Y.: Longman.

HACKER, HELEN MAYER. 1951. "Women as a Minority Group." *Social Forces*. Vol. 30 (October): 60–69.

HACKLER, TIM. 1979. "The Big City Has No Corners on Mental Illness." *The New York Times Magazine*. (December 19): A1.

HADLEY, JANET. 1996. *Abortion: Between Freedom and Necessity*. Philadelphia: Temple University Press.

HAFNER-EATON, CHRIS. 1994. "When the Phoenix Rises, Where Will She Go?: The Women's Health Agenda." In Pauline Vaillancourt Rosenau, ed., *Health Care Reform in the Nineties* (pp. 236–56). Thousand Oaks, Calif.: Sage.

HALBFINGER, DAVID M. and STEVEN A. HOLMES. 2003. "Military Mirrors Working-Class America." *The New York Times on the Web*. (March 30). [Online] http://www.resrearchnavigator.com/content/nyt/2003/03/30/82.htm Accessed September 8, 2003.

HALLINAN, MAUREEN T., and RICHARD A. WILLIAMS. 1989. "Interracial Friendship Choices in Secondary Schools." *American Sociological Review*. Vol. 54, No. 1 (February): 67–78.

HAMER, DEAN, and PETER COPELAND. 1994. *The Search for the Gay Gene and the Biology of Behavior*. New York: Simon & Schuster.

HANDGUN CONTROL, INC. 2001. [Online] http://www.handguncontrol.org/press/archive/march30-98.htm

HANEY, CRAIG, CURTIS BANKS, and PHILIP ZIMBARDO. 1973. "Interpersonal Dynamics in a Simulated Prison." *International Journal of Criminology and Penology*. Vol. 1: 69–97.

HARKEY, JOHN, DAVID L. MILES, and WILLIAM A. RUSHING. 1976. "The Relation between Social Class and Functional Status: A New Look at the Drift Hypothesis." *Journal of Health and Social Behavior*. Vol. 17, No. 2: 194–204.

HARPSTER, PAULA, and ELIZABETH MONK-TURNER. 1998. "Why Men Do Housework: A Test of Gender Production and the Relative Resources Model." *Sociological Focus.* Vol. 31, No. 1 (February): 45–59.

HARRIES, KEITH D. 1990. *Serious Violence: Patterns of Homicide and Assault in America.* Springfield, Ill.: Charles C. Thomas.

HARRINGTON, MICHAEL. 1962. *The Other America: Poverty in the United States.* Baltimore: Penguin.

HARRIS, DAVID R., and JEREMIAH JOSEPH SIM. 2002. "Who Is Multiracial? Assessing the Complexity of Lived Race." *American Sociological Review.* Vol. 67, No. 4 (August): 614–27.

HARVEY, DAVID. 1973. *Social Justice and the City.* Baltimore: Johns Hopkins University Press.

HAUB, CARL. 2002a. "Has Global Growth Reached Its Peak?" *Population Today.* Vol. 30, No. 6 (August–September): 6.

———. 2002b. "How Many People Have Ever Lived on Earth?" *Population Today.* Vol. 30, No. 8 (November–December): 3–4.

HAVINGHURST, ROBERT J., BERNICE L. NEUGARTEN, and SHELDON S. TOBIN. 1968. "Disengagement and Patterns of Aging." In Bernice L. Neugarten, ed., *Middle Age and Aging: A Reader in Social Psychology* (pp. 161–72). Chicago: University of Chicago Press.

HAWKINS, J. DAVID, DAVID P. FARRINGTON, and RICHARD F. CATALANO. 1998. "Reducing Violence through the Schools." In Delbert S. Elliott, Beatrix A. Hamburg, and Kirk R. Williams, eds., *Violence in American Schools: A New Perspective* (pp. 180–216). New York: Cambridge University Press.

HENDERSON, DAMIEN. 2003. "Cannabis Cafes Face Ban on Smoking." *The Glasgow Herald.* [Online] http://www.theherald.co.uk (May 29). Accessed September 4, 2003.

HENLEY, NANCY, MYKOL HAMILTON, and BARRIE THORNE. 1992. "Womanspeak and Manspeak: Sex Differences in Communication, Verbal and Nonverbal." In John J. Macionis and Nijole V. Benokraitis, eds., *Seeing Ourselves: Classic, Contemporary, and Cross-Cultural Readings in Sociology,* 2nd ed. (pp. 10–15). Englewood Cliffs, N.J.: Prentice Hall.

HERDT, GILBERT H. 1993. "Semen Transactions in Sambian Culture." In David N. Suggs and Andrew W. Miracle, eds., *Culture and Human Sexuality* (pp. 298–327). Pacific Grove, Calif.: Brooks Cole.

HEREK, G. M. 1991. "Myths about Sexual Orientation: A Lawyer's Guide to Social Science Research." *Law and Sexuality.* Vol. 1, No. 1: 133–72.

HERMAN, DIANNE F. 2001. "The Rape Culture." In John J. Macionis and Nijole V. Benokraitis, eds., *Seeing Ourselves: Classic, Contemporary, and Cross-Cultural Readings in Sociology,* 5th ed. (pp. 38–46). Upper Saddle River, N.J.: Prentice Hall.

HERRNSON, PAUL S. 1998. "Parties and Interest Groups in Postreform Congressional Elections." In Allan J. Cigler and Burdett A. Loomis, eds., *Interest Group Politics,* 5th ed. (pp. 145–68). Washington, D.C.: CQ Press.

HERRNSTEIN, RICHARD J., and CHARLES MURRAY. 1994. *The Bell Curve: Intelligence and Class Structure in American Life.* New York: Free Press.

HEWLETT, SYLVIA ANN, and CORNEL WEST. 1998. *The War against Parents.* Boston: Houghton Mifflin.

HILSMAN, ROGER. 1999. *From Nuclear Military Strategy to a World without War: A History and a Proposal.* Westport, Conn.: Praeger.

HIMES, CHRISTINE L. 2001. "Elderly Americans." *Population Bulletin.* Vol. 56, No. 4 (December). Washington, D.C.: Population Reference Bureau.

HINRICHSEN, G. A., N. A. HERNANDEZ, and S. POLLACK. 1992. "Difficulties and Rewards in Family Care of Depressed Older Adults." *Gerontologist.* Vol. 32: 486–92.

HIRSCHI, TRAVIS. 1969. *Causes of Delinquency.* Berkeley: University of California Press.

HIXON, ALLEN L. 1999. "Preventing Street Gang Violence." *American Family Physician.* Vol. 59, No. 8 (April 15): 2121–24.

HOCHSCHILD, ARLIE, with ANNE MACHUNG. 1989. *The Second Shift: Working Parents and the Revolution at Home.* New York: Viking.

HODKINSON, PAUL, and MARTIN BLOOMER. 2001. "Dropping Out of Further Education: Complex Causes and Simplistic Policy Assumptions." *Research Papers in Education.* Vol. 16, No. 2 (July): 117–41.

HOFFMAN, BRUCE. 1998. *Inside Terrorism.* New York: Columbia University Press.

HOGE, WARREN. 2002. "Britain to Stop Arresting Most Private Users of Marijuana." *The New York Times.* (July 11). [Online] http://www.researchnavigator.com Accessed September 4, 2003.

HOLDEN, KAREN C., and PAMELA J. SMOCK. 1991. "The Economic Costs of Marital Dissolution: Why Do Women Bear a Disproportionate Cost?" *Annual Review of Sociology.* Vol. 17: 51–78.

HOLLINGSHEAD, AUGUST B., and FREDERICH C. REDLICH. 1958. *Social Class and Mental Illness: A Community Study.* New York: Wiley.

HOLMES, ELLEN RHOADS, and LOWELL D. HOLMES. 1995. *Other Cultures, Elder Years,* 2nd ed. Thousand Oaks, Calif.: Sage.

HOLMES, MALCOLM D., HARMON M. HOSCH, HOWARD C. DAUDISTEL, DOLORES PEREZ, and JOSEPH B. GRAVES. 1993. "Judges, Ethnicity and Minority Sentencing: Evidence among Hispanics." *Social Science Quarterly.* Vol. 74, No. 3 (September): 496–506.

HOLMES, RONALD M., and STEPHEN T. HOLMES. 1993. *Murder in America.* Newbury Park, Calif.: Sage.

———. 1998. *Serial Murder,* 2nd ed. Thousand Oaks, Calif.: Sage.

HOLMES, STEVEN A. 1996a. "U.S. Reports Drop in Rate of Births to Unwed Women." *The New York Times* (October 5): 1, 9.

———. 1996b. "For Hispanic Poor, No Silver Lining." *The New York Times* (October 13): Sec. 4, p. 5.

HOLMSTROM, DAVID. 1994. "Abuse of Elderly, Even by Adult Children, Gets More Attention and Official Concern." *Christian Science Monitor.* (July 28): 1.

HORTON, HAYWARD DERRICK, BEVERLY LUNDY ALLEN, CEDRIC HERRING, and MELVIN E. THOMAS. 2000. "Lost in the Storm: The Sociology of the Black Working Class, 1850 to 1990." *American Sociological Review.* Vol. 65, No. 1 (February): 128–37.

HOUSING AUTHORITY OF NEW ORLEANS. 2002. [Online] http://www.hano.org Accessed October 4, 2003.

HOWELL, JAMES. 1996. "The Myth of Related Youth Gang Homicides and Drug Trafficking." *Juvenile and Family Justice Today.* (Summer): 12. [Online] http://www.cdc.gov/nchstp/hiv_aids/pubs/facts/hivrepfs.htm Accessed May 8, 1999. http://www.cnnsi.com Accessed July 4. 1998. http://www.thc.nl/Countries/nl/lawlex.htm Accessed April 19, 2000.

HSIN, HONOR. 2003. "Episode II." *Harvard International Review.* Vol. 25, No. 3 (Fall): 15–16.

HUBER, CHRISTIAN. 1994. "Needle Park: What Can We Learn from the Zurich Experience?" *Addiction.* Vol. 89, No. 5 (May): 413–517.

HUD. 1999. Press Release, No. 99-258 on Homeless in America (December 8). [Online] http://www.hud.gov/pressrel/pr99-258.html Accessed February 24, 2000.

HUDSON, KEN. 1999. "No Shortage of 'Nonstandard' Jobs: Nearly 30% of Workers Employed in Part-Time, Temping, and Other Alternative Arrangements." Economic Policy Institute Briefing Paper. [Online] http://www.epinet.org/briefingpapers/hudson/hudson.html Accessed December 10, 2000.

HUDSON, MICHAEL C. 1992. "The Middle East Under Pax Americana: How New, How Orderly?" *Third World Quarterly*. Vol. 13, No. 2: 301–16.

HUESMANN, L. ROWELL. 1986. "Psychological Process Promoting the Relation between Exposure to Media Violence and Aggressive Behavior by the Viewer." *Social Issues*. Vol. 42: 125–39.

HUFFMAN, MATT L., STEVEN C. VELASCO, and WILLIAM T. BIELBY. 1996. "Where Sex Composition Matters Most: Comparing the Effects of Job versus Occupational Sex Composition of Earnings." *Sociological Focus*. Vol. 29, No. 3 (August): 189–207.

HUGHES, MATTHEW. 1998. "The World Trade Center Bombing." In *Encyclopedia of World Terrorism*. Vol. 3 (pp. 540–41). Armonk, N.Y.: M. E. Sharpe.

HUNT, GEOFFREY, and ANNA XIAO DONG SUN. 1998. "The Drug Treatment System in the United States: A Panacea for the Drug War?" In Harold Klingemann and Geoffrey Hunt, eds., *Drug Treatment Systems in an International Perspective: Drugs, Demons, and Delinquents* (pp. 3–19). Thousand Oaks, Calif.: Sage.

HYMOWITZ, CAROL. 1995. "World's Poorest Women Advance by Entrepreneurship." *Wall Street Journal* (September 9): B1.

IGNATIEV, NOEL. 1995. *How the Irish Became White*. New York: Routledge.

INCIARDI, JAMES A., ed. 1990. *The Drug Legalization Debate*. Newbury Park, Calif.: Sage.

———. 1992. *The War on Drugs II: The Continuing Epic of Heroin, Cocaine, Crack, Crime, AIDS, and Public Policy*. Mountain View, Calif.: Mayfield.

———. 1996. *Drug Control and the Courts*. Thousand Oaks, Calif.: Sage.

———. 2000. *Elements of Criminal Justice*, 2nd ed. New York: Oxford University Press.

INCIARDI, JAMES A., DOROTHY LOCKWOOD, and ANNE E. POTTIEGER. 1993. *Women and Crack-Cocaine*. New York: Macmillan.

INCIARDI, JAMES A., and DUANE C. MCBRIDE. 1991. "The Case against Legalization." In James A. Inciardi, ed., *The Drug Legalization Debate* (pp. 45–79). Newbury Park, Calif.: Sage.

INSTITUTE FOR STRATEGIC STUDIES. 2003. *The Military Balance: 2003–2004*. London: Oxford University Press.

INTER-PARLIAMENTARY UNION. 2003. "Women in National Parliaments." [Online] http://www.ipu.org/wmn-e/classif.htm and http://www.ipu.org/wmn-e/world.htm Accessed June 30, 2003.

ISAY, RICHARD A. 1989. *Being Homosexual: Gay Men and Their Development*. New York: Farrar, Straus, & Giroux.

JACKSON, SHERI, and SUE SCOTT, eds. 1996. *Feminism and Sexuality: A Reader*. New York: Columbia University Press.

JAGAROWSKY, PAUL A., and MARY JO BANE. 1990. *Neighborhood Poverty: Basic Questions*. Discussion paper series H-90-3. John F. Kennedy School of Government. Cambridge, Mass.: Harvard University Press.

JAGGER, ALISON. 1983. "Political Philosophies of Women's Liberation." In Laurel Richardson and Verta Taylor, eds., *Feminist Frontiers: Rethinking Sex, Gender, and Society*. Reading, Mass.: Addison-Wesley.

JANUS, CHRISTOPHER G. 1996. "Slavery Abolished? Only Officially." *Christian Science Monitor* (May 17): 18.

JASINSKI, JANA L., and LINDA M. WILLIAMS. 1998. "Introduction." In Jana L. Jasinski and Linda M. Williams, eds., *Partner Violence: A Comprehensive Review of 20 Years of Research* (pp. ix–xiv). Thousand Oaks, Calif.: Sage.

JENCKS, CHRISTOPHER, MARSHALL SMITH, HENRY ACLAND, MARY JO BANE, DAVID COHEN, HERBERT GINTIS, BARBARA HEYNS, and STEPHAN MICHELSON. 1972. *Inequality: A Reassessment of the Effect of Family and Schooling in America*. New York: Basic Books.

JENKINS, J. CRAIG, and MICHAEL WALLACE. 1996. "The Generalized Action Potential of Protest Movements: The New Class, Social Trends, and Political Exclusion Explanations." *Sociological Forum*. Vol. 11, No. 2 (June): 183–207.

JENKINS, PHILIP. 1994. *Using Murder: The Social Construction of Serial Homicide*. New York: Aldine De Gruyter.

JENNESS, VALERIE. 1993. *Making It Work: The Prostitutes' Rights Movement in Perspective*. New York: Aldine de Gruyter.

JENNESS, VALERIE, and RYKEN GRATTET. 2001. *Making a Hate Crime: From Movement to Law Enforcement*. New York: Russell Sage Foundation.

JOHNSON, CATHRYN. 1994. "Gender, Legitimate Authority, and Leader-Subordinate Conversations." *American Sociological Review*. Vol. 59, No. 1 (February): 122–35.

JOHNSON, DIRK. 1991. "Census Finds Many Claiming New Identity: Indian." *The New York Times* (March 5): A1, A16.

JOHNSON, JACQUELINE, SHARON RUSH, and JOE FEAGIN. 2000. "Doing Anti-Racism: Toward an Egalitarian American Society." *Contemporary Sociology*. Vol. 29, No. 1 (January): 95–110.

JOHNSON, KEVIN. 2000. "Serious Crime Down Again: 7% Dip in '99." *USA Today*. (May 8): A1.

JOHNSON, KIRK, and THOMAS L. LUECK. 1996. "Region's Economy in Fundamental Shift." *The New York Times*. (February 19): A1.

JOSEPHY, ALVIN M., JR. 1982. *Now That the Buffalo's Gone: A Study of Today's American Indians*. New York: Alfred A. Knopf.

KADLEC, DANIEL. 2002. "Everyone, Back in the (Labor) Pool." *Time*. Vol. 160, No. 5 (July 29): 22–31.

KADUSHIN, CHARLES. 1983. "Mental Health and the Interpersonal Environment." *American Sociological Review*. Vol. 48, No. 2 (April): 188–98.

KAIN, EDWARD L. 1990. *The Myth of Family Decline: Understanding Families in a World of Rapid Social Change*. Lexington, Mass.: Lexington Books.

KALB, CLAUDIA. 2001. "Can This Pill Stop You from Hitting the Bottle?" *Newsweek*. (February 12): 48–50.

KALDOR, MARY. 1999. *New & Old Wars: Organized Violence in a Global Era*. Stanford, Calif.: Stanford University Press.

KAMINER, WENDY. 1997. "Demasculinizing the Army." *New York Times Review of Books* (June 15): 7.

KANE, CAROL C. and HORST LOEBLICH. 2003. "Physician Income: The Decade in Review." In *Physician Socioeconomic Statistics, 2003*. Chicago: American Medical Association.

KANTOR, GLENDA KAUFMAN, and JANA L. JASINSKI. 1998. "Dynamics and Risk Factors in Partner Violence." In Jana L. Jasinski and Linda M. Williams, eds., *Partner Violence: A Comprehensive Review of 20 Years of Research* (pp. 1–43). Thousand Oaks, Calif.: Sage.

KANTROWITZ, BARBARA, and PAT WINGERT. 1993. "The Norplant Debate." *Newsweek.* (February 15): 37–41.

———. 2001. "Unmarried with Children." *Newsweek* (May 28): 46–52.

———. 2003. "What's at Stake." *Newsweek* (January 27): 30–7.

KAPLAN, DAVID E., and MICHAEL SCHAFFER. 2001. "Losing the Psywar." *U.S. News & World Report* (October 8): 46.

KAPLAN, ELAINE BELL. 1997. *Not Our Kind of Girl: Unraveling the Myths of Black Teenage Motherhood.* Berkeley: University of California Press.

KATSURA, HAROLD M., RAYMOND J. STRUYK, and SANDRA J. NEWMAN. 1989. *Housing for the Elderly in 2010: Projections and Policy Options.* Washington, D.C.: The Urban Institute Press.

KATZ, GARY. 2003. "Getting to Trial." CBC News, August 13. [Online] http://www.cbc.ca/news/indepth/lockerbie/trial.htm Accessed November 20, 2003.

KATZ, MICHAEL B. 1986. *In the Shadow of the Poorhouse.* New York: Basic Books.

———. 1986. *The Undeserving Poor: From the War on Poverty to the War on Welfare.* New York: Pantheon.

KAUFMAN, WALTER. 1976. *Religions in Four Dimensions: Existential, Aesthetic, Historical and Comparative.* New York: Reader's Digest Press.

KAUKAS, DICK. 1999. "The Poor Struggle for Transplants." *Louisville Courier-Journal* (June 6): A1, A14.

KAUSLER, DONALD H., and BARRY C. KAUSLER. 1996. *The Graying of America: An Encyclopedia of Aging, Health, Mind, and Behavior.* Chicago: University of Chicago Press.

KEISTER, LISA A. 2000. *Wealth in America: Trends in Wealth Inequality.* Cambridge: Cambridge University Press.

KEISTER, LISA A., and STEPHANIE MOLLER. 2000. "Wealth Inequality in the United States." *Annual Review of Sociology.* Vol. 26: 63–81.

KEITH, PAT M., and ROBERT B. SCHAFER. 1994. "They Hate to Cook: Patterns of Distress in an Ordinary Role." *Sociological Focus.* Vol. 27, No. 4 (October): 289–301.

KELLERT, STEPHEN R., and F. HERBERT BORMANN. 1991. "Closing the Circle: Weaving Strands among Ecology, Economics, and Ethics." In F. Herbert Bormann and Stephen R. Kellert, eds., *Ecology, Economics, and Ethics: The Broken Circle* (pp. 205–10). New Haven, Conn.: Yale University Press.

KELLY, KATE. 2001. "Lost on the Campus." *Time.* Vol. 157, No. 2 (January 15): 51–3.

KEMP, JACK. 1994. "A Cultural Renaissance." *Imprimis.* Vol. 23, No. 8 (August): 1–5.

KEMPE, C. H., F. N. SILVERMAN, B. F. STELE, W. GROEGEMUELLER, and H. K. SILVER. 1962. "The Battered Child Syndrome." *Journal of the American Medical Association.* Vol. 181: 17–24.

KENNICKELL, ARTHUR B., MARTHA STARR-MCCLUER, and BRIAN J. SURETTE. 2000. "Recent Changes in U.S. Family Finances: Results from the 1998 Survey of Consumer Finances." [Online] http://www.federalreserve.gov/pubs/bulletin/2000/0100lead.pdf Accessed April 7, 2000.

KENT, MARY MEDERIOS. 1999. "Shrinking Societies Favor Procreation." *Population Today.* Vol. 27, No. 12 (December): 4–5.

KENT, MARY M., and MARK MATHER. 2002. "What Drives U.S. Population Growth?" *Population Bulletin.* Vol. 57, No. 4 (December): 3–40.

KENTOR, JEFFREY. 1998. "The Long-Term Effects of Foreign Investment Dependence on Economic Growth, 1940–1990." *American Journal of Sociology.* Vol. 103, No. 4 (January): 1024–46.

———. 2001. "The Long-Term Effects of Globalization on Income Inequality, Population Growth, and Economic Development." *Social Problems.* Vol. 48, No. 4 (November): 435–55.

KESSLER, RONALD C., KATHERINE A. MCGONAGLE, SHANYANG ZHAO, CHRISTOPHER B. NELSON, MICHAEL HUGHES, SUZANN ESHLEMAN, HANS-ULRICH WITTCHEN, and KENNETH S. KENDLER. 1994. "Life-Time and 12-Month Prevalence of DSM-III-R Psychiatric Disorders in the United States: Results from the National Comorbidity Survey." *Archives of General Psychiatry.* Vol. 51: 8–19.

KEY, SANDRA, with MARYCLAIRE LINDGREN. 1999. "Action against Missed Opportunities to Prevent Heart Disease in Women Urged." *Women's Health Weekly.* (May 17): 8–9.

KIEFER, CHRISTIE W. 1990. "The Elderly in Modern Japan: Elite, Victims, or Plural Players?" In Jay Sokolovsky, ed., *The Cultural Context of Aging: Worldwide Perspectives* (pp. 181–95). New York: Bergin & Garvey.

KILGORE, SALLY B. 1991. "The Organizational Context of Tracking in Schools." *American Sociological Review.* Vol. 56, No. 2 (April): 189–203.

KINKEAD, GWEN. 1992. *Chinatown: A Portrait of a Closed Society.* New York: HarperCollins.

KINSEY, ALFRED, ET AL. 1948. *Sexual Behavior in the Human Male.* Philadelphia: Saunders.

———. 1953. *Sexual Behavior in the Human Female.* Philadelphia: Saunders.

KIRN, WALTER. 1998. "Crank." *Time.* Vol. 153, No. 24 (June 22): 25–32.

KITMAN, JAMIE. 2003. "Tort Reform for Dummies." *Automobile.* (April): 145.

KLEIN, JOE. 2003. "How the Supremes Redeemed Bush." *Time.* Vol. 162, No. 1 (July 7): 27.

KLEINMAN, ARTHUR. 1997. "Intimations of Solidarity? The Popular Culture Responds to Assisted Suicide." *Hastings Center Report.* (September–October): 34–36.

KLUGER, JEFFREY. 2001. "A Climate of Despair." *Time.* Vol. 157, No. 14 (April 9): 30–36.

KNIGHT, ROBERT H. 1998. "How Domestic Partnerships and 'Gay Marriage' Threaten the Family." In Robert T. Francoeur and William J. Taverner, eds., *Taking Sides: Clashing Views on Controversial Issues in Human Sexuality,* 6th ed. (pp. 196–206). New York: Dushkin/McGraw-Hill.

KONIGSBERG, E. 1992. "S*M*A*S*H: Don't Fix Those Deadly Veterans Hospitals. Abolish Them." *Washington Monthly.* Vol. 24, No. 5 (May): 31–4.

KONO, CLIFFORD, DONALD PALMER, ROGER FRIEDLAND, and MATTHEW ZAFONTE. 1998. "Lost in Space: The Geography of Corporate Interlocking Directorates." *American Journal of Sociology.* Vol. 103, No. 4 (January): 863–911.

KONTOS, PIA C. 1998. "Resisting Institutionalization: Constructing Old Age and Negotiating Home." *Journal of Aging Studies.* Vol. 12 (Summer): 167–84.

KOONTZ, STEPHANIE. 1992. *The Way We Never Were: American Families and the Nostalgia Trap.* New York: Basic Books.

KOSBERG, J. I. 1988. "Preventing Elder Abuse: Identification of High Risk Factors Prior to Placement Decisions." *Gerontologist.* Vol. 28: 43–50.

KOSTERLITZ, JULIE. 1997. "When We're 64." *National Journal*. Vol. 29, No. 39 (September 27): 1882–85.

KOTKIN, JOEL. 2001. "Cities Must Change to Survive." *Wall Street Journal*. (October 24): A22.

KOZOL, JONATHAN. 1988. *Rachel and Her Children: Homeless Families in America*. New York: Crown.

———. 1991. *Savage Inequalities: Children in America's Schools*. New York: Crown.

———. 1992. *Savage Inequalities: Children in America's Schools*, reprint ed. New York: Harper Perennial.

KRATCOSKI, P., and L. L. KRATCOSKI. 1986. *Juvenile Delinquency*. Englewood Cliffs, N.J.: Prentice Hall.

KRAUTHAMMER, CHARLES. 1995. "A Social Conservative Credo." *The Public Interest*. Vol. 121 (Fall): 15–22.

KRISTOF, NICHOLAS D. 1996. "Baby May Make Three, but in Japan That's Not Enough." *The New York Times*. (October 6): A3.

KROMAR, MARINA, and PATTI M. VALKENBURG. 1999. "A Scale to Assess Children's Moral Interpretations of Justified and Unjustified Violence and its Relationship to Television Viewing." *Communication Research*. Vol. 26, No. 5 (October): 608–35.

KRYSAN, MARIA. 2002. "Community Undesirability in Black and White: Examining Racial Residential Preferences through Community Perceptions." *Social Problems*. Vol. 49, No. 4 (November): 521–43.

KUGLER, JACEK, and A. F. K. ORGANSKI. 1989. "The Power Transition: A Retrospective and Prospective Evaluation." In Manus I. Midlarskky, ed., *Handbook of War Studies* (pp. 171–94). Boston: Unwin Hyman.

KUNSTLER, JAMES HOWARD. 1996. "Home from Nowhere." *The Atlantic Monthly*. Vol. 278 (September): 43–66.

KUTTY, NANDINEE K. 1998. "The Scope for Poverty Alleviation among Elderly Home-Owners in the United States through Reverse Mortgages." *Urban Studies*. Vol. 35, No. 1 (January): 113–30.

LABATON, STEPHEN. 2000. "You Don't Have to Be Old to Sue for Age Discrimination." *The New York Times*. (February 16): A7.

LACAYO, RICHARD. 1999. "The Brawl over Sprawl." *Time*. Vol. 153, No. 11 (March 22): 44–48.

LAFREE, GARY. 1998. *Losing Legitimacy: Street Crime and the Decline of Social Institutions in America*. Boulder, Colo.: Westview Press.

LANGBEIN, LAURA, and ROSEANA BESS. 2002. "Sports in School: Source of Amity or Antipathy?" *Social Science Quarterly*. Vol. 83, No. 2 (June): 436–54.

LAPPÉ, FRANCES MOORE, and JOSEPH COLLINS. 1986. *World Hunger: Twelve Myths*. New York: Grove Press/Food First Books.

LAPPÉ, FRANCES MOORE, JOSEPH COLLINS, and DAVID KINLEY. 1981. *Aid as Obstacle: Twenty Questions about Our Foreign Policy and the Hungry*. San Francisco: Institute for Food and Development Policy.

LAUMANN, EDWARD O., JOHN H. GAGNON, ROBERT T. MICHAELS, and STUART MICHAELS. 1994. *The Social Organization of Sexuality: Sexual Practices in the United States*. Chicago: University of Chicago Press.

LAVELLA, MARIANNA. 2002. "Payback Time." *U.S. News & World Report*. Vol. 132, No. 7 (March 11): 36–40.

LAWTON, M. POWELL. 1995. "Forward." In Jon Phnoos and Phoebe S. Liebig, eds., *Housing Frail Elders: International Policies, Perspectives, and Prospects*. Baltimore: Johns Hopkins University Press.

LEACOCK, ELEANOR. 1978. "Women's Status in Egalitarian Societies: Implications for Social Evolution." *Current Anthropology*. Vol. 19, No. 2 (June): 247–75.

LEAF, A. 1973. "Getting Old." *Scientific American*. (September): 291–99.

LEE, DEBORAH. 2000. "Hegemonic Masculinity and Male Feminisation: The Sexual Harassment of Men at Work." *Journal of Gender Studies*. Vol. 9, No. 2 (July): 141–55.

LEE, FELICIA R. 2002. "Long Buried, Death Goes Public Again." *New York Times*. [Online] www.researchnavigator.com Accessed November 2, 2002.

LEINWAND, DONNA. 2001. "A Strange New World of Teenage Drug Use." *USA Today*. (August 28): 6D, 7D.

LEMERT, EDWIN M. 1951. *Social Pathology*. New York: McGraw-Hill.

———. 1972. *Human Deviance, Social Problems, and Social Control*, 2nd ed. Englewood Cliffs, N.J.: Prentice Hall.

LENGERMANN, PATRICIA MADOO, and RUTH A. WALLACE. 1985. *Gender in America: Social Control and Social Change*. Englewood Cliffs, N.J.: Prentice Hall.

LÉONS, MADELINE BARBARA, and HARRY SANABRIA. 1997. "Coca and Cocaine in Bolivia: Reality and Policy Illusion." In Madeline Barbara Léons and Harry Sanabria, eds., *Coca, Cocaine, and the Bolivian Reality* (pp. 1–46). Albany: State University of New York Press.

LERNER, SHARON. 1999. "Insurers Shortchange Bulimics and Anorexics." *Village Voice*. Vol. 44, No. 15 (April 20): 25.

LESSER, IAN, BRUCE HOFFMAN, JOHN ARQUILLA, DAVID RONFELDT, and MICHELE ZANINI. 1999. *Countering New Terrorism*. Washington, D.C.: RAND.

LEVAY, SIMON. 1993. *The Sexual Brain*. Cambridge, Mass.: MIT Press.

LEVINE, SAMANTHA. 2003. "Playing God in Illinois." *U.S. News & World Report*. Vol. 134, No. 1 (January 13): 13.

LEVY, FRANK. 1987. *Dollars and Dream: The Changing American Income Distribution*. New York: Russell Sage.

LEVY, LEO, and LOUIS ROWITZ. 1973. *The Ecology of Mental Disorders*. New York: Behavioral Publications.

LEWIN, TAMAR. 2000. "Now a Majority: Families with Two Parents Who Work." *The New York Times*. (October 24): A20.

LEWIS, OSCAR. 1961. *The Children of Sanchez*. New York: Random House.

———. 1966. *La Vida*. New York: Random House.

LI, JIANG HONG, and ROGER A. WOJTKIEWICZ. 1992. "A New Look at the Effects of Family Structure on Status Attainment." *Social Science Quarterly*. Vol. 73, No. 3 (September): 581–95.

LIAZOS, ALEXANDER. 1982. *People First: An Introduction to Social Problems*. Boston: Allyn & Bacon.

LICHTER, DANIEL T., and MARTHA L. CROWLEY. 2002. "Poverty in America: Beyond Welfare Reform." *Population Bulletin*. Vol. 57, No. 2 (June): 3–34.

LICHTER, ROBERT S. 2002. "TV Not So Fast and Furious Anymore." [Online] http://www.cmpa.org Accessed June 23, 2002.

LIN, GE, and PETER ROGERSON. 1994. Research reported in Diane Crispell, "Sons and Daughters Who Keep in Touch." *American Demographics*. Vol. 16, No. 8 (August): 15–16.

LINDEN, EUGENE. 1994. "More Power to Women, Fewer Mouths to Feed." *Time*. Vol. 144, No. 13 (September 26): 64–65.

LINDLAW, SCOTT. 2002. "President Signs Education Bill." *Yahoo! News*. [Online] http://www.yahoo.com/news Accessed January 8, 2002.

LINDSAY, LINDA. 1994. *Gender Roles*, 2nd ed. Englewood Cliffs, N.J.: Prentice Hall.

LINO, MARK. 2003. *Expenditures on Children by Families, 2002*. U.S. Department of Agriculture, Center for Nutrition Policy and Promotion. Miscellaneous Publication No. 1528-2002. Washington, D.C.: U.S. Government Printing Office.

LIPSET, SEYMOUR M. 1994. "The Social Requisites of Democracy Revisited: Presidential Address." *American Sociological Review*. Vol. 59, No. 1 (February): 1–22.

LIPSKY, DOROTHY KERZNER, and ALAN GARTNER. 1997. *Inclusion and School Reform: Transforming America's Classrooms*. Baltimore: Paul H. Brookes Publishing.

LITTLEJOHN-BLAKE, S. M., and C. A. DARLING. 1993. "Understanding the Strengths of African American Families." *Journal of Black Studies*. Vol. 23, No. 2 (June): 460–71.

LIVINGSTON, KEN. 1997. "Ritalin: Miracle Drug or Cop-Out?" *The Public Interest*. No. 127 (Spring): 3–18.

———. 1999. "Politics and Mental Illness." *Public Interest*. Vol. 143 (Winter): 105–9.

LOGAN, JOHN, and HARVEY MOLOTCH. 1987. *Urban Fortunes: The Political Economy of Place*. Berkeley: University of California Press.

LOMBROSO, CESARE. 1911 (orig., 1876). *Crime: Its Causes and Remedies*. H. P. Horton, trans. Boston: Little, Brown.

LORD, MARY. 2001. "Good Teachers, the Newest Imports." *U.S. News & World Report*. Vol. 130, No. 13 (April 9): 54.

———. 2002. "A Battle for Children's Futures." *U.S. News & World Report*. Vol. 132, No. 6 (March 4): 35–6.

LORENZ, KONRAD. 1966. *On Aggression*. New York: Harcourt.

LOSEKE, DONILEEN R. 1999. *Thinking about Social Problems: An Introduction to Constructionist Perspectives*. New York: Aldine de Gruyter.

LOTT, JOHN R., JR. 2000. *More Guns, Less Crime: Understanding Crime and Gun Control Laws*, 2nd ed. Chicago: University of Chicago Press.

LOVELESS, TOM. 1999. "Will Tracking Reform Promote Social Equity?" *Educational Leadership*. Vol. 56, No. 7 (April): 28–32.

LOWNEY, KATHLEEN S., and JOEL BEST. 1995. "Stalking Strangers and Lovers: Changing Media Typifications of a New Crime Problem." In Joel Best, ed., *Images of Issues: Typifying Contemporary Social Problems*, 2nd ed. (pp. 33–57). New York: Aldine de Gruyter.

LUKAS, J. ANTHONY. 1997. *Big Trouble*. New York: Simon & Schuster.

LUKER, KRISTEN. 1984. *Abortion and the Politics of Motherhood*. Berkeley: University of California Press.

LUND, DALE A. 1989. "Conclusions about Bereavement in Later Life and Implications for Interventions and Future Research." In Dale A. Lund, ed., *Older Bereaved Spouses: Research with Practical Applications* (pp. 217–31). London: Taylor-Francis-Hemisphere.

———. 1993. "Caregiving." In *Encyclopedia of Adult Development* (pp. 57–63). Phoenix, Ariz.: Oryx Press.

LYONS, LINDA. 2003. "School Confidence Low after Decades of Reform." *Gallup Poll Tuesday Briefing*. (July 2).

MCBROOM, WILLIAM H., and FRED W. REED. 1990. "Recent Trends in Conservatism: Evidence of Non-Unitary Patterns." *Sociological Focus*. Vol. 23, No. 4 (October): 355–65.

MCCABE, JAMES D., JR. 1970 (orig., 1872). *Lights and Shadows of New York Life*. New York: Farrar, Straus, & Giroux.

MCCARTHY, TERRY. 2001. "L.A. Gangs Are Back." *Time*. Vol. 158, No. 9 (September 3): 46–49.

MCCLELLAN, DAVID. 1985. *Karl Marx: Selected Writings*. New York, Oxford University Press.

MACCOBY, ELEANOR EMMONS, and CAROL NAGY JACKLIN. 1974. *The Psychology of Sex Differences*. Palo Alto, Calif.: Stanford University Press.

MACCOUN, ROBERT J. 2001. "American Distortion of Dutch Drug Statistics." *Society*. Vol. 38, No. 3 (March–April): 23–26.

MCDONALD, PETER. 2001. "Low Fertility Not Politically Sustainable." *Population Today*. Vol. 29, No. 6 (August–September): 3, 8.

MCFADDEN, ROBERT D. 2002. "Conviction Voided on Second Officer in Louima Attack." *The New York Times*. (March 1): A1, A20.

MCGEARY, JOHANNA. 1998. "Nukes . . . They're Back." *Time*. Vol. 151, No. 20 (May 25): 34–42.

MCGURN, WILLIAM. 2002. "Philadelphia Dims Edison's Light." *Wall Street Journal* (March 20): A22.

MACIONIS, JOHN J. 1978a. "Intimacy: Structure and Process in Interpersonal Relationships." *Alternative Lifestyles*. Vol. 1, No. 1 (February): 113–30.

———. 1978b. "The Search for Community in Modern Society: An Interpretation." *Qualitative Sociology*. Vol. 1, No. 2 (September): 130–43.

———. 2001. "Welcome to Cyber-Society." In John J. Macionis and Nijole V. Benokraitis, eds., *Seeing Ourselves: Classic, Contemporary, and Cross-Cultural Readings in Sociology*, 5th ed. (pp. 62–67). Upper Saddle River, N.J.: Prentice Hall.

———. 2001. *Sociology*, 8th ed. Upper Saddle River, N.J.: Prentice Hall.

MACIONIS, JOHN J., and LINDA GERBER. 2003. *Sociology: Fourth Canadian Edition*. Upper Saddle River, N.J.: Prentice Hall.

MACIONIS, JOHN J., and VINCENT R. PARRILLO. 2004. *Cities and Urban Life*, 3rd ed. Upper Saddle River, N.J.: Prentice Hall.

MACKINNON, CATHARINE A. 2001. "Pornography: Not a Moral Issue." In John J. Macionis and Nijole V. Benokraitis, eds., *Seeing Ourselves: Classic, Contemporary, and Cross-Cultural Readings in Sociology*, 5th ed. (pp. 294–301). Upper Saddle River, N.J.: Prentice Hall.

MCLANAHAN, SARA. 2002. "Life without Father: What Happens to the Children?" *Contexts*. Vol. 1, No. 1 (Spring): 35–44.

MCLAREN, PETER L., and JAMES M. GIARELLI, eds. 1995. *Critical Theory and Educational Research*. Albany: State University of New York Press.

MCNAUGHT, WILLIAM. 1994. "Realizing the Potential: Some Examples." In Matilda White Riley, Robert L. Kahn, and Ann Foner, eds., with Karin A. Mack, ed. assoc., *Age and Structural Lag* (pp. 219–36). New York: Wiley-Interscience.

MCNEAL, RALPH B. JR. 1999. "Parental Involvement as Social Capital: Differential Effectiveness on Science Achievement, Truancy, and Dropping Out." *Social Forces*. Vol. 78, No. 1: 117–41.

MCNEIL, DONALD G., JR. 1991. "Should Women Be Sent into Combat?" *The New York Times* (July 21): E3.

MCNULTY, PAUL J. 1994. "Who's in Jail and Why They Belong There." *The Wall Street Journal* (November 9): A23.

MCUSIC, MOLLY S. 1999. "The Law's Role in the Distribution of Education: The Promises and Pitfalls of School Finance Litigation." In Jay P. Heubert, ed., *Law and School Reform: Six Strategies for Promoting Educational Equity* (pp. 88–159). New Haven, Conn.: Yale University Press.

MALTHUS, THOMAS ROBERT. 1926 (orig. 1798). *First Essay on Population 1798*. London: Macmillan.

MANCALL, PETER C. 1995. *Deadly Medicine: Indians and Alcohol in Early America*. Ithaca, N.Y.: Cornell University Press.

MANHEIMER, RONALD J., ed. 1994. *Older Americans Almanac: A Reference Work on Seniors in the United States*. Detroit: Gale Research.

MARABLE, MANNING. 1995. *Beyond Black and White: Transforming African-American Politics*. New York: Verso.

MARCHAK, PATRICIA. 1999. *God's Assassins: State Terrorism in Argentina in the 1970s*. London: McGill-Queen's University Press.

MARE, ROBERT D. 1991. "Five Decades of Educational Assortative Mating." *American Sociological Review*. Vol. 56, No. 1 (February): 15–32.

MARKS, ALEXANDRA. 1999a. "Few Signs That Media Violence Is Abating." *Christian Science Monitor*. Vol. 91, No. 209 (September 23): 2

———. 1999b. "Police Brutality Trial Reaches a Turning Point." *Christian Science Monitor*. Vol. 91, No. 125 (May 26): 4.

———. 2001. "U.S. Shelters Swell—With Families." *Christian Science Monitor*. [Online] http://www.csmonitor.com Accessed December 4, 2001.

MARTIN, DOUGLAS. 1997. "The Medicine Woman of the Mohegans." *The New York Times*. (June 4): B1, B7.

MARTIN, PHILIP, and ELIZABETH MIDGLEY. 2003. "Immigration: Shaping and Reshaping America." *Population Bulletin*. Vol. 58, No. 2 (June). Washington, D.C.: Population Reference Bureau.

MARULLO, SAM. 1987. "The Functions and Dysfunctions of Preparations for Fighting Nuclear War." *Sociological Focus*. Vol. 20, No. 2 (April): 135–53.

MARX, KARL. 1959. 1964 (orig., 1844). *Economic and Philosophic Manuscripts of 1844*. New York: International Publishers.

———. 1985 (orig., 1847). "The Communist Manifesto." In David McClellan, ed., *Karl Marx: Selected Writings* (pp. 221–47). New York: Oxford University Press.

MARX, KARL, and FRIEDRICH ENGELS. 1959. *Marx and Engels: Basic Writings on Politics and Philosophy*, Lewis S. Feurer, ed. Garden City, N.Y.: Anchor.

MASSEY, DOUGLAS S., and NANCY A. DENTON. 1988. "Suburbanization and Segregation in U.S. Metropolitan Areas." *American Journal of Sociology*. Vol. 94, No. 3 (November): 592–626.

———. 1989. "Hypersegregation in U.S. Metropolitan Areas: Black and Hispanic Segregation along Five Dimensions." *Demography*. Vol. 26, No. 3 (August): 373–91.

MASTERS, WILLIAM H., VIRGINIA E. JOHNSON, and ROBERT C. KOLODNY. 1988. *Human Sexuality*, 3rd ed. Glenview, Ill.: Scott, Foresman/Little, Brown.

MATTHEWS, MERRILL, JR. 1995. "Health Care for Vets Should Be Privatized." *Human Events*. Vol. 51, No. 1 (January 13): 22.

MATTHIESSEN, PETER. 1984. *Indian Country*. New York: Viking Press.

MAURO, TONY. 1997. "Ruling Likely to Add Fuel to Already Divisive Debate." *USA Today*. (January 7): 1A, 2A.

MAUSS, ARMAND L. 1975. *Social Problems of Social Movements*. Philadelphia: Lippincott.

MEADOWS, DONELLA H., DENNIS L. MEADOWS, JORGAN RANDERS, and WILLIAM W. BEHRENS, III. 1972. *The Limits to Growth: A Report on the Club of Rome's Project on the Predicament of Mankind*. New York: Universe.

MEDINA, JOHN J. 1996. *The Clock of Ages: Why We Age, How We Age, Winding Back the Clock*. Cambridge: Cambridge University Press.

MELTON, G. B., and F. D. BARRY. 1994. "Neighbors Helping Neighbors: The Vision of the U.S. Advisory Board on Child Abuse and Neglect." In G. B. Melton and F. D. Barry, eds., *Protecting Children from Abuse and Neglect* (pp. 1–13). New York: Guilford.

MENDELSON, JACK H., and NANCY K. MELLO. 1995. "Alcohol, Sex, and Aggression." In James A. Inciardi and Karen McElrath, eds., *The American Drug Scene: An Anthology* (pp. 50–62). Los Angeles: Roxbury.

MERTON, ROBERT K. 1938. "Social Structure and Anomie." *American Sociological Review*. Vol. 3, No. 6 (October): 672–82.

———. 1968. *Social Theory and Social Structure*. New York: Free Press.

METZGER, KURT. 2001. "Cities and Race." *Society*. Vol. 39, No. 1 (December): 2.

MEYER, MADONNA HARRINGTON, and MARCIA L. BELLAS. 1995. "U.S. Old-Age Policy and the Family." In Rosemay Blieszner and Victoria Hilkevitch Bedfore, eds., *Handbook of Aging and the Family* (pp. 263–83). Westport, Conn.: Greenwood.

MEZEY, GILLIAN, and MICHAEL KING. 1989. "The Effects of Sexual Assault on Men: A Survey of 22 Victims." *Psychological Medicine*. Vol. 19, No. 1 (February): 205–9.

MILBRATH, LESTER W. 1989. *Envisioning A Sustainable Society: Learning Our Way Out*. Albany: State University of New York Press.

MILKMAN, HARVEY, and STANLEY SUNDERWIRTH. 1995. "Doorway to Excess." In James A. Inciardi and Karen McElrath, eds., *The American Drug Scene: An Anthology* (pp. 12–22). Los Angeles: Roxbury.

MILLER, BERNA. 1997. "Population Update for April." *American Demographics*. Vol. 19, No. 4 (April): 18.

MILLER, G. TYLER, JR. 1992. *Living in the Environment: An Introduction to Environmental Science*. Belmont, Calif.: Wadsworth.

MILLER, WALTER B. 1970 (orig., 1958). "Lower Class Culture as a Generating Milieu of Gang Delinquency." In Marvin E. Wolfgang, Leonard Savitz, and Norman Johnston, eds., *The Sociology of Crime and Delinquency*, 2nd ed. (pp. 351–63). New York: Wiley.

MILLET, KATE. 1970. *Sexual Politics*. Garden City, N.Y.: Doubleday.

MILLS, C. WRIGHT. 1956. *The Power Elite*. New York: Oxford University Press.

———. 1959. *The Sociological Imagination*. New York: Oxford University Press.

MINISTRY OF HEALTH, WELFARE AND SPORT. 1998. "Policy on Soft Drugs and Coffee Shops." *Drug Policy in the Netherlands: Continuity and Change*. [Online] http://www.thc.nl/Countries/nl/VWSdrugs.htm Accessed May 10, 1999.

MIROWSKY, JOHN, and CATHERINE ROSS. 1983. "Paranoia and the Structure of Powerlessness." *American Sociological Review*. Vol. 48, No. 2 (April): 228–39.

———. 1984. "Mexican Culture and Its Emotional Contradictions." *Journal of Health and Social Behavior*. Vol. 25: 2–13.

MITCHELL, DOUGLAS E., TOM DESTINO, RITA T. KARAM, and ANAIDA COLON-MUNIZ. 1999. "The Politics of Bilingual Education." *Educational Policy*. Vol. 13, No. 1 (January–March): 86–104.

MOAKLEY, TERRY. 1999. "The Thanks of a Grateful Nation?: The Numbers Don't Lie When It Comes to VA Shortfalls." *WE Magazine.* Vol. 3, No. 5 (September–October): 106.

MOLANDER, ROGER C., and PETER A. WILSON. 1994. "On Dealing with the Prospect of Nuclear Chaos." In Brad Roberts, ed., *Weapons Proliferation in the 1990s: A Washington Quarterly Reader* (pp. 3–23). Cambridge, Mass.: The MIT Press.

MONTAGU, ASHLEY. 1976. *The Nature of Human Aggression.* New York: Oxford University Press.

MONTO, MARTIN. 2001. "Prostitution and Fellatio." *Journal of Sex Research.* Vol. 38, No. 2 (May): 140–46.

MOORE, WILBERT E. 1977. "Modernization as Rationalization: Processes and Restraints." In Manning Nash, ed., *Essays on Economic Development and Cultural Change in Honor of Bert F. Hoselitz* (pp. 29–42). Chicago: University of Chicago Press.

———. 1979. *World Modernization: The Limits of Convergence.* New York: Elsevier.

MORA, JILL KERPER. 1999. "An Analysis of Proposition 227." [Online] http://coe.sdsu.edu/people/jmora/Prop227/227YearTwo.htm Accessed September 27, 2003.

MORAN, JOHN S., S. O. ARAL, W. C. JENKINS, T. A. PETERMAN, and E. R. ALEXANDER. 1989. "The Impact of Sexually Transmitted Diseases on Minority Populations." *Public Health Reports.* Vol. 104, No. 6 (November–December): 560–65.

MORRIS, CHARLES R. 1996. *The AARP: America's Most Powerful Lobby and the Clash of Generations.* New York: Time Books Random House.

MORRIS, DAVID C. 1997. "Older Adults' Perceptions of Dr. Kevorkian in Middletown, U.S.A." *Omega.* Vol. 35, No. 4: 405–12.

MORSE, JODIE. 1999. "Cracking Down on the Homeless." *Time.* Vol. 154, No. 25 (December 20): 69–70.

———. 2002. "Learning While Black." *Time.* Vol. 159, No. 21 (May 27): 50–52.

MOUW, TED. 2000. "Job Relocation and the Racial Gap in Unemployment in Detroit and Chicago, 1980 to 1990." *American Sociological Review.* Vol. 65, No. 5 (October): 730–53.

MOYNIHAN, DANIEL PATRICK. 1993. "Toward a New Intolerance." *The Public Interest.* No. 112 (Summer): 119–22.

MULRINE, ANNA. 2002. "Risky Business." *U.S. News & World Report.* Vol. 132, No. 18 (May 27): 42–49.

MURDOCK, GEORGE PETER. 1965 (orig., 1949). *Social Structure.* New York: Free Press.

MURRAY, CHARLES. 1984. *Losing Ground: American Social Policy 1950–1980.* New York: Basic Books.

———. 2001. "The British Underclass: Ten Years Later." *The Public Interest.* Vol. 145. (Fall): 25–37.

MURRAY, HARRY. 2000. "Deniable Degradation: The Finger-Imagining of Welfare Recipients." *Sociological Forum.* Vol. 15, No. 1 (March): 39–63.

MURRAY, STEPHEN O., and WILL ROSCOE, eds. 1998. *Studies of African Homosexualities.* New York: St. Martin's Press.

MYERHOFF, BARBARA. 1979. *Number Our Days.* New York: Dutton.

MYERS, DAVID G. 2000. *The American Paradox: Spiritual Hunger in an Age of Plenty.* New Haven, Conn.: Yale University Press.

———. 2001. *Psychology,* 6th ed. New York: Worth.

MYERS, NORMAN. 1991. "Biological Diversity and Global Security." In F. Herbert Bormann and Stephen R. Kellert, eds., *Ecology, Economics, and Ethics: The Broken Circle* (pp. 11–25). New Haven, Conn.: Yale University Press.

NADELMANN, ETHAN. 1995. "Switzerland's Heroin Experiment." *National Review.* Vol. 47, No. 13 (July 19): 46–47.

NAGEL, JOANE. 1996. *American Indian Ethnic Renewal: Red Power and the Resurgence of Identity and Culture.* New York: Oxford University Press.

NASH, J. MADELEINE. 2002. "Cracking the Fat Riddle." *Time.* Vol. 160, No. 10 (September 22): 50–5.

NATIONAL CENTER FOR ELDER ABUSE. 1998. [Online] http://www.elderabusecenter.org/ Accessed February 21, 2004.

NATIONAL COALITION FOR HOMELESS VETERANS. 2000. "Policy Issues." [Online] http://www.nchv.org/policy.html Accessed March 11, 2000.

NATIONAL EDUCATION ASSOCIATION. 2003. "Teacher Shortage 2003." [Online] http://www.nea.org/teachershortage/03shortagefactsheet.html

NATIONAL GAY AND LESBIAN TASK FORCE. 1998. Press release. "NGLTF Urges Greater Federal Action to Curb Hate Crimes." Washington, D.C. (January 9). [Online] http://www.ngltf.org/pub.html Accessed March 15, 2000.

NATIONAL INSTITUTE ON DRUG ABUSE. 1999a. "Cigarettes and Other Nicotine Products." NIDA Infofax (March 4). [Online] http://www.nida.nih.gov/infofax/tobacco.htm Accessed April 12, 1999.

———. 1999b. "Steroids (Anabolic)." NIDA Infofax. [Online] http://www.nida.nih.gov/Infofax/steroids.html Accessed May 4, 1999.

NATIONAL INSTITUTES OF HEALTH. 2002. "College Drinking Hazardous to Campus Communities; Task Force Calls for Research-based Prevention Programs." [Online] http://www.nih/gov/news/pr/apr2002/niaaa-09.htm Accessed July 26, 2003.

Nation's Health. 1998. "Fetal Alcohol Exposure Linked to Mental Illness." (May–June): 23.

NAVARRO, MIREYA. 2000. "Puerto Rican Presence Wanes in New York." *The New York Times* (February 28): A1, A20.

NEUGARTEN, BERNICE L. 1977. "Personality and Aging." In James E. Birren and K. Warner Schaie, eds., *Handbook of the Psychology of Aging* (pp. 626–49). New York: Van Nostrand Reinhold.

———. 1982. *Age or Need in Public Policies for Older People.* Beverly Hills, Calif.: Sage.

———. 1996. "Retirement in the Life Course." In Dale A. Neugarten, ed., *The Meanings of Age: Selected Papers of Bernice L. Neugarten* (pp. 221–37). Chicago: University of Chicago Press.

NEWMAN, RICHARD J. 2002. "Hunters and Hunted." *U.S. News & World Report.* Vol. 132, No. 2 (January 21): 30.

NEWPORT, FRANK. 2003. "Americans' Mood Drops as Economy and War Dominate Concerns." *The Gallup Poll Tuesday Briefing.* (February): 102–4.

NOCK, STEVEN L., JAMES D. WRIGHT, and LAURA SANCHEZ. 1999. "America's Divorce Problem." *Society.* Vol. 36, No. 4 (May–June): 43–52.

NOEL, PETER. 1997. "Were Cops Trying to Kill Abner Louima?" *Village Voice.* Vol. 42, No. 38 (September 23): 47–49.

NORC. 1999. *General Social Surveys, 1972–1998: Cumulative Codebook.* Chicago: National Opinion Research Center.

———. 2003. *General Social Surveys, 1972–2002: Cumulative Codebook.* Chicago: National Opinion Research Center.

NORD, MARK, MARGARET ANDREWS, and STEVEN CARLSON. 2002. "Household Food Security in the United States: 2001." U.S. Department of Agriculture, Economic Research Service.

NORTON, ELEANOR HOLMES. 1985. "Restoring the Traditional Black Family." *The New York Times Magazine.* (June 2): 43–98.

NOVAK, VIVECA. 1999. "The Cost of Poor Advice." *Time.* Vol. 154, No. 1 (July 5): 38.

———. 2001. "New Ritalin Ad Blitz Makes Parents Jumpy." *Time.* Vol. 158, No. 10 (September 10): 61–2.

OAKES, JEANNIE. 1982. "Classroom Social Relationships: Exploring the Bowles and Gintis Hypothesis." *Sociology of Education.* Vol. 55, No. 4 (October): 197–212.

———. 1985. *Keeping Track: How Schools Structure Inequality.* New Haven, Conn.: Yale University Press.

OAKLEY, ANN. 1984. *The Captured Womb: A History of the Medical Care of Pregnant Women.* New York: Oxford.

OCHOA, RACHEL. 1999. "Bilingual Education Challenged Again." *Hispanic.* Vol. 12, No. 10 (October): 12–13.

OFFICE OF NATIONAL DRUG CONTROL POLICY. 2003. *Drug Data Survey.* Washington, D.C.: U.S. Executive Office of the President.

OGDEN, RUSSEL D. 2001. "Nonphysician-Assisted Suicide: The Technological Imperative of the Deathing Counterculture." *Death Studies.* Vol. 25, No. 5 (July): 387–402.

O'HARE, WILLIAM P. 2002. "Tracking the Trends in Low-Income Working Families." *Population Today.* Vol. 30, No. 6 (August–September): 1–3.

OLESEN, VIRGINIA L. 1997. "Who Cares? Women as Informal and Formal Caregivers." In Sheryl Burt Ruzek, Virginia L. Olesen, and Adele E. Clarke, eds., *Women's Health: Complexities and Differences.* Columbus: Ohio State University Press.

OLIN, DIRK. 2003. "The Tracking System." *The New York Times.* (September 28). [Online] http://www.researchnavigator.com

ONE WORLD. 1998. Data from Web site. [Online] http://www.oneworld.org

O'NEILL, BRIAN, and DEBORAH BALK. 2001. "World Population Futures." *Population Bulletin.* Vol. 56, No. 3 (September): 3–40.

ORFIELD, GARY and CAROLE ASHKINAZE. 1991. *The Closing Door: Conservative Policy and Black Opportunity.* Chicago: University of Chicago Press.

ORGANIZATION FOR ECONOMIC COOPERATION AND DEVELOPMENT. 2003. *Education at a Glance: OECD Indicators 2003.* Paris: OECD.

OWEN, CAROLYN A., HOWARD C. ELSNER, and THOMAS R. MCFAUL. 1977. "A Half-Century of Social Distance Research: National Replication of the Bogardus Studies." *Sociology and Social Research.* Vol. 66: 80–98.

PADGETT, TIM. 2002. "Taking the Side of the Coca Farmer." *Time.* Vol. 160, No. 6 (August 5): 8.

PAKULSKI, JAN. 1993. "Mass Social Movements and Social Class." *International Sociology.* Vol. 8, No. 2 (June): 131–58.

PALLONE, NATHANIEL J., and JAMES J. HENNESSY. 1998. "Brain Dysfunction and Criminal Violence." *Society.* Vol. 35, No. 6 (September–October): 20–27.

PALMORE, ERDMAN B. 1979. "Predictors of Successful Aging." *The Gerontologist.* Vol. 19, No. 5 (October): 427–31.

———. 1998. "Ageism." In David E. Redburn and Robert P. McNamara, eds., *Social Gerontology* (pp. 29–41). Westport, Conn.: Auburn House.

PARCEL, TOBY L., CHARLES W. MUELLER, and STEVEN CUVELIER. 1986. "Comparable Worth and Occupational Labor Market: Explanations of Occupational Earnings Differentials." Paper presented to the American Sociological Association, New York.

PARENTI, MICHAEL. 1995. *Democracy by the Few,* 6th ed. New York: St. Martin's Press.

PARK, ROBERT E., and ERNEST W. BURGESS. 1970 (orig., 1921). *Introduction to the Science of Sociology.* Chicago: University of Chicago Press.

PARLER, KAREN F., and MATTHEW V. PRUITT. 2000. "Poverty, Poverty Concentration, and Homicide." *Social Science Quarterly.* Vol. 81, No. 2 (June): 555–70.

PARRILLO, VINCENT N. 2003. "Updating the Bogardus Social Distance Studies: A New National Survey." Revised version of a paper presented at the annual meeting of the American Sociological Association (August 17, 2002). Provided by the author.

———. 2003. *Strangers to These Shores,* 7th ed. Boston: Allyn & Bacon.

PARSONS, TALCOTT. 1942. "Age and Sex in the Social Structure of the United States." *American Sociological Review.* Vol. 7, No. 4 (August): 604–16.

———. 1954. *Essays in Sociological Theory.* New York: Free Press.

———. 1964 (orig., 1951). *The Social System.* New York: Free Press.

———. 1966. *Societies: Evolutionary and Comparative Perspectives.* Englewood Cliffs, N.J.: Prentice Hall.

PAUL, ELLEN FRANKEL. 1991. "Bared Buttocks and Federal Cases." *Society.* Vol. 28, No. 4 (May–June): 4–7.

PEAR, ROBERT. 1997. "Expense Means Many Can't Get Drugs for AIDS." *The New York Times.* (February 16): A1, A14.

PEAR, ROBERT, WITH ERIK ECKHOLM. 1991. "When Healers Are Entrepreneurs: A Debate over Costs and Ethics." *The New York Times* (June 2): 1, 17.

PEASE, JOHN, and LEE MARTIN. 1997. "Want Ads and Jobs for the Poor: A Glaring Mismatch." *Sociological Forum.* Vol. 12. No. 4 (December): 545–64.

PEDERSON, DANIEL, VERN E. SMITH, and JERRY ADLER. 1999. "Sprawling, Sprawling. . . ." *Newsweek.* (July 19): 23–27.

PERAINO, KEVIN, and EVEN THOMAS. 2003. "Father, Where Art Thou?" *Newsweek.* (January 27): 54–56.

PERLSTEIN, GARY R. 1998. "The Oklahoma City Bombing and the Militias." In *Encyclopedia of World Terrorism.* Vol. 3 (pp. 545–50). Armonk, N.Y.: M. E. Sharpe.

Peters Atlas of the World. 1990. New York: Harper & Row.

PETERSILIA, JOAN. 1997. "Probation in the United States: Practices and Challenges." *National Institute of Justice Journal.* No. 233 (September): 4.

PETERSON, J. L. 1992. "Black Men and Their Same-Sex Desires and Behaviors." In Gilbert Herdt ed., *Gay Culture in America: Essays from the Field.* Boston: Beacon.

PHILADELPHIA, DESA. 2001. "Rookie Teacher, Age 50." *Time.* Vol. 157, No. 14 (April 9): 66–68.

PHILLIPS, ANNE, ed. 1987. *Feminism and Equality.* New York: New York University Press.

PHILLIPS, MELANIE. 2001. "What about the Overclass?" *Public Interest.* No. 145 (Fall): 38–43.

PHILLIPSON, CHRIS. 1982. *Capitalism and the Construction of Old Age.* London: Macmillan.

PILLEMER, KARL. 1988. "Maltreatment of the Elderly at Home and in Institutions: Extent, Risk Factors, and Policy Recommendations." In U.S. Congress. House, Select Committee on Aging and Senate, Special Committee on Aging. *Legislative Agenda for an Aging Society: 1988 and Beyond.* Washington, D.C.: U.S. Government Printing Office.

PIQUERO, ALEX R., JOHN M. MACDONALD, and KAREN F. PARKER. 2002. "Race, Local Life Circumstances, and Criminal Activity." *Social Science Quarterly*. Vol. 83, No. 3 (September): 654–70.

PITTMAN, DAVID. 2001. "Memories of Rape." [Online] http://www.1gc.apc.org/spr Accessed April 13, 2001.

PIVEN, FRANCES FOX, and RICHARD A. CLOWARD. 1971. *Regulating the Poor: The Functions of Public Welfare*. New York: Vintage Books.

PLECK, ELIZABETH. 1987. *Domestic Tyranny: The Making of Social Policy Against Family Violence from Colonial Times to the Present*. New York: Oxford University Press.

POLGREEN, LYDIA, and ROBERT F. WORTH. 2003. "Children with Foster Parents Found Starving in New Jersey." *International Herald Tribune Online*. (October 28) http://www.ith.com/articles/115312.html Accessed October 28, 2003.

POLLOCK, PHILIP H., III, and M. ELLIOT VITTAS. 1995. "Who Bears the Burdens of Environmental Pollution: Race, Ethnicity, and Environmental Equity in Florida." *Social Science Quarterly*. Vol. 76, No. 2 (June): 294–310.

POLSBY, NELSON W. 1959. "Three Problems in the Analysis of Community Power." *American Sociological Review*. Vol. 24, No. 6 (December): 796–803.

POPENOE, DAVID. 1988. *Disturbing the Nest: Family Change and Decline in Modern Societies*. New York: Aldine de Gruyter.

———. 1991. "Family Decline in the Swedish Welfare State." *The Public Interest*. No. 102 (Winter): 65–77.

———. 1992. "The Controversial Truth: Two-Parent Families are Better." *The New York Times*. (December 26): A21.

———. 1993a. "American Family Decline, 1960–1990: A Review and Appraisal." *Journal of Marriage and the Family*. Vol. 55, No. 3 (August): 527–55.

———. 1993b. "Parental Androgyny." *Society*. Vol. 30, No. 6 (September–October): 5–11.

———. 1999. *Life without Father: Compelling New Evidence That Fatherhood and Marriage Are Indispensable for the Good of Children and Society*. Cambridge, Mass.: Harvard University Press.

POPENOE, DAVID, and BARBARA DAFOE WHITEHEAD. 1999. *Should We Live Together? What Young Adults Need to Know about Cohabitation before Marriage*. New Brunswick, N.J.: The National Marriage Project.

Popline. 2001. "Terrorist Attacks Spur Unseen Human Toll." Vol. 23 (December): 1–2.

POPULATION REFERENCE BUREAU. 1999. *1999 World Population Data Sheet*. Washington, D.C.: Population Reference Bureau.

———. 2002. *2002 World Population Data Sheet*. Washington, D.C.: Population Reference Bureau.

———. 2003. *World Population Data Sheet, 2003*. Washington, D.C.: Population Reference Bureau.

Population Today. 2000. Vol. 28, No. 5 (July): 7.

PORTES, ALEJANDRO. 2000. "The Hidden Abode: Sociology as Analysis of the Unexpected." *American Sociological Review*. Vol. 65, No. 1 (February): 1–18.

PORTES, ALEJANDRO, and LEIF JENSEN. 1989. "The Enclave and the Entrants: Patterns of Ethnic Enterprise in Miami before and after Mariel." *American Sociological Review*. Vol. 54, No. 6 (December): 929–49.

POSNER, RICHARD A. 1995. *Aging and Old Age*. Chicago: University of Chicago Press.

POSTEL, SANDRA. 1993. "Facing Water Scarcity." In Lester R. Brown et al., eds., *State of the World 1993: A Worldwatch Institute Report on Progress toward a Sustainable Society* (pp. 22–41). New York: Norton.

POWELL, COLIN L., with JOSEPH E. PERSICO. 1995. *My American Journey*. New York: Random House.

POWELL, LAWRENCE ALFRED, KENNETH J. BRANCO, and JOHN B. WILLIAMSON. 1996. *The Senior Rights Movement: Framing the Policy Debate in America*. New York: Twayne.

PRESSER, HARRIET B. 1993. "The Housework Gender Gap." *Population Today*. Vol. 21, No. 7/8 (July–August): 5.

PURCELL, PIPER, and LARA STEWART. 1990. "Dick and Jane in 1989." *Sex Roles*. Vol. 22, Nos. 3–4: 177–85.

PURDUM, TODD S. 1999. "Suburban 'Sprawl' Takes Its Place on the Political Landscape." *The New York Times*. (February 6): A1, A12.

PYNOOS, JON, and PHOEBE S. LIEBIG, eds. 1995. *Housing Frail Elders: International Policies, Perspectives, and Prospects*. Baltimore: Johns Hopkins University Press.

QUILLIAN, LINCOLN, and DEVAH PAGER. 2001. "Black Neighbors, Higher Crime? The Role of Racial Stereotypes in Evaluations of Neighborhood Crime." *American Journal of Sociology*. Vol. 107, No. 3 (November): 717–67.

RAGAVAN, CHITRA. 2002. "Coming to America." *U.S. News & World Report*. Vol. 132, No. 5 (February 18): 16–24.

RALEY, R. KELLY. 1996. "A Shortage of Marriageable Men? A Note on the Role of Cohabitation in Black-White Differences in Marriage Rates." *American Journal of Sociology*. Vol. 61, No. 6 (December): 973–83.

RAMO, JOSHUA COOPER. 2001. "America's Shadow Drug War." *Time*. Vol. 157, No. 18 (May 7): 36–44.

RANDALL, VICKI. 1982. *Women and Politics*. London: Macmillan.

RANKIN, SUSAN R. 2003. "Campus Climate for Gay, Lesbian, Bisexual, and Transgender People: A National Perspective." National Gay and Lesbian Task Force. [Online] http://www.ngltf.org/news/release.cfm?releaseID-538 Accessed May 6, 2003.

RATNESAR, ROMESH. 1999. "Not Gone, but Forgotten?" *Time*. Vol. 153, No. 15 (February 8): 30–31.

RAYMOND, JOAN. 2001. "The Multicultural Report." *American Demographics*. Vol. 23, No. 11 (November): S1–S6.

RECER, PAUL. 1999. "Teen-age Smoking Harms Lungs Forever, Study Says." *Louisville Courier-Journal*. (April 7): A8.

RECKLESS, WALTER C. 1973. *The Crime Problem*. New York: Appleton-Century-Crofts.

RECKLESS, WALTER C., and SIMON DINITZ. 1972. *The Prevention of Juvenile Delinquency*. Columbus: Ohio State University Press.

RECKLESS, WALTER C., SIMON DINITZ, and E. MURRAY. 1956. "Self Concept as an Insulator against Delinquency." *American Sociological Review*. Vol. 21, No. 5 (October): 744–56.

———. 1957. "The 'Good Boy' in a High Delinquency Area." *Journal of Criminal Law, Criminology, and Police Science*. Vol. 48: 18–25.

RECTOR, ROBERT. 1998. "America Has the World's Richest Poor People." *Wall Street Journal* (September 24): A18.

REEVE, SIMON. 1999. *The New Jackals: Ramzi Yousef, Osama bin Laden and the Future of Terrorism*. Boston: Northeastern University Press.

REIMAN, JEFFREY. 1998. *The Rich Get Richer and the Poor Get Prison: Ideology, Class, and Criminal Justice*. Boston: Allyn & Bacon.

REMY, JACQUELINE. 1996. "Interview with Agnes Fournier de Saint-Maur, Interpol Police Lieutenant." For *L'Express*. Reprinted in *World Press Review* (November): 7.

RENNER, MICHAEL. 1993. *Critical Juncture: The Future of Peacekeeping*. Washington, D.C.: Worldwatch Institute.

REVKIN, ANDREW C. 2002. "Can Global Warming Be Studied Too Much?" *New York Times* (December 3): D1, D4.

RICHARDSON, LAUREL. 1988. *The Dynamics of Sex and Gender: A Sociological Perspective*, 3rd ed. New York: HarperCollins.

RICHE, MARTHA FARNSWORTH. 2000. "America's Diversity and Growth: Signposts for the 21st Century." *Population Bulletin*. Vol. 55, No. 2 (June).

RILEY, M. W., and R. SUZMAN. 1985. "Introducing the Oldest Old." *Milbank Memorial Fund Quarterly*. Vol. 63: 177–86.

RIMER, SARA. 1998. "Blacks Carry Load of Care for Their Elderly." *New York Times* (March 15): 1, 22.

RITTER, MALCOLM. 2003. "Children–TV Violence Link Has Effect." *Yahoo! News*. [Online] http://www.yahoonews.com Accessed March 9, 2003.

RITZER, GEORGE. 1993. *The McDonaldization of Society: An Investigation into the Changing Character of Contemporary Social Life*. Thousand Oaks, Calif.: Pine Forge Press.

———. 1998. *The McDonaldization Thesis: Explorations and Extensions*. Thousand Oaks, Calif.: Sage.

ROBERTS, J. TIMMONS. 1993. "Psychosocial Effects of Workplace Hazardous Exposures: Theoretical Synthesis and Preliminary Findings." *Social Problems*. Vol. 40, No. 1 (February): 74–89.

ROBERTS, ROBERT E. 1980. "The Prevalence of Psychological Distress among Mexican Americans." *Journal of Health and Social Behavior*. Vol. 22: 394–400.

ROBINSON, JOHN P., PERLA WERNER, and GEOFFREY GODBEY. 1997. "Freeing Up the Golden Years." *American Demographics*. Vol. 19, No. 10 (October): 20–24.

ROBINSON, LINDA, and PETER CARY. 2002. "Princely Payments." *U.S. News & World Report*. Vol. 132, No. 1 (January 14): 24–7.

ROCHE, TIMOTHY. 2000a. "The Chief and His Ward." *Time*. Vol. 156, No. 2 (July 10): 82–3.

———. 2000b. "The Crisis of Foster Care." *Time*. Vol. 156, No. 20 (November 13): 74–82.

ROGERS, RICHARD G., REBECCA ROSENBLATT, ROBERT A. HUMMER, and PATRICK M. KRUEGER. 2001. "Black-White Differentials in Adult Homicide Mortality in the United States." *Social Science Quarterly*. Vol. 82. No. 3 (September): 435–52.

ROOSEVELT, MARGOT. 2001. "The War against the War on Drugs." *Time*. Vol. 157, No. 18 (May 7): 46–7.

ROSCIGNO, VINCENT J., and MARTHA L. CROWLEY. 2001. "Rurality, Institutional Disadvantage, and Achievement/Attainment." *Rural Sociology*. Vol. 66, No. 2 (June): 268–92.

ROSE, LOWELL C., and ALEC M. GALLUP. 2003. "The 35th Annual Phi Delta Kappa/Gallup Poll on the Public's Attitudes toward the Public Schools." *Phi Delta Kappan*. Vol. 85, No. 1 (September): 44.

ROSEGRANT, MARK W., XIMING CAI, and SARAH A. CLINE. 2002. *World Water and Food to 2025: Dealing with Scarcity*. Washington, D.C.: International Food Policy Research Institute and International Water Management Institute.

ROSENFIELD, SARAH. 1989. "The Effects of Women's Employment: Personal Control and Sex Differences in Mental Health." *Journal of Health and Social Behavior*. Vol. 30: 77–91.

ROSENTHAL, ELIZABETH. 1991. "Canada's National Health Plan Gives Care to All, with Limits." *The New York Times* (April 30): A1, A16.

ROSS, CATHERINE E., JOHN MIROWSKY, and WILLIAM C. COCKERHAM. 1983. "Social Class, Mexican Culture, and Fatalism: Their Effects on Psychological Distress." *American Journal of Community Psychology*. Vol. 11: 383–99.

ROSS, JOHN. 1996. "To Die in the Street: Mexico City's Homeless Population Boom as Economic Crisis Shakes Social Protections." *SSSP Newsletter*. Vol. 27, No. 2 (Summer): 14–15.

ROSTOW, WALT W. 1960. *The Stages of Economic Growth: A Non-Communist Manifesto*. Cambridge: Cambridge University Press.

———. 1978. *The World Economy: History and Prospect*. Austin: University of Texas Press.

ROTHENBERG, BESS. 2002. "The Success of the Battered Woman Syndrome: An Analysis of How Cultural Arguments Succeed." *Sociological Forum*. Vol. 17, No. 1 (March): 81–103.

ROWLES, G. D. 1993. "Evolving Images of Place in Aging and 'Aging in Place'" *Generations*. Vol. 17, No. 2: 65–70.

ROY, ROGER. 2003. "Death, Injury, Illness Toll at 10,000 for U.S. In Iraq." *Seattle Times*. (November 29): A1.

RUESCHEMEYER, DIETRICH, EVELYN H. STEPHENS, and JOHN D. STEPHENS. 1992. *Capitalist Development and Democracy*. Chicago: University of Chicago Press.

RULE, JAMES, and PETER BRANTLEY. 1992. "Computerized Surveillance in the Workplace: Forms and Delusions." *Sociological Forum*. Vol. 7, No. 3 (September): 405–23.

RUSHING, W. 1969. "Two Patterns in the Relationship between Social Class and Mental Hospitalization." *American Sociological Review*. Vol. 34, No. 4 (August): 533–41.

RUSSELL, CHERYL. 1995a. "Are We in the Dumps?" *American Demographics*. Vol. 17, No. 1 (January): 6.

———. 1995b. "True Crime." *American Demographics*. Vol. 17, No. 8 (August): 22–31.

RUSSELL, CHERYL, and MARCIA MOGELONSKY. 2000. "Riding High on the Market." *American Demographics*. Vol. 22, No. 4 (April): 44–54.

RYAN, WILLIAM. 1976. *Blaming the Victim*, rev. ed. New York: Vintage Books.

RYBCZYNSKI, WITOLD, and PETER D. LINNEMAN. 1999. "How to Save Our Shrinking Cities." *The Public Interest*. Vol. 135 (Spring): 30–44.

ST. JEAN, YANICK, and JOE R. FEAGIN. 1998. *Double Burden: Black Women and Everyday Racism*. Armonk, N.Y.: M. E. Sharpe.

SADKER, DAVID. 1999. "Gender Equity: Still Knocking at the Classroom Door." *Educational Leadership*. Vol. 56, No. 7 (April): 22–26.

SADKER, DAVID, and MYRA SADKER. 1986. "Sexism in the Classroom: From Grade School to Graduate School." *Phi Delta Kappan*. Vol. 67 (March): 512–15.

———. 1994. *Failing at Fairness: How America's Schools Cheat Girls*. New York: Scribner.

SAGAN, CARL, and RICHARD TURCO. 1990. *A Path Where No Man Thought: Nuclear Winter and the End of the Arms Race*. New York: Random House.

SAID, EDWARD. 1981. *Covering Islam: How the Media and the Experts Determine How We See the Rest of the World*. New York: Pantheon.

SALE, KIRKPATRICK. 1990. *The Conquest of Paradise: Christopher Columbus and the Columbian Legacy*. New York: Alfred A. Knopf.

SAMPLES, FAITH, and LARRY ABNER. 1998. "Evaluations of School-Based Violence Prevention Programs." In Delbert S. Elliott, Beatrix A. Hamburg, and Kirk R. Williams, eds., *Violence in American Schools: A New Perspective* (pp. 217–52). New York: Cambridge University Press.

SAMUELSON, ROBERT J. 2003. "The Rich and Everyone Else." *Newsweek* (January 27): 57.

SANTOLI, AL. 1994. "Fighting Child Prostitution." *Freedom Review.* Vol. 25, No. 5 (September–October): 5–8.

SAUDI ARABIA EMBASSY. 1999. "Saudi Arabia: Economy & Industry." [Online] http://saudiembassy.net/profile/industry/saudi-economy-industry.html Accessed November 19, 1999.

SCANLON, JAMES P. 1992. "The Curious Case of Affirmative Action for Women." *Society.* Vol. 29, No. 2 (January–February): 36–42.

SCHECTER, SUSAN. 1982. *Women and Male Violence: The Visions and Struggles of the Battered Women's Movement.* Boston: South End Press.

SCHICK, FRANK L., and RENEE SCHICK, EDS. 1994. *Statistical Handbook on Aging Americans.* Phoenix: Oryx Press.

SCHILLER, BRADLEY. 1994. "Who Are the Working Poor?" *Public Interest.* Vol. 155 (Spring): 61–71.

SCHLOSSER, ERIC. 2001. *Fast Food Nation: The Dark Side of the All-American Meal.* Boston: Houghton Mifflin.

SCHLUMPF, HEIDI. 1999. "Babes in Arms." *U.S. Catholic.* Vol. 64, No. 12 (December): 34–38.

SCHMALZ, J. 1993. "Poll Finds an Even Split on Homosexuality's Cause." *The New York Times.* (March 5): A14.

SCHNEIDER, JODI. 2003. "Getting Nurses Back on Board." *U.S. News & World Report.* Vol. 135, No. 3 (July 28–August 4): 20.

SCHOEN, ROBERT, ANN MARIE ASTONE, KENDRA ROTHERT, NICOLA J. STANDISH, and YOUNG J. KIM. 2002. "Women's Employment, Marital Happiness, and Divorce." *Social Forces.* Vol. 81, No. 2 (December): 643–83.

SCHOOFS, MARK. 1999. "The Deadly Gender Gap." *Village Voice.* Vol. 63, No. 53 (January 15): 34–36.

SCHULZ, JAMES H. 1997. "Ask Older Women: Are the Elderly Better Off?" *Journal of Aging & Social Policy.* Vol. 9, No. 1.

SCHUR, EDWIN M. 1984. *Labeling Women Deviant: Gender, Stigma, and Social Control.* Philadelphia: Temple University Press.

SCHWARTZ, JOE. 1992. "Everybody Loves a Drunk." *American Demographics.* (March): 13.

SCHWARTZ, MARTIN D. 1987. "Gender and Injury in Spousal Assault." *Sociological Focus.* Vol. 20, No. 1 (January): 61–75.

SCOMMEGNA, PAOLA. 1996. "Teens' Risk of AIDS, Unintended Pregnancies Examined." *Population Today.* Vol. 24, No. 8 (August): 1–2.

———. 2002. "Increased Cohabitation Changing Children's Family Settings." *Population Today.* Vol. 30, No. 7 (July): 3, 6.

SCOTT, JOHN, and CATHERINE GRIFF. 1985. *Directors of Industry: The British Corporate Network, 1904–1976.* New York: Blackwell.

SEAGER, JONI. *The State of Women in the World Atlas.* New revised 2nd ed. New York: Penguin Group, 1997.

SEAMAN, BARRETT. 2001. "No Hands, No Harm." *Time.* Vol. 157, No. 12 (March 26): 61.

SECCOMBE, KAREN. 1999. *So You Think I Drive a Cadillac? Welfare Recipients' Perspectives on the System and Its Reform.* Boston: Allyn & Bacon.

SEGAL, MADY WECHSLER, and AMANDA FAITH HANSEN. 1992. "Value Rationales in Policy Debates on Women in the Military: A Content Analysis of Congressional Testimony, 1941–1985." *Social Science Quarterly.* Vol. 73, No. 2 (June): 296–309.

SEGE, R., and W. DIETZ. 1994. "Television Viewing and Violence in Children: The Pediatrician as Agent for Change." *Pediatrics.* Vol. 94, pp. 600–607.

SENNETT, RICHARD. 1998. *The Corrosion of Character: The Personal Consequences of Work in the New Capitalism.* New York: Norton.

THE SENTENCING PROJECT. 2000. [Online] http://www.TheSentencingProject.org Accessed April 2000.

SHAPIRO, JOSEPH P., and JOANNIE M. SCHROF. 1995. "Honor Thy Children." *U.S. News & World Report.* Vol. 118, No. 8 (February 27): 39–49.

SHEA, RACHEL HARTIGAN. 2002. "The New Insecurity." *U.S. News & World Report.* Vol. 132, No. 9 (March 25): 40.

SHEEHAN, MICHAEL A. 2000. "Post-Millenium Terrorism Review." Speech at the Brookings Institution. Washington, D.C. (February 10). [Online] http://www.state.gov/www/policy_remarks/2000/000210_sheehan_brookings.html Accessed March 13, 2000.

SHIELDS, J., L. HESTON, and H. GOTTESMAN. 1975. "Schizophrenia and the Schizoid: The Problem for Genetic Analysis." In R. Fieve, D. Rosenthal, and H. Brill, eds., *Genetic Research in Psychiatry* (pp. 167–97). Baltimore: Johns Hopkins University Press.

SHILTS, RANDY. 1987. *And the Band Played On: Politics, People, and the AIDS Epidemic.* New York: St. Martin's Press.

SHLAES, AMITY. 1998. "A Chance to Equip My Child." *The Wall Street Journal.* (February 23): A22.

SHUPE, ANSON, WILLIAM A. STACEY, and LONNIE HAZLEWOOD. 1987. *Violent Men, Violent Couples: The Dynamics of Domestic Violence.* Lexington, Mass.: Lexington Books.

SIEGEL, LOREN. 1997. "The Pregnancy Police Fight the War on Drugs." In Craig Reinarman and Harry G. Levine, eds., *Crack in America: Demon Drugs and Social Justice* (pp. 249–59). Berkeley: University of California Press.

SIERRA CLUB. 1999. "Toxic Waste Is a Terrible Thing to Mind" *Sierra Club Newsletter.* (May). [Online] http://louisiana.sierraclub.org/acadian/may99.html Accessed November 29, 2003.

SILVERBERG, ROBERT. 1991. "The Greenhouse Effect: Apocalypse Now or Chicken Little?" *Omni* (July): 50–54.

SIMON, JULIAN. 1981. *The Ultimate Resource.* Princeton, N.J.: Princeton University Press.

———. 1995. "More People, Greater Wealth, More Resources, Healthier Environment." In Theodore D. Goldfarb, ed., *Taking Sides: Clashing Views on Controversial Environmental Issues,* 6th ed. Guilford, Conn.: Dushkin.

SIMON, ROGER W. 2002. "Revisiting the Relationship among Gender, Marital Status, and Mental Health." *American Journal of Sociology.* Vol. 107, No. 4 (January): 1065–96.

SIMPSON, SALLY S. 1989. "Feminist Theory, Crime, and Justice." *Criminology.* Vol. 27 (November): 605–31.

SINGER, RENA. 2001. "A Sadly Mounting Ritual." *U.S. News & World Report.* Vol. 130, No. 16 (April 23): 34.

SIPRI (STOCKHOLM INTERNATIONAL PEACE RESEARCH INSTITUTE). 2003. *SIPRI Yearbook 2003.* Stockholm. Data provided courtesy of Mikael Eriksson, The Upsala Conflict Data Program.

SIVARD, RUTH LEGER. 1988. *World Military and Social Expenditures, 1987–1988,* 12th ed. Washington, D.C.: World Priorities.

SKIBA, RUSSELL. 2000. "No to Zero Tolerance." *The Louisville Courier-Journal.* (January 16): D3.

SLOAN, ALLAN. 2002. "Bad Boys Club." *Newsweek.* (July 1): 44–6.

SMAIL, J. KENNETH. 2004. "Let's *Reduce* Global Population!" In John J. Macionis and Nijole V. Benokraitis, eds., *Seeing Ourselves: Classic, Contemporary, and Cross-Cultural Readings in Sociology*, 6th ed. Upper Saddle River, N.J.: Prentice Hall, pp. 422–6.

SMART, TIM. 2001. "Not Acting Their Age." *U.S. News & World Report*. Vol. 130, No. 22 (June 4): 54–60.

———. 2003. ". . . and Those Who Came When Called." *U.S. News & World Report*. Vol. 133, No. 25 (December 30–January 6): 48.

SMITH, ADAM. 1937 (orig. 1776). *An Inquiry into the Nature and Causes of the Wealth of Nations*. New York: The Modern Library.

SMITH, DOUGLAS A. 1987. "Police Response to Interpersonal Violence: Defining the Parameters of Legal Control." *Social Forces*. Vol. 65, No. 3 (March): 767–82.

SMITH, DOUGLAS A., and CHRISTY A. VISHER. 1981. "Street-Level Justice: Situational Determinants of Police Arrest Decisions." *Social Problems*. Vol. 29, No. 2 (December): 167–77.

SMITH-LOVIN, LYNN, and CHARLES BRODY. 1989. "Interruptions in Group Discussions: The Effects of Gender and Group Composition." *American Journal of Sociology*. Vol. 54, No. 3 (June): 424–35.

SMOCK, PAMELA J. 2000. "Cohabitation in the United States: An Appraisal of Research Themes, Findings, and Implications." *Annual Review of Sociology*. Vol. 26: 1–20.

SMOLOWE, JILL. 1994. "When Violence Hits Home." *Time*. Vol. 144, No. 1 (July 4): 18–25.

SNOW, DAVID A., and LEON ANDERSON. 1993. *Down on Their Luck: A Study of Homeless Street People*. Berkeley: University of California Press.

SNYDER, SOLOMON H. 1980. *Biological Aspects of Mental Disorder*. New York: Oxford University Press.

SOMMERS, CHRISTINA HOFF. Lecture at Kenyon College, April 7, 2003.

SONENSTEIN, FREYA L., GARY J. GATES, STEFANIE SCHMIDT, and NATALYA BOLSHUN. 2002. *Primary Child Care Arrangements of Employed Parents: Findings from the 1999 National Survey of America's Families*. Washington, D.C.: The Urban Institute, 2002. [Online] http://www.urban.org Accessed September 12, 2002.

SOWELL, THOMAS. 1981. *Ethnic America*. New York: Basic Books.

———. 1987. "Preferential Treatment," in *Compassion versus Guilt and Other Essays* (pp. 197–99). New York: William Morrow.

———. 1990. *Preferential Policies: An International Perspective*. New York: Morrow.

———. 1994. *Race and Culture*. New York: Basic Books.

———. 1995. "Ethnicity and IQ." In Steven Fraser, ed., *The Bell Curve Wars: Race, Intelligence and the Future of America* (pp. 70–79). New York: Basic Books.

———. 1999. "Random Thoughts." *New York Post*. October 1: 33.

SPECTER, MICHAEL. 1997a. "Deep in the Russian Soul, a Lethal Darkness." *The New York Times* (June 8): Sec. 4, pp. 1, 5.

———. 1997b. "Moscow on the Make." *The New York Times Magazine* (June 1): 48–55, 72, 75, 80, 84.

SPECTOR, MALCOLM, and JOHN I. KITSUSE. 1977. *Constructing Social Problems*. Menlo Park, Calif.: Cummings.

SPENDER, DALE. 1989. *Invisible Women: The Schooling Scandal*. London: Women's Press.

SPILLMAN, BRENDA C. 2002. "New Estimates of Lifetime Nursing Home Use: Have Patterns of Use Changed?" *Medical Care*. Vol. 40, No. 10 (October): 965–1006.

SPITZER, STEVEN. 1980. "Toward a Marxian Theory of Deviance." In Delos H. Kelly, ed., *Criminal Behavior: Readings in Criminology* (pp. 175–91). New York: St. Martin's Press.

SROLE, LEO. 1972. "Urbanization and Mental Health: Some Reformulations." *American Scientist*. Vol. 60: 576–83.

———. 1975. "Measurements and Classification in Socio-Psychiatric Epidemiology: Midtown Manhattan Study I (1954) and Midtown Manhattan Study II (1974)." *Journal of Health and Social Behavior*. Vol. 16: 347–64.

SROLE, LEO, T. S. LANGNER, S. T. MICHAEL, M. K. OPLER, and T. A. C. RENNIE. 1962. *Mental Health in the Metropolis: The Midtown Manhattan Study*. New York: McGraw-Hill.

STACEY, JUDITH. 1990. *Brave New Families: Stories of Domestic Upheaval in Late Twentieth-Century America*. New York: Basic Books.

———. 1993. "Good Riddance to 'The Family': A Response to David Popenoe." *Journal of Marriage and the Family*. Vol. 55, No. 3 (August): 545–47.

STACK, CAROL B. 1975. *All Our Kin: Strategies for Survival in a Black Community*. New York: Harper & Row.

STANLEY, WILLIAM D., and THOMAS J. DANKO. 1996. *The Millionaire Next Door: The Surprising Secrets of America's Wealthy*. New York: Pocket Books.

STAPINSKI, HELENE. 1998. "Let's Talk Dirty." *American Demographics*. Vol. 20, No. 11 (November): 50–56.

STAPLES, R., and L. B. JOHNSON. 1993. *Black Families at the Crossroads: Challenges and Prospects*. San Francisco: Jossey-Bass.

STARES, PAUL B. 1996. *Global Habit: The Drug Problem in a Borderless World*. Washington, D.C.: Brookings Institution.

STARR, ALEXANDRA. 2003. "What McCain-Feingold Really Means." *Business Week Online*. http://www.businessweek.com Accessed August 15, 2003.

STARR, PAUL. 1982. *The Social Transformation of American Medicine*. New York: Basic Books.

STEELE, SHELBY. 1990. *The Content of Our Character: A New Vision of Race in America*. New York: St. Martin's Press.

STEIN, JOEL. 2002. "The New Politics of Pot." *Time*. Vol. 160, No. 19 (November 4): 56–62.

STERN, JESSICA. 1999. *The Ultimate Terrorists*. Cambridge, Mass.: Harvard University Press.

STETS, JAN E., and MURRAY A. STRAUS. 1989. "The Marriage License as a Hitting License: A Comparison of Assaults in Dating, Cohabiting, and Married Couples." In Maureen A. Priog-Good and Jan E. Stets, eds., *Violence in Dating Relationships: Emerging Social Issues* (pp. 161–80). New York: Praeger.

STEVENS, HELEN. 2003. "Declining Biodiversity and Unsustainable Agricultural Production: Common Cause, Common Solution?" Research Paper No. 2, 2001–2002 Department of the Parliamentary Library, Australia, 2002. [Online] http://www.aph.gov.au/library/pubs/rp/ 2001-02/02RP02.pdf Accessed October 31, 2003.

STODGHILL, RON, II. 1998. "Where'd You Learn That?" *Time*. Vol. 151, No. 23.

STONE, BRAD LOWELL. 2000. "Robert Nisbet on Conservative Dogmatics." *Society*. Vol. 37, No. 3 (March–April): 68–74.

STONE, CLARENCE N. 1998. "Linking Civic Capacity and Human Capital Formation." In Marilyn J. Gittell, ed., *Strategies for School Equity: Creating Productive Schools in a Just Society* (pp. 163–76). New Haven, Conn.: Yale University Press.

STONE, ROBYN, GAIL LEE CAFFERATA, and JUDITH SANGL. 1987. *Caregivers of the Frail Elderly: A National Profile.* Washington, D.C.: U.S. Department of Health and Human Services.

STOUT, DAVID. 2003. "Supreme Court Splits on Diversity Efforts at University of Michigan." *Yahoo! News.* [Online] http://www.yahoo.com/news Accessed June 23, 2003.

STRATTON, LESLIE S. 2001. "Why Does More Housework Lower Women's Wages? Testing Hypotheses Involving Job Effort and Hours Flexibility." *Social Sciences Quarterly.* Vol. 82, No. 1 (March): 67–76.

STRAUS, MURRAY A., and RICHARD J. GELLES. 1986. "Societal Change and Change in Family Violence from 1975 to 1985 as Revealed by Two National Surveys." *Journal of Marriage and the Family.* Vol. 48, No. 4 (August): 465–79.

STROM, STEPHANIE. 2000. "In Japan, the Golden Years Have Lost Their Glow." *The New York Times.* (February 16): A7.

STRONG, BRYAN, and CHRISTINE DEVAULT. 1994. *Human Sexuality.* Mountain View, Calif.: Mayfield.

SUDNOW, DAVID N. 1967. *Passing On: The Social Organization of Dying.* Englewood Cliffs, N.J.: Prentice Hall.

SULLIVAN, ANDREW. Lecture given at Kenyon College, 2002.

SULLIVAN, BRIAN. 1996. "International Organized Crime: A Growing National Security Threat." *Strategic Forum.* No. 74 (May). Washington, D.C.: Institute for National Strategic Studies.

SUTHERLAND, EDWIN H. 1940. "White Collar Criminality." *American Sociological Review.* Vol. 5, No. 1 (February): 1–12.

SZASZ, THOMAS S. 1961. *The Manufacturer of Madness: A Comparative Study of the Inquisition and the Mental Health Movement.* New York: Dell.

———. 1970 (orig., 1961). *The Myth of Mental Illness: Foundations of a Theory of Personal Conduct.* New York: Harper & Row.

———. 1994. "Mental Illness Is Still a Myth." *Society.* Vol. 31, No. 4 (May–June): 34–39.

———. 1995. "Idleness and Lawlessness in the Therapeutic State." *Society.* Vol. 32, No. 4 (May–June): 30–35.

TABB, WILLIAM K. 1992. "Vampire Capitalism." *Socialist Review.* Vol. 22, No. 1 (1992): 81–93.

TANNAHILL, REAY. 1992. *Sex in History.* Scarborough House.

TANNENBAUM, FRANK. 1946. *Slave and Citizen: The Negro in the Americas.* New York: Vintage Books.

TATARA, T. 1993. "Understanding the Nature and Scope of Domestic Elder Abuse with the Use of State Aggregate Data: Summaries of Key Findings of a National Survey of State APS and Aging Services." *Journal of Elder Abuse & Neglect.* Vol. 5, No. 4: 35–57.

TAVRIS, CAROL, and CAROL WADE. 2001. *Psychology in Perspective,* 3rd ed. Upper Saddle River, N.J.: Prentice Hall.

TAYLOR, LAWRENCE. 1984. *Born to Crime: The Genetic Causes of Criminal Behavior.* Westport, Conn.: Greenwood.

TAYLOR, STEVEN J. L. 1998. *Desegregation in Boston and Buffalo: The Influence of Local Leaders.* Albany: State University of New York Press.

TERKEL, STUDS. 1974. *Working.* New York: Pantheon.

THERNSTROM, ABIGAIL. 1999. "Courting Disorder in the Schools." *The Public Interest.* Vol. 136 (Summer): 18–34.

THIGPEN, DAVID E. 2002. "The Long Way Home." *Time.* Vol. 160, No. 6 (August 5): 42–44.

THOMAS, EVAN. 2003. "The War over Gay Marriage." *Newsweek.* (July 7): 38–44.

THOMAS, EVAN, JOHN BARRY, and CHRISTIAN CARYL. 2003. "A War in the Dark." *Newsweek.* (November 10): 24–31.

THOMAS, EVAN, and MICHAEL HIRSH. 2000. "The Future of Terror." *Newsweek.* Vol. 135, No. 2 (January 10): 34–37.

THOMPSON, MARK. 1997. "Fatal Neglect." *Time.* Vol. 150, No. 17 (October 27): 34–38.

———. 1998. "Shining a Light on Abuse." *Time.* Vol. 152, No. 5 (August 3): 42–43.

THOMPSON, WILLIAM E., and JACKIE L. HARROD. 1999. "Topless Dancers: Managing Stigma in a Deviant Occupation." In Henry N. Pontell, ed., *Social Deviance: Readings in Theory and Research,* 3rd ed. (pp. 277–87). Upper Saddle River, N.J.: Prentice Hall.

THORNBERRY, TERRANCE, and MARGARET FARNSWORTH. 1982. "Social Correlates of Criminal Involvement: Further Evidence on the Relationship between Social Status and Criminal Behavior." *American Sociological Review.* Vol. 47, No. 4 (August): 505–18.

TIERNEY, KATHLEEN J. 1982. "The Battered Women's Movement and the Creation of the Wife Beating Problem." *Social Problems.* Vol. 29, No. 3 (August): 207–20.

TILLY, CHARLES. 1978a. "Collective Violence in European Perspective." In T. R. Gurr, ed., *Protest, Rebellion, Reform, Vol. 2 of Violence in America: The History of Crime.* Newbury Park, Calif.: Sage.

———. 1978b. *From Mobilization to Revolution.* Reading, Mass.: Addison-Wesley.

Time. 1992. "Closed: Needle Park." Vol. 139, No. 7 (February 17): 53.

TIPPIT, SARAH. 2001. "Poll: One Teen in Five Took Weapon to High School." *Yahoo! News.* [Online] http://www.yahoo.com/news Accessed April 2, 2001.

TJADEN, PATRICIA. 1997. "The Crime of Stalking: How Big is the Problem?" *National Institute of Justice Research Preview.* Washington, D.C.: U.S. Department of Justice.

TJADEN, PATRICIA, and NANCY THOENNES. 1998. "Stalking in America: Findings from the National Violence against Women Survey." *National Institute of Justice Centers for Disease Control and Prevention Research in Brief.* Washington, D.C.: U.S. Department of Justice.

TONER, ROBIN. 1999. "Doctors Fault HMOs in Survey." *The New York Times.* (July 29): A4.

TONRY, MICHAEL H. 1995. *Malign Neglect: Race, Crime and Punishment in America.* New York: Oxford University Press.

TOTTHAM, JYOTI. 2003. "Where the Good Jobs Are Going." *Time.* Vol. 162, No. 5 (August 4): 62–65.

TRATTNER, WALTER I. 1980. "Social Welfare." In Glenn Porter, ed., *Encyclopedia of American Economic History,* Vol. III (pp. 1155–67). New York: Scribner.

TREAS, JUDITH. 1995. "Older Americans in the 1990s and Beyond." *Population Bulletin.* Vol. 50, No. 2 (May). Washington, D.C.: Population Reference Bureau.

TREBACH, ARNOLD S., and JAMES A. INCIARDI. 1993. *Legalize It? Debating American Drug Policy.* Lanham, Md.: University of America Press.

TROIDEN, RICHARD R. 1988. *Gay and Lesbian Identity: A Sociological Analysis.* Dix Hills, N.Y.: General Hall.

TUCKER, DAVID. 1998. "Responding to Terrorism." *Washington Quarterly.* Vol. 21, No. 1 (Winter): 103–17.

TYLER, S. LYMAN. 1973. *A History of Indian Policy.* Washington, D.C.: United States Department of the Interior, Bureau of Indian Affairs.

UDRY, J. RICHARD. 2000. "Biological Limitations of Gender Construction." *American Sociological Review.* Vol. 65, No. 3 (June): 443–57.

———. 2001. "Feminist Critics Uncover Determinism, Positivism, and Antiquated Theory." *American Sociological Review.* Vol. 66, No. 4 (August): 611–18.

UNITED NATIONS DEVELOPMENT PROGRAMME. 1994. *Human Development Report 1994*. New York: Oxford University Press.

———. 1995. *Human Development Report 1995*. New York: Oxford University Press.

———. 1996. *Human Development Report 1996*. New York: Oxford University Press.

———. 1998. *Human Development Report 1998*. New York: Oxford University Press.

———. 1999. *Human Development Report 1999*. New York: Oxford University Press.

———. 2000. *Human Development Report 2000*. New York: Oxford University Press.

———. 2001. *Human Development Report 2001*. New York: Oxford University Press.

———. 2002. *Human Development Report 2002*. New York: Oxford University Press.

———. 2003. *Human Development Report 2003*. New York: Oxford University Press.

UNNITHAN, N. PRABHA, LIN HUFF-CORZINE, JAY CORSINE, and HUGH P. WHITT. 1994. *The Currents of Lethal Violence: An Integrated Model of Suicide and Homicide*. Albany: State University of New York Press.

UNRAU, WILLIAM E. 1996. *White Man's Wicked Water: The Alcohol Trade and Prohibition in Indian Country, 1802–1892*. Lawrence: University of Kansas Press.

UNRUH, JOHN D., JR. 1979. *The Plains Across*. Urbana: University of Illinois Press. U.S. Bureau of Economic Analysis. 1999. *Foreign Direct Investment in the United States. Country Detail for Selected Items*. Washington, D.C.: The Bureau.

U.S. BUREAU OF JUSTICE STATISTICS. 1999. *Substance Abuse and Treatment, State and Federal Prisoners, 1997*. Washington, D.C.: U.S. Government Printing Office.

———. 2000. *Capital Punishment 1999*. Washington, D.C.: The Bureau.

———. 2000. *Criminal Victimization 1999: Changes 1998–99 with Trends 1993–99*. Washington, D.C.: The Bureau.

———. 2000. *Sourcebook of Criminal Justice Statistics 1999*. Washington, D.C.: The Bureau.

———. 2001. *Intimate Partner Violence and Age of Victim, 1993–99*. Washington, D.C.: The Bureau. [Online] http://www.ojp.usdoj.gov/bjs/pub/pdf/ipva99.pdf Accessed December 4, 2001.

———. 2002. *Homicide Trends in the United States*. Washington, D.C.: The Bureau.

———. 2003. *Prevalence of Imprisonment in the U.S. Population, 1974–2001*. Washington, D.C.: The Bureau.

U.S. BUREAU OF LABOR STATISTICS. 2002. *Highlights of Women's Earnings in 2001*. Report 960. Washington, D.C.: The Bureau.

———. 2003. *Employment and Earnings*. Vol. 50, No. 5 (June 2003). Washington, D.C.: The Bureau.

———. 2003. *Employment and Earnings*. Vol. 50, No. 6 (June 2003). Washington, D.C.: The Bureau.

———. 2003. *Union Members in 2002*. February 25. (News release).

U.S. CENSUS BUREAU. 2000. *Educational Attainment in the United States: March 2000 (Update)*. Current Population Reports, P20–536. Washington, D.C.: U.S. Government Printing Office.

———. 2000. *Health Insurance Coverage 1999* (P60-211). Washington, D.C.: The Bureau.

———. 2000. *Historical Income Tables: Families*. Table F-3. Mean Income Received by Each Fifth and Top 5 Percent of Families (All Races): 1966 to 1999. [Online] http://www.census.gov/hhes/income/histinc/f03.html

———. 2000. *Housing Vacancies and Home Ownership: Annual Statistics: 1999*. Table 20. [Online] http://www.census.gov/hhes/www/housing/hvsannual99/ann99t20.html

———. 2000. *International Data Base*. [Online] http://www.census.gov/ipc/www/idbprint.html

———. 2000. *Metropolitan Area Population Estimates for July 1, 1999, and Population Change for April 1, 1990, to July 1, 1999*. Washington, D.C.: The Bureau.

———. 2000. *Money Income in the United States 1999*. Current Population Reports P60-209. Washington, D.C.: U.S. Government Printing Office.

———. 2000. *Poverty in the United States 1999*. Current Population Reports P60-210. Washington, D.C.: U.S. Government Printing Office.

———. 2000. *Projections of the Total Resident Population by 5-Year Age Groups and Sex with Special Age Categories: Middle Series*. [Online] http://www.census.gov/population/projections/nation/summary/np-t3-?.pdf

———. 2000. *Statistical Abstract of the United States 2000*. Washington, D.C.: U.S. Government Printing Office.

———. 2000. Table F-1. Income Limits for Each Fifth and Top 5 Percent of Families (All Races): 1947 to 1999. [Online] http://www.census.gov/hhes/income/histinc/f01.html

———. 2000. Table F-2. Share of Aggregate Income Received by Each Fifth and Top 5 Percent of Families (All Races): 1947 to 1999. [Online] http://www.census.gov/hhes/income/histinc/f02.html

———. 2000. Table F-7. Type of Family (All Races) by Median and Mean Income: 1947 to 1999. [Online] http://www.census.gov/hhes/income/histinc/f07.html

———. 2000. Table P-28. Years of School Completed: Workers 18 Years Old and Over by Mean Earnings, Age, and Sex: 1991 to 1998. [Online] http://www.census.gov/hhes/income/histinc/p28.html

———. 2000. Table P-31. Years of School Completed: Workers 18 Years Old and Over by Mean Earnings, Age, and Sex: 1974 to 1979. [Online] http://www.census.gov/hhes/income/histinc/p31.html

———. 2001. Historical Income Tables: People, Table P-10. [Online] http://www.census.gov/hhes/income/histinc/p10.html

———. 2001. *Resident Population Estimates of the United States by Sex, Race, and Hispanic Origin: April 1, 1990, to July 1, 1999, with Short-term Projections to November 1, 2000*. [Online] http://www.census.gov/population/estimates/nation/intfile3-1.txt

———. 2002. *Custodial Mothers and Fathers and Their Child Support*. (Current Population Reports, P60-217) Washington, D.C.: The Bureau.

———. 2002. Historical Income Tables. Table 36-b. "Full Time, Year-Round White, Non-Hispanic Workers by Median Income and Sex: 1987–2001." [Online] http://www.census.gov/hhes/income/histinc/p36e.html

———. 2002. Table NC4. "Renter Subsidized Housing by Selected Household Characteristics, Hispanic Origin, and Poverty Status: 2001." Washington, D.C.: U.S. Government Printing Office.

———. 2002. "Voting and Registration in the Election of 2000." *Current Population Reports* P20-542. Washington, D.C.: U.S. Government Printing Office, p. 7.

———. 2002. "Voting and Registration in the Election of November 2000." Current Population Reports P20-542. Washington, D.C.: U.S. Government Printing Office.

———. 2003. *Disability Status, 2000*. Washington, D.C.: U.S. Government Printing Office.

———. 2003. "POV:04 Families by Age of Householder, Number of Children, and Family Structure, Below 100 Percent of Poverty." Last revised September 26, 2003. [Online] http://ferret.bls.census.gov/macro/32003/pov/new_04_100_03.htm and http://ferret.bls.census.gov/macro/32003/pov/new_04_100_05.htm Accessed December 8, 2003.

———. 2003. *Poverty in the United States 2002*. Current Population Reports P-60-222. Washington, D.C.: U.S. Government Printing Office.

———. 2003. Table F1. Family Households, by Type, Age of Own Children, Age of Family Members, and Age, Race and Hispanic Origin or Householder: March 2002: Total Family Households, Asians and Pacific Islanders. [Online] http://www.census.gov/population/socdemo/hh-fam/cps2002/tabF1-api.p Accessed June 12, 2003.

———. 2003. Table F-23 Families by Total Money Income, Race, and Hispanic Origin of Householder: 1967–2001. [Online] http://www.census.gov/hhes/income/f-23.html Accessed June 11, 2003.

———. 2003. Table MS-2. Estimated Median Age at First Marriage, by Sex: 1890 to Present. [Online] http://www.census.gov/population/socdemo/hh-fam/tabMS-2.pdf Accessed June 12, 2003.

U.S. CENTERS FOR DISEASE CONTROL and PREVENTION. 1997. "Youth Risk Behavior Surveillance: National College Health Risk Behavior Survey, United States, 1995." *Mobility and Mortality Weekly Report*. Vol. 46, No. SS6 (November 14): 38.

———. 2002. "Abortion Surveillance: United States, 1999." *Morbidity and Mortality Weekly Report*. Vol. 51, No. SS-9 (November 29): 12.

———. 2002. "Alcohol Use among Women of Childbearing Age." *Morbidity and Mortality Weekly Report*. Vol. 51, No. 13 (April 5): 274.

———. 2002. *HIV/AIDS Surveillance Report*. Vol. 13, No. 2: 18, 20, 24.

———. 2002. *Sexually Transmitted Disease Surveillance, 2001*. Atlanta, Ga.: The Centers.

———. 2003. *Genital Herpes*. [Online] http://www.cdc.gov/nchstp/dstd/fact_sheets/facts_genital_herpes.htm Accessed August 18, 2003.

———. 2003. "Prevalence of Current Cigarette Smoking among Adults and Prevalence of Current and Some Day Smoking, United States, 1996–2001." *Morbidity and Mortality Weekly Report*. Vol. 52, No. 1 (April 11): 303.

U.S. DEPARTMENT OF HEALTH and HUMAN SERVICES. 1995. *Substance Abuse and Mental Health Services Administration. National Household Survey on Drug Abuse: Main Findings, 1995*. National Household Survey on Drug Abuse Series: H-1. Washington, D.C.: U.S. Government Printing Office.

———. 1999. *Mental Health: A Report of the Surgeon General—Executive Summary*. Rockville, Md.: U.S. Department of Health and Human Services.

———. 2000. *Administration for Children and Families. Temporary Assistance for Needy Families (TANF) Program: Third Annual Report to Congress, August 2000*. Washington, D.C.: The Administration.

———. 2002. *National Institute on Drug Abuse. Marijuana Abuse. Research Series*. Rockville, Md.: U.S. Department of Health and Human Services.

———. 2003. *Substance Abuse and Mental Health Services Administration. Results from the 2002 National Survey of Drug Use and Mental Health: Detailed Tables*. Rockville, Md.: U.S. Department of Health and Human Services.

———. 2003. *Substance Abuse and Mental Health Services Administration. Lifetime Use of Specific Stimulants in 2000 and 2001, National Household Survey on Drug Abuse*. Rockville, Md.: U.S. Department of Health and Human Services.

U.S. DEPARTMENT OF JUSTICE. 1993. *Drug Enforcement Administration. Briefing Book*. Washington, D.C.: U.S. Government Printing Office.

———. 1994. Bureau of Justice Statistics. "Two-Thirds of Women Violence Victims Are Attacked by Relatives or Acquaintances." BJS 202-307-0784. Washington, D.C.: U.S. Government Printing Office.

———. 1997. Bureau of Justice Statistics. *Sourcebook of Criminal Justice Statistics-1997*. Washington, D.C.: U.S. Government Printing Office.

———. 1999. Bureau of Justice Statistics. "Drugs and Crime Facts, 1994." [Online] http://www.ojp.usdoj.gov/bjs/pub/ascii/dcfacts.txt Accessed May 8, 1999.

———. 2000. *Compendium of Federal Justice Statistics, 1998*. Washington, D.C.: U.S. Government Printing Office.

———. 2001. "Nearly Three Percent of College Women Experienced a Completed Rape or Attempted Rape During the College Year, According to a New Justice Department Report." [Online] http://www.ojp.usdoj.gov/bjs/pub/press/svcw.pr Accessed February 15, 2001.

———. 2002. Bureau of Justice Statistics. "Two-Thirds of Former State Prisoners Rearrested for Serious Crimes." [Online] http://www.ojp.usdoj.gov/bjs/abstract/rpr94.htm (June 2). Accessed June 25, 2003.

U.S. DEPARTMENT OF LABOR. 2000. *International Comparisons of Hourly Compensation Costs for Production Workers in Manufacturing, 1975–1999*. Supplementary tables for BLS News Release USDL 00-254, September 7, 2000. Washington, D.C.: The Bureau.

———. 2003. Bureau of Labor Statistics. Tables from *Employment and Earnings*. [Online] http://www.bls.gov/cps/#annual Accessed August 30, 2003.

———. 2003. Bureau of Labor Statistics. *International Comparisons of Hourly Compensation Costs for Production Workers in Manufacturing, 2002*. [Online] http://www.bls.gov/fls Accessed September 30, 2003.

U.S. DEPARTMENT OF STATE. 2000. "Patterns of Global Terrorism: 1998, The Year in Review." [Online] http://www.state.gov/www/global/terrorism/1998Report/review.html

———. 2000. *Patterns of Global Terrorism 1999*. Washington, D.C.: The Department.

———. 2003. *World Military Expenditures and Arms Transfers 1999–2000*. [Online] http://www.state.gov/documents/organization/18738.pdf Accessed December 28, 2003.

U.S. DEPARTMENT OF TRANSPORTATION. 2002. National Highway Traffic Safety Administration. Traffic *Safety Facts, 2001: Alcohol*. Washington, D.C.: U.S. Government Printing Office.

U.S. DEPARTMENTS OF EDUCATION AND JUSTICE. 2002. *Indicators of School Crime and Safety 2002*. Washington, D.C.: U.S. Government Printing Office.

U.S. FEDERAL BUREAU OF INVESTIGATION. 2000. *Crime in the United States 1999*. Washington, D.C.: The Bureau.

———. 2001. *Crime in the United States 2000*. Washington, D.C.: The Bureau. [Online] http://www.fbi.gov/ucr/cius-00/ Accessed November 11, 2001.

———. 2002. *Crime in the United States 2001*. Washington, D.C.: The Bureau.

———. 2003. *Crime in the United States: Uniform Crime Reports 2002*. Washington, D.C.: U.S. Government Printing Office.

U.S. FEDERAL ELECTION COMMISSION. 2000. "18-Month Summary on Political Action Committees." News release, September 27. [Online] http://www.fec.gov

———. 2003. "FEC Issues Semi-Annual Federal PAC Count." News release. (August 29, 2003).

U.S. HOUSE OF REPRESENTATIVES. 2001. Committee on Government Reform. Special Investigations Division. Minority Staff. "Abuse of Residents Is a Major Problem in U.S. Nursing Homes." Prepared for Rep. Henry A. Waxman. Washington, D.C.: The Staff.

U.S. IMMIGRATION AND NATURALIZATION SERVICE. 2002. *Legal Immigration, Fiscal Year 2000.* Washington, D.C.: The Service. [Online] http://www.ins.usdoj.gov/graphics/aboutins/statistics/IMM2000AR.pdf Accessed August 13, 2002.

U.S. NATIONAL CENTER FOR EDUCATION STATISTICS. 1999. *Dropout Rates in the United States: 1997.* Washington, D.C.: The Center.

———. 2002. *Digest of Education Statistics 2001.* Washington, D.C.: U.S. Government Printing Office.

———. 2003. *Digest of Education Statistics 2002.* Washington, D.C.: U.S. Government Printing Office.

———. 2003. *Overview of Public Elementary and Secondary Public Schools and Districts; School Year 2001–02.* Washington, D.C.: U.S. Government Printing Office.

U.S. NATIONAL CENTER FOR HEALTH STATISTICS. 1999. *Current Estimates from the National Health Interview Survey 1996.* Series 10, No. 200. Hyattsville, Md.: The Center.

———. 1999. *National Vital Statistics Report.* Vol. 47, No. 25 (October 5).

———. 2001. *National Vital Statistics Report.* Vol. 48, No. 18 (February 7, 2001). [Online] http://www.cdc.gov/nchs/data/nvsr/nvsr48/nvs48_18.pdf

———. 2002. *National Vital Statistics Report.* Vol. 50, No. 5 (February 12).

———. 2002. *National Vital Statistics Report.* Vol. 50, No. 6 (March 21).

———. 2002. *National Vital Statistics Report.* Vol. 50, No. 12 (August 28).

———. 2002. *National Vital Statistics Report.* Vol. 50, No. 14 (September 11).

———. 2002. *National Vital Statistics Report.* Vol. 50, No. 15 (September 16).

———. 2002. "Births: Final Data for 2001." *National Vital Statistics Report.* Vol. 51, No. 2 (December 18): 44.

———. 2002. *National Vital Statistics Report.* Vol. 51, No. 3 (December 19, 2002).

———. 2003. "Deaths: Preliminary Data for 2001." *National Vital Statistics Reports.* Vol. 51, No. 5 (March 14): 17.

U.S. NATIONAL INSTITUTE ON MENTAL HEALTH. 2003. *The Numbers Count: Mental Disorders in America.* Washington, D.C.: The Institute.

U.S. OFFICE OF JUVENILE JUSTICE AND DELINQUENCY PREVENTION. 2003. *Highlights of the 2001 National Youth Gang Survey.* Washington, D.C.: U.S. Government Printing Service.

U.S. SUBSTANCE ABUSE AND MENTAL HEALTH SERVICES ADMINISTRATION. 2003. *Results from the 2002 National Survey of Drug Use and Health: Detailed Tables.* Rockville, Md.: The Administration.

U.S. VETERANS ADMINISTRATION. 2003. *Facts about the Department of Veterans Affairs.* (April). [Online] http://www1.va.gov/opa/facts/docs/vafacts.htm Accessed December 3, 2003.

VALDEZ, A. 1997. "In the Hood: Street Gangs Discover White-Collar Crime." *Police.* Vol. 21, No. 5 (May): 49–50, 56.

VALLAS, STEPHEN P., and JOHN P. BECK. 1996. "The Transformation of Work Revisited: The Limits of Flexibility in American Manufacturing." *Social Problems.* Vol. 43, No. 3 (August): 339–61.

VAN BIEMA, DAVID. 1994. "Parents Who Kill." *Time.* Vol. 144, No. 20 (November 14): 50–51.

VAN DEN HURK, ARIE. 1999. "Europe: Drugs, Prisons, and Treatment." In *THCi: The Netherlands Law.*

VAN DER LIPPE, TANJA, and LISET VAN DIJK. 2002. "Comparative Research on Women's Employment." *Annual Review of Sociology.* Vol. 28: 221–41.

VAN EVERA, STEPHEN. 1999. *Causes of War: Power and the Roots of Conflict.* Ithaca, N.Y.: Cornell University Press.

Vanity Fair. 1998. "There's Something about Mary." Vol. 461 (January): 63.

VEBLEN, THORSTEIN. 1953 (orig., 1899). *The Theory of the Leisure Class.* New York: The New American Library.

VILLAROSA, LINDA. 2002. "To Prevent Sexual Abuse, Step Forward." *The New York Times.* (December 3): D5, D8.

VIOLENCE AGAINST WOMEN ONLINE RESOURCES. 2001. [Online] http://vaw.umn.edu Accessed April 24, 2001.

VITO, GENNARO F., and RONALD M. HOLMES. 1994. *Criminology: Theory, Research, and Policy.* Belmont, Calif.: Wadsworth.

VOGEL, EZRA F. 1991. *The Four Little Dragons: The Spread of Industrialization in East Asia.* Cambridge, Mass.: Harvard University Press.

VOGEL, LISE. 1983. *Marxism and the Oppression of Women: Toward a Unitary Theory.* New Brunswick, N.J.: Rutgers University Press.

VOYDANOFF, PATRICIA., and BRENDA W. DONNELLY. 1990. *Adolescent Sexuality and Pregnancy.* Newbury Park, Calif.: Sage.

WAITE, LINDA J., and MAGGIE GALLAGHER. 2000. *The Case for Marriage: Why Married People Are Happier, Healthier, and Better Off Financially.* New York: Doubleday.

WALDMAN, STEVEN. 1992. "Deadbeat Dads." *Newsweek.* (May 4): 46–52.

WALKER, LENORE. 1984. *The Battered Woman Syndrome.* New York: Springer.

———. 1989. *Terrifying Love: Why Battered Women Kill and How Society Responds.* New York: HarperPerennial.

WALLACE, HARVEY. 1996. *Family Violence: Legal, Medical and Social Perspectives.* Boston: Allyn & Bacon.

WALLACE, STEVEN P., and JOHN B. WILLIAMSON, with RITA GASTON LUNG. 1992. *The Senior Movement: References and Resources.* New York: G. K. Hall & Co.

WALLERSTEIN, IMMANUEL. 1974. *The Modern World-System: Capitalist Agriculture and the Origins of the European World-Economy in the Sixteenth Century.* New York: Academic Press.

———. 1979. *The Capitalist World-Economy.* New York: Cambridge University Press.

———. 1983. "Crises: The World Economy, the Movements, and the Ideologies." In Albert Bergesen, ed., *Crises in the World-System* (pp. 21–36). Beverly Hills, Calif.: Sage.

———. 1984. *The Politics of the World Economy: The States, the Movements, and the Civilizations.* Cambridge: Cambridge University Press.

WALTON, JOHN, and CHARLES RAGIN. 1990. "Global and National Sources of Political Protest: Third World Responses to the Debt Crisis." *American Sociological Review.* Vol. 55, No. 6 (December): 876–90.

WARF, BARNEY, and CYNTHIA WADDELL. 2002. "Heinous Spaces, Perfidious Places: The Sinister Landscapes of Serial Killers." *Social and Cultural Geography.* Vol. 3, No. 3 (September): 323–46.

WARSHAW, CAROLE. 1990. "Limitations of the Medical Model in the Care of Battered Women." *Gender & Society.* Vol. 3, No. 4: 506–40.

WASHBURN, PHILO. 1986. "The Public School as an Agent of Political Socialization." *Quarterly Journal of Ideology.* Vol. 10, No. 2: 24–35.

WATKINS, T. H. 1993. *The Great Depression: America in the 1930s.* New York: Little, Brown.

WATTEL, H. 1958. "Levittown: A Suburban Community." In William Dobriner, ed., *The Suburban Community* (pp. 287–313). New York: Putnam.

WEBER, MAX. 1958 (orig., 1904–5). *The Protestant Ethic and the Spirit of Capitalism.* New York: Scribner.

WEBSTER, PAMELA S., TERRI ORBUCH, and JAMES S. HOUSE. 1995. "Effects of Childhood Family Background on Adult Marital Quality and Perceived Stability." *American Journal of Sociology.* Vol. 101, No. 2 (September): 404–32.

WEEKS, JEFFREY. 1985. *Sexuality and Its Discontents.* London: Routledge

WEIDENBAUM, MURRAY. 1995. "The Evolving Corporate Board." *Society.* Vol. 32, No. 3 (March–April): 9–20.

WEIL, ANDREW T., and WINIFRED ROSEN. 1983. *Chocolate to Morphine: Understanding Mind-Active Drugs.* Boston: Houghton Mifflin.

WEINBERG, GEORGE. 1973. *Society and the Healthy Homosexual.* Garden City, N.Y.: Anchor.

WEINRICH, JAMES D. 1987. *Sexual Landscapes: Why We Are What We Are, Why We Love Whom We Love.* New York: Scribner.

WEISNER, THOMAS S. 1981. "Cities, Stress, and Children." In Ruth H. Moore, Robert I. Monroe, and Beatrice B. Whiting, eds., *Handbook of Cross-Cultural Human Development* (pp. 783–803). New York: Garland.

WEISS, CAROL H. 1972. *Evaluation Research: Methods for Assessing Program Effectiveness.* Englewood Cliffs, N.J.: Prentice Hall.

WEISS, R. D., M. L. GRIFFIN, and S. M. MIRIN. 1992. "Drug Abuse as Self-Medication for Depression: An Empirical Study." *American Journal of Alcohol Abuse.* Vol. 18, No. 1: 121–29.

WEITZ, ROSE. 1996. *The Sociology of Health, Illness, and Health Care: A Critical Approach.* Belmont, Calif.: Wadsworth.

WEITZMAN, LENORE J. 1985. *The Divorce Revolution: The Unexpected Social and Economic Consequences for Women and Children in America.* New York: Free Press.

———. 1996. "The Economic Consequences of Divorce Are Still Unequal: Comment on Peterson." *American Sociological Review.* Vol. 61, No. 3 (June): 537–38.

WEITZMAN, LENORE J., DEBORAH EIFLER, ELIZABETH HODAKA, and CATHERINE ROSS. 1972. "Sex-Role Socialization in Picture Books for Pre-School Children." *American Journal of Sociology.* Vol. 77 No. 6 (May): 1125–50.

WELCH, SANDY, MYRNA DAWSON, and ANNETTE NIEROBISZ. 2002. "Legal Factors, Extra-Legal Factors, or Changes in the Law? Using Criminal Justice Research to Understand the Resolution of Sexual Harassment Complaints." *Social Problems.* Vol. 49, No. 4 (November): 605–23.

WELLNER, ALISON STEIN. 2000. "Generation Z." *American Demographics.* Vol. 22, No. 9 (September): 60–64.

WESTERN, BRUCE. 2002. "The Impact of Incarceration on Wage Mobility and Inequality." *American Sociological Review.* Vol. 67, No. 4 (August): 526–46.

WHITE, JACK E. 1999a. "Prejudice? Perish the Thought." *Time.* Vol. 152, No. 8 (March 8): 36.

———. 1999b. "The White Wall of Silence." *Time.* Vol. 153, No. 22 (June 7): 63.

WHITE, JASON M. 1991. *Drug Dependence.* Englewood Cliffs, N.J.: Prentice Hall.

WHITEHEAD, BARBARA DEFOE. 1997. *The Divorce Culture.* New York: Alfred A. Knopf.

WHITELAW, KEVIN. 2003. "In Death's Shadow." *U.S. News & World Report.* Vol. 135, No. 2 (July 21): 17–20.

WIARDA, HOWARD J. 1987. "Ethnocentrism and Third World Development." *Society.* Vol. 24, No. 6 (September–October): 55–64.

WICKHAM, DEWAYNE. 2000. "Homeless Receive Little Attention from Candidates." [Online] http://www.usatoday.com/usatonline Accessed October 24, 2000.

WIERSMA, D., R. GIEL, A. DEJOND, and C. SLOOF. 1983. "Social Class and Schizophrenia in a Dutch Cohort." *Psychological Medicine.* Vol. 13, pp. 141–50.

WILCOX, CLYDE. 1992. "Race, Gender, and Support for Women in the Military." *Social Science Quarterly.* Vol. 73, No. 2 (June): 310–23.

WILL, GEORGE F. 1999. "An Ironic Agony for the Ivory Tower." *New York Post.* (April 25): 53.

WILLIAMS, DAVID R., DAVID T. TAKEUCHI, and RUSSELL K. ADAIR. 1992. "Socioeconomic Status and Psychiatric Disorder among Blacks and Whites." *Journal of Health and Social Behavior.* Vol. 33: 140–57.

WILLIAMS, PATRICIA J. 2000. "Without Sanctuary." *The Nation.* Vol. 270, No. 6 (February 14): 9.

WILLIAMSON, CELIA, and TERRY CLUSE-TOLAR. 2002. "Pimp-Controlled Prostitution: Still an Integral Part of Street Life." *Violence against Women.* Vol. 8, No. 9 (September): 1074–93.

WILSON, EDWARD O. 1975. *Sociobiology: The New Synthesis.* Cambridge, Mass.: Belknap Press of the Harvard University Press.

———. 1991. "Biodiversity, Prosperity, and Value." In F. Herbert Bormann and Stephen R. Kellert, eds., *Ecology, Economics, and Ethics: The Broken Circle* (pp. 3–10). New Haven, Conn.: Yale University Press.

WILSON, JAMES Q., and RICHARD J. HERRNSTEIN. 1985. *Crime and Human Nature.* New York: Simon & Schuster.

WILSON, WILLIAM JULIUS. 1987. *The Truly Disadvantaged: The Inner City, the Underclass, and Public Policy.* Chicago: University of Chicago Press.

———. 1996a. *When Work Disappears: The World of the New Urban Poor.* New York: Alfred A. Knopf.

———. 1996b. "Work." *The New York Times Magazine* (August 18): 26–31, 40, 48, 52, 54.

WINSLOW, RON. 1997. "Long-Term Economic Hardship Can Be Detrimental to Your Health, Study Finds." *The Wall Street Journal.* (December 26): B11.

WINTERS, REBECCA. 2002. "Trouble for School Inc." *Time.* Vol. 159, No. 21 (May 27): 53.

WINZER, MARGARET A. 1993. *The History of Special Education: From Isolation to Integration.* Washington, D.C.: Gallaudet University Press.

WIRTH, LOUIS. 1938. "Urbanism as a Way of Life." *American Journal of Sociology.* Vol. 44, No. 1 (July): 1–24.

WISE, DAVID A. 1997. "Retirement against the Demographic Trend: More Older People Living Longer, Working Less, and Saving Less." *Demography.* Vol. 34, No. 1 (February): 83–95.

WISEMAN, JACQUELINE. 1978. *Stations of the Lost: The Treatment of Skid Row Alcoholics.* Englewood Cliffs, N.J.: Prentice Hall.

———. 1991. *The Other Half: Wives of Alcoholics and Their Social-Psychological Situation.* New York: Aldine de Gruyter.

WITKIN, GORDON. 1998. "The Crime Bust." *U.S. News & World Report.* Vol. 124, No. 20 (May 25): 28–40.

WOLFGANG, MARVIN E., and FRANCO FERRACUTTI. 1967. *The Subculture of Violence: Towards an Integrated Theory of Criminology.* London: Tavistock.

WOLFGANG, MARVIN E., TERRENCE P. THORNBERRY, and ROBERT M. FIGLIO. 1987. *From Boy to Man, From Delinquency to Crime.* Chicago: University of Chicago Press.

Women's International Network News. 1999a. "U.N. Survey Finds AIDS Is Devastating Sub-Saharan Populations." Vol. 25, No. 1 (Winter): 1.

———. 1999b. "Why Girls in Rural Areas of India Drop Out of School." Vol. 25, No. 1 (Winter): 15.

WOODWARD, C. VANN. 1974. *The Strange Career of Jim Crow.* 3rd rev. ed. New York: Oxford University Press.

THE WORLD BANK. 1993. *World Development Report 1993.* New York: Oxford University Press.

———. 2000. *Entering the 21st Century: World Development Report 1999/2000.* New York: Oxford University Press.

———. 2002. *World Development Report, 2001/2002.* Washington, D.C.: The World Bank.

———. 2003. *2003 World Development Indicators.* Washington, D.C.: The World Bank.

WORLD HEALTH ORGANIZATION. 1946. *Constitution of the World Health Organization.* New York: World Health Organization Interim Commission.

———. 1998. *The World Health Report, 1998: Life in the 21st Century, A Vision for All, Report to the Director-General.* Geneva, Switzerland: Office of World Health Reporting.

———. 2001. *Global Water Supply and Sanitation Assessment 2000 Report.* Washington, D.C.: World Health Organization. [Online] http://www.who.int/docstore/water_sanitation_health/globalassessment/GlobalTOC.htm Accessed October 31, 2003.

———. 2002. *The Tobacco Atlas.* Brighton, U.K.: Myriad Editions.

WREN, CHRISTOPHER S. 1996. "Study Poses a Medical Challenge to Disparity in Cocaine Sentences." *The New York Times.* (November 20): A1.

———. 1997. "Maturity Diminishes Drug Use, a Study Finds." *The New York Times.* (February 2): Sec. 1, p. 27.

WRIGHT, JAMES D. 1989. "Address Unknown: Homelessness in Contemporary America." *Society.* Vol. 26, No. 6 (September–October): 45–53.

WRIGHT, QUINCY. 1987. "Causes of War in the Atomic Age." In William M. Evan and Stephen Hilgartner, eds., *The Arms Race and Nuclear War* (pp. 7–10). Englewood Cliffs, N.J.: Prentice Hall.

WRIGHT, RICHARD A. 1994. *In Defense of Prisons.* Westport, Conn.: Greenwood.

WRIGHT, ROBERT. 1995. "Hyperdemocracy." *Time.* Vol. 145, No. 3 (January 23): 15–21.

WYATT, EDWARD. 2000. "Tenure Gridlock: When Professors Choose Not to Retire." *The New York Times.* (February 16): D11.

YANDLE, TRACY, and DUDLEY BURTON. 1996. "Reexamining Environmental Justice: A Statistical Analysis of Historical Hazardous Waste Landfill Siting in Metropolitan Texas." *Social Science Quarterly.* Vol. 77, No. 3 (September): 477–92.

YIN, SANDRA. 2002. "Wanted: One Million Nurses." *American Demographics.* Vol. 24, No. 8 (September): 63–65.

YORK, RICHARD, EUGENE A. ROSA, and THOMAS DEITZ. 2002. "Bridging Environmental Science with Environmental Policy: Plasticity of Population, Affluence, and Technology." *Social Science Quarterly.* Vol. 83, No. 1 (March): 18–34.

ZAKARIA, FAREED. "Bigger than Both of Them." *Newsweek* (January 19, 2004): 39.

ZANINI, MICHELE. 1999. "Middle Eastern Terrorism and Netwar." *Studies in Conflict & Terrorism.* Vol. 22, No. 3 (July–September): 247–56.

ZERNIKE, KATE. 2000. "A Gap in Test Scores Becomes a Talking Point." *The New York Times.* (August 13): A3.

———. 2001. "Antidrug Program Says It Will Adopt a New Program." *The New York Times.* (February 15): A1, A23.

ZHOU, MIN, and JOHN R. LOGAN. 1989. "Returns of Human Capital in Ethnic Enclaves: New York City's Chinatown." *American Sociological Review.* Vol. 54, No. 5 (October): 809–20.

ZICKLIN, G. 1992. "Re-Biologizing Sexual Orientation: A Critique." Paper presented at the Annual Meeting of the Society for the Study of Social Problems, Pittsburgh, Pa. (August).

ZIGLER, E., and S. STYFCO. 1994. "Head Start: Criticisms in a Constructive Context." *American Psychologist.* Vol. 49, No. 2: 127–32.

ZIMBARDO, PHILIP G. 1972. "Pathology of Imprisonment." *Society.* Vol. 9 (April): 4–8.

ZIMMER, MICHAEL. 2001. "Explaining Marital Dissolution: Explaining the Role of Spouses' Traits." *Social Science Quarterly.* Vol. 82, No. 3 (September): 464–77.

ZIMRING, FRANKLIN E. 1998. *American Youth Violence.* New York: Oxford University Press.

ZIMRING, FRANKLIN E., and GORDON HAWKINS. 1997. *Crime Is Not the Problem: Lethal Violence in America, Studies in Crime and Public Policy.* New York: Oxford University Press.

ZOGBY INTERNATIONAL. 2001. Poll reported in Sandra Yin, "Race and Politics." *American Demographics.* Vol. 23, No. 8 (August): 11–13.

ZUBERI, TUKUFU. 2001. *Thicker Than Blood: How Racial Statistics Lie.* Minneapolis: University of Minnesota Press.

ZUBOFF, SHOSHANA. 1982. "New Worlds of Computer-Mediated Work." *Harvard Business Review.* Vol. 60, No. 5 (September–October): 142–52.

PHOTO CREDITS

Steve McCurry/Magnum Photos, Inc., ii.

CHAPTER 1: © Paul Marcus, *Saturday*, Studio SPM Inc., xxxii; Alan Weiner/Getty Images, Inc.–Liaison, 2; AP/Wide World Photos, 5, 6; The Granger Collection, 8 (*left*); Myrleen Ferguson Cate/Photo-Edit, 8 (*right*); Jacob A. Riis/Museum of the City of New York, 11; Reuters/Rafiqur Rahman/Getty Images, Inc.–Hulton Archive Photos, 12; Eric Grigorian/Polaris Images, 14; Jay Dorin/Omni-Photo Communications, 19; Michael Newman/PhotoEdit, 21 (*left*); Greg Smith/Corbis/SABA Press Photos, Inc., 21 (*right*).

CHAPTER 2: © Paul Marcus, *Upstairs–Downstairs*, Studio SPM Inc., 26; Wally Santana/AP/Wide World Photos, 28; S. Liss/Corbis/SABA Press Photos, Inc., 37; Bob Rowan/Corbis/Bettmann, 38; Patrick Bennett/Getty Images, Inc.–Stone Allstock, 39; H. William Tetlow/Hulton/Archive, 41 (*left*); Cecil Stoughton/Corbis/Bettmann, © Corbis, 41 (*right*); Esbin-Anderson/The Image Works, 44; Monkmeyer Press, 45; Reuters/Jay Gorodetzer/Archive Photos, 47; David R. Frazier/David R. Frazier Photolibrary, Inc., 48.

CHAPTER 3: © Paul Marcus, *Musical Chairs*, Studio SPM Inc., 54; Getty Images, Inc.–PhotoDisc Inc., 56; Gary Buss/Getty Images, Inc.–Taxi, 57; Corbis/Bettmann, 59; AP/Wide World Photos, 62; Kevin Flemming/Corbis/Bettmann, 63; AP/Wide World Photos, 64; Seattle Bureau/Brown Brothers, 66; Stuart Franklin/Magnum Photos, Inc., 70; Mark Peterson/Corbis/SABA Press Photos, Inc., 74; Justin S. Parr; AP/Wide World Photos, 81 (*left, right*).

CHAPTER 4: © Paul Marcus, *The Glass Box*, Studio SPM Inc., 84; Lynsey Addario/Corbis/Bettmann, 86; D. Maillac/REA/Corbis/SABA Press Photos, Inc., 94 (*left*); Mark Richards/PhotoEdit, 94 (*right*); © Janet Wishnetsky/Corbis, 97; © Underwood & Underwood/Corbis, 101 (*left*); Adam Smith/Getty Images, Inc., 101 (*right*); The Granger Collection, 102; J.P. Williams/Getty Images, Inc.-Stone Allstock, 105.

CHAPTER 5: © Paul Marcus, *The Mourning After*, Studio SPM Inc., 110; Jim Noelker/The Image Works, 116; Tony Freeman/PhotoEdit, 117; Lester Sloan/Woodfin Camp & Associates, 119; Robert Brenner/PhotoEdit, 123; Richard Scheinwald/AP/Wide World Photos, 125; AP/Wide World Photos, 126; Penny Tweedie, 129.

CHAPTER 6: © Paul Marcus [detail from] *Yvonne's Story—Maze of AIDS*, Studio SPM Inc., 134; Brian Philips/Syracuse Newspapers/The Image Works, 136; Richard Lord/The Image Works, 140; B. Seitz/Photo Researchers, 143; Keith Brofsky/Getty Images, Inc.–Photodisc, 146; Ed Betz/AP/Wide World Photos, 147; Mark Richards, 149; Steve Lehman/Corbis/SABA Press Photos, Inc., 150; David Young-Wolff/PhotoEdit, 154; Michael Newman/PhotoEdit, 157; Pictor/ImageState/International Stock Photography Ltd., 159.

CHAPTER 7: © Paul Marcus, *Quality Time*, Studio SPM Inc., 164; Yellow Dog Productions/Getty Images, Inc.–Image Bank, 166; Mark Richards/PhotoEdit, 167; Greg Gilbert/Corbis/Bettmann, 169; Joe Raedie/Newsmaker/Getty Images, Inc.–Liaison, 171; Bettmann/Corbis/Bettmann, 172; Daniel Laine/Corbis/Bettmann, 177; Bob Daemmrich/The Image Works, 181; AP/Wide World Photos, 183.

CHAPTER 8: © Paul Marcus [detail from] *Maze of AIDS*, Studio SPM Inc., 190; Corbis/Bettman, 192; Kinsey Institute for Research–Sex, Gender, and Reproduction, 191; Ezio Peterson/Corbis/Bettmann, 199; Obed Zilwa/AP/Wide World Photos, 209; Toby Talbot/AP/Wide World Photos, 211; Jim Bourg/Reuters/Corbis/Bettmann, 213.

CHAPTER 9: © Paul Marcus, *Junk in the Hole*, Studio SPM Inc., 218; Courtesy of The National Library of Medicine, Bethesda, 220; Ray Ellis/Photo Researchers, Inc., 222; Carl D. Walsh/Aurora & Quanta Productions, Inc., 227; Jeff Greenberg/Rainbow, 229;

Ferdinando Scianna/Magnum Photos, Inc., 232; Hank Morgan/Photo Researchers, Inc., 234; Nascimento/REA/Corbis/SABA Press Photos, Inc., 237 (*left*); Sjoerd Van Delden/AP/Wide World Photos, 237 (*right*); Larry Kolvoord/The Image Works, 239.

CHAPTER 10: © Paul Marcus, *Look, Sweetie Look!*, Studio SPM Inc., 244; Barbara Reilly, 247; © Peter Turnley/Corbis, 250; Stephen McBrady/PhotoEdit, 253; David Young-Wolff/PhotoEdit, 255; Tony Freeman/PhotoEdit, 258; Adam G. Sylvester/Photo Researchers, Inc., 260; Jerry Cooke; Photo Researchers, Inc., 263; Ferdinando Scianna/Magnum Photos, Inc., 267.

CHAPTER 11: © Paul Marcus *Capital Dunking*, Studio SPM Inc., 272; Alexander Platz/Polaris Images, 274 (*left*); Ricardo Teles/D. Donne Bryant Stock Photography, 274 (*right*); Courtesy of the Library of Congress, 279; AP/Wide World Photos, 281; Jack Kurtz/New York Times Pictures, 282; Damian Dovarganes/AP/Wide World Photos, 285; Matt Heron/AP Wide World Photos, 286; AP Wide World Photos, 287; Mug Shots/Corbis/Bettmann, 289.

CHAPTER 12: © Paul Marcus, *You Deserve A Smile*, Studio SPM Inc., 296; Andrew Sacks/Getty Images/Time Life Pictures, 298; David Sams/Stock Boston, 300; Adam Lubroth/Getty Images, Inc.–Stone Allstock, 304; Richard Pasley/Stock Boston, 308; Brown Brothers, 310; Donnie Kamin/PhotoEdit, 314; Peter Morgan/Reuters/Getty Images, Inc.–Hulton Archive Photos, 317.

CHAPTER 13: © Paul Marcus, *Picnic In The Bronx*, Studio SPM Inc., 322; The WB/Greg Schwartz/Photofest, 324; Bruce Ayers/Getty Images, Inc.–Stone Allstock, 326; Will Hart/PhotoEdit, 327; Corbis/Sygma, 335; Andrew Hall/Getty Images, Inc.–Stone Allstock, 336; Dan Bosler/Getty Images, Inc.–Stone Allstock, 339.

CHAPTER 14: © Paul Marcus, *There's Public, Then There's Public*, Studio SPM Inc., 344; Mark Richards/PhotoEdit, 346; Courtesy of the Library of Congress, 348; Carol Iwasaki/Getty Images/Time Life Pictures, 354; Jose L. Pelaez/Corbis/Stock Market, 356; T. Lindfors/Lindfors Photography, 357; Will Faller, 362; David Martin/AP/Wide World Photos, 364.

CHAPTER 15: © Paul Marcus, *Flying*, oil on panel, Studio SPM Inc., 370; The Granger Collection, 372; Lester Lefkowitz/Corbis/Bettmann, 374; Courtesy of the Library of Congress, 378 (*top left*); *Baxter Street Court*, circa 1898, Museum of the City of New York, The Jacob A. Riis Collection, 378 (*top right*); Jacob A. Riis, *Family in Poverty*, Courtesy of the Museum of the City of New York, 378 (*bottom right*); AP/Wide World Photos, 379; Lee Snider/The Image Works, 386; AP/Wide World Photos, 389.

CHAPTER 16: © Paul Marcus, *Crossing the Rio Grande*, 1999, Studio SPM Inc., 394; Leah Melnick/Estate of Leah Melnick, 399; The Granger Collection, 402; Paul W. Liebhardt, 407; Lemoyne/Getty Images Inc.–Liaison, 408; North Wind Picture Archives, 410; Francis Li/Getty Images, Inc.–Liaison, 414; Mark Edwards/Peter Arnold, Inc., 418.

CHAPTER 17: © Paul Marcus, *Day Dreaming*, Studio SPM Inc., 422; Malcolm Fife/Getty Images, Inc.-PhotoDisc, 424; Pierre Roussel/Getty Images, Inc.–Liaison, 427; AP/Wide World Photos, 429; © 1999 Daniel Beltra/Greenpeace, 435; Ben Osborne/Getty Images, Inc.–Stone Allstock, 437; Alan S. Weiner, 438; Louis Psihoyos, 441.

CHAPTER 18: Francisco Goya, *Los fusilamientos del 3 de mayo*, 1808, Museo Nacional del Prado, Madrid, 446; United States Marine Corps, 451; Brennan Linsley/AP/Wide World Photos, 453; AP/Wide World Photos, 455, 456; Mario Tama/Getty Images, Inc.–Liaison, 458; AP/Wide World Photos, 459, 460; Reuters/Mike Segar/Corbis/Bettmann, 464.

George Breithaupt, 503

ABOUT THE AUTHOR

John J. Macionis (pronounced ma-SHOW-nis) was born and raised in Philadelphia, Pennsylvania. He earned a bachelor's degree from Cornell University and a doctorate in sociology from the University of Pennsylvania. His publications are wide-ranging, focusing on community life in the United States, interpersonal intimacy in families, effective teaching, humor, new information technology, and the importance of global education.

Macionis is best known for twenty-five years of work as a textbook author, and his books are the most popular in the discipline. *Sociology* and *Society: The Basics* (both from Prentice Hall) are lively introductions to sociology, and Macionis collaborates on various international editions of these texts. He and Nijole V. Benokraitis have edited the anthology *Seeing Ourselves: Classic, Contemporary, and Cross-Cultural Readings in Sociology*. In addition, Macionis and Vincent Parrillo are authors of the urban studies text: *Cities and Urban Life* (Prentice Hall). The latest on all the Macionis textbooks, as well as information and dozens of Internet links of interest to students and faculty, are found at the author's Web site http://www.macionis.com or http://TheSociologyPage.com. Additional information, instructor resources, and online student study guides are found at the Prentice Hall site, http://www.prenhall.com/macionis.

John Macionis is Professor and Distinguished Scholar of Sociology at Kenyon College in Gambier, Ohio. During a career of twenty-five years at Kenyon, he has chaired the Sociology Department, directed the college's multidisciplinary program in humane studies, and presided over the campus senate and also the college's faculty, and, most important, taught sociology to thousands of students.

In 2002, the American Sociological Association named Macionis recipient of the Award for Distinguished Contributions to Teaching, citing

S. Georgia Nugent, president of Kenyon College, congratulates John Macionis on his receiving the Philander Chase medal for twenty-five years of teaching at Kenyon.

his innovative use of global material as well as new technology in the textbooks.

Professor Macionis has been active in academic programs in other countries, having traveled to some fifty nations. During his last study tour, he directed the global education course for the University of Pittsburgh's Semester at Sea program, teaching 400 students on a floating campus that visited twelve countries as it circled the globe.

Macionis writes, "I am an ambitious traveler, eager to learn and, through the texts, to share much of what I discover with students, many of whom know so little about the rest of the world. For me, traveling and writing are all dimensions of teaching. First and foremost, I am a teacher—a passion for teaching animates everything I do." At Kenyon, Macionis offers a wide range of courses, and regularly teaches social problems. In fact, much of the planning and the content of this text was inspired in the classroom. Macionis enjoys extensive contact with students and each term invites members of his classes to enjoy a home-cooked meal.

The Macionis family—John, Amy, and children McLean and Whitney—live on a farm in rural Ohio. In his free time, John practices yoga and enjoys swimming and bicycling through the Ohio countryside. During the summer, he is a competitive sailor, and year-round, he enjoys performing oldies rock and roll and playing the Scottish bagpipes. Professor Macionis welcomes (and responds to) comments and suggestions about this book from faculty and students. Write to the Sociology Department, Palme House, Kenyon College, Gambier, Ohio 43022, or direct e-mail to MACIONIS@KENYON.EDU

NAME INDEX

SUBJECT INDEX